Terje Oestigaard is Senior Researcher, Nordic Africa Institute, Uppsala, Sweden, and Docent, Department of Archaeology and Ancient History, Uppsala University. He has a doctorate in archaeology from the University of Bergen, where he was also a researcher in the Department of Geography. His books include *Water, Christianity and the Rise of Capitalism* (I.B.Tauris, 2013), *Religion at Work in Globalised Traditions* (2014), and *Water and Food: From Hunter Gatherers to Global Production* (co-ed. with T. Tvedt, I.B.Tauris, 2016).

'Oestigaard is a rising star with spatial, temporal, and topical breadth akin to that of the insightful and exacting scholarship of Joseph Campbell. Oestigaard's use of archaeology, documents, and ethnography is a clever, contemporary way to link great religious traditions and the human perception of the Divine.' – Carole L. Crumley, Professor Emerita, Department of Anthropology, University of North Carolina at Chapel Hill

THE RELIGIOUS NILE

WATER, RITUAL AND SOCIETY SINCE ANCIENT EGYPT

TERJE OESTIGAARD

Published in 2018 by
I.B.Tauris & Co. Ltd
London • New York
www.ibtauris.com

Copyright © 2018 Terje Oestigaard

The right of Terje Oestigaard to be identified as the author of this work has been asserted by the author in accordance with the Copyright, Designs and Patents Act 1988.

All rights reserved. Except for brief quotations in a review, this book, or any part thereof, may not be reproduced, stored in or introduced into a retrieval system, or transmitted, in any form or by any means, electronic, mechanical, photocopying, recording or otherwise, without the prior written permission of the publisher.

Every attempt has been made to gain permission for the use of the images in this book. Any omissions will be rectified in future editions.

References to websites were correct at the time of writing.

ISBN: 978 1 78453 978 8
eISBN: 978 1 78672 242 3
ePDF: 978 1 78673 242 2

A full CIP record for this book is available from the British Library
A full CIP record is available from the Library of Congress

Library of Congress Catalog Card Number: available

Typeset in India by Integra Software Services Pvt. Ltd.
Printed and bound by CPI Group (UK) Ltd, Croydon, CR0 4YY

Contents

List of Illustrations — vi

Preface — ix

1 Sources of Religion — 1

2 The Source of the Blue Nile and Lake Tana in Ethiopia — 64

3 From Lake Victoria to Murchison Falls in Uganda — 128

4 The Sources in the Sky and Rainmaking — 196

5 The River Civilization in the Desert — 258

6 Water and World Religions Along the Nile — 327

Notes — 392

Bibliography — 428

Index — 449

List of Illustrations

1. John Hanning Speke at Ripon Falls and the Source of the White Nile, 28 July 1862. Photo: Terje Oestigaard.   2
2. Omugga Kiyira – the Source of the White Nile in between the two islands. Photo: Terje Oestigaard.   5
3. The religious Nile from the sources to the sea. Map: Henrik Alfredsson.   12
4. The Nile at Aswan today. Photo: Terje Oestigaard.   16
5. The annual inundation of the Nile. Photo: Lehnert & Landrock, 1924.   26
6. *The Deluge*, Genesis 7: 23. From Gustav Doré, *The Bible Gallery* (1880).   35
7. Jaja Bujagali. Photo: Terje Oestigaard.   39
8. The life-giving rains after the 2011 drought in Tanzania. Photo: Terje Oestigaard.   45
9. Gish Abay – the source of the Blue Nile. Photo: Terje Oestigaard.   77
10. The holy water is blessed by priests at Manbebya Kifle Church, 2009. Photo: Terje Oestigaard.   84
11. 'Tis Abay' or the 'smoking waters'. Photo: Terje Oestigaard.   86
12. Tana Kirkos in Lake Tana. Photo: Terje Oestigaard.   90
13. The sacrificial pillars believed to have an Old Testament origin. Photo: Terje Oestigaard.   90
14. The baptismal pool at Meskel Square. Photo: Terje Oestigaard.   98
15. Woyto water-world. Photo: Terje Tvedt.   108

LIST OF ILLUSTRATIONS

16. Praying to Abinas before sacrifice. Photo: Gedef Abawa Firew. 111
17. The Great Sacrifice. Photo: Gedef Abawa Firew. 117
18. The Ripon Falls as documented by Speke in the *Journal*. 138
19. Jaja Bujagali. Photo: Terje Oestigaard. 146
20. Kiyira, or the very source, flowing against the Nile's current. Photo: Terje Oestigaard. 152
21. Jaja Kiyira in his compound. Photo: Terje Oestigaard. 154
22. Shrines for spirits on the islands just across from the source of the River Nile. Photo: Terje Oestigaard. 157
23. Itanda Falls. Photo: Terje Oestigaard. 160
24. Mary Itanda praying to Itanda. Photo: Terje Oestigaard. 164
25. Visitors in Nfuudu's compound reading his sign. Photo: Terje Oestigaard. 169
26. Murchison Falls and Wang Jok. Photo: Terje Oestigaard. 185
27. Who controls the life-giving rains – God or ancestors? Photo: Terje Oestigaard. 211
28. Rainmaking pot in Usagara. Photo: Terje Oestigaard. 218
29. Lifting an exhausted animal during drought in Kenya. Photo: Marcel Rutten. 226
30. Replica of the royal palace, King's Palace Museum-Rukari, Rwanda. Photo: Terje Oestigaard. 229
31. Nuer dug-out canoes. Photo: John M. Lee, 1920–8. Copyright Pitt Rivers Museum, University of Oxford (1998.204.11.1). 239
32. The Bor Dinka rainmaker, Biyordit Dinka. Photo: Charles Gabriel Seligman. Copyright Pitt Rivers Museum, University of Oxford (1967.26.166). 247
33. Dinka fishing party. Photo: Godfrey Lienhardt, 1947–51. Copyright Pitt Rivers Museum, University of Oxford (2005.51.312.1). 249
34. Dinka girl milking. Photo: Godfrey Lienhardt, 1947–51. Copyright Pitt Rivers Museum, University of Oxford (2005.51.118.1). 250
35. Shilluk shrine of Nyakang. Photo: Charles Gabriel Seligman, 1910. Copyright Pitt Rivers Museum, University of Oxford (1967.26.128). 252

36. The inundation and the life-giving water with the pyramids at Giza. Photo: Lehnert & Landrock, 1924. 261
37. King Zer's tomb with subsidiary graves. From Petrie, *Royal Tombs of the Earliest Dynasties II* (1901). 270
38. Horus the Falcon. From the Temple of Edfu. Photo: Terje Oestigaard. 282
39. Osiris. Temple of Seti I, Abydos. Photo: Terje Oestigaard. 294
40. The confluence of the White Nile and the Blue Nile in Khartoum. Photo: Terje Oestigaard. 303
41. The sacred pool at Karnak. Photo: Terje Oestigaard. 313
42. The dead's journey to eternity. From the Dendera Temple. Photo: Terje Oestigaard. 316
43. *The Wilbour Plaque* probably depicting Akhenaten and Nefertiti. Brooklyn Museum, US. Photo: Nils Billing. 335
44. Saint Virgin Mary's Coptic Church or the Hanging Church in Old Cairo. Photo: Terje Oestigaard. 345
45. The divine breast milk. From the Dendera Temple, Egypt. Photo: Terje Oestigaard. 351
46. The Virgin Mary breastfeeding Jesus, Daga Istafanos Monastery. Photo: Terje Oestigaard. 353
47. Al-Azhar mosque, Cairo. Photo: Kjersti Gravelsæter Berg. 360
48. The Roda Nilometer in Cairo. Photo: Terje Oestigaard. 362
49. Baptism in the Nile close to the source. Photo: Terje Oestigaard. 380
50. Gandhi symbolically overlooking the Nile as the river flows by. Photo: Terje Oestigaard. 388

Preface

Without me knowing it, this book started in 2004 just after I completed my doctoral dissertation. After a period of eight years studying death and life-giving waters in Nepal, India and Bangladesh along the holy rivers, one of my supervisors, Professor Terje Tvedt, advised me to change continent and focus on the Nile. 'There are many more possibilities there and less done from your perspective', he said, and I am indeed indebted to him for this advice, and, of course, he was right. As the saying goes, although in different forms, 'if you drink from the Nile you will always come back', and since then the Nile has been part of my life and career. My postdoctoral project 'An archaeology of the Pharaonic Nile and the rise of the Egyptian civilization: comparing religious water-worlds in history' (project number 171313) was funded by the Research Council of Norway, for which I am very grateful, and it resulted in the book *Horus' Eye and Osiris' Efflux: The Egyptian Civilisation of Inundation ca. 3000-2000 BCE* (2011). Chapter 5 builds on this work in a shorter and restructured version. Parallel to this work, I also had different positions at the Nile Basin Research Programme at the University of Bergen. During the 2008 spring semester I worked as the research coordinator for the research group 'Water, Culture and Identity', and edited the book *Water, Culture and Identity: Comparing Past and Present Traditions in the Nile Basin Region* (2009), focusing on cultural and religious aspects of the Nile. During 2008–9 I was also a Research fellow at The Centre for Advanced Study (CAS) at the Norwegian Academy of Science and Letters, University of Oslo and part of the research group 'Understanding the Role of Water in History and Development' led by Terje Tvedt, continuing working with water and religion. Throughout the period 2001–16, I worked in close cooperation with Terje Tvedt on the nine-volume series *A History of Water*, which has also shaped my direction of water studies. I am therefore extremely grateful for the long and stimulating work with Terje over the years – without his constant support and inspiration this book would never have materialized. I will also thank in particular the director of the Nile Basin Research Programme (NBRP), Dr Tore Saetersdal, for his support and friendship for more than two decades, and also Professor Randi Håland, who was my main supervisor in my early years, directing me not only to an anthropological approach in archaeology but also to the wider world and a global and comparative archaeology. I would also like to thank Professor Tim Insoll, who at the time was at the University of Manchester (now at the University of Exeter), where I had the opportunity to spend a short semester in 2007 studying the Nile and ancient Egyptian civilization.

Since 2000, I have worked primarily at the Centre for Development Studies at the University of Bergen, which in the following decade changed names and structure a number of times. The academic and administrative staff has to be thanked for constant support. In 2010 I moved from Bergen and started working at the Nordic Africa Institute in Uppsala, continuing with water and the Nile. In 2009 I had my first trip to Ethiopia and the source of the Blue Nile, which, again without knowing it, turned out to define my future research direction for years. Not only did I work in close cooperation with my good friend Gedef Abawa Firew, and together we published the book *The Source of the Blue Nile: Water Rituals and Traditions in the Lake Tana Region* (2013), but it also stimulated my continuing research in Ethiopia, and other places along the Nile. In Ethiopia, most of the fieldwork was conducted in August/September 2009 and in January and March 2010, with additional follow-up inquiries in 2011 and 2015 on specific topics being pursued during the process of writing. I would like to thank Professor Yacob Arsano at Addis Ababa University and the members of the History Department at Bahir Dar University, Ethiopia, whose help was instrumental. Parts of chapters 2 and 6 build on this work in a restructured form.

At the Nordic Africa Institute I was part of the 'Rural and Agrarian Change, Property and Resources' cluster, led by Professor Kjell Havnevik. I am grateful for Kjell Havnevik's support and trust in my work, also when things did not turn out as planned, which happened with my next and main project about rainmaking and globalization in Tanzania. The main fascination with ethnographic fieldwork, and the greatest frustrations as well, is that it never turns out as expected. Despite initial difficulties, I ended up on the southern shores of Lake Victoria, which resulted in the book *Religion at Work in Globalised Traditions: Rainmaking, Witchcraft and Christianity in Tanzania* (2014). The fieldwork was carried out in 2011 and during the drought in the Horn of Africa. I would like to thank my interpreter Simeon Mwampashi whose personal and social skills opened up many doors during the course of the fieldwork. I would also like to express my gratitude to Jumanne Abdallah, Sokoine University of Agriculture, Tanzania, and the nuns at Nyakahoja Hostel.

Since I had been working with the source of the Blue Nile and the Sukuma on the southern shores of Lake Victoria, it led naturally to my next focus: the historic source of the White Nile in Uganda on the northern shores of Lake Victoria. I conducted fieldwork there from 2012 to 2014 (and a short fieldwork in 2017) in parallel with other projects, and during the autumn of 2014 I had a more or less complete manuscript ready to be published as a book with the title *The Source of the White Nile*, directly referring to *The Source of the Blue Nile*. At this time, the idea of working on *The Religious Nile* had developed, although without having any clear idea of how to proceed. I had sent the manuscript to Terje Tvedt for comments, and during a dinner in Oslo in September 2014 we talked about my future plans, and I briefly mentioned that I had been thinking about the religious Nile covering most of the basin. Then he gave me a piece of advice, obviously not the one I wanted at that time, but, as usual, he was right: cancel the book about the source of the White Nile! Thus, from the satisfaction of having almost a new book completed, I had none. However, from then on it was clear what to do and I knew how to write this book. As part of the cancelled book, I had also written about dam discourses, and I took that part out and published it as a small book, *Dammed Divinities: The Water Powers at Bujagali Falls, Uganda* (2015). The main ethnography from the unpublished manuscript about the source of the White Nile was hence the axis which this book developed around.

In Uganda, I would in particular thank the healers Jaja Kiyira, Jaja Bujagali and Jaja Itanda. Although it is not common to name informants, it is done in this case since they are public figures and easily identified, although the necessary anonymization is done when needed. Special thanks are due to Richard Gonza and Waguma Yasin Ntembe for putting me in touch with key informants. Oki Simon provided invaluable help as a translator and Moses Mugweri, my assistant throughout, deserves special thanks. Henni Alava provided me with the quote about the Ugandan martyrs in Gulu. A research project like this does not take place only in the field. The Nile Basin Research Programme (NBRP) at Makerere University also assisted me, and I particularly thank Professor Edward Kirumira and Margaret Kyakuwa. The Uganda National Council for Science and Technology provided me with a research permit (SS 3202), and otherwise I would like to thank John Baptist Sseppuuya for excellent driving as well as help with other practical matters.

In 2013, I became docent in archaeology at Uppsala University and from 2016 affiliated at the Department of Archaeology and Ancient History, and I would like to extend my gratitude to professors Anders Kaliff, Paul Lane, Neil Price and Paul Sinclair. In 2017, I started on a project in Bergen again, which somehow completed the circle of this book.

I would like to express my sincere thanks to all the informants who generously gave of their time and answered my questions, and without their generosity this book – or any of the others – would not have been possible to write. While it is always a danger writing acknowledgements, thanking some and forgetting others, I hope I am excused since there are too many involved in a project like this who have supported me in one way or another throughout the years, and I am grateful to all. I would also like to extend my gratitude and a general thanks to the staff at the Nordic Africa Institute. The friendly staff at the British Library and SOAS have been very helpful during different phases of my work during the last 15 years. Lastly, I will thank my 'own' super-librarian Pernilla Bäckström for her invaluable help with library loans, and for support and everything else that matters in life.

At various stages, Francesca de Châtel and Peter Colenbrander have commented on language and academic un-clarities, and I will also thank the Pitt Rivers Museum, University of Oxford, Terje Tvedt, Marcel Rutten, Kjersti Gravelsæter Berg and Nils Billing for allowing me to use some of their photographs. Tore Saetersdal also let me use the transcripts of one of their films on rainmaking and Nils Billing gave me valuable literature suggestions regarding Egypt. I would also like to express my gratitude to the Satterthwaite Colloquium.

While this book is more than ambitious, given that the Nile basin covers almost one-tenth of the African continent and the time span covers 5,000 years of history, and indeed I have had many second thoughts regarding if it was a good idea to embark on this project at all during the writing process, there are obviously periods and areas that are not covered in the same depth as others. In particular, Burundi, Kenya, Rwanda, Sudan (primarily today's South Sudan) and Tanzania are covered less than Egypt, Ethiopia and Uganda, and are to a large extent based on existing literature. This I hope is justified, since, in particular, in the upper Nile region rainmaking is a dominant cosmology and there are many structural similarities, which are discussed in Chapter 4. Still, with the focus on the sources, rainmaking, the spiritual world along the Nile, the Egyptian civilization, and the role of water in the monotheistic religions in a comparative context, including parts of the classical sources, I believe that many of the most central parts of the religious Nile are covered, and sufficiently documented for theoretical discussions of water and religion.

Regarding references, I have to a large extent tried to minimize the literature focusing as much as possible only on the Nile basin as such, given that the comparative reference literature is unlimited in practice, although in many cases it has been necessary to extend the knowledge base beyond the basin. Still, the references are voluminous enough and I have used endnotes to make the text more readable, and, I hope, to use a water metaphor, more flowing.

A last note about the terminology of the chronology is necessary. It has been a challenge to choose the nomenclature of years since the religious Nile includes Christianity, Islam, Hinduism and Judaism, and not least the African indigenous religions. The Western system of dating uses BC and AD, 'before Christ' and the Latin phrase *anno domini*, 'in the year of our Lord'. The Islamic calendar starts in AD 622 in the year when Muhammed fled from Mecca, and is labelled 1 AH and signifies the Hijri year or era, and the Islamic year follows the lunar calendar and hence the year is slightly shorter than the years used in the Gregorian calendar. One way of solving this is to use BCE and CE – 'Before Common Era' and 'Common Era' – which is in any case linked to Christianity and the birth of Christ, since these two calendars coincide with the same starting point. A last option is the strict archaeological C14 dating method BP – 'Before Present' – which was introduced in 1950. The latter system would make the text unreadable or at least complicate matters too much without being more precise; for example, that Jesus was born in the year 1950 BP. The Islamic calendar, given that the years are shorter than the other calendars and the calendar starts later, in addition to the fact that water in Islam occupies only a smaller part of this book, makes this calendar less optimal in this analysis. Christianity in Ethiopia does, however, have a central part, and the Ethiopian Orthodox Church has indeed its own calendar following the Julian calendar, and for instance the year 2015 is 2008 in Ethiopia. Moreover, the Ethiopian New Year starts 11 September (or in leap years 12 September) signifying several important happenings, including the end of the rainy seasons (see Chapter 2).

There cannot be one dating system that will be optimal throughout all periods given that this book covers a 5,000 year span and numerous religions. Not only because of simplicity and comparison, BC and AD are used with notably exceptions, since large parts of the Nile basin are now Christianized and also traditional African religions most often use this system. In Chapter 5, which discusses ancient Egypt, BCE and CE are used, since this civilization developed millennia before Christianity. On certain occasions, when relevant, however, the Islamic calendar will also be used, but then correlated to AD to make the years comparable.

Throughout this journey I have tried my utmost to be guided by what the informants have told me and the narratives and interpretations of earlier travellers and scholars, but of course I am solely responsible for any mistakes and misinterpretations in this book.

1 Sources of Religion

APPROACHING SOURCES

One hundred and fifty years after John Hanning Speke came to the outlet of Lake Victoria in Uganda and identified it as the source of the White Nile in 28 July 1862, I came for the first time to this historic place. Approaching the source of the Nile, on 21 July 1862, Speke writes:

> I told my men they ought to shave their heads and bathe in the holy river, the cradle of Moses – the waters of which, sweetened with sugar, men carry all the way from Egypt to Mecca, and sell to the pilgrims. But Bombay [the assistant], who is a philosopher of the Epicurean school, said, 'We don't look on those things in the same fanciful manner that you do; we are contented with all the commonplaces of life, and look for nothing beyond the present. If things don't go well, it is God's will; and if they do go well, that is His will also.'[1]

When coming to the outlet of Lake Victoria on 28 July 1862, the search for the source was over (fig. 1). Speke concludes in his *Journal of the Discovery of the Source of the Nile*: 'The expedition had now performed its functions. I saw that old Father Nile without any doubt rises in the Victoria N'yanza, and, as I had foretold, that lake is the great source of the holy river which cradled the first expounder of our religious belief.'[2] He continues:

> I now christened the 'stones' Ripon falls, after the nobleman who presided over the Royal Geographical Society when my expedition was got up; and the arm of water from which the Nile issued, Napoleon Channel, in token of respect to the French Geographical Society, for the honor they had done me, just before leaving England, in presenting me with their gold medal for the discovery of the Victoria N'yanza.[3]

The importance of finding the source has to be seen in conjunction with the history of the searches for the sources in Europe and the global relevance

1. John Hanning Speke at Ripon Falls and the source of the White Nile, 28 July 1862. Painting at Speke Hotel, Kampala.

of the Nile from the nineteenth century onwards. Moreover, in European mythology, the Nile had a special role. Speke writes, 'the N'yanza is the great reservoir that floated Father Moses on his first adventurous sail – the Nile'.[4] The Nile had a fundamental role in the Old Testament and hence in the history of Christianity, giving it special importance in the European context. Still, unlike Gish Abay, the source of the Blue Nile, which is a remote spring in the highlands of Abyssinia, the source of the White Nile documented by Speke at the outlet of Lake Victoria has been seen as a colonial construct and allegedly devoid of indigenous cultural and religious importance. Gish Abay, by contrast, has strong cultural and religious significance. It is believed that the heavenly River Gihon flows directly from Paradise to this specific spring, thus linking heaven and earth and making the water and the river deeply holy.[5] In the written history to date, the source of the White Nile is not invested with comparable cosmological significance by any religion. Instead, it is generally held that there is not much to report about the water at this place in terms of culture and religion. This could not be further from the truth. In the river, innumerable spirits reside, some more powerful than others, and the most important of them is located only 8 km from the source at Bujagali Falls. This spirit is part of a wider water cosmology, which includes the source as the second most important and powerful water spirit in the Busoga Kingdom and cosmology at the outlet of Lake Victoria.

In discussing sources of rivers, in particular of the Nile, it is important to note that a source can be many things simultaneously, some partly overlapping and others partly contradictory. *Hydrologically*, a source is the remotest spring or discharge point of a river – the very starting point for measuring the river's length. Thus, although rivers have innumerable sources or small tributaries forming larger tributaries and so on, in terms of ultimate length there will only be one source. *Religiously*, a source can originate at any place along the river's course, but most often it is a fountain, a waterfall or some subterranean source, which may also be a link in one way or another to all the flows of cosmos in the celestial realms. From a religious point of view, river sources can be unrelated to the hydrological sources. Given the aim of studying the role and importance of water and religion in history, these religious sources are of utmost importance, since many hydrological sources are often found and documented quite late in history, and often lack religious significance. In many cases it is the religious sources and not the hydrological ones that have defined history, or at least the mythology that has shaped history. *Historically*, some sources are historical places given major importance in the history of ideas and development. The history of the source of the White Nile has, to a large extent, been constructed by the British since Speke's discovery in 1862. But, as will become evident, this source is also a religious source, and even a hydrological source, even though it is not the remotest spring upstream in the Nile Basin.

Although Speke labelled the outlet of Lake Victoria as the source of the White Nile, most likely he did not see the real source, which existed, and still exists, there. At the historic source of the Nile documented by Speke there are two small adjacent islands. The Western Island is the main tourist destination for visitors coming to see the source, and there is a blue sign on which is written: 'The source of R. Nile. Jinja. World's longest river.' Few visitors pay much attention to the other seemingly irrelevant island just a stone's throw to the east. At the southernmost end of this island stand some huge trees. Because of the extremely rich bird life, all these trees and the nearby ground have been whitened by countless droppings. Next to the trees there is a small opening on which can be found a few apparently unspectacular remains of pots and minor wooden structures. But the importance of these islands is not because Speke in 1862 identified Ripon Falls as the source of the Nile, but because there is indeed a very powerful source of the Nile flowing between the islands at this point.

Today, the source of the Nile is not much celebrated in the guidebooks: 'a visit to this once lovely site is now a disappointment [...] the site looks basically at a passing river'.[6] True, the Ripon Falls are gone because of the Owen Falls Dam that was opened in 1954, and today the name marks the place where visitors embark in tourist boats to the small islands now seen as the source. When standing at this spot, one inevitably looks at the large billboard proclaiming 'Welcome to the source of the great river Nile – Jinja, Uganda.' This billboard is worthy of comment. Written in huge letters are the words 'Uganda's heritage'. These do not, however, refer to the Nile or its source. Rather, they advertise the sponsor of this billboard, Bell Lager Beer. Below, one reads: 'On the western bank of the river is an obelisk marking the spot where Speke stood for hours when he saw the source of the River Nile, making it known to the outside world.'

The abovementioned islands are located in the bay named by Speke after Napoleon III, as the billboard records: 'The bay behind this billboard through which the waters of Lake Victoria funnel in the Nile is called the Napoleon Gulf.' But it is barely possible to see the bay or the islands because of the size of the billboard. Nevertheless, whatever the billboard's other shortcomings, there is one intriguing and important piece of information on it: '"Omugga Kiyira" is the local name for the River Nile.' Thousands of visitors have read these words without knowing what they mean, but behind this seemingly trivial information there lies a whole cosmology, which certainly makes the source of the White Nile an actual source, and a very important one, but also a very different source from the one Speke found. And this source has utmost importance today, being part of the greater water cosmology of this area among the Busoga.

In 2012 I read the text on this billboard as most tourists do, without knowing what it meant or the implications. The next year when I was back I did not make a discovery: it was the boatman, who is also named Moses, who told me what it means.

When standing next to the 'The source of R. Nile' sign and looking carefully across to the other small island and towards Lake Victoria, one may notice something peculiar about the water. There is a current at this spot. At first it may be difficult to see what is special unless one pays close attention, but the water flows the wrong way!

The two small islands are called Obuzzinga Nalubale, meaning the two small islands of the Lake God (fig. 2). The two islands are located in the gulf where all of the waters of Lake Victoria – the second largest lake in

2. Omugga Kiyira – the source of the White Nile in between the two islands. The tourist island is to the right and the sacrificial island to the left.

the world after Lake Superior – leaves the lake and starts flowing north before eventually reaching Egypt and the Mediterranean Sea. But at the very source, in the middle of the river between the two small islands, something in the water creates a current flowing southwards. The water from the lake is forced back at this point, and one may see banana leaves floating in both directions: some following the flow of the Victoria Nile northwards and some in the opposite direction, southwards. Moreover, while the water in the Nile coming from the lake is rather muddy and polluted, the colour of the water flowing southwards is crystal clear and tastes perfect. Even its temperature feels cooler.

The reason for this strange occurrence is that the source of the White Nile here is literally a source, not only geologically but also spiritually and religiously. If one looks carefully along the shores of the tourist island while standing near the sign, one clearly sees that fresh water is welling up from below. At this spot, there is an underground source of fresh water. Not only is this water crystal clear, but it is also very powerful. The volume and force of this water is uncertain, but it is obviously very forceful, since it actually pushes back the rest of the water in the Nile at this point. The force of this source would have been perceived as even mightier before the Owen Falls Dam was constructed. Just downstream from the source, the Ripon Falls would have offered powerful visual and aural evidence of the tremendous intensity of the water. And whereas all the other river water would have turned into thundering cascades northwards, the water from the source would have flowed the other way.

'Kiyira' is the name of the specific spirit coming from the source. In the local language, 'Kiyira' means river and 'Omugga' means coming from below. This river god or spirit is nothing other than the waters welling up at the very source of the Nile and forcing the water from Lake Victoria backwards. And this water spirit is very powerful. Sacrifices are made to it on the other small island just across from the tourist island. In the river and all around there are numerous other spirits, and the small wooden structures on this island are some of the shrines to them, including Kiyira. Thus, the source of the Nile is very special not only in the European tradition, but also in local cosmology, for it is the home of innumerable spirits and of river gods, and in particular Kiyira.

Thus, this place is definitely a source from a religious point of view, but not in a conventional sense of a river's most remote spring or origin. This source is more like a fountain, but a very special fountain since it is subterranean in the middle of the outlet of Lake Victoria. Although Speke claimed that the 'lake is the great source of the holy river which cradled the first expounder of our religious belief', these beliefs at the source of the White Nile have little to do with Christianity and European tradition. The source is a fountain of wealth and a fundamental part of the Busoga kingdom's water cosmology. But the spirits also enable witchcraft. In many cases, it is difficult to distinguish between propitiation of water spirits and witchcraft, and to some extent the difference is in the eye of the beholder. Christians condemned all these practices as witchcraft and even among the Busoga healers they are perceived with ambivalence, since those who can bring the betterment may also bring malevolence. Still, Speke was also right, and even today among Christians in Uganda the historic source of the White Nile has a special importance precisely because it links Christians in Uganda with the Nile and Moses as described in the Bible (see Chapter 6).

In the traditional cosmology, the role and importance of the source at Ripon Falls has to be seen in relation to Bujagali Falls and Itanda Falls and to the associated hierarchy of water spirits. Bujagali Falls and Itanda Falls are respectively approximately 8 and 30 km north of the source following the Nile. Among the Busoga, all three falls have special religious significance. In each of the falls resides a river spirit or god. In fact, there are innumerable spirits, but there are three main spirits. Today, the spirits in the Ripon and Owen Falls have been flooded, but the underground water fountain at the source is as mighty as ever. These three spirits at the source, Bujagali and Itanda incarnate themselves in human form as a traditional healer or diviner. The Budhagaali spirit in Bujagali Falls is the supreme god and is seen as the father or elder brother of the other two. This is due to the force of the falls, naturally and hence spiritually. The Bujagali Falls were the largest. Thus, the force and sound of the rapids testifies to the presence and power of the spirits: they can remove any malignance or misfortune, or be malevolent if devotees are disobedient.

Because the spirit is embodied in them, traditional healers can transfer and mediate the spirit's power. Believers or clients come to the healer with requests for wealth and success or health and prosperity for their children. The healer as medium asks the spirit or god to respond to these requests, and if there are successful physical or spiritual outcomes, the believer will fulfil his or her promise and obligation to the god. This may include making sacrifices to the river of a goat or a sheep or in accordance with the promises made when the healer procured the necessary medicines. These sacrifices are not part of annual or cyclical rituals, but occur when the believers achieve the outcome sought in the rite. Sacrifices at the source of the Nile therefore take place irregularly depending on how many have consulted the healer and taken part in his rituals and if the spirit has granted their wishes. And the human embodiment or the healer of the spirit at the source – Jaya Kiyira – conducts at least one sacrifice to the spirit annually. The water spirits at all three falls are part of the same water cosmology, and in the river live innumerable other spirits. On land, there are numerous healers, but only three main healers use water: in order of importance, they are the Bujagali healer, the source of the Nile healer and the Itanda healer.

Speke has been criticized because he did not discover anything that had not been known for millennia by local people living along the Nile's shores. Hastings Banda, Malawi's first president, for instance, found the idea that Europeans 'discovered' anything insulting and absurd: 'There was nothing to discover,' he said, 'we were here all the time.'[7] Academics have also argued along these lines. Nwauwa says: 'It seems absurd to continue to credit European explorers with the "discovery" of African peoples, rivers, lakes, waterfalls, mountains, and creeks when Africans themselves knew about the existence of these things.'[8] Although it is obviously true that indigenous people knew their waters, they did not know about the hydrology and that the waters from the lake flowed to the Mediterranean. In fact, it seems they did not care or want to know. Not only did the term mzungu ('someone who roams around aimlessly') originate as a description of these explorers, their search for the sources made no sense. When Livingstone asked about the source and course of a local river, one chief answered: 'We let the streams run on, and do not enquire whence they rise or whither they flow', and another chief declined to discuss the topic, since it was 'only water – nothing to be seen'.[9] Where the river flowed after passing through a chiefdom was not relevant or worth bothering about. However, one should doubt the local people perceived it only as water and nothing to be seen; although it might be true that they did not worry about where it flowed, as seen with the source and the falls along Victoria Nile water, the spirits residing there are of utmost importance. In fact, everywhere water has cosmological importance, but in very different and specific ways at each place.

Still, it is true that Speke did not discover a waterfall or an outlet from a lake that the indigenous people did not already know. What Speke did discover, however, which became evident later, was that the mighty river connected the great and mysterious lake in the interior of Africa with the river passing through Cairo to reach the Mediterranean. His geographical and scientific quest enabled new understanding of the African continent, an understanding that was crucial to the forthcoming colonization of this part of Africa. Not only was the British discovery of Uganda connected with Egypt through the Nile, but a scientific and hydrological understanding emerged of utmost importance to British expansion in Eastern Africa. This expansion linked the different parts of the Nile Basin in ways that are still of fundamental geopolitical importance. It is in the context of river systems linking Lake Victoria to the Mediterranean that Speke's claim of discovering the Nile's source is to be understood. And it is only in this context that Speke claimed to have made a discovery. Still, Speke's discovery was contested back in England at the time.

In 1848, Frederick Ayrton wrote that anyone claiming to find the sources of the Nile should be met with the utmost scepticism and criticism. Not only had 'the question, as is well known, had an interest long anterior to the time of Ptolemy the geographer', but 'Sesostris, Cambyses, Alexander, Ptolemy Philadelphus, Cæsar, Nero, and not a few besides, who have sought to leave for the chaplet of their future fame a record of their discovery of the sources of the Nile, have failed in attaining this object of their ambition'.[10] In the last decade alone some 50 individuals had appeared as rivals in the search for the source. Still, 'Caput Nili quærere', Ayrton says, 'has so long been accepted as a phrase of the futility of attempts to discover the sources of the famous river of Egypt, that, perhaps, one ought not to be surprised that a sudden announcement of success, even though professing to be founded upon the positive testimony of personal observation, should be met by incredulousness'.[11] The Romans had even a saying for searching for the sources of the Nile – 'Quaere fonte Nili' – which is equivalent to 'looking for the needle in a haystack'. With this background, Samuel W. Baker, who was the first westerner seeing Lake Albert, started his narrative by summarizing the Nile quest in one paragraph:

> In the history of the Nile there was a void: its Sources were a mystery. The Ancients devoted much attention to this problem; but in vain. The Emperor Nero sent an expedition under the command of two centurions, as described by Seneca. Even Roman energy failed to break the spell that guarded these secret fountains. The expedition sent by Mehemet Ali Pasha, the celebrated Viceroy of Egypt, closed a long term of unsuccessful search. The work has now been accomplished. Three English parties, and only three, have at various periods started upon this obscure mission: each has gained its end. Bruce won the source of the Blue Nile; Speke and Grant won the Victoria source of the great White Nile; and I have been permitted to succeed in completing the Nile Sources by the discovery of the great reservoir of the equatorial waters, the Albert N'yanza, from which the river issues as the entire White Nile.[12]

From Khartoum in 1863, on his way back to England, Speke sent his famous telegram: 'The Nile is settled',[13] and although Baker proclaimed that the issues were settled in the late 1860s, it was finally confirmed by Stanley in 1875 when he proved that there are no other outlets from Lake Victoria than the one Speke documented in 1862. Thus, in a historic perspective the Nile quest has to be seen in relation to the legendary status of the Nile sources for more than 2,500 years, and these legends were to a large extent religious in nature, including perceptions of different types of divine waters. Undiscovered in the nineteenth century when the rest of the world was largely explored and documented (and partly colonized), it was 'the problem of ages' in science and geography as Sir Roderick Murchison, the President of the Royal Geographical Society in London, said in 1863.[14]

After Burton and Speke's expedition (1857–9), when Speke made a detour and for the first time saw the southern reaches of Lake Victoria, there remained as many unanswered questions as before, although new knowledge had been gained. One such question was whether the monsoon that gave rise to the annual flooding of the Blue Nile reached as far south as Speke claimed. 'The solution of this question alone is worthy of the labours of another expedition,' Colonel Sykes commented. He went on:

> The work is only half accomplished, and the reputation of our country demands that it should be completed. My own opinion is, that independent of any commercial advantages or sordid considerations, the Society ought, for the simple investigation and verification of physical truths, to use its best endeavours to induce the Government to send out a second expedition. For the good name of England; let us have the doubt removed. We have an inkling of the truth; let us have the whole truth.

He was specifically preoccupied with the Mountains of the Moon and whether the western source of the Nile issued from lakes below the mountains, as described by Ptolemy 1,700 years earlier.[15]

Claudius Ptolemy began his studies in Alexandria in the early second century and he was the main geographical authority onwards to the discovery of America.[16] Ptolemy's *Geography* was rediscovered in Europe and the translated Latin version in 1406 by Jacopo d'Angelo representing a landmark in Western cartography. In 1475 it was printed without the maps, but two years later the maps were included, and from then on *Geography* was printed in many editions.[17] Ptolemy's sources of the Nile have, however, even a longer history, and it directs the attention to the knowledge in antiquity and ancient Egypt. What did they know about the sources, but also and perhaps more important: what is a source? This is also a question about knowledge systems – hydrology or mythology. A hydrological understanding of the sources may not coincide with religious perceptions of sources, because sources are much more than hydrology and geography – they are about cosmology and the ultimate sources of life.

RELIGIOUS QUEST

The Nile quest is practically ended,' Harry Johnston wrote in 1903.[18] Every important branch, affluent or lake-source in the Nile Basin had been identified and mapped, with some few exceptions. Still, as it was said already in 1884:

The Nile, which during thousands of years has attracted much attention from the intelligent portion of mankind, yet remains in many respects the most interesting of the great rivers of the globe. Its sources, which for so long a time were a mystery, have within the last quarter of a century been rediscovered; but that rediscovery has only rendered it more interesting, and more worthy of study.[19]

While the historic era of explorers and discoveries was over, with new knowledge the role and importance of the Nile grew, then as now.

The religious Nile is a little-explored theme. In the current political discourse and the struggle for water, although perceived as important, culture and identity – and religion as a supra structure guiding beliefs and being – has gained less significance. The Nile Basin Initiative, an intergovernmental partnership launched in 1999 by the riparian countries, has the overall objective 'to achieve sustainable socio-economic development through equitable utilization of, and benefit from, the common Nile Basin water resources'. Still, at the very beginning of the first State of the River Nile Basin Report from the Nile Basin Initiative, the religious role of the Nile was emphasized by the chairperson and ambassador and minister of natural resources in Rwanda, Stanislas Kamanzi: 'The Nile is commonly regarded as the most important river in the world, and occupies an important place in the tradition of many of the world's religions, including Judaism, Christianity, and Islam.'[20] Even in contexts where water is a contested resource, a river like the Nile is much more than mere shares of water.

A focus on water and religion directs the attention to what matters most for the majority of the people living in the Nile Basin; water for wealth and prosperity. Religion structures this and the other worldly realms – and how they relate, spiritually as well as physically. The same waters pouring out from the sources or rains at the Ruwenzori mountains eventually flow to Egypt, linking people and perceptions, and particular beliefs – even in world religions like Christianity and Islam – relate to and are understood in specific local contexts and water-worlds along the Nile. In fact, in many cases it is the local particularities and peculiarities of specific types of water that are the sources for religious understanding and how these are understood and being integrated into larger religious structures and cosmologies, and even partly defining them.

This book will present a history of the religious role of water and the Nile in the rise and constitution of societies and civilizations in

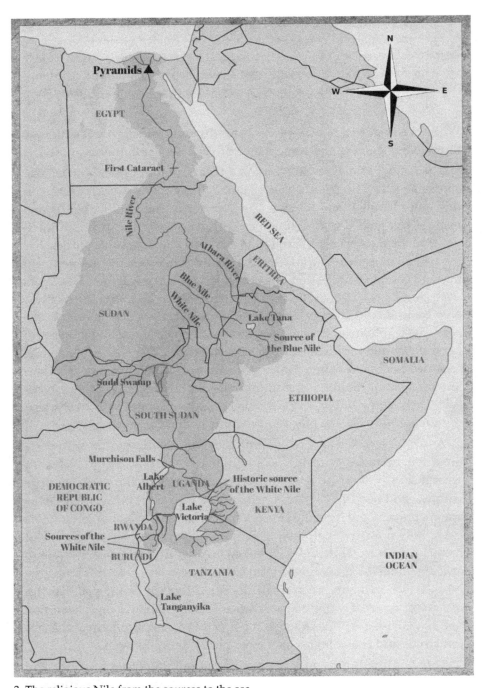

3. The religious Nile from the sources to the sea.

the past and present (fig. 3). Thus, the book has two overall objectives, which are intimately connected and dependent on each other.

On one hand, it is an empirical quest by following the religious Nile from the sources to the sea in the past and present. While all water in the Nile is the same in one way, it is also in very different forms and amounts in time and space, and among the main types or bodies of water are rivers, rains and lakes. The specific forms and particularities of water at a given place are essential parts of livelihoods and worldviews for the people living there, whether it is in a desert or rainforest, and hence part of their religions.

On the other hand, it is a theoretical quest of how to gain more knowledge of religion as process and structure by using water as an approach, since not only does it link secular and profane spheres, but water is also the very basis for all human well-being, which are also divine concerns or incorporated into spiritual realms. The theoretical challenge thus has to combine living religion in practice in specific ecologies with theology, exegesis and cosmology in the world beyond or parallel to the daily, practical matters. Local beliefs or parts of traditional religions including specific features of nature and ecologies or water-worlds are often not in contradiction to other supra structures like world religions, rather the contrary: they constitute them, which unite the empirical and theoretical quests.

Hence, water and religion are fundamental in the origin and development of societies and civilizations. As Dawson wrote: 'The great civilizations of the world do not produce the great religions as a kind of cultural by-product; in a very real sense, the great religions are the foundations on which the great civilizations rest.'[21] Water is not only the basis for agriculture and all livelihoods, but the forces and generative processes enabling health and wealth are fundamental parts of cosmological worldviews. And in all religions, water comes from somewhere – physically and spiritually – giving sources in its various forms particular importance before the flows of rivers continue to the sea. Life starts from the sources, literally and metaphorically.

SOURCES AND NATURAL PHENOMENA

'Much that once was is lost, for none now live who remember it […] And some things that should not have been forgotten were lost', the opening sequence in *The Lord of the Rings* starts. 'History became legend. Legend became myth. And […] two and a half thousand years' ago, Herodotus, the Father of History, inquired about the sources of the Nile, without knowing where they were. Herodotus wrote:

> I could not gain any information about the nature of the river from the priests or anyone else. I was particularly eager to find out from them why the Nile starts coming down in a flood at the summer solstice and continues flooding for a hundred days, but when the hundred days are over the water starts to recede and decrease in volume, with the result that it remains low for the whole winter, until the summer solstice comes round again. No one could in Egypt give me any information about this at all, when I asked them what it was about the Nile that made it behave in the opposite way from all other rivers.[22]
>
> As for the question where the Nile rises, no Egyptian or Libyan or Greek I have spoken to claimed to have the definitive answer, except the scribe of the treasury of Athena in the city of Saïs in Egypt – and I got the impression that he was joking when he said that he knew the answer for certain. But what he said was that there were two mountains with sharply pointed peaks between the cities of Syene in the Thebaïd and Elephantine, which were called Crophi and Mophi; between them, he said, rise the springs of the Nile, which are bottomless, and half of their water flows north towards Egypt, while the other half flows south towards Ethiopia [...] Now, if this story of the scribe's was true, all he proved, to my mind, was that there are strong whirlpools and counter-currents there.[23]

His *Histories* incorporated Egyptian legends, which were 2,500 years old when he wrote about them. Although the knowledge of the sources of the Nile was history at one time, it survived only as mythology, but the mythology turned into history like the Nile itself – ever flowing and ever changing, but still the same and different. The mythologies became sources for creating new histories and along the Nile religions developed around the mighty artery of life-giving waters flowing from the interiors of Africa to the Mediterranean Sea. Still, Herodotus has another curious passage where he also writes that the soil in Egypt is 'black and friable, which suggests that it was once mud and silt carried down from Ethiopia by the river'.[24] In other words, it seems that he knew that the sources came from Ethiopia, since he connected the fertile fields in Egypt with the silt coming from Ethiopia. It seems that in antiquity, there were no contradictions perceiving the Nile as coming both from the cataracts and Ethiopia at the same time. Philostratus says, 'This country supplies Egypt with the river Nile, which takes its rise at the cataracts (*Catadupi*), and brings down from Ethiopia all Egypt, the soil of which in flood-time it inundates.'[25]

The waters in the River Nile are binding all people throughout time together; the waters flowing in the Egyptian Delta watering the fields have their ultimate origins in the sources of the Nile in Ethiopia and Uganda, and beyond; in Burundi and Rwanda and the Ruwenzori Mountains and elsewhere in Tanzania and Kenya, since there are innumerable sources and each and every single tributary in the catchment area can be seen as a source flowing downstream. In fact, without all these innumerable sources there would not have been a River Nile, but some sources are more important than others.

Natural phenomena are integrated into the religious realm, in particular when it is something beyond the obvious 'natural', like the origin of river and springs, as Dickson says, 'That pure water should spring from the earth and form into rivers to sustain mankind is a phenomenon that challenges the imagination.'[26] Thus, at the outset there are two crucial aspects – the mysteries at the very source itself from where it originates out of nothing, or from elements like rocks or soils from where the water trickles, and the ways they are forming mighty rivers like the Nile and sustaining whole civilizations. That the ancient philosophers devoted much time and thinking about the sources is no wonder and in particular natural phenomena that were counter-intuitive gave rise to speculation and mysticism. Religious sources have not always been identical with the hydrological sources defining lengths of rivers, or in other words, that the most remote spring is the source of a river. Other hydrological phenomena seemingly counter-intuitive or counter natural – unnatural nature – have also been seen as sources, in fact more important than the mere flow of a river downstream from the most distant origin.

In the ancient Egyptian religion the Nile had its source at Elephantine and the First Cataract where it flowed from a subterranean origin (see Chapters 5 and 6). Herodotus has, as quoted, one intriguing passage where he says that half of the water flows northwards towards Egypt and half southwards towards Ethiopia. This seemingly puzzling information may hint that there was a source in the middle of the river and that there also was a counter-flow running southwards, like the source of the White Nile in Jinja at the outlet of Lake Victoria. A great number of early travellers reported nothing unusual about the river, but a chief engineer of the Egyptian Sudan, M. Chélu, published a book in 1891. He documented all physical features such as the rapids, the cataracts, their beds and measured the extent of the fall of each. He mentions that there was a counter-current, and a very powerful and violent one, which stretched as far as 50 km south. It is remarkable that no other travellers or early geographers have stressed this, if it existed, and it might have been seasonal. However, Herodotus also mentioned that there were strong whirlpools, and one was even commemorated as late as in the 1950s as 'The Whirlpool of Osiris'. Nordén, a Swedish traveller, noted in 1737 that at this place in the Nile it is very 'dangerous to pass on account of the stones which embarrass the channel of the river'.[27] William F. Albright also pointed this out in an article:

> Evidently the prehistoric Egyptians, whose knowledge of the Upper Nile was very limited, noted this fact, and jumped to the conclusion that there were two Niles, rising at the cataract and flowing in opposite directions. In modern times the Maelstrom has been explained in just as naïve a way.[28]

If there was a counter-current or strong whirlpools south of the First Cataract, today nobody can know for sure since, if such natural phenomena existed, it has been flooded by the Aswan High Dam (fig. 4). What is sure, however, is that such extraordinary natural phenomena would most likely have been ascribed with special importance and religious qualities, or at least have been seen as something unnatural or counter-intuitive in all senses of understanding. The ancient Egyptians obviously knew that

4. The Nile at Aswan today.

waters of the Nile flowed from lands further south of Aswan and the First Cataract, but that was not the point from a religious perspective. A religious source can originate, literally, in the middle of a river – in the falls or cataracts at Aswan, for instance. This was also the place where the water abyss came from the subterranean regions in Egyptian cosmology. In Egypt, the name for water abyss was Nun or the proper 'inundation', indicating that different types of water could have the same signification but visualized differently, and the two Nile sources were expressed in hieroglyphs as two serpents pouring water from their mouths.[29]

Thus, at the outset it seems that the scholars in antiquity and the ancient Egyptians had different worldviews with regards to what a proper source was; the former emphasizing hydrology and the latter cosmology. Moreover, it seems likely that during antiquity onwards it was realized by the ancient geographers that there were at least two sources of the Nile – one flowing from the Abyssinian highlands and another from the interiors of Africa. Pliny mentions no less than seven Greek and Roman explorers who travelled in the regions south of Meroe, including the ones sent by Emperor Nero. Pliny had several sources of information, and the fact that the famous expedition sent by Nero probably reached the Sudd indicates that the ancient geographers believed that there were other sources of the Nile than the one coming from the Ethiopian highlands. Hence, Ptolemy's Nile system and his famous map is not an invention of his own, but builds on centuries of knowledge and explorations.[30]

In retrospect, it seems that Strabo was one of the ancients who had most accurate knowledge about the actual flood in Egypt, and implicitly where the source(s) was. He may himself have been travelling as far as the borders of Ethiopia and travelling increased knowledge, although he was surprised that his contemporaries were not aware of the summer rains in the Ethiopian highlands. According to Strabo:

> The ancients relying for the most part on conjecture, but subsequently men having seen for themselves, perceived that the Nile was filled with summer rains when upper Ethiopia flooded, particularly in the most distant mountains; then when the rains stopped, the river flood gradually dies down.[31]

In antiquity, there were numerous popular and competing theories about the Nile flood and all of them had their proponents. One theory emphasized the etesian winds (northerly summer winds of the Mediterranean) in different variants. Thales believed that it drove back the water itself and thereafter it started to accumulate and thereby caused the flood. Euthymenes favoured this interpretation in combination with an oceanic source whereas Thrasyalces argued for a combination with a rain-cloud theory. Pliny shows that these theories continued to flourish centuries later, as he says:

> People have advanced various explanations for the rising of the Nile, but the most likely are either the backflow caused by the Etesian winds which blow against the current river at that time of the year – the sea outside being driven into the mouths of the Nile – or the summer rains in Ethiopia.[32]

A second theory was that the source of the Nile in fact was the ocean, which could cause unseasonable flooding, and this position was favoured by Dicaearchus, Euthymenes and possibly also Juba. A third theory proposed by Anaxagoras was that the flood originated when snow on the high mountains in remote Ethiopia melted. A fourth position was held by Herodotus that the flood was caused by the sun in one way or another. The last category of explanation was favoured by many philosophers like Thrasyalces, Aristotle, Callisthenes, Eratosthenes and Agatharchides, namely that the flood had its origin in the tropical rains. Strabo dismissed all but the latter explanation without arguing why, simply by stating: 'Whereas the fact that the river risings come from rain did not need investigation.' Although we know today that this is the correct explanation, it is unclear how he arrived at that conclusion; in particular, since not only were there many contradicting theories among his contemporaries, but these theories continued to flourish for a long time after Strabo. In any event, Strabo stressed the need for investigating why the rains occurred during the summer and not during the winter as it does on the northern shores of the Mediterranean, and why the rains fell in the southern regions.[33]

Thus, a part of the struggle and confusion in antiquity with regards to the sources of the Nile was how to relate hydrology and mythology. Although the Greeks and Romans also believed in religious water, their cosmologies were different, but more important in this context was the different emphases on hydrological or scientific understanding and measurements of the river's flow and its source. Religiously, however, this is not the most important, unless the hydrological source coincides with the religious one, as with Gish Abay or the source of the Blue Nile. In African cosmologies, 'water is power. It is never dead, in the sense of being unusable or spent. It is life-water when it purifies, it is death-water when it soils,' Diadji says. 'I speak of water as a sign of life, and as a sign of death, but always of water full of Existence, because there is no non-being in water. Thus water is always and everywhere imbued with spirituality.'[34]

Consequently, local sources or bodies of water within a given cosmology are given specific meaning for the people living next to these. In many respects, the search for and knowledge of distant sources are more important for downstream users and countries than for those living nearby, who may not know that the river flows downstream for thousands of kilometres to other people and lands who depend on it in unimaginably different ways – such as Egypt, located in a desert – then as now. Still, the importance of a source goes beyond the basin and is not restricted to people living next to them ascribing specific meanings to these waters, or to ancient Egyptians and even Greeks and Romans in antiquity. Throughout history, apart from scientific and geographical quests, sources and, in particular, the sources of the Nile, had also fundamental importance in Christian mythology and cosmology. Throughout the history of Christianity, the link between the Garden of Eden and earthly Paradise has been established, but not exactly where. In Genesis it is written (Gen. 2:8–14):

> Now the LORD God had planted a garden in the east, in Eden; and there he put the man he had formed. The LORD God made all kinds of trees grow out of the ground – trees that were pleasing to the eye and good for food. In the middle of the garden were the tree of life and the tree of the knowledge of good and evil. A river watering the garden flowed from Eden; from there it was separated into four headwaters. The name of the first is the Pishon; it winds through the entire land of Havilah, where there is gold. (The gold of that land is good; aromatic resin and onyx are also there.) The name of the second river is the Gihon; it winds through the entire land of Cush. The name of the third river is the Tigris; it runs along the east side of Ashur. And the fourth river is the Euphrates.

In the Bible, the term 'living water' is usually seen as 'water of life', and referred to as 'running', 'fresh' or 'springing' water, including 'a well of springing water' and 'living fountains of water'.[35] In the Old Testament, the waters of life have a prominent place, including at least four domains or types of creation waters:

The fountain of the garden of Eden and its connection with the primitive waters of the deep, the flood and the destructive potential of the deep, the crossing of the Red Sea and the sustenance of the chosen people by Horeb's water, and lastly the *fons signatus* of the garden of the Canticles.[36]

In Western poetry and literature, God has been described as 'the great Source, or Fountain', or, for example, as Coleridge wrote in his notebook in 1796: 'Well-spring – *total* God'. In Christian mythology and symbolism, the fountain thus represents the fountain of eternal life;[37] it is not only water, but also divine grace and a spiritual source for heaven. 'When Adam and Eve are expelled from the garden, they lose the tree of life and the waters of life; in the fullness of time, at the very end of the narrative of cosmic history, the tree and waters of life are restored to a redeemed mankind,' Dickson writes. 'This imagery was understood by Renaissance readers to constitute a pattern describing an essential Christian tenet, the renewal or regeneration of the believer made possible by Christ's intervention of time.'[38] As described by John, 'Except a man be born of water and of the Spirit, he cannot enter the kingdom of God' (John 3:5), pointing out that the regenerative water is Christ who is the fountain of living waters,[39] in this context having a fundamental role for baptism as a sacrament:

> The fountain of Eden, therefore, represented the temporal source of life, not only because it was the source of the four great rivers, but most importantly because it was connected with the waters of the deep and hence with creation. Furthermore, its privileged position at the very beginning of the biblical narrative [and when] God proclaims that he will be a fountain of living waters to his people [...] we can expect that the image of the fountain in Eden would be recalled along with other types of the regenerative waters of life.[40]

The divine waters were not limited to the rivers from Eden, but included also wells and deep underground streams. Christ proclaimed to the Samaritan women that he was the true fountain of life, as written by John: 'But whosoever drinketh of the water that I shall give him shall never thirst; but the water that I shall give him shall be in him a well of water springing up into everlasting life' (John 4:14). In fact, Messiah means the 'anointed one'. William Fulke, a biblical scholar and meteorologist, described the rivers from Paradise as such:

> But this river flowing out not of the earth, nor out of the temple of Jerusalem, but oute of the throne of God almighties and of his Christ, doth minister joys of eternall life most aboundantly to the Citizens of the new Jerusalem. They therefore never feare death, which drincke dayly of the river of the water of life.[41]

The cosmological importance of this divine water and river cannot be underestimated, and the Gihon River from Paradise was believed – then as now – to be the source of the Nile. This is the source Gish Abay in Ethiopia. Moreover, the divine qualities of these waters are also partly reflected in the etymology of 'nature' itself and water has thus a fundamental place in Christianity as in most other religions.

WATER AND QUALITIES OF NATURE

Roy Williams once said that 'culture' is one of two or three of the most difficult words to define, because it is a concept fundamental to numerous non-compatible disciplines – perhaps only 'nature' is more difficult to define. Consequently, the concepts of culture and nature have a history of diverse and mutually contradictory ideas,[42] and they have numerous definitions. In this regard, it can be fruitful to search for the original meaning of 'nature', which in this context reveals important aspects of water as an element of nature, but also of the role of water in religion.

The etymology of the word 'nature' comes from Latin – *nasci* – which means 'to be born', 'to spring from', 'to arise' or 'to be produced':[43]

> Nature, then, is the creative matrix from which all things arise and to which they return, the complexity of orders of powers by which these things are upheld and by which each of them, or each type of them, attains its own peculiar attributes and capabilities.[44]

And that water as a peculiar element of nature had special characteristics was without any doubt in antiquity, although different cosmological meanings could be ascribed. According to Seneca:

> All standing and enclosed water naturally purges itself. For, in water that has a current, impurities are not able to settle; the force of the current sweeps them along and carries them away. Water which does not emit whatever settles in it more or less boils. As for the sea, it drags from the depths dead bodies, litter, and similar debris of shipwrecks, and purges itself of them, not only in storms and waves, but also when the sea is tranquil and calm.[45]

Water is always in a flux. The fluid matter changes qualities and capacities wherever it is, and it always takes new forms. This transformative character of water is forcefully used in ritual practices and religious constructions. Water represents the one and the many at the same time, and the plurality of ritual institutionalizations and religious perceptions put emphasis on water's structuring principles and processes in culture and cosmos. Water is hence a medium which links or changes totally different aspects of humanity and divinities into a coherent unit; it bridges paradoxes, transcends the different human and divine realms, allows interactions with gods, and enables the divinities to interfere with humanity. Water is a medium for everything – it has human character because we are humans; it is a social matter but also a spiritual substance and divine manifestation with immanent powers; and, still, it belongs to the realm of nature as a fluid liquid.[46]

The 'natural' characters of water are quite different from other properties in nature, perhaps with the exception of fire.[47] Bachelard writes:

> [Water] can be cursed [...] evil can put it in active form [...] what is evil in one aspect, in one of its characteristics, becomes evil as the whole. Evil is no longer a quality but a substance [...] Clear water is a constant temptation for a facile symbolism of purity [...] it is the one that constantly breathes new life into certain old mythological forms. It gives life back to forms by transforming them, for a form cannot transform itself. It is contrary to its nature for a form to transform itself [... but] water is the most perfect liquid, it is the one from which all other solutions get their fluidity.[48]

From an ecological and religious point of view water can thus be described as benevolent or malevolent, where the former is seen as a blessing or divine gift and the latter as a curse or collective penalty for moral or ritual misconduct resulting in harvest failures, famines and death. Malevolent waters normally occur as devastating floods, too much precipitation such as prolonged rains, the fimbulwinter of snow or the lack of rain; and unsuccessful rainmaking rituals or deliberately withholding the rain is generally seen as evil or as a consequence of malevolent and malignant powers.

In his *Natural History*, the Roman author and philosopher Pliny the Elder writes: 'My subject, the natural world, or life (that is life in its most basic aspects), is a barren one,'[49] and one may add both physically and spiritually. This is one of the fundamental characteristics of water in religion: it gives life and it is about life. Fresh water represents deep ontological relations, and the water-worlds in a society create opportunities for all kinds of constructions. The hydrological cycle links all places and spheres together, and the physical character of water combined with its role as a historical agent enables the medium to link the past with the present and the future.[50]

Also, Pliny's view is interesting from another perspective, since it transcends the dichotomy of culture and nature. Nature is life; a quality of living – growing, germinating, and being – and hence also culture and religion. Water is life and a quality and essence of being human, since the body consists of some 60 per cent water and without it everyone will die within a few days. The extreme power of water as a life-giving force is experienced by all; when somebody faints or almost dies due to absolute thirst, water re-generates strength immediately – no other element has such intrinsic powers.

Thus, water has a unique place in culture, nature and religion. Pliny writes later:

> What could be more amazing than water standing in the sky? [...] This same water falls back to earth and, if one considers the matter, becomes a source of all things that grow out of the earth – thanks to the miracle of Nature [...] Consequently we are bound to admit that all earth's powers are due to the gift of water.[51]

At the outset then, the original Latin definition of 'nature' and its inherent qualities of nature bears many similarities to the qualities of water, or more precisely, nature cannot be understood without a focus on water.

As Eliade pointed out with regards to water on a general level, 'it existed at the beginning and returns at the end of every cosmic or historic cycle; it will always exist, though never alone, for water is always germinative, containing the potentiality of all forms in their unbroken unity'.[52] Or in the words of Victor Turner: 'For African thought [...] embeds itself from the outset in materiality, but demonstrates that materiality is not inert but vital.'[53] Not only is spirituality embedded in materiality, but it is also active and transcending the materiality. Thus, following Eliade again, 'The prototype of all water is the "living water" [...] Living water, the fountains of youth, the Water of Life [...] are all mythological formulae for the same metaphysical and religious reality: life, strength and eternity are contained in water.'[54] The ancient Greeks believed that their gods drank ambrosia – immortality – and Aristotle said that whoever did not drink ambrosia became mortal, because otherwise, how could gods be eternal if they needed food?[55]

From a human perspective, eternal life or existence is hardly possible in this worldly domain, and for humans, Hocart says, immortality is not as we usually perceive it, 'but freedom from premature death and the diseases that cause it and the renewal of this vigorous life hereafter'.⁵⁶ The ritual specialist employing water is often a traditional doctor. That a traditional healer also works as a doctor using medicines is logical given that rituals and medicines traditionally work in very much the same ways. Hocart goes on:

> Ritual has appeared throughout as a method of achieving life. Ritual has at the bottom the same end as medicine, but medicine has a more specialized purpose. Ritual promotes life by promoting everything on which life depends: crops, cattle, children – and also what these depend on: rain and sunshine. Medicine confines itself to what directly affects the body and concentrates on curing illness.⁵⁷

Water, on the other hand, sharing many of the properties medicines have, is more total and encompassing than anything else, and medicines without water are traditionally not working.

These wonders of nature, in particular in relation to life and agriculture, were pointed out by many thinkers in antiquity. In antiquity, there were at least 56 Classical, Hellenistic and Roman authors writing about the properties and beneficiations of the Nile water.⁵⁸ Moreover, 'Creation is procreation, and therefore magical power must have some connection with sexual power.'⁵⁹

In *The Odyssey*, Homer (c. 850 BC) gave the river the name Aigyptos. The name Nile – or more precisely Neilos, seems to first appear in Hesiod's poem *Theogony* (c. 750–650 BC).⁶⁰ Heliodorus, Bishop of Tricca, himself a mysterious figure in history, is the author of *Æthiopica – The Ethiopian Story*. In the introduction he writes, 'Thus endeth the *Ætheiopian* historie of Theagenes and Cariclia [by] the author whereof is Heliodorus of Emesos a citie in Phænicia [descendent] from the Sunne.' In the Ninth Book he writes about the Nile at the feast celebrated by midsummer when the flood increased. The Egyptians believed Nylus (the Nile) to be a god, and the greatest of all Gods, equal to heaven, because he watered their country without clouds or rain that comes out of the air. Nylus is Osiris. They said that Nylus was nothing else but the year: 'Which opinion also the name approved, for if you divide the letters conteyned therein, into unities, if they be put together, will make three hundred sixty and five, and so many there bee days in the yeere.'⁶¹ Thus, an interesting feature of the name is the numerical value of the Greek letters used in it (50, 5, 10, 30, 70, 200), which add up to 365 or the total number of days in a year, indicating that the Nile was everything.⁶² Many ancient sources show the belief in mystical powers of number.⁶³ Heliodorus also wrote that the Nile is called 'Horus', 'the giver of life', 'the saviour of all Egypt, both Upper and Lower Egypt', 'the father of Egypt', 'the creator of Egypt', 'he who brings new mud each year'.

Seneca wanted to 'separate the Nile from ordinary rivers; it is unique and exceptional.'[64] He also said:

> There is another type of water which we Stoics like to think began with the universe. If the universe is eternal, this water, too, always existed. Or, if there was some beginning for the universe, this water also was set down along with everything else. You ask what water this is? The ocean and any sea from it that flows between the lands. Some judge that also the rivers whose nature is explicable take their beginning along with the universe itself; such as the Danube and the Nile, rivers so vast and so remarkable that they cannot be said to have the same origin as the other rivers.[65]

Moreover:

> This, then, is the classification of waters, as it seems to some: of the waters that are later than the ocean some are celestial, others are terrestrial. Celestial waters are discharged by the clouds. Some terrestrial waters swim on the surface, so to speak, and creep along the top of the ground; others are hidden.[66]

Seneca also pointed out:

> The idea appeals to me that the earth is governed by nature and is much like the system of our own bodies in which there are both veins (receptacles for blood) and arteries (receptacles for air). In the earth also there are some routes through which water runs [...] and nature fashioned these routes so like human bodies that our ancestors even called them 'veins' of water.[67]

According to Philostratus, among the Egyptians 'The Nile is the chief object of worship, for they regard this river as land and water at once.'[68] He continues:

> Nature has raised up this noblest of rivers before the eyes of man and has arranged it to flood Egypt at the very time the earth, especially parched by heat, may draw in the waters more deeply [...] It brings both the water and the soil to the sandy and thirsty ground [...] It aids the fields for two reasons: it both inundates them and coats them with mud [...] the remarkable characteristic of the river is that while other rivers wash away the land and exhaust it, the Nile, much larger than the others, is so far from eating away or rubbing away the soil that on the contrary it adds to the soil's vigour [...] Egypt owes to the Nile not only the fertility of the land but the land itself.[69]

All of Egypt was made up of the Nile: the silt created the land and the water gave it life – both qualities and outcomes of the flood, which created

5. The annual inundation of the Nile.

an extremely fertile environment (fig. 5). And the sources were religiously also well known to be located at the Cataracts at Elephantine or Aswan. In a conversation between Apollonius and Nilus, after Nilus inquired for how long a time Apollonius would stay among the naked sages, Apollonius answered:

> So long as the quality of their wisdom justifies anyone in remaining in their company; after that I shall take my way to the cataracts, in order to see the springs of the Nile, for it will be delightful not only to behold the sources of the Nile, but also to listen to the roar of its waterfalls.[70]

And Philo of Alexandria wrote:

> Egypt is a land rich in plains, with deep soil, and very productive of all that human nature needs, and particularly of corn. For the river of this country, in the height of the summer, when other streams, whether winter torrents or spring-fed, are said to dwindle, rises and overflows, and its flood makes a lake of the fields which need no rain but every year bear a plenty of crop of good produce of every kind.[71]

A 'river', Philo also said, 'is generic virtue, goodness. This issues forth out of Eden, the wisdom of God, and this is the Reason of God; for after that has generic virtue been made. And generic virtue waters the garden, that is, it waters the particular virtues.'[72] Moreover, 'For God willed that Nature should run a course that brings it back to its starting-point, endowing the species with immortality, and making them sharers of external existence.'[73]

Diodorus, too, stressed that 'the Nile surpasses all the rivers of the inhabited world in its benefactions to mankind.'[74] He also adds other qualities as a consequence of this noble river, if one is to believe his comparison of Egyptian farmers to those elsewhere:

> For since the water comes with a gentle flow, they easily divert the river from their fields by small dams of earth, and then, by cutting these, as easily let the river in again upon the land whenever they think this to be adventageous. And in general the Nile contributes so greatly to the lightening of labour as well as to profit of the inhabitants [...] For, generally speaking, every kind of field labour among other peoples entails great expense and toil, but among the Egyptians alone is the harvest gathered in with very slight outlay of money and labour.[75]

The flood was also a time of feasting and religious activities. Diodorus notes:

> The masses of the people, being relieved of their labours during the entire time of the inundation, turn to recreation, feasting all the while and enjoying without hindrance every device of pleasure. And because of the anxiety occasioned by the rise of the river the kings have constructed a Nilometer at Memphis, where those who are charged with the administration of it accurately measure the rise and despatch messagees to the cities, and inform them exactly how many cubits or fingers the river has risen and when it has commenced to fall. In this manner the entire nation, when it has learned that the river has ceased rising and begun to fall, is relieved of its anxiety, while at the same time all immediately know in advance how large the next harvest will be, since the Egyptians have kept an accurate record of their observations of this kind over a long period of terms.[76]

As will be seen later, from the earliest Egyptian dynasties, the records of the Nile were documented, and indeed at least in later periods the Nilometers were also shrines or temples.

In religion, nature in this sense – as life and what sustains life – is but one side of the coin. Life is what humans ultimately value, but life comes at a high and inevitable price: death. In order to maintain life, the life of other organisms is sacrificed on a daily basis, whether it is grains or animals.[77] Living necessitates death, and in the end death waits for all living creatures, humans included. Following Joseph Campbell

> we may say, then, that the interdependence of death and sex, their import as the complementary aspect of a single state of being, and the necessity of

killing – killing and eating – for the continuance of this state of being, which is that of man on earth, and of all things on earth, the animals, birds, and fish, as well as man – this deeply moving, emotionally disturbing glimpse of death as the life of the living is the motivation supporting the rites around which the social structure of the early planting villages was composed.[78]

Everyone has to kill to live and to maintain life. Not only animals have to be killed, but even harvesting plants and crops can also be perceived as killing. A sacrifice of a living being is conducted as an offering to a deity in exchange of some divine or supernatural gifts or favours, and essential in this understanding are the concepts of 'vital force' or 'energy',[79] but importantly, 'it is not the life of the animal that is at issue but rather the life in the animal'.[80]

Religiously, one may stress that it is not a worship of nature as such for two reasons. First, 'nature' as a whole is too broad and all-encompassing, including everything, so a worship of nature as a unity would imply that everything was holy or sacred, and thereby nothing. The holy or the sacred has meaning only in contrast to what are not holy or revered; the profane or the secular in one way or another. Trees, rocks, sand, air, water, etc. – or everything – cannot be equally religious. If that was the case, humans would live in a holy totality, and the closest we can imagine such an existence is for instance the Paradise of Eden. By definition, in heaven everything is holy, including water, and that is why the river Gihon flowing in paradise is utmost holy and the outlet of this river on earth at the source of the Blue Nile in Ethiopia – Gish Abay – is a direct link to heaven and God's grace (see Chapter 2). Second, as Hocart has emphasized, there is no such thing as 'nature worship'. It is not nature as such that is worshipped, even when a tree or a stone is venerated, but a tree in African religion is no more worshipped than the timber used in Christian Churches symbolizing the original cross on which Jesus was crucified. Contrary, the divine may embody and materialize *within* a stone, statue, tree or water, but the very stone, statue, tree or water has no soul as such; it is the mere presence of the divinity that is venerated.[81] Importantly, not everything has power or being imbued with power. As Hocart says, 'Ritual would be utterly pointless if everything were charged with power. It is based on the belief that some things have power and others have not.'[82] The natural world of religion is *differentiated*, which is also essential for the analysis of religion as a social process.[83]

A divinity may choose to embody a person like a healer, or a stone or waterfalls, but without this divine embodiment, the stone or the person is simply just any stone or person. Importantly, even if a divinity chooses to manifest in a stone or in water, it is not only there, in the same vein as Christians believe in Jesus everywhere despite worshipping him in churches. The gods are obviously invisible, Obeyesekere argues, but still visible:

> Not only are they present in a particular community, but they may be present if invoked in other communities and shrines at the same time. They must be in this place, and that, in the then and the now. They therefore obviously cannot be present *in person*; rather, they are there in *essence*.[84]

Or as Campbell wrote: 'A god can be simultaneously in two or more places – like a melody, or like the form of a traditional mask. And wherever he comes, the impact of presence is the same: it is not reduced through multiplication.'[85]

Still, the perception of veneration or worship of nature has caused many misconceptions throughout the history of religion, such as idolatry, but in Christianity and traditional religions alike there is a difference between sign and signifier. A god may be visible or comprehensible through the forces of nature, whether it is successful harvests or plentiful rains, and some gods or spirits have defined and restricted forces in certain spheres, like controlling rain but not rivers' inundation. However, weather phenomena, for instance, are testimonies of the powers of certain invisible divinities, but not the essence of the divinities themselves. In this regard, the almighty Christian God works in the same way; the Deluge was a testimony of his powers, but the Deluge *was not* God. From another perspective, in this world gods and divinities have few other options than to work through nature and materiality in a broad sense, in one way or another. Apart from transferring humans straight to heaven, all divine revelations or interventions on earth have a material dimension from penalty and suffering of the body (or the release of it), the life-giving rains and successful harvest, plagues or the Deluge, and so on. Or in other words, 'Religion is fundamentally material in practice'[86] and water plays a fundamental role in religious practices, precisely because it is life, and those who control the sources of all human life – whether divinities or not – have utmost power.

Nevertheless, the role of water has largely been omitted in religious or theological studies, and part of the reason is that life in this realm on earth is just a prelude to an eternal existence in one way or another in the other world from a religious perspective. This life is just a means, although a very important one, towards a greater goal from a Christian or Muslim perspective, or at least a more permanent or enduring existence in traditional religions. Hence, cosmologies are predominantly occupied with the other world and not so much with the life-giving properties of water on this side defining religious practices. Still, the varying water-worlds are important for humans and consequently included in their own perceptions of religion. Herein lies also some challenges of defining religion. If culture and nature have been difficult to define, religion has been even more so. From a religious perspective, culture and nature can be seen as parts of religion, but inferior since religion signifies a larger whole in time and space – cosmos – existing both before and after this world, with all its culture and nature: religion is a supra-entity without external boundaries beyond and above this world governed by more powerful structures or divinities.

However, by claiming that the religious world is often believed to be greater than this world does not mean the worldly matters are beyond the realm or importance of the divinities in whatever form, rather the contrary. Apart from the gods, divinities or ancestors, in many religions although not all, humans are at the epicentre of the religious world, for the better or worse, or so it is often believed and perceived by the believers themselves since religions ultimately are about their lives in a broad sense. This directs the attention to the history of religions and how scholars have approached religion, and more often than not gods and divinities and their works have not necessarily been the focus, and as a consequence, the divine or life-giving qualities or properties of water given by the divinities have often been neglected.

THEORIES OF RELIGION WITHOUT WATER[87]

The history of religion or the sociology of religion may start with many great thinkers, but there are several reasons why Georg Wilhelm Friedrich Hegel (1770–1831) is a fruitful point of departure, as Merleau-Ponty stressed: 'All the great philosophical ideas of the past century [nineteenth century] – the philosophies of Marx and Nietzsche, phenomenology, German existentialism, and psychoanalysis – had their beginnings in Hegel.'[88] Hegel's perception of African history, religion included, shaped large parts of the nineteenth- and early twentieth centuries' discourses. Hegel stated that Africa 'is no historical part of the World; it has no movement or development to exhibit. Historical movements in it – that is in its northern part

– belong to the Asiatic or European World.'[89] Africans were not only perceived as barbaric and as having evolved behind the rest of humanity, but Africans were 'capable of no development or culture, and as we see them at this day, such have they always been'.[90] However, the ancient Egyptian civilization represented a 'problem' with regards to understanding how such astonishing developments could have taken place in Africa. This 'Egyptian problem' was solved by excluding the civilization from black Africa. According to Hegel: 'Egypt will be considered in reference to the passage of the human mind from its Eastern to its Western phase, but it does not belong to the African Spirit.'[91] Even the distinguished Oxford professor Hugh Trevor-Roper wrote as late as 1965 that Africa has no history: 'at present, there is none, or very little: there is only the history of the Europeans in Africa. The rest is largely darkness, like the history of pre-European, pre-Columbian America. And darkness is not a subject for history.'[92] Samuel W. Baker (1821–93), who was the first white explorer coming to Lake Albert and seeing the Murchison Falls, claimed in 1867 that the Nilotic people had no religious belief at all: 'Without any exception they are without belief in a supreme being, neither have they any form of worship or idolatry; nor is the darkness of their minds enlightened by even a ray of superstition.'[93] From seeing Africans as having no religion, in the following anthropological discourse Africans were credited with religion, but for a long time it was seen as 'primitive religion', and indeed, still is by some Christian pastors and preachers, being African or not. Later, Africans have been perceived as 'notoriously religious', yet another cliché separating Africans from other believers, although also held by Africans.[94]

Although debated and discussed, Hegel's idealism and dialectics have generally been seen as reverted or turned upside down by Karl Marx (1818–83) and his materialism, and Marx' thoughts were firmly rooted in the Hegelian tradition. Although Marx did not write much about religion, he is famously renowned for the phrase that religion is 'the opium of the people'. The following sentence is, however, more telling and illustrates Marx' view about religion, although most often omitted in discussions of Marx: 'The abolition of religion as the illusory happiness of the people is required for their real happiness.'[95] For Marx, religion was ideology, and the ideology was legitimating exploitation and structures of dominance. Marx did not use the pyramids as examples supporting his view, although today it is estimated that a pyramid like the one of Khufu was built by some 30,000 men over a period of 30 years.[96] Others have, on the other hand, used the pyramids as examples, and Pliny the Elder was particularly harsh about the pyramids in Egypt:

> They are a pointless and absurd display of royal wealth, since the general view is that they were built either to deny money to the kings' successors and the rivals plotting against them, or else to keep the people employed. These men showed much vanity in this enterprise. The remains of several unfinished pyramids survive.[97]

Or as Rudyard Kipling wrote, maintaining the stereotype of Egypt, 'Egypt is one big undertaker's emporium.'[98]

Today, Pliny's approach can firmly be analysed within Marxism or materialism as an approach. Not only does it omit the religious role and importance of the pyramids and the role of the Nile in the Egyptian cosmology (Chapter 5), but the ancient Greek and Romans' curiosity and questions have also been challenged. They were visiting Egypt when the tradition was living and they could have asked all kinds of interesting questions and solved some of the largest mysteries in the world. Why did they not ask *why* the pyramids were built? And when they did, why did they accept seemingly pointless answers? The nineteenth-century French Egyptologist Auguste Mariette was particularly furious about Herodotus: 'I detest this traveller [...] [he] tells us gravely that a daughter of Cheops built a pyramid with the fruits of prostitution. Considering the great number of mistakes in Herodotus, would it not have been better for Egyptology had he never existed?'[99] Although Herodotus writes in other places that he does not believe the stories he was told or that they are foolish tales, with regards to the evilness of Cheops prostituting his own daughter it seems that he retold them in good faith. Not only that, according to what he was told the pharaoh's daughter also wanted to be remembered, and everyone who had intercourse with her had to give her one stone, as well as other payments. Of these stones were her pyramid built and each side measured 150 ft.[100]

The Great Pyramid of Khufu is the world's largest pyramid and the last of the existing seven ancient wonders of the world. The enormous monuments thus point to the role of materiality in religion and Marx' emphasis on the 'production of material life' conditioning or determining ideology and social structures, religion included. From another perspective, Herodotus is attributed with the most famous phrase 'Egypt is the gift of the Nile', but most probably it stems from Hecataeus of Miletus who travelled through Egypt almost a century before Herodotus.¹⁰¹ In any event, the paramount importance of the Nile as the artery of life for all welfare and prosperity in Egypt is without any doubt. This also raises questions regarding the roles of different water-worlds in shaping perceptions of religion, and whether it is a form of determinism to include nature and water in religious explanations, or whether it is the contrary, that water is at the very core of the substance of religion in practice?

The German sociologist Max Weber (1864–1920) did not work in the Hegelian tradition and his works, including those of Durkheim, were challenging historical materialism. Max Weber's *The Sociology of Religion* has been seen as '*the* most crucial contribution of our century [twentieth century] to comparative and evolutionary understanding of the relations between religion and society, and even of society and culture generally'.¹⁰² According to Weber:

> To define 'religion', to say what it is, is not possible at the start of a presentation such as this. Definition can only be attempted, if at all, at the conclusion of the study. The essence of religion is not even our concern, as we make it our task to study the conditions and effects of a particular type of social behavior.¹⁰³

Two of Weber's central aspects in his analyses were rationalization and theodicy. The notion of rationalization implied both an increasing systematization of ideas and religious beliefs and a decline of magic and mysticism. In *The Protestant Ethic and the Spirit of Capitalism*, Weber argued that the Protestant ethic created a capitalistic spirit because magic was eliminated from the sacraments.¹⁰⁴ Although this process to a large extent took place with Protestantism, it does not fully apply to religious water, and varying concepts of the powers and capacities of holy water continued to exist even within Protestantism.¹⁰⁵

What is more important along the Nile, even today the mysterious powers of water not only flourish within traditional African religions, but also within Christianity and Islam. Despite possible rationalizations in other aspects of religion, the divine or magical qualities of water continue. Still, nature and the water-world were included in Weber's thoughts, at least implicitly. The elect could be measured in terms of success and accumulation of wealth based on the belief that obedience to God's law and commandments would ensure prosperity. As Thomas says, 'the course of worldly events could [...] be seen as the working-out of God's judgments. This was but a refinement of the more basic assumption that the material environment responded to man's moral behaviour.'¹⁰⁶ Here the water-worlds are part of the picture, since devastating floods or withholding the precious and life-giving rains have also been seen as God's penalty for sinful behaviour. This points to the other central aspect of Weber's thoughts: theodicy. God is almighty and has unlimited powers over his creation, but why then is God allowing both good and evil at the same time? While the almighty God may penalize his children by withholding the life-giving waters or creating floods like the Deluge, it is within the believed sphere of a just God (fig. 6), but there are still other realms where water is in the domain of evil, like the properties of the devil or witches.[107] In short, Weber aimed to explain religious conditions and effects of certain types of social behaviour, and his approach has been described as 'methodological individualism', since he emphasized individuals and their social actions rather than social structures, although not as functions but as meaning and causes.[108]

If Max Weber's approach can be described as methodological individualism, the sociologist Émile Durkheim (1858–1917) can be seen as working within the framework of methodological collectivism. Apart from that, his influence on social sciences and anthropology is undisputed, and scholars like Mary Douglas, Victor Turner, Edmund Leach and Claude Lévi-Strauss have worked within the tradition he founded, although there are disagreements with regards as to what extent. Durkheim's approach to religion can partly be understood by his own beliefs, or more precisely, his absence of religious beliefs. Evans-Pritchard pointed out that Durkheim was not only an unbeliever, but a militant atheist and propagandist.[109] His famous *The Elementary Forms of Religious Life* (1915) rests on the same premises that he put forward in *The Rules of Sociological Method*, first published in 1895, that social facts can only be explained by other social variables.[110] Natural variables and the physical world were left out as research topics in the humanities and social sciences. C. P. Snow later characterized this scientific divide as the 'two cultures' – a universe of humanities as opposed to the natural sciences.[111] The approach that social facts can only be explained by other social facts has been a dogma in sociology and from this perspective water in general, and water and religion in particular, has been omitted, simply because water has been seen as a natural variable; at best given subordinate relevance if seen as a social construction. That said, also given his atheist stand, Durkheim was more positive to the variety of 'other' religions than Christianity than many of his contemporaries. In *The Elementary Forms of Religious Life*, Durkheim writes:

In reality, then, there are no religions which are false. All are true in their own fashion; all answer, though in different ways, to the given conditions of human existence. It is undeniably possible to arrange them in a hierarchy [...] [but] All are religions equally, just as all living beings are equally alive, from the most humble plastids up to man [...] So when we turn to primitive religions it is not with the idea of depreciating religion in general, for these religions are no less respectable than the others. They respond to the same needs, they play the same role, they depend upon the same causes; they can also well serve to show the nature of the religious life, and consequently to resolve the problem which we wish to study.[112]

6. *The Deluge*, Genesis 7:23. Gustav Doré, 1880.

Whereas Durkheim worked within (and established) the sociological tradition explaining religion as and with social factors, yet others have focused on more psychological perspectives. Sigmund Freud (1856–1939) analysed religion from a psychoanalytical approach focusing on, among other factors, the Oedipus complex and relations to the (patient's) father.[113] While this approach is fundamentally reductionist in its basis and not very useful in comparative religious analyses, the psychological experiences in religious minds are equally undeniable. Still, others have gone beyond psychology as a discipline. Rudolf Otto (1869–1937) emphasized precisely the religious experience and stressed what he called the 'numinous' – the experience of the sacred or the holy.[114] Mircea Eliade (1907–86) too stressed the irreducible character of religion and religious experiences, which are impossible to grasp or reduce to explanations by means of physiology, psychology, sociology, etc.[115] Eliade's phenomenological approach is to understand religion on its own terms: 'Understanding is ecstatic and contemplative, not reductionist and analytical. Understanding is given to us, from somewhere within ourselves or from the outside, but it is not known through thinking.'[116]

This approach is quite the contrary of Durkheim as an atheist and makes religious studies difficult for non-believers, if not impossible. Nevertheless, although one may be sympathetic to this position where one aims to understand religion on religious criteria only, all religious phenomena are historical and all data are conditioned and consequently religious phenomena cannot be understood outside of its 'history'.[117] From another perspective, 'Religious beliefs are not immune from explanation in nonreligious terms,' Kevin Schilbrack says. 'Religious communities speak and act in ways that can be redescribed in terms of what they take as true, a redescription that makes certain kinds of explanation and evaluation possible.'[118] And history is not only His Story in a strict religious sense, but more importantly in the daily life is the water-world people live and inhabit, which is the source of all life.

Although the origins of religion might be before, behind or beyond history from a religious point of view, all religions are historically situated in time and space among humans and consequently need to be understood on these premises as well. In the real world the metaphoric and symbolic world is omnipresent and open for interpretation, and religion can also be seen as a model *of* 'reality' and a model *for* 'reality', as Clifford Geertz (1926–2006) said. Thus, religion defines the 'rules of the game', at least in terms of cosmic and final answers and solutions, most often expressed in complex systems of symbols, and how humans should live a moral life. But as he also pointed out, 'no one, not even a saint, lives in the world religious symbols formulate all of the time, and the majority of men live in it only at moments', highlighting the challenges of distinguishing secular and profane spheres and how religion is part of culture and social structures, or the other way around. In 'Religion as a Cultural System', Geertz argues that there have been no theoretical advances of major importance in the study of religion since Durkheim, Weber, Freud or Malinowski, because 'no one even thinks of looking elsewhere – to philosophy, history, law, literature, or the "harder" sciences – as these men themselves looked, for analytical ideas.'[119] Water is one such area where one has to search, not because it is also within the domain of hard sciences, but because it is both nature and culture and the universal and the particular at the same time, and it constitutes large parts of religious belief systems and practices. More important than that, water may challenge academic dogmas; water is fundamentally about human life and hence a human concern since time immemorial. As a universal concern for humans, water has also been incorporated in the divine realms as believed by people themselves.

The reason for this short tour in the history of the sociology of religion, which is incomplete not only with regards to the scholars presented and their thoughts, but also all others who could have been included, is to illustrate parts of complex and varied approaches to the study of religion, even before any definitions or attempts to define religion have been put forward. The aim here is not to criticize these respective scholars, with the exception of Hegel's view of Africa and African history, which has been thoroughly criticized in post-colonial theory, but to point out that all these theories are reductionist in one way or another, and therefore, they are also partly right on their own premises and equally insufficient. In order to get a broader and more comprehensive understanding of religion, one needs all these perspectives and new ones. With water as a point of departure and in this case the River Nile, one may attempt to approach a more holistic understanding of religion.

JAJA BUJAGALI AND THE POWERS OF THE GODS

When the Bujagali Dam located only 8 km north of the source of the White Nile eventually was inaugurated in 2012, it was delayed for more than a decade and the final price tag was almost one billion US dollars. Apart from the general and global anti-dam activism against large dam construction and corruption allegations which terminated the first phase of the project, a unique aspect of this dam project was that to a large extent it was the powerful river spirit in the Bujagali Falls that blocked the construction of the dam. Although the name of the spirit in Bujagali Falls has various spellings, 'Budhagaali' will be used when referring to the spirit and Jaja Bujagali in referring to the medium or healer. Since this dam was partly dependent upon World Bank funding, the construction had to incorporate social and environmental assessments, and the Budhagaali spirit was at the core of this. From 2001 to 2011 no less than three grandiose appeasement and relocation ceremonies took place, but they were not conducted by Jaja Bujagali, but another healer, Nfuudu (see Chapter 3).

Jaja Bujagali, who is one of the most renowned and powerful traditional healers, said in one interview before the dam was constructed:

> If they want to relocate [spirits] to another place, will they carry the whole river or falls to that place? [Do] they really think that a [spirit] is like a goat that can be transferred from place to place? [...] The spirits would never allow the dam to be built.[120]

If the dam was built, people would die, he argued. Moreover, he stressed that a river spirit could not be moved except of its own free will (fig. 7). The powers of water and water spirits in the profane sphere are evident when one spirit through its medium could block an almost billion dollar dam for years. The process and the ritual drama behind the dam and its relation to other water spirits along the Nile in the Busoga cosmology will be elaborated on later, but as an introduction to the abovementioned theoretical approaches to religion, it can illustrate some points.

From Marxism or materialism as an approach, the dam contractors would probably agree that 'the abolition of religion as the illusory happiness of the people is required for their real happiness', or in other words, electricity, industrialization and modernization are the sources for development, wealth and prosperity leading people out of the poverty trap, not the local medicines provided and made efficient by a powerful

7. Jaja Bujagali.

healer. And although a partly privately financed dam controls the modes of productions and hence could be criticized from other Marxist perspectives, the mere fact that a dam could be blocked by an invisible spirit is from this perspective an illusion.

Following Weber, 'the essence of religion is not even our concern, as we make it our task to study the conditions and effects of a particular type of social behavior.' The social and political consequences of Jaja Bujagali and the way he conveyed the spirit's messages, according to him, is clear – the dam was delayed for a decade although he failed to terminate it once and for all. And although Weber argued that modernization and rationalization would lead to a decline of magic and mysticism, these were very much present in the twenty-first century at the Bujagali Falls, and such perceptions were even favoured by contemporary anti-dam activists.

The sociological tradition from Durkheim onwards explaining religion as and with social factors and variables alone cannot account for a water spirit like Budhagaali. Although the spirit itself is invisible, as all spirits and consequently understood as a social construct, it was the force and the powers of the waterfall that gave testimonies to the supremacy of the spirits. Without the thundering cascades of explosive waters as external nature, the perceptions of the water spirit would not have originated.

While a Freudian perspective aimed at understanding why and how a spirit may speak to and embody a healer, partly based on the life-histories of the healer, is important and valuable, it cannot explain the specific forms and the ecology of the water spirits.[121] The perspectives of Otto and Eliade, where religion can only be experienced and not rationally understood, also holds true. As Jaja Bujagali explained to officers from the World Bank, 'the Spirit speaks through him. Non-believers may view this response as nonsense, believing that spiritual mediums are speaking for themselves.'[122] This is, however, not a dialogue, but when the spirit embodies the healer he becomes possessed. From yet another perspective, Geertz is also right when he says that religion can be seen as a model *of* 'reality' and a model *for* 'reality'. More than anything else the spirit shaped the reality of the dam construction with all its delays and grand ceremonies, and even global dam discourses between dam developers and anti-dam campaigners. Studies of symbolism are obviously important in religious studies and the healers' compounds are full of ritual paraphernalia believers hardly know the full meaning of, since they are not initiated and not supposed to know.

As all these brief examples show, the above theoretical perspectives are perfectly fruitful for studying aspects of religion depending upon the questions asked. While studying the totality of religion is probably not possible, and perhaps not even desirable since the complexity of empirical realities is so great and varied that it will be a form of reductionism because one has to choose some aspects, by bringing water into the picture it may open up new possibilities for understanding practices at work and how religion works. With the Budhagaali spirit as an example, everything centres on water and the waterfalls in particular. Similar scenarios exist all along the Nile and a water and religion perspective is therefore not a substitute for other approaches, but a possible entrance to combine the fluidity of other perspectives while being sensitive to the empirical realities on the ground or literally found in water. Following the Nile from the sources to the sea may enable such an approach.

WATER AND RELIGION – FUNCTION OR SUBSTANCE?

While there is no general accepted definition of what religion is, the problem of trying to define religion has nevertheless played a central role in developing the sociology of religion as a discipline since it has enhanced knowledge of religion.[123] On a general level, religion focuses on answering three main questions: 1) What becomes of us after death? 2) How should we lead a moral life? and 3) How and why were the universe, life, and human beings created?[124] These are, however, overall, existential questions, and do not help much in defining religion and are relevant for non-religious people as well.

In 1913, Henry S. Nash struggled with defining 'religion':

> To attempt in these days a definition of religion may seem like taking a wanton risk of intellectual confusion. Even a rough classification of religions is difficult. The mass of data is so vast, the varieties of religion so manifold, that no sooner has a scheme of classification been established itself than it begins to sag under the weight of material thrown upon it. But, as things are with us, no classification is better than a working hypothesis into which, as the constituent element, enters the knowledge of its own mortality.[125]

One century later, defining religion was as difficult as before, despite all the scholarly developments and discussions. In his book *Religion Without God* from 2013, Ronald Dworkin defines religion, as the title of the book suggests, without God: 'Religion is deeper than God. Religion is a deep, distinct, and comprehensive worldview: it holds that inherent, objective value permeates everything, that the universe and its creatures are awe-inspiring, that human life has purpose and the universe order',[126] and within such a perspective the belief in a god is but one alternative.

Broadly, religion and definitions of religion can be seen from functional or substantive approaches. Functional or pragmatic approaches identify cultural phenomena as religious when certain problems are seen as belonging to or possible to be solved by the divine spheres. Durkheim belongs, for instance, to this category. This approach focuses on what people get out of religion and what types of problems religion can solve. Substantive approaches focus on the ontological reality of certain phenomena, like the existence of gods, divinities and ancestors, and the beliefs and rituals concerning the interaction between this and the other world. Augustine is clearly in the latter category when he said that religion means 'worship of God'[127] and also Edward Tylor when he wrote that a minimalist definition of religion is 'belief in spiritual beings'. Otto and Eliade also belong to this category.

Although the different positions have caused a heated scholarly debate for more than a century, it is possible, as Schilbrack argues, to combine these two positions, not because of convenience but because it grasps the religious phenomena in a better way. If one rematerializes religion in this worldly sphere, one may distinguish between realities that are available and visible to our senses, and those that are not. The empirical realities, like suffering and drought, are equally as real as the non-empirical realities for believers, like the belief in God's forgiveness or judgement at Doomsday. Schilbrack thus defines religion as 'forms of life predicated upon the reality of the superempirical [...] Religious communities are those that adopt values they do not believe depend on human or other empirical forms of agency',[128] which may function as a working definition and analytical approach, although no definitions should be seen as absolute.

Whether particular African river spirits or transcendental divinities like God in Christianity or Allah in Islam, they are all clearly substantive or ontological while at the same time may fulfil functional tasks benefiting humans and local communities, if they want, but they may also choose not to do so. Bruce Trigger distinguishes between transcendental religions such as Judaism, Christianity and Islam and cosmogonic religions, and African traditional religions may partly fit in the latter category in this classificatory scheme. In the former 'the omnipotence of a single god renders that god's existence totally independent of his creation, [and] sacrifice becomes merely a token of individual and collective human gratitude for the deity's favours'.[129] 'Cosmogony', on the other hand, is derived from two Greek words, *kosmos* and *genesis*. *Kosmos* refers to the order of the universe and/or the universe as order and *genesis* to the process of coming into being.[130] Importantly, individual deities in cosmogonic religions are generally viewed as dependent on humans and supported by humans through sacrifices. In short, humans and gods depend on each other.[131] This has salience for the types of rites being conducted, specifically sacrifice or prayer, the two fundamental acts of worship. Broadly speaking, sacrifice is more common in cosmogonic religions and prayer in transcendental religions, although both types of worship may occur in both religious types.[132] Still, it is difficult to label many traditional African religions as strictly cosmogenetic religions, since these divinities may also exist independently of their own creation.

More importantly, perhaps, is that it is possible to combine the functional and substantive approaches to religion not only from an academic perspective, but also from a religious one as perceived by the believers. That gods and divinities work and may interfere in this world among humans for the better or worse is indisputable, so the functional approach is obviously correct on certain premises. But these divine engagements in the human world are dependent upon the substantive approach, that the gods and spirits exist ontologically and that it is possible for humans to intervene with them in an asymmetrical and inferior relationship. Thus, in practice, a substantive approach can exist without a functional approach, but a functional approach cannot work unless the spirits and divinities exist.

Although supreme gods like God and Allah are independent of their own creation, this goes to a large extent also for African traditional divinities and ancestral spirits, but in varying degrees. Indeed, some also argue that African traditional religion is simultaneously monotheistic and polytheistic at the same time, since there most often is one supreme and unrivalled supreme being, often the creator of the universe and all living beings, and at the same time innumerable other spirits and ancestors in multiple forms.[133]

Among the Sukuma along the southern shores of Lake Victoria in Tanzania, for instance, there is a Supreme Being. Although he is not almighty and supreme in the Western sense or in Islam, everything is contingent on his force despite the fact that he is not responsible for maintaining the world, including procuring the life-giving rains in response to rainmaking rituals. He is basically too superior to bother with mundane things and the well-being of humans. He is mainly concerned with nature as a whole and not controlling humans and natural fluctuations, which are the realms of the ancestors and the non-ancestral spirits. Consequently, humans cannot contact the Supreme Being directly (the non-ancestral spirits and the ancestors may), but they can intervene very much and easily with the ancestral spirits, which after all were their descendants and the ancestors as spirits want to be remembered and respected.[134] This is an important difference, not only from a water perspective, but in all realms of human life. The ancestors have historically been very active and in close contact with their descendants. The ancestors are superior to humans – ever existing regardless what humans do – but they are commonly believed to have the power to actively intervene in the here and now for the better or worse.

A fundamental part of African traditional religions and their cosmologies is *power*. The power of and in cosmos is nevertheless generally ambivalent and ambiguous; it is neither good nor bad, but both, and it is a constant struggle to balance the various forms of power. The very same source of power can thus be a source for good and bad, depending upon the intent of the practitioners; it can heal a person but it can also inflict malevolence upon the same being:

> Power is both spiritual and material and often explicitly so. Spiritual power is believed to lead to material power – political influence and wealth [...] Overall, spirit power is assumed to permeate the material world, which makes this world both something to be wary of and something that can be used in interaction with the spirits.[135]

It is a common feature in most religions that the superior divinities are believed to care for humans and their believers in one way or another, although the ways this happen may largely be concealed or imperfectly understood by the believers. During the drought in the Horn of Africa in 2011, in a village outside Mwanza on the southern shores of Lake Victoria in Tanzania, I met an old woman who had become a Christian. According to her, this was one of the three worst droughts she had experienced in her whole life. Despite being a Christian, she still believed in the ancestral tradition of rainmaking and recalled that in the old days it worked and provided the life-giving rains. But rainmaking traditions had largely disappeared in this area and it was quite impossible to conduct these rituals anymore, not only because of the sacrifices and the expenses involved, but also since hardly anyone believed in the powers of the traditional rituals anymore it was difficult to find a proper rainmaker these days. As a hungry Christian starving during the drought, she went to the Church where the priests prayed for food and prosperity. But as she laconically commented, they left the Church more hungry than when they came. The Christian God did not deliver rain and food; the former ancestral and rainmaking tradition was believed to do so (fig. 8).[136]

This poignant example, and there are many others, illuminates parts of the cosmic principles and differences between transcendental gods and other divinities with regards to the ways they may or may not interact and intervene in the daily lives and what matters the most for agriculturalists: the precious life-giving rains for bountiful and successful harvests. The fact that religions are believed to work and function in one way or another is unquestionable. Concepts such as 'work' and, in particular, 'function' have, however, as part of the criticism of structural functionalism, gained negative connotations in the history of anthropological thought and largely been abandoned. In *Ritual and Religion in the Making of Humanity*, Roy Rappaport stressed that 'neither religion "as a whole" nor its elements will, in the account offered to them, be reduced to functional or adaptive terms'. He continued:

8. The life-giving rains after the 2011 drought in Tanzania.

> An account of religion framed, a priori, in terms of adaptation, function or other utilitarian assumptions or theory would [...] paradoxically, defeat any possibility of discovering whatever utilitarian significance it might have by transforming the entire inquiry into a comprehensive tautology.[137]

While there are legitimate reasons why functionalism, and in particular in religious studies, has been dismissed (since the functionalism of the 1950s and 60s was based on flawed premises), one should not confuse academic exegesis with real perceptions and aims of believers praying or conducting sacrifices. The religious aspects of function is more consequential, as it is said in Deuteronomy (4:40):

> You shall therefore keep His statutes and His commandments which I command you today, that it may go well with you and with your children after you, and that you may prolong your days in the land which the Lord your God is giving you for all time.

It is not a function humans decide, but a consequence of God, but as it is emphasized here too, God *may* – whatever God decides is uncertain and it partly depends on human obedience and piety. In other words, the divine consequences may have functions, but these functions and consequences are often quite different from humans' intentions or the consequences they wish and pray for.

That the Christian God is fully capable of providing both rain and food is undisputable. In the Old Testament, rainmaking was the utmost testimony of the powers of the gods. In the battle between the Jews and the Baal worshippers on Mount Carmel (1 Kings 16–45), the ultimate proof regarding which god was superior and indeed the only one was through rainmaking.[138] In the desert, the Baal-worshippers failed, whereas when Elijah prayed and sacrificed, Yahweh let the precious rain fall. Being a supreme divinity, God may also use his powers to completely bypass the hydrological cycle and provide food miraculously. One of the most famous passages in the New Testament is when Jesus fed the 5,000 hungry with two fish and five bread (John 6:1–14). Thus, the question is not whether gods and divinities work, function and can provide everything the believers pray or ask for, but the structures of different belief systems in which these interventions are believed to take place and on which premises humans are thought to actively partake and potentially bend the divine powers for their own benefits, or why the divinities choose not to intervene and let people starve or die. All these interactions take place within overall cosmological frameworks where the asymmetrical relationships between divinities and humans establish religious hierarchies and worldviews combining how the Otherworld is related and integrated into this world, which in daily life is rather practical. Water is fundamental in the daily and practical life, but so are many other things as well, and therefore it is important to understand why and under which circumstances some fundamental matters are ritualized and elevated above all other important and fundamental issues.

While the criticism of functionalism has been massive, I think there is one important aspect which has not been discussed sufficiently, which Lord Raglan mentioned briefly in a sentence in the foreword to Arthur Maurice Hocart's book *Social Origins*: 'if all customs and beliefs [...] had been evolved by them in response to their own needs, we should expect them to be far more tenacious than they actually are'.[139] In other words, they should be much more uniform, but one could also anticipate that if only function was the function, so to speak, there would be limits to symbolic elaboration and mythic developments, since functionally speaking, there would not be any need to complicate things and make extensive mythologies and metaphors beyond the mere function. Nothing could be further from truth, and it also shows the futility of reducing or criticizing any functional aspect of ritual as functionalism.

Weber points out, at least implicitly, that gods may also choose to change the divine gifts according to culture and social developments. Rain 'was one of the rewards promised by Yahweh to his devotees, who were at that time primarily agriculturalists [...] God promised neither too scanty rain nor yet excessive precipitation or deluge.'[140] And while he emphasizes 'that any particular economic conditions [being] prerequisites for the emergence of a belief in spirits does not appear to be demonstrable', he nevertheless cannot escape the economic foundation of religion. In Egypt the regulation of the Nile was the source of the king's strength:

> In the desert and semiarid regions of the Near East this control of irrigation was indeed one source of the conception of a god who had created the earth and man out of nothing and not merely fashioned them [...] A riparian economy of this kind actually did produce a harvest out of nothing, from the desert sands. The monarch even created law by legislation and rationalization, a development the world experienced for the first time in Mesopotamia. It seems quite reasonable, therefore, that as a result of such experiences the ordering of the world should be conceived as the law of a freely acting, transcendental and personal god.[141]

Thus, Weber seems to acknowledge economy in a broad sense as a basis for religious development although rejecting a narrow understanding. In Hinduism, Lakshmi is the goddess of wealth, fortune and prosperity, which include not only material wealth but also spiritual wealth. In some symbolism, she is even portrayed holding a jar with money. Although Hinduism is not a money religion, it emphasizes, as do most religions, human wealth in a broad sense, including spiritual enlightenment. In other words, the specific administration and organization of wealth does not create religion, but wealth in general is intrinsic to social understanding of religion in general. As Thomas Piketty says:

> The truth is that economics should never have sought to divorce itself from the other social sciences and can advance only in conjunction with them. The social sciences collectively know too little to waste time on foolish disciplinary squabbles. If we are to progress in our understanding of the historical dynamics of the wealth and distribution and the structure of social classes, we must obviously take a pragmatic approach and avail ourselves of the methods of historians, sociologists, and political scientists as well as economists.[142]

From a social perspective, it can be seen as what Marcel Mauss said with regards to the gift: it is a 'total social phenomenon' because it involves legal, economic, moral, religious, aesthetic and other dimensions.[143] Or as Weber stressed, 'the nature of a stratum's religiosity has nowhere been *solely* determined by economic considerations',[144] but on the other hand, as he showed in *The Protestant Ethic and the Spirit of Capitalism*, religion may create specific conditions for further economic developments and in particular mentalities having feedback mechanisms shaping the whole economy and development.[145]

The social aspect of work in Africa and more particular in rural Kenya is elaborated by Shipton:

> Work in equatorial Africa is something you do with others if you can, alone if you must, and in midday sun only when desperate. Sharing work can be conceived in more than one way. It can be seen in an economic idiom as exchanging labor, in a social and experiential one as keeping company, or in a political one as practicing some sort of solidarity or making a statement about ideology. It is a sign and a seal of religious commitment, since much work on farms is done by church groups, and whether or how often you show up can count you in or out.[146]

Importantly for this study, thus, agriculture as a livelihood from the cradle to the grave and beyond in ancestral realms cannot be compared to Wall Street economy. In other words, religion does not arise from economy seen as free from culture and society, but religion may include economy because it is part of grander concepts of wealth. Thus, in religion, the economic part of wealth can be seen as one part of cosmic generative forces. But this relates also in another way to the study of the role of water and religion in agricultural societies and the development of religion. Weber once pointed out that the religion of peasants has often been looked down upon; in fact, the early Christians perceived the rustic as the heathen (paganus), and the peasants were basically Christians of a lower rank according to the doctrine of the medieval church. Religious thinking and development took place in monasteries and urban churches.[147] This has implications for this study. Although baptism is a church practice, the religious water-worlds analysed here have partly developed apart from the main doctrines, in particular in water contexts based on farmers' understanding and changing lives. Still, all these partly different and partly overlapping and similar perceptions have mutually influenced each other, and today also agrarian rituals are part of the official doctrines.

Water is at the heart of agricultural economies, but religious water is much more and has never been reduced to mere substance and survival: it is life in the broadest sense. In other words, water in traditional agriculture represents completely different beliefs than for people selling groceries at the supermarket, although it is about food in both settings. Hocart writes about cosmic rites:

> The rituals [...] have as their purpose to produce or increase the necessaries of life. They are acts of creation. They create more [...] buffaloes, more clouds, or whatever desired objects may be. The cosmic rites create more of everything that man may need, and as the food supply depends on the proper working of the whole world, such ceremonies create the world.[148]

Or more particularly with regards to agriculture, 'the essence of these rites is that increase of food is secured by identifying men and objects with the food it is intended to produce or something that has power over that food.'[149] Life, and water as life, should not be reduced to function, but to meaning, and as meaning of life there are no limits to the depths of mythology and symbolism of water and the elaborateness of cosmologies.

On a general level, local deities and cosmologies are often believed to better be able to solve any kind of practical problems here and now than transcendental religions and divinities, despite the latter being omnipotent and omnipresent. Still, in a cosmology like the Busoga at the source of the White Nile, there are many spirits that are not particularly active (see Chapter 3), but there are always other spirits that it is possible to engage with for any specific and practical purpose. Some spirits are believed to be more powerful and deliver the particular wishes of the devotees if the appropriate rituals are conducted, and from a practical point of view it makes sense to engage with the spirits and healers who have the greatest reputation for being powerful and deliver what is urgently needed for prosperity and betterment. Such practical strategies by the believers and practitioners have to be included in cosmological worldviews, because daily life is full of miseries or mundane problems that have to be solved. Religion is about life, but not only life after death.

Barth argues that the most fruitful way to approach cosmology is to perceive it as 'a living tradition of knowledge – not as a set of abstract ideas enshrined in collective representations'.[150] Tradition can be seen as 'the transmission of customs or beliefs from generation to generation, or the fact of being passed on in this way [...] a long-established custom or belief that has been passed on from one generation to another'.[151] From this perspective, what matters the most for farmers is the arrival of the annual rains in the right amounts at the right time. Agriculturally, the arrival of the rains is a hydrological matter from a profane perspective, but if this sphere is part of religious or cosmological realms, the life-giving rains are often part of rainmaking rituals. As a point of departure, this may exemplify structural premises and processes of the relations between local and transcendental religions in practice and the ways they work.

Healers or conjurers not only work differently than gurus or priests in world religions, as Barth points out, but their knowledge transfers are quite opposite with different cumulative effects on how traditions are transmitted. The conjurer initiates his novices into sacred knowledge, not necessarily articulated, but often performed. The novices are supposed to be transformed through participation in the rite itself, and as such the knowledge becomes embodied. The guru, on the other hand, teaches, explains, instructs and elaborates – he *shares* his knowledge. Moreover, he always needs more or new knowledge to share. Thus, the guru's knowledge is radically decontextualized and logical, and represents a different way of knowing.[152] Similarly, the local environments in which the world religions originated are equally decontextualized when the religions develop and spread across continents, and in this process new meaning and importance is ascribed to the ecologies and water-worlds.

Despite that a local healer may claim that his or her powers or the powers bestowed upon him or her by various spirits are unlimited and almighty, in practice they are restricted and limited to certain areas defined geographically and spiritually, or more precisely by the specific water-world. The respective healers may claim that their particular spirit or spirits are the most powerful in the world and beyond, but so do many healers, and in the next kingdom, chiefdom or ethnic group there are other local spirits believed to be equally strong. Often the local spirits work within bounded territorial units, whether it is a chiefdom or an ethnic group. While this limits the powers on one hand, the spatial demarcation of the geographical spread of the powers of various local spirits seems to enforce the very powers within that territory; they may solve anything and everything, including weather modification and enable different forms of witchcraft for the better or worse. In such contexts, the local environment is to a large extent incorporated into the cosmology since this is the primary context of life and living. Local spirits are often seen as more powerful and practical than transcendental gods in daily life.

In world religions like Christianity or Islam, following Barth's knowledge transfer by the guru, the most important knowledge is distributed and shared by all, ideally by each and every one on the planet. The knowledge is not necessarily abstract, rather the contrary – it is very specific, such as the Ten Commandments – but it is a shared knowledge with relevance for all regardless of whether believers live in deserts, rainforests or in the arctic. A world religion works partly above and beyond the local environments since it covers all and cannot privilege one specific ecology or waterworld over another; for example, emphasizing rainmaking. Still, during the Old Testament times when the religion was still a rather local religion and located to desert environments, water had a strong and more prominent role. In the Hebrew Bible there are more than 580 direct references to water and many more to rain, rivers, wells and dews. Similarly, in the Qur'an the word 'water' occurs more than 60 times, 'rivers' over 50 and 'the sea' over 40, whereas 'fountains', 'springs', 'rain, 'hail', etc. occur less frequently.[153] But when religions grew out of their specific ecological contexts of origin, the role of particular environments and water-worlds were downplayed in favour of more theological exegesis or divine events that could include all, such as the crucifixion of Jesus. In academic terms, religion changed focus from practice to theology or from function to substance, broadly speaking, although the works of God were evident in other spheres, like the creation from *ex nihilio* in Genesis.

However, despite worldwide theology, universal eschatology and cosmic soteriology, even world religions have to relate their beliefs and practices to local contexts, since believers live in specific contexts and these water- and life-worlds are where religion operates. This has several implications. Holy water coming from heaven or the source Gish Abay in Ethiopia is given great importance and has become a place of pilgrimage. Apart from various divine places where holy water pours out, also rain and the weather are within the religious realms, but this water is not holy as such. Priests in Tanzania and Ethiopia and elsewhere may also pray to God for the life-giving rains when it is desperately needed, but the absence is understood differently in transcendental religions than within rainmaking cosmologies both with regard to the actual inherent qualities of water and the divine processes at work. This directs the attention to divine waters or water in religion in its many facets.

DIVINE WATER AGENCY AND HOLY, SACRED AND NEUTRAL WATERS

The term 'holy water' is so commonly used that it is often more concealing than revealing because the divine waters are so complex and take so many forms, and very few of them are 'holy' in a strict sense, of course depending upon definitions. Still, more than mere theoretical exegesis, it is worthwhile to explore what 'holy water' means and its religious implications. In order to understand the religious role of water, one could distinguish between 'holy' and 'sacred'. In general, 'holy' and 'sacred' are often seen as identical and used interchangeably, but the terms imply different relationships to the divine. Most people say 'holy water', but not 'sacred water', and this difference is important. Theoretically, as Oxtoby pointed out, 'holiness' refers to the divinity and what is derived from the divinity as attributes, whereas 'sacredness' points to consecrated items, 'respected or venerated objects but not the divine itself and not to persons as individuals'. Moreover, one says 'the holy Bible', but the 'sacred books of the East',[154] and this relates directly to the ways and by whom the divine revelations are revealed. The difference lies in whether the scriptures are truly seen as divine revelations or as being compiled and written by sages and priests at a later stage; the content might be the same, but the religious authority differs.

'Holy water' thus implies a special and particular relationship to the divine: it is identical with the divine, at least partially. In Hinduism, Mother Ganga is truly a holy river encompassing everything in the religion, and the water itself *is* the goddess. This perspective is fundamental to understanding the role of holy water in religions. The water may be the very divinity itself and Hinduism is a water religion *per se*. On the other hand, holy water may take numerous forms, even in Christianity. As will be discussed in Chapter 2, in the Ethiopian Orthodox Church water is seen as holy. The beliefs in the holiness of water among the vast majority of the people in the Lake Tana area may be linked to Gihon as the divine river in heaven and in the baptism of Jesus by John the Baptist in the Jordan River. Gihon as a divine river is mentioned in both the Bible and the Qur'an. When Jesus was baptized in the Jordan River, he transferred holiness to the water as a substance, and hence, all water is holy. Gods and divinities may transfer holiness to any kind of substance, but water is the most common form. Such water, although holy, is different from, for instance, Ganga, which is solely a water goddess, and not all divine powers and qualities are embodied in water in Christianity. Nevertheless, the actual baptism of Jesus and the role of baptism have made water holy in Christianity, because the sacrament was institutionalized by Jesus through his immersion in water. Still, the function and use of holy water in whatever profane sphere may differ, despite the fact that certain types of water in both Christianity and Hinduism are holy. Even holy water may be conditioned on this worldly side; it might be used as holy in a Christian baptism when officiated by a priest, but it may not bless animals or cure infertility of cattle, although the latter is also important for farmers living of their husbandry. The mere fact that a certain item or in this case water is invested with direct divine qualities does not imply that humans can use it for whatever purposes apart from the original function as believed to be defined by God himself. That humans do so, however, is another thing, and throughout European history holy baptismal water has been stolen from churches for other means, including apotropaic purposes. This points to the fluidity of the qualities of holy water in particular; if it works in one defined sphere it might also work in another, devotees may believe, since it is holy, despite that priests say it is a sacrilege.[155]

Even in Christianity there are many types of waters and all of them are part of the divine sphere in one way or another. The purifying waters (by torturing) like the Deluge or in Hell are neither holy in the common sense nor sacred, although they are invested with cosmological properties. Holy water enabling divine grace like the holy (Catholic) water used in baptism is in a different category. On the other hand, in Protestantism and Calvinism, the water in baptism is not holy, but the spiritual outcome is the same since the Word works parallel to the sacraments (although Luther himself saw the water as holy). Precious rains for successful harvests, wealth and well-being is yet another category of water. It is neutral in essence as mere water, but the spiritual grace is the very presence of the right amount at the right time: God lets the rain fall and there are numerous references that he has and can withhold it too, if he wishes, and the same principles are testified to in Islam as well. In arid areas, this bears similarities to more traditional rainmaking practices, but with the notable exception that in local cosmologies this is believed to work in practice and that transcendental gods seldom intervene in such daily or yearly water issues (see Chapter 4).

Importantly, all the above qualities and divine processes with regard to water appear in ecologically more 'water neutral' contexts in the sense that these do not refer to specific natural phenomena – for example, particular springs, annual inundations, irregular rains among different villages, forces of waterfalls, etc. – although ecological differences are incorporated on a broader scale, such as the difference between the barren deserts in Egypt dependent upon the Nile and the life-giving rains in Israel. Thus, at the outset, then, by using Christianity as an example, there is on one hand a whole water cosmology unrelated to specific ecologies (such as the creation waters or the rivers in Paradise), but, on the other, there are yet other cosmologies directly relating to specific phenomena of the Nile, such as Gish Abay (see Chapter 2) or the divine miracles of the annual flooding in Egypt in Christianity (see Chapter 6). If transcendental religions like Christianity and Islam have at least two parallel cosmological perceptions working hand in hand, one ecologically context free and the other originating from specific water features in nature, then it is no wonder that this relation is even more intimate in local or traditional religions, which have developed in particular ecologies where all life and well-being depended upon specific water types and their changing relations throughout the year.

The source of the White Nile originating in the middle of the river at the outlet of Lake Victoria, and possibly also the Nile at First Cataract in ancient Egypt, are particular phenomena in nature which cosmological meaning is ascribed to. There are yet other dimensions to this. It seems that at least from the later periods of the Egyptian civilization even the divine water originating from the abyss at the First Cataract changed cosmological qualities and properties as it flowed downstream towards the sea.[156] This represents another form of holy water – even the character of the holiness or the divine waters may change qualities and properties as the water flows, and subsequently enable different purposes and rituals.

A last challenge is how to conceptualize water spirits or deities living in water without the water itself being holy. Again, the goddess Ganga unites all these perceptions and she is somehow the most perfect water deity: she is water and water is Ganga, at least at the most cosmologically auspicious places like Varanasi, and hence the water is holy. The Christian God, on the other hand, is not a water God, but the almighty may transfer some of his powers to water, like in the Catholic conception of the baptismal waters. Thus, some water, but not all, and only in particularly ritualized contexts, is holy. Then there are other spirits living in water like the Budhagaali spirit in the Bujagali Falls or Nalubaale in Lake Victoria, and innumerable other spirits along the course of the Nile and its lakes. The force and sound of the Bujagali Falls give testimonies to the powers of the Budhagaali spirit and it is truly a river spirit. Still, it moves freely around on land and wherever it wants; after all – gods are gods, spirits are spirits, and humans are humans, but unlike transcendental gods like God or Allah who 'live everywhere', the Budhagaali spirit has its 'home' in water and particularly in the Bujagali waterfalls, or today in the reservoir after the dam was completed. And although he too is 'almighty' in his local context, this is not because the water is holy as such, but because he is a powerful spirit. The forces of the waterfalls proved the power of the spirit, but according to the healer embodying this spirit – Jaja Bujagali – the spirit is still as strong as before, even though the falls have been dammed and it now lives in the reservoir. A spirit's power is not dependent upon physical materialization, since spirits are spirits, but the force of a waterfall may visualize and convince the adherer of the spirit's power.

A study of the religious Nile from the sources to the sea may hence start with a concept of 'holy water' as a point of departure and analytical approach for probing into the rich variety of water perceptions, mythologies and cosmologies. However, as with the very term 'religion' having a certain bias, water in religion and divine spheres take numerous forms and functions transcending other definitions of religions and the concept of 'holy water'. The concept of holy water works best in the major world religions, but as seen with Christianity, even in this religion there are many types of religious water that are not holy in a strict definition. Importantly, even though the waters in, for instance, the Bujagali Falls cannot be labelled 'holy' in the same way as the waters originating at the spring Gish Abay in Ethiopia, that does in no way imply a derogatory view of local cosmologies, rather the contrary for a number of reasons.

Since the very same waters may have many varying qualities and properties depending upon where, when and used by whom – holy, sacred, neutral, and even evil – it is the differences and changing divine powers and consequences that are the central focus in the different water cosmologies. Water is a unique element in the sense that it is always both *universal* and *particular* at the same time, 'and shared ideas of water seem to have encouraged religious beliefs and practices, making it possible to identify underlying structures in the use and beliefs of water'.[157]

It is also about how religious ideas and conceptions flow like water, following the river or the hydrological cycle, or not – in many cases the spread of beliefs have not followed the water courses but on foot on land. Often as the water or the perceptions of water flow, they change meaning and cosmological importance. While the water at the source of the Blue Nile is utmost holy at the very spring, this particular holiness is limited to the source and the water further downstream is not imbued with the same holiness. The Nile is not a holy river all along its course in Christianity because it consists of much more and very different waters. The absence of making the whole river holy when the source as the origin is holy, is yet another peculiar phenomenon of the Nile. In other cases one single drop of holiness can transfer holiness to the greater whole, but not in the Christian or Hindu Nile. In Bradford in the UK the River Aire, a polluted and industrial river in the city, was in 2002 turned into 'a sort of holy Ganges in Bradford' where the ashes of the departed could be immersed. It became a 'substitute' river for the Ganges. While this was possible in Britain, it was not possible in Jinja at the source of the White Nile (see Chapter 6). Thus, the very same origin water, in this case the Ganges, may have different ritual and religious functions far away from the source.

It is the totality of all these different religious conceptions and beliefs that make the Nile the legendary river that it is. Although the Nile quest and the searches for the sources since antiquity onwards enhanced the fame and mystery of this most celebrated river, it did not end with the Western rediscoveries of the sources. The legacy continues, and then, as now, the mythological greatness of the Nile is inseparable from the religious role water has had and still has from the sources to the sea.

CHALLENGES AND CONTENTS

After this rather lengthy introduction to water and religion, it is time to follow the religious Nile from the sources to the sea. This is not, however, a straightforward task. Before Speke came to the source of the White Nile in 1862, 'The usual and most methodical mode of describing a river [was] to commence at its source, and to follow its course down the entire stream, noting its various tributaries as they consecutively join in,' Beke wrote in 1847. But, he commented, 'this method is [...] forbidden us in the case of the Nile',[158] primarily because of the challenges in the Sudd in Sudan. Although the hydrology is now well-known, concepts of the religious Nile do not always follow the hydrological flow in time and space, and today, for instance, Christianity is prevalent in the whole Nile basin and consequently in many cases it is necessary to include a broader perspective when discussing particular places and bodies of water in their various forms.

The very character of water itself is also complicating the procedure and narrative. While the searchers for the sources have primarily emphasized the most remote source of a river giving the total length in a hydrological perspective, from antiquity onwards it has been explicitly clear and discussed that the ultimate sources of the Nile, and rivers in general, is the rain from the sky or heaven. Thus, one approach could have been to start with the rains in the Ruwenzori Mountains, and then turn the emphasis to Lake Victoria and the proper Nile successively, but rain is important everywhere from the sources to the sea, even in the barren deserts in Egypt where there is hardly any. Explaining the absence of rain, and the exceptional occasions when it comes, is also within cosmological spheres, and in order to gain a broader picture of water and religion throughout the basin it is the relation between the different main types of water – sources, lakes, rivers and rain – that must be emphasized and analysed.

Then there are the empirical and chronological challenges. This is not a problem as such, since 'data' comes from Latin meaning 'what is given',[159] and the empirical data at hand is what one has to use, and new data and perspectives later enables other histories and interpretations. Still, the empirical base is uneven and scattered in time and space. Parts of the Buganda lake history were first documented and written by Speke and Grant during their 1860–3 expedition and for larger parts of the following century it was other explorers, colonial administrators and missionaries documenting most of the oral traditions. Regarding the source of the Blue Nile and the Lake Tana traditions in Ethiopia, there have been scant references to the religious practices throughout the centuries since the first Portuguese missionaries came there around 1615. As a consequence, the empirical material of both the sources of the Blue and White Nile is to a large extent based on my own fieldwork. This gives the analysis a contemporary emphasis although with longer historical trajectories linking the current perceptions and practices with religious and mythological pasts. To some extent this also highlights the importance of the religious Nile, since today's relevance and pervasiveness of beliefs build on centuries and even millennia of traditions.

Egypt, on the other hand, represents quite the opposite. From the ancient Egyptian civilization going back five thousand years and throughout the millennia with changes of religions, not only is the material culture extremely rich, but so are the written sources. Together, these empirical limitations and possibilities make it impossible to strictly follow the Nile as it flows in time and space. Moreover, since the Nile basin covers an area of almost one-tenth of the African continent, some areas, types of water and time periods are covered and discussed more than others. Still, given the legendary and mythological status of the Nile River, I attempt to discuss the most important and interesting aspects of the religious Nile by following the river's flow from the sources to the sea as much as the data allows, although the religious beliefs and practices literally flow back and forth in time and space along the river.

The interpretative challenges are obviously huge when it comes to water and religion, particularly in the past. Unlike hydraulic structures like a dam or canal, which are clearly material, to a large extent the religious aspects of water are in its *use*, and by definition, the actual use of fluid water leaves very few traces since the water flows away. The next three chapters focus therefore on ethnography, either documented primarily by myself or others, bearing in mind that these are living traditions having long historic trajectories which may span hundreds and perhaps even thousands of years back, although having been constantly changed and renegotiated throughout history. Then the journey moves further back in history by using archaeological and other historic sources.

Chapter 2, 'The Source of the Blue Nile and Lake Tana in Ethiopia', starts with Gish Abay – the divine source from which the waters of Paradise flow – thus linking heaven and earth. In particular, this source has a special role in Christian mythology and cosmology, but also Lake Tana has been ascribed with great religious significance. The monastery islands in the lake were core areas of the Christianization process in this part of Ethiopia and, according to legend, the Holy family visited Lake Tana after staying in the deserts of Egypt. Today, the religious perceptions of holy water have a prominent role in the Ethiopian Orthodox Church, and the celebration of the Timkat festival or the commemoration of the importance of Jesu baptism is the most important festival. Still, the same waters also have other cosmological meanings. The source of the Blue Nile was also a stronghold for the traditional religion in the area and lavish ox sacrifices were conducted. Nowadays animal sacrifices to the river still take place, but it is a disappearing tradition. Among the indigenous group the Woyto, water is everything and their cosmological beliefs are structured around their river and lake lives. In the river lives their main and benevolent spirit Abinas, providing everything for his devotees and in the recent past an omnipresent hippo-cult was part of Abinas' realm.

Chapter 3, 'From Lake Victoria to Murchison Falls in Uganda', addresses the various water spirits from the lake through the outlet and along the Nile to Murchison Falls. Starting with a historic description of the nineteenth century among the Buganda and Lake Victoria, there seems to have been a strong continuity in the living traditions of the river spirits up to today. A detailed ethnographic description is presented of the healers and their spirits in the Busoga cosmology from the source to Bujagali and Itanda Falls. This is put in the context of dams destroying the waterfalls where the major Busoga spirits live. The Bujagali Dam and the rituals aiming to appease or relocate the Budhaagali spirit is discussed and also the fierce rivalry between the healers Jaja Bujagali and Nfuudu who both claimed to be the spirit's embodiment. In traditional religion, however, as in many others, there are also darker sides, and the role of witchcraft and extreme sacrifices aiming to please the water spirits are analysed. The spirits are not only benevolent, but they might be malevolent and bloodthirsty too; neither good nor bad, but both. This is also evident in the Murchison Falls, which has a very special place in Uganda's recent history and the civil war. The water spirits held court at the falls and instructed Alice Lakwena, a local Acholi healer who became possessed by the

Christian spirit Lakwena, to take up arms and stop the war. Although she failed and eventually was defeated, the spirits at these falls are still powerful and represent a source of utmost spiritual powers, including witchcraft.

Chapter 4, 'The Sources in the Sky and Rainmaking', starts with the Upper Nile basin and the Ruwenzori, directing the attention to rain in Congo, Rwanda, Burundi and Kenya, and Tanzania south of Lake Victoria and in Sudan. While rain drains into the streams forming the Nile River proper, the majority of the people in the basin do not live along the main river courses. In sub-Saharan Africa, then as now, smallholder and subsistence agriculture is the main basis of livelihood. This puts specific emphasis on the arrival of the annual rains at the right time and in right amounts for a successful harvest. However, in these regions there is not only great inter-annual variability in precipitation, but also within a year and from villages to villages. This unpredictable agro-water availability has throughout history been attempted to be controlled by invoking the ancestors and spirits. Rainmaking is thus not an ecological technique procuring rain, but a religious practice whereby the ancestors or divinities provide the life-giving waters if appropriate propitiations and sacrifices are made or if the ancestors are pleased with their heirs and the community at large. Rainmaking has also to be seen in larger cosmologies controlling the flows of energy in cosmos, which is not restricted to only rain. Blocking the vital forces of life may have violent consequences, and examples from Rwanda and historic Sudan are used to exemplify how societies are structured around controlling the life-giving forces and waters. This directs the attention to Egypt.

Chapter 5, 'The River Civilization in the Desert', analyses the ancient Egyptian kingdoms from a water perspective in relation to the sun cult in a chronological perspective going back to the origin of the civilization. During the first two dynasties there were massive human sacrifices as part of the kings' funerals, which bear similarities to sacrificial killings in a rain cosmology. With the Pyramid age it seems that a religious change took place where everything was focused on the Nile and the yearly inundation. By using the material culture and the monumental architecture, the analysis aims to combine mythology and ecology by looking at the Nile itself. The Nile was the artery of life in Egypt. The living King and Pharaoh was Horus, and when he died he became Osiris, the dead King of the

Nether World. Osiris also appeared as the divine power immanent within the Nile, and particularly within the waters of the flood. This embodiment of the Nile was believed to be real and intimately connected to death, and in fact, the waters were the divine blood and life-juices from which everything and all life arose. The inundation was seen as the liquids running from Osiris' decaying corpse. The Nile and, in particular, the flood was designated as Osiris' efflux or discharge, which directs the attention to the colours of the Nile. Although the two main branches of the Nile are usually called the White and the Blue Nile, these colour descriptions are not accurate for the physical properties of the river during the inundation: in Egypt the river was green, red and white, and the different properties and qualities of the hydrological Nile are analysed in a religious perspective.

Chapter 6, 'Water and World Religions Along the Nile', also starts with Egypt, but with the later periods and the continuities in beliefs structured around the Nile and its annual flood with an emphasis on the origin of monotheistic religion and the role of Moses. Following Egyptian beliefs, early Christianity continued many of the same perceptions and practices, but the life-giving qualities and properties were Christianized and seen as miracles of God. In the following periods, Muslims also continued these practices and perceptions, but then as part of Islam, and as late as the nineteenth century there were many rituals, although changed throughout the millennia, that had strong similarities to those in ancient Egypt. Thus, the waters of the Nile shaped also important parts of Christianity and Islam. These religious beliefs and perceptions spread across the Mediterranean Sea to Europe and beyond, but rather than following the religious Nile out of the African continent, the analysis will return to the sources. Not only Christianity and Islam are important religions along the Nile, but there are Hindus too, and parts of the ashes of Gandhi were immersed at the source of the White Nile. While the Nile is not a holy river among the Hindus, water is, and the analysis concludes by a comparative discussion of water and religion in traditional cosmologies, Christianity, Islam and Hinduism.

The religious Nile is thus a source to understanding origins and developments of religion over time as perceived and practiced by believers without a strong focus on scriptural or interpretative theology and eschatology. Water matters and the life-giving waters are not only a human concern, but in many cases they are the utmost testimonies of active gods and spirits and the most precious gift they can provide to their devotees. The water of the Nile flows as it always has done, then as now, but at the same time the river has been continuously changing – in velocity, amount, duration of the inundation and colours. And all along the river's course there have been particular water phenomena in nature; counter flows, sources in the middle of the river, sudden sources originating in hills to disappear as miraculously as they came, gentle and havocking rains, silent and violent waterfalls, and much more. While this analysis will mainly stand on land where people live emphasizing water and the river, since it is impossible from an academic perspective to embody the river and follow its flow throughout the ages, a poet may, on the other hand, imagine how it would be. While not emphasizing the divine qualities of the water as such, as I do in this book, James Thomson in his poem *A Voice from the Nile* takes a stance and perceives how it would be for the Nile to see endless numbers of people and different religions along the banks throughout history and how they have related to the river's life-giving waters. Different religions come and go, but the Nile remains and all religions are shaped by the river. James Thomson writes:

> [...] The pyramids and Memnon and the Sphinx,
> This Cairo and the City of the Greek
> As Memphis and the hundred-gated Thebes,
> Sais and Denderah of Isis queen;
> Have grown because I fed them with full life,
> And flourish only while I feed them still.
> For if I stint my fertilising flood,
> Gaunt famine reaps among the sons of men
> Who have not corn to reap for all they sowed,
> And blight and languishment are everywhere;
> And when I have withdrawn or turned aside
> To other reals my ever-flowing streams,
> The old realms withered from their old renown,
> The sands came over them, the desert-sands
> Incessantly encroaching, numberless
> Beyond my water-drops, and buried them,
> And all is silence, solitude and death,
> Exanimate silence while the waste winds howl
> Over the sad immeasurable waste.

Lo, I look backward some few thousand years,
And see men hewing temples in my rocks
With seated forms gigantic fronting them,
And solemn labyrinthine catacombs
With tombs all pictures with fair scenes of life
And scenes and symbols of mysterious death [...]
[...] Tremendous hieroglyphs of secret things;
I see embalming of the bodies dead
[...] Then I flow forward some few thousand years,
And then see new temples shining with all grace,
Whose sculptured gods are beautiful human forms.
Then I flow forward not a thousand years,
And again see a woman and a babe,
The woman haloed and the babe divine;
And everywhere that symbol of the cross
I knew aforetime in the ancient days,
The emblem then of life, but now of death.

Then I flow forward some few hundred years,
And see again the crescent, now supreme
On lofty cupolas and minarets.
Whence voices sweet and solemn call to prayer.
So the men change along my changeless stream,
And change their faiths; but I yield all alike
Sweet water for their drinking, sweet as wine,
And pure sweet water for their lustral rites [...]

[...] And I through all these generations flow
Of corn and men and gods, all-bountiful,
Perennial through their transientness, still fed
By earth with waters in abundancy;
And as I flowed here long before they were,
So may I flow when they no longer are,
Most like the serpent of eternity:
Blessed for ever be our Mother Earth.[160]

2 The Source of the Blue Nile and Lake Tana in Ethiopia

MOUNTAINS OF THE MOON IN ABYSSINIA AND THE SOURCE OF THE NILE

In Antiquity, there were many authors writing about the snows feeding the Nile. Aeschylus (525–456 BC) wrote of 'Egypt nurtured by the snow', Anaxagoras (c. 500–428 BC) and Euripides (c. 484–407 BC) reported that the Nile flood came from snow melting upstream, and Ptolemy (c. AD 150) spoke of the 'Mountains of the Moon' where snow fed the lakes at the sources of the Nile. But were these lakes in the interior of Africa south of Equator or perhaps in Abyssinia? The first visitor to Ethiopia discussing snow was the sixth-century Egyptian monk Cosmas. At Adolis, the port on the Red Sea, he described an inscription on a stone chair where a third-century Aksumite king speaks of the Semien as a land of mountains, 'difficult to access and covered with snow, where the year is all winter with hailstorms, frosts and snows into which a man sinks knee-deep'.[1]

Although most writers, historians and geographers from the nineteenth century onwards have argued and agreed that Ptolemy's Mountains of the Moon were the Ruwenzori Mountains, there are still others who have argued in favour of Abyssinia and Ethiopia, based on Medieval theories, and that the lakes Ptolemy described were Tana and Ashangi.[2] According to fifteenth century travellers, Prester John had sent an expedition to discover the sources of the Nile, and Prester John has throughout history been associated with Abyssinia. This was, however, a difficult task, because Prester John had to produce a race of men who could entirely live on fish. Apparently this expedition reached the Mountains of the Moon and saw the Nile pouring out of a hole in the rocks. However, some of the scouts refused to come down again while others refused to tell what they had seen, so the whole expedition failed. One of the problems the medieval theorists aimed to solve was with regards to the Earthly Paradise, and how it escaped the flood. Obviously, it survived the flood if it was located on high mountains, and Abyssinia was such a place where the alleged Mountains of the Moon could be feeding the lakes. Moreover, some of the fourteenth- and fifteenth-century maps show one of the sources of the Nile as a tributary called Gihon, believed to descend from *paradiso terreno* and hence the Earthly Paradise was located in Abyssinia.[3] From as far back as written sources testify, the source of the Nile was connected with heaven and God, whether this god was the Christian one or not. And from one point of view, sources have most often been identified with the divine and notions of eternal life, and hence, the searches for the sources were also searches or pilgrimages to God.

In particular the mythology about Prester John fascinated the Europeans. Rumours circulating among the Crusaders about this pious Christian monarch, Prester John, prompted the Portuguese to mount expeditions to find this Christian kingdom in Abyssinia. Here they arrived in 1520 and stayed for six years. Father Alvarez was part of this embassy.[4] Later, the Christian rulers of Abyssinia were forced to appeal to Portugal for help against the famous general Mohammed Gragn and the Muslim Moors. Gragn's Arabic name was Imam Ahmad Ibn Ibrahim, but he is commonly known as Ahmad Gragn, *gragn* meaning 'left-handed'.

Four hundred and fifty Portuguese went with Christopher da Gama to assist the Christian Abyssinian rulers against Gragn in 1541.[5] Da Gama commanded an army of 12,000 badly armed Abyssinians together with the Portuguese musketeers, whereas Mohammed Gragn had 1,000 horsemen, 500 more men on foot and 50 Turkish musketeers. Da Gama won the first battle in 1542, but was bested in 1543. The defeated Portuguese were brutally treated by Gragn, and da Gama himself was beheaded. Three hundred of the Portuguese escaped the fatal battle, and fled to Jew's Mountain in Semien province.[6]

The first Europeans to visit the source of the Blue Nile were probably the Portuguese sent to Ethiopia with Christopher da Gama in 1541. Exactly when they initially set eyes on the source is uncertain, since they did not document the event. However, some of the Portuguese remained in Ethiopia and finally settled at Nanina, which is only about 50 km from the source.[7]

The first European to visit and document the source of the Blue Nile was the Portuguese Jesuit priest Pedro Paez. The date of his visit is variously given as 21 April 1618 or 1615 or 1613. In the book by the Portuguese Jesuit, Father Lobo, the year 1613 is given, but James Bruce argues with reference to native Abyssinian chronicles that Paez' visit was probably in 1615. The Jesuit Athanasius Kircher, who in 1652 published the *History of Ethiopia*, a Latin version of Paez' journal account of his travels, gives the date 21 April 1618.[8] Whatever the exact date, Paez was the first European to describe the source:

> The river, at this day, by the Ethiopians is called the Abaoy; it rises in the kingdom of Gojam, in a territory called Sabala, whose inhabitants are called Agows. The source of the Nile is situated in the west part of Gojam, in the highest part of a valley, which resembles a great plain on every side, surrounded by high mountains. On the 21st of April, in the year 1618, being here, together with the king and his army, I ascended the place, and observed everything with great attention; I discovered first two round fountains, each about four palms in diameter, and saw, with greatest delight, what neither Cyrus king of the Persians, nor Cambyses, nor Alexander the Great, nor the famous Julius Caesar, could ever discover. The two openings of these fountains have no issue in the plain on the top of the mountain, but flow from the foot of it. The second fountain lies about a stone-cast from the first.[9]

Father Lobo visited the source in around 1629, and he described it thus:

> This spring, or rather these two springs, are two holes, each about two feet in diameter, a stone's cast distance from each other. The one is but about five feet and an half in depth [...] Of the other, which is somewhat less [...] we could find no bottom, we were assured by the inhabitants that none ever had been found. It is believed here that these springs are the vents of a great subterranean lake.[10]

Lobo's manuscript was translated into English and published by the Jesuit Father Balthazar Tellez in London in 1670.[11] Father Lobo also described the annual sacrifice:

> On the top of this mountain is a little hill which the idolatrous Agaus have in great veneration; their priest calls them together at this place once a year, and having sacrificed a cow, throws the head into one of the springs of the Nile; after which ceremony, every one sacrifices a cow or more, according to their different degrees of wealth or devotion. The bones of these cows have already formed two mountains of considerable height, which afford a sufficient proof that these nations have always

paid their adorations to this famous river. They eat these sacrifices with great devotion, as flesh consecrated to their deity. Then the priest anoints himself with the grease and tallow of the cows, and sits down on a heap of straw, on the top and in the middle of a pile which is prepared; they set fire to it, and the whole heap is consumed without any injury to the priest, who while the fire continues harangues the standers by, and confirms them in their present ignorance and superstition. When the pile is burnt, and the discourse at an end, every one makes a large present to the priest, which is the grand design of this religious mockery.[12]

The latter ritual, described where the priest sits in the middle of a heap of straw put on fire without being injured, indicates that specific and extraordinary events took place, but given the sparse and perhaps inaccurate information it is difficult to elaborate on the role and meaning. In any event, the Portuguese were horrified by the Abyssinians and their Christian practices. In Lobo's words: 'The Christianity professed by the Abyssinians is so corrupted with superstitions, errors, and heresies, and so mingled with ceremonies borrowed from the Jews, that little besides the name of Christianity is to be found here.'[13]

Another Jesuit, the Portuguese Father Manoel de Almeida, wrote the *History of High Ethiopia or Abassia* between 1628 and 1646. Almeida does not state that he actually visited the Nile's source, but his description is more precise and differs from Paez', so it is likely that he was there and saw it with his own eyes:

> This [is a] pool [...] where one sees clear and limpid water. The people who live near say that they are unfathomable and some of them have tested this by putting lances in up to 20 spans without finding the bottom. The water flows from this pool underground but the course it takes can be told from the grass. First it flows eastwards for a musket shot and then turns to the north. About half a league from the source the water comes to the surface in sufficient quantity to make not a very big stream, but others soon join it, which lose their own names when they do so, while the Nile begins to have that of a river.[14]

Almeida then describes how the water becomes muddied with black earth before it runs into the great lake named Dambeâ. He then proceeds to elaborate on the different flows of the Nile.

The explorations for the source of the Blue Nile did not follow the Nile from Egypt to Sudan and further into Ethiopia because of the difficulties presented by the canyons in the mountainous areas. With one exception, all the Portuguese explorers journeyed to the highlands from the shores of the Red Sea, arriving first at Massawa before reaching their headquarters close to Axum. However, the old Greek road from Adulis to Axum, reputedly the best along with the route from Halai and Dixa, seems not to have been used by the Portuguese en route to Abyssinia. Following the Portuguese expulsion in 1633, no Europeans were present in Abyssinia, with the exception of the physician Poncet, who visited in 1699, prior to Bruce's visit in 1770.[15]

James Bruce, who was born in 1730 at Kinnaird in Scotland, was an explorer who travelled from Cairo to the source of the Blue Nile. When Bruce finally reached Gish Abay on 4 November 1770, he believed – or at least claimed when he published his accounts – that he was the first European to visit the spring. Bruce published his *Travels to Discover the Source of the Nile: In the Years 1768, 1769, 1770, 1771, 1772, and 1773*, in five volumes in 1790.[16] Bruce claimed that Paez' account of his visit to the source was a modern interpolation, and he dedicates a number of pages in his third volume to disprove that Paez ever visited the source.

One may assume that Bruce became aware that Paez and Lobo had seen the source before him and that he became very bitter when he learned of this and hostile to the memory of the two men. As we have seen, Bruce travelled between 1768 and 1773. In 1772, the French geographer D'Anville published a map of the Nile based on the Portuguese descriptions. When Bruce met D'Anville in Paris on his way back to Britain, the geographer informed Bruce that the source of the Nile had been made known to Europe from the journeys of Paez and Lobo. D'Anville also tried to convince Bruce that the Blue Nile was not the main source of the Nile, and that at least two-thirds of the Nile mystery remained unsolved.[17] Thus:

> Not being aware that he had been forestalled, [Bruce] thought he had discovered the source of the Blue Nile, and not only that, but of the White Nile as well, and was much disappointed when, on his return to Europe, he was disillusioned by Monsieur D'Anville in Paris on both points.[18]

Bruce suffered from ill health after his expedition, but this information may account for the 17-year delay in the publication of his *Travels*.[19]

He really wanted to be recognized as the explorer who had discovered the source of the river, of life itself, after more than two millennia of Nile quest. In his own words:

> Far in antiquity as history or tradition can lead us, farther still beyond the reach of either [...] begins the inquiry into the origin, cause of increase, and course, of this famous river. It is one of the few phenomena in natural history that ancient philosophers employed themselves in investigating, and people of all ranks seemed to have joined in the research with a degree of perseverance very uncommon; but still this discovery, though often attempted under the most favourable circumstances, has as constantly miscarried; it has baffled the endeavours of all ages, and at last come down, as great a secret as ever, to these latter times of bold and impartial inquiry.[20]

Bruce is here expressing his feeling of taking part in history, and indeed of defining it by accomplishing a marvellous act that he believed no one before him had succeeded in doing:

> It is easier to guess than to describe the situation of my mind at that moment – standing in that spot which had baffled the genius, industry, and inquiry of both ancients and moderns, for the course of near three thousand years. Kings had attempted this discovery at the head of armies, and each expedition was distinguished from the last, only by the difference of the numbers which had perished, and agreed alone in the disappointment which had uniformly, and without exception, followed them all. Fame, riches, and honour, had been held out for series of ages to every individual of those myriads these princes commanded, without having produced one man capable of gratifying the curiosity of his sovereign, or wiping off this stain upon the enterprise and abilities of mankind, or adding this desideratum for the encouragement of geography. Though a mere private Briton, I triumphed here, in my own mind, over kings and their armies [...] 'Strates', said I, 'faithful squire, come and triumph with your Don Quixote at the island of Barataria where we have wisely and fortunately brought ourselves; come and triumph with me over all the kings of the earth, all their armies, all their philosophers, and all their heroes.'[21]

At the source, Bruce made a number of toasts to the good health of King George III and a long line of princes, as well as to 'a more humble, but still sacred name – here is to Maria!' Strates, his assistant, was hesitant about all the toasts Bruce proposed, and asked if the last was to the Virgin Mary. Bruce replied, 'In faith, I believe so, Strates.'[22] Strates responded:

> As for king George I drank to him with all my heart, to his wife, to his children, to his brothers and sisters, God bless them all! Amen; – but as

for the Virgin Mary, as I am no Papist, I beg to be excluded from drinking healths which *my church* does not drink. As for our happy return, God knows, there is no one wishes it more sincerely than I do, for I have been weary of this beggarly country. But you must forgive me if I refuse to drink any more water. They say these savages pray over that hole every morning to the devil, and I am afraid I feel his horns in my belly already.[23]

Bruce accused Strates of being peevish, but Strates replied:

Peevish, or not peevish, a drop of it never again shall cross my throat [...] there is no jest in meddling with devil-worshippers, witchcraft, and inchantments, to bring some disease upon one's self here, so far from home [...] No, no, as many toasts in wine as you please, or better in brandy, but no more water for Strates.[24]

Bruce then proposed a toast to Empress Catherine of Russia, which Strates also drank while defying the Devil and keeping trust in St George.

In fact, the Mary Bruce toasted was not the Virgin, but a Scotswoman he had become engaged to before he started his journey. It seems Bruce seriously expected that she should wait for him, even though for 12 years she had received no letters or news from him. On his way back to Europe, he learned she had married an Italian aristocrat, Marchese Filippo d'Accoramboni, and was living in Rome.[25]

PRE-CHRISTIAN PRACTICES AT GISH IN 1770

Although Bruce's description is a child of its time in terms of his vivid language and style, he gives a good account of the rituals and beliefs. Bruce documented elaborate ceremonies, but it is easy to see why he became distrusted back in Britain when he told of these sacrifices and banquets where meat was eaten raw. These sacrifices, however, were structured around the source and the divine or mythological powers of the water itself. The source was of utmost importance in the pre-Christian era:

The water from these fountains is very light and good, and perfectly tasteless; it was at this time most intensely cold, though exposed to the mid-day sun without shelter, there being no trees nor bushes nearer it than the cliff of Geesh on its south side, and the trees that surround Saint Michael Geesh on the north, which, according to the custom of Abyssinia, is, like other churches, planted in the midst of a grove.[26]

When Bruce approached the bog where the sources arise, he had to take off his shoes. 'We were allowed to drink the water, but make no other use of it. None of the inhabitants of Geesh wash themselves, or their cloaths, in the Nile, but in a stream that falls from the mountain of Geesh down into the plain.'[27]

Bruce gives great attention to the importance and holiness of the Nile and its source, in particular to the cult of sacrificing oxen. The source itself is called 'God of Peace', indicating the particular holiness of this spot:

> The Agows of Damot pay divine honour to the Nile; they worship the river, and thousands of cattle have been offered, and still are offered, to the spirit supposed to reside at its source [...] all the tribes [...] meet annually at the source of the river, to which they sacrifice, calling it by the name of the *God of Peace*.[28]

Thus, it was a true water cosmology where the most important rituals and sacrifices were the ones conducted to The God of Peace – the source. The ox sacrifices are then described:

> Upon the rock in the middle of this plain, the Agows used to pile up the bones of the beasts killed in sacrifice, mixing them with billets of wood, after which they set them on fire. This is now discontinued, or rather transferred to another place near the church, as they are at present indulged in the full enjoyment of their idolatrous rites, both under Fasil and Michael.[29]

There seems to have been a relationship between the star Sirius and the rituals, which may have origins going back to the ancient Egyptians. In the Egyptian religion, the Nile was believed to start rising with the helical rising of Sirius. If there is a connection between these belief systems, it may indicate that knowledge of the annual flood coming from the Blue Nile and that the river's source was in Abyssinia must be very old. Still, it might just be a coincidence that two different water cosmologies – one at the headwaters in Ethiopia and the other at the outlet of this mighty river in Cairo and the Delta in Egypt – used the same astrological marker in the major rituals along the same river:

> It is upon the principle fountain and altar, already mentioned, that once a-year, on the first appearance of the dog-star, (or, as others say, eleven days after) this priest assembles the heads of the clans; and having sacrificed a black heifer that never bore a calf, they plunge the head of it into this fountain, they then wrap it up in its own hide, so as no more to be seen, after having sprinkled the hide within and without with water from the fountain. The carcase is then split in half, and cleaned with extraordinary care; and, thus prepared, it is laid upon the hillock over the first fountain, and washed all over with its water, while the elders, or considerable people, carry water in their hands joined (it must not be in any dish) from the

two other fountains; they then assemble upon the small hill a little west of St Michael, (it used to be the place where the church now stands) there they divide the carcase into pieces corresponding to the number of the tribes.[30]

The Christians opposed these rituals in vain, as is evident from Beke's descriptions of the same sacrifices at a later date. Following Bruce:

> After having ate this carcase raw, according to their custom, and drunk the Nile water to the exclusion of any other liquor, they pile up the bones on the place where they fit, and burn them to ashes. This used to be performed where the church now stands, but [the missioners] demolished their altar where the bones were burnt, and built a church upon the site.[31]

Bruce's descriptions of raw meat being eaten shocked the Europeans back home and furnished his critics with arguments to discredit his integrity, although raw beef is seen as a delicacy in Ethiopia:

> After they have finished their bloody banquet, they carry the head, close wrapt from sight in the hide, into the cavern [...] The Abyssinians have a story, probably created by themselves, that the devil appears to them, and with him they eat the head, swearing obedience to him upon certain conditions, that of sending rain, and a good season for their bees and cattle: however this may be, it is certain that they pray to the spirit residing in the river, whom they call the Everlasting God, Light of the World, Eye of the World, God of Peace, their Saviour, and Father of the Universe.[32]

The dual nature of the river Bruce describes is of importance, and has survived up until today, as will be evident in the later ethnographic account of the river, the waterfalls at Tis Abay and the indigenous Woyto. The river represented both God and the Devil, in particular when the rain failed – often attributed to the malignant powers in the river – and sacrifices were made during rainmaking rituals for securing the life-giving waters. As noted earlier, when Bruce made numerous toasts to the world's dignitaries when he first arrived at the source, his assistant Strates was reluctant to partake of the waters because of their associations with malignant powers and indeed the Devil. On the other hand, the divinities who procure rain and the life-giving waters are seen as benevolent and divine:

> Our landlord, the Shum [priest of the river], made no scruple of reciting his prayers for seasonable rain, for plenty of grass, for the preservation of serpents, at least of one kind of this reptile; he also deprecated thunder in these prayers, which he pronounced very pathetically with a kind of tone or song; he called the river 'Most High God, Saviour of the World'.[33]

Bruce then asked the Shum or river priest what the spirit looked like:

> He said he was of a very graceful figure and appearance; he thought rather older than middle age; but he seldom chose to look at his face; he had a long white beard, his cloaths not like theirs, of leather, but like silk, of the fashion of the country. I asked him how he was certain it was not a man? He laughed, or rather sneered, shaking his head, and saying, No, no, it is no man, but a spirit. I asked him then what spirit he thought it was? He said it was of the river, it was God, the Father of mankind.[34]

This duality between good and evil powers associated with the water divinity was also emphasized by the river priest:

> I then decided to know why he prayed against thunder. He said, because it was hurtful to the bees, their great revenue being honey and wax: then, why he prayed for serpents? he replied, Because they taught him the coming of good or evil.[35]

These latter were directly related to the life-giving waters in the forms of rain and river. When Bruce and Strates were leaving, they were encouraged to take care of this river god:

> I took my leave of Kefla Abay, the venerable priest of the most famous river in the world, who recommended me with great earnestness to take care of his god, which, as Strates humorously enough observed, meant nothing less than he hoped the devil would take me.[36]

The duality in the forces in the Abay, with both benevolent and malevolent characteristics and capacities, is also seen in other beliefs along the river.

DR BEKE AND MAJOR CHEESMAN AT THE SOURCE

Very little ethnographic research has been done into the rituals, beliefs and traditions along the Blue Nile. Among the few who visited Gish Abay and documented the ritual practices and beliefs apart from Bruce were Beke and Cheesman.

Charles T. Beke visited the source of the Blue Nile twice in 1842, and he was the first to scientifically document the course of that river. Moreover, he gives important descriptions of the source and the ritual practices conducted at that time. His first visit to Gish Abay was on 26 March. About five yards distance from the principal source, he was shown another source. He asked about a third source, but was told no other sources existed. Of particular interest are the rituals that took place:

On questioning my guides as to the celebration of religious ceremonies, they scorned the idea of their performing anything of the sort, being Christians; but they admitted that yearly in the month of Hedár, or Tahsás (about the end of November), after the rainy season, and when the ground is sufficiently dry to allow it, an ox is slaughtered on the spot by the neighbouring Shum, and its blood is allowed to flow into the spring, its flesh being eaten on the ground. I could not learn that any particular ceremonies accompany this act. Also at the close of the Abyssinian year (the beginning of September), on the eve of St John, sick persons are brought hither and left for seven days, which they say ensures their recovery. Logs of wood have from time to time been laid around the source to serve as a bed for these sick visitants [...] These practices are evidently remains of a higher degree of veneration paid to the spot at a period when the inhabitants of the country were not converted to Christianity.[37]

Beke returned to Gish Abay on 23 December in quite different circumstances. Due to the unusual amount of rain, the whole area was saturated and he constantly sank up to his ankles in mud. Upon his arrival he sent for a priest, who told him that the church was known by three names: A'shihi St Michael, Abái minch (source) St Michael and Gíesh St Michael. The priest had brought his cross from the church, and with this he blessed the water before Beke could drink it:

On my inquiring what form of words he used, he was reluctant to answer. I asked, 'Do you say, In the name of the Father, Son, and Holy Ghost?' 'Yes.' 'Nothing else?' 'Nothing else.' But this assertion is not to be relied on, and I may remark that I found him apparently averse to answer any questions.[38]

Again, there were different perspectives on the qualities of the water and the rituals being conducted. 'The slaughtering of cattle at the spring, [the priest] says, has ceased. Whilst the custom continued the head and horns of the beast were thrown into the source,' Beke writes. He adds: 'A countryman told me that it is customary to pour milk into the spring, in order to ascertain whether the person so doing will soon die or not. If it turns to blood, he will soon die; if it retains its natural colour, he will live.' During Timkat, the Ark from the neighbouring church was brought to the source and 'much water is then consumed, without it having any effect on the level of the spring; and they said that if a 1000 people were to drink of it; it would still remain the same'.[39]

The length of the source was 6 ft and with a large rod Beke measured its depth. At 7 ft and 6 ins he struck a stone, but was able to push past it through the mud a further 18 ins or 2 ft. The priests and the countrymen, on the other hand, said the spring had no bottom, and that without the intervening mud and stones it would be possible to find a way through to the cave under Mount Gish.[40]

Major R. E. Cheesman made several trips to Lake Tana, his first two expeditions being in 1927 and 1929. In 1932–3 he was surveying the Lake Tana monasteries and his wife joined him at the source.[41] When Cheesman visited Gish Abay, he inquired about Zerabruk. The church at Gish Abay is dedicated to both St Michael and Zerabruk. Some have suggested that the name Zerabruk was a corruption of Bruce's name, for Bruce mentions only St Michael Gish in his book. The priests at Gish Abay, however, told Cheesman Zerabruk was a saint, but according to him, they had no idea who he was.[42] However, Zerabruk has a specific meaning, and in Amharic *zarburuk* means 'blessed seed'.[43] It is interesting to note that in the 1930s the priests had no theological explanation regarding the origin and history of Zerabruk, which indicates that the process of Christianizing this place has been very protracted and that combating the pre-Christian beliefs about the water-world has continued to this day. This is also evident in the perceptions of the dangers the water from the source represents. Moreover, Cheesman's observations remind us of mythologies in the making, and that no religions are static and unchanging.

Cheesman received holy water from a priest, but when the latter learned he had already eaten that day, he insisted that Cheesman had to wait until the next day and drink the water before breakfast. The water, it is held, loses its healing power if it is taken after food, but more importantly, it can be deadly. Several people who had ignored this warning and drunk the holy water after a meal had died. Similarly, when Cheesman visited the source with his wife in 1933, the priests took them to the spring. When she touched the water with the end of her stick, the surrounding pilgrims shouted: 'Don't let her touch it, she is a woman.' She asked the priest what evil would befall her if she bathed in the spring, and he replied, 'You would die.'[44]

When Cheesman inquired about the history of the church, a priest and several of his parishioners agreed that it was founded in the reign of Yohannes Kadus or John the Holy (John I, 1667–82). Apparently, the church was built using money donated by a woman named Bujet from Gonder. Her mother Iniya had brought Bujet to Gish to drink the water from the spring in the hope she would be cured of complaints her doctor could not relieve. Bujet recovered and fell in love with the chieftain of Sakala, whom she married, and refused to return to Gonder. Subsequent to Cheesman, there are no other references to Bujet or Iniya, but near Gish there is a small tributary to the Abay called the Bugeta, which may commemorate Bujet and her marriage.[45]

THE HEAVENLY GISH ABAY

In the pre-Christian era the source has very different religious meanings and attributes than when Christianized. According to the Shum or the river priest, following Bruce, in the water there lived a mighty spirit who was the father of mankind. Thus, it seems that it was the power of the embodying spirit rather than the water itself that was powerful, although they were intimately related. This directs the attention to holy water, since the borders between gods or spirit living in water and the water itself being invested with divine qualities are literally fluid.

Philo of Alexandria in the first century AD pointed this out:

> That the food of the soul is not earthly but heavenly, we shall find abundant evidence in the Sacred Word. 'Behold I rain upon you bread out of heaven, and the people shall go out and they shall gather the day's portion for a day, that I may prove them whether they will walk by My law or not' (Exod. xvi. 4). You see that the soul is fed not with things of earth that decay, but with such words as God shall have poured like rain out of the lofty and pure region of life to which the prophet has given the title of 'heaven'.[46]

As indicated in Chapter 1, rain in itself is seldom perceived as holy, since it is everywhere; it is often the gift from gods or divinities, and as such part of the divine sphere, but not holy in a similar vein as specific bodies of water. Sources in particular, on the other hand, are often believed to be utmost holy. Not only are they coming from somewhere, but because of this fact, they are connections between this world and otherworldly realms, such as heaven.

The Gish Abay spring is believed to be the source of the Blue Nile coming from Paradise and hence holy (fig. 9). In the area around the small town of Bicolo, the river is also named Bicolo Abay, a name adopted during the Italian occupation period, *bicolo* meaning 'small' in Italian. However, the name of the local area was changed by Haile Selassie to Wetet Abay or Milk Abay, and the river is also called Milk or Wetet Abay. The source of the Nile is protected by the Gish Mikael monastery, and the water from the spring is believed to be of utmost holiness and to possess healing powers. Close to

THE SOURCE OF THE BLUE NILE AND LAKE TANA IN ETHIOPIA

9. Gish Abay – the source of the Blue Nile.

the spring there is another holy trio of springs, from which, it is believed, the Father, Son and Holy Spirit emerge. The holiness of Gish Abay has its origin in both Old and New Testament contexts. In Genesis it is written:

> A river watering the garden flowed from Eden; from there it was separated into four headwaters. The name of the first is the Pishon; it winds through the entire land of Havilah, where there is gold. The name of the second river is the Gihon; it winds through the entire land of Cush. The name of the third river is the Tigris; it runs along the east side of Asshur. And the fourth river is the Euphrates. (Genesis 2:11–14)

Apart from religious explanations, there is one intriguing question which is impossible to answer, but nevertheless relates to the millennia-long quest for the sources of the Nile: why was the river Gihon mentioned by Jews so far back in history? Although throughout history there have been different suggestions where the river Gihon is located, it is only in Ethiopia there is a living tradition connecting the river and its source with the Bible. Given that there seems to have been a tradition going back to the Old Testament era connecting the river with Cush, it also relates to the legends of Queen Sheba and the presence of the Beta Israel in Ethiopia, which will be discussed later, as well as Moses in Egypt (see Chapter 6).

In Ethiopia today the Blue Nile is called Abay, but before its name was Gihon. Gihon, one of the four rivers from heaven and the Garden of Eden, has its earthly outlet at Gish Abay. Hence, Gish Abay is the direct source from heaven and is a physical conduit to the divine spheres whence the life-giving waters come. According to the priests, 'Gihon feeds heaven', 'Gihon has served heaven' and 'Gihon has rotated the world seven times and has fed the water for heaven, and has come back to Ethiopia.' The river is always moving and circulating. It feeds heaven in the east and it emerges in Ethiopia. All water in different forms, such as rain and small streams, join the Nile and represent a circle. Heaven was the first place where Adam and Eve and hence humanity lived. Thus Gihon has always served humanity. In heaven, when Adam and Eve lived there, Gihon was a life-giving river in Paradise, and when humanity was expelled, Gihon flowed from heaven to earth. Thus in Ethiopia, Gihon may also be seen as a source of Christianity, of being a Christian and as a path to heaven. Since humans are dependent on the Nile and its water for survival, the water can be seen as a covenant between humans and God, since God penalizes people with too little or too much water if they are sinful and disobedient.

There are two particular religious stories with regard to the holiness of the Nile on earth, one relating to Gihon and the other to Abay and Gish Abay. According to the first story, following the Bible, the four divine rivers in heaven have different qualities and characteristics: one consists of honey, another of oil, the third of wine and Gihon of milk. When these rivers are flowing on earth, they do not carry these divine substances. Instead, the holy waters appear as clear and normal water. According to the priests of Gish Abay, when Jesus was born, all the earthly counterparts of these divine rivers assumed their divine qualities for one day. The Gihon River turned into milk, hence its name Milk Abay. The day after Jesus' birth, all the divine rivers reverted to their earthly characteristics, namely normal, clear and holy water.

The other story is about the introduction of Christianity to this area, the miracles of Zerabruk and why the Nile is called Abay and its source Gish Abay. Abune Zerabruk was born of Kidus Deme Christos (father) and Kidist Mariam Mogessa (mother) at the end of the eighth century AD. Kidus and Kidist literally connote the male and female variants of the term 'blessed'. Before his birth, one of his forefathers is said to have foretold that a man would be born from his seventh generation in the maternal line who with his prayers and sacrifices would save the world.

Zerabruk was a man of religious character from his early days. At about the age of seven, the abune prayed to God to blind him so he could not see the evil deeds of the secular world. Accordingly, he lost his vision for

12 years. From then on, the abune went to different places for religious education and eventually to monasteries. During this period, he is said to have performed a number of miracles and religious deeds. He also prayed for about 30 years at the source of the River Abay, which was to become Gish Abay.

According to the legend of the church, the abune received from God the power to cure people of their physical diseases and spiritual sins by using water. Before he could do so, he had to bless the Gish Abay stream in the name of the Father, the Son and the Holy Spirit. People using this water would also gain eternal life. Even people not yet baptized could be considered so from that time on, since they had used the water from Gish Abay, or Gihon, as the river was then called.

Owing to his growing fame for his religious deeds and powers, the abune eventually faced difficulties with regional rulers. Prior to his stay near Abay/Gihon, he was forced to leave Tsima because of political resistance to his religious teachings. At Gish Abay, he was eventually arrested by the king's soldiers. Before he was arrested, the abune stood at the source of Gihon River and prayed, and finally consigned his seven sacred books to the source of the river. It is also said that God told him to give the books to the river. He was imprisoned for five years, during which time destructive events were said to have occurred in the jail. As a result, the king released the abune. After two more years of teaching and preaching in different places, the abune finally returned to the source of Abay where he had left his books. The abune prayed intensively and devotedly to God and asked the river to bring forth the books he had given in to its custody when he was imprisoned.

Gish means 'bring forth', and when Zerabruk stood at the source of the Nile where he had deposited the sacred books seven years earlier, he called out *gish*. Then the river brought forth the books, which were undamaged after being hidden in the water. Surprised and pleased by the miracle, the abune asked his old disciple Aba Zerufael to behold the miracle. He said 'Aba Eyi' in Amharic, which means 'Father, look', directing the disciple's attention to the miracle of the undamaged books. 'Aba Eyi' became *Abay*, which is the Ethiopian name for the Blue Nile. Hence, the name of the holy river and in particular its source – Gish Abay – derives from this religious event. After this miracle, the river's name changed from Gihon to Abay and the river got a masculine character, indicated by the term 'Aba Eyi' – 'Father, look'. Lobo later wrote that the natives called the Nile Abavi, 'that is, the Father of Waters'.[47]

'Abay' normally implies greatness, strength and splendour, hence the river's masculine association and status as a male river. However, in Geez, the old church language still in use, Abay may also connote 'big' or 'great' in terms of women or the feminine, or the quality of being a woman and hence motherhood and fertility. It can also be a female name and may indicate a girl as well as a woman, whereas Abei signifies a man or boy. Thus, after the miracles of Zerabruk, Abay acquired a particular etymology signifying 'motherhood' or the 'feminine', and as a mother of her devotees, she is a life-giver providing wealth, prosperity and everything bountiful. Still, the feminine association is not the primary one, and the Blue Nile is first and foremost seen as masculine and as a male river. As Tafla argues, the Nile was simply the river or the father of rivers, and the Geez adjective 'Abbawi' means 'fatherly'. Ethiopian lexicographers believe that one reason the river is described as father is because it unites so many tributaries, like a father gathering together his children.[48] One may also add that in the language of the Agows, *gish* means 'dig', and thus Gish Abay becomes 'Dig father'.

Gish Abay is believed to be the source of both secular and spiritual life. It is generally held that people who are baptized or sprinkled with water from the Gihon River in the name of the holy water of Abay/*Ye Abay tsebel* are cured of sins, sicknesses and misfortunes. This is because, the church claims, the abune once again prayed at Gihon for many years. On the behalf of the abune, it is believed that God bestowed all his mercy on up to 70 generations of the descendants of the devotees who used the water of this river and prayed at its source.

Abune Zerabruk died at the age of 482 and was buried at Tsima Silasie, where he previously had prayed, healed and performed miracles. His seven sacred books have since his death been kept in the monastery at Gish Abay as most auspicious and sacred treasures. They are accessible to neither the public nor the monks. Today, only one living priest has seen them, and the books are still in perfect condition. Since the holy books are not accessible to anyone but of the utmost religious importance, the monastery sells an edited Amharic version of the sacred books, which the above account is partly based on.

Thus, the river has a double religious, institutional function in the Christianity of this area. The source of the river marked the birth of Jesus, and the miracles of Zerabruk coincided with the introduction of Christianity in this part of Ethiopia. Still, when Christianity was introduced here, people were reluctant to accept the new religion because they wished to continue to worship the river and its old spirit. The priests devised a compromise, and said that 'we will believe in Abay again' and 'we will believe in Abay in the name of Jesus Christ'. According to their version, they destroyed the former bad spirits in the river and the places where they lived. Henceforward, the river and the former beliefs associated with it were converted to Christianity, and the water worship continued in order to secure acceptance of Christianity as the new religion. The priests' rationale for this stratagem was that if Christianity could first be established and institutionalized, the older pre-Christian beliefs and rituals could gradually be changed and displaced.

The continuity of the older rituals conducted at Gish Abay has been pervasive. Next to the church of Zerabruk, where the water from the source forms the stream that later becomes the Nile, it was common to conduct sacrifices to the river, a tradition that has disappeared only by the turn of the millennia or so. Devotees praying to be healed of sickness and suffering would swing a chicken three times around their heads before throwing it into the river. Similarly, women praying for fecundity would pass a Bible three times around their heads. Today, following church practice, priests bless the water used by people and offer prayers in accordance with Orthodox teaching.

Particular places with unique waters are often some of the most important pilgrimage sites, and Gish Abay is a major pilgrimage site. On the way to Gish Abay there is a small church where pilgrims and devotees give money either en route to the source or on their return. It is not only local people who attend the services at the source to collect and be blessed by the holy water, but pilgrims from all over the country. According to a traditional Ethiopian proverb, 'The son of the Nile thirsts for water', and there are water pilgrimage sites all over Ethiopia. Apart from Gish Abay, one of the most famous place for water rituals is Fasilidas' bath in Gonder from the seventeenth century. The pool measures 50 m by 30 m and is fed from the Qaha River by a small canal and it is a central pilgrimage place during the Timkat festival.[49] The centrality of these places can best be understood by emphasizing the role of religious water whether it is holy or it is through the water rituals officiated by priests securing the divine outcomes. In another context, sources of a holy river have been called 'sin-destroying localities'.[50] Hence, the water and the associated rituals have a double power; not only are the very rituals enabling purification, but the water itself has also this capacity, and consequently, 'pilgrimage to crossing places may put humans where divine beneficence and even release – are more readily approached'.[51] And Gish Abay is the most important pilgrimage place because of the divine waters.

The most important festival, attracting the most pilgrims, is the holy day of Zerabruk, which falls on 13 January (Ethiopian calendar). The main ceremony takes place in St Mikael Church, which houses the arks of both Michael and Zerabruk. The service starts early in the morning. St Mikael's is located on the upper hill, from where the devotees, after attending the church services and praying, descend the slope to the source of the Blue Nile. Within a small compound there are two churches. The source itself is located in the small church named after Zerabruk. However, the real source is also believed to be another church, just a few metres away but at a slightly higher elevation. To this church only priests are given admittance, but it is the Zerabruk Church that is generally perceived to be the most important.

Before approaching the source, the devotees must be in a pure condition, despite the fact they will use the holy water to cleanse themselves of impurities and sins. If a person brings impurity to the source, this is a triple sin. First, if a person defiles the holiness, he is desecrating God; second, as a consequence, God will punish the person not only in another existence, but possibly in the form of an accident such as a snake bite that will endanger his own life; and finally, desecrating the source reduces its holiness for other devotees who will then be less purified by the holy water. Therefore, the implications of bringing impurity to the holy water are not restricted to the relationship between God and the sinner, but also to the community of Christians who believe in the divine powers of Gish Abay. In practice, this means that everyone who approaches the source has to have fasted, not for many days, but by eschewing breakfast or any food on the day of the visit. Moreover, the source is only accessible to Christians, meaning Ethiopian Orthodox Christians, and anyone who is not a Christian will by their very presence pollute the holy water. Finally, wearing shoes is also a source of contamination and all those entering the sanctuary to take the full ablution are barefooted.

While visiting the source in 2009, some pilgrims took full ablution whereas others queued in front of the church with plastic bottles and cans. Devotees taking the full ablution and ritual baths at the source within the church do not need the assistance of priests or monks. There are two entrances to the source, each covered by a cloth. Women use the left entrance and men the right. Depending upon the devotees' circumstances, the purification process may be felt as an exorcism of evil spirits from the body. On one occasion in 2009, a woman screamed out loudly several times 'I am burning!' as the water chased the evil out of her. Thus, the water has the power to cast out evil spirits and demons if devotees truly believe it has this capacity. This was further testified in 2015 when we visited the source again. On this particular Sunday in late August, there were a huge number of patients suffering from mental diseases, or, religiously interpreted, from being attacked by the Devil. The huge crowd of pilgrims were at unrest and the atmosphere was tense, and the mere presence of Westerners far from the source and any water was seen as a threat to the holiness of the water. The possibility of defilement of the water was a serious matter since the stakes were high; the great number of people attacked by the Devil sincerely needed the divine water for their healing. The great number of exorcisms taking place testified to the deep beliefs that the utmost holiness of the heavenly waters are the most efficient in the cosmic drama and battle between good and evil.

On more ordinary occasions, the water is used for blessings and cleaning lesser sins or evils. Devotees wanting to collect holy water for later use do not have direct access to the source. Church attendants and assistants fill the bottles and cans, which are later blessed by priests. After the devotees have collected the water or taken full ablutions within the church, everyone proceeds to the Manbebya Kifle Church, literally meaning 'reading room'. Here, preaching and the blessing of the water take place. The water is holy in itself, but when it is blessed by the priests it acquires additional holiness (fig. 10). The blessing takes place after a priest has preached about moral decay and degeneration among people and in society and that the only hope for salvation is believing in God and following the righteous Christian path. When the priest has finished, devotees give him money and collect their bottles and cans of holy water, which are then collectively blessed and rendered even more holy than before. Then the people are blessed by priests who sprinkle water on their torsos, which are partly uncovered. These

10. The holy water is blessed by priests at Manbebya Kifle Church, 2009.

rituals and procedures take place each morning, but on Sundays, when people have more time and do not have to work, the sermons are longer.

The holy water is healing and life-giving, and cleanses devotees of sins and any kind of sickness or malignance. After drinking the water, the effects may be immediate, but it may also take days, months and even years before the prayers are fulfilled. The effects of the holy water are not limited to the actual pilgrims praying at Gish Abay, but may work miracles for their descendants up to 70 generations. The holy water is also given to pilgrims or devotees unable to come to Gish Abay, for instance people living close to the Sudanese border and even further afield.

The powers of holy water are unquestionable, but it is not a ritual to be done without commitments. By the turn of the twentieth century, it was documented a noteworthy feature of being sprinkled with holy water by the church in general. The water should not be spilled on the ground, since it was a symbol of regeneration, but on the devotee's head and garments. Then the priest would say:

> If you think that I have now cleansed your garments and purified your bodies, and yet continue to cherish hatred and malice in your hearts, I tell you that the body of Christ will prove to be a burning fire to consume you, and His blood a bottomless sea to drown you.[52]

Although the water had cleansing and purifying powers, it was also a symbol of the religious pact with severe consequences if broken. Thus, as an initiation, the use of water was much more than a mere ritual in the liturgy; it could open the gates to heaven, but also to hell. The experiences of exorcisms may also be understood from this perspective.

TIS ABAY AND THE 'SMOKING WATERS'

Although the Ethiopian Orthodox Church is one of the oldest Christian denominations in the world and the Lake Tana region is central to Christianity in Ethiopia, there are still an amalgation of pre-Christian beliefs and practices existing when it comes to water and the Nile. When Father Lobo saw the waterfalls, he did not refer to them as Tis Abay and he writes:

> Fifteen miles farther, in the land of Alata, it rushes precipitately from the top of a high rock, and forms one of the most beautiful water-falls in the world: I passed under it without being wet; and resting myself there, for the sake of the coolness, was charmed with a thousand delightful rainbows, which the sunbeams painted on the water in all their shining and lively colours. The fall of this mighty stream from so great a height makes a noise that may be heard to a considerable distance; but I could not observe that the neighbouring inhabitants were at all deaf. I conversed with several, and was as easily heard by them as I heard them. The mist that rises from this fall of water may be seen much farther than the noise can be heard. After this cataract the Nile again collects its scattered stream among the rocks, which seem to be disjoined in this place only to afford it a passage.[53]

Nor did Bruce describe the waterfalls as Tis Abay, but as the noble cataract of Alata:[54]

> The cataract itself was the most magnificent sight that ever I beheld [...] The river, through swelled with rain, preserved its natural clearness, and fell, as far as I could discern, into a deep pool, or bason, in the solid rock, which was full, and in twenty different eddies to the very foot of the precipice, the stream, when it fell, seeming part of into run back with great fury upon the rock [...] in a noise like the loudest thunder, to make the solid rock (at least as to sense) shake to its very foundation, and threaten to tear every nerve to pieces, and to deprive one of [the] other senses besides that of hearing. It was the most magnificent sight, that ages, added to greatest length of human life, would not deface or eradicate from my memory; it struck me with a kind of stupor, and total oblivion of where I was, and of every other sublunary concern.[55]

These 'smoking waters' have always fascinated visitors who come to the waterfalls, and the common understanding of 'Tis Abay' – 'smoking waters' – is that it refers to these cascades (fig. 11). However, villagers at Tis Abay give another story about why the place is so named. This may help to explain why Lobo and Bruce did not refer to the waterfalls as Tis Abay, since the name is more recent.

According to elders currently living in the village, the earlier name of the area was Genji, but that changed following an event that took place more than a century ago. The Abo Monastery, named after the Egyptian Abune Gebre Menfes Kidus, was located close to the village of Tis Abay in an area covered by dense forest. Annually, three major ceremonies were held in the monastery, which took place on 5 July, 5 October and 5 March (Ethiopian calendar), and were attended by pilgrims from neighbouring villages. According to the elders in Tis Abay, after the July ceremony in 1898, pilgrims from the other villages asked how they could establish whether those living in Tis Abay had survived the summer and whether there would be a ceremony in October. Heavy rain and landslides made the area dangerous and summers can be a difficult and hazardous time. The villagers from Tis Abay answered that if everything had gone well

11. 'Tis Abay' or the 'smoking waters'.

and they had all survived through July and August, they would light a huge fire to indicate that the October ceremony would proceed. The fire would create dense smoke – *tis* – that would serve as the signal. In due course, the fire was lit close to the Abay and so the village came to be called Tis Abay.

Thus, the 'smoking waters' do not refer to the waterfall, but to the villagers' promise to signal their survival through the summer and to confirm the holding of the next ceremony. This is what gave rise to the name of the village, and since the waterfall is close to the village, it was also named Tis Abay. Therefore, as the elders stressed, the name Tis Abay was not taken from the waterfall, but the other way around.

It is particularly intriguing that there seem to be no important religious beliefs associated with the waterfall itself. Despite the power and roar of the falling water, these physical characteristics have not been afforded special religious significance. This is quite contrary to other places along the Nile and in particular the waterfalls coming from the source of the White Nile in Uganda, which will be elaborated in Chapter 3. The Christian waters at Tis Abay are ascribed with different meaning, although there might have been different pre-Christian perceptions. Or, as the elders say, it is the same water above the fall as below, and the holy Abay and the heavenly Gihon are identical.

There is, however, one important Christian association with the falls. During the summer rains the water in the river is full of silt and mud. Although the water is clear in the months from January onwards, the amount of water is very small. From October to January, on the other hand, there is an abundance of clear water, which makes a wonderful rainbow, in particular from around 9.00am to 11.00am. This is called *Yemariam mekenet*, the Virgin Mary's scarf, similar to the scarves women in their traditional folk costumes tie around their hips. This relates directly to Noah's fear and destiny after the deluge. The sinful acts of humanity prompted God's wrath, and all animals and humans not aboard the Ark were killed with boiling water. When the water receded, Noah was fearful of leaving the Ark since God had shown no hesitation in killing everything and everyone. He said to God that humans cannot be free from sin and will commit sins in future, and then they will become extinct again through the boiling water. God answered that he repented the act and would never extinguish humanity again, and as a sign of the promise and the new covenant with his children a rainbow appeared. The rainbow was made in the name of Virgin Mary, who is above all other women in the world. Today, the colours in the Ethiopian flag, red, yellow and green, are also seen as symbolizing this covenant and the rainbow of St Mary.

CHRISTIANITY IN THE LAKE TANA REGION AND TANA KIRKOS

It is generally held that the Ethiopian Orthodox Church, which was established in the Axumite state during the reign of Ezana, did not suffer persecution during its expansion. This conclusion is, however, not entirely correct and one may rather argue the opposite. There is substantial evidence that the process of Christianization encountered strong local opposition and hostile sentiment. The pre-Christian religions were strong, and the Nine Saints in their time faced considerable opposition. These hostile attitudes seem to have increased after the decline of Axumite power, and when the church spread further southward, particularly during the fourteenth and fifteenth centuries, it ran into huge difficulties.[56] Many different religious practices existed at the time, with people worshipping the sky, springs, rivers, lakes, hills, trees and fire. As late as the mid-fifteenth century, there were also references to the probable earlier practice of human sacrifice. Traditional African priests had comprehensive powers and controlled all natural phenomena: rain and drought, famine and epidemic, good and evil.[57]

The Tana region was the political and religious centre of the Christian empire in the period between the collapse of the Zagwe dynasty in the late thirteenth century and the establishment of Gonder as the permanent capital in the early seventeenth century. In this period, the Lake Tana monasteries played a fundamental role. In late-medieval Ethiopia, there were two major phases of the spread of Christianity in the central highlands. The first phase is associated with the rule of Amda-Seyon (1314–44). Before this time, Christianity was in a weak position and the small isolated communities were dependent on the mercy of local chiefs. The Christians faced persecution, churches were burnt down and entire Christian villages were destroyed. Church communities in the south had little hope of military assistance from the Christian kings to the north, but this changed dramatically during the reign of Amda-Seyon.[58]

Amda-Seyon has been seen as a defender of the church and a champion of its expansion. His local chiefs were obliged to protect priests and monks within their districts, but this does not mean there was no opposition to the Christians. Numerous reports tell of monks being ambushed by militant groups, with heavy casualties. Even though non-Christians were defeated militarily, resistance to the new religion remained strong. The conflict between the religions was bitter, since Christian monks, protected by the king, insisted on building their churches on the sites of non-Christian sanctuaries, thus destroying the old sacred grounds. The non-Christian resistance was strongest in Gojjam, which was almost completely non-Christian until the beginning of the fifteenth century. The initial spread of Christianity into this region was most probably through the Tana Kirkos Monastery in Lake Tana (fig. 12), which seems to have been established in the Zagwe period (c. 1137–270). The monastery islands appear to have attracted many hermits at the beginning of the fourteenth century, but the Christian offensive and conquest took place with Amda-Seyon.[59]

According to the monks at Tana Kirkos recalling the mythology of the monastery, the island became a religious centre in 4518 BC, and there are a number of pieces of evidence as to the holiness of this island. Of particular importance is the presence of sacrificial stones, believed to have been used in Old Testament times when cows and calves were sacrificed (fig. 13). The myths vary, but one priest told that they were erected in 982 BC. Another fundamental event in the island's history is the Ark of the Covenant. The Ark is believed to have stayed at the very spot where the sacrificial pillars lie for up to 800 years before being transferred to Axum around AD 400, and in the rocks just next to the pillars there are cracks interpreted to be pot-holes where the poles carrying the tent covering the Ark was erected. According to mythology, the Ark was carried from Jerusalem by 12,000 Jews, also explaining why the Jewish Beta Israel diaspora has existed ever since. It also explains, according to legends, why Ethiopians as Africans are not as black-skinned as others. The Jews married Ethiopian ladies and hence the Ethiopians got lighter skins. However, the integration was not without frictions. When the Ethiopians became Christians, the Jews continued to worship the Ark and became segregated as the Falasha. Given the religious divide, the future of the Ark was uncertain. The location on the island far away was seen as an optimal place initially, but then grew suspicions that the Jews wanted it, and the Axumite king ordered the Ark to Axum where it has resided ever since.

12. Tana Kirkos in Lake Tana.

13. The sacrificial pillars believed to have an Old Testament origin.

There are yet other reasons for the holiness of Tana Kirkos. The first abune of the Ethiopian Orthodox Church – Abune Selama – baptized devotees at this place. Although Selama preached and worked in the fourth century, his presence on the island is seen as relating to older Old Testament practices. St Yared – the first and the most famous Ethiopian composer of religious songs and hymns – wrote his greatest works on this island, apparently using a cup-mark engraving on one of the sacrificial stones to prepare the ink he used for writing. There are also other connections to Jerusalem and the Old Testament. The main church on the monastery island is differently constructed from the other churches in the region, and according to the monks it follows the same architectural plan as King Solomon's Palace.

From the New Testament period, the most holy remains are evident. On the mountain rim where the sacrificial pillars and the evidence of the Holy Family are located, there are also nine invisible churches. In a sacred museum are stored the Holy Books together with relics from the monastery's history. Among the latter are the crowns of several kings, glass from Emperor Menelik and the metal cross used by Abune Selama. But the most important of all are the material remains and traces of the Holy Family. Virgin Mary with her family, including Jesus and Joseph, spent three months and ten days on the island after they had fled from the persecution of Herod first to Egypt and then to Ethiopia. There are several items of physical evidence of their stay at the mountain rim where the sacrificial pillars and invisible churches are. One is a big stone bearing a mark believed to be the footprint of Jesus. Next to this stone there is a mark in poor condition on the mountain rim believed to be the footprint of St Mary. A little further away on the rim stands a small chapel covering marks on the ground held to be the traces from Mary's dress when she rested there.

The material imprint of the Virgin Mary is the most sacred feature on the island,[60] but all of these features together are of vital importance to the Ethiopian Orthodox Church. They testify to and legitimize this island's status as one of the oldest and greatest religious centres in Ethiopia, and for Christians bear witness to their salvation at the end of the world, or so the monks on the island believe. This long continuity and the tradition of sacrifices, ritual worship and praying have increased the holiness of this spiritual centre. In Old Testament times, the place of sacrifice was used for sacrifices of bullocks and cows, and sacrifices could only take place at this spot, otherwise devotees would be punished. There were two main reasons for sacrifices. It was believed that if a person had sinned grievously, God would punish the sinner directly and physically. Moreover, it was believed sinners would be marked with a sign on their skins and thus become alienated from their people and treated as an outcast. To repent and erase the sign, the sinner would make a sacrifice and give the blood to the cup-mark on the 'stone chair', *Ye dingie menber*, one of the sacrificial pillars. Then, a fire would appear from the sky and usurp the blood, thereby signifying that the True God had received the sacrifice and that the sinner was cleansed of sin. In addition, any person could make a sacrifice even if they were not marked on the skin as a sinner. This practice continued until Abune Selama arrived in the fourth century and replaced the older Christian rituals with New Testament traditions.

These sacrifices were different from those performed by indigenous groups to the Abay. The Christians at Tana Kirkos made sacrifices in the name of the True God whereas, according to the Christians, those sacrificing to the Abay did so in the name of the 'bad spirit'. The Christians making sacrifices were people of the *Krubel* – 'messengers of God' – who carried the spirit of God from the area where Jesus was born. In this light, one of the most significant religious events was the actual visit of Jesus with his family to the island, which also had implications for the perceived holiness of the water in Lake Tana.

After the Virgin Mary, along with Jesus and her family, were persecuted by Herod in Jerusalem and fled to Egypt, she stayed in the mountainous desert for two years. One day Jesus pointed with his small finger towards Ethiopia, and when Mary asked what country that was, he said 'Ethiopia'. Then the Virgin Mary, Jesus and Joseph, together with Mary's sister Salome, invisible saints and five lions started to walk from Egypt to Ethiopia. They passed through Eritrea on their way to Axum before they reached Waldiba, which is a monastery north of Gonder. The lions remained at this monastery when the rest of the group continued on their travels. From Waldiba they came to Tara Gedam, which is a monastery south of Gonder, before continuing southwards to Tana Dar and then Tana Ampa. At Tana Ampa, there is a stone imprint where St Mary rested awhile. The group continued to Gibtsawit Anbesamit Mariam in the Dera District, which Mary thought was similar to Egypt. They proceeded to Marefit Mariam monastery, located at the edge of Lake Tana near Rema, whence they crossed the lake by papyrus boat to Tana Kirkos.

The island of Tana Kirkos was called Saf or Tsion, which are Old Testament or Jewish terms: the church in Axum, for instance, is called Axum Tsion. With the arrival of the Virgin Mary with her family, the island's name was changed to Tana Kirkos. Jesus was five years old when they came to the island, where, as already noted, they stayed for three months and ten days.

One day St Orael (Urael?) appeared and ordered them to return to Israel because Herod had died. St Mary, however, refused to leave the island and such a wonderful country where she had found safety and warm hospitality. In Israel, she had experienced war and Herod's persecution and in Egypt she had suffered from hunger and thirst in the desert. By contrast, on Tana Kirkos she had enjoyed the peaceful and bountiful pleasures of the island. The saint, on the other hand, eventually convinced her that Jesus as the Son of God would come to teach the gospel to the people and in the end would be crucified and thereby take on humanity's sins for their salvation. When St Mary was told about Jesus' destiny and religious importance, she said 'carry us' and they were taken up in the clouds and transferred back to Egypt. When they left Ethiopia, they blessed the country, all parts of it – east, west, south and north – and that is how, according to the Ethiopian Orthodox Church, Ethiopia came to be mentioned in the Bible.

In Geez, *tseane* means 'covered by', referring to the clouds on which Virgin Mary together with Jesus, Joseph and their followers where carried on their divine flight back to Egypt. The clouds carried the group in secret to Debra Qusquam Monastery in Egypt, whence they continued to Nazareth. Thus, the name of the lake –Tana – has its origins in this religious event.

In the historical literature, the name of Lake Tana is more in accordance with the original word from which it is derived. Beke referred to Lake Tzána[61] and Lake Tsána,[62] and Budge to Lake Sānā.[63] The names of the lake were also discussed after Cheesman's paper 'The Upper Waters of the Blue Nile' (1928) had been read at the Royal Geographical Society in his absence, since he was on his way back to Abyssinia. One of the questions concerned the name of the lake. The Permanent Committee on Geographical Names had decided that Tana and not Tsana was the correct translation of the name from Amharic into English.[64] The earlier Portuguese usually called Lake Tana Dambia (or Dembea), the latter being the name of the fertile floodplain east of Lake Tana, which is flooded annually. The Portuguese also called the lake Sena, which is similar to Bruce's Tsana,[65] and probably refers to the story of Jesus and his family being borne back to Egypt in the clouds. In any event, the name of Lake Tana derives from this holy event and the water in the lake has a specific holiness.

Water is holy, and the long religious continuity and practices at Tana Kirkos have further blessed the waters of Lake Tana. The religious beliefs and views regarding the holiness of this water held by the monastic community on this island differ from those among Christians living along the Abay and shores of the lake. Gish Abay as the source from heaven is not highlighted by the former when they explain particular sanctity of Lake Tana's waters. On the other hand, there are several other important religious events that bestow special holiness on the water. First, the lake is holy in itself because streams with holy water run into it from the four cardinal corners. Second, Christos Semra, who was a devoted Christian, immersed her body in Lake Tana for 12 years while praying. Third, Elijah, Moses and John the Apostle brought with them a yellow cup with yellow water, which was given from the sky in the name of God, and they gave this water to the lake, thus adding a holy substance to the already sacred Lake Tana. Finally, although Jesus was not baptized in the lake, he, together with St Mary, Joseph, Sister Salome and the invisible saints, bathed in the lake, further increasing the holiness of its water.

Thus, for the monks living at Tana Kirkos, the lake has utmost holiness. Depending upon where other people live, there are varying understandings of the degrees of holiness of the water in the rivers and lake and in the form of rain. Still, for all Christians the use of holy water in their rituals is of cardinal cosmological importance, and water is an intrinsic part of the most important rituals and celebrations of the Ethiopian Orthodox Church. In Ethiopia there are numerous festivals throughout the year and the Ethiopian Orthodox Church celebrates a number of them in a manner and form unique within Christianity. Common to many of the festivals is the emphasis on and importance of water in the rituals, but also of the outcome of successful rains at the right time and the ensuing plentiful harvest and prosperity. The most important festival is the Timkat, which were observed in Bahir Dar along the shores of Lake Tana.

TIMKAT – RE-COMMEMORATING BAPTISM

The main aim of Timkat is to celebrate the importance for humanity of the sacrament of baptism, which Jesus institutionalized. Baptism defined Christianity, specifically how to become a Christian and to follow the divine path laid down by God. The ceremony is a gift of grace for the people and Timkat means 'immersion' in Amharic. This celebration is unique to the Ethiopian Orthodox Church and is the equivalent of Epiphany ('manifestation' in Greek) in the Western Christian tradition. In the West, Epiphany is celebrated on 6 January and commemorates the revelation of the infant Jesus to the Gentiles. Timkat, on the other hand, celebrates Jesus' baptism in the Jordan River at the age of 30 (some say 31), thereby revealing him to humanity. Timkat is celebrated on 18 and 19 January, and, with regard to St Michael, continues on 20 January. The main ceremony is in the morning of 19 January, but the festival starts the previous afternoon when the *tabot*s are carried from the various churches to the body of water where the baptisms will take place the next day. Timkat is celebrated throughout Ethiopia, and there are local traditions and adaptations within the overall set of prescribed religious practices. The following presentation is based on the celebrations in Bahir Dar in 2010.

Jesus' baptism was not for himself but for humanity. It was an act of mercy enabling humans to partake of Christ and the Kingdom of God. It was a salvation rite for humanity and an instructional code for Christians, as is shown in the baptism of Jesus. Originally, John the Baptist refused to baptize Jesus and argued that Jesus could not be baptized by an inferior servant. Jesus, on the other hand, replied that baptism is an act of obedience and teaches how the rich, wealthy and powerful should serve the less fortunate. Jesus offered humanity the opportunity to partake of this grace and the Kingdom of God. Water is a medium through which initiates may reach heaven, and the very act Jesus institutionalized is celebrated during the Timkat festival.

Timkat is celebrated each year to commemorate the bountifulness and prosperity Jesus' baptism promised humanity. The festival is similar to the Israelites' celebration of God when they praise his deeds and greatness: not only had God made humans, he had also made everything they needed. Timkat acknowledges what God has provided and enabled for humanity and what God is and represents. It testifies to the importance of baptism, which enables salvation for Christians. In Matthew, baptism is celebrated to acknowledge the greatness of God and to praise the bountifulness, prosperity and wealth God provides.

For Western churches, the celebration of Epiphany is directly and solely related to the Angel Gabriel's annunciation to the Virgin Mary that she would be the mother of the Messiah, Jesus Christ (Luke 1:26–38). The Epiphany has the same meaning for the Eastern Orthodox Church, but has another meaning in addition involving an unusual manifestation of the spirit of God in the baptism of Jesus.

In Western churches there is only one baptism and that baptism is a sacrament. The baptism of an infant or of an adult convert symbolizes entry into a new and eternal life of salvation and faith in God. The meaning of baptism is the same in the Ethiopian Church, and initiates are baptized in the name of the Father, the Son and the Holy Spirit. There is, however, an important difference between Eastern and Western churches with regard to the birth and baptism of Jesus. *Lidet* or Christmas Day is also celebrated in the Ethiopian Orthodox Church. However, from a religious perspective, the most important event along the path to salvation and eternity for each Christian is baptism as a sacrament institutionalized by Jesus, not his birth. Christmas Day is celebrated, but no holy water is used in this ceremony, and the commemoration takes place within families or among households, with several households sometimes joining together and sacrificing an ox.

The Ethiopian Orthodox Church clearly states and underlines that baptism during the Timkat festival is not a sacrament, and hence the associated rituals and the immersion in holy water do not constitute rebaptism. The fundamental doctrine of Christianity is that there is only one Lord, one faith and one baptism (Eph. 4:5). Only infant baptism is a sacrament. Baptism during the Timkat festival is therefore not a new baptism or renewal of the original baptism, but commemorates the baptism of Jesus and the role this has for humanity. Being baptized as a child and initiated into the Kingdom of God does not, however, mean you cannot be baptized and immersed in water at a later stage of your life, but all other forms of baptism differ in function and religious meaning from the original infant baptism.

Thus, baptism in the Timkat celebration is not a sacrament and does not lead to salvation. It is a baptism of repentance and for healing. Timkat is in honour of the Lord and saviour Jesus Christ who was baptized to fulfil divine prophecy and reveal the Trinity. Through the baptism, Jesus showed his humility and submission to his Father.

The Timkat celebration serves a number of religious purposes. It celebrates the main function and outcome of baptism, initiation into the Kingdom of Heaven through baptism and thus being blessed. According to the Ethiopian Orthodox Church, Jesus' baptism revealed the Trinity as unity – the Father, the Son and the Holy Spirit as one. This essential truth was laid bare to believers in the year of revelation – *Yemegelet zemene*. The skies opened and the spirit of God descended as a Dove and the Trinitarian basis of Christianity was revealed. God the Father spoke, God the Spirit descended like a dove, and God the Son was evident in Jesus in person, fully God and fully human. This dual character is captured in the word *'Tewahedo'*, and the church in Ethiopia is consequently called the Ethiopian Orthodox Tewahedo Church.

When believers are baptized with the blessed and holy water during Timkat, they may also be healed of sickness. The water has particularly purifying, curative and divine qualities, and this use of holy water differs from the original baptism. When Jesus was baptized at the hands of John the Baptist, he served as a role model for Christians (John 13:15, Pet. 2:21) in a double sense. On one hand, when Jesus as the King was baptized by John, he showed obedience in the same way as when he washed Peter's feet. On the other, kings, nobles and authorities are shown that, whoever they may be, they should be baptized by the church and that everyone is under the King of Heaven and his power. When Jesus requested John the Baptist to baptize him, John asked how he could baptize Jesus since he baptized others in the name of the Father, the Son and the Holy Spirit. God answered that he would be a priest forever, and thereby institutionalized the practice of baptism and bestowed on the priesthood the power of baptizing and initiating humans into the Kingdom of God.

In baptism Jesus took on the sins of humankind. In Paradise, the Devil tempted Eve who offered Adam the forbidden fruits of the tree of knowledge and they both committed a sin. As a consequence, they and humanity were subsequently expelled from Paradise. As a penalty, Adam became the servant of the Devil and Eve the Devil's slave. One of them was sent to the River Jordan and the other to Hell. In order to rescue Adam and Eve and humanity from sin and suffering and enable salvation, Jesus institutionalized the essences of Christianity. By being baptized in the Jordan and not in another river, Jesus purified the sins perpetrated in Paradise. When Jesus was crucified and died on the cross, he took on the sins of humanity, thereby enabling devotees to escape Hell and gain eternal life and salvation in Heaven. In addition to the general aspects of baptism, there are also particular Ethiopian perceptions. The aim of Christ's baptism was to fulfil the prophecy of King David (Dawit in Amharic). In the prophecy, the sea and the River Jordan retreated, the mountains and the hills were shaken and turned to water, and these events would come to pass with the baptism of Jesus.

Turning to the actual celebrations witnessed in 2010, the Timkat festival started in the churches on the afternoon of 18 January. The day before Timkat is called *Ketera*, which refers to the damming of a stream to create a baptismal pool. This pool is also called the sea, and all bodies of water are viewed as equally holy, regardless of whether they take the form of a constructed pool, a flowing river or a lake.

Although Bahir Dar is located alongside Lake Tana and the Abay, nowadays the ceremony takes place at Meskel Square downtown (fig. 14). The square is a huge, open field upon which has been built a baptismal pool, Bahire Timiket, whose water is blessed by the bishop and splashed on the masses through pipes and a sprinkler system. In the past the rituals were

14. The baptismal pool at Meskel Square.

performed in Lake Tana and the Abay, but with growing urbanization and population pressure, there are now too many people in the city to allow for collective baptism along the waterfront. This change of venue to Meskel Square occurred in 1980 (Ethiopian calendar) for the sake of convenience and safety, but the move does not alter the religious significance of the ceremonies. There is no difference in the holiness of the water, because the water in the pool comes from Lake Tana and the Abay.

Nevertheless, some priests were not satisfied with this solution because they preferred to perform the ritual in the running waters of the Abay. The baptismal pool is artificial and, while it may be convenient, is less than ideal from a religious viewpoint, because it is unlike the original setting of Jesus' baptism, the Jordan River. In villages outside Bahir Dar people do perform the baptism in Lake Tana or in the Abay, depending upon which body of water is the closest to their settlements.

In Ethiopia, *tabot* strictly implies a container and therefore the Ark of the Covenant, as well as the Ark of Noah in the Ethiopian Bible. But in everyday use it is also commonly used when referring to the *sellat* or altar tablet, and hence supposed to refer to one or several of the tablets of the Law contained in the Ark. In practice it is believed that it represents both the Ark and the tablets of Moses.[66] During Timkat, the *tabot,* or replica of both the Ark and of the tablets of the law that Moses placed in the Ark, is taken out of the church. This is the only time during the liturgical year the *tabot*s leave the churches, other than during the annual celebration by individual churches of their saint's day. All churches are built around the Ark of the Covenant in the same way as the Jewish temple was organized around the Ark. When the Ark is taken out of the church during Timkat, the church is purified. The holiness of the *tabot* and the possibility for devotees to see it and get close to it during the festival make this day a special occasion for worshipping God. Devotees also change their clothes and put on their best and newest to symbolize a new covenant with Jesus. Dirt, filth and sin are exchanged for holiness, beauty and divine love, a process similar to being baptized in water.

The Ark is the home of the Lord and it is holy. According to tradition, the holiness and power of the Ark were manifested when St Iyasu carried the Ark through dry and barren deserts. Every area he visited with the Ark became wet and fertile. Moreover, every Ark contains the Greek signs alpha and omega, which symbolize that the Lord was here in the past, he is here now, and he will be here in the future, and consequently, that the Lord is alpha and omega.

On the eve of 18 January, the *tabot* is carried to the bank of a river or close to the baptismal pool, and devotees fast from dusk to the dawn of the following day. Before the *tabot*s are carried from their respective churches, there is a ceremony in each of them involving prayers for the safe return of the *tabot*. Then the *tabot*s are carried by priests accompanied by large processions to the baptismal pool. The *tabot*s are covered with gold and silver embroidered velvet clothes to protect them and seclude them from the public. Each church's head priest carried the *tabot* on his head while other priests protected it from the sun by holding ceremonial umbrellas. In Old Testament times, the Ark was borne on a stretcher, but with the New Testament and in the Orthodox Church, the *tabot* is carried on the head of a priest.

The procession started from the Bahir Dar Giorgioys, the main church in Bahir Dar, at around 3.30pm on 18 January, and it was led by older men bearing guns and blowing trumpets. Following behind the priests who carried and protected the *tabot* were singing Sunday school choirs. They in turn were followed by the laity and youths, who sang and danced. The procession is seen as symbolizing Jesus' journey from Galilee to the Jordan River (Matt. 3) and David's dancing around the Ark (2 Sam. 6). The road ahead of the procession was purified with water and swept with palm leaves in direct reference to Jesus' arrival in Jerusalem on Palm Sunday. The processions with the Arks from the different churches in the Bahir Dar area converged from various directions on Meskel Square and the priests with the Arks gathered at the baptismal pool, together with the bishop and other dignitaries.

When an Ark is carried to the river or any body of water, it symbolizes the baptism of Jesus in the River Jordan. The patriarch, bishop or priest who blesses the water performs the same role as John the Baptist did when he baptized Jesus. The Ark is the most holy and venerated object in the Ethiopian Orthodox Church. Jesus went to the Jordan River and was baptized. Since the Ark embodies the Lord's presence on earth, the Ark is carried to the water to be baptized in a way similar to what happened with Jesus. The Ark *is* the home of the Lord, and consequently this act commemorates the original baptism of Jesus whereby he blessed and made all water holy. The presence of the Ark at any body of water

– a pool, a river, lake or the sea – recreates the original ritual by which Jesus enabled salvation for humanity by being baptized in holy water.

The Arks were not immersed in the baptismal pool, but their very presence in a tent nearby was seen as identical to the immersion of Jesus in the River Jordan. These Arks were blessed by the bishop in the same way Jesus was blessed by John the Baptist. In the past, when there were fewer people, the Arks were brought close to the given body of water. However, since there are now so many people participating in the Timkat festival, the Arks were held in the tent throughout the ceremony for security reasons and to avoid damage. This did not, however, have any significance for the blessings and ceremony, since the mere presence of the Arks in the tent close to the pool made the water holy.

Altogether 17 Arks were brought to Meskel Square, and when all had arrived, the ceremony started. First there was a short introduction regarding practicalities, and then there were prayers followed by the singing and dancing of Sunday School students. Then the bishop, Abune Barnabas, who was the head of the Ethiopian Church of West-Gojjam, preached and prayed from the podium of the baptismal pool and the main ceremony for the evening was finished. The priests carrying the Arks left the baptismal pool and brought them to the tent arranged in the form of a village church, a mobile church if you like, where the Arks remained overnight securely guarded. The main ceremonies at Meskel Square lasted from about 4.00pm until 6.00pm that evening.

After the Arks were safely secured, the celebrations continued. Timkat is a collective festival celebrated with joy and great pomp. Various church and Sunday School communities sang and danced in the streets of Bahir Dar, some only during the evening, others throughout the night, and many people stayed at Meskel Square for the start of the further ceremonies early next morning. They had been fasting, but could now eat. In rural areas it has been common for a meal to be prepared by the river for the men and boys – women cannot partake – and during Timkat cattle are often sacrificed, although this is not the case in towns.

Early in the morning of 19 January, devotees gathered around the tent were the Arks had been kept overnight. Some had been at Meskel Square the whole night, and others began to stream into the area. Before the dawn a huge crowd of people had gathered and were praising, praying and singing towards the Arks. When the sun started rising, attention turned to the baptismal pool. At around 7.00am the main ceremony began and an area in front of the baptismal pool was prepared for donations.

The bishop, together with other high priests and dignitaries, climbed the stairs on the eastern side of the baptismal pool and then took up their seats on the western side. The main consecration and blessing of the holy water in the baptismal pool took about two and a half hours of continuous prayer and religious songs. As the ceremony started to draw to an end, three burning candles were put on a plate and placed on the water's surface, symbolizing the Trinity of the Father, the Son and the Holy Spirit. Thereafter the bishop and a procession of clerks walked around the baptismal pool and the bishop blessed each of the cardinal points of the pool by quoting passages from the four Gospels. These blessings had to be repeated three times. After blessing the cardinal points, the bishop returned to the western side of the pool and again blessed the water with his large cross. This blessing was to commemorate the baptism in Jordan and to bear witness to the tradition and the importance of holy water. The blessing did not alter the quality of the water because it is always holy and blessed, and in Amharic blessed is *kidus*. Another priest then filled up a bottle with water from the pool, which he gave to the bishop. The bishop baptized the high priests next to him by sprinkling holy water on them, and at the very moment when these priests had been baptized, the sprinkler system around the baptismal pool was turned on and spouted water over the crowd.

People flocked around the sprinkler system so that the holy water fell on their faces and bodies, and many tried to get access to the baptismal pool itself. Some got close enough to the pool and sprinkled themselves with the water, but the guards tried their best to keep the huge crowd away because if everyone reached the baptismal pool there would be an enormous and dangerous crush. That is why the sprinkler had been set up in such a way as to spout the water from the pool over as many people as possible. In fact, the water pressure in the sprinkler was so strong that for a short time it had to be turned off.

How many people attended the Timkatfestival this year is hard to tell, but no less than 10,000 would appear to be a reasonable estimate. The whole of Meskel Square was packed with people, and the growing number of attendees has necessitated changes in the ritual performances associated with the celebration. However, the religious significance is the same as if the baptisms had taken place in Lake Tana or the Abay, because the very same holy water is involved.

When everyone had been baptized with the holy water, the Timkat ceremony was over. The Arks were brought back to their respective churches in processions similar to those seen arriving in Meskel Square the day before. The only Ark left guarded in the church tent was the Ark of St Michael. St Michael's Day is 20 January and those church communities which have St Michael as their saint take the Ark back home in similar processions on that day. Thus, the Timkat festival may last for two or three days, depending upon which saint the church community is associated with, and the Arks will not be taken out of their churches again before the next Timkat or the celebration of specific name days.

The Ethiopian Timkat ceremony has in the past often been misunderstood and misinterpreted by the Western Church as a real rebaptism, and therefore as sinful. The Jesuits in Ethiopia were horrified at the Epiphany, not only because they believed it to be a rebaptism, but also because of the promiscuity involved. In the words of Bruce:

> The baptism, Alvarez says, began at midnight, and the old tutor dipt every person under water, taking him by the head, saying, 'I baptise thee in the name of the Father, of the Son, and of the Holy Ghost.' It was most thronged at sunrise, and ended about nine o'clock; a long time for an old man to stand in frozen water. The number (as women were promiscuously admitted) could not be less than 40,000; so that for even the nine hours this baptism-general officiated, he must have had exercise enough to keep him warm, if 40,000 (many of them naked beauties) passed through his hands.[67]

On the other hand, Bruce corrects Alvarez' interpretation of Epiphany as a rebaptism:

> [T]he whole account of Alvarez is a gross fiction; that no baptism, or any thing like baptism, is meant by the ceremony; that a man is no more baptised by keeping the anniversary of our Saviour's baptism, than he is crucified by keeping his crucifixion. The commemoration of our Saviour's baptism on the epiphany, and the blessing the waters that day, is an old observance of the eastern church, formerly performed in public in Egypt as now in Ethiopia.[68]

With regard to the nakedness, Bruce was also shocked, perhaps even stunned:

> The Abuna, the king and the queen, were the three first baptised, all three absolutely naked, having only a cotton cloth round their middle. I am sure there never could be a greater deviation from the manners of any kingdom, than this is from those of Abyssinia. The king is always covered; you seldom see any part of him but his eyes, The queen and every woman in Abyssinia, in public and private, (I mean where nothing is intended but conversation) are covered to the chin.[69]

In particular, the naked women were promiscuous, and in Bruce's mind this must have tempted the priest to behave non-religiously. In his vivid language, he wrote:

> The women were stark naked before the men, not even a rag about them. Without some such proper medium as frozen water, I fear it would not have contributed much to the interests of religion to have trusted a priest (even an old one) among so many bold and naked beauties, especially as he had the first six hours of them in the dark.[70]

If Bruce is to be believed, one must assume that the cold water early in the morning of Timkat ensured that the celebration was performed according to prescribed religious orthodoxy. But as long as Christianity has been in the region, it has fiercely opposed other water beliefs and cults, which relate to the indigenous religion and practices, including the Beta Israel or the Ethiopian Jews.

THE BETA ISRAEL

The Ethiopian Christianity bears many resemblances to Jewish traditions, and the questions of how and when Jewish influences came to Ethiopia, and some may even say if, have been discussed for decades, and Steven Kaplan argues that these do not appear before the first centuries AD. Moreover, Egypt is not the obvious cradle for these influences, and Judaized communities of southern Arabia and the Red Sea are a likely source to the early Jewish influence.[71] The presence of Ethiopian Jews known as Beta Israel is another enigma and in 1868 it was estimated that their number was between 150,000 and 200,000.[72] When the Jews came to Ethiopia is uncertain, and if it is assumed that the Jewish introduction was pre-Christian, even fourth to sixth century AD is too late.[73] The majority of the Beta Israel has traditionally lived in the Lake Tana region. For how long a time they have been in Ethiopia nobody knows. In Numbers 12:1 it says: 'Then Miriam and Aaron spoke against Moses because of the Ethiopian woman whom he had married; for he had married an Ethiopian woman.' Not only is the Ethiopian Orthodox Church one of the oldest Christian denominations in the world, but according to biblical mythology there is also an Ethiopian connection from the times of Moses, since he married an Ethiopian wife.

The founding myth of Ethiopia is Queen Sheba and Ethiopia's role and place in the Old Testament. According to an old tradition, the Abyssinians descended from Ham, who was the second son of Noah. Together with his brothers Shem and Japhet, they were born before the flood. Following legend, the sons of Ham were the fathers of different people: Kush in Nubia, Misraim in Egypt, Put in Libya and Kenaan in Phaenicia, and the Abyssinians stemming from Kush.[74] In the book *The Glory of the Kings*, it is said about the Queen of Ethiopia:

> This Queen of the South was very beautiful in face, and her stature was superb, and her understanding and intelligence, which God had given her, were of such high character that she went to Jerusalem to hear the wisdom of Solomon; now this was done by the command of God and it was His good pleasure. And moreover, she was exceedingly rich, for God had given her glory, and riches, and gold, and silver, and splendid apparel, and camels, and slaves, and trading men.[75]

When Queen Sheba listened to King Solomon while he told about his God, the Queen said:

> From this moment I will not worship the sun, but will worship the Creator of the sun, the God of Israel. And that Tabernacle of the God of Israel shall be unto me my Lady, and unto my seed after me, and unto all my kingdoms that are under my domination.[76]

After six months she wished to return to her country and sent a message to Solomon when she was about to depart. Solomon was pondered in his heart and said, 'A woman of such splendid beauty hath come to me from the ends of the earth! What do I know? Will God give me seed in her?' As it is widely known, Solomon was a lover of women, and he married beautiful women from wherever. It has been said that he had 400 queens and 600 concubines. This was not for the sake of fornication, but the wise intent of the remembering of what God said to Abraham: 'I will make thy seed like the stars of heaven for number, and like the sand of the sea.' And he said in his heart: 'What do I know? Peradventure God will give me men children from each of these women [...] My children shall inherit the cities of the enemy, and shall destroy those who worship idols.'[77] The child King Solomon got with Queen Sheba was Menelik I. And according to legend, it was Menelik who brought the Ark of the Covenant to Ethiopia, and this religious relic has an extremely important place in the Ethiopian Orthodox Christianity.

Menelik I, the son of Queen Sheba and King Solomon, made Axum the centre for worshipping the God of Noah and the Kings David and Solomon of Israel. According to priests:

> Ham begot Kush, Kush begot Aethiopis, after whom the country is called Aethiopia to this day. Aethiopia was buried in Axum, and his grave is known there to this day [...] Aethiopia begot Aksumawi [... the] six sons of Aksumawi became the fathers of Aksum.

Thus, Ethiopia took her name from an unknown ancestor and Axum from his son.[78] According to legend, then, the origin of Ethiopia has its roots in the Old Testament stories and the Jewish connections, but this equally explains the particular character of the Ethiopian Orthodox Church.

The Beta Israel was perceived by others as a low status occupational caste group, working as blacksmiths, potters and weavers, and tenant farmers, and they had been banned from owning agricultural land since the fifteenth century when Emperor Yeshaq (1413–30) declared 'May he who is baptized in the Christian religion inherit the land of his father; otherwise let him be uprooted from his land and be a stranger.'[79] Although the Beta Israel were not baptized as Christians and perceived as low-caste, they themselves had other perceptions, and in fact were more obedient and observed the fast and ritual purity stricter than their Ethiopian Christian counterpart. Although the Ethiopian Orthodox Church prescribed more days of fasts than other Christian denomination, on average 180 days per year, the Beta Israel observed at least 150 days, and whereas the orthodox could eat after lunch during days of fast, among the Beta Israel usually no food was permitted. Moreover, water and healing springs where devotees took baths and water was sprinkled was a central part for the Falasha, although seen as religious deviation by orthodox and other Christian missionaries.

Ritual purity was central to the Beta Israel, and in Judaism the ritual bath or mikvah is used for physical ritual cleanliness. As opposed to in Israel, there were no constructed bath houses in Ethiopia, and this ritual state was achieved by ablutions in streams and rivers.[80] 'The Falashas themselves,' one author wrote, 'believe that they look like the rest of the Ethiopian population; indeed, one Falasha informed me that Ethiopians say that they can recognize a Falasha only by the heavy mineral odor of water which clings to him as a result of his incessant ritual ablutions.' The special ablutions and characteristic smell was attributed by Amhara to ye-ouha falasha or 'water Falashas'.[81] Although both Ethiopian Christians and Beta Israel observed the Saturday Sabbath, the Beta Israel perceived that they observed it in a more orthodox way; not only did they not light fire or work, but they could not even cross bodies of water.[82] Thus, water and rituals had a central role in the religious life of the Beta Israel, but also in their relations to the Christians and their segregation from the rest of society. In fact, their purity was fundamental. Intermarriages with other groups were strictly forbidden, and Beta Israel would not allow others to enter their house or touch their clothes. If some impure touched their clothes, they would wash it in running water, and therefore they always lived close to a spring or river. Even money received for their crafts when sold on markets was received in a dish full of water.[83]

Water symbolism includes blood as a fluid. The Beta Israel had an ambivalent social and ritual position. As smiths, they were perceived by others as being descendants of the smiths making the nails for Christ's crucifixion and hence referred to as 'may his blood be upon you'. On the other hand, the issue of blood also distinguished the Christians and the Jews. The Beta Israel saw their Christian neighbours as consumers of blood not only because of Eucharist, but also due the practice of eating raw meat, which they looked upon with disgust.[84]

The long continuity and isolation of the Beta Israel from Judaism in Israel is a mystery. In fact, when the Beta Israel first met European Jews in the nineteenth century they were surprised when they found out that they were not the only Jews in the world. Given that they had been cut off from mainstream Judaism for centuries they were unaware of the Talmudic law.[85] After a scrutinizing process, however, it was acknowledged that the Beta Israel or Falasha were indeed Jews. In 1975 it was decided that the Beta Israel had the right to emigrate to Israel in accordance with the religious 'law of return'. From 1979 to 1982 only a small number of Ethiopians migrated, but from 1983 to 1985 a massive transport called 'Operation Moses' took place where some 17,000 Beta

Israel came to Israel and with some 8,000–10,000 famine affected left behind in Ethiopia and Sudan.[86] 'Operation Solomon' in 1991 when most of the remaining Beta Israel were flown out of Ethiopia to Israel brought an end to this long tradition of Jews in Ethiopia,[87] and one of the few remaining indigenous groups along Lake Tana is the Woyto.

THE RIVER SPIRIT ABINAS AMONG THE WOYTO

The Woyto today embody most of the extant indigenous traditions, although other traditional practices also survive, including Christian and Muslim syncretic practices. James Bruce's above described rituals and sacrifices at Gish Abay have to be seen in light of the rich pre-Christian tradition existing in the Lake Tana region, and although the ones Bruce described belonged to another group, it shows the omnipresence of different beliefs structured around water and sacrifices in this region. The Woyto represents another tradition, although this one too is decaying and will probably soon disappear (fig. 15).

The Woyto or Negedie Woyto still live in Bahir Dar and they have been displaced several times. They are believed to have their origin in Egypt and to have followed the Nile southwards through Sudan before ending

15. Woyto water-world.

up in the Bahir Dar region of Ethiopia. According to another legend, the Woyto accompanied the Queen of Sheba up the Nile when she visited King Solomon.[88] They attribute their displacement to a war that occurred while they were still living in Egypt. In the course of this war, they came near the river and their war leader, the king, ordered his people to drink from it and then to follow him again. However, the Woyto drank too much river water so they could not accompany the king and his army further, and they remained along the river, as they have ever since.

Yet there are also other legends. Elders of the community unanimously state that wherever there is *Bahir* (literally meaning Sea), there are the Woyto. For the Woyto, Lake Tana in general and Abay in particular are their life, society and religion. It is all about water. This indicates how their life and entire survival is linked to the Lake and its water resources. Following their oral history, even the origin of the name Woyto is strongly associated with water. They explained that the name Woyto is derived from an ancient event. When the king of the Woyto was defeated and chased by Egyptian Pharaohs, he sank into the water of the lake to hide himself. Hence, according to the Woyto elders, the name Woyto is literary similar to the Amharic word *watow*, meaning swallowed by the water. The Woyto has then settled around the water in Lake Tana and the water has remained their mainstay of survival. The Woyto has also another origin myth where they argue that they are the people of the sea (Lake Tana). The birthplace of their people is the sea and like fish they cannot survive without water. In fact, some elders explained that 'We are like fish' and 'We are the son of the fish.' Being totally dependent upon the lake, not only have they to live close to the shores, but all their life and well-being come from this inland sea and therefore they have to make sacrifices. And as they explained the reason for making sacrifice, 'unless you give it something, it cannot give you anything'.[89]

The Woyto are believed to be the first arrivals in Bahir Dar. Traditionally, they have been seen as river people and fishermen. As noted by Blundell in 1906, Wattu (Woyto) boatmen and lakeshore dwellers were viewed by the Gallas and Amharas as inferior and, to some extent, unclean on account of their eating hippopotamus and elephants, etc.[90] The situation is very much the same a century later, although they no longer eat these animals. Another reason for these attitudes is the Woyto's sacrifices to the Nile and the worship of Abinas. The Christians view them as pagan, in part because as fishermen living off the resources of the Blue Nile and Lake Tana, they have eaten hippopotamus and species of fish, such as catfish, that Christians perceive as unclean and sinful.

The Woyto, long suppressed by Christians and treated as outcasts, converted to Islam, but mainly in name only so they would be left alone by the Christian majority. The Woyto do not know when they converted, but claim that their roots are in Islam. By the time Hormuzd Rassam wrote his *Narrative of the British mission to Theodore, king of Abyssinia: with notices of the countries traversed from Massowah, through the Soodân, the Amhâra, and back to Annesley Bay* in 1869, the Woyto were already Muslims. In the 1930s, when Cheesman visited the Lake Tana monasteries, he was transported by the Woyto, who, at that time, claimed that Islam was their religion and Amharic their language.[91] Their Muslim heritage may be a consequence of historical events in the sixteenth century. The Woyto made an alliance with Gragn Mohammed, who conquered and ruled Abyssinia, including the Portuguese, and they may have adopted Islam then. When he was defeated, all those who had supported him were exiled to the lake.[92] There is, however, one problem with this interpretation: Almeida did not refer to them as 'Moors', and neither Orthodox Christians nor Muslims would eat the flesh of the hippopotamus.[93]

Orthodox Muslims do not accept the Woyto as proper Muslims, and although they officially are Muslims, their whole belief system still revolves around water: as one elderly Woyto man put it, 'the water of the Nile is everything and we give everything to the Nile'. Indeed, the Muslim community opposes their traditional rituals and beliefs. However, they continue with their worship of the Nile and sacrifices to Abinas, admitting that their relationship with Islam is superficial because for them the Nile is everything. Nevertheless, their perceptions of the river and Abinas have come to be strongly influenced by Islam and the Muslims over the centuries.

According to tradition today, when the spirits divided the territories at Tis Abay, they decided their faith in front of Allah. It is also said that it was actually Allah who initiated and enabled the 40 spirits to divide all the territories among themselves on the island. In the Islamized version of Abinas, he has a human character. Abinas is not a water spirit but a god who resides in the Abay. Some elders today compare Abinas with Christian saints such as St Gabriel or St Mary, and he works as a mediator. Thus, they perceive Abinas to be a mediator with Allah just as Christian saints are seen as mediators with God in the Orthodox Church. Today, they believe

Allah gave Abinas the position and role of protector of the river on account of his religious standing. Furthermore, Abinas also protects people against Aganent, the Devil, who has a more spiritual character than Abinas, with his human character. The very spot where the Great Sacrifice occurs is also believed to have been revealed by Allah. Lastly, in the Islamized perceptions of Abinas, he is also called Che Abinas, Sheik Abinas (fig. 16).

Thus, the indigenous water cult and animistic religion have been influenced by Islam, but the influence has also been the other way around. The water-world and cosmology of the Abay and Lake Tana have influenced local perceptions among Muslims. Muslims in Bahir Dar also worship water, which is an intrinsic aspect of Islam. For the ablutions performed five times a day, clean water from a river or stream cleanses both body and soul, externally as well as internally. Water in general is perceived as holy because it is given by Allah. The Nile or Abay is particularly holy because it comes from heaven and this water has healing and medicinal powers. Orthodox Muslims deny, however, that Muslims make sacrifices to the Nile. Even though the Woyto are Muslims, they are not seen as proper or strict Muslims because of these sacrifices, but also because they drink alcohol and deviate from other Muslim practices. Nevertheless, Muslims along the Little Abay and in the villages around the outlet from Lake Tana

16. Praying to Abinas before sacrifice.

do sacrifice calves, a practice that testifies to their incorporation of rituals and beliefs from the original cosmology of the region, as has been the case with Christianity as well.

The religion of the Woyto is solely based on water, specifically the Blue Nile and Lake Tana. The primary belief is in the power of the Blue Nile. Abinas is the god of the Blue Nile or the spirit of the Abay, and he is a male spirit. He is the source of everything: it is from him that the Woyto receive wealth, health, prosperity, natural resources and all that they need. A central element in their religious practice is making sacrifices to the Abay, but also to Lake Tana. The sacrifices are performed by individuals, families or community groups. Personal and family sacrifices to the river may be made at any time of the year. Individuals may sacrifice hens and cocks as well as sheep and goats on various occasions, but calves are only sacrificed at the community level and traditionally on the day before Lent, the last day Christians eat meat before the fast begins. This is the main sacrifice and most important ritual among the Woyto.

The sacrifice before Lent takes place on the eastern shore of the Abay close to the outlet from Lake Tana and it is a collective ritual. The bullock that is offered should not be fertile and mature, but clean and uncontaminated, in other words, it should not have procreated. Before the sacrifice, money is collected to defray the costs of the ritual, which include both the calf and other ingredients and ritual items. If certain people from the community cannot take part in the ritual – for instance, they are away on that particular date – they still have to contribute money for the sacrifice, because the ritual is for the prosperity of the whole group. When calves and sheep are sacrificed, their blood is given to the river so that Abinas can drink of it directly.

The prosperity and destiny of the Woyto are totally dependent on Abinas and the gifts of the Nile. Before a sacrifice, the Woyto thank the river and make a wish for the future; for instance, fecundity for a wife who has not yet conceived. Then they promise the river that if their wishes are granted, they will return the next year in gratitude and make a sacrifice that includes specific commitments. When the sacrifice is completed, the wish is repeated. However, if their wishes are not fulfilled, it is believed that Abinas was not satisfied with the previous sacrifice, so that they must return to sacrifice more. Moreover, misfortune, malignance or even catastrophe that befall individuals and collective groups are generally believed to be a punishment from Abinas or the spirit of the Blue Nile for moral misconduct. In such cases, people have to make sacrifices to the river in order to propitiate the spirit that has inflicted these calamites.

According to the Woyto, there are several examples of Abinas penalizing them harshly when they have not fulfilled their ritual commitments and made sacrifices to him. Since they are officially Muslim, the Islamic authorities, like their Christian counterparts, see these beliefs and ritual practices as pagan and have attempted to abolish them. In 1989 (Ethiopian calendar), the Muslim community imposed stringent restrictions on these ritual practices and the Woyto were unable to worship and make sacrifices to the river as before. As a direct result, seven or eight of their people died, some of them by drowning, and for the Woyto this was clear proof of the consequences of not worshipping Abinas and making sacrifices. Consequently, as the elders say, they cannot at any cost stop believing in and making sacrifices to the Nile. Although the younger generation would like to change or to abandon these traditions, the elders argue that the Abay is the central pillar of their religion and they cannot stop believing in it or making sacrifices to it, despite Muslim restrictions and if necessary in utmost secrecy.

Christians also oppose Woyto practices and beliefs and they are consequently stigmatized. Debre Maryam Monastery is one of the oldest in the Lake Tana region. According to a priest, Debra Mariam Church on Debra Mariam Island was founded by Abuna Thadeos in the reign of Amda Seyon (1314–44), the grandson of Yekuno Amlak. This was once a famous monastery. When Abuna Thadeos first went to the island to establish the church, it is believed that he divided the waters and walked on dry land, just as Moses had done when he crossed the Red Sea.[94] The location of the monastery at the source of the Nile had implications for Woyto and other non-Christian practices. This area is also one of the most important for the worship of the river and for making sacrifices. The church calls the old river spirit that, for instance, the Woyto worship, *baed amlko* – 'bad spirit' – in reference to the practice of not believing in and worshipping the True God. If Christians worship the river, they also fall prey to *baed amlko*. Once, a young man with pain in his back prayed for good health and offered coffee to the river. Other people along the river mocked and ridiculed him for his 'pagan' practices, and more generally the Woyto are seen as 'poor' and 'dirty'. Thus, there is strong social and religious pressure by Christians and Muslims on the Woyto individually and collectively on account of their religion and practices.

If someone dies in the river or lake, it is the Woyto who, as river people, collect the corpse. The Woyto believe that the Blue Nile and Lake Tana will not take their own lives since they are obediently making sacrifices to the river, and the water spirit does not wish to harm its own people. However, when one of their members drowns in the river or lake, the Woyto believe this is because they have not been sufficiently obedient and made the appropriate sacrifices. Consequently, new and more elaborate sacrifices are called for.

There are no priests among the Woyto and the ceremonies and prayers are led and conducted by male elders. The main sacrificial site was located along the western shore of the Abay just south of the outlet from Lake Tana and below the bridge in the area called Kebele 10, but now it is a residential area. In 2009, the Woyto still used to make their sacrifices here for fecundity, wealth and prosperity. Thursdays, Saturdays and Sundays are the preferred days for sacrifices since the spirit is believed to be most accessible on these days. When sacrifices are made, Abinas must always have the first taste. The blood is drunk by the river spirit when the animal dies, and before those who make the sacrifice taste the coffee, liver and finally the meal, each item must be given to Abinas. As the people say: 'The spirit of the water should taste first', or 'the Nile spirit should taste first', otherwise the spirit will be offended and attack and endanger them. The power of the Nile is ubiquitous and if something goes wrong during the ritual or proper procedure is not followed, danger could ensue. Once, when only one person went down to the river to make the offerings, the others present said 'he should not go alone', indicating that the Abay has special powers that can cause harm and jeopardize prosperity if people are not careful and obedient.

In Woyto religion and cosmology, sacrifices to the river spirit to ensure well-being are of utmost importance, and Abinas is the supreme deity. The water has healing powers, but the water in the Abay is holier than that in Lake Tana. Even so, since water from the Nile is found in the lake, it also holds the spirit, but to a lesser degree. Hence, this spirit is known as Sher Abinas, which means minor or less powerful than Abinas in the Blue Nile.

Abinas is the spirit of the Nile. Mythologically, the role of Abinas as the river spirit goes back to a meeting among all the indigenous gods of the area. Originally, there were 40 spirits of non-Christian origin (or 44, as well as 44 Christian Arks) in the regions nearby, in particular in the area around the outflow from Lake Tana. The presence of all these spirits increased the holiness of the river at this place, although the church claims this particular area has no extraordinary holiness. According to legend, the 40 spirits gathered on an island south of Tis Abay. The island was not at the waterfalls, but was secluded and secure from people. Otherwise it is not clear why this spot was chosen. While the 40 spirits were discussing among themselves which divine realms each of them should get, the spirit who later became Abinas had gone to the river to collect water for all of them. By the time he returned, they had divided the realms and territories over which they would rule among themselves, but had forgotten Abinas, who was then given the river as his realm. Today, the other gods have disappeared or enjoy only minor importance in local cosmologies, but Abinas is the omnipotent spirit for the Woyto. He was given the right to supervise and protect the river and this is reflected in his very name: Abay is the river, *in* means 'position' and *yaz* is 'to control', hence Abinas.

Following his appointment as guardian of this mighty river at the meeting of the 40 spirits, Abinas has only lived in the Abay. There is, however, another divinity in Lake Tana named Meshiha. He was not among the original 40 and has less power than Abinas and enjoys less popularity. Nevertheless, the Woyto pray to him for safety while they are on the lake, especially if they encounter problems with their papyrus boats.

Although the church believes the waters of the Abay and Lake Tana have healing and miraculous powers that are a gift from the True God and a sign of his grace, it views Woyto's belief in the power of the Abay as a separate deity as profoundly pagan. However, until a couple of decades ago even Christian priests believed in the Nile and accepted the worship of it and sacrifices to it, including calves. However, when school- and elite-educated priests, seen by many as fundamentalists, came to the area, they actively campaigned against these indigenous practices. Some decades ago, Sunday School priests threw stones at and chased away the Woyto as they were preparing for their main sacrifice before Lent. Today, although they still strongly oppose the worship of the Nile, the priests are less aggressive and more tolerant and the Woyto take the view that if the Christians interrupt, Abinas may seek revenge and cause them harm.

Due to the strong Christian influence in this region, several Woyto rituals coincide with similar Christian rituals. During the five days of the 13th month before New Year, the Woyto collect rain water, which they use for the ritual ablution of their bodies. They celebrate New Year's Day, 12 June, which is the day of St Mikael, and they also celebrate 12 November, the day of St George. During these celebrations they conduct sacrifices to the Nile. Over Lent, they make no sacrifice, since the Christians do not eat meat during these 40 days. However, due to the Christian suppression of Woyto practices, which have made it difficult for these people to conduct their rituals in strict accordance with their traditions and religion, these rituals occurring simultaneously with Christian feasts are not as strongly rooted as before.

On the other hand, among Christians it was also common practice to make sacrifices to the river and make offerings of chickens. These rituals did not take place on specific dates or during specific ceremonies, but whenever it was believed they were necessary to reduce misfortune or as repentance for sins that had caused hardship. Even now, the offering of sacrifices of poultry and sheep continues, but only at home.

The Ethiopian Orthodox Church does not approve of sacrifices, dismissing them as 'pagan practices' or 'bad practices', since prayers in church are the only acceptable ritual for approaching God. Although the church has absorbed many pre-Christian practices and beliefs in transfigured form into Christianity, such practices in their original form or in the way they have continued up to today are to be combated as heresy or paganism. Similarly, although Muslims are a minority and latecomers to Bahir Dar, they also strongly oppose any water cult that deviates from their own teachings and beliefs. The Ethiopian Orthodox Church calls Abinas or the Nile spirit *aganent*, which has associations with or is the equivalent of the Devil or Satan, and thus views Abinas as a truly pagan and 'bad' spirit. The Woyto, on the other, perceive their animistic deity as wholly good and as a totally dependable source of everything they need. Consequently, they associate the Abay and Abinas with heaven.

THE 'GREAT SACRIFICE'

The main Woyto sacrifice takes place before the Lent starts, and sacrifices are conducted on both the Saturday and Sunday prior to the Christian fasting period. In 2010, the Great Sacrifice took place on 7 February. The festival is simply called the 'Great' and involves sacrifices made by both family and community. The family sacrifices take place first, in the morning. Numerous hens and cocks are sacrificed and are afterwards cooked and consumed. These fowl are sacrificed in the same manner as described above. It is worth noting that the appearance of the chicken is important.

Preferably, the comb of the bird should be thick, a sign that the animal has charisma and is powerful. If the comb is small, thin or single, the chicken is believed to have fewer of these qualities. If, however, chickens with small combs are sacrificed, then one egg has also to be sacrificed to the river.

Where devotees are unable to secure a calf, they may sacrifice chickens or sheep, although this is not ideal. The calf should be clean, with no physical blemishes on its body or horns. The sacrificial calf may be white or red, but never black. The reason a calf is preferred to a mature bull is that the sacrificial blood should be clean, and the Woyto believe that the blood of a young animal is cleaner than that from an older beast. Abinas will not accept the sacrifice of a mature bull, and will be offended. The sacrifice takes place at Abay Ras, the source of the Abay where it leaves Lake Tana. This spot is called Cherechera, a name with no specific meaning.

The Great Sacrifice is the calf sacrifice performed after the chickens have been offered. Women may not participate in the Great Sacrifice, although one woman made the preparations for the coffee and bread ceremony before leaving the area. This was in accordance with Woyto tradition, although no one could give an explicit answer as to why women cannot participate in the sacrifice and meal.

The Great Sacrifice is for the whole community (fig. 17). The calf's throat was slit with a knife and the blood was collected in a plastic cauldron and

17. The Great Sacrifice.

given to the river. While the sacrifice was taking place, a young man read from a book with Muslim poetry describing the benefits and delights of plentiful harvests and good fortune. After the calf had been sacrificed, a meal was prepared and eaten by the devotees and the rest of the meat was divided among the male participants.

Importantly, it was not only the Woyto who came to the source of the Nile for this annual sacrifice. Families from remote rural villages came to the river and sacrificed chickens. These were Christians, but they followed the same rituals, except that even the devotees who did not sacrifice washed their hands and feet. According to the Woyto, Abinas was very satisfied that day because much blood had been offered to him. The sacrifice protected people from disease and provided good fortune to society. If, by contrast, no sacrifice had been made, the people would have been punished with misfortune and calamity. The role of Abinas is, however, not restricted to annual or even irregular sacrifices made at individual or household levels, but the cosmology involved all important parts of life, where the hippo had a crucial place in the traditions of the Woyto, although this culture and cosmology is rapidly disappearing in the modernizing world.

THE HIPPO-CULT AMONG THE WOYTO OF LAKE TANA[95]

The Woyto confidently state that since their life, birth and growth are by Lake Tana and the river Abay – the Blue Nile – they cannot be consumed or endangered by these waters even when they enter deep into the waters of the lake and the river on their papyrus boats, or even when they swim far out and deep into the lake. The Woyto of Lake Tana, whose traditions and ways of life depend entirely on water, has different values and belief systems associated with big animals and fishes in the lake and Abay such as the hippo and catfish. The Woyto's economy and main source of living have been structured around hunting and fishing in Lake Tana and the Blue Nile.

Due to the very close dependence on the lake resources for their livelihood for centuries or perhaps even millennia, the Woyto cosmology has developed a strong ritual and religious significance to hippos and catfish in the lake and the Blue Nile River. The hippo-cult and the water-traditions in general are widely recognized as parts of their living heritage, but this tradition is slowly dying and disappearing in the modern world. Cheesman noted in his descriptions from the 1930s that a Woyto man could not marry before he had killed a hippopotamus. At that time, the Woyto were already a small and marginalized group. He estimated that there were only some 200 to 300 Woyto living in scattered villages along the shores of Lake Tana, and that they were most numerous in the south where the papyrus grew.[96]

Fish in general but in particular the catfish (*Ambaza*) has been ascribed with important cultural or ritual values among the Woyto of the Lake Tana region. According to Woyto informants, the catfish is considered distinctively different and special compared to other fish species in the lake and the surrounding rivers. The catfish has been associated with a number of specific cultural and ritual values and powers. Fat from the catfish is believed to, as with the hippos, enhance fertility of infertile women. If an infertile woman eats fat from a catfish in the days immediately following menstruation, she may become pregnant.

The big catfish which they call *sorz* is highly appreciated for this and other rituals. Since the Woyto believe in the ritual values and spiritual power of this fish, people even keep parts of its meat at home for ritual purposes. The way the fish is prepared and conserved has ritual significance. The fish should be washed and cut into pieces without slaying its hide and thereafter dried and kept in the homes. If the catfish is prepared in this way, it has the power to protect the household from malignant spirits causing harm and suffering for people.

As with the hippos, it is also believed that the catfish works as medicine in numerous ways. It is regarded as the best medicine for intestinal pains and worms. It can also cleanse the body and it is seen as protecting the beauty of a person's skin. Moreover, the bile of the catfish is believed to have qualities and supernatural powers which can be used for magical purposes. More pragmatically in a secular context, the role of the fish diet among the Woyto is considered as the most preferred way of building and maintaining a strong body and staying in good health.

Thus, both hippos and big catfish (*tiliku ambaza*) share ritual and religious similarities. According the Woyto elders, hippos and big catfish are chiefs or masters of the sea (*Yebahir Aleka*) because of their big size compared to the other species living in the lake and the river. They are also ascribed as spirits of the sea and as such sacred animals and fishes with particular ritual and religious powers and capabilities. Therefore, their meat and flesh and other parts of their bodies such as the hippo teeth are seen as invested with spiritual powers which keep away malignant spirits who otherwise would have caused misfortune and disasters.

According to the Woyto elders, the hippo is seen as a sacred animal which has spiritual power that structures the social, cultural and economic life of the Woyto society. In particular the hippo teeth, meat, hide and waste have in different ways great spiritual value and ritual importance for the Woyto of Lake Tana. Hippo teeth protect people from attacks by bad and malignant spirits. They are also regarded as having the power to protect the god spirit (*Kole*). A hippo tooth or part of it is thus kept in the households for the protection against malevolent spirits and the benevolence of the god spirit. Hippo meat is used as medicine in a number of ways for different treatments. Fat from the hippo may be smeared on the body for curative purposes. It is believed that hippo meat cures malaria and people suffering from malaria are therefore advised to eat raw hippo meat. Raw meat of hippo was also seen as enhancing fertility and reproduction. It is believed that an infertile woman who eats the raw meat of the hippo will give birth.

Similarly, the hippo hide is assumed to increase the fertility and reproductivity of animals and create wealth and prosperity for people and society. The Woyto made their cattle taste or eat the hippo hide by spraying salt on the inside or on the fleshy sides of the hide. This would protect the well-being of the cattle and increase their fertility and productivity. Even infertile women could eat or taste the hippo hide to become fertile. The waste of the hippo released after coagulation was also considered to have the same spiritual power, enhancing the fertility of the cattle.

It was not only the flesh of the hippo that could bring prosperity and well-being. When the hippo was heard crying or making loud sounds early in the morning, it was considered as a sign of good fate or fortune. These beliefs and practices were not restricted to the Woyto only, but also shared by the surrounding non-Woyto societies of the Lake Tana area. The non-Woyto farmers of Gorgora at the northern shores of Lake Tana described the significance of the hippo meat for the well-being of cattle. The meat of hippo was together with finger millet baked as bread, fed to oxen, fattening them, and making the animals strong for ploughing and other farming activities.

Culturally and ritually, hippos have had a fundamental role in initiation rites and marriage among the Woyto. Until the recent past, it was a tradition among the Woyto that unless young men killed a hippo and brought the tail of the animal back to the village community as a proof of the successful hunt, they could not get married.

The institution of marriage has been a great and important part of the social life of the Woyto. Choosing the right bride was a long process and not just any woman would be considered suitable for marriage by the groom's side. The forthcoming husband's family thoroughly studied and investigated the potential bride and her family. Marriage is a unification of two families and therefore it involves everybody and not only the couple. If the groom's family accepted the potential bride as a good woman with the necessary deeds and qualities for being a wife, the elders from the forthcoming husband's family would go to the bride's family and discuss the prospects and possibilities of marriage. After negotiations and common understanding, the two families would come to an agreement and accept the coming marriage. However, the coming bride and groom could not live together or have sex before the forthcoming husband had killed a hippo.

This *rite de passage* was so important and culturally fundamental that young women did not dare to marry a person who had not killed a hippo. Therefore, the Woyto youth went hippo hunting after being blessed by elders for the successful hunt in an elaborate ritual. In this ceremony a capon or a white chicken was sacrificed and bread and ponded oil seeds were also offered and eaten. The parents to the groom prayed to Abay that the hunt would become successful and that the river would bless their son so that he would not become old before getting married. Thus, by the prayers to Abay and the blessings of the elders, the novice would be prepared to start the hunt of a hippo.

Hunting hippo is a very challenging and difficult task because the hippo can sense people's body odour from far distances. The hunter should therefore be very cautious regarding the wind direction and avoid making any noises while approaching the animal. Moreover, as a novice who has not hunted a hippo before, he would be guided by an elder with experience regarding how and when to shoot the animal. In the hunt, the novice is accompanied with his members of family and others from the village. Traditionally the hippo was killed by shooting an arrow, but in more recent times hippos have also been killed by shooting bullets with guns. As part of this ritual kill, the importance is put on the novice to shoot the first and fatal shot. Thereafter, the rest of the group could help him in killing the hippo.

As a *rite de passage*, killing a hippo was not an easy task for everyone, and unsuccessful novices could spend several years in vain trying to get a hippo successfully killed. If a man was an unsuccessful hunter he was a shame for his family and an insult for society. Killing the hippo would unite the two families and an unsuccessful hunter would hinder this social institution. In such cases where the novice brought disgrace upon his family, the best hunter in the family would assist him and shoot the animal for him, restoring the family's honour. If the young hunter had failed repeatedly, even his father or grandfather could help him in the hunt.

When the hunter succeeded in killing the hippo in the lake, together with other villagers he would bring the dead hippo to the shore of the lake using the *tankua* (papyrus boat). If it was killed on land or in Abay, the ceremony of the successful hunt would start there. At the same spot where the hippo was brought on the shore, the tent for his wedding would be erected. The successful novice was offered beer and butter was smeared on his head.

The meat of the hippo was divided into two parts. The novice, who was going to marry and had shot the hippo, was first given half of the animal and its flesh. The second part was shared among the group who assisted him in the killing. People would come and gather at the place along the shore where the hippo was shot. There the groom's family would start feasting and eat the hippo meat together with beer drinking and consumption of other food. This was a lavish ceremony. The marriage tent would be erected at this very spot at the shore and people would come and break calabash of butter and eat the meat of the hippo until it was finished. This could take from a few days up to ten days. This major ritual was also associated with the spirit of Abinas and his relation to the hippo and the successful kill.

The importance of having killed a hippo was fundamental to the Woyto. During the ceremony after the successful hunt, only men who themselves had killed a hippo were allowed to eat the hippo meat. Hippos could be hunted at any time in secular contexts, and a successful hunter could have killed up to ten hippos or more in his lifetime, but the first killing by the novice as part of becoming married was the most important. When the novice killed the hippo, he would be very proud and happy to marry. By the killing, he had removed the social constrains which were imposed on him. If he failed, he had insulted both families and was seen as a disgrace. However, if a man was unsuccessful as a hunter for his whole life, it was seen as the will of an unspecified god and nothing anyone could do anything about.

It was only hippos that had this ritual and religious importance. Other big animals, such as lions, were not ascribed with any such significance. The exact reason as to why hippos had this predominant role in culture and cosmology is uncertain. Still, the elders point out the fact that marriage as an institution is a big thing, and that hippos are big too, so it symbolizes the greatness, the importance and the fundamental role of marriage and being married. Moreover, the killing of the hippos is also a huge challenge and a big thing, thus strengthening the symbolism between this act and the act of being married.

After the hippo had been killed, the successful young hunter would cut off the hippo's tail and wrap it around his left arm, signalling that he killed the animal. The tail was called *ado*. He would keep the tail around his arm for several days or sometimes months, symbolizing and signalling that he had become a successful hunter and killed a hippo. According to the Woyto elders, this tradition of killing a hippo as part of the marriage ritual has existed since time immemorial and been passed down through the generations.

When a killing of a hippo was successful and the marriage tent erected, the rumours of the event spread quickly in the community, and people from all over would come and present gifts. The forthcoming bride and her family would also bring butter to the tent. Some elders said that the male members of the bride's family would also partake in the feast, eating hippo meat, whereas others denied that they ate hippo meat during the ceremony. By breaking and discharging a calabash of butter as a sign of success in his hippo hunting, the novice would be gladly accepted and invited by the forthcoming father-in-law to marry his daughter. As part of the marriage ceremony, at the shore where the tent was erected, an immature calf would be sacrificed to Abay. Back at the bride's family, another ox would be sacrificed, although it was not mandatory that this ox should be an immature calf.

The ritual and religious significance of the hippos was closely related to water and Abay. According to one legend, which even all the elders do not agree upon, the sacredness of the hippos are related to the very founding myth of the Woyto when they escaped from Egypt. The Woyto king was hiding in the lake and, according to one story, the horse of the Egyptian pharaoh when he searched for the Woyto king, became a hippo when it sank into Lake Tana.

In general, the hippo was seen as the spirit of Abinas or *Kole*, which is a good spirit. The hippos were seen as the *kole* of the sea and Abay. The hippos are believed to be protectors of Abinas and as such the animals are highly sacred. When the water in the lake and the river decreases, the hippo nevertheless stays there and protects Abinas. And as with Abinas, the hippos are perceived to be invisible or difficult to be seen by humans, only surfacing in the water from time to time.

There are also other reasons why the hippos were seen as sacred animals. It was considered as a different creature than all other animals, which is not only related to the size. Cattle have two cloves on their legs whereas the hippos have four, and as such there are eight cloves on the hippos' forelegs. Cattle have four stomachs whereas the hippos have eight, it was pointed out. The hippo teeth are also very sharp and can cut through any kind of material, unlike other teeth. Thus, hippos were seen as having special powers compared to all other animals. Moreover, hippos were also perceived as pure, clean and friendly animals. Unlike other animals, which roam around destroying crops and fields, the hippos do not eat from the farms or harm the farmers. In sum, the hippos were seen as truly unique creatures compared to other animals and they were therefore sacred.

Today, however, most of the tradition has disappeared. Hunting hippos, and in particular for marriage, was practised in the Haile Selassie era, but after the 1970s they have not been allowed to kill hippos. Moreover, eating hippos was considered taboo among the Christians living in the Lake Tana region and the Woyto's practice of killing and eating hippos was one of the reasons why they have been displaced several times and seen as outcasts. The young generation today will not be associated with these traditions and distance themselves from them; indeed, they will not listen to the elders when they tell about their old rituals and traditions. The old traditions will simply disappear.

The elder Woyto still believe in the ritual and religious powers of Abay or the river, which is more powerful than the water in the lake. Abinas is the head of all water and Abay governs Lake Tana. This is evident, it was explained, by the physical character of the river and the lake. All the mud and silt in the lake is transported away by Abay, thus signifying the strength and importance of the river. There is a saying that 'Lake Tana without Abay cannot survive'. Abay is the collector of all – including both the physical characters and aspects of the Nile, but also the spiritual.

Abay is the spirit or power, and the hippo is the spirit of Abinas and Abay. Thus, the hippos are a quality of Abay: it is the spirit of Abay. This is, however, a cosmology soon gone, but it gives a glimpse into the rich water cosmologies that have existed in the Lake Tana era from time immemorial, including the pre-Christian traditions at Gish Abay.

RELIGIOUS WATER FROM GISH ABAY TO TIS ABAY

Although there are some 60 rivers flowing into Lake Tana, the source at Gish Abay has a peculiar and particular role not only in Ethiopia but also in Christianity. The origins and reasons for the strong pre-Christian cult at this spring will remain shrouded in mystery, and most likely one will never know if or to what extent people living in the vicinity had knowledge about this source being the source to the mighty Nile flowing in Egypt several thousand kilometres away. On one hand, from antiquity onwards there was knowledge about Ethiopia and some sources of the Nile, whether one of them was located at Gish or not, and on the other, the knowledge and reputation of such a mighty cultic place as documented by James Bruce in the pre-Christian era must have been widespread. Although it is impossible to know how far away and downstream knowledge of the cult-place at Gish spread, it is without doubt that it was well recognized in the Lake Tana area. The Portuguese missionaries with biblical references to the Gihon River flowing from Paradise came there in the sixteenth or seventeenth century and Christianized the source, even without knowing that it actually flowed to Egypt by following the river itself through the canyons. There exists, however, at least one very intriguing source about the close connection between Egypt and Ethiopia in pharaonic times, which will be discussed in Chapter 6.

From the perspective of the religious Nile, one may address different roles, qualities and capacities of the very same water flowing from Gish Abay to Lake Tana and further to the waterfalls at Tis Abay. On one hand, it is the same waters, but it is also different waters both in volume, texture and force. While the crystal clear water from the source flows into a larger tributary, where other sources and rainwater merge, in Lake Tana the composition of the water is further mixed with more silt from other tributaries before the waters turn into cascades at Tis Abay. It is the same, but different water, and throughout history it has been invested with various religious and cosmological meaning.

The Christian perception of the water at Gish Abay is by definition holy: the water flows from heaven. By following this holy water in changing forms from the source through Lake Tana to Tis Abay, it also shows the complexity of holy water in ritual, practice and theory. As a source of water for benevolent and healing purposes, the quality of the water at Gish is more intense or divinely accessible or 'activated', since it is believed that the actual water may bring blessings to devotees up to 70 generations after originally used or consumed. That this mythology in practice is probably not generally believed since it would limit the need for other pilgrimages and rituals, is another question, but it testifies to the immanent powers of this particular water at the source.

While the role of baptism in Ethiopia concurs with general notions of opening the gates to heaven and being initiated into the kingdom of God, the water used during the Timkat festival as commemorating baptism has yet additional function. In the above discussed case, it was Lake Tana water piped and sprinkled on the devotees, but it was nevertheless believed to have healing and miraculous powers. Thus, the ritual itself enhanced the holiness and its purposes, and while some monks on the monastery islands proclaim that all water is holy since it comes from Gish, others generally believed that the actual water coming directly from heaven was even more holy. As such, the water at the waterfall Tis Abay is also holy, but particular local phenomena like the water vapour creating the rainbow symbolize Virgin Mary's scarf and the pact God made with the Ethiopians.

This points to a fundamental aspect of holiness in general and holy water in particular, and the role of religious water in traditional African cosmologies. Although sounding paradoxical at the outset, one may argue that holiness restricts and limits the use and omnipresence compared to non-holy water in water cosmologies. Apart from heaven, which by definition is holy in its totality, on earth there is only limited holiness and the holy can only exist in opposition to the profane. As seen with Christianity, although there are general concepts that the Nile is holy, there are grading scales of holiness and some places and water are more holy than others, like Gish Abay. Used in rituals during Timkat, even sprinkled water can be seen as holy, but regular tap water in Bahir Dar is not believed to be holy. Everything cannot be equally holy, and holiness implies exclusiveness and seclusiveness.

The Woyto water-world represents the opposite. Not only may the same water inhabit different sprits and various groups creating completely opposite cosmologies, but different perceptions of Christian holy water and spirits living in and embodying water further testifies to the role of water in societies and religions. In analyses of water and religion, although not a prominent field of research, the main interest has been on holy water and rivers while the role of cosmologies where spirits live in water has been more neglected, partly because the water itself has not been seen as holy. This is probably due to implicit Christian biases and Western research horizons where it has been more academically interesting to study the holy than the profane, and because it has been difficult to conceptualize the role of water in cosmologies where the water is not holy.

It is difficult to say anything conclusive about the extent and spread of the pre-Christian cult at Gish, but, as Bruce documented, there cannot be any doubt that the spirit of the source was extremely powerful; benevolent but also terrifying. The role of water in the Woyto cosmology, on the other hand, is easier to comprehend. As one informant said, 'the water of the Nile is everything and we give everything to the Nile'. From the point of view of holiness, such a belief approaches total and inclusive holiness, but since it is impossible to live in a world where everything is equally holy, an alternative is that none of the waters in the water-world is holy. The latter perception does in no way limit or decrease the importance of water in society and cosmology because when the Nile is everything, nothing can be bigger, greater or beyond. Within this cosmology is Abinas – the spirit of this encompassing totality of water and the Nile. In a cosmology where everything is the Nile and in its water resides the omnipresent spirit Abinas, controlling not only the welfare of people and society, but also the order in this world and beyond, the water cosmology is complete.

Thus, from one perspective it is possible to argue that one may better grasp the significance and importance of water in society and religion by emphasizing cosmologies where water is not perceived as holy, if the most powerful spirits and deities are associated with or reside in different forms and types of water. In African traditional religions this holds very much true, which will be seen with rainmaking in Chapter 4, but also with the rich water cosmologies in Uganda from Lake Victoria to Murchison Falls. And at the source of the White Nile and the successive waterfalls there is a particular strong water cosmology.

3 From Lake Victoria to Murchison Falls in Uganda

A LAKE FULL OF SPIRITS

Since time immemorial, there seems to have been water cults structured around the major rivers and lakes of the Lake Victoria region. With regard to Buganda, Richard Reid writes:

> The lake, rivers and streams [...] formed the organs and veins of the country [...] Human life, and, with it, social communities grew up along the rivers and streams of the region, and on the edges of the great lake from which so much was taken. As the water flowed, so did the progress of human society; political economy in Buganda was at the origin born of proximity to water, be it for the sustenance of the plantation or for fishing. Rivers bound communities, districts and ultimately, the kingdom together. The political and economic importance of rivers was reflected in Ganda culture by the nineteenth century. Each river had its own deity, to be appeased, thanked, entreated for the produce and prosperity so vital to the survival and growth of communities. On one level these were the blood cells of the nineteenth-century corpus.[1]

Speke did not document any particular river spirits at the source of the White Nile, or in the Ripon and Owen Falls. Neither did he document anything about the Bujagali Falls, which he may have seen, since they are only 8 km from the source. According to oral tradition, the current Jaja Bujagali is the 39th incarnation of the Budhagaali spirit. Thus, one of his predecessors should have been there at the time Speke passed on his way northwards in 1862. Speke stayed only a few days at Ripon Falls before proceeding northwards. On 1 August, when he left them, the party halted 'after marching an hour, as there was now no need for hurrying,' as Speke wrote, and he used the time for hunting. Speke does not mention spirits at Bujagali Falls in his *Journal*. That such a river spirit existed at that time is, however, without doubt, since Speke describes a spirit of this sort at Karuma Falls a bit further north:

> The name given to the Karuma Falls arose from the absurd belief that Karuma, the agent or familiar of a certain great spirit, placed the stones that break the waters in the river, and, for so doing, was applauded by his master, who, to reward his services by an appropriate distinction, allowed the stones to be called Karuma. Near this is a tree which contains a spirit whose attributes for gratifying the powers and pleasures of either men or women who summon its influence in the form appropriate to each.[2]

Moreover, there were certainly very powerful water spirits in the lake. In Buganda, the term Nalubaale literally means 'the place or mother of lubaale', meaning the place of gods. In the nineteenth century the Ssese Islands dominated the ritual world in this inland ocean.[3] When Speke sojourned in the Buganda kingdom, he took part with the king in an outing on the lake. The king, Speke wrote:

> Finally directing the boats to an island occupied by the Mgussa, or Neptune of the N'yanza, not in person, for Mgussa is a spirit – but by his familiar or deputy, the great medium who communicates the secrets of the deep to the king of Uganda. In another sense, he might be said to be the presiding priest of the source of the mighty Nile, and as such was, of course, an interesting person for me to meet.

But before they met him, they picnicked on the shore. Beer was brought to the king and the whole party enjoyed themselves thoroughly, until one of the royal wives, 'a most charming creature, and truly one of the best of the lot', picked a fruit and offered it to the king as a token to please him. The king, however, became furious, since this was the first time a woman had had the impudence to offer him anything. He ordered his servants to seize, bind and lead her off to be executed. All the women begged on their knees for the king to forgive their sister, but 'the more they craved for mercy, the more brutal he became, till at last he took a heavy stick and began belabour the poor victim on the head.' This was too much for Speke:

> Hitherto I had been extremely careful not to interfere with any of the king's acts of arbitrary cruelty, knowing that such interference, at an early stage, would produce more harm than good. This last act of barbarism,

however, was too much for my English blood to stand; and as I heard my name, Mzungū, imploringly pronounced, I rushed at the king, and, staying his uplifted arm, demanded from him the woman's life. Of course I ran imminent risk of losing my own in thus thwarting the capricious tyrant; but his caprice proved the friend of both. The novelty of interference even made him smile, and the woman was instantly released.[4]

After this the party proceeded to the Mgussa medium's hut, which was decorated with many mystic symbols, including a paddle and his badge of office. As they chatted, they drank beer. He was not a very old man, and wore a white goatskin apron decorated with numerous charms and had a paddle as a mace or walking stick. The king looked at Speke and humorously joked to the medium 'What do you think of them?' Then the Mgussa medium beckoned several of the officers towards him, and 'in a very low tone, he gave them all the orders of the deep, and walked away. His revelations seemed unpropitious, for we immediately repaired to our boats and returned to our quarters.'[5]

The relationship between the Buganda king and Mukasa (Mgussa) was ambivalent. Robert Ashe, a missionary, wrote in 1895: 'The great god Mukasa is lord of Sesse, and kills any person intruding on his dominions. He calls the king of Uganda his slave and the king when he sends to perform religious rites, must do so through his chiefs.' Moreover, the king's eldest sister was considered the wife of Mukasa, and the god's medium referred to the king as a 'son-in-law'. When Mutesa fell seriously ill, it was believed this was caused by the lake. The god's medium also had the power to decree an end to all canoe traffic on the lake and thereby block Arab traders and missionaries from taking the easiest route to the coast. Another missionary, MacKay, argued with Mutesa about who ruled over Buganda: 'I said that this Mukasa was practically causing rebellion in the country, for he disobeyed Mtesa's orders, and asserted his right over the lake as before that of the king.' Yet another missionary, Wilson, commented that the 'person who is the representative or personification of the god has an enormous influence over the minds of the people and chiefs, and thus indirectly exercises an important control over the government of the country'.[6]

It has been suggested that the complex relationship between king and diviners was one reason Speke was so well received at the king's court. What was Mutesa expecting of Speke? Bridges says:

It is said that he interpreted the first visit of a white man to Buganda as a sign that he was the rightful king; his coronation began soon after Speke had left. Put it another way, this may mean that Speke was used as some kind of pawn in a game that the *kabaka* [king] was playing to establish his position as a complete despot.

He goes on to ask:

> Was it, for example, merely a sight-seeing tour when Speke was taken on a visit to the shrine of the lake god Mukasa? Mukasa was one of the most important of the *balubaale* [spirits], yet the *kabaka* treated the god's medium with a good deal of contempt.[7]

The Ssese Islands were the cult centre of Mukasa, and the god was among other things the main spirit for fishermen. The cult centre was a place of great danger, and the natives there were reputed to be cannibals.[8] The islanders, however, believed that even further out in the lake there were yet more islands, and that the people there were cannibals. The dangers of the water and the lake were also the source of other cannibal accusations:

> Because of their white skins, people were concerned that [...] Europeans were the red sons of Mugasa who had lived on the Sese Islands and had refused to marry black women. Indeed it was believed strongly by some people that these Europeans had emerged from the Sese Islands and were white-skinned because they lived underwater like fish.[9]

Northrop wrote in 1891:

> Their great object of superstitious dread is a sort of water-spirit, which is supposed to inhabit the lake, and to wreak his vengeance upon those who disturb him. Like the water-spirits of the Rhine, this goblin has supreme jurisdiction, not only on the lake itself, but in all rivers that communicate with it; and the people are so afraid of this aquatic demon, that they would not allow a sounding-line to be thrown into the water, lest perchance the weight should happen to hit the water-spirit and enrage him. The name of this spirit is M'gussa.[10]

The name Mukasa may hint at the god's characteristics. Mu is the singular prefix, and what kasa means is not completely clear. When the word appears in Luganda, it signifies 'sharpness', 'the capacity to draw blood' or 'bloodiness', among other meanings. Mukasa could appear in the shape of a giant python and there are stories of an enormous 'sea python' in Lake Victoria, like the Loch Ness monster. On the lake, people used to make offerings to Mukasa and cut a finger and sprinkle blood on the water to appease the serpent deity.[11]

Mukasa controlled not only the rain, but also the increase in the fish and was responsible for granting the birth of twins. He was also associated with iron and smelting. One manifestation of Mukasa was a large meteoric stone, and in the temple on the Ssese Islands there was a very large iron hammer. This association with smithing and iron is also linked to sexuality and lordship, as well as violent weather and weather control.[12]

This information was seemingly confirmed by Speke. According to him the Arabs said 'that thunder accompanies nearly all the storms, and the lightning there is excessive, and so destructive that the King of Uganda expresses the greatest dread of it – indeed his own palace has been often destroyed by lightning'.[13] When the rain fell, it was considered a good omen, and everybody 'declared the king mad with delight'. On another occasion, the king wanted medicine to propitiate the lightning.[14] Speke also describes the characteristics of this religion:

> The new moon seen last night kept the king engaged at home, paying his devotions with his magic horns or fetishes [...] The spirit of this religion – if such it can be called – is not so much adoration of a Being supreme and beneficent, as a tax to certain malignant furies – a propitiation, in fact, to prevent them bringing evil on the land, and to insure a fruitful harvest.[15]

Regarding Mukasa's character, there seem to be have been differing, although not necessarily incompatible, perceptions. On one hand, in 1911 John Roscoe described the god, who had his chief temple on Bubembe Island in Lake Victoria, thus:

> Mukasa held the highest rank among the gods of Uganda. He was a benign god; he never asked for the life of any human being, but animals were sacrificed to him at the yearly festivals, and also at other times when the King, or a leading chief, wished to consult him. He had nothing to do with war, but sought to heal the bodies and minds of men. He was the god of plenty; he gave the people an increase of food, cattle and children.[16]

The sacrifices to Mukasa were described. While one priest slaughtered the animals, another

> caught a little of the blood from each, and poured it into a large wicker water-proof receptacle which stood near, while the rest of the blood flowed down the channel into the lake. Watchers at the lake announced in a loud

> voice when the blood first reached the water; they called: 'He has drunk it,' and their cry was taken up by all hands. Afterwards the priests went into the enclosure, and killed the animal which had been tied to the temporary temple [... the chief priest] placed the vessel containing the blood in the temple of the god. He alone entered the temple, while the other priests remained standing in the enclosure; when the chief priest entered he knelt down, and asked the god to accept the blood, and to grant an increase of children, cattle, and food.[17]

On the other hand, among malignant spirits, the principal devil was called Mukasa, and he resided in Lake Victoria. Many Buganda had met their deaths in the lake, which can be very rough and stormy. Mukasa was presented with sacrifices for commercial and military purposes, and fishermen also appeased the spirit with banana offerings. The rule of Mukasa included all. When the king planned his regular predatory expeditions, Mukasa's representative had to be consulted to establish whether the time was favourable, and most often it was not. The expeditions were frequently postponed for considerable lengths of time, during which precious offerings had to be made. The sacrifices included cattle, sheep or goats, and possibly also humans, according to one early twentieth-century writer, but contrary to what Roscoe said. Lightning, too, was greatly feared. Witchcraft was ubiquitous and charms, often cowrie shells, were worn by all. The priests were also doctors and prophets, predicting the future and detecting bewitchers.[18] Thus, it seems the water spirit was rather bloodthirsty in one way or other, whether or not human sacrifices took place. Importantly, the sacrifices were restricted to certain spirits, not all.

At the turn of the twentieth century, Mukasa's medium was a woman who remained in office until her death. She lived in secrecy and seclusion, except for her female temple slaves, and was not allowed to speak to any man except the high priest:

> Mukasa, as god of the lake, controlled the storms, and gave the increase of fish; he also gave good passages to people travelling by water. The boatmen sought his blessing before they set out on a voyage, and called to him when in danger from a storm [...] Sometimes childless women made vows to give Mukasa a child if he would grant their request and cause them to become mothers.[19]

Another deity, Wamala, who also had a woman as a medium, sat down one day on a hill to rest, placing the water-skin by his side; by some mishap the water escaped and tricked down the hill. A spring burst forth from the hill where the water flowed, became a river which ran down onto the valley, and formed the lake known as Lake Wamala.

This deity was also bloodthirsty:

> Human sacrifices were made to Wamala; the victims were clubbed to death on the lake shore, and afterwards speared, and thrown into the lake. The water is said to have become quite crimson with the blood of the victims by the time that the sacrifices were ended.[20]

In Lake Victoria, the male lake god Mukasa was the most important of all the deities among the Buganda, and manifested himself in various forms and symbols.[21] In the Luo language, Lake Victoria is called Nalubaale, 'Lake of the Goddess', hence a female deity.[22] Thus, the same body of water as well as different bodies of water may take on various divine forms and be perceived accordingly. This once again directs our attention to the importance of studying the role of water in history and society. Moreover, the internal hierarchies and relative superiority and powers of the deities may at the outset seem contradictory, since they change according to context. Among the Buganda, there was one god or supreme being called Katonda, not perfect but absolute. At the same time, the lake god Mukasa was the most important of all deities – in a sense he was the lake and was symbolized by nautical symbols such as pythons, canoe paddles and the unique Ugandan canoe. Mukasa is masculine, but, as noted above, Lake Victoria has also been seen as feminine in the form of Nalubaale: lubaale is the generic word for 'deity', indicating a female spirit. The lake, as a mother, is whence the gods emerged, but Mukasa was seen as the lake itself or at least as residing in it.[23]

Also in 1911, Condon noted that:

> The religion of the Basoga Batamba is a vast conglomerate of more or less ridiculous superstition. However, notwithstanding this, they admit the existence of invisible beings superior to man, which beings are generally termed lubale [...] These lubale or gods are either belonging to those who bring good or blessing to man, or to those whose only work is to shower evils upon humanity. Each lubale has its earthly representatives, who pretend to be in touch with their respective gods. These representatives are always willing, for a trifle, to act as mediums between the gods and people. If any evil befalls a person, then the god of that evil is consulted through his earthly representative.[24]

Condon then provides an example. Once when a chief fell seriously ill, his relatives came to the medium, who demanded four goats for the god. However, the chief eventually died, whereupon the medium had the audacity to claim that he would have lived if more goats had been provided. Divination was common, and many innocent people were accused of terrible crimes, including witchcraft. With regard to deaths, if the cause was natural and apparent, it was acknowledged as such, but as a rule death was seen as being caused by witchcraft and the spirits.[25]

In the main rivers there were resident spirits, which had powers of good and evil.[26] *All the major spirits could transform themselves into giant pythons when visiting each other.* Roscoe mentions one medium living along a river where a python had been tamed and lived in the healer's compound. The medium brought daily milk from sacred cows to the python. Occasionally on the banks of the river the medium tied fowls and goats, which the python devoured. These sacrifices were made when the medium wished for a successful fishing expedition, since the python was believed to possess all the powers of the river and the fish that lived in it. Pythons were also responsible for procuring human offspring.[27] The use of water was also imbued with taboos:

> No woman was allowed to wash in the same water or to use the same bath as a man used except his wife, and no woman would allow any man to use the pot which she washed in except her husband. A transgressor against either rule was at once judged to be guilty of immoral conduct.[28]

Moreover, crossing a river on an unsafe bridge was a dangerous enterprise, and

> if a person made a false step, and went down, he was caught by the current, and was almost certain to lose his life [...] Such accidents were attributed to the Spirit of the River, and no one attempted to assist a person who had gone under, because it was thought that the Spirit needed him, and would wreak vengeance upon the would-be rescuer.[29]

Although Uganda is a country of good rains and plenty of water, scarcity also occurs, and particular wells and springs were protected through certain proscriptions. The well from which the king fetched water was for his sole use, apart from a few of his wives. Throughout the country, some wells were famous and protected by particular water spirits. The sacredness of these wells demanded sacrifices, and newly appointed chiefs might sacrifice humans, even their own children, to them. On more regular occasions commoners made offerings of animals to the wells, the animals afterwards being eaten as sacred meals. Menstruating women were prohibited from approaching wells, to prevent them from drying up and even their own deaths. Similarly, fetching water with dirty hands could also dry up the wells. Consequently, women with dirty hands would stop at some distance and ask their friends to bring water so that they could wash their hands before approaching the well to draw water.[30]

'POLITICS OF THE BELLY' AND 'THE NILE IS WEALTH'

In sub-Saharan Africa the 'politics of the belly' have been an intrinsic part of many societies where hunger has been widespread and a social and political reality, and being well-fed or corpulent is a sign of wealth and power. A green place is a good place.[31] But as Thomas suggests, it is not only about the belly, but also the womb, creating 'politics of the womb'. Reproductive struggles are part of material resources and imbued with moral aspects, since reproduction more than anything else constitutes the social and links the flows of cosmos with the body.[32] Cosmology can literally and metaphorically be seen as a vast machinery of consumption and digestion structured around exchanges, flows and transformations of various substances such as water, milk, blood and semen, which are interlinked at three levels: the king's body, the social body and the cosmos, as Heike Behrend argues:

> Act of consumption, digestion and shared substances are seen as central to the operations of power, domination and violence [...] these practices of eating and being eaten [provide] the basis for [...] relations of power and violence in colonial and postcolonial encounters.[33]

Thus, whereas life is identified with breath, fat is a common life-giving substance identified with health.[34]

There are different forms of incorporation. Eating is the most common and by the very practice the external world is incorporated into the body. By eating, the boundaries collapse between the body and the outer world and the body takes or attempts to take control over the outer world. This may represent opposite qualities and processes. On one hand, it may create or recreate the unity of the eaters with what is eaten, but on the other, it may also be an aggressive and destructive act annihilating what is consumed. Sex is another form of incorporation, although it can also be seen as an incomplete process, like a locus or cooking pot for further life. Spirit possession is yet another form of incorporation, although most often limited in time and space to when the spirit takes part of a person's body or a medium before it leaves.³⁵

In the Kingdoms of Bunyoro and Tooro, the body of the deceased king was dried by a slow fire and a pot was placed under the corpse and the pyre collecting the liquids from the dead body. These liquids were mixed with food and presented during the new king's ascension ceremony so both the new king and the people could partake in the dead king and be said to have 'eaten their king':³⁶

> The king was not only the centre of an asymmetrical exchange system but also formed part of a cosmology that centred on his body as a conduit through which liquids flowed. The king's body formed a vessel to be filled with liquid, above all milk, and, to a lesser degree, solid food. His body was part of and represented the body politics of the kingdom; it was a metonym of the entire cosmos, and the king's health and prosperity ensured the health and prosperity of the kingdom and its inhabitants.³⁷

The very same principles applied to rainmakers in general, although sometimes to a lesser degree, since the rainmaker worked on behalf of the king or chief, and in any case the chiefdom or community, representing and interacting with cosmos on behalf of the people.

In the colonial era, as today, the Busoga is a natural rich area with picturesque masses of rocks, vegetation and fully brought under cultivation.³⁸ In the Busoga Kingdom, there is a Lusoga proverb that 'The Nile is Wealth.'³⁹ Jinja's municipal armorial bearings contain the same motto, in Luganda *Kiyira bwe bugagga*, and this motto and image are also on the billboard where the tourist boats depart for the source of the Nile. In 1963, the official presentation and interpretation of the emblem was:

> The hippopotamus is representative of the fauna of the district. The rock, or stone, is a reference to the name Jinja which in Luganda means the stone and is thought to have historical significance. The wavy bar [...] denotes the river Nile at the source of which Jinja stands. The cotton plants refer to one of the principal crops of Busoga District in which Jinja is situated and the cogwheel and flash of lightning allude to industrial development and the Owen Falls Hydro-electric scheme on the Nile, which is the source of energy for the industry and the country in general. The group of a shield, spears, drums and an antelope's head is a representation of the badge used by the Busoga African Local Government.⁴⁰

18. The Ripon Falls as documented by Speke in the *Journal*.

If water and food is one form of wealth controlling the flows of cosmos, another way of physically controlling the flow of water is by dams. According to Stanley, the natives living along the falls called Lake Victoria the 'Mother of the River at Jinja', and apparently there was also the perception that the lake would dry up but for the very powerful river.[41] The first ideas of damming Lake Victoria were put forward by Stanley, as he writes in 1878 when he stood at the Ripon Falls (fig. 18), where there were four separate falls:

> I thought what an immense difference might be effected in the level of the Victoria Falls if Mtsea were assisted by engineers. He might by a couple of charges of dynamite, and the destruction of the two islands between which the surplus water rushes into the Victoria Nile, reduce the lake by 12 feet; or he might, by employment of the vast labour at his disposal, dam up the gaps which nature has created, and soon extend the lake thousands of square miles![42]

Standing at the Ripon Falls, it was worth a visit just for the beauty of the place, Winston Churchill wrote in 1908. But more importantly:

> It is possible that nowhere else in the world could so enormous a mass of water be held up by so little masonry. Two or three short dams from island to island across the falls would enable, at an inconceivably small cost, the whole level of the Victoria Nyanza.[43]

Owen Falls dam was inaugurated in 1954 and started the dam building era in Uganda, which continues with full force in the twenty-first century. Controlling water and the flows of life has always been important in Uganda; but with dams, technology and cosmology clash when dammed divinities oppose the destruction of the waterfalls where they reside.[44]

A RIVER SPIRIT BLOCKING AN ALMOST USD 1 BILLION DAM

The Bujagali Dam, located only 8 km north of the source of the White Nile and the Owen Falls dam, was inaugurated in 2012. It has been seen as one of the most controversial dams in world history. More dams are planned along the Nile, including Itanda or Kalagala, the next waterfall north of Bujagali and some 30 km from Jinja. Apart from the general criticism of dams, the Bujagali Dam was unique in the sense that the controversies surrounding it related to the major water spirit in the culture of the Busoga, whose home was to be flooded. In fact, the dam was postponed for years because of this spirit and the fierce disputes between two healers claiming to be the water spirit's representative or embodiment; Jaja Bujagali and Nfuudu. But this water spirit – Budhagaali – is part of a wider water cosmology, in which, as noted earlier, the source of the White Nile is itself second, and in some contexts and mythologies, first in importance.[45]

The Budhagaali spirit has attracted much international attention, for better or worse. In the *New York Times* it was reported in 2001 that traditional spirits were blocking a USD 500 million dam, although the final price tag in 2012 was estimated at USD 902 million. Following the media coverage, the dam constructor conducted a study which filled seven volumes, including mitigation strategies for cultural heritage. In the report, a map showed where the numerous trees and rocks considered to be homes of the spirits were located. It reported that:

> A ceremony must take place at each site to move the spirit and another to introduce it to another resting spot. Each ceremony requires livestock for slaughter as well as local millet and banana brews. Additional ceremonies must take place at each grave site near the dam to properly transfer the remains of ancestors to another location. Two mass ceremonies are also planned to appease the spirit that resides in the water, one gathering for each of the rival clans that claim to be in touch with the Jaja.

The cultural strategy of the project was 'focused on closure, relocating, or appeasing the spirits, compensating when necessary, documenting spiritual appeasement through signed certificates, and setting a finite timeline (originally six months in 2001)'.[46] Thus as regards cultural and religious matters, the solutions and approaches were practical, technical and mechanical:

> Dwelling sites of spirits important to the local community are being addressed through transfer and resettlement ceremonies. Ceremonies for

the Bujagali Rapids have been carried out, although additional activities are being discussed with the Busoga Kingdom. The project will result in flooding of household graves and amasabo (shrines). Where possible these have been relocated as part of the resettlement programme or through compensation payments. Remembrance services to commemorate those buried in the area will be completed. A structure or monument may be erected, either at the site of remembrance or elsewhere, in accordance with the wishes by local communities.[47]

Although there were innumerable spirits, the main focus was Dumbbell Island and the chief spirit Budhagaali. If the spirits were not appeased, they could become intensely wrathful. There was one major ceremony conducted to appease the main spirits, but this seems to have been a charade caught up in fraud and lies:

> On September 28, 2001 at the only large ceremony conducted to appease *'the Budhagaali community spirit'* an unspecified number of clan spiritual leaders, the *baswzi abadhagaali* and important dignitaries from all over Busoga were transported to the site at the Sponsor's expense. The followers of Budhagaali were concerned with the rumor that the construction of the dam would take place at their sacred site. They were satisfied, however, when it was revealed that the dam would not be constructed at the site but 3 kilometers downstream at Dumbbell Island.[48]

Neither the dam builder nor the non-governmental organizations present corrected this misunderstanding that the sacred sites would not be destroyed, and it seems that the truth of the location of the dam was not explicitly told.

In 2001, the project identified

> Lubaale Nfuudu as a diviner (muswezi) who asserts that the spirit Lubaale is the father of Nabamba Budhagaali spirit. He conducts occasional ceremonies with *buswezi* at the Bujagali Falls to communicate with Lubaale, one of the highest spirits within Busoga cosmology, but different from the Bujagali spirit.

The inspection panel thus concluded: 'This opens the possibility that Bujagali Falls, as a cultural property may be the site of two high spirits of the Busoga, not one.'[49] Moreover, the references to undifferentiated 'Bujagali spirits' makes 'it difficult to determine whether or not there are rival claims or just a rivalry between two spiritual mediums'.[50] While the dam project identified three custodians or diviners, rather than having three separate ceremonies for the appeasement of the Budhagaali spirit, it aimed for one and a co-signed certificate of appeasement, so that the matter could be resolved once and for all, but the diviners refused.[51]

Following the 28 September 2001 ceremony financed by the sponsor to relocate the Bujagali spirits, the builders claimed that all three mediums involved had agreed that the compensation had been adequate and that construction could proceed. They prepared a certificate of appeasement for signing, but at a 2 October meeting Jaja Bujagali withheld his endorsement.[52] According to Jaja Bujagali and Busoga spiritual logic, 'he could not sign the document for the Spirit. He also claimed that the ceremony on September 28, 2001, had been called not to conduct the ritual of appeasement but to consult his *buswezi Budhagaali*.'[53] Jaja Bujagali also handed over a memorandum to the World Bank inspection panel officers signed by 75 spiritual mediums stating that they had never been consulted in the dam process.[54] Moreover, Jaja Bujagali had from the very beginning opposed the dam on the grounds that if the spirits were not appeased, they would wreak havoc on the project through construction problems, and cause death and illness. He concluded: 'The spirits would never allow the dam to be built.'[55]

In early August 2006, the Busoga prime minister expressed concern that the spirits at the falls had not been properly released. At a meeting attended by nine of the 11 Busoga cultural leaders, all of them reconfirmed that the spirits and the shrines needed to be relocated. However, as the inspection panel also noted, although the dam builders to a great extent regarded this *kyabazinga* – or council of the Busoga kingdom – as an important guardian of Busoga cultural tradition, the council did not have the authority to speak on behalf of the spirits: this was the responsibility of the spirits' mediums.[56] Thus, there were uncertainties about the rituals and if they had worked, and the whereabouts of the spirit: was it still in the reservoir or in Nfuudu's compound? And was the spirit satisfied?

The next appeasement ceremony on 19 August 2007 was conducted only two days prior to the official ground-breaking for the dam, and as such cleared away the last hindrance to the Bujagali Dam. When President Museveni again laid the foundation stone during a ceremony on 21 August 2007, he said: 'You cannot claim to be protecting the environment when you are denying over 90 percent of the population access to electricity.' Development and industrialization were the priorities, not culture and indigenous religion.

A Ugandan newspaper characterized the ritual as 'bizarre'. '[T]he disturbing question was how the spirits could be resettled since they were not like the Internally Displaced People in northern Uganda who at least are given seeds, pangas and hoes to start a new life.' Moreover:

> Unusual as it may appear, the Busoga traditional healers bulldozed it and performed rituals at Bujagali in Jinja to relocate spirits from the falls [...] [However] the spirits had earlier already been 'removed' from the falls and kept by Jajja Nfuudu [...] only waiting to be resettled.

The developers had bought a new piece of land in accordance with the compensation agreement:

> The healers were called to perform at the exercise and one, Nfuudu was given all the necessary requirements which included, goats, sheep, cowries, clay pots, and beads to appease the gods [...] Nfuudu was mandated to take measurements for the shrines at the new site with respect to the cultures of the land as recommended by the Busoga Kingdom [...] the Kingdom officials prefer working with Nfuudu because the spirits 'acknowledged' him.

Still, not all the hereditary chiefs were satisfied with the ritual,

> arguing that the spirits will be missing the chance of 'enjoying' the water [...] they only agreed to relocate the spirits but not the site [suggesting that] the spirits would have been asked to choose a site because the eight kilometres from the falls [to the new shrines] seem like chasing the spirits from the water where they were 'created'.

The representative of Bujagali Energy Limited (BEL), on the other hand, Dr Florence Nangendo, was satisfied: 'We are here to resettle the spirits so that the dam can go on. The project respects cultural sites and cultural beliefs.'[57]

Jaja Bujagali was not satisfied at all. Not only had he deliberately not been invited, and hence not been there when the ritual was conducted, but as the Budhaagali incarnate proper, he would never have allowed this ritual to take place. In spiritual terms, the spirit would have informed Jaja Bujagali that it did not accept the ritual and that it was furious at what had happened. Then Jaja Bujagali would have conveyed the spirit's message to the world. Indeed, this was what Jaja Bujagali did. The next day he announced on a local radio station in Jinja that he had never authorized the relocation and no agreement had been reached with him.[58]

The transfer of the spirit was symbolic. Nfuudu placed a spear wrapped in bark cloth in the roaring waters of Bujagali Falls, holding the spear there for some time before pulling it out and later taking it to the new site at Namizi West, some 8 km from the falls, where the new shrines were not completed. This was the final relocation of the spirits, the healers agreed. 'The spirits have accepted to relocate. To prove that they were happy, there was rain as we relocated them. This will allow the construction and completion of the Bujagali hydropower project successfully,' said James Christopher Mutyaba, the leader of the healers. The chairman of the Busoga chiefdoms sacrificed three cows, 20 goats and chickens at the three new temporary shrines, which had been hurriedly built of brick. 'The blood sacrifice is to get the spirits embedded under the River Nile waters to relocate. This is a clear testimony that we are behind the project.' For three days the festivities went on:

> They sang, feasted on meat, matooke and drank local brew during the rituals that kicked off on Sunday and ended yesterday. Dressed in bark cloths and beads, joyful elderly men and women numbering about 30, smoked tobacco in long brightly decorated pipes as they danced at their new site worth over sh 11m. The whole relocation exercise cost about sh 21m. Project developers, Bujagali Energy Limited, purchased the site measuring 1.2 acres, following a compensation agreement.[59]

There was one last ceremony in this ritual drama. At the end of June 2011, Nfuudu again moved the Budhagaali spirit. The spiritual contestation between Jaja Bujagali and Nfuudu continued, and still does. In a newspaper, it was reported:

> The move, carried out last week, ended an impasse that had delayed the ritual for over three years [...] The conflict resulted in a stalemate until [...] Nfudu secured the blessings of the kingdom officials to conduct the event. The spirits were moved from the dam site to Namizi East village in Budondo sub-county in Jinja.[60]

Although Nfuudu claimed that the spirit resided in his compound, the ritual started by the river or the reservoir. As before, it was transported back to the new shrines in Namizi village, the place used in 2007 when the shrines were temporary. As the spirit was being moved for the third time, one must assume that it had been rather dissatisfied with the new shrines and at being moved around:

'We hereby certify that the construction of the shrines and associated features has now been completed to our satisfaction ...,' states a certificate of Completion of Namizi Shrines and Relocation of Budhagali Spirits, signed by the Busoga kingdom and the government. 'Today is an important day for Busoga and Uganda. Giving up our shrine [the waterfalls] was not easy – but for development's sake, we had to. The government should give our children jobs because the power project will benefit all of us. Busoga Kingdom should also get its fair share of the proceeds from the project,' the acting *Kyabazinga* (king) of Busoga kingdom, Kawunhe Wakooli said. Benedicto Nfuudu, the chief spirit medium, conducted the ritual, and while standing in front of a fire from which smoke arose, he declared: Ever since the spirits were temporarily kept at my home after the ground breaking ceremony for the power dam, I have not had peace. They have been nagging me for another home ... These new shrines are in honour of the Busoga. People will be coming here to worship the spirits of our dead who protect, direct and guide us. I pray and ask that the Busoga sacrifice a cow each year to appease the spirits.[61]

RELIGIOUS AFTERMATH

Despite the fierce fighting among the healers and the kingdom's support for Nfuudu, thereby leaving Jaja Bujagali out in the cold, things have changed. The 2011 ritual was the last straw and changed the kingdom's attitude towards Nfuudu, simply because it was not a ritual, and afterwards he became *persona non grata*. Today, he is no longer the chief healer in the kingdom and a new one has been appointed with no affiliation with the Bujagali Falls or the Budhagaali spirit.

It is now generally acknowledged that the 2011 ritual was a staged, pretend ritual – a charade. Nfuudu was not possessed when the rite was performed, and the ritual did not convince participants, with the consequence that Nfuudu was seen as a charlatan and Jaja Bujagali as having been right all along. The improper ritual performances convinced people that they had been deceived and the kingdom realized it had been fooled by Nfuudu. It was impossible to transfer the spirit in the first place, and consequently impossible to transfer it back or to the Namizi shrines.

Although it was claimed that Nfuudu moved the spirit in 2011, this claim was open to diverse interpretations. One is, of course, Nfuudu's version. Another is that this is proof that if he relocated the spirit it was not, by definition, in his possession – he was not the owner of the spirit or its incarnation. He could have been the custodian of the spirit for a short time, but he was not the proper Jaja Bujagali. Jaja Bujagali was the real and only medium of the Budhagaali spirit. Nfuudu was an imposter, and employing him as the healer for the rituals had fatal implications. The Budhagaali spirit was not pleased with what had happened. And when the kingdom realized that the 2011 ritual was a charade, the implication was that the rituals conducted in 2001 and 2007 were also staged and fake.

Chief Ntembe of the Busoga kingdom, who made the agreement with the contractor and the government allowing Nfuudu to perform the ritual transfer of the Budhagaali spirit in 2007, died 18 May 2009. He was a very old man and his death would sooner or later have been inevitable, but it was understood to be in consequence of Budhagaali's wrath. In the kingdom, it was generally acknowledged that he had been deceived and forced to accept the agreement allowing Nfuddu to perform the rituals paving the way for the dam, but that is no excuse in a divine perspective. Not only did his actions bring divine wrath, but they also had direct consequences in that the chief was harshly punished and killed by the Budhagaali spirit. The chief did not die of natural causes. This was evidently confirmed by his ancestors, who told of fatal demons in his head that were the work of the furious Budhagaali spirit. The old chief was killed by the spirit for not adhering to the cosmic rules.

Waguma Yasin succeeded Chief Ntembe, his father. A central feature of Busoga culture is reconciliation.[62] Jaja Bujagali has a reputation of being intensely hostile to his enemies, but also of sincerely loving and taking care of his devotees and friends. During the summer of 2013 Chief Waguma met Jaja Bujagali. Despite the bitterness and conflicts aroused by the dam project, and in particular the kingdom's choice of Nfuudu as its representative and not Jaja Bujagali, the custodian and embodiment of the spirit, Chief Ntembe was reconciled with Jaja Bujagali. Not only had money made everything worse and the wrong decision brought on the wrath of the Budhagaali spirit and the death of his father, but the experience of being deceived in what mattered most, namely religion, included

19. Jaja Bujagali.

the whole kingdom, with serious implications. Religion matters and the Budhagaali spirit is still the most important deity within the chiefdom, apart from the Christian and Muslim gods. Jaja Bujagali is its medium and Nfuudu is a charlatan. Thus, the cosmological order has been restored, not to where it was before the dam project started, because much water has flown in the river since then causing many upheavals, but to the extent that Jaja Bujagali is the undisputed medium of the Budhagaali spirit (fig. 19). And that spirit is one of the most important in the Busoga cosmology. Moreover, Jaja Bujagali has regained his central position in the kingdom as one of its main ritual specialists. On Saturday 13 September 2014, William Gabula Nadiope was enthroned as the new King (Kyabazinga) of Busoga. President Museveni was in attendance, as were many other dignitaries. In the ceremony, Busoga traditional culture also featured. Jaja Bujagali was instrumental in the impressive rituals associated the 'traditional' events, which included the spirit world and the intangible parts of Busoga heritage. This directs the attention to the role of these healers and their cosmologies, the role of the Nile and the waterfalls, and the stakes involved and the power of the spirits.

'THE MESSENGER OF GOD'

Although Speke does not mention specific water spirits at the source when he was there in 1862, Stanley did give one important piece of information when he wrote in 1878:

> Rounding the western end of Uvama we enter the Napoleon Channel, and after sailing up about 20 miles arrive at the outfall of the Victoria Nyanza, called by Captain Speke the Ripon Falls, but by the natives Namweni. The river is named Ki-ira, the lake, Nyanza. The east, or the Usoga side, is called Jinja, or the Stones; the west is called Ugungu.[63]

Thus, Stanley pointed out two spirits at the source, Kiyira and Namweni. The river was, as it is today, called Kiyira, and importantly, the river spirits still exist. Namweni was one important river spirit residing in the Ripon Falls, but the falls disappeared with the completion of the Owen Falls Dam in 1954.

When the Owen Falls Dam was constructed, the current Jaja Bujagali was the ritual specialist in charge of appeasing the relevant spirit when the dam flooded the falls, he said. He is at the centre of all waters and everything that concerns water. There is, however, another story. According to Nfuudu, it was his father who conducted the necessary ritual facilitating the Owen Falls Dam. This ritual took place in 1948 and involved the sacrifice of a goat. Thus, there are different accounts, and obviously only one of them can be correct. The involvement of Nfuudu's father in this ritual was challenged and denied by the Busoga chiefdom. Nfuudu and his father do not belong to the Busoga, but to the Luo of the Tororo district in eastern Uganda bordering Kenya. And apparently Nfuudu came alone to Busoga, and hence his father could not have been there at the time. In any event, this is only one of several instances where the stories differ greatly, and these controversies are a recurring theme: who embodies the powerful gods? The healers themselves strongly disagree about who the true incarnates are and these issues are largely decided by the believers and followers. After all, it is they who constitute the cosmology in practice and benefit from the healers as the spirits' embodiments.

What is undisputable is that water spirits are believed to be very powerful, and those residing in waterfalls are the most powerful of all.

Among the Busoga, diviners who are possessed by important spirits are called *basweezi*.[64] Being initiated as a diviner or healer (the terms will be used interchangeably) brings with it great responsibility and great danger. What is learnt must remain secret on pain of death, and it is no wonder nobody speaks of the darker side of their practices. As part of the initiation, an older priest or diviner will threaten the neophyte with a spear: 'This is how you will be speared, should you ever reveal the secrets of the diviners, especially what happens here in the bush.' In front of an imitation grave, the initiate is threatened again: 'This is the grave and the bark-cloth in which you will be buried the moment you reveal what happens here in the bush.' Thereupon the neophyte replies: 'This is the grave and the bark-cloth in which you will bury me in case I reveal the secrets of the diviners and whatever happens here in the bush.'[65]

An ancestor or a spirit may choose whoever he or she wants to take up the office of diviner. If the person chosen rejects or ignores the ancestors, the latter may punish and torture the chosen one for disobeying. One story goes thus:

> I would dream of my grandfather telling me to go to the bush and get herbs to treat the sick person. Being a Christian and a choir member, I did not want to have anything to do with spirits, so for some time I ignored the dreams. After some time, I felt sick. I had a persistent headache and I would always feel dizzy. Whenever I went to school, I would fall sick and people would take me back home. On account of this, my father consulted a number of diviners. He was told that the spirits which once possessed my grandfather, had chosen me to succeed him as a diviner [...] all of a sudden I got a terrible headache and felt as if I had become mad. So a senior diviner was invited to identify the cause of the sickness. He sensed the presence of divination spirits that needed to be installed and he later performed those rituals.[66]

Another story is very similar. A woman who had previously worked at a hospital was tortured by dreams and sickness. She recalled that when 'I was installed as a diviner priestess [...] that was the end of my mysterious sickness.'[67]

Strictly speaking, the body of a diviner or healer is an empty shell. Without being possessed, several healers stressed, they are just like any human. It is the gods or spirits who inhabit the healers' bodies and speak through their minds and mouths. Healers are merely mediums or bodily agents conveying the wishes and demands of the gods and facilitating devotees' requests, which the spirits may grant if they are pleased by the rites and offerings. In practice, though, this is not how it works. As the embodiment of the spirit, or rather, by having the ability to call upon a spirit and subsequently be incarnated by it, the healer may request that a devotee's troubles be resolved and convey the prescribed ritual actions to be taken, usually involving medicines or sacrifices, or both. By being closest to the spirits, healers are very powerful, and both respected and feared.

The spirits are both benevolent and malevolent. This duality is not the expression of arbitrary whims, but at the heart of most religions: the spirits provide and guarantee the cosmological order with particular consequences for human behaviour. If humans abide by the social order as established and supervised by the spirits, the gods will always be benevolent, but if they transgress and oppose the cosmic rules, divine wrath may be the consequence.

In many cases, the understanding of cosmology spans belief systems: being a Christian and adhering to traditional religious practices and beliefs is seen as unproblematic or as being two sides of the same coin, at least in an indigenous perspective. Even Catholics and many Muslims may accept this syncretism, depending on the orthodoxy of their religious upbringing. The Pentecostals are perhaps the most strongly opposed to a fusion of beliefs. Many adhering to indigenous practices see no contradiction between Christianity and African traditional religions, in this case the water cosmology of the Busoga. There is only one overall and supreme god – it is all one and the same. The god may have different names, but is the same true god. How to approach the god differs, but this is a matter of means and practice, not the essence. In church, believers pray and use the Bible; in traditional cosmology devotees use water and herbs and may conduct sacrifices to the river spirits.

JAJA KIYIRA

Jaja Kiyira is the healer of Kiyira, the spirit at the source of the White Nile. Omugga is the river and Kiyira is the god or spirit. The Nile itself may also be seen as having given birth to Kiyira. Thus the water itself is the very origin of everything, mythology included. There are only three strong diviners along the Nile among the Busoga in Uganda. In the hierarchical order of the spirits, these are Budhagaali, Kiyira and Itanda, and each has a healer as a human embodiment. Thus, there are only three main healers directly related to the water spirits in the Nile, whereas there are numerous healers on land. One central healer said there were more than 3,000 among the Busoga, but this should be seen as a qualified guess. Each year the healers try to come together to discuss important matters concerning their practices, but there is also a huge feast where they eat and enjoy themselves.

Jaja Kiyira had been working as a permanent healer for 15 years (in 2014), but he could have been working as a healer before that without knowing, he said, but he had only been an active healer for 15 years. This points to an important aspect of the ways the spirits work, also stressing the fact that it is the spirits who choose their human embodiments with or without their knowing. A spirit may embody a person without that person knowing and long before he or she has become a healer and been acknowledged as such. The presence of a spirit may be more or less active, and what seems to be a normal person may perform miracles without knowing. This is also one of the ways a spirit and a healer becomes identified; either they themself or other people realize that there is something special going on. For Jaja Kiyira's part, the first time he realized that there was something special going on was when the spirits told him not to eat fish or pork. Other traditional healers were then consulted and by means of spiritual ways they agreed that he was the chosen one by the Kiyira spirit. His family was at first frightened by this fact, because since he was still rather young they feared that it would be difficult for him to fulfil all that the spirit demanded. Being a healer is at times a dangerous life filled with commitments, and being chosen by such a powerful spirit carries with it a lot of responsibilities. Before being chosen he was a Muslim, but that was not seen as negative by the family and the community, and later they welcomed this and felt privileged that such a mighty spirit had chosen him. The spirit does not refuse him to go to the mosque, or for other healers the church if that was their previous religion, although Jaja Bujagali's spirit may not allow him partly due to all the sacrifices he has done.

The perceived powers of the water spirits relate to the visible force and size of different types of water. The more powerful the waters, the more powerful the spirits, and Bujagali Falls testify to the force of the spirit residing there. Thus, on one hand, relations between the spirits are determined by their respective powers, which serve as the basis for ranking them hierarchically, although the rankings are disputed by the healers and some spirits are more powerful than others in specific contexts. On the other hand, the mythological genealogy and relationship between spirits are not directly related to the spirits' power and importance: for instance, a son may be stronger than the father-spirit. However, given that the other spirits descend from the original spirit or spirits, their relative importance is not merely judged by the power of the water. Perceptions of these relations also change.

In some mythologies, Mesoké – the god of rain and thunder – was the first incarnation of Kiyira, and Budhagaali the second. As a perceived incarnation of Kiyira, the Budhagaali spirit is a kind of son to Kiyira. In other mythologies, however, the Budhagaali spirit is superior and has other positions in the genealogical and cosmological order. Budhagaali is like the founding father of all the other spirits, and knows everything.

The current Jaja Kiyira is the fourth or sixth incarnation of the Kiyira spirit. There may have been intervening incarnations that died because they were unable to perform the rituals and sacrifices in the prescribed way and were consequently killed by the spirit.

Kiyira is a very potent spirit and will never disappear, because it is *the* source of the river (fig. 20). As such, the river originates with this spirit. The water rises to the surface under great pressure, and appears to boil when it reaches the surface. And this very underground source of water is the river spirit where the river starts, hence its name. Before the river was known as the Nile, it was called 'Irita', meaning the 'River of the Gods'. From this, the name 'Kiyira' is derived.

Hydrologically water flows, but mythologically, although water spirits also move around on land according to their own will, their presence is enabled and restricted by their water bodies. This is exemplified by the Nalubaale spirit in Lake Victoria and the Kiyira spirit at the source. As powerful water spirits, there is not a huge difference between Kiyira and Nalubaale since they are both mighty and reside in water. There are also innumerable other spirits living in the lake, of whom Mukasa is one. Mukasa, as Nalubaale, is always in the lake, and Nalubaale is like a leader or the more powerful of the two (and Nalubaale is a general name for both male and female gods). As water spirits or gods, Nalubaale and Kiyira do more or less the same thing, but the difference between them

20. Kiyira, or the very source, flowing against the Nile's current.

lies in the body of water they hold. Consequently, Nalubaale is the more powerful, since the lake is very large. However, the Nalubaale spirit is a Buganda spirit, and the healer who is its incarnation belongs to the Buganda, whereas Kiyira, Budhagaali and Itanda are Busoga spirits. Consequently, Nalubaale is a lake spirit only, despite the size of the lake, and, more importantly, is a Buganda spirit. Although the Victoria Nile is hydrologically connected to Lake Victoria, mythologically and cosmologically the Busoga lake spirit ends where the Busoga river spirit begins. Therefore, the Nile – or Kiyira – starts at the source, because different spirits embody different water bodies.

As lake or river, the water moves differently. Not only does the water flow in both directions at the source, but the thunderous cascades just below the source also testify to the different character of the spirits, and there are many spirits in this part of the river. The Kiyira river spirit is potent and has specific powers, because the river is wide at this point. Strong winds move across the water and the spirits use them to move around, unlike the spirits on land. In Uganda, people do not freeze, but they do experience fog and mist, particularly in summer, when the whole area and the river can be covered in low cloud. When it is foggy, the spirits prefer to move on water. And in the waters from the source to the Ripon and Owen Falls, there are innumerable spirits, even though the falls have gone.

The name of the female river spirit in the Owen Falls is Nambaga, which can be translated as 'honour to her husband'. Nambaga is the wife of Kiyira and she resided in Ripon Falls. This spirit was ritually appeased by Jaja Bujagali when the Owen Falls Dam was constructed, in contrast to his exclusion from the rituals associated with Bujagali Dam, even though Nambaga had chosen not to embody a healer as her medium. This demonstrates another aspect of the spirits: not only do they choose whoever they want as a healer or human embodiment, if they choose anyone at all, but they may also accept a healer from another waterfall to conduct the necessary rituals, or so it is believed.

One reason Nambaga has no embodied healer is precisely because she is married to none other than the spirit of the source itself – Kiyira. Usually a female river spirit will choose a woman as her embodiment and a male spirit a man, but not always. The Kiyira spirit can choose a woman as his healer if he wishes. As husband and wife, these two spirits are both different and represent a unity. They move on the water – away from the falls and the source – and can travel around Lake Victoria if they wish. As such, they may also be labelled Lubaale. However, only Kiyira speaks to and through the healer at the source. Still, if the wife has particular requests, she communicates them to Jaja Kiyira through her husband. Thus, although Jaja Kiyira is strictly only embodied by the spirit of the source, other spirits may also convey their messages through him. This function is reflected in his name. The healer's common name is Jaja Kiyira, but he is also known by another, Jaja Muwereza, 'muwereza' simply meaning 'messenger'. Thus Jaja Kiyira is the messenger of God. And the spirits may convey their messages in different ways.

In Jaja Kiyira's compound, clients sit on goatskins from earlier sacrifices, and also on the skin of a python. Part of the ritual paraphernalia includes a ring of cowrie shells to enable the birth of twins. While calling up the spirit, Jaja Kiyira smokes a pipe containing specially purified tobacco, and also shakes his gourds to attract the spirit's attention. In his compound, Jaja Kiyira has two large cowrie shells. In these, ancestors may reside, but more importantly they are the residences of the river spirits Kiyira and Nambaga. Kiyira resides in the cowrie shell to the healer's right and Nambaga in that to left side (fig. 21).

The healer usually becomes possessed by the spirit in his compound after calling for it, but the spirit may appear in different guises to

21. Jaja Kiyira in his compound. The Kiyira spirit may reside in the cowrie shell to the left of the picture and his wife Nambaga in the cowrie shell to the right.

deliver messages at other times as well. One preferred way is to come as a python. The spirit may also come in the shape of a cobra or black mamba. Although these snakes are highly dangerous to other humans, they bring him no harm, even when they appear under his bed as he sleeps at night. The snakes, when they are empowered by the spirit and bring his message, are always gentle. Moreover, anyone bitten by these snakes can easily be cured by the healer.

Although Kiyira is married to Nambaga, who resides in the water where the Owen Falls were, there was one particular spirit residing in the Ripon Falls. Stanley mentioned in 1875 that this spirit was called Namweni. Jaja Kiyira had also heard of this spirit, although he could not trace its origin and where it came from. At that time, the falls were very strong and nobody could sacrifice close to them, and Namweni would point out a place where they could do so. Namweni is a female spirit but very different from Kiyira's wife. Today, Namweni is not prominent in the cosmology and few know about her. This in no way alters her ontological status as a spirit and her existence, but it does point to another aspect of the divine world. There are innumerable spirits, some of them known and others not; some are active among humans while others are concerned with different issues. This is not for humans to question. What humans can and must do is to comply with the spirits whenever and in whatever way they make their will evident through the healers. The powers of these other spirits are uncertain: they may be great, but as long as they do not bother too much with the human world, they are seemingly not that important, at least for the time being. The Budhagaali, Kiyira and Itanda spirits are, however, very active in the human realm. Not only do they lay down rules of morality and good conduct for believers, but devotees may also approach them for their own betterment.

Like humans, the various spirits are believed to have different characteristics. In particular, some are more wrathful and fearsome than others. This is partly a divine matter and inherent in the character of the spirits, but it is also the outcome of the ways the healers fulfil their commitments and the obedience of common people to the rules laid down by the divinities. If people do not adhere to cosmic rules, the river spirits may avenge themselves harshly, including killing people if social rules are transgressed and proper sacrifices are not made. Still, the spirits may differ in their particular attitudes and anger – and powers. Kiyira is generally seen as more benevolent than Budhagaali. The latter is also a benevolent spirit, but is seen as more dangerous and unpredictable, and given that it is the most powerful, it is both held in awe and feared. In the end, there is nothing humans can do about this: gods are gods and humans are humans, and that is the cosmological order. Humans have to obey the gods, whether good or bad. When people drown by accident, for instance, it is believed a particular water spirit has taken them, for whatever reason. Malign events, whatever they may be, do not challenge the omnipresence and power of the spirits. On the contrary, malignity proves that the spirits are alive and active, and as a consequence one should be devoted to them and abide by their wishes and rules. And when devotees do so, they might be well rewarded if the spirits are pleased. Sacrifices to the spirits are tokens of gratitude and respect, particularly when the spirits grant devotees' wishes.

Clients coming to have the healer work upon their bodies approach him obediently and humbly, like devotees attending church and praying. The healer gives the client special herbs. These are suspended in water and used on the body or sprinkled about. Spirits in the river or the wind are invisible, but they can see you. During the consultation in the compound the spirit is present, supervising the healer as well as judging and instructing the believer. Most people ask for health for their children and prosperity from the spirits. The spirit decides whether to accede, and refusal of requests does not mean the spirit does not work, but that there is unsettled business between spirit and believer. If the gods grant the wishes, devotees must fulfil the gods' wishes. If a person pledged a goat, he has to bring the goat; if he promised a cow if the rites were successful, he has to fulfil his commitment.

The healer can only request the river spirit for specific help, like the well-being of children, fertility for barren couples, or wealth and health for people. Although there are innumerable spheres for which the healer can request the spirit for help, there are also spheres beyond the spirit's influence. For farmers dependent upon rain-fed agriculture, the arrival of the annual rains in the right amount at the right time is a matter of plenty or famine, and ultimately life or death. Kiyira, although a water spirit residing in the river, has no control over water in the form of rain. According to Jaja Kiyira, rainmaking is impossible because this power is in the hands of Almighty God, meaning the Christian God. Making rain is beyond the power of the river god: he cannot help his people when the sun heats and desiccates the land. On the other hand, other healers on land can cure the barrenness of the fields by procuring rain, and some spirits control the rain, like the Mesoké spirit, which also resides in Itanda Falls.

The number of sacrifices to the river spirit depends on how many people come to ask for favours of the spirits: in some years there may be only one sacrifice, whereas in others there may be five or more. The healer Jaja Kiyira also gives sacrifices to the river – at the very source – at least once a year. Sometimes these are only small, like a chicken or a goat, and may involve lighting a bonfire. On special occasions, he sacrifices a sheep. Chicken and goats are lesser sacrifices, whereas a sheep is always special: even in the Bible a sheep is a special sacrifice.

Sacrifices to Kiyira take place on the small island next to the tourist island with the sign 'The source of the R. Nile.' When sacrifices are made, whether of chickens, goats, cows or bulls, the blood of the animal has to be poured directly into the river without any being spilled on land. The blood is given to the waters and to the very source originating underground: the spirit then receives the sacrifice. On this island, there are several shrines to various spirits, including Kiyira (fig. 22). However, although this is the spot where the spirit is believed to reside, or where it and the source of the Nile originate, the spirit's powers are omnipresent and may work far away from the source.

Jaja Kiyira has shrines at the riverside, but most rituals and healing take place in his compound. His compound is in Namalere village, some 30 km from Jinja by car, but nearer as the crow flies, since the spirit does not follow the road. Although Jaja Kiyira lives far from the river, he was chosen by the river spirit and not a hill spirit. Even the water spirits, Budhagaali included, visit the homes of other divinities on land, in particular Kagulu Hill.[68] Thus, distance from the source is immaterial, and even in Kampala Jaja Kiyira can be in touch with the spirit, and he regularly goes to the capital to sell herbs and medicines. During a normal week, from seven to 20 people may come to him in his compound for his services. Including those he treats outside the compound, he may see about 50 persons a week. Christians and Muslims believing in the source also come to him as their healer, since he embodies the powerful Kiyira spirit.

22. Shrines for spirits on the islands just across from the source of the River Nile.

The importance of the river spirit, its role in indigenous cosmology, people's visits to the healer and sacrifices to the spirit are not decreasing despite modernization and missionary activities. When a person who has been worked upon by the healer has experienced successful outcomes, he will go back to his village and tell of what has happened. News of the success spreads and more people learn of the power of these gods, and so more come to the source and its healer.

This also includes fishermen, mainly living in the fishing village called Chikondo, who seek the healer's services in catching fish. If they have a successful catch, they give him fish as gifts. However, as the incarnation of Kiyira, the healer is prohibited from eating fish, since fish are seen as the spirit's brothers and sisters, or its children or grandchildren. This taboo includes all healers associated with water, but also other healers embodying hill and forest spirits, since they know that the main powers come from the river spirits. This taboo does not apply to commoners, and there is no contradiction in the healer securing good catches for the fishermen even though fish are children of the river spirit. As Jaja Kiyira says, fishing is unproblematic and more like harvesting fruit from a garden, although overfishing or harming the lake by killing small fish is a bad practice. Fishing in general does not offend him, because some eat fish and others not, but as a healer whose powers come from the spirit he cannot eat the children of the river.

Even though traditional cosmology coexists with Christianity and Islam, and the healer at the source is also a Muslim, today indigenous people and their beliefs face challenges from those Christians who say that such rituals are against God's laws and actively denounce such traditional religions as pagan. In traditional Busoga cosmology, it was said that there is little difference between Christianity and the traditional religion, and only the names of the supreme divinity differ. While a true Christian goes to church and asks the Almighty for wealth, success and prosperity for his or her children, a member of the clan can go to the spirit and do the same. The powers are also similar: what one can ask for in church, one can also ask of the river. Still, there are differences in beliefs and practices. A person who has been bewitched and gone mad can go to the healer, and through the relevant rituals the water spirit will release him from his spell and cure him.

When Christians hear of this, on the other hand, they are offended and may start throwing stones, and may also withhold the rain, it is claimed. The cosmology of the source belongs to traditional religion whereas rainmaking is in the realm of the Christian and Almighty God. Thus, there are two powers: one the Almighty Christian God, the other the spirit at the source, which includes the clan, the tribe and someone's totem.

The power of the Christian God is seen by believers as coming from one true source. They also see all other spirits as nonexistent or pagan. This is not so with traditional cosmology. In water and on land there are numerous spirits. Some are local and work at the clan level, others like the Budhagaali spirit are for the Busoga. Still, although there are omnipresent and omnipotent princely spirits working for the well-being of the whole population, each spirit, including even Budhagaali, is also highly particular and bound to a local place. This was evident in the discussions back and forth about the relocation of the Budhagaali spirit. One attempted solution was moving one of the primary shrines to the Kalagala or Itanda Falls. Although Kalagala is the extremely holy home of numerous spirits and rituals are conducted there, this stratagem led to other problems, and the whole idea was abandoned. Kalagala Falls with its spirits are on Buganda land to the west of the Nile whereas Itanda Falls and its spirits are on Busoga land to the east of the river. Neither Busoga nor Buganda want another's spirits on their land.[69] Among the Busoga, this is in any case an impossibility. The Budhagaali spirit resides in the Bujagali Falls and nowhere else. It does not belong at Itanda Falls: the spirits live in their own waterfalls, even if their powers and presence transcend these waters. And in Itanda Falls, there are numerous other deities, all of them important in Busoga cosmology.

JAJA ITANDA

'Itanda' means 'power', signifying the characteristics of the spirit, and the waterfalls are a manifestation of these powers (fig. 23). According to Mary Itanda, who is the spirit incarnate, she is the only healer at these falls on the Busoga side, although another female healer had once tried to convince other healers that she was the true Itanda incarnate. Those other healers favoured Mary Itanda and the cosmological order was re-established. Still, there are numerous spirits in the waterfalls. The Kalagala spirit is a Buganda spirit and different from the Busoga

23. Itanda Falls.

Itanda spirit. However, if she needs something extra or special advice, she can contact the Kalagala healer on the other side of the falls and even visit Jaja Bujagali to discuss religious matters.

Jaja Itanda is the sixth incarnation and was installed around 2003. Before she was chosen by the spirit as its embodiment, Dada Itanda was married. Marriage is no impediment to being a healer and chosen by the spirit, but if she had been unmarried at that time, the spirit would have chosen for her an appropriate spouse and life companion, or refused to allow her to get married.

One day when she was at home, she suddenly realized that she had been chosen and taken to the river by the spirit. If a land spirit in the forest had made the choice, she would have been taken to the hills. By the shores of the river, the Itanda spirit took her to a huge rock in the middle of the river. The other villagers witnessing the occurrence had to make sacrifices on the shore, and the spirit, being pleased with the sacrifices and, more importantly, with her, secured her safe return to the shores.

The Itanda spirit is an intrinsic part of the river's pantheon. According to Mary Itanda, a close relationship exists between the Kiyira, Budhagaali and Itanda spirits. Kiyira is like the founding father and Budhagaali and Itanda are like sons. But just as sons differ, so do spirits. The Budhagaali and Itanda spirits are different and may do different things. The former has more power and can be seen as a president, and Jaja Bujagali has the power to sit on water. By this means, it is believed, the Budhagaali spirit can through its medium perform miracles impossible for others. The Itanda medium cannot do this, and its main function and quality is providing wealth.

Among the numerous water gods or spirits in the river and the waterfalls of Itanda are Mesoké and Walumbe. Mesoké is the rain and thunder god. Mesoké and Walumbe are brothers and almost alike, distinguished only by their tempers and wrathfulness. Mesoké is always angry and dangerous whereas Walumbe is more peaceful, despite being the spirit of death. Bad luck is traditionally believed to come from Walumbe.[70] He is also believed to inhabit certain pythons, so killing a python is strictly forbidden, since it will annoy the spirit of death and have consequences for the perpetrator.[71] Although invisible, Kiyira is also believed to take the form of a python, and it is an impressive sight to see a huge python swimming in the waters close to the source knowing who, cosmologically speaking, has made his presence visible. Christians too may believe in the powers of Kiyira, including his various embodiments like a python.

Whenever short-tempered Mesoké requests something, whatever that may be, it is wise to comply promptly. He may bear a person to the rock in the middle of the falls, and the safe return of that person necessitates a sacrifice. These brothers or twins are individually and jointly very powerful and born with their respective capacities. It is beneficial for couples wanting children or health and prosperity to make sacrifices to these spirits.

Although the sun shines most of the time, apart from the rainy seasons, the annual precipitation in Jinja is about 1,300 mm per year. The weather changes suddenly and dramatically. Heavy clouds may form rapidly or drift in; the skies may open and pour down heavy rain for a limited time, not only in a very local area, but the clouds may disappear as quickly as they arrived, giving way to sunshine and humidity. Thunderstorms appear the same way: under a clear, starry night sky, one may see lightning at a distance striking at the land and waters. When the lightning tears open the sky and moves around on the lake or visits numerous different villages and communities, it bears impressive witness to the literal arrival of the rain and thunder god Mesoké. He has a very powerful physical presence: he is here and now and roams where he wants with immense force. Whether his visits are because of rainmaking rituals for life-giving waters, or as punishment for sinful people and villages in the form of too much heavy rain with lightning and storms, is a matter of belief, but his visual presence and power is easy to apprehend. Moreover, lightning is different in form, shape and intensity – it is a very living and moveable spirit. And when intense lightning strikes one village and not others, it is easy to understand why the question arises – why is Mesoké striking this particular village? What have the villagers done or is it because of the sinful conduct of specific individuals? While it is not unusual that it rains, rather the contrary in most places, the extreme and varied irregularities are, however, although usual from one point of view, also unpredictable phenomena from another perspective.

Both Mesoké and Walumbe have wives. Mesoké is married to Nalwogga and Walumbe to Kasulo. The couples had children who also begat children. One grandson of these original spirits is Katigo, who became in turn one of the most powerful of them all, like an overlord to many spirits. Whatever he says or decides is of utmost importance. He emerges from the water and can walk on land. His appearance is not human, for he is an invisible, powerful force and can come and strike anyone anywhere.

Although in addition to the two brothers and Katigo there is a huge number of other spirits, all spirits (or mediums) agree that Itanda is the most powerful. He is like a human who once died, and is also seen as the spirit controlling and directing Mesoké and the other spirits. Consequently, he is like the father of the family.

The Itanda and Mesoké spirits have the greatest impact on the daily lives and mundane affairs of humans. Itanda gives wealth. Mesoké, too, gives wealth, but in the form of rain: he can be categorized as a rain and thunder god. Importantly, Mesoké always gives clean rain, which also works as a shield and blocks bad weather such as hail, which is due to witchcraft. As such, Mesoké protects his people. The spirit moves on land and in water, everywhere giving rain, but may also strike at particular places. However, if there are periods of drought and no rain appears, it is a sign that the people have not been obedient and sacrificed to Mesoké. Likewise, if there is too much sun, heat or rain, people have not sacrificed adequately. Despite being fearsome and angry, Mesoké is a good spirit, but needs sacrifices to be pleased, and if these are not conducted in the prescribed manner, the life-giving rains may be withheld.

There are various sacrifices that may be offered to the spirit, ranging from chickens and goats to sheep and cows. Sacrifices always take place by the falls, since this is where the spirit resides. Such sacrifices can take place as needed and when devotees feel they are appropriate. Nowadays, sacrifices to the rain-god are declining. Many Christians condemn the traditional ways by saying they do not work and are not worth performing.

Itanda, Mesoké and Walumbe are all gods, and it is possible to bring them together by calling attention to them through huge festivities, including dancing and sacrifices. Both the Itanda and Mesoké spirits may talk through Mary Itanda, who is thus the embodiment of both. According to her, it is possible to be incarnated as two or more spirits, but not simultaneously. If the Itanda spirit appears to her, she cannot be possessed by Mesoké, and vice versa. However, after Itanda has left her body, she may be embodied by Mesoké, and the spirits speak directly to and through her. Itanda and Mesoké are the main spirits that approach her, but if there are urgent needs, other lesser water spirits like Navalongo, the wife of Itanda, and Meru and Walumbe may use her to convey their messages.

Part of being a healer is being able to have a dialogue with the ancestors in order to resolve questions of witchcraft, such as who has been bewitched by whom. Some of the ancestral spirits also live in water. They may live in the river or the falls or in trees or caves, or wherever they like to reside. Thus, as a healer, one may be in touch with numerous spiritual forces in one way or other. But spirits are independent and highly localized, at the same time as being ubiquitous. Spirits choose whoever they want as their embodiment, and only that healer, when possessed, has a spirit's power. Consequently, although spirits and healers are very powerful, Jaja Bujagali, for instance, has no power from the Itanda Falls. His powers derive from the Budhagaali spirit only. Still, it was he who conducted the appeasement ceremonies when the Owen Falls Dam was built, and consequently had the approval of the spirits to do so. Thus, spirits do what they want, as usual, and if they approve other healers or choose the same healer as their embodiment, then that is the way it is, or so it is believed.

Traditional healers have an important role in people's everyday lives and problems. If commoners lack wealth and success, are barren and childless, or encounter difficulties at school or work, they may turn to Jaja Itanda, and Itanda is the spirit who may solve all these problems (fig. 24). Compared to Mesoké, who also provides wealth but in the form of rain, which is most needed by farmers, Itanda is more universal and may deal with most other kinds of misfortune. Thus, although other powerful spirits reside in the falls, they may not be engaged too much in the daily

24. Mary Itanda praying to Itanda.

world of the living. Consequently, spirits like Itanda who can resolve any kind of human misfortune are perceived as the most powerful.

One of Jaja Itanda's compounds is on the hill next to the falls and many clients prefer to visit her close to the roaring water itself, since they can more readily experience the presence and power of the river spirits. In a normal week, she may see up to ten clients. As with Jaja Kiyira, she has another compound some distance from the water where she lives. In her compounds, before the consultations and rituals start, she sets out to attract the spirit's attention by using gourds and smoking a pipe: the sound and smell alert the spirit and direct it to her. She is dressed in bark cloth embroidered with cowrie shells. This attire is necessary for the spirit to be embodied in her, and is a sign that she will serve her people. The tree bark is holy and only those chosen by the spirits may wear this ritual paraphernalia. She will work on the clients with herbs and powerful water.

As with the spirit at the source and at Bujagali Falls, devotees may make sacrifices to the river, depending on the requested outcome and the seriousness of the matter at hand. Not all consultations end with a sacrifice. Indeed, they are quite rare, occurring perhaps twice a month or five times a year. The animal sacrificed will depend upon the graveness of the problems and the solution being sought through the healer. Thus, chickens, goats or sheep may be offered, but if the stakes are higher, a bull or a cow. In the end, the sacrifice and choice of animal depend on devotees' perceptions of their problems and life situations, and their appreciation of how the problems were solved by the spirits. If the spirits were very benevolent and secured the expected and extraordinary solution or gift, a proper sacrifice is in order. When sacrifices are conducted, the animal's throat is cut and the blood is spilled into the river whereupon the meat is prepared and eaten on the shore afterwards. The sacrificial place at Itanda Falls lies next to the river by a sacred tree. Shrines can be built anywhere a spirit resides or visits. This particular tree is a shrine where Jaja Itanda also prays to the spirits.

There are no graves at Itanda Falls, but ancestors and spirits may choose to live there. When people drown in the falls, it is believed the spirits have taken them. The powers of the waters and falls are celebrated not only in indigenous tradition and belief, but also by Christians. No baptisms occur in the Itanda Falls because of the force of the river – or of the spirits – and they have to take place in calmer waters. Still, Christians and non-Christians carry water in jerry cans from the falls, and use it as holy water for different purposes, whether for prayers or mixed with herbs as medicine. Thus, the power of the water transcends cosmologies and the benevolent uses of water are for the many. These powers, however, are double-edged, and have serious consequences when believers and healers are disobedient.

Being a healer involves numerous taboos, and violating them may be lethal. Like Jaja Kiyira and Jaja Bujagali, Jaja Itanda may not eat fish, since they live in the water and are seen as children or grandchildren of the river. Moreover, chicken is prohibited and she may only eat goat and beef. As a healer, she cannot cut her hair. This taboo applies to several but not all healers, and both Jaja Kiyira and Nfuudu (Jaja Lubaale) have cut their hair and are bald. The spirits must approve the hair cutting and various spirits have specific requests and criteria. If she wishes to cut her hair, she has to perform a major sacrifice. If she does so without permission, the spirit will become very angry and will kill her. But it is not only this that may evoke the spirits' wrath with possible lethal consequences – so does dam building.

Despite the Ugandan government's promise as part of the overall negotiations for Bujagali Dam that the Kalagala/Itanda Falls should not be developed for hydropower but remain pristine, the situation has changed. Plans for a dam at Kalagala Falls were now officially on the table in 2014 when I discussed the matter with her. If a dam is built there, the spirits will most likely be very angry. How this wrath will be expressed and with what consequences is not known, but repercussions there will be, Jaja Itanda believed. However, it may be possible to mitigate these consequences if everything is done in the right and proper way.

As a traditional healer, she would have to ask the spirits what they require to accept the dam, and most likely this will be costly for the dam builders. Lavish sacrifices are mandatory, the construction of new shrines likewise, and it is of utmost importance that the spirits will be pleased. In such a process, being the embodiment of the spirit carries huge responsibilities, and the first person likely to experience the spirits' wrath if she is unable to please the spirits in an appropriate way is the medium herself. Thus, if the dam is rushed and she is unable to conduct the necessary rituals, she fears for her life, since she is responsible for the spirits' well-being in this world. This was her main concern: if the process is rushed and the builders abruptly try to remove the spirits without the proper rituals, there will be divine wrath. On the other hand, if they are consulted and their requirements are satisfied, Mary Itanda believes the spirits could easily allow the dam to be built.

If the government rides roughshod by blasting the falls, rather than adopting a conciliatory approach by allowing her to negotiate with the spirits, there will be serious repercussions. As she admitted, she has not power enough to stop the government, and the politicians lack knowledge of spiritual matters. Currently, she is protected by the spirits, but if inappropriate steps are taken, such as disturbing the waterfalls without the spirits' acceptance, the spirits may accuse her of failing to perform her duties satisfactorily. Having in mind the story of the old Chief Ntembe, who was killed by the Budhagaali spirit for allowing Nfuudu to conduct the mock rituals, I asked why the spirits would kill her as a devotee rather than any of the dam builders or members of the government, since it was they who would either build or allow the dam to be built, and thus destroy the waterfalls. The question provoked much laughter, but the answer was serious, and sheds more light on the workings of the spirits and the role of the healer as medium. As a follower, she said, she would always be condemned for being unable to stop the dam. Because she was a medium, she was trusted by the spirits, who would accuse her, the first person linking the gods and humans, of not having done all in her power to prevent it. Moreover, the spirits do not personally know anyone in the government, and she is the one tasked with attending to the divinities' daily affairs in this world. Thus, she is the first person the spirits will strike and kill, but they may also kill some in the government as well. In any event, all this could be avoided if she is acknowledged as the appropriate healer who is able to engage in dialogue and negotiation with the spirits to secure their interests and welfare. However, by 2014 nobody in government had contacted her, and the only information she had was what she had heard in the news as well as from rumours that a dam would be built.

I was back in Uganda in 2017 and visited Mary Itanda. There were no new plans for a dam at these falls. However, the next waterfalls north of Itanda had been dammed – the Isimba Falls. Although the Itanda waterfalls were safe for the time being, the future of the waterfalls was uncertain. If the Isimba reservoir is filled to its maximum potential, the reservoir's tail end may flood parts of the surrounding settlements and even impact the Itanda or Kalagala waterfalls themselves. According to Mary, the gods were furious, not only the spirits at Bujagali and Isimba Falls, but also those residing in the Itanda Falls. Thus, the Bujagali history may be repeated at Itanda Falls and at all the other falls where dams are planned. But if there were general concerns among healers about the possible negative impacts of these dam projects, there was one healer who saw things quite differently and had other views – Nfuudu.

BENEDICTO NFUUDU

Among the learned and laymen of the community, it was not obvious why Nfuudu had been chosen by the kingdom to represent the Budhagaali spirit in place of Jaja Bujagali, the man acclaimed as the spirit incarnate. Benedicto Nfuudu provided the obvious answer: he was the only true incarnation of the Budhagaali spirit. Not only that, he is also the embodiment of Jaja Lubaale, and visitors to his compound are met by a sign clearly stating this. Jaja Bujagali says Nfuudu takes many of his clients by pretending to be Budhagaali incarnate, but according to Nfuudu the reverse is true. So they are bitter enemies as regards who is the true incarnation of the Budhagaali spirit, the flow of clients and the money lost or gained.

Within the realm of magic and mystery, seclusion and exclusion are strategies that enhance a spiritual aura. Whereas an increasing number of healers choose to be more visible and accessible by living along roads where they can easily attract more clients, Nfuudu has opted for a more secret location. Although he is widely known, very few knew where he lives or his telephone number, and many other famous healers have never met him. Although it turned out he lived not far away, in fact close to Jaja Bujagali, my interpreter and local friends had to inquire of numerous people to establish where to find him. When I got to his compound, he was surprised that I had been able to locate him, and more importantly, that his reputation had reached the other side of the world.

His compound is next to a military training camp for young recruits. Before reaching his compound, visitors have to pass through road-blocks and checkpoints. This location has certain strategic advantages in the occult business. With the change in the kingdom after the last chief died, he has not been given the ritual responsibilities he wants and claims the right to. Still, the number of clients coming to him now is the same as it used to be before the dam was built. Soldiers being sent to dangerous areas to fight rebels, including Joseph Kony's Lord's Resistance Army (see below), seek protection and he provides them with the necessary medicines. The proximity to the military camp guarantees a steady supply of needy clients, and there were even rumours that the government wants soldiers to use witchcraft in hunting the rebels so as to secure its own power. When a healer needs medicines for this purpose, spirits in the bush will guide him to the plants and trees from which the necessary medicines can be obtained. Although other healers have a spouse, whether husband or wife, Nfuudu has an invisible spirit as his wife. If he wanted a human wife, the spirits could provide him with one.

At the age of 70 (in 2013), Nfuudu had worked as a healer for 51 years. In his compound, there were 15 main shrines and a large number of spirits and ancestors live there (fig. 25). As the caretaker, he looked after these spirits well. The materiality of the compound also testifies to the power of the healers. A large portfolio of ritual paraphernalia, including spears and shields, impresses visitors, who may not understand the full meaning of all the sacred objects. But the mere presence of a rich and varied material culture gives the impression that the healer is well equipped and skilled in the realm of the occult and the otherworld. And, as being both Jaja Bujagali and Jaja Lubaale, he is supreme among healers or diviners.

According to him, nothing can be done concerning the water and the spirits there except by him. He is the strongest of all healers. Nfuudu says there are not two Bujagali healers. There is only one, and he is that healer: he is like a king of water, in fact, the king of gods, he said. Everything concerning

25. Visitors in Nfuudu's compound reading his sign: 'Nabamba Bujagali. Mzee Nfuudu Benedicto Badru. Jjaja Wa Lubaale Kimaka.'

water in the Busoga kingdom is within his realm. Like Jaja Lubaale, he is in charge of all waters, including the Nile. The Budhagaali spirit is the most important of all the spirits, and he is responsible for the Busoga kingdom. Mythologically, though, Kiyira or the source of the Nile was originally superior. Kiyira was like a grandfather, but nowadays he is more like a son, after Budhagaali took over the main responsibilities. According to Nfuudu, since he embodies both Budhagaali and Lubaale, he controls all water of whatever form and appearance. Nfuudu can also work as a rainmaker, including performing rain-stopping rituals. If there is drought, he can perform the necessary rituals to ensure the life-giving rains arrive, and can also stop harmful rain, activities that, according to Jaja Itanda, lie within Mesoké's realm.

If a dam is built at Itanda Falls, this will not cause problems, Nfuudu said. Itanda is like a son of Budhagaali, and he can also perform the necessary rituals enabling the relocation of this spirit to ensure a safe and successful process. Nobody died during the construction of Bujagali Dam, which is unusual in constructions of this massive size. According to Nfuudu, this was because he had conducted specific rituals that pleased the river spirit. With the consent of the spirit, the work proceeded well. As long as he is in charge, everything will be fine.

While the dam was being constructed, the spirit resided in his compound. During the construction and the filling of the reservoir, the very spot in the river where the Budhagaali spirit lived was destroyed, and to ensure its well-being, the spirit was located by him in his compound. During the time the spirit was at his place, he took great care of it, making sacrifices and looking after it in the best possible way. When the construction was completed, he safely returned the spirit in 2011 and today everything is as it used to be, according to him.

When asked if construction of dams caused cultural or religious challenges and problems among the Busoga, Nfuudu answered in the negative. As long as he is in charge and in power, there would be no problems, since he can appease the spirits and undertake the necessary rituals. And although other healers argue the contrary, there will, according to Nfuudu, be no difficulties if he is consulted. He can resolve any issues concerning water, in particular with the spirits of the water. The spirits exist whatever happens, he said, a view shared by all. He added that before he transferred the Budhagaali spirit there had been difficulties, but he gave the spirit whatever it demanded and by adhering to and pleasing the spirit, all the spirits in Busoga cosmology were satisfied. Therefore, with his powers and capacities, there will be no problems in relocating the Itanda spirit and others.

Other healers, though, just laughed at this, saying he was bragging and aiming to impress me. When I asked Mary Itanda about Nfuudu's claim that he can easily relocate the Itanda spirit, she sneered and promptly replied 'he is only talking!' He can do nothing unless he is incarnated as Jaja Itanda, which he is not. She, on the other hand, as Itanda's embodiment, can negotiate with the spirit. She used the Namizi shrines as an example. When Nfuudu tried to build new shrines for the spirits, they refused to leave the water. In the eyes of other healers, this undermined Nfuudu's claim that he was the Budhagaali spirit. In fact, she argued, he is not incarnated by any spirits since he claims that he is Jaja Nalubaale, Jaja Bujagali and Jaja Itanda, and others – he is everywhere! He does not even have a proper site where the spirits reside. This is, of course, disputed by Nfuudu, and ironically Jaja Bujagali's and Nfuudu's compounds are not far apart and once upon a time these two men were on good terms.

JAJA BUJAGALI

Although Jaja Bujagali is internationally famous for opposing Bujagali Dam and his fierce conflict with Nfuudu, this is not why his reputation is well established in Busoga culture. It is, however, difficult to separate rumour from reality. Jaja Bujagali was the 39th incarnation of Budhaagali, and there are two dominant legends or stories about Jaja Bujagali. One central story is that Jaja Bujagali used to sail on bark cloths to Dumbbell Island to perform his rituals, and his ability to float on water is truly seen as evidence of his divine powers. The other is the terrifying story about human sacrifices and, in particular, child sacrifices taking place in the waterfalls where humans are sacrificed and given to the river spirit Budhagaali. The mythology of Jaja Bujagali is not solely related to the current healer, but relates to the embodiment of this water spirit. As was often pointed out, many of the current healer's predecessors were more powerful and famous than he is, and the Busoga administration claimed that the previous incarnations conducted better rituals than the current incumbent. Thus, in talking of Jaja Bujagali, it is difficult to separate the institution, the predecessors and the current healer, since past perceptions influence current views of Jaja Bujagali.

In any event, Jaja Bujagali is seen as a highly dangerous man and the Budhagaali spirit is not necessarily seen as only a benevolent god. In the past, the healer had enormous powers and was greatly feared wherever he visited. Some did not even dare to look at him and ran away upon his approach. None objected when he arrived in villages and demanded a cow to eat. What he demanded was freely given, even daughters as wives. If a farmer had ten cows, the healer could be given five, since he was the most potent among spirits.

Thus, perceptions of healers vary. Some see Jaja Bujagali as a truly good healer, others are more frightened. Rumours of what some Budhagaali incarnations may have done influence perceptions of the existing Jaja Bujagali. Being a medium is being in between. When Jaja Bujagali becomes possessed of the spirit, he communicates the messages of the river god without knowing what he conveys, and when the spirit leaves him for the time being he is just an ordinary human being. Thus, although the Budhagaali medium is just like any other person when not possessed, by being the medium he has great powers since he can invoke the spirit, even if only for his own betterment.

The healer has to follow the spirit's orders and conduct the necessary rituals in a satisfactory way. He is in no position to tell the gods what to do, but the gods tell him and all the other believers what they have to do. By honouring the spirits and behaving kindly, things go well; otherwise the spirits intervene and everybody will be dead, including the healer.

Thus, although the spirit and healer are feared, no human may challenge their existence, regardless of whether they are perceived as benevolent or not. And precisely because he is the embodiment of the most powerful spirit, many people come to Jaja Bujagali. Even Christians and Muslims visit him during the dark evenings for secret consultations. When couples come to him asking for fecundity and a healthy child, they are obliged to come back with their child to Jaja Bujagali. He will then bless the child and cut its hair. Everyone from highest to lowest comes to him for the spirit's benefits. Kenyatta from Kenya once came to him, he told me, but otherwise he can tell no names, but there are many politicians, musicians and other important persons, including engineers and dam builders. Their precise identity must remain secret. If he divulges this, people will start gossiping and many of those visiting him will officially deny that they still believe in the powers of witchcraft, or simply adhering to the cosmic rules of Budhagaali.

There are several myths regarding the twin aspect of the Budhagaali spirit. On one hand, the spirit has a twin brother called Nabamba. As mythological twins, they are still distinct, and whereas Budhagaali resides in the falls, Nabamba is believed to live in Mabira rainforest between Lugazi and Jinja. In this indigenous rainforest, one of the last in Uganda and the largest in the central part of the country, Nabamba is believed to be a fearful spirit. Malevolent occurrences take place there, including fatal accidents and apparent human sacrifices, and the Budhagaali spirit wants his twin brother to return to the river. Allegedly, however, the Nabamba spirit was hostile to the clan and therefore abandoned. It appears as a large python and is evidently seen by many people on the main highway through the forest. This account parallels the story of the twin brother Waibira or Mabira. The believed sacrificial practices in Mabira forest also reflect upon Jaja Bujagali, since the spirits are twins. Thus, the Budhagaali cosmology is not restricted to the waterfalls, but also includes what happens in the rainforest.

And the hot-tempered Nabamba or Mabira spirit in the rainforest is believed to demand frequent human sacrifices. Among commoners, there are different perceptions of this spirit. Some believe that humans are still sacrificed there, whereas others argue such sacrifices are no longer performed since they are prohibited by government. Still, the twin deity is believed to be bloodthirsty, and some claim that, rather than demanding human sacrifices, the spirit just takes humans as needed. This has its rationale in the frequent fatal road accidents on the road through the forest. When such deaths occur, some perceive them as the spirit taking its share of blood.

Although the Mabira or the twin spirit of Budhagaali is primarily a spirit belonging to the Buganda pantheon of spirits, there are yet other connotations, which even includes Kiyira as an ancestral spirit. The Mabira spirit belongs to the Mabiro clan, which is etymologically related to *okubira*. Okubira refers to foam or boiling, or boiling over like milk, with white foam, similar to the waters in the falls and hence they are twin spirits. On one hand, Okiyira denotes the roaring sound and can be seen as 'he who makes the sound', and from this mythology it is the falls giving the name to the river as Kiyira. On the other, at the very source itself, the water looks like boiling when it comes up from beneath, strengthening this connection of the roaring and boiling character of the waters. Thus, this double connotation which takes different forms are applicable to and testimonies of different spirits, which are specifically located or living where these phenomena of nature occur. Moreover, water is always in plural and is never just one phenomenon. The powers of waterfalls are manifested in the foaming and roaring qualities like boiling or strong counter-currents.

When I asked Jaja Bujagali about the Budhagaali spirit's twin, while wondering where I had come across these stories, he replied that there is hardly any difference, because they are twins. Indeed, there are indications that he is the healer embodying both. Chief Waguma Yasin said that the Budhagaali spirit is also known as Nabamba – and both names are used by Jaja Bujagali. Moreover, he is known as Waibira, and as the oracle of the Budhagaali spirit he comes from the Waguma clan.[72]

As twin spirits, they perform the same functions, Jaja Bujagali said. But he doubted that the spirit lives in or visits the Mabira forest. They are twin brothers, but there is only one incarnation, himself, he said. This has implications, but what they are is difficult to tell because this is a sensitive topic. When the twins want to perform something or communicate with humans, they have to go to Bujagali Falls, not the forest: the twin spirit comes to Bujagali. And if there are numerous stories about human sacrifices to the bloodthirsty spirit in Mabira forest, most of these rumours revolve around Bujagali Falls. The spirits' blood thirst is partly connected to the diviner's hair.

There are beliefs that if Jaja Bujagali wishes to cut his hair, the sacrifice of a child is mandatory. These children have been stolen from other places. According to stories, the Bujagali incarnate has occasionally cut his hair in the past, although this is now taboo. As the most powerful, the Budhagaali spirit and its healer are enveloped in many such stories. Grown-ups today recall that when they were young, they widely feared the Jaja Bujagali healer – and do so today. In former times, children did disappear and elders still recall that such sacrifices took place, or were believed to. The ritual was not annual, but occurred at irregular intervals of from five or ten years, depending on the spirits' demands. Rumours circulate today that child sacrifices still occur, although nobody can be sure where and when, and which healer is responsible. More recent history recalled by elders suggests that such sacrifices took place in their early lives. All these rumours and beliefs are based on speculation, in the sense that none of the disappearances of children can be explicitly linked to actual sacrifices at Bujagali Falls by the spirit himself and his healer.

Even newcomers to Jinja from other regions or neighbouring countries are quickly exposed to this Busoga mythology, specifically Jaja Bujagali's ability to sit on water and the rumours that children are sacrificed to the river spirit. These stories are shared and feared by everyone, old and young, farmers and fishermen, priests and prostitutes. The reality is another issue, what matters is the mythology about Jaja Bujagali and his powers. All these stories mean the healers were truly seen as very powerful and dangerous. Hence, except in extraordinary circumstances, it was believed that it was preferable not to engage with them and their powers. Perhaps the rumours are stronger than actual facts, and in practice such rumours help to create the healers' reputations and aura. But is there evidence of such sacrificial practices, and how is it part of the overall cosmology?

HAIR-CUTTING SACRIFICES AND BLOODTHIRSTY SPIRITS

The Busoga kingdom was displeased with Jaja Bujagali's numerous complaints against the dam contractor and it seems the kingdom was particularly dissatisfied with the way Jaja Bujagali acted and lived: not only did he have many wives and ate meals in public, including dishes he was not allowed to consume, but his short hair was also noted.[73] In a study of traditional religion among the Busoga by the Cultural Research Centre in Jinja, these points were stressed. Jaja Bujagali is not allowed to eat fish or chicken; he is not allowed to share matoke with others except those possessed of the Nabamba spirit and confirmed to be so (and Jaja Bujagali is called the 'one who eats alone'); each new moon he must sleep alone without his wife for four days, and – he is not allowed to cut his hair.[74]

Where healers have unfinished business with the spirits, cutting one's hair is a great sacrilege. Jaja Itanda said that if she cut her hair, her spirit would immediately strike her dead to the ground. Being a healer is thus both a blessing and also dangerous work, and one must obey divine laws and provide what the spirits demand. If cutting hair is certain death for the healer, there is one possible substitution for his or her own death. This is the ultimate human sacrifice, and in particular the sacrificing of a child to the river spirit. Among the Busoga there are many rumours and fears about these sacrifices.

According to Jaja Bujagali, there were two main healers conducting the mock ritual in 2007, and Nfuudu stole his identity by claiming that he was the proper Jaja Bujagali. This was plausible since Jaja Bujagali is not supposed to cut his hair, and the resemblance convinced people that Nfuudu was the proper incarnation of the Budhagaali spirit. Today, Nfuudu has boldly shaved his hair. If it is correct that his long hair allowed Nfuudu to claim that he was the proper incarnation of the Budhagaali spirit, because he also had long hair, his apparent lack of long hair since, including his performance in the 2011 ritual, is striking.

Thus, if such extreme rituals have been conducted recently, and there are widespread rumours that they have, but no evidence, there is no single and obvious candidate. Importantly, these dark sides of spirituality and witchcraft are not meant to be public but to remain shrouded in mystery. People may believe in this reality, but for obvious reasons no outsider may participate in them, since then they would become witnesses to murder and hence accomplices. Obviously, inquiring about human sacrifices is difficult because of the sensitivity and illegality of such practices, and nobody will admit to conducting them. Thus, the evidence is at best circumstantial, but the words of the healers may have more weight than the rumours among commoners, since the healers know at least in part the practices associated with the cosmology.

Healers do not share their secrets with anybody, not even other healers, so what Jaja Bujagali does is not shared with Jaja Kiyira, for instance. Hence, there is much secrecy, and no one tells when and if dangerous and prohibited sacrifices occur. Still, the healer's status would not increase unless others know that such rituals take place, without knowing. Thus, when such a sacrifice is made, a healer may hint that they have been conducted. It is implicitly understood that he refers to human sacrifices, and that the actual ritual is conducted in utmost secrecy. Consequently, not even other healers know the full truth. However, one centrally positioned healer in the cosmology confirmed that the last human sacrifice to Bujagali Falls that he knew of had been in 1987, although he did not witness it and thus this information is based on second-hand sources. If this and perhaps later sacrifices did occur, it is by no means certain they were conducted by Jaja Bujagali, since these falls are central to the cosmology of many healers.

Following Jaja Kiyira, sacrifices of children have never taken place at the source. Mary Itanda strongly objected to this line of inquiry, or more precisely, she said, only witchdoctors perform this practice. She is a traditional healer and herbalist, and proper healers do not engage in or encourage such sacrifices. They employ only water and herbal medicines, and gratitude to the spirits involves only animal sacrifices when devotees' problems are resolved.

According to other healers, Jaja Bujagali has allegedly not fulfilled all the obligations demanded by the Budhaagali spirit. In the past when he cut his hair, sacrifices of children were made. These are no longer taking place, and the older people tell of how in the past children were also secretly sacrificed because the river demanded blood. Humans are humans, and hence human blood is the most valuable, I was told. Moreover, there were stories that when chiefs or other important personages were buried in the past, their funerals were accompanied by human sacrifices, with the chosen victims being buried alive. Past times were dangerous, but this has now changed. Still, the mythology surrounding the importance of the healers' hair lingers.

Although there are strong religious taboos regarding the cutting of hair, these restrictions affect specific healers and depend upon the associated spirits. Whether shaving off hair is permitted is also testament to the relationship between the spirit and his embodiment, and different spirits have in varying degrees specific restrictions for each and every medium. Whereas the cutting of Jaja Bujagali's and Mary Itanda's hair would have resulted in the spirit's wrath and their own deaths if the necessary rituals were not performed, both Jaja Kiyira and Jaja Lalubaale have cut their hair. There is thus a distinct difference between healers who can cut their hair and those who cannot, not because of their own spiritual capacity but because of the differences among the spirits and their plans for their healers and for humans. Some spirits are more demanding than others.

Another healer argued that Jaja Bujagali has not fulfilled all the divine requests and commitments, and there are still obligations to be met. Whether this is because some of the spirit's demands are beyond the capabilities of a singular human incarnation, is yet another question. In any event, a healer is in an asymmetrical reciprocal relationship with his/her spirit, and the healer's well-being and ritual powers are a matter of choice by the spirits, not something they can decide on their own. The hair is the ultimate symbol of the fulfilment of ritual obligation. During the initiation of a healer, lavish sacrifices are made, but these are not a full sacrifice. As part of the initiation, a healer may promise not to cut his hair before a full sacrifice, and the uncut hair is therefore a token of the moral obligation and indebtedness of the healer to the spirit.

According to Jaja Kiyira, he has served his spirit and the river god is well pleased with him. More precisely, he has inherited his ritual and spiritual status from his forefathers, who fulfilled all the necessary commitments. Thus, his ritual status today is largely the outcome of the founding fathers and how they solved the original issues. As the incarnation of Kiyira, he is fortunate that his predecessors cleared all the ritual obligations, which would otherwise have imposed taboos and restrictions on him. Consequently, sacrifices of children or humans do not occur at the source whereas healers like Jaja Bujagali may have to make a full sacrifice if they are to cut their hair.

Thus, there are several processes at work. First, it was claimed that if Jaja Bujagali is to be set free as a healer, he needs to conduct lavish sacrifices to the spirit, which may include a cock, a sheep, five goats and a bull, and ultimately a human. Such sacrifices would set him free once and for all and allow him to cut his hair, but currently he cannot afford such a major sacrifice, one healer argued. But if it is correct that child sacrifices took place occasionally in the past, this may indicate that the Budhagaali spirit was only temporarily pleased. Jaja Bujagali as a healer was not set free; perhaps the spirit will never set him free.

This points to another aspect. The spirits have different qualities and characters. Some are fiercer and more malevolent than others; humans can only pay homage and be even more obedient. And as shown in Buganda ethnography from the late nineteenth and early twentieth centuries, some spirits were more bloodthirsty, demanding human sacrifices. Other spirits did not, and this was, so to speak, a matter of taste among spirits. The Budhagaali spirit is more demanding than, for instance, Kiyira and Itanda, and partly for this reason is seen as more powerful. Thus, the most important spirits demand blood, but not all demand human blood. Spirits may demand blood exclusively through sacrifices conducted by the healer, since he or she embodies the spirit and as such has a unique responsibility. The spirits may also demand blood from commoners, since as spirits they are, after all, supreme. There remains one last sphere in which blood sacrifices are intrinsic to the spirits and their believers, and that is witchcraft, although witchcraft does not necessarily demand blood.

WATER AND WITCHCRAFT

There are many definitions of witchcraft.[75] Busoga Catholics define it thus:

> Witchcraft is the manifestation of a hidden destructive power emanating from a person. This power may be innate, inherited or acquired in a variety of ways. Some people practice witchcraft without being aware of it or having control of it. Witchcraft is mostly used in secret for destructive purposes, but sometimes used to protect oneself, one's family and one's property.[76]

For the Busoga this is a good definition since it is broad but captures the realities as they are perceived by people themselves. Whether witchcraft or not, diviners enable encounters with invisible and non-vocal spirits.[77]

Evidence of the existence of witchcraft takes many forms for the Busoga, among whom belief in witchcraft is ubiquitous. As the Busoga say: 'witchcraft is a reality and every human being a potential witch'.[78] Practically all misfortunes, including death, are directly or indirectly related to witchcraft. For the Busoga, a 'natural' death is almost unthinkable, and they have a proverb that 'a person cannot die unless bewitched'. There is always somebody behind a death, and 'one who has not been bewitched, does not fit in the grave'.[79] Everything malignant can be explained by witchcraft:

> Misfortune is the result of bad luck or witchcraft. When one has a long sickness, when a young man fails to get a spouse, when a woman fails to bear children, when yields are poor, when one gets an accident, when one is struck by lightning, when children fail to perform well in class and above all when someone dies, witchcraft is considered to be the prime cause. The immediate thing that comes to mind is that someone has caused the misfortune through witchcraft.[80]

Moreover, Busoga believe that in creating the universe

> God appointed some power to nature, which is seen as something put at human service. So, the Basoga use nature to enhance the quality of life. This explains why Africans bend nature to their will by using herbs of witchcraft. Therefore, whilst we say that God is the origin of all power, nature created by God, is looked upon as a source of witchcraft on account of being manipulated for selfish tendencies.[81]

Rain-stopping is a particular category of witchcraft. Witches withholding rain may not do so on their own account, but may feel compelled to do so by the ancestors. If they do not, the ancestors may punish them with sickness, poverty and even death. Some rain-stoppers do, however, act on their own initiative and for selfish motives, for instance, when someone takes another's wife. Brick makers are believed to employ such rituals since rain will destroy their business, and when the Chinese built a bridge they were believed to have used anti-rain witchcraft, because no rain fell for a very long time. During funerals too, relatives may use witchcraft to stop the rain from disturbing the mourners. Initiation into and the practice of rain-stopping is performed at night in secret. If there is a long drought and if people believe they know who is responsible, they may beat up the rain-stopper, as reported in one village: 'One Saturday morning, I met people in [the] village beating up an elderly man, accusing him of withholding the rain and making their crops fail. People burnt all his belongings and chased him from the village. The following morning it rained.'[82] Although one way to end the problem is to chase away the alleged rain-stopper, another is to visit a diviner who calls upon the spirits that have caused the rains to fail and orders them to leave the person withholding the rains. However, even if the spirits follow this advice, they may possess another clan member to stop the rain, since it is believed that the spirits stopping the rain are bound by clan affiliation.[83]

By contrast:

> Rainmakers are deeply religious people who spend a lot of time praying to the god of rain, Musoké, to give their people rain [...] They don't make rain as the term seemingly suggests. They only pray for it and perform certain rituals after which they inform the people when it is going to rain.[84]

This also highlights the dual aspect of the gods and the use of witchcraft. There are people who can send hailstorms, and others who can send lightning by manipulating nature to bring harm to others to their own advantage. 'A witch causes lighting to strike his/her adversary by using [certain] seeds mixed with other herbs [...] while invoking Musoké (the god of lighting) and other spirits ordering them to strike the victim.'[85] While Mesoké is a benevolent god, he can also be malevolent when invoked through witchcraft. And rainmaking too may involve the darker side of witchcraft. A rain spirit existed called Kaghango to whom sacrifices were made to procure rain. During droughts, a diviner would choose a crippled man to be sacrificed by placing him in front of a pit where Kaghango was believed to reside. People would say: 'You, Kaghango, if it is you who keeps the rain away, accept this offering and let it rain. If it is not you, then give this man strength to get up and walk back to us.' Then they would wait to see if the man rose and walked towards them. If he fell into the pit, they would sacrifice a goat and the rains would come.[86]

Witchcraft is a religion, it was claimed, and Christianity is a religion, and although the Christians want to eradicate witchcraft, witchcraft has always existed and was there long before Christianity. From the church's perspective, the practice of witchcraft is 'an enemy of life'. Although witchcraft is believed to ease problems, it may also cause harm and evil, and often money is a main driver for such practices, whether in terms of the client's needs or the healer's advantage. Although the early missionaries labelled all African practices devilish, the church now accepts the use of herbs and healing for benign purposes. If witchcraft is an enemy of life, it is an inherent quality in everyone, since all humans have the potential to inflict harm on others in varying degrees.

According to some, witchcraft is everywhere and used by everyone – from the poorest to the richest, from the humble to the mighty. When someone is bewitched, a healer may tell that person to wash the evil away in the middle of the river. The water is strongest in falls such as Bujagali Falls or Itanda Falls. Any sickness, evil or witchcraft can be removed from the person by forceful water flows. A person afflicted with evil may also go to the river in his ordinary clothes, take them off and give them to the river before fully immersing himself in the water, whereupon he will arise free of his sicknesses or the malevolence besetting him. In other cases, the bewitched may use the river water to wash their face and head to erase the evil. Witchcraft can also be used to obtain wealth. Whereas most people work hard in the fields and do their best to provide for family and friends, some resort to diviners or healers to secure greater riches through witchcraft, whether in the fields, in school or in business. One healer pointed out a paradox: 'Many people consult us in order to win in political campaigns or to retain their social positions; yet these same politicians advocate banning our activities.'[87] Witchcraft may even work as a much cheaper option to doping in sports. Some coaches and players visit diviners before a match to secure extra strength and divine advantage, and the healers accommodate such requests.[88]

Still, there is also anxiety and fear about consulting a diviner or healer, because dabbling in the occult also has drawbacks. Among the Busoga there are sayings like 'Going to diviners breeds witchcraft' and 'Fortune-telling leads to practising witchcraft': by only seeking positive advantages one may become a witch oneself.[89]

Given that the spirits are also bloodthirsty in differing measure, they may provide for a devotee's requests in return for sacrifices. At this point, there is little difference between seeing the indigenous spirits as divinities that take care of their believers and serious witchcraft, since many of the same processes are at work. From a positive religious perspective, the spirits may secure health, wealth and the safety of children, whereupon the parents may sacrifice an animal as a token of gratitude and respect. For greater wealth and immense riches, bigger sacrifices are necessary, including humans, or so it is often believed. And although it was commonly held that the spirits are important because they are the guardians of morality and social conduct, it also seems that they may allow human sacrifices when they provide huge benefits and riches to the few. Thus, the spirits are not always to be trusted, but that does not alter their cosmological position and power as divine mechanisms operating and structuring society. If spirits can be pleased with blood sacrifices, others may use the prescribed practice for their own betterment and protection as well.

Although Nfuudu claimed that nobody died during the construction of the Bujagali Dam because he had conducted rituals to propitiate the spirit, there were rumours that humans had been sacrificed as part of the project. Huge structures, particularly those made of concrete such as dams, bridges and hotels, are often believed to involve human sacrifices to be successful. Based on belief, rumour, and newspaper reports, there is a fear that children will be sacrificed and buried alive in the concrete. When construction accidents occur on such projects, it is often believed that healers play a part. Consequently, rumours about human death and sacrifices flourish. Construction workers testify to the fact that people disappear in ways difficult to explain, and people read newspaper reports telling of contractors being convicted of sacrificing humans as part of the building process.

Human sacrifices are not restricted to rural lives. In towns and in industry, working with heavy machinery may be dangerous work. If workers are killed by unsafe machines, the perception that the machines eat up people easily takes hold. The machines' need for blood can be counteracted by sacrifices involving humans so as to avoid further deaths in the factory. Which healer to contact to prescribe the actions required to safeguard the workers is another question, and nobody knows for sure. However, the most likely candidates are those believed to be the most powerful, whether they base their powers on spirits on land or in the water, for water is also an intrinsic part of witchcraft.

The healer through his practices mystifies and obscures matters, and because of that is seen as eccentric, exclusive and important. The theatrical performances create fear and awe, respect and obedience. The complex process of achieving the right ritual performance adds to the mystery and importance of the rite and the healers' believed powers. For instance, sacrificial animals must not be spotted. Unspotted chickens are not readily available, and pure white sheep, seen as a more valuable sacrifice, are even more difficult to obtain. The sacrificial victim is also a reflection of the power and importance of the gods or spirits, and by implication the healer. The more serious the problems, the bigger the sacrifice, and sacrificial rites culminate with human sacrifice. More serious problems and misconduct can be resolved by using goats as sacrificial animals. For even graver issues a sheep may be mandatory. The spirits may punish a sinner who has behaved malevolently, and the sacrifice may cleanse him of his misdeeds. Next in the hierarchy is a cow or bull, which is very costly, but also indicates the gravity of the misconduct or wished-for outcome. The final sacrificial offering is the human being. When humans are sacrificed, it is believed the spirits will be extremely pleased. This sacrificial hierarchy is common to most healers, who can perform benevolent healing as well as dangerous witchcraft. Some healers, however, are seen as more likely to instigate and perform such sacrifices than others. Moreover, there is a strong belief that human sacrifices take place, particularly when people aim for quick and immense riches as well as the success of huge construction projects. And although everyone knows human sacrifice is wrong and murder and comparable to corruption, it does and will persist because it is believed to bring benefits.[90]

There are several reasons children are preferred as human sacrifices. One pragmatic reason is that they are more vulnerable and helpless, and are thus easy prey. Ritually, they are also preferable. A young child is perceived as pure and blameless, whereas a child with pierced ears is seen as contaminated. And adults, who for instance may have had sex, are even more unclean. Grown-ups are more likely to have sinned in one way or other and hence are impure, and by extension, not desirable as sacrificial victims. In this region, there is a general fear of witchcraft and rumours that children have been abducted and sacrificed in secret have compelled parents to follow their children closely to school and elsewhere.

What is rumour and what reality in regard to the healer's practices is hard to determine. But what is certain is that rumour, wild or not, significantly shapes the reputations of the healers. The dark magic, illegal practices and human sacrifices conducted in utmost secrecy – or believed to have been conducted – add to the mystical aura surrounding the healers' powers and menace, and this is true for both specific healers and healers in general.

In the dark shadows of witchcraft, it is worth returning to Jaja Bujagali and Nfuudu to compare their practices. Many mythologies surround Jaja Bujagali and, as noted, it is impossible to tell what he has done or not, and equally impossible to ask questions directly. He was averse to answering probing questions about the twin spirit of Budhagaali and what the spirit does.

If it is generally believed that Bujagali's incarnation cannot cut his hair unless he has conducted a full sacrifice, one may wonder why Nfuudu did so. There are several possibilities. Since he sees himself as superior to all others, as the king of water, he may see himself as having fulfilled all his obligations and commitments to various spirits. He is thus so clean he can cut his hair without problem. The spirit Jaja Lubaale, whom he is perceived to embody, may also have allowed him to cut his hair. Or he may have conducted serious sacrifices. Nobody knows.

Other healers generally accused Nfuudu of liking money too much, and of not performing good rituals. Generally, healers earn more for dangerous witchcraft rituals than for benevolent rituals involving white magic. The healer's material benefits and prospects of earning big money play a role in blood sacrifices. By staying next to a military camp and having large groups of soldiers in need of protection as clients, from an outside analytical perspective Nfuudu in his practices walks a fine line between protective medicines and witchcraft. Again, in terms of dark witchcraft it is impossible to know who is doing what – that is the whole point of the secrecy surrounding witchcraft. What is clear, though, is that the spiritual world opens up possibilities for benevolent practices for the needy and malevolent interventions for the greedy. And the river spirits themselves have their own agendas, and they too can be both benevolent and malevolent, with major consequences for society.

MURCHISON FALLS AND FIGHTING SPIRITS

Among many of those believing in traditional cosmology it was perceived that the Budhagaali spirit was infuriated by the misconduct associated with the dam, and avenged himself by killing those who allowed the project to proceed. Although Jaja Bujagali had consistently predicted these consequences, nobody listened to him or did not care. From a religious understanding of the wrath of the spirits, it seems that history may repeat itself, probably at Kalagala or Itanda Falls, and maybe also at Murchison Falls, where preliminary studies have indicated a hydropower potential of 642 MW.[91] If and when this dam is built, is uncertain.

The water spirits at Murchison Falls have played a prominent role in Uganda's history, with serious repercussions up to today, even if one does not believe in spirits and the indigenous cosmology (fig. 26). Alice Auma, an Acholi in northern Uganda, was born in 1958 at Bungatira

26. Murchison Falls and Wang Jok.

and the Holy Spirit of Lakwena took possession of her when she was 27 years old in 1985. There existed a strong cult at Bungatira at that time centred around a sacred rock with a mysterious footprint. After Alice had a childless marriage, she was considered a 'loose woman', and her father, Severino, asked a dozen healers to cure her, but all were in vain. Alice was once labelled 'a lunatic prostitute turned witch'. The Christian God sent the spirit Lakwena to Uganda on 2 January 1985. The spirit Lakwena spoke 74 languages. On 15 May of that year, Lakwena violently possessed Alice Auma, Lakwena meaning 'messenger' in the Acholi language. The spirit ordered her to a place called Wang Jok by Murchison Falls, where she stayed for 40 days. It is unclear to what extent this move sprang from Alice's conviction or her father's persuasiveness, but this spirit was important to her later life story.[92] On 29 May, the spirit held court on the water, and at its command the water in the falls stopped flowing. Lakwena asked: 'Water, I am coming to ask you about the sins and the bloodshed in this world,' whereupon the spirit in the falls answered:

> The people with two legs kill their brothers and throw the bodies into the water [...] I fight against the sinners, for they are the ones to blame for the bloodshed. Go and fight against the sinners, because they throw their brothers in the water.[93]

The spirit convinced Alice that the reason the country was being torn apart by civil war was because of the pervasiveness of witchcraft at all levels, involving personal greed and power over one's opponents. The battle was seen as a preliminary Last Judgment to purify the world of evil. Death and being killed did not undermine her belief system, since they were viewed as justifiable punishment for the sins. On 6 August 1986, Lakwena instructed Alice to give up her local medicine practice and to become a military commander. Alice formed the Holy Spirit Movement with the aim of ending the civil war and cleansing Uganda of sin and formed an army called the Holy Spirit Mobile Forces. And she was by no means alone in this project. Some 7,000 to 10,000 Holy Spirit Soldiers joined the ranks along with 140,000 spirits, and even bees, snakes, rivers, stones and mountains. Although the soldiers were armed with stones and guns, water was also prominent as a weapon and source of protection in the fight, for the spirit had said: 'There is nothing greater than water,' and 'Whatever it is, it will be washed away by water!'[94] A report the Holy Spirit Movement provided to missionaries in June 1987 stated:

> The good Lord who sent Lakwena decided to change his work from that of a doctor to that of a military commander for one simple reason: it is useless to cure a man today only that he be killed the next day. So it is an obligation on his part to stop the bloodshed before continuing his work as a doctor.[95]

When one women named Celina, who was diagnosed with hysteria by a doctor, heard about Alice for the first time:

> The people in the villages thought that what she did was right, and, although some were forced, many believed. Her followers came to the hospital. They said that the Holy Spirit had come from under the waters, and that Alice was one of seven. Others would come later with more power than hers. People should pray very much [...] Towards the end a strange thing happened that made me wonder. The message came from the bush that the hospital would be closed, and all the staff sent away, before it actually happened. Two weeks before it happened. We were surprised to hear it. When I heard it I thought it was a lie. Then a week

later the soldiers arrived to remove everyone. It made some people think that Alice was really a prophet.[96]

Lakwena was not an indigenous spirit in the traditional sense. According to one soldier:

> Lakwena is a holy spirit. Now being a spirit he is not visible. Nobody has seen [...] Lakwena and we should not expect to see him anyway. Being a spirit he has no relatives on earth. He speaks 74 languages including Latin [...] When the Holy Spirit is addressed he should be called 'Sir'.[97]

Lakwena was the supreme commander, but there were other spirits as well. All of the spirits in the Holy Spirit Movement were in fact 'foreign' or 'alien' spirits in the local cosmology. Lakwena was the spirit of an Italian captain who had died during or after the World War II near Murchison Falls. Another account has him drowning in the Nile during the World War I. Then there was the Wrong Element spirit, from the United States; the Franko spirit from Zaire; the Ching Poh spirit from China or Korea; and a number of alien Christian and Arab spirits.[98]

Nowadays, Severino, Alice's father, tells another story with regards to Lakwena. The Italian soldier was one of several spirits who embodied Alice, but Lakwena itself is the Holy Spirit, so these two spirits could be different from each other. Indeed, Severino sees himself as merely being the body containing the spirit of God. Moreover, the political and religious roles are intimately intertwined, which is evident in the very concept of *jok* itself. It is neither but at the same time both and goes beyond the very distinctions we make. While the early missionaries unsuccessfully tried to link *jok* with the Christian God, it has rather been associated with evil, Satan and witchcraft by Christians.[99] In this sense, Alice combines both the early Christian perceptions and the traditional.

Despite that the movement enjoyed initial success, it was defeated by the National Resistance Army led by Yoweri Museveni. Thus, during the civil war Museveni fought against movements prompted by a river spirit that urged the Acholi to take up arms. It is perhaps no wonder that Museveni would not allow a river spirit at Bujagali Falls to halt his plans for a hydroelectric dam: he had fought against stronger water spirits before with more lethal consequences. Given the bloody civil war and its spiritual roots in the water spirit at Murchison Falls, one should not hold one's breath that the preservation of indigenous religion and water spirits will be a high priority if a dam is built at this place.

Although Alice Lakwena set out to combat the evil of witchcraft, witchcraft accusations also became her fate. Despite her being a prophet, there was distrust in the ranks. When the Holy Spirit Mobile Forces reached Busoga en route to Kampala, Lakwena instructed the soldiers not to use the bridge to cross the Nile, but to walk on the water like Jesus. Only 300 were allegedly pure enough for this, and sinners would remain on the shore. This caused disbelief among the soldiers, some of whom deserted. After the defeat by the National Resistance Army, many former Holy Spirit soldiers lost faith in Lakwena. Some claimed she was a witch; others that she was a prostitute with AIDS who did not want to die alone, and had recruited the army so that as many as possible would die with her. In Kampala, other rumours flourished among opponents of the movement: Museveni had recruited another witchdoctor to give National Resistance Army soldiers strong medicines to enable them to defeat their Holy Spirit adversaries.[100] Whatever its truth, in a same vein Nfuudu is allegedly providing medicines to soldiers fighting against rebel groups on the borders of the Congo, including the Lord's Resistance Army.

And it was precisely on the ruins of the Holy Spirit Movement that Joseph Kony built the Lord's Resistance Army, one of the most brutal armed movements in modern history. Kony claimed to be a cousin of Alice. He too became possessed by a particular spirit, named Juma Oris, who had been a minister under Idi Amin. This spirit became Kony's chief spirit and chairman, and ordered Kony to liberate humanity from disease and suffering. It also held that healing was meaningless when those healed were killed. Kony did not inherit Alice's spirits, but introduced a range of completely new and unknown ones.[101] Nevertheless, even Kony was also possessed by Lakwena and many other minor spirits. What is certain, however, is that among the Acholi there were beliefs that there was something special with this family. Even years later, sometimes Severino, Alice and Kony were referred to as the Trinity; Kony equated with the son, Severino Lukoya with the father, and Alice with the Holy Spirit. Those joining Kony's movement had to be cleansed from witchcraft and sorcery, and they were sprinkled with water and shea-butter, transforming them into angels.[102]

In 2005 the International Criminal Court issued an arrest warrant for Kony, charging him with 12 counts of crimes against humanity and

21 counts of war crimes. The ideology with which he was associated had started 20 years earlier with the prophecies of one healer and on the orders of the water spirits at Murchison Falls.

Thus, one sees a complex interplay between spirits, actors and factors. Lakwena was not a river spirit, but he guided Alice to Murchison Falls were she received her instructions from other spirits. Thus, Lakwena, a foreign and Christian spirit, cooperated closely with local, indigenous spirits. Although Lakwena as an independent spirit demanded that Alice took up arms, it was the miseries explained by the water spirits that prompted the movement. Kony too used water in his possession, but he included a wide range of spirits unrelated to the Nile in his cult. However, through the Holy Spirit Movement, the Lord's Resistance Army also originated in part in the Nile spirits in Murchison Falls.

From a cultural heritage perspective, Lakwena presents more challenges and paradoxes than easy answers for the preservation of indigenous religion and water spirits in an era of dam building. All these examples, including the now offended Budhagaali spirit who wreaks havoc on society, clearly show that spirits are believed to have independent powers and agency, and are not necessarily good or bad, but both. Regardless of whether the spirits objectively exist or not, their presence is a matter of faith and belief, and Christians obviously reject it. 'The essence of religion is not even our concern, as we make it our task to study the conditions and effects of a particular type of social behavior,'[103] Max Weber said. Thus, the fact that some believe that spirits exist may have unexpected and at times devastating consequences, as the history of Alice Lakwena exemplifies. What will happen if the Itanda spirit is offended, nobody knows. And given the history of spirits at Murchison Falls, the religious interpretation of the ravaging spirits' needs and concerns may have serious consequences in the secular sphere. These may be felt far away from the healers who become possessed, for the spirits may work together and water spirits have to be seen in relation to all the other spirits in a given cosmology.

In a film called *Fighting spirits* (2010), made by Meier and Offerman, they follow Severino, offering a detailed and visual documentation of his works and deeds.[104] Severino, whose last name is Lukoya, was a healer and preacher at the New Jerusalem Tabernacle Church, Gulu. He explains before a ceremony:

This case, bad spirits had sent fire which was burning her body. It was burning her up. I have poured water on her head, then I have put her in the water. So she can get well from the legs upwards. The fire should stop. To remove bad spirits from her. So her body can remain free. The hot thing that burns her body like fire will not be there.

In the traditional Acholi perspective, violence is an invasion of spirits and hence needs spiritual healing. In the broad category of violence are also personal misfortunes and societal problems, and different forms of violence need separate solutions. 'Human beings fight human beings, spirits fight spirits. You cannot fight a spirit,' as one told. Wild spirits, 'jok', invade people and may harm or heal and the wild spirits may cause bad things like drought, infertility, epidemics and bloodshed. And in this battle no other than God is the strongest and most supreme.

Professor Isaac Ojok, a follower of Alice and Severino, recalled the civil war:

And it was an awesome warfare between what is called 'The holy Mobile Forces' and all the other forces that were fighting; killing innocent people. And it was all directed to the re-establishment of the Kingdom of God. It was not Alice herself fighting but the angels of war who were deployed by God himself. They were the ones who were fighting. So every soldier, everybody who was going to be involved in this war, had to be purified. There should be no sin, no quarrel, no anything [...] any grudge, and you should be spiritually prepared. Water became the most important element for purification.

The Professor said to Severino when he met him: 'you have to have the revelation of God yourself to understand who is talking in him. You'll find that in most cases it is the spirit of God speaking through him and not he himself the one speaking, and it can be very confusing.' Severino himself proclaims his divine status:

I am the father who first sent Jesus Christ. Afterwards, I sent Alice Lakwena as covenant. Because of the level at which the world had gotten spoilt, I sent Alice Lakwena for a covenant, having seen that the world had gotten spoilt. Alice was possessed by a spirit called Lakwena [...] From heaven. I sent that spirit.

On the pathway to Murchison, Severino said:

The world has become rotten. People are just killing each other. Even those who I asked to keep my people have become killers [...] All is right! Rise, and raise their hearts, and return them all down. Rise, and raise their hearts of all the people and return them down forever.

By the falls, standing with the arms out and with a stick in the right arm, Severino said: 'I am alive, I want to change the seeds [...] This is black soil that I created long ago. It contains dark hearts. I want their work to end completely. River, the work of the soil should end completely. It should be replaced with new seeds.' Taking the dark seeds in his hand throwing them into the falls, saying 'Amen! We welcome you! Come, let's change these new white seeds.' White hearts, white hearts,' taking the new white seeds from his bag. 'I want white heart which will put people together, to live together. The black ones have no more use.' He puts the white seeds in a small pot with water, stirs and throws them into the falls. 'Amen!' Then he proclaims:

> Come, come we go. Come, we go to work! Come, we go to work! To plant new seeds, in a new field, in a new field, in a cool soil full of happiness. I will take care of all of them, because of love, because of respect. Peace should remain in the Nile. I want new seeds called Elijah to come here. The throne of leadership of Uganda, I am the one responsible. No one should begin to go and kill my people. I want this world to cool down. The seat of power of Uganda should cool down. The fire has stopped. Amen!

The powers of Murchison Falls are still there. And while many Christians see this place as evil where the dark forces and spirits of witchcraft reside, these beliefs are, as shown, easily merged into a Christian cosmology. And the spiritual force of this place is testified by the physical force of the waterfalls.

Murchison Falls is a spectacular place which mesmerizes the spectator and perhaps the most beautiful along the whole course of the Nile. The river gradually narrows to only some 6 m where it cuts through the rocks and falls some 30 m in cascading thunders and torrents. The mere forces of water rushing through the narrow gorge are strong testimonies of raw power and brute force. Apart from thunderstorms and flaring lightning, which occur irregularly and are also included in the religious sphere as various forms of rain and storm divinities, the forces of Murchison Falls is perhaps the strongest and most forceful natural phenomena possible to observe in this region. Active volcanoes – for instance, on the Congo-Rwanda border – are yet other extreme phenomena of nature, but as a distinct and unique phenomena of nature the Murchison Falls, as all other falls (if not dammed), has one important and particular characteristic: it is permanent all year around – the force is *there*. From hydrological and geological perspectives this is as natural as it can be given the size of Lake Victoria. From a religious perspective, compared to other testimonies of nature, the amount of water exploding in the narrow gorge is brutal force and the sound and intensity of the water here is more than 'natural', in the sense that it is 'supernatural'. Or that it is water and nature as elsewhere, but many times more intensive than other places. It is simply just extremely more nature and power. The permanency of the intense and brutal forces of water is an omnipresent and constant source of power. If spirits and divinities are power, there are no other places where the powers are so strong, visible and accessible as Murchison Falls.

The Victoria Nile separates the Acholi on the northern side from the Bunyoro on the southern side. Among the Acholi, the very falls or just where it starts its most powerful revelation is called Wang Jok, and seen as the 'Eye of God', the 'Place of God', the 'Manifestation of God' or alternatively as the 'Eye of the Devil'. This place epitomizes the concept of the almighty and all powerful God, but also visualizing very specific powers and characteristics. Wang Jok is hence also seen as a 'place of witchcraft' or a 'source of witchcraft'.

There are innumerable river spirits in the Murchison Falls and although there are overlapping perceptions, there are also differences between the spirits at the Acholi and Bunyoro sides. Compared to the source or Bujagali Falls, for instance, where there is only one healer who can embody the respective spirits, Murchison is an epicentre for many healers among the Acholi and Bunyoro. The spirits may call upon any healer from these kingdoms or the healers may come there of their own accord. The Murchison Falls National Park is almost 4,000 km^2 and none of the healers live in the park itself. Today, the healers come in secret and do not announce that they are going to the falls to obtain power from the spirits. When a spirit calls upon a healer to come, and it is not an option to refuse coming if the spirits have decided so, the healer is protected by the spirits when they walk through the park in dangers of facing lions, elephants or buffaloes. Being protected by the spirits, no harm or danger is afflicted upon them and at the falls they make sacrifices in gratitude and for receiving strength and powers.

Healers have permits allowing them to be healers and they can openly perform any kind of benevolent rituals, and even start new churches if they are Christian. From the believers' point of view, the crucial aspect is whether the rituals work or not, and the distinction between traditional religion and Christianity is in many cases blurred. Often the believers are satisfied when the rituals work, but Christians may also get upset if they realize that the pastor had received the powers from Wang Jok and not the Christian God. Even healers working within the indigenous religions may not tell where they have derived their powers from, and the place of propitiation and receiving power is conducted in utmost secrecy partly because of the history of Murchison Falls in Uganda. Still, despite the extreme powers and potentially dark forces, as far as I was told, there were no rumours of human sacrifices to the falls, but other regular sacrifices do take place.

There are several reasons why this place is shrouded in mystery and secrecy. When Alice came to Murchison, she was open about her mission and told that she went there on the spirits' instructions. The history that followed after Alice's visit to the falls is one reason that nobody wants to be associated with Alice and her movement and the civil war. Apparently Joseph Kony was also on his way to the spirits in Murchison Falls, but he was stopped by the army. Apart from the fact that the park restricts the access, Christianity would not officially allow such practices. Still, the powers are there and healers and some pastors continue as they have always done, even with Christianity as a disguise. The resilience of tradition is pervasive, and even feared, but if the powers are used benevolently the successful outcomes may be seen as more important than from where the powers derived from. Although Christianity is officially the currency of the day, it exists in combination with the traditional religion and its spirits, which makes the combination so powerful, and manifested by the very powers of the falls themselves.

In Uganda and elsewhere, spirits take action during times of crises, which was what happened with Alice Lakwena. When spirits embody themselves in humans they have become mediums of Jok or the highest divinity. And here is perhaps why the source of the White Nile will be of greater importance in the future than it is today. There are innumerable healers in Uganda and some are believed to be more powerful than others, and their alleged power is always under pressure to be proven and hence constantly negotiated. Some have already started to question Jaja Bujagali's powers now that the falls have disappeared. If the Itanda Falls are also dammed, others may start to challenge Mary Itanda's powers. What is certain, however, is that the spirits still exist and will continue to do so: spirits are spirits, and humans are humans. And humans die, but not spirits, and after death humans become part of the ancestral world of the spirits. What is also certain is that people and believers choose the healers they perceive to be the most powerful ones in engaging with the ancestors and spirits, or witchcraft. Even if individual spirits lose some powers because the waterfalls are gone, as some commoners believe, the water cosmologies along the Nile in Uganda still exist. With thousands of healers engaging with the various spirits, there are always other healers who can provide and guarantee divine intervention – and deliver outcomes. And, as shown, despite being princely, the Budhagaali spirit may be seen as being inferior to other spirits, and there is always huge contestation between the healers about the superior status of the divinities embodying themselves.

Thus, rather than dams along the Nile causing cultural death or the extinction of beliefs, it is more likely they cause a transfer of power and alteration of hierarchies among healers and their spirits. If Jaja Bujagali and Jaja Itanda lose some of their powers in the near future, the source is likely to gain in importance in the water cosmology. The source will continue to burst forth in the middle of the currents as it has always done. Dams further downstream may alter the water-world of the other spirits, but the source is still the source. Thus, Jaja Kiyira may become a more powerful healer and a larger body of clients and believers may seek the spiritual powers of the source when other waterfalls are gone. Precisely because the Nile is wealth, the source of the White Nile will continue to be of the utmost importance in the future.

In any case, the beliefs in the existence of spirits or the presence in God is evidently very strong, but this is not because of mere beliefs but also personal experiences, and very violently and redeeming experiences. Just as an anecdote, it was the Itanda spirit that made the greatest impression on me, and perhaps vice versa. During one interview with Mary Itanda, we were sitting in her compound next to the falls. When the interview was over and we were ready to set off for Jinja, the Itanda spirit suddenly decided to enter the scene. Although it had witnessed the whole interview, it now chose to make its presence visible. Jaja Itanda became violently possessed: she screamed, her body shook, and she truly seemed to be in pain. The spirit seemed to be physically beating and molesting her. It was indeed an unforgettable experience: the onlookers, including me, were mesmerized and astonished, indeed half-paralysed by what truly seemed to be an experience not from this world. If Mary was acting, her performance was worth an Oscar. There can be no doubt that such experiences provide all the proof people need to believe that spirits exist. After about a minute, the spirit left Mary Itanda's body as suddenly as it had come, and the healer disclosed what the spirit had said. Although the experience was dramatic, the message was not. The spirit just wanted to welcome me and thank me for the good questions, and wished me a safe trip home.

Apart from this small personal experience, which undoubtedly was something extraordinary, an important difference excluding me from the cosmology was that I was not a believer. In similar vein to Mary Itanda being possessed by the good spirit, people can also be possessed by bad ones. Whether belonging to traditional religion or, in particular, Pentecostal Christianity, people are regularly possessed by malignant spirits, demons and even Satan. The ways people experience these forces are strikingly similar regardless of which religion people adhere to, and so are the ways and means used in the expulsion of these very same forces, which most often include water, although the use of a cross is not part of the healers' paraphernalia. Being possessed by malignant forces is an extremely physical and mental exhaustion; probably some of the most bodily violent and worst experience a devotee goes through in his or her life. Not only does it happen quite often in a village, but the very experience, whether personal or observed in the community, become evidences and testimonies of the forces at work and the stakes involved. These experiences are transferred individually and collectively as tradition, and many of the younger community members will experience the same at one point in life. It is thus difficult to separate traditional indigenous religious practices from Christianity in actual experiences, but it also creates continuity in traditional religion although it may change at the surface, become Christianized and other words, means and rituals may be used, but essentially it has strong cultural and religious resemblance to the past and pre-Christian practices. Traditional religious practices are deep-rooted because they are based on experiences. Another such century and even millennium long ritual practice and belief system is rainmaking, and the experience of seeing the life-giving rains arrive when it is desperately needed create long historical trajectories. And from one perspective, the ultimate sources of the Nile are in the sky falling down as rain.

4 The Sources in the Sky and Rainmaking

THE SOURCES BEFORE THE SKY

One of the southernmost sources of the White Nile was discovered by Burchardt Waldecker on 12 November 1937, although it is also claimed that the actual source was 12 miles further west.[1] In Burundi, the source of the Nile lies at an altitude of 2,050 m, and when Burchardt Waldecker came to the ravine from where a thin trickle of water flowed, he claimed that this was the source of the grand river. At this spot, he set up a stela to mark the spot and he built a small stone pyramid on the nearest hilltop symbolizing that these waters would reflect the great pyramids in Egypt.[2] Just below this spring, the stream being locally known as Kasumo, Waldecker scrawled in the rock wall in Latin: CAPUT NILI MERIDIANISSIMUM – the southernmost source of the Nile. Still, there is yet another source giving the length of the river another 36 miles. Below the summit of Mount Bigugu, which is part of the Congo-Nile watershed east of Lake Kiwu, springs another stream which joins the Lukarara River. However, these differences are so small that they become a curiosity, and both these streams have no dramatic watershed and the springs arise from otherwise undistinguished hills among many others in this area.[3]

On 31 March 2006, *National Geographic* explorers determined, by using GPS, that the remotest source of the Nile is in Nyungwe Forest in Rwanda. In the same vein as earlier explorers, the British co-leader of the team, Neil McGrigor, said: 'The Egyptians sent whole armies to discover its source [...] In the 1800s it became almost a British Imperial obsession to find the source. All the greatest names failed – until now.' He continued:

Speke thought he had solved one of the greatest mysteries of 19th-century geography. What he didn't know was that for the Nile to be the longest river in the world, the longest tributary leading into Lake Victoria from the south had to be added to its length.[4]

Although the team may have documented the southernmost hydrological source, it was certainly wrong to state that Speke was unaware that the hydrological source was not the outlet of Lake Victoria. More importantly, early explorers agreed that the ultimate sources were the rains, since the mountains received the rains and hence being 'river-makers'. This directs the attention to rainmaking and its historic role in societies along the Nile, and the history of the Nile rains is as long as history itself.

In the *Odyssey*, Homer does not describe the Nile by this name, but as the river of Aegyptus. This river is described as 'the heaven fed stream of Egypt' or 'Egypt's waters [... the] heaven-descended stream',[5] clearly indicating the divine origin. According to Homer and the Greek cosmology, Zeus is the sky who brings rains and snow. Rivers can be 'swollen by rain and melted snow'. Still, the Nile in Egypt was different and not fed or swollen by rain according to him, not knowing were the ultimate sources were. Thus, it seems that Homer's phrase was describing a 'river flying in the sky', or in other words, a 'celestial river'.[6] This fitted with the later notions of the Mountains of the Moon.

STANLEY AND MOUNT RUWENZORI

The Mountains of the Moon and a lake on the Equator was documented on several Arab maps, including a map prefixed to Rasm (AD 835) and Abui Hassan (AD 1008).[7] The Arab geographer Dimisqi (died 1326) wrote that the Nile waters:

> Come from the Mountains of the Moon, which separate the habitable part of the earth from the part scorched by the sun of which we have no knowledge. Its sources are ten rivers [...] They all flow into two great lakes, separated one from the other by a distance of four day's journey.[8]

The Arabic name for 'Mountains of the Moon' is 'Djabal al-Qoumr', and 'Djabal' means 'mountain' and 'Qoumr' anything which shines or glistens and even the 'moon'. Earlier, Aristotle spoke about the Nile rising in the 'Silver Mountains', which can be seen in relation to the Arab notion of shining mountains. It thus seems that the Mountains of the Moon had cosmological significance in the same manner as the Atlas Mountains were supposed to have had in Antiquity, and the Atlas Mountains were believed to support the vault of heaven keeping heaven and earth asunder.[9] And the terrestrial paradise in Christian beliefs was situated on high mountains, but no foreigners had seen or could give a precise description of its location and hence the legends of the Nile and its heavenly origin continued to flourish century after century.

In Henry M. Stanley's *Darkest Africa* (1890), he gives in detail descriptions of the previous and current status of the Nile and the searches for the sources.[10] He elaborates in length from a manuscript which was in the possession of H. E. Ali Pasha Moubarek, the then Minister of Public Instruction in Egypt. The author of the work was not known, but it was given the date AD 1686:

> As for the Nile, it starts from the Mountain of Gumr (Kamar) beyond the equator, from a source from which flow ten rivers, every five of these flowing into a separate lake, then from each one of these two lakes two rivers flow out; then all four of these rivers flow into one great lake in the first zone, and from this great lake flows out the Nile. The author of the book called 'The Explorer's Desire,' says that 'this lake is called Lake of Likuri [Victoria Nyanza, Lake of Likuri, so called after a tribe named the Wakuri, or Wakori, on the north shore of Lake Victoria].'

Stanley continues quoting:

> Others say that the Nile flows from snowy mountains, and they are the mountains called Kaf [...] It is said that a certain king sent an expedition to discover the Nile sources, and they reached copper mountains, and when the sun rose, the rays reflected were so strong that they were burnt. Others say that these people arrived at bright mountains like crystal, and when the rays of the sun were reflected they burnt them.[11]

Stanley also quotes old Muslim perceptions of the water of the Nile:

> Historians relate that Adam bequeathed the Nile upon Seth his son, and it remained in the possession of these children of prophecy and of religion, and they came down to Egypt (or Cairo) [...] After them came a son [and then several sons] and his son Hermes – that is Idrisi the prophet. [Idrisi went to Nubia and Abyssinia] [...] He even calculated the volume of the water and the rate of flow. He is the first man who regulated the flow of the Nile to Egypt. It is said that in the days of Am Kaam, one of the Kings of Egypt, Idrisi was taken up to heaven, and he promised the coming of the flood, so he remained [on] the other side of the equator and there built a palace on the slopes of Mount Gumr. He built it of copper, and made

eighty-five statues of copper, the waters of the Nile flowing out through the mouths of these statues and then flowing into a great lake and thence to Egypt. Idyar el wadi says, 'the length of the Nile is two months' journey in Moslem territory, and four months' journey in uninhabited country. That its source is from Mount Gumr beyond the equator, and that it flows to the light coming out of the river of darkness, and flows by the base of Mount Gumr.' Mohammed, the Prophet of God, says: 'The Nile comes out of the Garden of Paradise, and if you were to examine it when it comes out, you will find in it leaves of Paradise.'[12]

Thus, in Muslim perceptions the Nile also originated in Paradise, and more specifically the Mountains of The Moon, which differ from the biblical source Gish Abay in Ethiopia, although this source too is seen in Islam as flowing from Paradise.

Numerous Arab geographers shared this notion, reflecting the beliefs at that time. Stanley writes:

> Other explorers have said that the four rivers, Gihon, Sihon, the Euphrates, and the Nile arise from one source – from a dome in the gold country, which is beyond the dark sea, and that the country is a part of the regions of Paradise, and that the dome is of jasper. They also say that Hyad, one of the children of Ees, prayed to god to show him the extreme end of the Nile. God gave him power to do this, and he traversed the dark river, walking upon it with his feet over the water which did not stick to his feet, until he entered that dome. This legend I have taken from El Makrisi's book.[13]

Stanley also refers to Scheabeddin, an Arab geographer who wrote around AD 1400:

> In this isle is also the source of that great river which has not its equal upon the earth. It comes from the mountain of the moon which lies beyond the equator. Many sources come from this mountain and unite in a great lake. From this lake comes the Nile, the greatest and most beautiful of the rivers of all the earth.

In an even older Arab description, Abdul Hassan Ali, who was born in Bagdad and came to Cairo in AD 955, writes:

> I have seen in a geography a plan of the Nile flowing from the Mountains of the Moon – Jebel Kumr. The waters burst forth from twelve springs and flow into two lakes like unto the ponds of Bussora. After leaving these lakes, the waters re-unite, and flow down through a sandy and mountainous country. The course of the Nile is through that part of the Soudan near the country of the Zenj (Zanzibar).[14]

The first Westerner who could have seen the legendary Mountains of the Moon was Samuel W. Baker, but he did not. What he saw, however, was Lake Albert, and hence, according to himself, concluded the Nile Quest. On 14 March 1863 Baker crossed a deep valley and hurried to the summit: 'The glory of our prize burst suddenly upon me! There, like a sea of quicksilver, lay far beneath the grand expanse of water, – a boundless sea horizon on the south and south-west, glittering in the noon-day sun.' The feeling of triumph was beyond words. 'It is impossible to describe the triumph of that moment; here was the reward for all our labour – for the years of tenacity with which we have toiled through Africa. England had won the sources of the Nile!' Baker had long planned three cheers in honour of the discovery, but standing at that spot overlooking the lake, he changed his mind:

> I had been the humble instrument permitted to unravel this portion of the great mystery when so many greater than I had failed, I felt too serious to vent my feelings in vain cheers for victory, and I sincerely thanked God for having guided and supported us through all dangers to the good end.

The Nile was too important for individual triumph:

> I looked down [...] upon that vast reservoir which nourished Egypt and brought fertility where all was wilderness – upon that great source so long hidden from mankind; that source of bounty and of blessing to millions of human beings; and as one of the greatest objects in nature, I determined to honour it with a great name. As an imperishable memorial of one loved and mourned by our gracious Queen and deplored by every Englishman, I called this great lake 'the Albert N'yanza.' The Victoria and the Albert lakes are the two sources of the Nile.[15]

Standing on the shores of Lake Albert, he proclaimed:

> No European foot had ever trod upon its sand, nor had the eyes of a white man ever scanned its vast expanse of water. We were the first; and this was the key to the great secret that even Julius Cæsar yearned to unravel, but in vain. Here was the great basin of the Nile that received *every drop of water*, even from the passing shower to the roaring mountain torrent that drained from central Africa towards the north. This was the great reservoir of the Nile![16]

Stanley writes about Baker:

> It is quite a mysterious fact that from the localities reached by Sir Samuel Baker, Ruwenzori ought to have been as visible as St. Paul's dome from Westminster Bridge [...] [However, the mountains are] obscured by

the dense clouds and depths of mist under which for about 300 days of the year the great mountain range veils its colossal crown. Then again, its classical history: the fables that have been woven about it, its relation to the dear old Nile, the time-honoured Nile – the Nile of the Pharaohs, of Joseph, Moses, and the Prophets, its being the source whence so many springs of the Nile issue [...] the very mountain before whose Alexander and Cæsar would have worshipped, if the poets may be believed.

History and mythology apart, Stanley also emphasized the life-giving qualities of the Nile and the utmost dependence for people living downstream:

> Another emotion is that inspired by the thought that in one of the darkest corners of the earth, shrouded by perpetual mist, brooding under eternal storm-clouds, surrounded by darkness and mystery, there has been hidden to this day a giant among mountains, the melting snow of whose tops has been for some fifty centuries most vital to the peoples of Egypt. Imagine to what a God the reverently-inclined primal nations would have exalted this mountain, which from such a far-away region as this contributed so copiously to their beneficent and sacred Nile. And this thought of the beneficent Nile brings another. In fancy we look down along that crocked silver vein to where it disports and spreads out to infuse life to Egypt near the pyramids, some 4,000 miles away, where we beheld populous swarms of men – Arabs, Copts, Fellahs, Negroes, Turks, Greeks, Italians, Frenchmen, English, Germans, and Americans – bustling, jostling, or lounging; and we feel a pardonable pride in being able to inform them for the first time that much of the sweet water they drink, and whose virtues they so often exalt, issues from the deep and extensive snow-beds of Ruwenzori or Ruwenjura – 'the Cloud King'.[17]

That the view was breathtaking is without any doubt, but it was much more according to Stanley, it was a religious experience:

> The superb Rain-Creator or Cloud-King, as the Wakonju fondly termed their mist-shrouded mountains, fill the gazer with a feeling as though a glimpse of celestial splendor was obtained [...] These moments of supreme feeling are memorable for the utter abstraction of the mind from all that is sordid and ignoble, and it is utter absorption in the presence of unreachable loftiness, indescribable majesty, and constraining it not only to reverentially admire, but to adore in silence, the image of the Eternal. *Never can a man be so fit for Heaven as during such moments, for however scornful and insolent he may have been at other times, he now has become as a little child, filled with wonder and reverence before what he has conceived to be sublime and Divine.*[18]

However, in the history of what Stanley did, his own personal religious feeling of looking at a mountain could probably not repent the atrocities he committed in Uganda and later in Congo.[19]

THE MOUNTAINS OF THE MOON AS THE RAINMAKER

Stanley, who did not pretend to be linguistically trained, has been accused of being misled when recording African place-names when in fact the interpreters replied 'don't know' when he inquired about the names of certain places. However, in many places in Africa there is a particular difficulty in giving a whole-course name to a river. Many local inhabitants have challenged the very exercise and utility of giving a standing name to water that flows away, which would carry off with its name in it, and hence a waste of words.[20]

Stanley inquired the local Ankole people about what they called these mountains, and it was Ruwenzori – 'the place whence the rain comes'. Stanley, as opposed to other explorers, accepted this name, which he translated as 'Rain-Maker'.[21] It is also argued that the name Ruwenzori is somewhat a distorted form of the name Ruwenjara, meaning 'the rainy mountain',[22] and there are also other different names and perceptions structured around the fluid capacities of water.

The Ruwenzori as the 'Rain-Maker' is intrinsically linked to the specific rainfall-patterns in this region where there are up to some 300 days each year with rain. Rainfall in the Nile Basin is highly uneven and seasonal, and characterized by huge differences in time and space. Only the Equatorial zone has two distinct rainy seasons and most of the basin has only one, or none, like Sudan and Egypt. The Rwenzori Mountains are wetter than the other East African Mountains, and the annual precipitation varies with altitudes and ranges normally from 2,000 to 3,000 mm in the habitual areas,[23] and perhaps even more than 3,000 mm on the eastern slopes.[24] The Senecio rain forest just below the Ruwenzori glaciers, located at between 12,500 and 15,000 ft, is one of the wettest regions in the world. Although there are limited data available from meteorological stations in the higher regions, recent precipitation modelling suggests that some of the upper regions may receive as much as 7,000 mm of rain each year,[25] truly making the Ruwenzori worth its name as the 'rainmaker', even if the actual rainfalls might be less.

When Harry Johnston was on the Ruwenzori Mountains by the turn of the twentieth century, he wrote:

> The whole time of our stay on Ruwenzori the weather was, with very few and brief exceptions, atrocious. It rained constantly, and at high altitudes it snowed and hailed [...] The clouds would come rushing up the Mubuko valley like express trains one after the other, and they did not appear as vague mists, but as bodies of singular definiteness of outline which constantly seized and involved you as in a thick blanket. You might be sitting for a few minutes in brilliant, welcome sunshine, looking at the blazing white snowfields and the minutest detail of the rocks and boulders. Suddenly an awful greyish-white mass would come rushing at you, and everything would be blotted out.[26]

A rather vivid and descriptive characteristic was given by Captain Humphrey in 1927:

> That enchanted forest has a weird and grotesque effect that is all its own. In the mists and gloom of the frequent rainstorms it may suggest a nightmare caused by studying the illustrations of Paleolithic vegetation in some textbook. In the rare sunshine one may fancy oneself enveloped in the scenery of a Russian pantomime. The open glades bristle with the upright stalks of lobelias, green obelisks 12 feet high, like tombstones in a Turkish cemetery. They are mixed with scenarios, writhing stems, crowned my mops of spiky leaves, fit for a witch's broom. High up a white everlasting Helichrysum covers acres with a sheet of its silver or golden blossoms. On the precipitous slopes and ledges tree heaths drip with the perpetual moisture. Gaunt and grey, draped in preposterous masses of moss and lichen, they look like the vegetable ghosts of a departed world. You may be familiar with the Alps and the Caucasus, the Himalaya, and the Rockies, but if you have not explored Ruwenzori you have still something wonderful to see and do.[27]

Without knowing that he was more right than he could have anticipated, in Humphrey's imagination the mountains were fit for witches, they certainly were also places for witches in local cosmologies.

Among the Bashu, who occupy the Mitumba Mountains to the north-west of Lake Edward, south of Ruwenzori Mountains, Nyavingi was seen as a powerful female ancestor exclusively in the realm of the Babito chiefs. Nyavingi was seen as the 'mother of abundance' playing an active role of ending famines, and she was closely associated with the ritual functions of the chiefships legitimizing their authority. In their 'utopia of absolute health', there were several groups of healers. One group was in particular responsible for curing the illnesses of the land and they were the 'healers of the land'. Another group was the rainmakers, who could also drive away unwanted rains and storms, and some healers could perform both functions – healing the land and bringing rain, since these were connected.[28]

The Ankoli Kingdom stretched as far west as the shores of Lake Edward and on its borders other Bantu people lived, including the pastoral people Bahima. They believed in a vaguely defined all-powerful deity associated with rain, thunder and other weather phenomena. They made pottery and were smiths producing weapons and agricultural tools, although agriculture was held in contempt and for other groups to do.[29] Throughout this region, beliefs in rainmaking and the mountains as rainmakers have been prevalent, but there have also been other perceptions.

With regards to the name 'Ruwenzori', Reverend Fisher conducted a study by the turn of the twentieth century among various tribes and he said that speaking of the mountains as a whole was quite unknown to them. Each peak had its own name, and 'Ruwenzori' might be derived from 'Rwensozi' meaning 'the mountain of mountains' or 'Rwenseri' meaning 'the mountain over there' (in the direction referred to). More commonly, it was called Birika, which is the only name for 'snow' used by the mountain people. The Buganda, however, called it 'Gambalagala fumba biri' which means 'the leaf that cooks the clouds'. This refers to their practice of cooking all their food in banana leaves, and when the mists come down from the mountain-sides, they say it is the smoke from the 'cooking-pot'. In the Toro Kingdom north of Ankole, there is a chain of extinct volcanoes and in several of the craters there are lakes and dense vegetation growing on the sides. Although not knowing the geological processes in the late nineteenth century, the local people told the reverend that the craters were the dwelling places of witches or evil spirits. The craters were called 'Kaitabaloga', which means 'that which kills the witches'. Witches were believed to originate from these craters and evil spirits swallowed up men and cattle, and whenever a witch was found, she was thrown back into a crater.[30]

The reverend's conclusion of the people living on the slopes of the Ruwenzori was, however, less than flattering:

> I would say that what forced itself on me while living among these people of the western province is that deterioration is naturally stamped

everywhere, or, if we must admit evolution, it must be evolution of evil. Whether we speak of the general features of the country, or the spiritual, mental, and physical characteristics of the people in their natural condition, demoralization is the outstanding feature.[31]

This was the colonial and not the indigenous view. That the mountain spirits possessed powers over life and death was without doubt, and they were benevolent towards the good ones. The then President and later King of Rwenzururu, Isaya Mukirane, was the custodian of the spirits at the Mountains of the Moon. In the 1960s, in conflict with the government, he wrote them a letter saying that 'the God, King of Rwenzururu is sending down the Rwenzururu heavenly spirit with sharp swords which will slash down those who are disturbing and invading the innocent Country Rwenzururu!' His son, Charles Wesley, was 'King-over-the-water', highlighting the all-encompassing powers of the spirits.[32] Since rainmaking has been of utmost importance for people, it has always been part of politics – from local levels to conflicts in between areas and regions, and religions.

DAVID LIVINGSTONE, RAINMAKING AND WATER SYSTEMS

At the outset, there is a long way from African rainmaking cosmology, rainfed agriculture and Western popular music. In 1974 ABBA won the Eurovision song contest with 'Waterloo' and their destiny to eternal fame started. The single sold almost 6 million copies, making it one of the best-selling singles of all times. The record, with the same name, includes not only 'Honey, Honey', but also another groovy but less known song: 'What about Livingstone?' There they sang about the Nile explorers, and raised some questions:

What about Livingstone?
What about all those men?
Who have sacrificed their lives to lead the way
Tell me, wasn't it worth the while
Travelling up the Nile
Putting themselves on test
Didn't that help the rest?
Wasn't it worth it then?
What about Livingstone?

On 18 April 1974 ABBA released the French version of Waterloo, which commemorated Livingstone, who exactly 100 years earlier was given a state funeral in Westminster Abbey on 18 April 1874. On the south side of Livingstone's grave stone, it is written in Latin: 'So great is my love of truth that there is nothing I would rather know than the sources of the river, which lay hid for so many centuries,' which is a quote from the classical author Lucan.[33] On the base of a statue of Livingstone at Victoria Falls his motto is inscribed: 'Christianity, Commerce, and Civilization'.[34]

Was it worth sacrificing the life to find the Nile's sources? Captain Robert James Gordon, who set off for the sources in the early 1820s, said: 'If I should find it advisable for my purpose to travel as the slave of some black merchant, I will most gladly do so, for I feel there is no retreating from what I have undertaken – *en avant* is my motto, and trust to fortune!'[35] He died somewhere in Sudan, walking alone towards the sources in the south. Richard Burton was even more explicit: 'Everything – wealth, health, and even life – was to be risked for this prize.'[36] Livingstone paid that price and he was found dead on 1 May 1873. His assistants removed his heart and buried it in African soil, embalmed the body with salt and poured whiskey over his face and hands, before the long transport journey to Zanzibar started whereupon the corpse was carried back to England and Westminster Abbey.[37] Before his death, Livingstone wrote from the interior of Africa: 'I have lost nearly all my teeth, and am fast drifting into second childhood; this is what the sources have done to me.'[38]

With regards to the question if it was worth it, Livingstone was clear; there was one thing much more important than finding all the Nile sources together, and that was to end the terrible slave trade.[39] Although 'the final solution of this most ancient and most interesting problem would indeed be a geographical triumph,' as it was argued back in England, there was also a practical question: 'To what good can such a discovery be applied?'[40] Not only would commerce bring civilization to these regions, as argued, but it would also cut off the slave trade from the western regions and the coast. Livingstone himself was well aware of the power and status he would get if he became the discoverer of the Nile sources. According to him, the sources

> are valuable only as a means of enabling me to open my mouth with power among men. It is this power which I hope to apply to remedy an enormous evil [the slave-trade]. Men think I covet fame, but I make it a rule not to read aught written in my praise.[41]

So prominent was the quest for the Nile sources that it was believed that the one who found them would have such a status that he could influence significant developments on the African continent.

Commerce was believed to be essential in this civilizing process. Samuel W. Baker argued that

> The progress of civilization depends upon geographical position. The surface of the earth presents certain facilities and obstacles to general access; those points that are easily attainable must always enjoy a superior civilization to those that are remote from association with the world.[42]

The role of commerce in the civilization process was eloquently elaborated by John Stuart Mill: '[Commerce] is one of the primary sources of progress [...] rapidly rendering war obsolete, by strengthening and multiplying the personal interests which are in opposition to it.'[43] Or, in the words of Baker again:

> The philanthropist and the missionary will expend their noble energies in vain in struggling against the obtuseness of savage hordes, until the first step towards their gradual enlightenment shall have been made by commerce. The savage must learn to *want*; he must learn to be ambitious; and to covet more than the mere animal necessities of food and drink.[44]

And while ABBA praised the explorers, Africans and post-colonial scholars have challenged this view, since '*The explorer is the precursor of the colonist*; and the colonist is the human instrument by which the great work must be constructed – that greatest and most difficult of all undertakings – the civilization of the world,'[45] according to Baker.

Livingstone's book from his first mission to Africa – *Missionary Travels and Researches in South Africa* – sold over 70,000 copies and became one of the most widely read books on African travel.[46] Nothing could match Livingstone, not even the discovery of the sources of the Nile:

> Livingstone's impact on the course of history in Africa was immense, perhaps greater than that of any other individual of the nineteenth century. It did not stem, however, from the personal contacts which he made with African groups and individuals while in their territories, but from the impact his character and way of life made in Europe. He became a popular hero, the missionary and explorer par excellence.[47]

Johnston wrote that Livingstone 'died a martyr to that form of religion which we call science'.[48] Still, despite his legendary status, 'Livingstone appears to have failed in all he most wished to achieve. He failed as a conventional missionary, making but one convert, who subsequently lapsed. He failed as the promoter of other men's missionary efforts,' Tim Jeal points out in his biography, and despite some remarkable achievements a series of miscalculations deceived him into believing that he had found the source of the Nile when he was in fact on the upper Congo. There were other failures too: failure as a husband and father, failure to persuade the British Government to advance into Africa.[49]

Apart from geography and solving the enigma of the Nile, Johnston argues that it was biblical studies that drew Livingstone to Egyptology, and one of his reasons for searching for the source was his conviction that Moses was interested in Nile exploration. By discovering the sources, it seems that Livingstone also hoped, at least partly, to come across some archaeological traces of Egyptian influence.[50] Livingstone believed that he had found the ultimate source of the Nile, which was the source of the Lualaba River. Although he said that he was not 'cock sure' – he still had an itching feeling that it might be a tributary of the Congo (which later proved right) – this source was the source of the Nile, he claimed. As an irony of history, Livingstone and Stanley were in fact very close to the sources. Apart from one of Africa's most famous quotes, 'Dr. Livingstone, I presume', Stanley gave him at least two more years of life when he brought him much needed medicines and supplies. When Livingstone regained some of his strength, they had what Stanley described as a 'picknicking voyage to the north end of Tanganyika'.[51] What they did not know was that they were very close to one of the sources of the Nile.[52]

In this region, cannibal rumours flourished, but as Livingstone said: 'If I had believed one-tenth part of the horrible tales the traders and adjacent tribes told me, I might not have ventured to come among them.' Winwood Reade, for instance, in his *Savage Africa* (1864), writes probably with a twist of humour: 'A cannibal is not necessarily ferocious. He eats his fellow-creatures, not because he hates them, but because he likes them.'[53] As numerous studies have shown, the cannibal talk was largely a Western construct of the others, although similar perceptions are also prevalent in African witchcraft discourses today.[54] Indeed, British Victorian ethnologists formed a special branch of the Anthropological Society and called it 'The Cannibal Club', displaying a savage skeleton in its front window to great complaints of the Christian Union across the street in London. Richard Burton was their first president.[55] Alleged cannibals were not a problem for Livingstone, rather the contrary, his worst enemy was something else: the rainy season.[56] Water and the rain did not only cause Livingstone physical problems, but it was also the greatest challenge to his missionary success, where he failed.

Livingstone was successful in converting one, namely chief Sechele of the Bakwain tribe in the Limpopo area of today's border between Botswana and South Africa. Although Sechele did not stay chaste with only one of his wives, which was a moral blow to Livingstone since he had baptized the chief, the failure of stopping rainmaking rituals is interesting from a water systems perspective. The tribe blamed Livingstone for the prolonged drought after he had convinced Sechele in stopping rainmaking rituals, and in the end the chief was obliged to make rain again. The local tribe-men were also reluctant to receive baptism since, as Livingstone put it, there was a 'Satanic suggestion' that baptism meant 'being caused to drink men's brains'.[57]

Although Sechele converted to Christianity, 'all the friends of the divorced wives became opponents of our religion', Livingstone writes, and

> the chief Sechele was himself a noted rain-doctor, and believed in it implicitly. He has often assured me that he found it more difficult to give up his faith in that than in anything else which Christianity requires him to abjure.[58]

Livingstone's response to this dilemma can illustrate the fruitfulness of a water systems perspective. All water systems can be understood to consist of three interconnected layers. The first layer addresses the physical form and behaviour of actual waterscapes. This can include precipitation, evaporation, how rivers run within the landscape and how much water they contain at a given time of the year, the relationship between rivers and the sea, and the development patterns to which these physical structures may give rise. The second analytical layer addresses human modifications and adaptations to the actual waterworlds. The ways in which people in different societies have utilized water in the creation of social opportunity, and how modifications have limited the physical constraints of scarce water resources, have at all times structured societies and their future development. The third and final analytical layer addresses cultural concepts and ideas of water and water systems, including management practices and religious beliefs.[59]

Livingstone was soon to experience the pervasiveness and strength of rainmaking beliefs. Rain was precious but scarce, and he believed that if he could reduce the dependency of the rain and provide the water by alternative means it would weaken their traditional cosmology, enabling more people to convert to Christianity. Livingstone pointed out to Sechele that 'the only feasible way of watering the gardens was to select some good, never-failing river, make a canal, and irrigate the adjacent lands'. Livingstone's idea was well received, but modifying the actual water-scape could not be done where the tribe lived and soon they all moved to the Kolobeng stream some 40 miles away. As Livingstone says, 'the experiment succeeded admirably during the first year [...] But in our second year again no rain fell. In the third year the same extraordinary drought fell [...] The fourth year was equally unpropitious.'[60] The rain would simply not fall, and no dry irrigation channel or Christianity could mitigate the drought. The villagers believed that all this was because Livingstone had bound the rainmaker Sechele with some magic spell by being a Christian. Old village counsellors came to Livingstone requesting him to let Sechele make only some few showers. 'The corn will die if you refuse, and we will be scattered', they said, and if he let Sechele make rain, they could do Christian practices as Livingstone wished: 'we shall all, men, women, children, come to the school, and sing and pray as long as you please.'[61] The arrival and presence of the life-giving waters mattered more than the Christian God. Having sympathy not only with the people, but also to their logic and the limits of Western rationality, Livingstone summarized the arguments between him and the villagers in a fictitious dialogue. As he said, 'these arguments are generally known, and I never succeeded in convincing a single individual of their fallacy, though I tried in every way I could think of.' In order to show the logic of rainmaking, it is worth referring to parts of Livingstone's fictitious dialogue between a Rain Doctor and Medical Doctor – traditional African religion and nineteenth-century Western rationality:[62]

> *Medical Doctor*: So you really believe that you can command the clouds? I think that can be done by God alone.
>
> *Rain Doctor*: We both believe the same thing. It is God that makes the rain, but I pray to him by means of these medicines, and, the rain coming, of course it is then mine [...].
>
> *Medical Doctor*: But we are distinctly told in the parting of words of our savior that we can pray to God acceptably in his name alone, and not by means of medicines.
>
> *Rain Doctor*: Truly! but God told us differently [...]
>
> *Medical Doctor*: I quite agree with you on the value of the rain; but you can not charm the clouds by medicines. You wait till you see the clouds come, then you use your medicines, and take the credit which belongs to God only.

Rain Doctor: I use my medicines, and you employ yours; we are both doctors, and doctors are not deceivers. You give a patient medicine. Sometimes God is pleased to heal him by means of your medicine; sometimes not – he dies. When he is cured, you can take the credit of what God does. I do the same. Sometimes God grants us rain, sometimes not. When he does, we take the credit of the charm. When a patient dies, you don't give up trust in your medicine, neither do I when rain fails. If you wish me to leave off my medicines, why continue your own?

Medical Doctor: [...] God alone can command the clouds. Only try and wait patiently; God will give us rain without your medicines [...] I think you deceive both them and yourself.

Rain Doctor: Well, then, there is a pair of us (meaning both are rogues).

The rainmaking cosmology proved stronger than Christianity in the nineteenth century. Although medical doctors could cure individual patients with or without the help of God, the Christian God had little to offer during the consecutive years of drought. The rainmaker, on the other hand, worked collectively for the whole community, and while their gods did neither bring the rains when desperately needed, during droughts the traditional religion had still the upper hand when it failed; it included more and for the many as an ideal outcome – Christianity could not compete with that despite promises of an eternal life after death (fig. 27).

27. Who controls the life-giving rains – God or ancestors?

RAINMAKING OR DIVINE CONTROL?

One may consider rainmaking as an ecological technique, as many have done, at least as perceived by the practitioners, who respond to ecological crisis and political situations by performing rainmaking rituals.[63] But strictly speaking it is wrong to see rainmaking as an ecological technique for two reasons; first of all it is not rainmaking and consequently not an ecological technique. Although rainmaking as a term is commonly used in the literature, the rainmakers do not procure rains, which somehow may sound like a negative tautology. The point is that in Africa as elsewhere, the rainmaker himself or herself has no powers to make rain. They work as mediators between humans and divinities, and the presence and absence of rain is ultimately dependent upon the ancestors, spirits or gods in one way or another. The rainmaker may contact spirits or divinities and pray for rain, and be the intermediary facilitating this spiritual contact and engagement, but without the spiritual realms the rainmaker is as barren as the fields without rain. Thus, although technically the rainmaker does not procure rain, he or she is nevertheless often seen as the one bringing forth the precarious waters since as a ritual specialist he or she has the powers to interfere with the divinities in this and other matters.

In this analysis of rainmaking and rainmakers, I will not present meticulous descriptions of the actual rainmaking rituals and practices, since there are differences everywhere, and the skilled ritual specialists created the varied and distinct ritual dramaturgy. Among the Sukuma in Tanzania, for instance, rain ceremonies were not necessarily held each year, and were conducted when the rainmaker predicted a year of bad rain. When a famous rainmaker from another area was called to a village facing a shortage of rain, he would start by asking questions about the situation. Was the sun hot and what colour was it when setting? Were there strong winds and from which direction? Did a certain species of bird arrive? And so on. The rainmaker was a skilled observer of natural phenomena and could interpret signs in nature regarding the arrival or failure of rain. Importantly, he would frame his interpretations in ways that would enhance his status rather than undermine it if the rains failed. Rather than attributing the absence of rain to rainmakers more skilled and powerful elsewhere, he might blame the absence of rains on the inhabitants, accusing them of violating taboos, hiding the birth of twins or neglecting certain rituals and observances.[64] Thus, the focus here is on the social and societal roles of the rituals, and the role of the rainmaker as a ritual specialist with particular importance in the community. The background is that the life-giving rains are everything, as explained by Per Brandström with regards to the Sukuma:

> Disastrous droughts, epidemics and epizootics are not only hearsay and phantoms in the minds of the people but well-known facts of life. Life is precarious. Threatened by destruction through famine, sickness and death, life is always at risk. To stay alive is an achievement, something to work for incessantly through the whole array of technological, organizational and ideological means offered by culture and society: through cultivation and livestock-rearing, through cooperation with kin and neighbours and through the veneration of the ancestors.[65]

A common feature of many African cosmologies is the division of the world into two distinct realms. One is the visible or the manifest world, which is 'obvious' to all, and the other is the invisible or unseen world, which is nevertheless as real as the visible world. Indeed, it is more real in that it structures and defines the premises of this world. The visible world is the everyday world of living – farming, collecting water and fuel, political and economic matters, etc. The invisible world comprises the ancestors, God and the realm of witchcraft and the occult, among other spiritual forces. These two realms are intrinsically linked and the invisible forces largely determine outcomes in the visible world. The visible world is therefore shaped by a deeper, 'more real' reality, and consequently, it is of utmost importance to control the spiritual and occult forces that would otherwise harm society.[66]

In most cosmologies, humans facing problems turn to the ancestors or gods. Problems involving the wrong types of water or the absence of annual rains are divine concerns or within the realm of the ancestors, and for them to solve.[67] Religion works and may have practical consequences here and now. Importantly, the role of rainmaking and the life-giving rains are exclusively in this worldly realm. Water and food as successful harvests matter here and now; right now – today, this month and this year. Solutions to hunger and famines cannot be postponed to the next year, or in an eschatological perspective to the life in another existence after death. This is the essence of the importance of rainmaking: life and the continuity of life now.

SUKUMA COSMOLOGY AND RAINMAKING

The Sukuma are the largest ethnic group in Tanzania partly living along the southern shores of Lake Victoria, and are estimated to number more than 5 million people. The origins of the Sukuma as an ethnic group are shrouded in history and the Sukuma were traditionally agro-pastoralists and cattle were their main possession and form of storable wealth for procuring all of life's necessities. Although cattle still have importance in Sukuma society and cosmology, the role of farming has increased at the expense of cattle.

Wijsen and Tanner note that among the Sukuma 'religious practice originates from the misfortunes which they experience in their lives [...] they will not worship, any more than Westerners will worship, unless they feel that they are obtaining grace *ex opere operato*'.[68] *Ex opere operato* is the principle that sacraments work – they are holy and divine and work automatically since they are divine by excellence, as in the Roman Catholic theology.[69] They argue further that 'the Sukuma see religion in terms of the options it provides rather than the obligations it creates. They have periodic problems and their religious practices tend to be periodic.'[70] Thus, conversion to Christianity is not a straightforward displacement of one religion by another. Instead, it is a process of syncretism. The different religious systems offer different possibilities and solutions to various problems. This also results in hybrid and overlapping conceptions and parallel practices, since the worldly problems still exist and

> plans never turn out exactly as intended. The more people the plans involve, the more unintended consequences there are likely to be. In a sense a religion, like any other social movement, is bound to some extent to be a victim of its own success.[71]

The benefits of Christianity are also largely its main shortcoming – it does not solve the most acute problems here and now, the problems that *have* to be resolved. Consequently, religious solutions are sought elsewhere. This highlights the premises on which the Sukuma world works:

> Causation in their thinking is animate rather than inanimate. An event, particularly an unfortunate one, has to be caused by someone or something, living or dead, with malevolent intentions toward the sufferer. There are no pure accidents in Usukuma.[72]

Sukuma religious practices and beliefs have an individual, rather than a familial or communal, character. Indeed, 'Sukuma religion may be described as a "do it yourself" religion.'[73] More practically:

The success of the Sukuma religious system is that, in practice as well in theory, it is no system at all, except perhaps in very general terms, nor is the Sukuma cultural system so institutionalized that the rituals of the chiefly system imposed a religious structure on all who wanted to participate as citizens in that particular chiefdom.[74]

Moreover:

> When asked for their religion, traditionally minded Sukuma would reply: 'mimi ni msukuma tu' (I am just a Sukuma), meaning that they made no distinction in their own minds between religion and secular life; a word for religion did not even exist in the Sukuma language.[75]

Religious practices were not and still are not rigidly linked to institutions. In consequence, there are no communal shrines were regular worship takes place, an absence that relates to the Sukuma practice of 'living apart together'.[76]

Among the Sukuma, death is not an end but a continuation of life, uniting the living and the dead. The ancestors are dependent on their living relatives and the lack of children means both physical and spiritual extinction. Without a name, one is nobody, and the child borrows identity from his or her ancestors, thereby establishing links between living and dead.[77] Grandchildren have therefore been seen as the continuation of the self, representing a successful lifecycle, and 'the birth of grandchildren secures the link between the past and the present and establishes the bond between the living and the dead in the cult of the ancestors'.[78]

Importantly, the ancestors as humans are not good *or* bad, but good *and* bad.[79] Ancestors may be malevolent for different reasons. Sins such as incest between close kin may threaten both human fertility and the fertility of the land. If the descendants do not name their children after the ancestors, maladies may also result. Moreover, if ancestors are not properly remembered in prayers and propitiation, they may cause misfortune. People who die of unnatural causes are particularly dangerous, and if the corpse is lost, lineage unity is breached, exposing family members to more misfortunes and sickness:[80]

> The ancestors are considered specifically as the protectors of the family [...] Although so many of their troubles are thought to be due to ancestors, there does not appear to be any fear of them even when their descendants are suffering from their activities.[81]

The belief that propitiation of ancestors may cure illness and reduce malignance is based on a firm notion that the ancestors may take part or full control of their descendants.[82]

Although the Sukuma live in an arid area for half the year and despite the importance of rainmaking rituals, they have not developed other religious institutions and protective rituals for water resources. This may be because these resources have traditionally been adequate and that water-gathering has been the primary task of women rather than men, thereby making water difficult to include in the spiritual world of patrilineal ancestors.[83] In Sukuma cosmology, the religious concerns were for rain (and water springs) in the dry season. Few Sukuma have conducted religious practices except in relation to the agricultural cycle, being the responsibility of the chief.[84] The rains may come in different forms. If heavy showers arrive early, they may wash away all seeds. Excessive rain may prevent the crops from maturing properly, while delayed or patchy rain may cause drought and famine.[85]

Even as rain came to be seen as a gift from God, the chiefs, together with rainmakers, were responsible for performing the rituals necessary to ensure the life-giving rains. Disasters such as absence of rain, drought or destructive flood or storms were not seen as caused by God, but by evil spirits. In the 1960s, Balina et al. documented the following traditional prayer for rain:[86]

> O God, you come from Balang'hani, Bisugilo, Bakalwinzi and Bamazoya; you bring us prosperity; you continue westward to Ruhinda.
>
> - You take away evil, you put it into the lake.
>
> - We want to be peaceful, so that we may get good crops, many children, goats, cows and let rain come.
>
> O kind God come down, come down.

Hans Cory gave a detailed account of how a rainmaking ceremony was performed in the late 1940s and early 1950s:

> First two perfectly new cooking pots are obtained into which are placed two white stones, a small amount of rain water obtained from the first slight showers and mixed with *dawa* (medicine). On the day of calling down the rain a black goat and a white sheep are slaughtered. The blood from the goat is mixed with the other ingredients in the pots, and the blood of the sheep is boiled separately with other dawa and is used for

smearing the face of the Rain Doctor. The meat of the two animals is cooked and eaten by him, in addition to a dish of cooked food brought in to him by each of the villagers. The ceremony having been performed, the people return to their homes and the *Nfuti Mbula* (rainmaker) is left alone to hold communion with the 'spirits'. He makes a large fire of green grass from which arises dense clouds of smoke. From this day on he continues to call in a loud voice at regular intervals of the day to the 'spirits'. He is granted a period of a full month in which to achieve success.[87]

The ancestors were responsible for the rain, but their goodwill also depended on the villagers:

> By cooperating, spirits can bring rain to this world. Or they can withhold it. The options they choose at any given time depends, in the main, on the living: if the living are 'working together', 'cooperating', and 'living together harmoniously', this bodes well. Spirits will likely see this, be pleased, and bring rain. If, on the other hand, people quarrel, do not cooperate, and so forth, the ancestors will know, be angry, and withhold the rain.[88]

Among the Sukuma, people held the belief that the rulers must have power over Nature and her phenomena, and if the ruler failed to provide rain, he could be driven out.[89] According to Chief Charles Kafipa of the Bukumbi chiefdom of the Sukuma, who is a Christian, every chief had to know how to conduct the rainmaking rituals (interview in 2011). However, in this village the rainmaking tradition had disappeared decades ago, but he recalled the practice and the importance of the rituals (fig. 28).[90] If the chief did not know the proper practices and ways to secure rain, he could be expelled from his post. On the other hand, a successful outcome of the rainmaking rite legitimized the chieftain's position. Sukuma rainmaking rituals involved two fundamental aspects. First, they were based on belief in and prayer to God, and God's greatness and powers were attested to through his duties and deeds affecting people. Second, it was based on the belief that when humans died, they retained contact with those alive. The deceased were broadly classified in two categories: the 'good people', who had behaved well during their lives, and those who had a bad character while alive. The latter group were undesirable and not included in rainmaking rituals. The 'good people' were respected and had been accepted by God. Consequently these ancestors could be approached and propitiated by the descendants to seek favours from God.

28. Rainmaking pot in Usagara.

There were certain preconditions the rainmaker had to meet before commencing the ceremony. In Sukuma society, polygamy was widespread. The rainmaker had to be married and his first wife was the one most respected by the ancestors. He was allowed to see her before the ritual, but he had to abstain from intercourse with his other wives for five or six days beforehand. On the appointed day of the ceremony, the rainmaker would go to a sacred and secluded place early in the morning. This isolation and solitude were mandatory. In particular, no women were allowed to come across, because they could disturb his mind by awakening thoughts of relationships with women. He could prepare himself throughout the day and the only persons allowed to see him were a young boy and girl, who brought him water and food, and any other items he requested. He would start by fetching water and collecting a branch of special leaves. These were ground on a grinding stone with another stone. The grinding required full concentration and had to be done soundlessly. Any sound or noise would mean that the rainmaker had not been concentrating on his task, and he would have to throw away those leaves that had been improperly pulverized. The leaves are a link to water and rain, since they grow on plants needing both.

When the rainmaker conducted the ritual, he called upon the ancestors and requested them to make contact with God and present the issues at stake and ask for rain. The message the ancestors would be asked to convey would begin: 'God – who controls the east, north, west and south.' The rainmaker would call upon the ancestors by name, mainly those who were known and remembered, and in particular old rainmakers. He would then pray and sing traditional songs and the rain would come. The rainmaking rite was also part of other rituals for ensuring a successful harvest. Each year, before the planting, the chief would cut his hair in a ceremony involving the royal drums. He could cut his hair at other times of the year, but this particular ceremony had symbolic significance. The hair on the ruler's head would grow again, symbolizing the sprouting and growth of the seeds and thus the coming success of the harvest.

WATER AND BODY FLUID METAPHORS

The role of hair has had strong symbolic meaning, and if one follows religious testimonies, real powers throughout history. The biblical reference to Samson is well known: 'If I am shaven, then my strength will leave me, and I shall become weak, and be like any other man' (Judg. 16:17). A person's soul or power has often been seen as bound up in his hair,[91] which also include status and wealth.[92] Among the healers along the Nile in Uganda long hair was a very powerful symbol, and indeed a sign of ritual purity and reciprocal relation with the spirits. When the leaders or ritual specialists symbolize or unify society and cosmos through the body, growing and cutting hair can be parallel processes to the actual sowing and harvesting.

Hair is but one part of the body. The central aspect is that the bodily processes not only parallel the processes in nature, but indeed that they are identical, and even more: the bodily processes may control nature. This is most explicitly seen in the sexual metaphors and practices structured around the life-giving fluids and processes in body and nature. After all, the ultimate outcome of rainmaking is life in the broad sense, not only successful harvests, but life and people in general.

Although the sexual metaphors and mocking rituals are widely testified to in rainmaking ceremonies, documenting such rituals and getting good translations is a challenge, and perhaps there has never been so good documentation as the one Tore Saeteresdal, Liivo Niglas and Frode Storaas did among the chiefdom of Chadzuka, north of Manica city in

Mozambique. Albeit one cannot assume that similar expressions have been used elsewhere,[93] also since in some areas like among the Sukuma women did not participate and the rituals were conducted by men collectively or only by the rainmaker alone, it nevertheless gives an idea of cosmologies at work and how rainmaking is intimately connected to sexuality, fertility and reproductivity. In the film *If the Vagina had Teeth* women were mocking men and their male re-productive organs and processes. The quotes are from different songs sung by the women during the secret ritual, demonstrating obscene behaviours and inversing the social order:[94]

> You will burn from the penis [...] They are already open [...] climb on top king [...] climb there king climb there they are already open [...] be careful of farting the snuff is very good [...] you should have said farting with the penis, snuff! I do not fart from the snuff. Be careful when you sneeze you may fart. I want to fart a little bit [...] then you will fart [...] You have excreted [...] You have fart with your vagina, you have fart with your vagina, fart with your vagina, farting a little bit [...] Who is sneezing like that who has not done that before?

> The man miss and the soil gets into the penis [...] they are heavy [...] They are very heavy [...] No one is available to pick them up (the penis) [...] we cannot stand up because of the weight [...] they are angry (the penis). Are they angry? yes they are heavy [...] Stand up stand up.

> I am tired of holding the penis and the balls, I am tired. I am tired of holding the vagina and the balls.

> The owner of the penis. Has gone to pick up wild fruits. The owner of the penis has gone to pick up wild fruits.

> If the vaginas had teeth, the penises would be finished. If the vaginas had teeth, the penises would be finished.

> Did you hear that? Do you think she still has standing breasts? Hold tightly to the vagina [...] What is left is penetration those penises are being pulled out [...] They are being pulled, those penises are being pulled [...] Careful you might fart [...] I want the manhood to get in [...] Sorry [...] Too bad for you they have all released.

> I am tired mother I am tired. I am tired of holding the penis I am tired.

> They [probably referring to the penises] are heavy because they are full of soil [...] Forgive them the testicles have been cut and hung on the trees.

> What does the crow have, it has the penis [...] where were you when it was taken? [...] Excreting.

> That thing that is promiscuous kuchonyera *that thing that is fond of penetrating?* [...] My child's vagina came out. Chiro. That thing that is promiscuous. My child's vagina came out.
>
> Could not find the rope [...] take the penis and tie with it [...] Can you lend me the rope [...] Take the penis and tie with it [...] yeah yeah could not find the rope [...] Take the penis and tie with it [...] yeah yeah the rope my King [...] take the penis and tie with it.
>
> Vagina is tired of being on top of testicles [...] Vagina is tired of being on top of testicles.
>
> You should have said the vagina is longer than the penis [...] The vagina stinks/smells you adults [...] You have not seen its inside [...] the vagina stinks/smells you adults [...] .you have not seen its inside.
>
> What can I do with this vagina that wants a penis [...] The testicle is a burden [...] The testicle is a burden.

When the rituals were finished, the rains arrived. As a fertility ritual, rainmaking addresses the human reproductive forces. The reason for these sexually explicit songs and performances is because women are believed to be naturally wetter than men and therefore better equipped to attract rain. Women's watery composition is on account of their vaginas, whereas men have lean bodies and 'dry' penises, which are not a good thing at all.[95] With regards to women's wetness, it also included breast milk and the nurturing capacities, the most life-giving for any child, which will be discussed further with direct reference to the Nile and the ancient Egyptians in Chapter 5. Milk in general is also a prevalent feature in many water cosmologies since it is an essence of living, and a central aspect to pastoralists, for instance the Maasai (see below).

All these bodily expressions, where the body is not only part of cosmos, but also defining cosmos, has throughout history been a source of philosophy of the flesh.[96] And the body and all its reproductive processes as parallel and part of cosmological structures have also been fundamental in mythologies and webs explaining and understanding religious worlds, partly because if it relates to personal experiences and bodies, and having direct relevance and implications for these very processes, they make more intuitive sense, although not necessarily understood at an explicit or articulated level, but rather acted out ritually.

Religion contains both beliefs and practices, and the relation between myth and ritual is complex. Leach once argued that 'myth implies ritual, ritual implies myth, they are one and the same',[97] but most researchers argue that the relationship is more complex, and that myths and rituals possess qualitatively different aspects. Joanna Brück says that

> By acting practically upon the world in day-to-day life, people play out the beliefs and values that constitute their particular way of understanding the world. In other words, cosmologies are not abstract ideological or symbolic systems but enable people to understand the world and to get on in it by providing a logic for action and an explanation of the universe. Ideas about what constitute an appropriate economy strategy, for example, are part and parcel of these systems of value and meaning.[98]

Early anthropologists approached myths from a different angle and more direct way, suggesting 'that myths are not the creations of unbridled fancy, but in many cases at least are sober historical records',[99] and as a consequence, 'myths form the most important part of their traditions, not merely justifying and sanctifying all their rites and costumes, but being regarded as *in themselves a source of life*'.[100] Thus, water mythologies represent life in a double sense, not only are the myths creating and maintaining life and other aspects of cosmos, the water in the myths enhance these pro-creative forces and powers. Water myths are often some of the strongest, most pervasive and all-encompassing myths in religion or a cosmology. Moreover, water mythologies are not restricted to just water in itself, but include all aspects of flows giving life, milk, blood and the very flows themselves. Water myths are like water itself, fluid, and about all fluids that give life, or take life, either by being lethal or blocking the life flows.

Throughout the history of humanity, Joseph Campbell lists four essential functions of mythology. First, it elicits and supports a sense of awe before the mystery of being, or what Otto described as the numinous. The second function of mythology is 'to render a cosmology, an image of the universe that will support and be supported by this sense of awe before the mystery of a presence and the presence of a mystery'. The third function is to support the current social and political order, and finally, 'the fourth function of mythology is to initiate the individual into the order of realities of his own psyche, guiding him toward his own spiritual enrichment and realization'.[101] Myths evoke cultural resonance, often unconscious: 'Very deep is the well of the past. Should we not call it bottomless?' asked Thomas Mann in *Joseph and His Brothers* and quoted by Joseph Campbell:[102]

> For it is a fact that the myths of our several cultures work upon us, whether consciously or unconsciously, as energy-releasing, life-motivating and – directing agents [...] Mythology is not invented rationally; mythology cannot be rationally understood. Theological interpreters render it ridiculous. Literary criticism reduces it to metaphor.[103]

But they misunderstand the ways myths work:

The cosmological body of the rainmaker, as well as other healers, is the most potent as he or she embodies the process and through it the outcomes. As shown with the Sukuma case, the chief cut his hair when the seeds were planted, but the same growing and life-giving capacities can be embodied in different ways. By replicating the seasonal process in detail, being sexually active during the rainy season, less active in the cold season and abstinent in the hot, and keeping his hair and nails uncut throughout the rain period reflect the growth on the fields. When dead and buried properly, his powers and potency are captured and kept in the soil and the land, and the rain will always return. The rainmaker thus influences the cycle of nature through his own body and physicality, and

> this type of sympathetic magic is possible only because the body is as much a map of the territory as the territory is a map of the body: the land is the feminine source of life, the rain its male inseminator, and the land draws the rain to it as a woman draws a man.[104]

THE RAINBOW, THE PYTHON SNAKE AND MAKING RAIN

Rainmaking cosmologies show a great variety of specific perceptions and practices adapted to particular waterscapes. As shown in Chapter 3, the rain-god Mesoké also lives in the Itanda waterfalls and both Itanda and Mesoké can embody and possess Mary Itanda, although not at the same time. And while Mary is not a traditional rainmaker as such, she may also intervene in these matters.

In March 2017, I was back in Uganda again and visited Mary. The rains had been erratic the last four to five months and the harvests started failing, and it was natural to focus on the rain-god this time. The rainbow and the python snake are two common features in African rain-cosmologies, but I was also curious about understanding how a rain-god can live in the waterfalls as a river-god, which intuitively seemed like a contradiction representing two different water phenomena.

Mary did not only reveal the underlying logic, but it was literally a beautiful cosmology shining like the rainbow itself. The great African python snake is one of the world's sixth largest snakes. Water is its natural element, and when many gods want to move around, they may use the python as their vehicle. The python has a colourful shape and body like the rainbow, and they also connect and complete the hydrological cycle.

While a rain-god may provide the necessary and life-giving rains to his devotees, even the rain-god needs to make rain. When we see the rainbow, it is usually after rain on sunny days, but this represents only half of the cosmological cycle. The rains have been released from the sky, but before Mesoké can give the divine gifts, he himself has to bring the waters to the sky.

Every morning on clear days when the sun rises, it forms a perfect and beautiful rainbow rising from the Itanda waterfalls. These cascading torrents of water in the waterfalls splash the water high up in the air, and one can literally see that water-drops are dragged up to heaven. This is the works of Mesoké. Through the rainbow, he sucks and drags water up to the sky. The rainbow is like a reversed waterfall from the river filling the sky with the life-giving rains Mesoké later will give to his people. This happens each morning, and Mary also puts pots with water at her holy places for Mesoké, if he needs more and additional water.

Thus, the rainbow rising from the waterfalls like a python snake is a good and benevolent rainbow, whereas rainbows on dry land are bad and dangerous, since they empty the already dried land of water and moisture.

The rain-god Mesoké, the Itanda waterfalls, the rainbow and the python snakes complete the hydrological cycle. Even the rain-god must create rain, not by magic, but by literally filling heaven with physical water flowing in the river, which eventually will be returned to the catchment area and the river as rain. The force of the waterfalls testify to the immense powers of the rain-god and the python snake and the rainbow are links to heaven making the rains. The clouds need to be filled.

After having talked about Mesoké and the failing rains for quite some time, Mary Itanda suggested that it would be a good idea to sacrifice a goat to the rain-god; not only was I interested in her cosmology, but there were also needs for more rain. It was difficult to disagree with Mary in this regard. Soon after the sacrifice was conducted, dark clouds appeared on the horizon. Mary said Mesoké was very pleased with the sacrifice and cosmologically it secured the good rains in the forthcoming rain season.

MAASAI – 'THE LORDS OF THE PLAINS'

From a strict ecological point of view as a risk mitigation strategy in arid regions, low and erratic rainfalls may cause people to rely more on pastoralism than agriculture, since with pastoralism one may move the animals to where the water is whereas settled subsistence patterns are solely dependent upon if and when the precarious rains come.[105] Pastoralists are also dependent upon the rain and hence emphasize the utmost importance of rainmaking rituals, but they have one fundamental advantage compared to farmers; traditionally they have not been bound to one place and can take their cattle and follow the rain to fertile lands. As a farmer told me during the drought in Tanzania in 2011, without rain, there was nothing the farmers could do. One cannot move the land and farmers have to live where their land is, he said.[106] But water and land are more than mere subsistence strategies – food systems are inevitably part of larger cultural and cosmological structures.

Different food ways are associated with particular ways of feeling, thinking, being and behaving. Kenyan pastoralists have been described as the 'people of milk' and the most famous and legendary are the Maasai, once also called the 'lords of the plains'.[107] In another context it has been said that 'Our great bank is cattle,'[108] stressing the role of cattle and the wealth they represent, which directly relates to the importance of rainmaking and good grazing lands. Importantly, the wealth of cattle among pastoralists is also very real and material. A cow, which gives birth to a calf each year, implies a doubling of the original investment, which no bank can match.[109]

But this 'walking bank' was dependent upon rain and fodder, indeed, the whole wealth of the Maasai was traditionally and solely dependent upon the welfare of the beasts; without sufficient rain for grass the milk production would be jeopardized, and in worst cases the animals would suffer, starve, and eventually die (fig. 29).[110] Among the Maasai, certain families had unusual ritual powers enabling them to deal with

29. Lifting an exhausted animal during drought in Kenya.

any uncertainty and misfortune. These powers channelled through prophets were often highly specialized, and could involve rainmaking or capabilities to interpret specific natural phenomena.[111]

Among the Maasai, as many other pastoral groups, the close intimacy between human and animals structured the social and cosmological lives and worldviews. From the very origin of life, pro-creation is a natural and human phase. Semen or male 'blood' of young men has been seen as a powerful source both giving life and making social relations; it transforms girls to women and adult persons, creates fertile producers from barren women, and seals life-long unions between men. But semen is also potentially lethal if it flows in wrong directions and may weaken and endanger life, and sexual intercourse is strictly forbidden after the third or fourth month of pregnancy since the man's 'blood' may come in contact with the fetus.[112] Fluids in general, and in particular milk and blood, also being closely related to sexuality and nursing mothers, have also had other roles and parallels in the culinary diet of the pastoralists dependent upon their cattle.

Traditionally, the Maasai lived exclusively on a pastoral diet; milk, meat and blood – a dietary ideal that is not fully adhered to in times of hardship despite their loathing of plant food. The culinary code was also a social code where the food separated its members according to sex and age, but also social responsibilities, and one important differentiation was made between 'warriors' and 'elders'. Milk was the staple and daily food for all, and the cows were milked twice a day by girls and women. Men drank only milk from cows whereas women and children could also drink milk of the small stock if there was scarcity. Curdled milk was favoured by warriors and boiled by the elders, often nowadays flavoured with sugar and tea leaves. In particular warriors are supposed to keep the strict dietary ideal of milk, meat and blood, and milk are often reserved for the warriors. When elders or men in general are forced to eat gruel, milk added with water and maize, they still refer to the ideal as this being milk. In times of extreme milk scarcity, milk is mixed with blood, and although not seen as substituting milk, it rather symbolizes the close association with meat of slaughtered beasts. Meat in general is extraordinary food; cattle are never killed for food and only ceremonially at ritual occasions, although these restrictions are less strict for small stocks. Thus, whereas milk is ordinary food, meat is ritual food, also having a gender division; women provide milk and only men may slaughter animals; also reinforcing another dichotomy: milk is a symbol of life as it sustains and gives life and meat symbolizes death. As a consequence, drinking milk and eating meat at the same time is a taboo since it would bring together life and death in a union that has to be separated, and hence jeopardizing the cosmic order of life and wellbeing. This paradox is, however, overcome – that man is associated with death – by the fact that meat is not eaten raw but mediated by fire, making the difference between life and death, or more precisely between death and rebirth, a life-giving transformation: fire is a transformative agent, and only men generate fire.[113]

For Claude Lévi-Strauss, boiling, which is different from cooking, is a process which reduces raw food to a decomposed state similar to rotting, whereas roasting is a partial cooking.[114] By emphasizing the means used, boiling is a cultural product by the use of pots, but as the results obtained, it belongs to nature. According to Lévi-Strauss, roasting is always attached to high status as opposed to boiling: 'boiling provides a method of preserving all the meat and its juices, whereas roasting involved destruction or loss. One suggests economy, the other waste; the second is aristocratic, the first plebeian.'[115] Thus, although his analysis was not based on the Masaai, the very practices among this pastoral group bear many similarities and, importantly, food symbolism is expressed and often in close association to water symbolism and at many times inseparable. Such perceptions are intrinsically linked in various ways to the fluids and flows of cosmos throughout the Great Lakes region,[116] which can further be discussed with Rwanda as a case.

GENOCIDE AND FLOWS OF LIFE IN RWANDA

Christopher C. Taylor has analysed the genocide in Rwanda, including the deep motivational and cultural resonances which enabled the genocide to take the specific violent forms it did. Despite Rwanda's otherwise rich and fascinating history, the slaughter of almost 1 million predominately Tutsis in 1994 during a three-month period will always be a dark chapter not only in the country's history, but also for Africa and for the international community. The ethnic differentiation between the Hutus and the Tutsis was to a large extent a colonial construct and partly based on wealth and number of cows. The royal family and the dominant group were the Tutsis, but wealth and different degrees of poverty was not the only reason for the genocide. Mythology and cosmology played fundamental roles. On one hand, the Tutsis were seen as descending from Ham, connecting them to changing interpretations of the biblical stories. The myth about the Hamites comes from the Old Testament. Ham was one of Noah's three sons; the two others were Japheth and Shem – whose successors were the alleged Aryans and Semites respectively. In Genesis 10.6 it is written that the Hamites include Cush, Egypt, Put and Canaan. The interpretations of the Hamites have undergone several changes, and in the early nineteenth century the Hamites were seen as Caucasians – whites in black skin – they were not like the other Africans, thus linking the Egyptian civilization to the Bible and the Middle East. The Hamites became the great 'civilizers' of Africa.[117] In Rwanda, however, descending from Ham meant being a stranger and not belonging to the country, or as phrased in the pre-genocide propaganda, the Tutsis were 'cockroaches'.

Apart from the Hamitic myths, there were also other cosmological mythologies working at a deeper level directly related to rain-making practices and the king, with implications for all Tutsis, as the king embodied life and all well-being in Rwanda. Taylor argues that in order to understand the genocide one has to grasp the underlying logic of how ordinary Rwandans could commit such cruelty and how they perceived the internal other as threatening not only their personal integrity but also the cosmic order of the state. These symbolic structures go back at least to the nineteenth century and are related to the sacred kingship in pre- and early colonial times. Crucial in this logic is the notion of the king controlling or blocking the life-giving flows of cosmos. In Rwanda, *imaana* has often been translated as 'God' or the supreme being, but it could rather be seen as a generalized, creative and transformative force and vaguely defined fecundating fluid. The king was the supreme rainmaker of the kingdom and he mediated between the sky and the earth. He renewed the divine gifts of fertility and passed it down to his subjects, and, importantly, his body was seen as a hollow conduit through which the powers of celestial flows passed. The king was the most giving or 'flowing' being. Death, on the other hand, was associated with blocked flows, and flows of life in general, like old women no longer menstruating. One of the fundamental tasks of the king was to eliminate beings or processes that blocked the flows – in the kingdom and cosmos (fig. 30).[118]

This powerful symbolism, which will be elaborated later with regards to the killing of rainmakers among the Nilotic tribes in Sudan, was forcefully activated to the extreme. It cannot fully explain the magnitude of the atrocities, but it can be part of explaining the specific form it took and the particular excessive violence. In the propaganda cartoons during the genocide the Tutsis were put on poles and speared from their anus and women were impaled from anus to mouth with wooden or bamboo poles and much more. Historically, though, in royal rituals genitals and women's breasts were cut off victims and slain enemies. Without going into elaborate and

30. Replica of the royal palace, King's Palace Museum-Rukari, Rwanda.

macabre details of the brutalities and the mutilations, since this can be read elsewhere, it related to the role of the king. Taylor writes:

> The Rwandan monarchy manifested its control over flowing processes – rainfall, human fertility, bovine fertility, milk, and honey production – through its ritual capacity to catalyse or to interdict them. Kings thus encompassed the qualities of both 'flow' and 'blockage' and in that sense, were ambiguous, 'liminoid' beings, the embodiment of evil as well of good. At times of dire calamity to the polity as a whole, the king became the ultimate repository of ritual negativity, the ultimate 'blocking being' and in these instances, it was his blood that had to be sacrificially shed to reopen the conduits of *imaana*.

The events that led to and were included in the 1994 genocide incorporated much of the 'mythic logic' of king sacrifice, although applied to the whole group of Tutsis in a secular sphere rather than profane.[119]

Rivers and the flow of rivers played a vital role in this conceptual understanding of flows and blocks. Rivers used to be central in royal rituals, although they had lost ritual significance in the post-colonial period, but the mythologies were revitalized during the genocide. One of the leading Hutu extremists, Leon Mugesera, said before the genocide:

> [The Tutsis] belong in Ethiopia [referring to the Hamitic myth] and we are going to find a shortcut to get there by throwing them then into the Nyabarongo river [which flows northwards]. I must insist on this point. We have to act. Wipe them all out!

And it was in the rivers that many of the bodies ended up after the slaughter, thrown in the Nyabarongo River and then the Akagera River. Thousands of bodies were found floating in Lake Victoria washing up on the shores. As Taylor says:

> Rwanda's rivers became part of the genocide by acting as the body politic's organs, in a sense 'excreting' its hatred internal other. It is not much of a leap to infer that Tutsi were thought of as excrement by their persecutors. Other evidence of this is apparent in the fact that many Tutsi were stuffed in latrines after their deaths. Some were even thrown while still alive into latrines.[120]

It is without any doubt that the powers of rainmaking cosmologies, including society and cosmos widely, are extremely forceful, since the one controlling these forces controls life and death of all his subjects. As shown, this power or the beliefs that the forces were obstructed may have lethal consequences, and as the corpses were thrown in the Rwandan rivers floating into the southern parts of Lake Victoria, eventually some of the dead bodies ended up at the source of the White Nile and even in Bujagali Falls. There were stories that during the Rwandan genocide in 1994 Jaja Bujagali collected corpses that had floated across Lake Victoria. When asking Jaja Bujagali about this, he strongly opposed these stories. His purity prohibits him from being in contact with corpses and he never buried the genocide victims – this was done by the government. Although drowned people are seen as being taken by the river spirits in his cosmology, the water has to be protected since it is the abode of the spirits. The Budhagaali spirit was furious and ravaging about this atrocity. The victims of the genocide were crimes not only against humanity but also the spirits, because it also defiled the river and the spirit. As the human incarnation of the Budhagaali spirit, Jaja Bujagali has to stay pure and protect the purity of the river, and his purity is vital to his ritual obligations. In this case the mythology of Jaja Bujagali was larger than the man himself, in other cases perhaps not, for his ritual tasks may literally involve everything between heaven and earth, as with the Rwandan king. They both share, as do many other ritual specialists at the heart of the water cosmologies, huge responsibility and their purity are mandatory for their divine interaction and successful mediation. Obstructing the purity or the flow of these cosmic processes of life-giving fluids may have deadly consequences – for the ritual specialists or the responsible bodily mediums themselves or for their people.

What is without doubt is the pervasiveness and ontological depth of water cosmologies, including rainmaking beliefs, encompassing whole societies and in the case of Rwanda even nation-states. Far from being just 'myths' or postmodern constructions of fancy, those who believe in these myths and religious frames are dead serious because ultimately they are not only about life and death, but also construct and maintain the cosmological structure guaranteeing social life. Moreover, the seriousness and effectiveness of divine waters is not restricted to harvests and agriculture, but as seen above, include bodily and other fluid metaphors. In fact, water may work in any domain, and one area where water has had devastating effects is when water has been a central medium in wars, and there are several instances where such beliefs have shaped part of history.

THE ALLAH WATER CULT – WATER IN WAR AND VIOLENCE

The Maji Maji rebellion (1905–7) in Tanzania was a watershed in colonial resistance and probably inspired by the earlier Yakan cult and shared many of the same features and beliefs.[121] The Yakan or Allah Water cult built on former and existing notions at the time, which were reshaped and actualized in a given particular context, only to perhaps surface again almost a century later in a bizarre form during one of the darkest chapters in Africa's modern history.

The Lugbara are a Sudanic-speaking group living in north-western Uganda and north-east of the Congo. By the end of the nineteenth century, the Yakan or Allah Water Cult was acknowledged by the colonial administration. The core aspect of the cult was drinking sacred or magic water. The first reference seems to go back to 1883 when the Agar Dinka revolted and killed eight hundred troops after having drunk the 'water of Allah'. The cult spread as the Dinka were successful, which proved the powers of the waters. The cult reappeared among the Dinka in about 1920. Middleton writes:

> The drinkers of the water believed that certain things would happen to them after drinking. These were that the water would preserve them from death; that their ancestors would come to life; that their dead cattle would come to life; that they could flout government orders with impunity and need not pay tax; that they would be immune against rifles which would fire only water; and that they would obtain rifles to drive the Europeans from the country [...] Those who refused to drink the water were said to become termites when they died or to be carried away by a strong wind. These were the promises made on behalf of the water during the dry season of December 1918 to March 1919.[122]

The Yakan water cult seems to have continued for a long time, although at personal levels it may have taken more perverted forms being expressed in weird ways. Idi Amin grew up among the tribes around the western Nile in a world of witchcraft and superstitions, and he himself was a boy of 'the water of Yakan'. Probably he also learnt how to prepare the 'waters of Yakan' during cult ceremonies which he attended in his youth. The alleged magical powers of the Yakan waters are believed to come from a particular plant called *kamiojo* creating hallucinations, and somehow the LSD of central Africa in the second part of the nineteenth century.[123]

This close association with the Yakan cult has been explained as one reason for Idi Amin's bizarre and brutal practices, apart from him probably having syphilis. In Uganda, most people believed that he literally had a taste for blood, which was more direct than just the mere slaughtering of at least 150,000 Ugandans that were dumped in the Nile. Amin's tribe, the Kakwa, as many other warrior tribes, were reputed for practising blood rituals on slain enemies. This included the cutting of a piece of flesh from the slain body to subdue the spirit of the dead or tasting the blood to render the spirit harmless. Amin himself said on several occasions that he had eaten human flesh; in 1975 he said 'I have also eaten human flesh' and in 1976 'I have eaten human meat. It is very salty, even more salty than leopard meat.' Amin was also regularly going to witch doctors and on several occasions he also insisted being alone with the victims at the mortuaries, although nobody can of course know what he did when he was alone.[124] Whatever Idi Amin did or did not do, it is certain that this was not the mainstream and common aspects of the Yakan water cult, although there could have been some deep structures of mythological or cosmological triggering mechanisms through which these practices made sense from an individual point of view as personal symbols.

The regime of Idi Amin was a dark chapter in the history of the Nile. However, this chapter also illuminates the role and importance of the river gods. During this horrific episode, there were too many corpses and it was impossible to bury them. Idi Amin chose three dumping sites for the bodies: one was by the source just above Owen Falls Dam, another at Bujagali Falls and a third at Karuma Falls. How many were killed during these terrible years is difficult to say: the lowest estimates are around 100,000, but the figure was probably much higher. Keyamba observed:

> A boatman at Owen Falls works full-time removing corpses from the water. If he retrieved twenty corpses a day between July 1971 and my departure in April 1977 – a reasonable assumption – then, in round figures, this would amount to over 40,000 dead. But this figure doesn't include those that must have been eaten by crocodiles or swept through the dam – at least another 10,000. Moreover, Owen Falls was only one of three dumping areas.[125]

Multiplying the Owen Falls number by three, the total is at least 150,000, and many, many more were killed and abandoned at other places.

Jaja Kiyira and Jaja Bujagali, when asked about the Amin era, were filled with horror and contempt. Although the spirits are pleased with sacrifices, they were furious with the innumerable corpses from the massacres. Their divine wrath was provoked because the killings were mere slaughter. This is not how spirits work, since they are the custodians of the social and moral order. The spirits do not tolerate such atrocities, which are against religion. Moreover, the river and the spirits are about purity. All sacrifices have to be conducted in an appropriate manner, and it is the blood which is sacrificed. Although drowned people are seen as being taken by the river spirits, the water has to be protected as it is the abode of the spirits. Such appeasement ceremonies are also necessary when dams are built.

Whether the Yakan cult, the Maji Maji rebellion or Alice Lakwena and her family at Murchison Falls during civil war in Uganda, the water spirits have had and still continue to have extreme powers in society and for humans. The ways divine waters are part of society and cosmology may take numerous forms depending upon adaptation and what the life-giving waters are in a given community. However, it is also important to stress that not everything is about water, although individual power and prestige may have originated in controlling rain or from water spirits. As with Idi Amin, Alice or Kony, the spiritual powers may give legitimacy in other domains, including wars, since it is the very same spirits that give rain and other benevolent gifts, including the outcomes of witchcraft, who are also protecting and giving instructions in times of other hardships and problems. This is also evident in South Sudan and the unfolding emergency and civil war from 2013 onwards. President Salva Kiir and former vice-president Riek Machar consulted one powerful healer or prophet respectively, one favouring a more peaceful approach and the other a more violent one, and both being able to interfere and intervene in other domains as well, like rain.[126]

NILOTIC PEOPLE ALONG THE NILE AND PASTORALISM

In South Sudan lie the massive swamps of the Sudd. Sudd is an Arabic word for 'barrier' or 'blockage', and the massive floating vegetation and papyrus occasionally seals completely off the Nile to navigation, and it is also the reason why all searches for the Nile following the Nile southwards failed and why Livingstone, Burton and Speke started their searches for the source from the East Coast. The White Nile flows through the Sudd and it is estimated that the outflow of water (on average, 14 bcm annually) from the Sudd is only about half the inflow at Mongalla (27 bcm) coming from Lake Victoria and the other great lakes, the rest being lost.[127] The Sudd represents an enormous area and the width is approximately 1,300 km or about the same distance as from London to Vienna.[128] Measuring the size is difficult because of the extreme seasonal variations and fluctuations depending on the rains and the flood, but the maximum area of the catchment of the Sudd (Bahr el Jebel) is estimated by the Nile Basin Initiative to be around 169,665 km^2.[129] This ecology has thus given rise to specific adaptations and unique rituals structured around water.

The importance of rainmaking and of which types of water that are to be included in ritual and religious life cannot be properly understood except in a water and ecological context. In 1986, Douglas Johnson argued that the environment has to be included in Nilotic studies, which tend to be ahistoric in the sense that *why* an event happened *when* it did has been largely unexplained. In the swamps, as he says:

> The hydrology of the region is thus crucial to human settlement. If the river has a sustained rise in the wet season, then many riverine dry-season pastures may remain flooded and unusable for most or all of the year. A prolonged high level of flooding over several years can also make settlement sites near the river untenable or inaccessible, forcing people to move.

The variability in floods and rainfall implies that people have to move, not only as part of annual cycles, but also in both long- and short-term trends in relation to water distribution patterns and pasture availability:

> It is not pastoralism alone that keeps people moving. It is mainly the environment which has made movement and resettlement a constant fact of life. The historical pattern of flooding, which produces an ever-changing mosaic of water-logged and dry areas, continually draws people into and out of the eastern plains.[130]

In larger parts of the Nile basin the annual floods are the overall most important factor structuring most aspects of life, but flooding itself is an under-researched field (although discussed more in Chapter 5). Floods are unpredictable and ambivalent phenomena of nature; and in a similar vein as the appearance of the life-giving rains, the right amount at the right time may represent a fine line between life and death. Although not in the Sudd but in the Gambella region in Ethiopia, an area with heavy floods, an elderly person once commented on this deadly duality securing life: 'Flood is like a snake. You get medicine out of a snake, just like we make our livelihood by using the flood. All you have to know is how to handle it.'[131] This duality points to the benevolence, but also the dangers of the floods. Literally representing life and death in multiple ways, it is wise not only to aim for divine help in controlling these processes, but also to strictly adhere to the cosmic premises and the godly demands. Although the gods or spirits may take numerous forms and have different names, they are the ones controlling all spheres of life and death.

Among the Acholi in Uganda south of the Sudd, *jok* is applied to certain spiritual beings generally connected with particular places or objects, like big trees, but also in the shape and appearance of snakes – and waterfalls and hills. Then there were also *jok* having the form of hairy, large-headed dwarfs.[132] The rainmakers among the Acholi could come from any clan, and would possess the highest authority. Central in the ritual was rain-stones, and the stones could be called 'rain'. These stones were shaped crystals only found in rivers, and no commoner would touch them or even look at them, and if a person found such a stone by coincidence, it had to be brought straight to the chief and failing to do so could result in pain of death by dropsy. Young rain chiefs would not touch the rain-stones in fear of becoming sterile, but handed them over to an old wife of their father. The rain chiefs themselves had two or three pots containing 10 to 20 rain-stones, which were passed down from their forebears. If rain was the preferred outcome, the stone would be smeared with oil and water poured on them. Contrary, if rain was to be driven away, the stones would be put in a tree in the sun and even in the fireplace.[133]

The first of Evans-Pritchard's seminal books on the Nile basin was *Witchcraft, Oracles and Magic Among the Azande* from 1937. The Azande is living in the South Sudanese region close to the Congolese border receiving plenty of rain. The Azande had no knowledge of cattle and lived of cultivating their lands, killing animals, fishing and collecting roots and insects. Although this book is a milestone in witchcraft studies, he does also discuss rainmaking. However, in this region rainmaking was not an art to which great importance was attached, and the rainfall was normally heavy and regular. Those believed to have the power to procure rains did not receive rewards when making rain, and during periods of long droughts they got only corrections. Moreover, rainmaking was seen as a foreign art conducted by other tribes. People who were believed to withhold the rains were treated roughly, sometimes taken to a stream, washed, and then thrown into the river. Making the rain-stopper uncomfortable enabled the rains to come if there were dangers of droughts. Normally, however, every Azande knew how to prevent rain, even children, and this was done when people were threshing millet, holding a feast or travelling in the bush so the clouds would pass by. Since everybody knew these rites, they did not need to pay a magician to conduct the rituals. Still, rain medicines also existed.[134]

Among the Nuer living in the Sudd, where Evans-Pritchard wrote another seminal book with the same title (first published in 1940), rainmaking was much less important than among the Dinka and Shilluk. The ritual procedures were not fixed, and it seems that the belief in the efficacy varied greatly depending upon who the actual rainmaker was. The Nuer do not regard the sky or any other celestial phenomenon as God, which are testified by the expressions 'Spirits of the Sky' and 'Spirits who is in the sky'. Still, as with the water spirits such as Budhagaali, although the god is everywhere, the Nuer think that he is particularly in the sky and high up. In a similar vein, 'Rain may be said to be God but God cannot be said to be rain.'[135] Among the Nuer, although they could ask the leopard-skin priest to make sacrifice for rain or to put a hyena skull in water for the same purpose, it was not the most central rite. While some prophets' prayers and sacrifices were believed to be highly effective, any Nuer could pray to God to procure the life-giving rains. As one Nuer explained, 'Oh well, the leopard-skin priest may sacrifice a cow [probably a goat was meant] and pray to God for rain, and that is all; perhaps God will give it and perhaps he won't.'[136] Although rainmaking ceremonies could be conducted by any man from a tribe, the majority of successful rainmakers were prophets. Still, here too, it was the act and will of God letting the rain fall, and instead of saying 'it will rain', they said 'God falls'.[137] But as opposed to many other tribes, the rainmaker would not be ceremonially killed when he was no longer in use to his people.

Evans-Pritchard emphasized that a people having such a simple material culture as the Nuer is highly dependent upon their environment. Although they were pre-eminently pastoral, they were also growing some millet and maize, but horticulture was by all seen as forced upon them by the poverty of the stock. Cattle were everything, and they looked with profound contempt against people with few cows. Cattle were the most cherished possession and essential for food-supply, and all social processes and relationships were mostly defined in terms of cattle, even ritual and religious ones, including sacrifices. The value of the cows depended upon the amount of milk they gave, and the more milk, the more valued and cherished. Milk as a product does not need storage or transport, but is renewed daily. However, it depends directly on water and vegetation, forcing the herds to migration, and people to follow. Human needs were subordinate to the needs of the calves, which were given first priority if the herd was in danger. As Evans-Pritchard commented:

> It has been remarked that the Nuer might be called parasites of the cow, but it might be said with equal force that the cow is the parasite of the Nuer, whose lives are spent in ensuring its welfare [...] In truth the relationship is symbiotic: cattle and men sustain life by their reciprocal services to one another. In this intimate symbiotic relationship men and beast form a single community of the closest kind.[138]

And although the swamps have from a European perspective perhaps been seen as having no favourable qualities, the Nuer think they live in the finest country on earth. The surface water comes partly from rainfall and the rest from the river flooding the plains creating sufficient grass. But as Evans-Pritchard pointed out, rain was the most important:

> Scarcity of rain is probably more serious than low river water, but both may inconvenience the Nuer to the point of famine, because sufficient water may not be held up in the clay beds to enable the grasses to recover from firing; inland watercourses may quickly dry up and compel movement to lakes and rivers earlier than is desirable; and there may be a shortage of the marsh pasturage which is usually the mainstay of the cattle at the end of the dry season. Insufficient rain may also destroy the millet.[139]

In short, the life-giving rains were the ultimate source of the welfare of men and beasts alike, putting the emphasis on rainmaking as a ritual tradition. The problem of water was closely related to vegetation, and as part of the seasonal movement the Nuer searched for pastures and drinking-water and took their cattle to where they could find both (fig. 31). 'The early rains are the season of fatness, for then the grasses germinate, or renew their growth after the long drought, and the cattle can graze on the young shoots to their content,' Evans-Pritchard writes, but also pointing out rain being a double-edge sword:

THE SOURCES IN THE SKY AND RAINMAKING

31. Nuer dug-out canoes.

As the rains advance, grazing becomes more difficult, the ground being flooded and the vegetation rank, and in years of high water may be a serious problem. The cattle have to rely on the short grasses that prevail on village ridges: a further reason that compels Nuer to occupy these sites in rain.[140]

Rainmaking and rain-stopping rituals were hence of fundamental importance, since 'variation of water supplies and vegetation thus forces Nuer to move and determines the direction of their movements'.[141]

'WILLING THE SUN' OR MASTER OF DISASTER

In order to understand the particular and peculiar character of a river ideology and religion, which will be discussed in the next chapter, one may compare and contrast these practices and beliefs with rainmaking traditions. At a structural level these two belief systems and traditions share some fundamental ideas, namely that the king is responsible for the wealth and health of his people. However, a river religion may create a more stable ideology and a more powerful civilization than kingdoms ruled by rainmakers, which is particularly evident among the Nilotic kingdoms along the Nile. The unpredictability of the rain itself with often extreme variability and fluctuation gives non-reductionist premises, both possibilities and limitations, for organizing and controlling societies. It is not necessary to go to an extreme Marxist view where the control of the means of production is the essence, since controlling the means of production, including the labour, does not help much if there is nothing to produce because the rains have failed; no hoes, ox-ploughs or mills can mitigate a severe drought and harvest failure.

On the other hand, a society organized around controlling the rain may strengthen its ideology and beliefs even when the rains fail. Failure may indeed reinforce the beliefs of the system given the high stakes involved, basically since there is ultimately no rainmaking as such, but the benevolent rains are given by the ancestors, spirits or divinities mediated and enabled by a chief or a rainmaker. If the rain fails, it is not because there is something wrong with the system, in practice people's own ancestors and gods, but that there is something wrong with the leaders or the ritual specialists as mediators – or the community at large. Henceforth, the obvious solution has historically been to replace the ruler with another one better suited for the tasks. In African religions as elsewhere, blaming the gods or even worse, challenging their authority and accusing them of causing human misery unless it is due to divine repercussions for sinful behaviour, is simply an impossibility for believers adhering to these very cosmic principles. The system cannot be wrong since the religious principles are invented by the spirits and divinities themselves, and only fools would traditionally object to their own ancestors. Rulers and unsuccessful rainmakers, on the other hand, are another story, in particular if they were perceived as evil wanting to harm humans and herds, or just simply being incapable of fulfilling their duties.

In traditional African societies rainmaking has been a fundamental part of culture and religion, not necessarily because it has been an easy task, but because of the importance of the rain. I have met old rainmakers telling me with grave sincerity about the responsibility that they had on their shoulders in the past. If they failed, it would cause disasters for the community with possible deaths, and this was a huge burden not to take on lightly. This also reflected their decision, sometimes unwillingly, to become a rainmaker. If and when they realized that they had the skills and powers to intervene with the spirits in these matters, there was hardly a choice to refuse since this was also a divine gift passed on through the ancestors, and the community depended on them.

Rainmaking has thus closely been linked to ancestral propitiation and it was the forefathers and the deceased who provided the rain through the chieftain or the king as a medium, or through special rainmakers working for the chiefs in various ways. As such, the rainmakers have tried to *control* and *manipulate* nature through both physical and non-physical interventions, but ultimately it was in the realm of the ancestors,[142] and hence also reflecting the dire consequences if the rainmaker was unfit for the tasks or deliberately chose to withhold the rains. Enabling or failing to produce rain comes at a high price, and in all cases it involves lives, whether animals or not.

In the entire world 'the central practice of the sky- and fertility-religion is the sacrifice of the divine king, either in his own person or in that of a substitute,' Wainwright writes.[143] Being at the centre of this cosmology, the rainmaker most often faced a violent death if he could not provide sufficient water at the right time.[144] The rainmaker, who was normally the chief of the tribe, could also withhold the water as a political means to coerce people:

> To take the life of a fertility-king at the appointed time and in the appointed manner is to offer the highest sacrifice; to take it before the time in any other manner, unless as a punishment for failure, is to commit the foulest possible murder, indeed to strike at the prosperity of the whole country.[145]

In Equatorial Africa, the Bari people living along the Nile in Sudan commonly killed or severely punished the rainmaker if he did not produce sufficient rain or if it did not come at the right time.[146] Moreover, he could not only be killed if he failed to procure rain but also if the sun was shining too strongly. Prolonged sunshine was seen as the work of a malevolent rainmaker who was accused of 'willing the sun' and who could be put to death if the rains failed.[147] When the rains were absent, someone was always accused of having 'poisoned the sky', 'tied up the rain', or 'willed sun'.[148]

The whole ceremony aimed to ensure fertility and to banish diseases, as expressed in the following prayer:

> Make that water [come] so that it may fall, so that these people may cultivate, so that also their millet may ripen, so that these people can be contented, so that the people may bear and produce and their wombs grow large.[149]

Among the Bari and Lotuko, the rainmaker king was the Master of Disaster. The king's divinity was defined by his power to control disasters, which included the fertility of the fields, the health and wealth of humans and animals, epidemics, plagues, and safety from attacks by wild beasts, etc.[150] The relation between the king and his subjects was in equilibrium. The kings were believed to punish people collectively with drought and other ill fortunes while the people blamed the king for the disasters. Good rains and abundant harvests were seen as the work of the king.[151] However, killing the rainmaker was the ultimate measure taken if disasters were prolonged, and a common rationale was: 'He is killing us so why should we not kill him?'[152] In 1981 a rainmaker was killed after he was accused of scorching the land by deliberately 'putting the sun'. Four days after the rainmaker's killing and burial, it rained heavily, but the drought returned:[153]

> The extent of a King's power is determined by the reach of his clouds. Places where his rain or drought do not reach are per definition outside his power. As a corollary of a King's rain fortunes his 'clouds' may suddenly expand beyond the horizon, but they may just as easily contract. Rain careers were often ruined as quickly as they were built.[154]

It is not only people's disobedience which was thought to cause drought and low rainfall. The rainmaker could also threaten to stop the rain if his wishes were not fulfilled. However, if the king received gifts and his wishes were fulfilled, but the rain still did not come, then the accusations would bounce back to the king. If he demanded more, people would accuse him of being merciless and of blackmailing the community for his own interests. Thus, regicide was the only solution to end the drought:[155]

> The rain continuously forces King and people to redefine their relationship. The power of the rain is not just an ideological superstructure, justifying and mystifying a power relationship. It is the subject matter of daily transactions by which the King and people test the balance of power between them. The dramatic potential of the rain may be one of the deeper motives why Kings in the climatic zones of the tropical Africa depending on unpredictable rainfall are makers of rain.[156]

The power to control the weather makes the rainmaker a priest king who attains a divine status as a god incarnate here on earth. Consequently, he should not lose his powers as this endangers society. However, his powers can be renewed through magic as magic is part of the rainmaking process.[157] Ethnographically, the Nilotic rainmakers were similar to 'divine kings'. Among the Shilluk, the whole cosmology was incorporated into rainmaking and the divine sphere, and in prayers: 'you who give the rain. The sun is yours, and the river is yours', stressing that both water and the sun were within the realm of rainmaking.[158] Among the Dinka, 'every rainmaker has immanent in him the spirit of a great ancestor who has come to him down the generations,'[159] and as such they were divine rulers and kings.[160]

There are many similarities in the killing of rainmakers and divine kings. Kings were expected to commit suicide by taking poison when a disaster occurred or they had a natural physical defect such as impotence or infectious diseases, and Mashona chiefs could have their throat cut or be strangled if they were enfeebled by old age or sickness.[161] Rev. S. S. Doran reports that

> Among the Varozwe (Varozwi, a Shona tribe) the custom of killing the king prevailed. Absence of bodily blemishes was considered absolutely necessary in the occupant of the throne [...] If he showed any signs of physical decay, such as loss of teeth, grey hairs, failure of sight, or impotency – in fact, any of the indications of advancing age – he was put to death and a man was deputed to carry the resolution in effect.[162]

The health of the king embodied the people's prosperity. Among the Jukun, the new sovereign sums this up when he says: 'Our crops, our rain, our health and our wealth.'[163]

It is important to note that there was an intermediary period between the burial and the exhumation of the deceased king. During this period, it was still the deceased who was held responsible for rainmaking and droughts; the king-elect did not take up his duties before the former king was exhumed:

> Throughout this period the power of the dead King is believed to be more important than that of the King-elect or the regent. In fact, as far as rain is concerned, the dead rainmaker continues to rule. Just as during his life his rule may bring either blessings or disaster, but the power of the dead King is believed to be greater than that of the live one.[164]

The exhumation or the levelling of the tomb coincided with the end or beginning of a rainy season. The tomb had to be guarded during the exhumation so nobody would steal the rain. The king was believed to control the rain for at least one year after his death, and those who were closest to the king could be buried alive with him because the relationship was 'so close that it could be broken only in death'.[165]

RAINMAKING AND SACRIFICES OF DIVINE RAINMAKERS

Among the Bari, there were two overall groups; those who 'know water', or in other words rainmaking, and those who do not 'know water'. The rainmaker was literally 'chief of water' and sometimes called only 'rain-chief'. It is told about one great rainmaker that he never walked on the ground, and when he was on a journey, he was carried in a couch. The Bari were also expert iron-workers, but the smiths belonged to the class of slaves or despised people, at least from the perspective of the chiefs, whereas the smiths themselves denied this low status and claimed that they stood apart from the other classes in society. Moreover, the smiths are said not to cultivate or herd cattle and goats, being employed in all ceremonial and state errands, and they may even act in the place of a rainmaker when the latter was a child. Also, when a great rainmaker died, a slave or a smith could be buried with his master, and smiths could also be assistants to rainmakers.[166] The Bari rainmaker could be killed if he did not procure the rains. The killing of failed rainmakers decreased with the colonials, as what testified in one report: 'If you [the English] were not here, then we kill the rain-maker [but we do not now] because we fear the English. When the rain falls, then we do not kill, and when the sun shines strongly, then we kill.'[167] Prolonged sunshine was seen as the work of a malevolent rainmaker. Or his servants.

In the first quarter of the twentieth century it was difficult to grasp the idea of the main god Nun, and the Seligmans believed that the Bari were not as intensely religious as the Dinka. Nun was associated with rain and lightning. Regarding the rainmaker, he was in a very different position from that of the Shilluk or Dinka rainmaker who embodied a great ancestral spirit. The Bari rainmaker could be killed if he would not, or could not, produce the rain. A central aspect of the Bari rainmaker's ritual was the use of rain-stones:

> The rain-maker has certain green and white stones in a pot. He washes these with water and places them on a big stone [one of the old grindstones ...]. He smears the rainstones with simsin oil, he sacrifices a black goat near the stone, then he, his assistants, and 'all' the old men eat of this and the rain comes.[168]

The rain-stones may be old quartz labrets (or lip-plugs) or made of possible green garnet, or they may be pebbles with natural 'eye' marking and artificial perforations. Moreover, many if not all rain-stones were believed to possess sex or to be either male or female. These could be vague relations to ancestral spirits, but often the stones were in some way equated with specific persons or more likely their spirits. The rain-stones had not only sexes like male and female, but they could also be slaves and children, and long or pointed stones were male and short

THE SOURCES IN THE SKY AND RAINMAKING

were female. Rain-stones were not taken indoors, not even during rainy periods when they were not in use.[169] Also, the biography of rain-stones have been important; which important rainmaker had used them and how efficient they were, in addition to their status, gender and age.[170]

The role and function of the rainmaking ceremonies was to ensure fertility and banish disease and want, and one rainmaker named Pitia, who was a blacksmith, gave these instructions to his assistant when he sent him off to a distant village to act for him:

> Make that water (come) so that it may fall, so that these people may cultivate, so that also their durra may ripen, so that these people may be contended, so that the people may bear and produce and their wombs grow large.[171]

When a rainmaker died among the Bari, his body was submitted to a special treatment as soon as possible, because society was in danger and if the spirit of the rainmaker escaped, it could bring sickness to others and even become a lion or a leopard causing danger to people. As part of the treatment, all the orifices of the body were plugged, as documented:

> When the rain-maker is dead, he is plugged, his ears are plugged, his nose is plugged, his eye is plugged, his mouth is plugged, he is plugged, his fingers are plugged. And then thus so that [...] the spirits may not go out, so that the son may manage the father so that he obeys (him), so that the spirits obey the son.

Particularly during great famines, rainmakers were in danger of being accused of withholding the rains, and then they could be killed in violent ways. In a missionary report after a famine in 1859, the rainmaker was blamed and tried to run away:

> He escaped again, but was found in the neighbouring village of Tschuekir, and was struck down with blows from clubs and four spear-thrusts. His belly was slit open, and he was left for the vultures. So died Nigila, the great Nigila.

The treatment of deliberately killed rainmakers elsewhere has been described in much the same way:

> [If] a rain-chief has been killed because he has 'hidden the rain' his corpse is dragged near to water, his face is smeared with mud from the river bank, his body slashed, and his stomach ripen open, and he is left to the birds and scavengers. His old friends can go to the murderers, and by payment of cows purchase permission to bury him. He is then buried as a commoner, the apertures and cuts being left open.[172]

Among the Dinka, the God in the Firmament is known as Nyalic whereas the term Deng or Dengit means the 'great rain'. Nyalic has been seen as a god with no beginning or end and there are no legends concerning the origin of this god. The same holds true to a large extent for Dengit, although Deng or Dengit are somehow seen as an offspring or enumeration of Nyalic. Rain, and in particular the first rain, is connected with human procreation and with Divinity, as one said: 'This rain which falls, is it not Divinity? When it falls, the grass revives and cattle thrive and the earth becomes cool. And a man sleeps with his wife again and dreams of his child.' Deng is associated in any figure with rain, but it is not merely a 'personification' of rain and lightning:

> The name Deng re-creates for the Dinka the whole syndrome of experiences of these natural phenomena as they touch directly upon human life. Rain and its associated phenomena, for people like the Dinka whose subsistence economy makes them directly dependent upon the grass and the crops, do in fact mean life and abundance, just as their absence, or their presence at the wrong time or place, can mean death and misery.[173]

This relates to the very concept and being of life itself. The essence of life can be augmented or weakened, and a beast or man who is large and vigorous has more of it than one which is small and weak.[174]

Offerings to Dengit are made at certain rainmaking shrines, and although Nyalic is the creator, in ordinary affairs of life the *jok* is more important. The Dinka rainmaker was also a divine ruler and usually he lived longer than his Shilluk counterpart since they decided themselves when they were too old to continue in office and apparently there was no stress that they should be sexually active. One rainmaker told Seligman in 1910

> that his father and parental uncle had both been killed in the appropriate manner, the Niel custom being to strangle their rain-maker in his own house, having first prepared his grave. The power of the rain-maker is in theory, and to a very great extent in practice, absolute, and every care is taken to guard him from accident, but if he were thought to be dangerously ill he would be killed even if quite young, for should he die of illness it would prevent any of his sons from becoming rain-maker in his turn.[175]

The hereditary rainmaker was the most important man in the tribe, consulted on every occasion, and his word was law (fig. 32).[176] The Dinka who lived in the neighbourhood of Khor Adar, told this story:

Long ago, men and women of the 'river people' would sometimes come out of the river, marry, and settle down in the neighbouring villages. The description of the emergence of one of the 'river people' is curiously like the birth of a child; the river becomes agitated, and the waters rise up around a human being whose umbilicus is joined by a cord to a flat object beneath the water. The cord is cut, and bullocks are killed and thrown into the river; then the river-man or woman is brought with more sacrifices to the village. Their descendants should sacrifice on the bank, throwing a live cow into the river after giving it a pot of milk to drink into which the old and important men of the clan have spat.[177]

The omnipresence and importance of rainmaking rituals when they were really needed and the dangers mounting up is evident. This may also give clues to the role of water in religion, and misconceptions about 'how' religious Africans were and are, bearing in mind that the whole question is strongly flavoured by Christianity or monotheistic religions. It is simply impossible to say that a Muslim praying five times to Allah each day is more

32. The Bor Dinka rainmaker, Biyordit Dinka, outside his shrine-hut of the spirit Lerpio in his homestead, Gwala village, 1910.

religious than a Sukuma who may participate and support a rainmaking ritual once each second year when it is really needed and severe drought and hardship are replacing dark rain clouds on the sky. In a religious worldview the essence is the beliefs and sincerity when it matters the most, and since rainmaking has a clear functional effect right here and now if successful, it is an utmost powerful expression of the reality and spirituality of humans and divinities alike. Although many religious systems require continuous devotion throughout the days and years, even in good times of plenty and prosperity, this is but one solution. Powerful water cosmologies such as efficient rainmaking religions may suffice with only the most important – rain – whereas others may have more elaborate practices often wrongly described as idolatry in early missionary, colonial and ethnographic texts. In short, the depth and pervasiveness of religious logic in these communities should be sought in the centrality of rainmaking when absolutely needed, not in other practices when life was already secured (fig. 33).

Still, contrary to the Bari, which Seligman and Seligman wrote was not so religious:

> The Dinka, and the kindred Nuer, are intensely religious, in our experience by far the most religious people in the Sudan, their worship being directed to a high god dwelling in or associated with the firmament and to a host of ancestral spirits.[178]

If one agrees that it is difficult to identify some communities as more religious than others, and as Geertz pointed out in another context, 'no one, not even a saint, lives in the world religious symbols formulate all of the time, and the majority of men live in it only at moments',[179] different communities have been, however, religiously structured in a wide range of ways although sharing the same and most fundamental aspect: the life-giving rains. At the beginning of the rains among the Dinka, the householders in every village sacrificed a sheep to Dengit and to give him praise and thanks. Among the Dinka, every rainmaker embodied the spirit of a great ancestor who has descended through generations, in the same vein as every Shilluk king incarnated the god. It was this ancestor that made the rainmaker more far-seeing and wiser than the commoners, and the rainmakers could also be labelled divine rulers, although their rule was longer and they were not killed except when they decide so.[180]

Thus, it seems that it was a common Dinka custom to kill the rainmakers when they requested it themselves. This happened in different ways. One

33. Dinka fishing party.

was placed in the middle of the cattle hearth. The rainmaker was upon a mass of dried and burnt dung, and the people danced around for hours creating so much dust that the old man, who had chronic bronchitis, died. Others were strangled in their home after their grave had been prepared. The corpse was then washed and a bullock sacrificed in front of the house. The animal was skinned immediately and a couch was made of the skin, which was placed in the grave and the dead body laid upon. Another way of killing a rainmaker was by preparing the grave. He would be placed alive on a couch and surrounded by friends and family, even his younger children but never the older ones. He got food and water for hours, and now and then he talked to his people and recalled the past history of the tribe, how he had instructed and advised them, and also how they should live in the future. When he felt that it was time and that he had finished, he told them to cover the grave, and as the earth was thrown in the grave, he soon suffocated. Yet another way of killing the rainmaker in the grave was by building a roofed-in cell in the grave. The rainmaker's neck, elbows and knees would be broken; other times he would be strangled first with a cow-rope. On other occasions, he first eats some food, the cow-rope is placed around his neck, then the elbows and knees are broken, and he was given a sacred spear which helped him to rise when he became strangled.[181]

Bedri also reported about the killing of rainmakers among the Dinka, and a violent way

> is to hold him standing, cover the whole body with thick cow butter and vigorously stretch his legs, fingers, arms and privates, and press the testicles. They then break all the joints. Some people say they are broken before death but others say after. The question why the privates are stretched and the testicles pressed, is always an annoying one and is simply answered by a shrug with a prompt 'I don't know.'[182]

The importance of rain has also to be seen in relation to cattle and the role of pastoralism (fig. 34). Cattle are gifts from the Divinity and the Dinka look upon their non-Dinka neighbours who kill cattle merely for meat with contempt, and they have a saying 'Cattle are not just killed for nothing' and the expression 'eater of cattle' is a grave insult. When sacrificed in rituals, in compensating for the death of a cattle, a child is named after it and thus preserving its memory. Cattle as well as children are gifts from the Divinity and always ultimately belonging to the Divinity, the clan-divinity and the whole descent-group. Since all oxen are destined for sacrifice in the end, they all symbolized the social relationship of the sacrificing group.[183] And the sacrifice

34. Dinka girl milking.

of rainmakers has to be seen in relation to animal sacrifices, since they share many similar patterns symbolizing and embodying the processes at work.

The fate and burial of the rainmaker resembles the very rainmaking ceremony itself. Again, it was not the rainmaker making rain as such, but he intervened on behalf of the tribe contacting the spirits who procured the rain. When rain was wanted, the rainmaker sought rain from the spirit Lerpio (and in the case of the Bor Dinka of Gwala). Two bullocks were sacrificed to Lerpio to induce him to intercede with Dengit to send rain. While the sacrifice was prepared, people chanted: 'Lerpio, our ancestor, we have brought you a sacrifice, be pleased to cause rain to fall.' Then the rainmaker speared the bullocks and cut their throats.[184] The intimate relation between the way the rainmaker was killed and the way the rainmakers conducted the rainmaking rituals was further testified to among the Shilluk; partaking in rainmaking was partaking in cosmos on divine premises, which required a close intimacy between men and gods.

But it was not only the rain that was important having divine origin, but also rivers were believed to have strong powers, and there were stories about the old days that in the Bor area a very old woman got pregnant after having bathed in the river, and none other than the river spirits caused the pregnancy. After seven years she delivered a boy, but who had adult teeth, and since she had no milk in her breasts she fed him on cow milk.[185]

Among the Shilluk, there were two overall gods; Juok and Nyakang. Juok is the God in the Firmament, formless and invisible and like air everywhere at any time. Nyakang is the first king and founding father of their kingdom, and although Juok is far above Nyakang, nobody could sacrifice or approach Juok but through Nyakang. The Shilluk king (*reth*) was the supreme ruler reigning by direct descendant of Nyakang (fig. 35). The two most important ceremonies were the rainmaking rituals held before the rains at the new moon and the harvest festival held when the durra was cut or about when the rains ended, and the Shilluk king was a divine ruler responsible for the rains.[186]

More specifically, Howell points out:

> The *reth* is himself the medium through whom both Nyikang and, more vaguely, Juok are approached and is the human intercessor for mankind with God. Voluntarily by ritual acts, involuntarily by reason of his very existence, the *reth* affects the fortunes and fertility of the tribe and controls the natural phenomena which reacts upon crops and cattle. The *reth* is therefore the central figure of tribal religion as well as the symbol of political unity.[187]

35. Shilluk shrine of Nyakang with painted exterior of the hut called Kwayo (Duwad).

The Shilluk royal death ceremonies took place only during the dry season, which in this part of Sudan lasted from October to April/May. The second burial, which was the main event, took place at the beginning and at the height of the driest seasons, either in October or January/February.[188] The period between the king's death and the enthronement of the new king, which included the intermediate period and the second burial, was a time of danger – both politically and spiritually – for the whole tribe.[189] 'The King's power is believed to be most effective in the period following his death.'[190] The installation of the new Shilluk king should not take place before the crops are ripe and harvested, but the king should also be installed well before the start of the new rains, since the king is responsible for the rains.[191] The Shilluk kings are descendants from a line of kings who ultimately have divine origin on the parental side and related to the river and the crocodiles on the maternal side. According to mythology, one day Nyikang's father, Okwa, saw the daughters of the crocodile playing in the river, and he took one of them, Nyikaya, as his wife. When Okwa died, Nyikang and his half-brother quarrelled about who should be the king, and eventually Nyikang left the country with his supporters and later became the Shilluk tribe. The crocodiles are the agnatic kin of Nyikang's mother or the mother of the Shilluk royal clan.[192]

THE SOURCES IN THE SKY AND RAINMAKING

According to Shilluk beliefs, Nyikang, the first king and hero, did not die, which they strongly oppose, but he 'went like a wind' or 'he became wind'. Consequently, he still lives. In a similar vein, they do not say that the king has died, but rather that 'the world is lost', or 'the king has gone across the river'. Thus, nobody could really know if the king died naturally or was helped to die. 'With regards to the Shilluk, the notion that a king "must not die alone" is connected with a concern about the spirit of Nyikang and a desire to control its transfer from one king to another. It is said that according to sacred custom the reth is obliged to transfer the spirit to the Nile, which is the abode of Nyikang's mother Nyikaya.'[193]

However, the Shilluk kings were not rain-kings as such, or even rainmakers, since this was beyond their powers and control, which concurs with rainmaking in many places in Africa. According to one Shilluk chief when he was asked about the king's power over rain, he answered:

> The Reth begs Nyikang to send rain. He gives a bull and asks for rain. As we cleaned the village before we pray to Nyikang, we would get an answer. He asks God to bring rain. He has no power over the rain except to ask Nyiakang who asks God who sends rain.[194]

Hence, the Shilluk king is not believed to make rain, since this is ultimately the work of God. But since the king is the mediator between humans and supra-human powers, he has the power and capacity to communicate with them and thereby secure and influence 'rain-affairs'. This does not make the king's role less important, because often it may rain on the other side of the river on the Dinka side or fall down on the neighbouring settlements and leave the Shilluk territories dry. Hence, 'the Shilluk king as organizer and main actor – that is, as sacrifier – of the rain and harvest ceremonies helps to establish a ritual caesura of time – a caesura which brings society into a moral relationship with nature and which helps to organize the former'. Schnepel writes:

> The *reth* as sacrifier establishes a concordance between cosmic and social order by harmonizing socio-economic activities with changes of the physical environment or, put it differently, by co-ordinating work and ecological time. The rain and harvest ceremonies can be regarded as rites of passages in which the nation as a whole and every Shilluk individually is transferred into a new phase of socio-economic life.[195]

According to Seligman, the Shilluk king and the Dinka tribal chief must be classified as rulers being 'Divine Kings'. When the Shilluk king's health failed or his virility began to fail, or among the Dinka when the chiefs turned old, they would be ceremonially killed. The reason behind this practice was the belief that if the rulers became weak and senile, cattle would become sterile and the crops fail, and then people would die in increasing numbers.[196] This has to be seen in relation to what death represents among men and beasts alike. Following Schepel:

> For the Shilluk [...] death is not only a 'sacrilege' which has to be dealt with ritually; in the form of regicide death becomes the very objective of ritual. Ritual regicide represents a deliberate act leading to death and thereby to rituals which transfer Nyikang from the deceased to the new king and through which the Shilluk forcefully express and recreate the idea of their kingdom as a perpetual one. Thus, rather than just responding to the embarrassment of death, the Shilluk actively bring forth death. They seek life through death, rather than just life despite death.[197]

The excessive and extensive use of violence in some rainmaking cosmologies are at the outset difficult to explain. It does not take place in all cultures and cosmologies, but as shown in Rwanda and among the Nilotics, when the stakes are high and society and cosmos is threatened, lethal outcomes have been seen as a solution. In the contexts where ritual killings of kings and rainmakers have taken place, one may attempt an explanation based on the character and ontological status of the water itself. Since the rain is not holy – the water has no inherent properties and divine qualities which can be used for any kind of purposes – the sole and only function of the water is for drinking, harvests and pastures. As indicated, holy water and holiness in general implies restriction and exclusiveness. It is not for everything and everywhere – or for the totality of society in all its forms. On the other hand, the life-giving rains are for all here and now, and hence, from this perspective the rains are much more important than specific types of holy water, although the latter may secure individual blessings, redemption or salvation in the after-world. The stakes involved in the religious role of water in society and cosmos may have a greater importance when the water is not holy: the life-giving rains are everything.

The rains are divine and benevolent gifts, and precisely because the absence and the withholding of the life-giving waters testify to a broken relation between people and spirits, it is not only a matter impacting the welfare of humans and beasts, but also the cosmic flow and the regenerating forces sustaining everything within and beyond this world. This points to the lethal and dual character of kings and rainmakers embodying the flows of cosmos. While their social and divine status was legitimized because they are intermediators between gods and ordinary humans, and often interpreted failed rains as the laymen's collective sinful behaviour, they were still responsible. Commoners, on the other hand, interpreted it differently; the leaders have failed or lost their powers, jeopardizing society and cosmos. This ultimate threat had to be solved and mitigated, and historically the leader's death was an obvious and necessary solution. Thus, power comes at a high price.

Given that there is no necessary connection or relation between the importance of rainmaking rituals and the societal role creating wealth and prosperity, and the ontological status of the mediator whether this is a king or ritual specialist, different societies throughout history have organized these cosmic powers and structures in various ways. What seems to be the case, though, is that the more divine and godlike status the ruler providing life and death for his subjects has been given, the stronger and more enduring have these kingdoms and civilizations developed, including elaborate religious architecture and priesthoods, as will be discussed with ancient Egypt in the next chapter.

In this regard, from Sir James G. Frazer's *The Golden Bough* (1890–1915), the Shilluk has had a paradigmatic status as the 'divine kingdom' par excellence. Frazer was knighted in 1914 and received a string of honours, probably making him the most heavily decorated anthropologist of all times. *The Golden Bough* was at the time the most ambitious study ever undertaken attempting to gather data from all over the world throughout all time in a comparative perspective. At first it was enthusiastically received by the academic community, but as more editions came, the academic popularity waned as it became part of the Western popular consciousness, and, since the abridged edition from 1922, it has never been out of print.[198] Still, in the history of European thought and academia following Frazer, the Shilluk have been seen as evidence of a European motif in antiquity long gone. On the northern shores of Lake Nemi in Italia there was a sacred grove and the sanctuary of Diana Nemorensis. Frazer writes: 'Such was the rule of the sanctuary. A candidate for priesthood could only succeed to office by slaying the priest, and having slain him, he retained office till he was slain by a stronger or craftier.' But, as Frazer points out, 'The strange rule of this priesthood has no parallel in classical antiquity, and cannot be explained from it. To find an explanation we must go farther afield.'[199] The Shilluk was the prime example found in history throughout the world in his cross-cultural comparison, with direct relevance for the understanding of the Egyptian civilization.

FLOWS OF CONTINUITY IN EGYPT

Both anthropologists and archaeologists have emphasized the similarities between Nilotic kingdoms and the Egyptian civilization. Simon Simonse pointed out the striking similarity with ancient Egypt:

> In Egypt the dead and the living King ruled simultaneously. The dead King was equated with Osiris, who was responsible for the success of the agricultural seasons, and the living ruler was identified with Osiris's son Horus. The motor behind the annual flood and the regeneration of the crops was the power (*ka*) released at the King's death and equated with the divine power of Osiris, the dismembered King who was resurrected annually in the flood of the Nile.[200]

From an archaeological perspective, Henri Frankfort argues: 'The comparison of Ancient Egypt and Shilluk beliefs makes some problems connected with Osiris less embarrassing, since we can at least propose a solution by analogy.'[201]

As Robert Wenke notes:

> Studies of ancient Egypt have become almost geologically encrusted with interpretations that draw on other interpretations that drew on earlier interpretations, and so on, reaching from the dynastic Egyptians themselves to classical Greek historians, and then century after century to the present day.[202]

The continuity in practices and beliefs in relation to the Nile in Egypt has been emphasized by many, as once noted: 'As a whole, this land exhibits a singularly ancient adjustment of a people to their environment, one so clearly accomplished that there has been but little change in their customs or numbers for at least four millenniums.'[203] Or as Lady Duff Gordon wrote in 1863, even more explicitly:

> Nothing is more striking to me than the way in which one is constantly reminded of Herodotus [...] This country is a palimpsest in which the Bible is written over Herodotus, and the Koran over that. In towns the Koran is most visible, in the country Herodotus.[204]

Throughout history Egypt's climate favoured any kings who claimed divine power by controlling and predicting the flow of Nile.[205] With the unification of the Two Lands and the end of the Neolithic Wet Phase, 'The magic powers of the rainmaker were irrelevant in the Nile Valley, where the life-giving water came from the inundation and not from the heavens.'[206] Still, as Aldred argues, it is almost certain that the leaders used magic to ensure the Nile flood took place. This power came in the hands of the king who was thought to command the Nile.[207] Moreover, with the transformation of the Seth-ideology into the Horus-ideology, the sun cult did not necessitate sacrifices as demanded by the old religion,[208] 'but the old forms had to be adapted to new conditions of dependence upon the Nile, not upon the rain'.[209] Following Aldred again:

> The prehistoric rainmaker chieftain who was thought to keep his people, their crops and their cattle, in health and prosperity by exercising a magic power over the weather, is thus transformed into the Pharaoh, able to sustain and protect the nation and having command over the Nile in a rainless land. The never failing inundations of the river were more predictable in their occurrences, though not in their volume, and therefore more amenable to control than the weather.[210]

Thus, it is suggested that there was a change from a rainmaking cosmology to a river religion in ancient Egypt. After this preliminary introduction, it is time to analyse the rise and the resilience of the Egyptian civilization more systematically and chronologically from a water perspective by focusing on the first dynasties onwards to the building of the pyramids.

5 The River Civilization in the Desert

THE NILE AND THE EGYPTIAN GODS

The Great Pyramid of Khufu is the world's largest pyramid and the last of the existing seven ancient wonders of the world. Together with the pyramids of Khafren and Menkaure at Giza, Djoser's Step Pyramid in Saqqara, Sneferu's Pyramid in Meidum and his Bent and Red pyramids in Dashur, it has intrigued and haunted the imagination. Death has to be seen in relation to life, or more precisely water, because

> In these deserts the river was life itself. Had it failed to flow, even for one season, then all Egypt perished. Not to know where the stream came from, not to have any sort of guarantee that it would continue – this was to live in a state of insecurity where only fatalism or superstition could reassure the mind.[1]

Without water the population would soon have died of thirst in the extreme heat or hunger from failing harvests. Still, despite the Nile's fundamental and vital role in the Egyptian civilization, it never attained the status of a supreme deity. This place was reserved for the sun, which became ancient Egypt's greatest god:

> Although the Nile was the obvious giver of life to the early men of Egypt it was not the great river and its precious waters that first stirred thoughts of worship in their primitive minds. It was the sun, relentless bearer of death, that they supplicated.[2]

Ra was the sun and all the pharaohs were the Son of Ra – Horus. This seems paradoxical: why worship the sun in a desert environment where temperatures reach 50 °C in the summer months?

While it was never constant, the flood did occur every year and the river never failed entirely. Every year it came pouring out of the desert, rising from the south and flooding the Delta in September, the driest and hottest time of the year. In Egypt, the river ran through the harshest deserts without receiving water from a single tributary and hardly any rain.

The Egyptian civilization was entirely dependent upon the river and its annual inundation, but the secrets of the inundation and the river's sources were a mystery to the ancient Egyptians. While the inundation was worshipped, the Nile itself – as a uniform river or phenomenon – was not and there was no supreme Nile god or goddess. Compared to Hinduism's Mother Ganga or Saraswati, Yamuna or Indus, the Nile River acquired a unique religious status unlike any other river, but there never was a 'traditional' river god. And yet, in 1844 Champollion used the term 'Nile god'. The problem is that a number of figures belong to this group, either through their association with the Nile as a river or the inundation as a process. Hans Sethe was the first in 1918 to state explicitly in a short note that the term 'Nile god' was inappropriate or misleading. As John Baines argues, from then on most authors have discussed or alluded to the mistaken use of the term, but, at the same time, have continued to use it. He therefore introduces the term 'fecundity figures' instead of 'fertility figures', which can be equally misleading. The term 'fecundity figure' is used for what is usually referred to as 'Nile gods', and such figures are found from the Fourth Dynasty until the Roman period. 'Fecundity figures' are present on most of the major Egyptian antiquities in the form of hieroglyphic signs and depictions on temple reliefs, tombs, stelae, papyri, scarabs, furniture, as well as statues and statuettes in various materials. The most important context is the temple relief.[3]

In the Egyptian religion *Hapi* was closely associated with grain but not the Nile as such, although he is often referred to as a Nile or river god.[4] Following Hornung:

> There is a striking lack of personifications of waterways or stretches of water in the Egyptian pantheon. The so-called 'Nile gods', more recently termed 'fecundity figures', personify general concepts of abundance and its causes, among which the most prominent is the inundation [... but] they can scarcely be termed deities. There is neither a river god of the Nile (there are of course no other rivers in Egypt), nor deities of lakes [...] The only fecundity figure who takes on an independent existence as a deity is the inundation, Hapy.[5]

THE EGYPTIAN WATER-WORLD

The Egyptian civilization (c. 3000–332 BCE) developed in one of the largest and driest desert areas in the world, and this was only possible thanks to the Nile. During the Pharaonic period, the civilization was dependent on the Nile, and the summer inundation created an agricultural economy based on the annual floods. The three seasons formed the basis of the Egyptian calendar: *Akhet* (inundation), *Peret* (growing), and *Shemu* (drought), which was an ideal natural cycle.[6] The life-giving water was essential not only for the economy, but also as a constitutive part of the ancient Egyptian religious worldview. And yet, while the Nile was the very essence and basis of the civilization, the role of the river and water in ancient Egypt has been poorly understood. Traditionally, there have been two dominant theories regarding the rise of early civilizations. On the one hand, Karl Wittfogel argued in *Oriental Despotism* that large-scale irrigation systems gave rise to despotic and bureaucratic states. On the other hand, Robert Carneiro put forward the theory that a population increase in a restricted area such as the Nile Valley led to warfare and subsequently to hierarchies and the rise of civilization.[7] However, neither of these theories explains the empirical evidence and the historical development in Egypt (fig. 36).

Military generalship did not become intrinsic to the status of the Egyptian king before the second millennium BCE. Irrigation and agriculture were administered at a local rather than a national level; there was no centralized canal network and lifting devices were introduced late. In the Old and Middle Kingdoms, water was lifted manually with pots and buckets.[8] Irrigation was a local matter beyond government control, and in ancient times the only machine for irrigation was the simple *shaduf*. Images of the device can be found in tombs from the late Eighteenth Dynasty (c. 1350 BCE), in scenes depicting men watering gardens. In earlier scenes, water is carried in pairs of pottery jars, indicating that these pictures do not portray the irrigation of strategic crops, but the watering of minor vegetable plots and/or flowerbeds. It also further strengthens the argument that large-scale agriculture focused on a single crop that was dependent upon the yearly inundation.[9]

V. Gordon Childe proposed the hypothesis that the origin of civilizations in Egypt and Mesopotamia was a consequence of drier conditions, which forced people to migrate from the surrounding deserts:

> Enforced concentration in oases or by the banks of ever more precarious springs and streams would require an intensified search for means of

nourishment. Animals and man would be herded together round pools and wadis that were growing increasingly isolated by desert tracts and such enforced juxtaposition might almost of itself promote that sort of symbiosis between man and beast signified in the word 'domestication'.[10]

However, many scholars, like Barry Kemp, have argued against climatic and economic explanations:

> It has sometimes been thought that organized society – civilization – in Egypt and elsewhere arose from the need for collective effort to control rivers to allow agriculture to develop. In the case of Egypt one can state that this was not so. The origin of civilization is not to be sought in something so simple.[11]

Moreover, the Delta must in earlier times have been an unchannelled and undrained swamp, which is not likely to have fostered the birth of a high civilization.[12] Robert Wenke states that 'the Nile offered the same approximate natural resource for the whole period of evolving Egyptian social complexity. Thus in a sense the most interesting patterns of cultural changes are those that cannot be explained in terms of flood variations.'[13]

Still, even though simple economic explanations fail, it was a water civilization in the desert. The Nile was the artery in Pharaonic Dynasties, and environmentally there was a huge variation in the Nile floods both annually and throughout the millennia. The human responses to the changing

36. The inundation and the life-giving water with the pyramids at Giza.

landscape and water environment are therefore analytical entrances which may enhance the understanding of cultural processes and the rise and constitution of early civilizations. Water as an element in nature has rarely been incorporated and analysed as an agent in the construction of society and religion, but nevertheless, the materiality and spatiality of the water-worlds are entry points into the constitutive structures and mechanisms at work in history.[14]

The Egyptian state has its origin in the Naqada culture in Upper Egypt, and by *c.* 3050 BCE the Early Dynasty was firmly established. What is known as 'Dynasty 0' also took place around this time period.[15] The emergence of the Egyptian state is particularly interesting, not only because it is one of the oldest, but the formation of the state seems to have taken place in the absence of the most obvious factors. The population was relatively small and the natural resources so abundant that it is hard to believe that competition for resources out of sheer necessity was a primary drive in the emergence of political domination. Trade was neither a major force, nor an external military threat.

At the most basic level, political power is dependent upon economy, and hence, the control of the economy was crucial for the rulers of the First Dynasty. The resources were mainly of three types: human, agricultural and mineral. 'The dynamic for the growth of the state seems in many instances to lie inherent within the very fact of settled agriculture and the population increase which this allows',[16] or in the words of Adolf Erman, 'Agriculture is the foundation of Egyptian civilisation.'[17] The crucial principle structuring Egypt was 'food for the country'.[18]

Thomas K. Park has argued that in riverine societies early stratification occurred prior to population pressure due to the very characteristics of flood recession agriculture. Compared to other types of agriculture, unpredictable floods favoured the development of stratified systems. An economy of recession agriculture which is dependent upon a fluctuating flood creates a sharp distinction between riverbank lands, higher and rarely flooded land, the basic floodplains, and finally lands where only rain-fed agriculture is possible. If the inundation is low, large areas of land become marginal and uncultivated. Thus, a flood recession economy forms a type of common property where some have the right to exclude outsiders and exercise significant control over insiders. The weather and the world of water are chaotic and unpredictable, which implies that it is impossible to predict the future or forthcoming conditions. The variability of the flood has a major impact on the land that can be cultivated and consequently on production. On the one hand, a low inundation may flood little land whereas, on the other hand, a large flood may inundate more land than it is possible to cultivate. As a result, this type of economy favours social systems in which some people are given priorities over others since the availability of the best lands depends upon the volume of the flood, and with low floods some people will be marginalized. 'The chaotic quality of the flood and its regular range reinforce early prioritization or stratification in recession lands as well as the value of links to alternative means of production,' Parks argues, because

> the flood recession model suggests a dialectical form of causality. It is the relation between the initial social relations of production and the economic base that give rise over time to transformations in the social relation of production – the development of a significant degree of class stratification.[19]

Moreover, John Wilson has argued that the Nile's rebirth gave the Egyptians the belief that they also would conquer death and attain eternal life: 'True, the Nile might fall short of its full bounty for years of famine, but it never ceased altogether, and ultimately it always came back with full prodigality.'[20] Thus, the characteristics of the Nile also formed the basis for Egypt's religious beliefs. Before turning to the religious and mortuary monuments and practices from the Early Dynastic period and the Old Kingdom, I will therefore briefly address some aspects of the mythology.

THE PRIMEVAL WATERS – THE CREATION OF COSMOS

In theory, Egypt was where the Egyptians lived. In practice it was where the Nile was.[21] The Egyptian cosmos was Pharaonic culture, and

> it should be emphasized that the cosmos created is not cosmos in the sense of 'universe', nor in the sense of 'virgin' nature. The cosmos which was created for Horus is the place that is cultivated by man, the irrigation culture [...] a place of Egyptian civilisation.[22]

The Egyptians had no word for cosmos, but it may denote 'man's world' or the place of man's habitation. Chaos, on the other hand, may denote the ontological stage preceding cosmos. The landscape itself is not cosmos but chaos; it is the inundated and uncultivated soil. The temple is cosmos in the state of chaos. Chaos is characterized by two factors: it is dark and an aquatic landscape. The presence of water precedes the existence of the earth and it is through the inundation of the Nile that the earth becomes fertilized. When it is closed, the temple sanctuary is a nocturnal landscape representing the centre of the dark, watery cosmos, at least in the later periods.[23]

History is the period of time when the office of kingship is ruled by the pharaohs as opposed to gods or semi-gods.[24] The Egyptian sign of 'government' is the pharaoh holding the lash in his hand. This is identified with the 'regulation of waters'.[25] Thus, the Pharaonic government was intimately connected to the procurement of water and creating Maat, which the Egyptian religion through ritual and magic tried to preserve from the ever-present and threatening dangers of the still-existing waters of Nun lying on the edges of the world.[26]

As Ragnild Finnestad says, 'The creation texts do not merely relate a creation story: they represent creation.'[27] The problem of creation or origin was related to the actuality of human existence since the universe humans lived in had continued in an unchanged form since creation.[28] Creation did not happen *ex nihilo*, because before creation of the 'first time' there existed the amorphous 'Abyss' or 'Deep', known as Nun. Nun is described as the primitive water in which the creator god existed as a formless being. After the creator god created himself, he created a mound of land emerging from the waters:[29]

> The waters surrounding the Primeval Hill were, naturally, the waters of chaos; these personified in the god Nun, were still supposed to surround the earth, and inexhaustible reserve of latent life and fertility. And the subsoil water, as well as the Nile, was thought to flow out from Nun. Since the Primeval Hill was the place of sunrise and creation, and hence the place for rebirth and resurrection, the waters of Nun which surrounded it became those waters of death which, in the imagination of many people, separate the world of the living from the world of the dead.[30]

According to beliefs, in order to start creation the sun had emerged from the primeval ocean, Nun. Although Ptah was claimed to be the creator of the universe, he could not proceed on his own as he was an earthly being. The Ennead or the Nine Gods of Heliopolis consisted of the creator sun Atum, Shu (air) and Tefnut (moisture). The children of this couple were Geb (earth) and Nut (sky), and their children were Osiris and Isis, Seth and Nephthys. The first five gods represent cosmology and the creation; the latter four established a bridge between nature and humans through kingship.[31]

Ptah was equated with the Eight who served at Hermopolis as a conceptualization of cosmos. Hence, the Eight existed before the sun as they brought him forth from the primeval waters. They were known as 'the fathers and mothers who made light' and even 'the waters that made the light'. The creation of the universe or the rising of Order from Chaos could only be induced by the sun through the waters. The sun created the Primeval Hill as an island of dry land in the primeval waters, which became the centre of the universe. The first land which emerged from Chaos was believed to possess vital powers, and each temple and funerary tomb was believed to stand on this hill. The hieroglyph for 'hill' is the shape of a step pyramid.[32] The pyramids were built on the edge of the course of the annual flood. Hence, the land on which the pyramids were built was the first to emerge from the flood when the waters receded, representing the Primeval Hill. In the *Pyramid Texts* (Pyr. 1652–3) the sun god Atum, and not Ptah, is described as the Creator. He was standing on the Primeval Hill in the middle of the water of Chaos, creating from himself the first pair of gods – Shu and Tefnut – and vitalizing them by transferring his Ka to them.[33] Similarly, Geb is described as 'for you are the essence of all the Gods. Fetch them to yourself, take them, nourish them, nourish [Osiris] the King' (Pyr. 1623).

Thus, the cosmogonical system was based upon two of Egypt's fundamental and pervading natural features:

> The overwhelming importance of the Nile and its annual flooding and the ever-present sun as a continuing source of light and heat. The first surely accounts for both the insistence on the origin of everything in the primitive waters of Nun and the emergence of the mound or island of creation. The second stimulated, in all likelihood, the appearance of the sun as either the creator god or his principal creature in Egyptian cosmogonic schemes.[34]

When the annual flood subsided and land emerged, plant shoots were evident, and the rising of the sun after a cold night, cosmogonic processes that were repeated day after day, year after year, over and over, must have inspired Egyptian cosmologists. The Nile flood was the most impressive act of fertilization known to the Egyptians; it is viewed as the prototype of all later inundations when the earth emerged from the 'Lake'.[35]

Finally, if the world and cosmos originated from chaos, it will eventually return to chaos and the abyss. In the *Book of the Dead* (Spell 175) there is a description of what will happen at the end of time. Atum will revert to his primitive form as a serpent and the world will return to its state of undifferentiated chaos. Atum tells Osiris that only the two of them will remain when he destroys the creation and returns to snake forms:

> [I will] destroy all that I have made; the earth shall return to the Abyss, to the surging flood, as in its original state. But I will remain with Osiris, I will transform myself into something else, namely a serpent, without men knowing or the gods seeing.[36]

This was the inevitable end, but it was also the continuous cosmic threat before the end of time. Hence, it was the pharaoh's duty to ensure stability and harmony on earth and in cosmos in order to guarantee the welfare and prosperity of humans and gods for as long as possible. This was the cosmic stability and result of rituals which ensured the upholding of Maat, the core of Egyptian civilization. The realization of Maat included pacifying or satisfying the divine realm as well as guaranteeing justice in the human realm.[37] Everything was structured around the cosmic waters and the process of creating cosmos out of chaos in a desert environment.

FIRST DYNASTY AND ABYDOS

The emergence of the first kingship seems to have been an event which the Egyptians were very well aware of: they recognized a first king of a first dynasty – Menes (or Narmer) – who was preceded by an Upper Egyptian king, 'Scorpion'.[38] The strong institutional government of Menes or his immediate successors led to centralization of all religious functions of the local chiefs together with their political functions into one person – the king. Herodotus records (Histories II.99) that the Egyptian priests believed that King Menes diverted the River Nile and built the city of Memphis. Frankfort writes:

> The perfect consonance between the new political and the established cosmological conceptions gave to his creation a compelling authority. A state dualistically conceived must have appeared to the Egyptians the manifestation of the order of creation in human society, not the product of a temporary constellation of power. It was in this respect that Menes' victory differed from any other conquest which earlier kings, like Scorpion, had made.[39]

Both the red and the white crown seem to have originated in Upper Egypt. Although the red crown was in historic times associated with

Lower Egypt, it appears to have its origin among Predynastic rulers of Naqada. The red crown is depicted on a vessel from Naqada, which probably dates to late Naqada I (c. 3600 BCE). This is by far the oldest occurrence of the red crown as royal regalia, and it may have been used by the local ruler. The white crown originated at a later date and appears in the late Predynastic period on two royal artefacts. The first evidence of the double crown may stem from a rock-cut inscription of Djet in the western desert, although normally it is attributed to the famous Abydos label of Den. The Narmer Palette indicates that the white crown was superior to the red since the king depicted with the white crown is considerably larger than when he is wearing the red crown. The presumed superiority of the white crown may lie in its close association with the royal line of Hierakonpolis, which played a crucial role in the unification.[40]

According to tradition, the first major irrigation work was conducted by King Menes, the founder of the First Dynasty around 3000 BCE, who dammed the Nile somewhere near Memphis to protect the city. Moreover, the macehead of King Scorpion, the last of the Predynastic kings, depicts an irrigation work he supervised. The basin irrigation system was designed to capture the waters from the flood for the cultivation of a single winter crop. As early as the Old Kingdom there were attempts to enlarge the area of land with the aim of producing two crops a year, which was possible in areas where the subsoil had a plentiful supply of water. From the Early Dynastic periods it is here the ancient capitals of Egypt were made; the finest subsoil water in Egypt was at Abydos; Memphis had a very good supply, and also Thebes had good subsoil. Good subsoil was a major force in wealth accumulation. One crop a year produced sufficient food supplies for the population, but not a substantial surplus.[41]

The division of Egypt into nomes happened at some point before the beginning of the Third Dynasty.[42] During the First and the Second Dynasties the sun god Ra was not as dominant as he became in the Old Kingdom,[43] and Hornung has suggested that an evolution of the gods took place in the two first centuries of the third millennium whereby the gods were perceived and depicted in human form rather than as animals.[44] Still, it seems that the situation was more complex as the gods could be seen in animal and human form or in a mixture of both. Nevertheless, the constitution of the ancient Egyptian civilization took place in the Early Dynastic period, and among others, Flinders Petrie has maintained that all the significant traits of Egyptian culture had evolved before the end of the Third Dynasty.

The Early Dynastic period includes either the First and the Second Dynasties or the First to the Third Dynasties. The construction of the first pyramid under the reign of Djoser is seen as a major turning point and development in Egypt's history, and consequently starts the Pyramid Age, which today is more commonly described as the Old Kingdom. Culturally, however, it seems that the Third Dynasty had more in common with the two preceding ones than with the Fourth Dynasty, placing it within the Early Dynastic period and placing the start of the Old Kingdom in the Fourth Dynasty. The pharaohs of the three first dynasties were:[45]

First Dynasty (c. 3000–2890 BCE)	Second Dynasty (2890–686 BCE)	Third Dynasty (2686–13 BCE)
Narmer	Hetepsekhemwy	Netjerikhet (Djoser)
Aha	Nebra	
Djer (Zer)	Ninetjer	Sekhemkhet
Diet (Zet)	Weneg (Nubnefer)	Khaba
Merneith	Sened	Sanakht
Den	Peribsen (Sekhemib)	Huni
Anedjib	Khasekhem(wy)	
Semerkhet		
Qaa		

The first Egyptian kings were buried at Abydos, and 'It is usually an axiom of archaeology that treasure means trouble.'[46] In 1899–1900 Flinders Petrie conducted a rescue excavation at the royal cemetery. Abydos had been plundered by tomb robbers as well as excavated by Amélineau before Petrie started his work, and very few bodies were actually left in the subsidiary graves. According to Petrie:

> It might have seemed a fruitless and thankless task to work at Abydos after it had been ransacked by Mariette, and been for the last four years in the hands of Amélineau [...] My only reason was that the extreme importance of results from there led to a wish to ascertain everything possible about the early royal tombs after they were done with others [...] to rescue for historical study.[47]

Despite the unfavourable conditions of preservation and the disturbances, this cemetery contained invaluable finds from the very constitution of the Egyptian civilization. In 1921, Petrie conducted further investigations of graves at Abydos. About a mile from the Royal Tombs a line of graves from the First Dynasty was found, and Petrie organized excavations at the site. He found three great squares of graves belonging to the time of King Zer, King Zet and Queen Merneit.[48]

The royal cemetery at Abydos is called Umm el-Qaab, the Arabic for the 'Mother of Pots' due to the richness of surface finds. Apart from the burials of the kings themselves, and more importantly from a cosmogonic water perspective, are the subsidiary graves. Petrie called the group of graves the 'Tombs of the Courtiers'. They consist of three groups of brick-lined graves.

There are hundreds of subsidiary burials associated with each king in the beginning of the First Dynasty, declining to some dozens at the end of the dynasty. The courtiers were buried all at once because the brickwork was yet soft and had slipped down over many of the burials. The killing of the court upon the king's death ensured the preservation of an orderly government. Nobody could survive the king, and everybody knew that.[49] Around each royal tomb, a large square pit is surrounded by rows of subsidiary graves. These great squares of graves enclosed large areas, which were probably used for ceremonies. The enclosure of Zer alone equals that of four of the Royal Tombs with all the subsidiary graves (fig. 37). Hence, if these enclosed spaces were used for ceremonies, they can be seen as an early stage of what later became the lower temple of pyramids in the Fourth and the Fifth Dynasties. Aha's mortuary complex comprises of a series of 34 subsidiary burials.[50] Djer's mortuary comprises of 318 subsidiary burials. In his 1925 publication Petrie refers to the whole complex including both the upper and lower cemeteries. Petrie sums up the subsidiary burials as follows: 'The graves connected with Zer are 326 above and 269 below, total 595; of Zet 174 + 154 = 328; of Merneit 41 + 80 = 121 and a few lost; of Den 121, of Azab 63; of Semerkhet 69; of Qa 26.'[51]

According to Petrie's own interpretation, those who were most intimate with the king were buried around him where only those who were closest to the king could worship, whereas members of the court staff were buried on the edge of the desert in places that were open to all royal worshippers.[52]

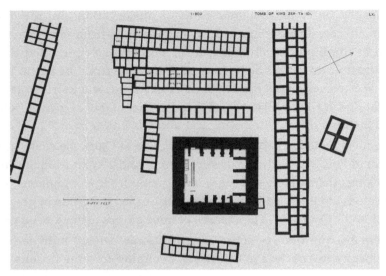

37. King Zer's tomb with subsidiary graves.

A striking feature of the burial of Narmer compared to that of Aha and the kings who succeeded him in the First Dynasty is the absence of any subsidiary or retainer burials. The average age of those who followed Aha in death was under 25 years, which strongly suggests that they were killed or committed suicide as part of the king's funeral. The absence of any subsidiary graves in Narmer's burial has parallels to the former Predynastic funerals.[53]

It is important to determine whether some or all of those buried were ritually killed prior to, or as part of, their funeral. The number of graves is too high for those buried to all have died a natural death. There are several indications that they were ritually killed and buried a short time after the king died or as part of the royal ritual itself. More than 20 men between the ages of 20 and 30, or under 25 years, were buried in Aha's tomb, a group too uniform to have died naturally.[54] Moreover, there are clear evidences that many of the dead were buried alive. With regards to the subsidiary graves of Zer, Petrie writes:

> In [grave] 537 the position is most peculiar; the heels have been tied tight back to the hips to prevent action; the body was thrown in, chest down, over a large boulder in the soil; the head has been twisted round upright, and at right angles to the spine literally; the left arm has been thrust up from below with the hand before the face [...] the skull rested truly on the atlas vertebra, and that all the vertebrae of the neck were in articulation down to the straight

line of the spine. The double twist of the head at right angles was entirely made while the body was fresh [...] the position proved that this man had been endeavouring to raise his head above the earth as the grave was being filled [...] 544 is another example suggesting, by the outstretched fore-arm, and the other hand outspread, that there was some consciousness at burial.[55]

This pattern is also similar in the burials around the tombs of Qa and of Khasekhemwy. One feature which caught Petrie's attention were the walls built of soft bricks and in a hurry, and the burials of the courtiers took place within a few days. In the words of Petrie:

> This hasty burial of a large number of bodies at one time showed that the persons had been intentionally killed at the funeral of the king. The burials now described confirm this by evidence that some were partly conscious at burial. From the absence of any broken bones, and the signs of partial consciousness, it seems likely that they were stunned (perhaps by a sand-bag) and buried before coming to. This would be the most rapid and painless death possible.[56]

Semerkhet's tomb, however, showed a change from the previous generations. The subsidiary burials were arranged next to the main burial chamber, and the location may indicate that these burials could have been covered by the same superstructure as the king's. This strongly suggests human sacrifices. The dead in these subsidiary graves were most likely the king's retainers and probably also women from the harem. Since they were buried at the same time as the king, they must also have died more or less at the same time and at least before the funeral was closed, and hence, this suggests ritual killing was part of the ritual. Qaa's tomb followed the same plan as that of his predecessor, which then also suggests the practice of retainer sacrifice.[57] Thus, numerous human sacrifices took place in the royal cult throughout the First Dynasty, although one cannot say that all those who were buried in the subsidiary graves where sacrificed during the kings' funerals. Nevertheless, this practice would have ensured not only that all the servants were loyal and faithful to the king, but also that they would have defended the king from outsiders by any means, including their own lives.[58]

SECOND AND THIRD DYNASTIES

The history of the Second Dynasty rulers is little known and obscure, with regards to both the order and number of rulers. There might have been internal tensions during the middle of the dynasty since

Seth appears in the royal titulary under Peribsen. The power could have been divided between kings in the north and the south, and as documented on the Palermo stone, the significant lower inundation as a consequence of ecological factors may have been important in the apparent tensions. This is also evident in the royal titularies.

The burial of Hetepsekhemwy broke with the royal tradition of being buried at Abydos, and the relocation of the royal funerals to Saqqara represents a fundamental change. Moreover, the architecture of the royal tomb was entirely new, and these changes must have had a historic importance, although it is difficult to say exactly what. Peribsen chose to replace the Horus-falcon surrounding the *serekh* with the Seth animal, and he was buried with the kings of the First Dynasty at Abydos, but his mortuary cult seems to have taken place at Saqqara. It is possible that he descended from the First Dynasty's royal family, but he may as well have intended to attest legitimacy, and these changes may suggest new developments in the ideology of kingship as well as religion. The town Sethroë in the north-eastern Delta was in later times known to have been the cult centre of Seth. Hence, although not proven, the town could have been part of Egypt and Peribsen may have established the Seth cult during his reign, with the consequence that he must have ruled both Upper and Lower Egypt.[59]

Khasekhem(wy) was the last of the kings in the Second Dynasty. At the beginning of his reign he adopted the Horus name Khasekhem, which means 'the power has appeared'. Later he added the Seth animal and changed his name to Khasekhemwy: 'the two powers have appeared'. Of special interest is the fact that the Seth animal on the top of the serekh wears the red crown whereas the Horus falcon wears the usual double crown. Khasekhemwy was buried at Abydos in a mortuary construction in which both design and symbolism point towards the Step Pyramid.[60]

In the Third Dynasty five rulers are recorded in both the Abydos king list and the Turin Canon, but there are difficulties in the correlation of both the names and the order. However, the archaeological evidence favours Netjerikhet (Djoser) as the first king of the Third Dynasty and hence Khasekhemwy's direct successor. The equation of Netjerikhet and Djoser does not appear on any contemporary material, but appears on the much later Sehel Famine Stela. Importantly, the first pyramid, the

Step Pyramid, was built by Djoser.[61] Thus, the 'Pyramid Age' started with Djoser, and this tradition became a watershed in the history of Egypt and the world. But monumental architecture does not appear in an ideological vacuum, and the watershed has to be seen in relation to the River Nile itself and the mythology and cosmology it created.

SETH IN HISTORY AND MYTHOLOGY

'In hot countries the sun is generally regarded as an evil, and in cold as a beneficent being.'[62] Thus, the Egyptian context seems at the outset to represent something different and extraordinary. The environment is drier and, from a rainmaking perspective, one would not expect sun worship in a desert, but rather an extreme focus on the life-giving waters in the form of the river or rain, and in particular the Nile. Still, 'there is sufficient to show that the fertility duties of the pharaohs were double ones, originally concerning the rain but later the Nile'.[63] One must therefore approach the processes and transformations of the life-giving waters in their various forms, but first and foremost consider the change from a rain ideology to a river ideology. The Narmer palette represents the Upper Egyptian victory over Lower Egypt under the patronage of Horus the Falcon. This also represents the replacement of the Seth ideology with the Horus mythology as a sun ideology. As will be shown, this is also when the change from a rainmaking religion to a river religion took place. Hence, the rise of the ancient Egyptian civilization went hand in hand with the constitution of a new religion in a new water-world which coincided with the end of the Neolithic Wet Phase ending around 3000 BCE or a bit later.

Seth was a traditional sky fertility god because 'he was a god of rain, storm, lightening, thunder, and earthquakes; meteorites and thunder-bolts symbolized his strength, his power to open the earth and to fertilize it, and also his power of destruction.'[64] Rain itself or the Sky from which it originates as the Giver of Life is often developed into a god, and the sky gods are often the supreme ones.[65] The rain-god Seth fits very well into this scheme: in rainmaking ideologies there is always an interplay between rain and the sun since it is their combination that gives life. Thus, Horus as a Sky god would have had the role of the sun god in relation to the rain-god Seth. Contrary to what one might have expected, with the change from a rain-ideology to a river-ideology in Egypt, it seems that the river god remained celestial instead of becoming terrestrial: the former sun god Horus incorporated all of the river's ideological qualities and capacities in the form of the sun. Hence, the river god was visualized in the old rainmaking cosmology as the sun, but the life-giving waters had changed from rain to the River Nile. The images of the divine continued, but their contents and cosmic functions had been transformed. It is in this light that one must see the development of the Osiris mythology.

In Pharaonic times Naqada was an important centre for the cult of Seth. Seth was closely associated with the king when the state formation took place; he was a local god at Naqada. The Seth animal is first found on the Scorpion macehead, symbolizing either a provincial deity or an aspect of royal power. 'The association between a major early archaeological site (Nagada) and the cult of one of the gods most closely associated with kingship (Seth) is encouragingly neat.'[66] Hierakonpolis, a second early site, also contains the essence of a similar association but this time with Horus, and it is much more complex.[67] Moreover, Seth was a royal and divine titular in the earliest dynasties together with Horus. 'She who sees Horus and Seth' is a queen's title in the First Dynasty, according to a seal found by Petrie[68] and the Second Dynasty Pharaoh Khasekhemwy was addressed 'Horus and Seth: the two powers have arisen; the two lords are at peace in him' (Khasekhemwy-nebwy-hetep-imef).[69] 'References in the Pyramid Texts to the incorporation of Horus and Seth in the king [is] a fact which doubtless represent an historical theological standpoint,'[70] and Horus and Seth also appear as representatives of Lower and Upper Egypt respectively on fragments of a statuette of Kephren from the Fourth Dynasty.[71]

According to Sethe, Egypt was unified twice in Predynastic times, and the conflict between Seth and Horus was political. The first unified kingdom was conceived under Osiris, the god of Busiris. Osiris was, following Sethe, originally a king, but he was deified and became the god of the nome, Andjety. Upper Egypt rebelled under the patronage of Seth. Lower Egypt crushed the rebellion and formed a second united kingdom with Heliopolis as its capital. However, as Griffiths has noted, the problem with this theory is:

> If the conflict of Horus and Seth represents a Predynastic war, it will have to be dated, it seems, to the era previous to the Predynastic union, since the two deities were apparently associated in an Upper Egyptian alliance in the period before the union under Menes.[72]

Emerey has argued, on the other hand, that Seth was the original god of Egypt and remained so even though the dynastic people who invaded Egypt were worshippers of Horus. Thus, the struggle between Seth and Horus reflects a religious conflict irrespective of whether there was an invasion or not.[73]

'Egypt' (*Kmt*) literally means 'black land', probably referring to the black soil of the alluvial plain of the Nile in contrast to the 'red land' of sand and rocks in the desert. This division goes mythologically back to the partitioning between the gods Horus and Seth where the whole of the Black Land was given to Horus and the Red Land to Seth.[74] Hence, the presence of Seth constituted parts of the Egyptian worldview throughout history, and Seth played a constitutive part of the Egyptian society from the rise and unification of the civilization. However, the Narmer palette shows the unification of Upper and Lower Egypt under the patronage of Horus where Upper Egypt was the dominant part. Although Seth's political role in the formation and unification of Egypt is uncertain, he undoubtedly played an important religious role.

Originally, Seth was a rain and storm god – 'a god of the blessed yet dangerous storms'.[75] This fits with Neolithic Wet Phase, but as the rain became rarer everything from the desert became sinister to the peasants, and Seth eventually became the personification of evil. There is a variation in the relation between Horus, Seth, and Osiris, which may be seen as four stages in the development of this relation. Firstly, in certain spells Horus and Seth are identified with the king, and Osiris who is hardly mentioned, has no royal associations. Secondly, in other spells Horus and Seth are closely connected with the king, but not identified as such, and Osiris has no associations to the king. Thirdly, the deceased king is closely associated and identified with Osiris. Horus and Seth are described as cooperating with the king. Finally, the deceased king is identified with Osiris and Seth is the enemy and slayer of the Osiris-King. Following Griffiths, 'It is quite possible that this inconsistency is not due to any mythological fusion; it may rather reflect a change in the political position of Seth.'[76]

Although Osiris is not attested by name before the Fifth Dynasty, the pairing of Horus and Seth which is crucial in the later Osiris myth, is found from the middle of the First Dynasty, 'antedating the first attestations of Osiris by six centuries or more'.[77] One of the emblems associated with Osiris, the Djed pillar, was found as two ivory objects in the grave goods in a tomb at Helwan dated to the First Dynasty.[78] During the late Second Dynasty, Seth gained a particular prominence, temporarily replacing and rejoining Horus, and a stone slab from Helwan dated to the late Second Dynasty, which belonged to a royal priest, has the inscription calling him 'Seth is beautiful'.[79] Thus, Seth was venerated and seen as the most important god, which provides the background and forms the point of departure for understanding the conflict with Horus.

Seth has two contrasting roles, one of which is positive. In the solar myth he fought together with the sun god. Standing at the prow of the sun barque he pierced the dragon Apopis with his mighty spear. The dragon, who had swallowed a huge amount of water, gushed forth all the water from his body when he was pierced. Ra used death in the fight against the absolute destruction, personified by Apopis.[80] Seth's role was also related to water rituals. Osiris or Osiris King is carried in the water, and Seth's role is that of a ship in the funerary voyage.[81] On the other hand, Seth is perceived as evil. Wainwright argues:

> As the rains grew rarer and the Egyptians came to rely more and more on the Nile, which they were in a process of taming, so Seth slipped from his ancient high estate. He, his rain and fertility rites, became a nuisance and an offence to his people until by the end he had become the personification of all evil, the very Devil himself.[82]

THE HORUS-SETH FEUD

In the original Horus-Seth feud the gods were brothers, which is similar to the Osiris-Seth feud where Seth is Osiris' brother. In the former myth and feud Horus and Seth are equal in power whereas in the latter Horus is initially inferior as a child, but in both myths he turns out superior. 'Unlike Horus, Seth is not given a double parentage. He is the brother of Osiris and the son of Geb and Nut [...] he is sometimes called the brother of Horus, and this is the salient discrepancy.'[83] The child Horus in the Osiris myth is a different god from the strong Horus who violates Seth, and it is plausible that the Hathor-cow as depicted on the Narmer palette was the mother of the Horus-falcon, but when the myth became Osirianized the genealogy was adjusted and Isis became his mother. Thus, it seems that Horus did not originally belong to the Osiris myth.[84]

In the *Pyramid Texts* the quarrel between Horus and Seth without references to Osiris is more frequent in the earlier pyramids of Wenis and Teti in the Fifth Dynasty than in those later ones of Pepi I, Merenre and

Pepi II in the Sixth Dynasty, but the difference is not great. In those cases where Seth is mentioned by name, he is more frequently related to Horus, but in the cases in which he is coupled with Osiris, he is more hostile. In the two earlier pyramids there are only a few allusions to the Seth-Osiris feud where Seth is Osiris' enemy, but it becomes fairly frequent in the three later pyramids. The myth of the conflict between Horus and Seth was the earliest; later it was absorbed by the Osirian myth so that the story became more complex. The fundamental change is that the deceased king was identified with Osiris, an idea which seems to have coexisted with the notion that the living king was Horus.[85] However, the Osiris myth seems never to have been a coherent whole, but rather served as a source of allusions for other religious texts:[86]

> When the deceased King was first identified with Osiris, the work of the living King or Horus gradually caused, by means of spells and offering-rites, the fusion of the Horus myth and the Osiris myth. Since Horus, now as son of the deceased king, becomes the son of Osiris, henceforth the enemies of Horus are to be the enemies of Osiris; the stolen eye, snatched back from Seth, is now presented to Osiris.[87]

In the *Pyramid Texts* there is actually only one reference that Horus killed Seth in revenge in the Osiris mythology: 'He has smitten for you him who smote you as [an ox], he has slain for you him who slew you as a wild bull, he has bound for you who bound you' (Pyr. 1977). Similarly, it is also difficult to find a definite reference to the murder of Osiris. However, the vague allusions indicate that the murder of Osiris was a fundamental part of the myth, but there are also indications that he was not entirely destroyed which relate to his revivification. Moreover, Seth is also believed to have drowned Osiris. Seth's penalty was to carry Osiris in what apparently is a water ritual: 'Horus has driven him off for you, for you are greater than he; he swims bearing you, that your strength is greater than his, so that they cannot thwart you' (Pyr. 588), which is followed by 'Horus comes and recognizes his father in you, you being young in your name of "Fresh Water"; Horus has split open your mouth for you' (Pyr. 589). Thus, it seems Seth was perceived as a benevolent god who, after having repented for the evil wrought by him, was cooperating with Horus for the benefit of the deceased king. Seth's carrying role is mainly that of a ship in a funerary voyage.[88] Traditionally, Seth also has a ritual role in the 'baptism of the Pharaoh', but he is not widely known for his sympathetic, cosmogonic and constructive aspects, rather the contrary.

Seth had three meanings: instigator of confusion, deserter and drunkard. These antisocial and dangerous qualities characterize Seth as a god. His followers were allegedly tortured and killed, and their blood drunk: 'Seize them, remove their heads, cut of their limbs, disembowel them, cut out their hearts, drink of their blood' (Pyr. 1286). Seth was homosexual (in relation to Horus), he was a murderer (killing Osiris), and he was repelling the Apopis snake. Seth was also perceived as a foreign god or lord of foreign countries. Seth revealed himself in the form of Ash, the chief god of the Libyans, Baal who was the chief god of the Western Semites, and Teshub, who was the chief god of the Hittites. All these gods were rain-, storm- or thunder-gods, which implies that the Egyptians were familiar with rain-gods, which no longer existed in Egypt, and therefore Seth was repelled. He was the lord of foreign countries where he gave rain and water, but not in Egypt, which must have been seen as a heinous act not worthy of a mighty Egyptian god, and consequently, over the course of history he was seen as a personification of evil and the Devil himself. However, Seth once was a fertility god who particularly had great sexual strength through, for example, rain, which he controlled by promoting the growth of plants.[89] He lost these powers, which were transferred to and transformed by Horus, which is dramatically expressed in the mythology of the original feud between Seth and Horus the Elder.

SETH'S TESTICLES AND HORUS' EYE

Horus' Eye plays a central role in both feuds of Horus-Seth and Osiris-Seth. As an oppositional pair 'wet' and 'dry' signify life and death: liquids are alive and dryness represents dying. When there is a finite and limited amount of goods like health and wealth, one person's health, wealth and gain can only come at the expense of others. One drinks 'health', which means that somebody else lacks the vital source:

> In symbolic terms, a pair of eyes may be equivalent to breasts or testicles. A single eye may be the phallus (especially the glans), the vulva, or occasionally the anus. The fullness of life as exemplified by such fluids as mother's milk or semen can thus be symbolized by the eye. Accordingly, threats to one's supply of such precious fluids can appropriately be manifested by the eye or eyes of others.[90]

What aspect of Ra or Horus' Eye does Seth want to rob or injure? The sun god is always victorious, but wounded during battle. It seems that the belief in Horus' Eye relates to or is the origin of the later belief known as the evil eye. The belief in the evil eye is the belief that it is possible to project harm by looking at another's property or person. The belief originated in the Near East in relation with the development of complex peasant-urban cultures and spread in all directions:[91]

> The evil eye is a fairly consistent and uniform folk belief complex based upon the idea that an individual, male or female, has the power, voluntarily or involuntarily, to cause harm on another individual or property merely by looking at or praising that person or property. The harm may consist of illness, or even death or destruction.[92]

Although the belief in the evil eye is associated with sorcery and witchcraft, its effects are different, and often include too little rain, destroyed crops, famines and accidents, and indeed, 'the most common effect of the evil eye is a *drying up* process'.[93] In Sumerian mythology, the evil eye took away the waters from the heavens and the storms sent no rain. In Spell 108 in the *Book of the Dead* one of the aspects to be feared from the demon of chaos was his malevolent eye. In P. Louvre 3239, a demon is described as follows: 'He is like Seth, the disturber, / the snake, the bad worm, the water in whose mouth / is fire, the one who comes with a furious face, / his eyes marked(?) with deceit, in order to do / great mischief [...].'[94] Seth's eyes seem to be most feared, but it is not in the usual sense of a permanent dread because Seth's eyes are bent upon evil among the gods rather than humans.

Importantly, the eye metaphors are often expressed sexually in terms of phalluses:

> If a healthy eye, that is, a phallus, can spit or ejaculate, then an unhealthy one cannot. Given this logic, it is not impossible to imagine that a larger, more powerful eye may rob a given eye of its ability to produce liquid, or of the precious liquid itself.[95]

Turning to the *Pyramid Texts* and Egyptian mythology, the symbolism surrounding the eye is closely related to sexual metaphors and the transference of power.

The feud between Seth and Horus contains of two parts: first Horus is violated sexually by Seth and loses one of his eyes to him, but on the other hand, Horus tears off one or both of Seth's testicles. The second part of the myth describes how Horus regained his wounded eye and restored its powers.

Seth violated Horus homosexually as evident in the *Kahun Papyrus* and in *The Contendings of Horus and Seth*, but there are also vague references to the episode in the *Pyramid Texts*.[96] It is through this violation that Horus' Eye became wounded, and hence, the equivalence of eye and phallus is found in the Horus-Seth feud. In the homosexual episode in which Seth violates Horus there is a discharge from the wound in the eye, which can either be interpreted as caused by a blow or a sexual act. 'After Seth had withdrawn' suggests that something is 'dragged out', 'pulled out' or 'flowed out', which may indicate Seth's finger or phallus, although these are not mentioned as direct objects. If the meaning is to flow out, Horus' Eye can drip: 'The Eye of Horus drips upon the bush of [...]' (Pyr. 133). Because of Seth's actions, the eye becomes small and loses its strength; the eye's discharge can be seen as tears.[97] There are also other versions. Seth trampled on the eye: 'O Osiris the King, take the Eye of Horus which Seth has trampled' (Pyr. 73) whereas in Pyr. 60, Osiris prevents Seth from trampling on the eye. Seth has also eaten of the eye (Pyr. 61), but a more explicit reference to the life-giving waters is found is in Pyr. 88: 'O Osiris the King, take the Eye of Horus, the water in which he has squeezed out'. Hence, the life-giving capacities of Horus' eye were wounded. In the *Pyramid Texts* there are references to Horus' two eyes, 'Take the two Eyes of Horus, the black and the white [...]' (Pyr. 33), and it is only one of the eyes which have been injured by Seth. The other was called *The Sound Eye*. Horus' right eye was the sun and his left eye the moon.[98] The Solar Eye was wounded whereas the left eye, the moon, which became Osiris, remained untouched.

In this battle between Seth and Horus, Horus abducts one or both of Seth's testicles. Several sky-gods have been castrated by others, and in general this represents the supplanting of one by another. Seth, as the storm god, suffered this at the hands of Horus.[99] 'Horus has cried out because of his Eye, Seth has cried out because of his testicles, and there leaps up the Eye of Horus, who had fallen on yonder side of the Winding Waterway, so that it may protect itself from Seth [...]' (Pyr. 594). The bull came to symbolize the storm-god and was Seth's animal; 'Horus fell because of his Eye, the Bull [Seth] crawled away because of his testicles; fall! Crawl away!' (Pyr. 418). Min, however, who also was a sky god, was saved from this fate and turned into a fertility god. In the Nineteenth and the Twentieth Dynasties a hymn addressing Min as the 'Great Bull' is preceded by 'opening the rain-clouds, the wind on the river'. Thus,

'While Min himself could be called "the King upon the rain-clouds", his Bull was said to be "opening the rain-clouds, the wind on the river".'[100]

The abduction of Seth's testicles does not always mean castration and Seth does not become a eunuch, but it can also be seen as theft of seed, leading to Seth's impotence:

> The wily theft of seed in the myth becomes castration by violence in the cult, because there is no other means of taking away the sexual power of the sacrificial animal than castration. This castration in the cult to present Horus' clever stealing of the semen, may be ancient.[101]

After the battle Seth was no longer seen and worshipped as the virile god of thunder, and Seth's homosexual act threatened the cosmic order:

> The sacrifice of the testicles to Seth, however, never takes place separately, as far as can be ascertained, but in the conjunction with the Eye of Horus. This means that the eye and testicles are sacrificed to a double-god; Seth no longer has an individual place of his own, but is integrated in Horus.[102]

Seth is pacified and Horus has gained the former rain god's power, but only after he regained his wounded eye. After the eye is injured it is filled up, and consequently, all the former rainwater was now contained in Horus' Eye (fig. 38). Moreover, the goddess of spinning and weaving clothes is known as Tayet, and her clothes are referred to as 'the woven eye of Horus', for instance in Pyr. 1202 where it says 'head-band of green and red cloth which has been woven from the Eye of Horus in order to bandage therewith that finger of Osiris which has become diseased'. Thus, this relates Tayet to the process of embalming and linking the life-giving waters to death and further life.[103] The deceased's thirst is an important metaphor in the funerary rituals, as will be discussed later. In the 'Opening of the Mouth' ceremony the dead received the Eye of Horus which wells up with water. The Eye contained the 'fluids of life'.[104]

There is a huge variation in symbolism with regards to Horus' Eyes, but one prominent aspect of this symbolism is the association to political power. Seth's castration implies the seizure of political power. Seth is, as mentioned, said to have eaten one of the eyes: 'O Osiris the King, take the Eye of Horus, for little is that which Seth has eaten of it' (Pyr. 61). In the *Cannibal Hymn* it is said that 'He [the King] has eaten the Red Crown, He has swallowed the Green one' (Pyr. 410). Seth ate the Egyptian crowns, and the white crown was sometimes called the green crown,[105] making him a threat to cosmic stability and Egypt. Thus, there is an important

38. Horus the Falcon. From the Temple of Edfu.

transference of power, with Horus being interpreted as the national god of Lower Egypt, which was pointed out by Pleyte as early as 1865.[106] According to the *Memphite Theology*, which presented the new religious teachings in Menes' new capital, the quarrel between Seth and Horus was eventually settled by a divine tribunal led by Geb. The text originated in an early stage of the Egyptian monarchy, but the extant copy dates back to the eighth century BCE,[107] although the trial is referred to in the *Pyramid Texts* as well:

> The Ennead gathered to him (Geb) and he separated Horus and Seth [...] He prevented them from quarrelling and installed Seth as Upper Egyptian king, in Upper Egypt, at the place where he was born, in Su [...] And Geb put Horus as Lower Egyptian king in Lower Egypt, at the place where his father was drowned, at the 'Half of the Two Lands' (probably near Memphis). And so Horus was in his place, and Seth was in his place; and they agreed with each other as regards the Two Lands in Ajan (opposite Cairo), which is the frontier

(or separation) of the Two Lands [...] It suited Geb's heart ill that the portion of Horus was like that of Seth, and so Geb gave his heritage (entirely) to Horus, that is, the son of his son, his eldest (literally, 'his opener-of-the-body').[108]

Thus, originally Egypt was divided between Seth in Upper Egypt and Horus in Lower Egypt. Horus became the king of the Two Lands not as a conqueror but as the rightful heir since he was Osiris' eldest son. A striking feature of Seth is that he is not destroyed or annihilated, but removed to be with the sun god in the sky where he can thunder, and according to *The Chester Beatty Papyri*, 'people will be afraid of him'.[109] Hence, as will be argued later, he cannot be annihilated because he has a fundamental cosmogonic role in the creation of cosmos and the constitution of society, or more precisely, in the dualism between chaos and cosmos since cosmos originates from chaos.

THE SUN AND WATER

From around 2600 BCE onwards, the king received the title 'son of Ra' and the sun cult was institutionalized with Djoser and the Step Pyramid.[110] Horus the Elder did not primarily represent the Sun, but encompassed everything: he was Horus the Falcon, the Lord of Heaven and the earthly king.[111] According to Wainwright, the former sky gods were either transformed into fertility gods or became solarized. Horus was solarized and gained absolute power; Min became a fertility god, whereas Seth lost all his powers and became the incarnation of evil.[112]

A transformation and transfiguration of power thus took place. The life-giving waters – from rain or river – were the object of the feud between Seth and Horus, which means the life and prosperity of all of Egypt were at stake. It is therefore necessary to focus on the key qualities and characteristics of the sun or the sun god. This will be elaborated more thoroughly later, but here follow some important features.

Movement and cosmic demarcation. The pharaoh's realm was often described as 'that which the sun encircles', or, in other words, the earth, while the name Ra means probably only 'the sun disc'.[113] The Egyptians described the sun and the moon as sailing round the world in boats, intimating that these bodies owed their power of movement, as well as their support and nourishment, to the principle of humidity. The two boats are a symbolic, polar opposite pair or dual unit of day and night/east and west, which comprise the total movement of the sun.[114] 'The divine power which is manifest in the sun thus appears, in its fullness, to surpass all and comprise all [...] the sun represents the divine in a form which far surpasses even the divinity of the kings.'[115]

Purity. The sun god is closely associated with ablutions and purity. Before the king could enter the temple, he was washed, and after death, he was washed before he could enter the kingdom of the sun god. The sun god was reborn every morning from the womb of the sky goddess, and underwent daily lustrations at dawn from sacred pools. The pharaoh underwent the same ritual washing after death as he did when alive in the 'House of the Morning'.[116] Thus, the immanent life-giving qualities of water were of utmost importance: 'This cold water of yours, O Osiris, this cold water of yours, O King, has gone forth to your son, has gone forth to Horus. I have come and I bring to you the Eye of Horus, that heart may be refreshed possessing it' (Pyr. 22). Cold water was life, but only through the Eye.

The Eye is water. A common theme throughout Egyptian mythology is that the Eye or the sun disc contains the life-giving waters and brings forth the Nile's inundation. 'O Osiris the King, take the water which is in the Eye of Horus, do not let go of it. O Osiris the King, take the Eye of Horus, the water in which Thoth has seen hrs-sceptre, a db3-sceptre and a mace' (Pyr. 43). In the New Kingdom the solar life-giving aspects were elaborately expressed in the descriptions and the qualities of Amun-Re.[117]

The Crown is the Eye. In Pyr. 410 Seth ate the red and the green/white crown, symbolically represented as eyes. There is thus a close metaphorical link between the eye and the crown:

> O King, the dread of you is the intact Eye of Horus, (namely) the White Crown [...] O King, I provide you with the Eye of Horus, the Red Crown rich in power and many-natured, that it may protect you, O King, just as it protects Horus [...] (Pyr. 900–1)

The king claims his rights as that of Horus through the Eye: 'My refuge is my Eye, my protection is my Eye, my strength is my Eye, my power is my Eye' (Pyr. 320). Importantly, as expressed in this spell, it is the control and access to the life-giving waters which give the king divine legitimacy to the throne and equips him as a god: 'O Osiris the King, take the water which is in the Eye of Horus. O King, fill your hand with the hrs-sceptre, that it may equip you as a god. Do not let go of it! Beware lest you let go of it! – a hrs-sceptre' (Pyr. 47). Thus, this seems to be a parallel to the divine rainmaker who gives the necessary life-giving water to his people; the one who has the crown is the controller of the water-worlds.

Warmth and heat. In some of the earlier allusions Seth seems to be the giver of light when he is transferred to heaven. More importantly, Seth is also seen as the power of the heat in the sun:[118] 'Your tomb(?), O Osiris, your shade which is over you, O Osiris, which repels your striking power, O Seth' (Pyr. 1487). Anthes has argued that Seth's character as his brother's murderer 'appears closely correlated with the hostility of the desert and its murderous heat, and the destruction of the testicles of Seth may recall the sterility of the desert'.[119] Qualities that we normally associate with the sun – warmth and heat – were actually qualities associated with Seth and not the sun disc. Thus, our normal conception of the sun's rays as heat-giving were not seen as an intrinsic quality of the sun; however, sun rays brought forth the life-giving waters in the form of blood or the most precious bodily fluid. As a preliminary summary, sun worship is not a worship of the sun as a warm and intensely burning disc as it appears in the sky – these are Seth's deadly qualities. On the other hand, the sun disc and the sun god represent numerous life-giving aspects expressed in water metaphors, which we initially would not have associated with the sun.

Hence, the sun is water and life and this has to be seen in relation to the original feud between Seth as a rain-god and Horus symbolized as the sun in an environment where the rain gradually disappeared and the civilization became totally dependent upon the annual inundation of the Nile. The life-giving waters were transformed from Seth into an already existing pantheon of gods in which Horus was the only supreme one left, and he was the Lord of Heaven, the Falcon, the Sun and the living king. The concept of the god as the ruler of the universe did not exist in Egypt before the kingship of Horus was established with the unification around 3000 BCE.[120]

SETH MURDERS OSIRIS

Although the conflict between Horus and Seth is closely linked with Osiris, they had separate origins and were only later merged together. Osiris is believed to have been an ancient divine king who reigned in the Delta.[121] The Osirian form was most likely developed in the Gerzean period (*c.* 3500–3200 BCE) in Egypt, characterized by hunting for food. With the unification and the rise of a temple priesthood, the Osirian rite was modified in accordance with the new political organization. It was purely agricultural and the great rite was solemnized at Abydos.[122] Osiris was the dead king *par excellence* and the ethical and judicial functions of the sun god were not given to him before the Sixth Dynasty when he becomes the judge of the dead.[123] As a result of the fusion of the Osiris and Horus myths, Seth's hostility was extended to Horus as the son of Isis. The reason that Osiris was identified with the deceased and not the living king is probably that Osiris in his original character was a god of the dead and since the first time Osiris appears in the religious literature, it is as a king of the dead.[124] On the other hand, it has been suggested that he originally was a god of vegetation in addition to being Moon God, King and Judge of the Dead. The Nile represented life and fecundity, symbolizing life surpassing death and consequently the victory of good over evil. Death and resurrection corresponded to the Egyptian agricultural year. However, Osiris is also perceived to have originated as human king, and normally depicted as a dead king. Thus, one may perceive Osiris in two ways: he originated as a king ruling over life and death, and hence was also attributed the role and realm of nature and vegetation; or on the other hand, he was accepted as a king because of his characteristics as a god of vegetation.[125] Therefore, Frankfort argues, 'It seems futile to inquire whether there are historical foundations for the myth and person of Osiris.'[126] I will, on the other hand, argue that it is still possible to shed new lights on these issues by a water perspective.

Following the mythology, the king was 'born in the Abyss before the sky existed, before the earth existed, before that which was to be made firm existed, before turmoil existed, before that fear which arose on account of the Eye of Horus' (Pyr. 1040) and in (Pyr. 1463) it is also referred to that the king 'was born before the Eye of Horus was gouged out(?), before the testicles of Seth were torn off'. In real life 'The crown prince, born a man, became Horus not before his father had become Osiris. Osiris and Horus were by their very nature the royal deceased father and his living royal son' and consequently, 'it was the king's transition from Horus into Osiris which confirmed his existence as an eternal being'.[127] Thus, according to Anthes, the two questions which the Egyptian sages solved by the Horus lineage were, first, how is it possible to understand the death of a god who has been a human being, and second, how is it possible to conceive the universal god.[128]

Seth murders Osiris by drowning, which is evident in the classical sources but also in the *Pyramid Texts* (see also Pyr. 24, 615), 'You [Isis] have come seeking your Brother Osiris, for his brother has thrown him down on his side in yonder side of Ghsty' (Pyr. 972), 'They have found Osiris, his brother Seth having him laid him low in Nedit [...]' (Pyr. 1256) and 'Osiris was laid low by his brother Seth, but He who is in Nedit moves, his head was raised by Re [...]' (Pyr. 1500).

According to the myth, Seth inflicted a wound on Osiris' leg from where the annual inundation poured out, and the leg was connected with Elephantine. In later versions of the myth, Osiris' body was dismembered into 42 parts identical to the 42 nomes of Egypt, which symbolized the body of Osiris, and Osiris is sometimes called 'the dismembered one'. The 42 districts were seen as the limbs of Osiris, and Egypt as his body. The ritual of embalming Osiris included and applied to the whole country and united, inspirited and renewed it.[129] Horus gave his father the Eye, which contained the rejuvenating powers, which in turn restored life to Osiris.

Assmann writes:

> In the context of the myth of Osiris, the dismemberment of the god's body has dual function and meaning, to which corresponds a dual tradition. Seth has not only killed his brother Osiris, but also, in a second act of violence, cut his corpse to pieces and thrown these into the water.[130]

The motif in this myth seems to present the same theme as presented in the original myth of the feud between Seth and Horus the Elder. Seth robs the life-giving water. In the older myth Horus the Elder snatched back his Eye and made Seth impotent, in the Osiris myth it is Horus the Son who killed Seth and restored the life-giving waters as the flood by giving his Eye to Osiris who was rejuvenated through the water.

Nile water was confounded with Osiris since he was drowned in the Nile. According to Herodotus, a person became holy if he was drowned in the Nile, which has to be seen in light of Osiris' death in the river. The floating of Osiris in the water rather than the drowning probably mirrored the cultivated land which submerged in the annual Nile flood.[131] Following the *Pyramid Texts*, 'Horus has assembled the gods for you, and they will never escape from you in the place where you have gone. Horus has mustered the gods for you, and they will never escape from you in the place where you were drowned' (Pyr. 615) and 'Receive the efflux which issued from you, for Horus has caused the gods to assemble for you in the place where you went. Receive the efflux which issued from you, for Horus has caused his children to muster for you in the place where you drowned' (Pyr. 766).

The drowning of Osiris in water may imply that water was seen as a symbol of death and chaos, but that this perception was changed to signify resurrection and rejuvenation. This is the crucial aspect of the Osiris myth, not the murder and dismemberment. 'Osiris is death from which life arises, and Seth is life which produces death.'[132] Osiris was resurrected, but he did not reascend to the throne. Hence, Seth's work was not entirely undone since he also had a vital function in the cosmic order.[133] The Osiris-Seth duality is that of life and death. Horus is the son who saves his father, but it is possible to see this relation more intimately:

> Since Horus was the living king and Osiris the deceased one, the slaying of Osiris was strictly speaking the slaying of Horus, who in consequence of his being slain, became Osiris [...] Horus, the son, felled Seth, regained the eye of Horus, and restored it to Osiris; for Osiris, who was Horus when he lost it, was its genuine owner.[134]

It seems that the concept of the eye was intimately connected with kingship rather than celestial notions, which may explain why it was necessary to connect as closely as possible the myth of Horus' Eye with the story of Horus as the son of Osiris.[135] Memphis was believed to have a special role in 'sustaining' Egypt because the interred body of Osiris was drawn ashore here by Isis and Nephthys. This 'finding' of Osiris, which is described as the recovery of his body by Isis and Nephthys, is ritually represented by the rite where a jar of fresh Nile water is lifted up. Moreover, it was believed that Osiris was buried in Memphis, and hence, it was a centre from which vital forces radiated and explained the extraordinary fertility of the region.[136] Horus became the king and received Egypt whereas Seth was driven out into the desert, hence he is not given the red land but he is driven away to it.[137]

THE CONTINUANCE OF SETH IN THE MYTHOLOGY

The feud between Horus and Seth and then Osiris and Seth not only enabled the divine kingship, but formed the very basis for the annual inundation. Cosmogonically, 'the death of a god signifies the transition from ontology to history. The divine enters the realm of human life and anticipates its pattern. The death of a god signals the integration of mankind into the mechanism of the cosmos.'[138] Therefore, Seth cannot be seen as evil in a strict sense since he is the one who takes the cosmic offering or scapegoat position of killing his brother, which enables the rise, unification and resilience of ancient Egypt. This task was assigned to a rain-god, because when the rain declined Seth as a god lost his importance as the life-giving source for the people and welfare of Egypt. One life-giving god gave room and enabled another – Horus – whose Eye had transformed and incorporated the former rain ideology into a river ideology; the Eye was a symbolic well of water from which the annual inundation originated. Nevertheless, this mythology was incomplete, and only through death and the transfiguration and rejuvenation of Osiris, in which the Nile was his exudation, did the river ideology become complete.

Still, one may ask why Seth continued to exist as a god when he did not fulfil his original role as a rain-god. In other contexts raingods who did not fulfil their function of procuring rain ceased to be perceived as divinities, and soon faded out of society and history since they could not procure the life-giving waters.[139] In Egypt, on the other hand, the mythology was built around Seth who enabled the annual flood through the murder of Osiris. Hence, he could not die and disappear in history. In a later context, Plutarch describes an important feature in this regard:

> Hence not unreasonably do they say in the myth that [while] the Soul of Osiris is eternal and indestructible, Typhon [Seth] often tears his Body in pieces and makes it disappear, and that Isis seeks it wandering and puts it together again. For the Real and Conceivable-by-the-mind-alone and Good is superior to destruction and change.[140]

The dismemberment of Osiris' body and the scattering across all of Egypt convey associations of ritual fertilization throughout the country. Plutarch refers to Osiris' body as *frequently dismembered*, which probably means it was annually dismembered. From a cosmogonic perspective this fits very well with the yearly inundation, and since the flood is Osiris' efflux, Osiris must be murdered each year to provide the life-giving waters. Consequently, Seth continued to play a fundamental role long after he lost his rainmaking powers because he guaranteed the yearly flood by murdering Osiris, and *the dismemberment is the flood* which covered all of Egypt. Finally, Egypt means 'black land' in contrast to the red and sterile desert, which belonged to Seth. Hence, Egypt itself as a fertile land was the antithesis of Seth and death. This dichotomy was necessary for the development of the river religion. Egypt was the land that was flooded by the Nile, and the black land was also the fertilizing silt which created prosperity and a fruitful harvest for the ancient Egyptians.

THE ANCIENT EGYPTIAN RELIGION AND *MAAT*

Approaching religion in Egypt is a challenge because there was no word for 'religion' in the ancient Egyptian language.[141] Nevertheless, 'religion' as a term will be used since it denotes a web of worldviews, cosmologies, beliefs and rituals. However, 'Egyptian religion does not consist of one connected logical system but is composed of a series of cults which have been roughly synthesized to fit, more or less harmoniously, into a general system.'[142] The *Pyramid Texts* highlight the Egyptian 'tendency to assemble an accumulated mass of material without synthesis. Contradictions are not solved but presented side by side.'[143] Since the discovery of the first texts, Egyptologists have debated the key question of whether the religion of the ancient Egyptians was monotheistic or polytheistic. One can argue that it was both and that neither of the concepts capture the true nature of the religion.[144] The dilemma was put precisely as early as 1880:

> Throughout the whole range of [ancient] Egyptian literature, no facts appear to be more certainly proved than these: (1) that the doctrine of one God and that of many gods were taught by the same men; (2) that no inconsistency between the two doctrines was thought of. Nothing, of course, can be more absurd if the Egyptians attached the same meaning to the word God that we do. But there may perhaps be a sense of the word which admits of its use for many as well as for one.[145]

On the one hand, the Egyptian word which is translated as 'god' has the form of *nutar* in earlier translations whereas present transcriptions give it the form *nṯr*. The Coptic language shows that at least for the latest phase of Egyptian religion, *nṯr* = *noute*, could be used in a monotheistic sense, and thus becomes synonymous with *theos*. Hence, the translation of *nṯr* as 'god' is justified although it had a variety of meanings in ancient Egypt. On the other hand, the intellectual foundation of Egyptian polytheism – insofar as it exists – is that the divine must be differentiated. Unity consists of diversity. Egypt is the unification of the 'Two Lands' or 'Upper and Lower Egypt'; space is 'sky and earth', totality is 'the existent and the non-existent', etc. In polytheistic religions it is common for each god to have a multiplicity of names, and Egypt is no exception. Apart from syncretism in general, gods could be linked to each other in at least three ways; firstly, kinship – a god could be married to another, son or daughter, etc.; secondly, a god (or king) could be an 'image' or 'manifestation' of another's *ba*, and thirdly, gods could be unified, and such unions mainly relate to Ra and Osiris.[146]

There were three crucial fundaments to the Egyptian ideology; firstly, there was continuity with the past; secondly, there was a mystical territorial unity over geographical and political subdivisions, and finally, there was stability and prosperity through the wise and pious government of the kings. Continuity is made explicit through the lists of deceased kings and 'the past was a cultural womb'[147] for religious and mythological narratives. In Egypt myths were sacred or culturally central narratives. Myths were incorporated in religious texts and hymns, and although usually without a narrative structure, they were often strongly literary. Contrary to many other religions, there are no narratives about the foundation of the civilization or 'heroic' phases or episodes in native Egyptian writings.[148] The myths hardly incorporate humanity, but are concerned with gods, the cosmos and the beginning or end of time. Therefore, myths have to be seen as historically important in society and not only referring to events which have taken place in the past. They are references to the basic constitution of the contemporary world.[149] The Egyptians did not distinguish between 'time' and 'eternity' or 'being' and 'becoming', which were more or less the same. Consequently, the original Creation was constantly repeated and interwoven into religious practice, and a fundamental source for existence was the non-existence and the yearly inundation.[150]

Religion in Egypt was cosmotheistic and throughout the Egyptian landscape there is the mythologically non-existent, especially in the desert, and hence, the whole environment and landscape is understood through mythology:

> For the Egyptians the entire extent of the existent, both in space and time, is embedded in the limitless expanses of the non-existent. The non-existent does not even stop short at the boundaries of the existent, but penetrates all of creation.[151]

The non-existent was present every day and at all times. It was not only an intellectual abstraction or imaginary concept, but it structured society and religious practice as human responses to the divine presence and transcendence.¹⁵² The state of non-existence before the Creation contained many negative and hostile elements, but there were also two positive and regenerative elements that constituted the state of non-existence: the limitless water or the primeval flood (Nun in Egypt), and the complete darkness. 'I was born in the Abyss before the sky existed, before the earth existed, before that which was to be made firm existed, before turmoil existed, before that fear which arose on account of the Eye of Horus existed' (Pyr. 1040).

Hence, the Egyptians encountered and faced the non-existent wherever they went. If they were digging foundations for a house, the groundwater that rose in the pit would remind them of the state before creation, and they poured sand to make a new 'primeval hill' so that existence might emerge from the primeval water. The yearly inundation brought the timeless non-existent back into the world of creation where, according to a Twenty-Fifth Dynasty text, 'the earth is Nun'. The primeval waters:

> In the natural cycle of the year the fertile land of the Nile Valley is also submerged in the primeval flood in the form of the inundation of the Nile, which 'forms (*msj*) that which exists', bringing to it new strength and fertility.¹⁵³

The sun god ruled the whole universe from the sky and the Duat, the netherworld. In the Duat the sun god underwent a transition whereby he died and was reborn the next day.¹⁵⁴ The positive aspect of the non-existent is the potential for fertility, renewal and rejuvenation. The sun dips into the primeval ocean daily. As it re-emerges from Nun it is purified and vivified. It was truly a rebirth giving life, and the world attained the perfection it had during the creation. 'Only through the non-existent does creation become possible, so that the gods and kings are especially dependent on it for the perpetual renewal of their work of creation and for the avoidance of lifeless finality', Hornung argues, 'In the Egyptian view the existent is in need of constant regeneration from the depths of the non-existent; only then can it maintain its living existence.'¹⁵⁵

Non-existence and disorder are hence at the very foundation of cosmos. 'Chaos is, in Egyptian thought, latent cosmos – hidden in the night and submerged in the inundation waters: it is potential cosmos.'¹⁵⁶ However, the forces of chaos and disorder must be controlled and tamed, which is the task of gods and people together. Through rituals they had to ensure that disorder did not overpower justice and order. This is what is understood as maintaining Maat. Although Maat is personified as a goddess, she is the underlying order structuring the world and the cosmos. It is the perfect state of everything, which human activities should be directed towards, and this is in accordance and in harmony with the creator god's intention. Maat represented the pristine state of the world, formed by the gods of creation even before any of the other gods and goddesses were born.[157] However, this state of Maat was believed to have been destroyed in the time of Osiris when he was murdered by Seth.

Te Velde has also argued that Seth was not just evil, but also a trickster. In the Egyptian language the opposite of Maat was confusion, and in Chapter 39 of the *Book of the Dead* Seth bragged that 'I am Seth the originator of confusion who thunders in the horizon of heaven.'[158] Maintaining Maat was the pharaoh's responsibility. Amenhotep III (c. 1390–53 BCE) strived 'to make the country flourish as in primeval times by means of designs of Maat',[159] which illustrates the structuring role of Maat. Humans were responsible for maintaining the original creation as it had been handed to them by the gods of creation. This cosmic cooperation explains the mixture of free will and predestination as justice in Egyptian thought since 'justice was part of an established order created by Re. Hence Re guards, protects, and vindicates his own work when he maintains justice. We must recall that Re's daughter is the goddess Maat.'[160] The 'unification of the Two Lands' was therefore not only the beginning of Egyptian history, but also a manifestation of a predetermined order which extended far beyond the political sphere and created a harmonious unity between society and nature.[161]

ALL WATERS ARE OSIRIS

The dismemberment of Osiris also works mythologically and physically at a deeper level relating directly to the qualities of the Nile. The Osiris mythology was built around the annual flood and its yearly changing character. The flood changed colours from clear or blue water to green, red and finally white before it returned back to the clear, blue colour which characterizes the Nile in Egypt today. These changes formed the basis for the mythology, which at a symbolical level, it will be suggested, also represented the time span of a pregnancy and thus associated the rebirth and rejuvenation of Osiris to the seasonal rhythms (fig. 39).

In later periods, Osiris was equated to every known body or type of water – the Aegean Sea, the Ocean, the Bitter Lakes, etc.,[162] although Plutarch refers to the sea as Seth, and to quote Plutarch again:

39. Osiris. Temple of Seti I, Abydos.

> But the more wise of the priests call not only the Nile Osiris, and the sea Typhon; but [they call] without exception every source and power that moistens, Osiris – considering [him] cause of generation and essence of seed, and Typhon everything dry and fiery, and of a drying nature generally and one hostile to moisture.[163]

This corresponds to the oppositional pair 'wet' and 'dry' meaning life and death.[164] Thus, Osiris is water in its many forms from moisture to the river and the sea, where each type has particular qualities and capacities. Nevertheless, the Nile was the most important water body, and the annual inundation was a vital phenomenon for the ancient Egyptians. Hence, the Nile and the inundation attained a unique place in ancient Egyptian religious thought and the cosmological world of metaphors.

The Nile was seen as originating from the first cataract at Aswan, 'O King, receive this pure water of yours which issued from Elephantine, your water from Elephantine' (Pyr. 864). Thus, Osiris may appear in the function of Nun, the primeval waters. These waters were also beneath the earth, and as the origin of everything that exists, it was an immeasurable source of fertility. Furthermore, the primeval waters were also seen as the source of the waters of inundation. This relation between Nun and Osiris leads to a situation in which Osiris is identified as the 'father' of the sun since he rises each morning from the waters of Nun.[165] Nun surrounds the earth, and if these waters are associated with Osiris and the Nile flood, then the sun rises from Nun/Osiris every morning as it did on the day of creation. Hence, Osiris can be a parent of Ra and he is designated and identified as the 'father' of Ra.[166] It is, however, strange that this identification and combination had no other cosmological consequences.[167]

The Nile water was supposed to have special life-giving virtues.[168] The vitality emerging from earth, either in the form of plants or the water of the Nile, was seen as a manifestation of Osiris. Moreover, the different types of waters had specific qualities, and in particular the inundation: 'The water of inundation which carried the silt was called the "pure water" or the "young water", and it is this water that was thought to be brought by Osiris or to emanate from him or to take its power from him.'[169] 'Horus comes and recognizes his father in you, you being young in your name of "Fresh Water"; Horus has split open your mouth for you' (Pyr. 589). Moreover, the earth became purified by the life-giving waters of Osiris: 'The cannals are filled, the waterways are flooded by means of the purification which issued from Osiris' (Pyr. 848). Thus, the inundation caused not only fertility, but also a religious purity of the arable land, linking agriculture to rituals and religion. This scene appears to also be depicted on the Scorpion macehead where the king is shown opening a canal in what seems to be an irrigation ceremony.[170]

The result of water and agriculture is a successful harvest or, in general terms, life in its broadest sense. 'Osiris is manifest in the life-giving waters rising from earth when land and people need them most.'[171] These immanent powers of procreation were celebrated and venerated, and there was a close intimacy in Egypt between kingship and nature's generative forces. The power of the buried king was seen as breaking forth from the earth where he rested; the plants sprouted from the earth, the Nile waters flooded the banks, and the moon and Orion rose above the horizon.[172] Osiris was killed but rejuvenated and the most important identification and character of Osiris was the relation between water and death. He was buried in the Nile, but

Osiris was also perceived as a personification of the Nile (Pyr. 1044–5). This embodiment of the Nile was believed to be real and intimately connected to death. In fact, the waters were the divine blood and life juice from which all life arose.

The inundation was thought to be made up of the liquids running from Osiris' decaying corpse. The Nile and the flood were the efflux of Osiris, which is confirmed by numerous spells and hymns in the *Pyramid Texts*: 'You have your water, you have your flood, the fluid which issued from the god, the exudation which issued from Osiris' (Pyr. 788) and 'Raise yourself, O spirit of this King! Your water is yours, your flood is yours, your efflux which issued from the putrefaction of Osiris is yours' (Pyr. 1360). In particular the flood was perceived as Osiris' discharge, which had its origin in heaven:

> Your water is yours, your flood is yours, your efflux which issued from Osiris is yours. The doors of the sky are opened for you, the doors of Nut are thrown open for you; the doors of the sky are opened for you, the doors of the firmament are thrown open for you. (Pyr. 1291)

The idea of the doors of the sky giving water has been related to ancient rain traditions which saw the waters as coming from heaven. Thus, the belief that the waters were simultaneously coming from heaven and Nut (the underworld) continued in the Osiris mythology.

The king possessed Osiris' bodily fluids; 'You have your water, you have your efflux, you have your flood which issued from Osiris' (Pyr. 2031), and it is also made explicit that the water is Osiris' blood: 'which issued from [...]. The King is the blood which issued from Re, the sweet which issued from Isis' (Pyr. 1263).

Thus, the Nile and its flood in particular were designated as Osiris' efflux or discharge. According to Plutarch, however, this belief was not limited to the inundation: 'And they call not only the Nile, but also without distinction all that is moist, "Osiris' efflux", and the water-vase always heads the processions of the priests in honour of the God.'[173] Lustrations using sacred waters from Elephantine had a ceremonial significance in the Pyramid Age if not earlier.[174] 'Thus, all the lustration- and libation-formulae, which identify the water with putrescence and exudations from the corpse, are Osirian, replacing the older solar formulae'[175] and creating a world in which everything was structured around the life-giving waters and the transformation of life from death.

The drowning of Osiris was a very concrete image of the fertilizing power of the flood in combination with an anthropomorphic figure. The earth's power to bring forth grain and prosperity vanish when the water in the river diminishes to a few channels in the riverbed. Osiris was drowned and thrown into the river by the hostile Seth. When the flood reappeared, fertility was restored, and Osiris was 'found' by Isis:

> If the recession of the Nile flood showed the diminution of the god's power in one sphere, it was merely as a prelude to an increased display of his vigour in another. For almost at once the freshly sown grain would start to sprout in the drying fields.[176]

Life had its origin in death. The Egyptian culture rebelled against death and did not accept it. Hence, the rebellion took the form of religion which created a counterworld, and these images did not reflect a distant 'next' world but a very real one in the here and now.[177] Isis saved Osiris by searching for his corpse, protecting it and endowing it with new life. According to Herodotus, the Egyptian embalming ritual took 70 days:

> The Pharaoh received his lunar *ka* [...] from Hathor and Isis but his solar *ka* from Osiris in a rite which followed his accession to the throne. Osiris in this context represented the Royal Ancestors, for the *ka* of every deceased king united with that of his Royal Ancestors in heaven.[178]

The body was seen as a puppet which was brought to life by using the heart and blood as a connective medium.[179] Moreover, 'Death was also part of the cosmic order; it did not threaten the cosmos from outside but only life from within.'[180] The inundation was the 'renewal' and 'rebirth' of the river, and even in the Old Kingdom these waters were called 'the new water'.[181] Hence, it is precisely because death is the source of further life that the flood is Osiris' discharge and the deceased is rejuvenated through it. In a desert environment in which the Nile was the only provider of water and life, its rejuvenating and regenerative powers were the axis on which cosmos was centred.

THE EYE AND THE EFFLUX

In Spell 943 in the *Coffin Texts* (CT VII, 157) the refrain 'I have appeared as the Eye of Horus, the Eye of Horus has appeared as I' occurs several times, indicating that 'the Eye of Horus and the deceased could be regarded as interchangeable.'[182] As indicated earlier, there is a very close relation between the Eye and the flood, which has its origin simultaneously in heaven and in the cosmic waters of Nun. The classical libation spell in Egyptian history is Spell 32 of the *Pyramid Texts* (Pyr. 22–3), which occurs about 100 times throughout all periods:[183]

Assmann's 2005 translation	Faulkner's 1969 translation
This your libation water, Osiris, this your libation water, O Wenis, has come out from your son, has come out from Horus.	This cold water of yours, O Osiris, this cold water of yours, O King, Has gone forth to your son, Has gone forth to Horus.
I have come to bring you the Eye of Horus, that your heart may be radiant by means of it. I have brought it beneath you, under your feet.	I have come and I bring you the Eye of Horus, That your heart may be refreshed possessing it; I bring it to you under your sandals.
Take the discharge that has issued from you, may your heart not be weary of it.	Take the efflux which issued from you, your heart will not be inert, possessing it.

The spell is divided in three parts. The first stresses that the water comes from Horus, seemingly restoring and cementing the bond between father and son – Osiris and Horus. The second part calls the water the 'Eye of Horus' aiming to make the deceased's heart 'radiant' or refreshed by restoring what was lost through death. The third part emphasizes that the water is the discharge of the deceased himself:

> A reference to the deceased in his mythic role as Osiris. If the deceased is Osiris, then the water poured out to him has flowed out of himself as Osiris. The water symbolizes life force as a life-fluid that has flowed out of the deceased and is restored to him by means of the libation.[184]

The libation aims to bring the dead water, which is a life-endowing substance. In many tombs from the Old and Middle Kingdoms devices led the libation water offered in the cult room down into the sarcophagus chamber. This spell is immediately followed in the *Pyramid Texts* by another libation spell (Spell 33, [Pyr. 24–5]) in which the dead are united with the gods through water.[185]

Assmann's 2005 translation	Faulkner's 1969 translation
Osiris Wenis, take your libation! May it be cool for you with Horus in your name 'He-who-came-from-the-cool-place.' Take the discharge that issued from you.	O King, take this cold water of yours, for you have coolness with Horus in your name of Him who issued from cold water; take the efflux which issued from you.
Horus has caused the gods assemble for you at the place to which you have gone. Horus has caused the Sons of Horus to gather for you at the place where you were drowned.	Horus has caused the gods to assemble for you at the place where you have gone, Horus has caused the Children of Horus to muster for you at the place where you drowned.
Osiris Wenis, take your incense, that you may become divine, for Nut has cause that you be divine for your enemy in your name of 'God'. Horus the rejuvenated has recognized you in your name 'Rejuvenated-water'.	O Osiris the King, take your natron that you may be divine, for Nut has caused you to be a god to your foe in your name of God; Har-renpi recognizes you, You being young in your name of Fresh Water.

Thus, it is a cyclical water-world in which the libation is the life substance that originates from and returns to the god and, consequently, the pharaoh. 'Divine bodily secretions of the gods, tears and sweat specifically, were then consumed by other gods and literally became *self-sustaining* substances. The god ate themselves.'[186] The spell refers to the myth in which Seth killed Osiris and threw him into the Nile. The flood is made up of the exudation of Osiris' corpse and the water of the inundation is described as 'rejuvenated' or 'fresh' water. The spell ends by connecting the dead with Osiris, from which it can be deduced that the life-giving inundation flowed from the pharaoh's own body:

> The idea of a cycle is crucial to this association of ideas. With the water, life-fluid is returned to the deceased, life-fluid that has flowed out of him, out of Osiris. The water is a discharge that is returned in the offering. The concept of 'rejuvenation' results from this idea of a cycle.[187]

THE GREEN, RED AND WHITE NILE

How does the cyclical concept and belief in rejuvenation relate to the River Nile itself? The level of the inundation could vary dramatically from one year to another, and even though the Nile flowed throughout the year, it shows a significant variation with regards to the amount of water, and the flood has throughout history carried huge amount of silts. Not only referred the antique authors to the silt, but today's climate analysts use the different levels of sedimentation as indicators of Nile flows and hence climate change.

The very name 'Blue Nile' is a misnomer and misleading, and indeed an incorrect translation of the Arabic name 'Al Bahr al Azraq', which means the 'dark' Nile because of the reddish-brown colours of the sediments during the flood.[188] The Blue Nile and the Atbara contribute respectively with about 68 per cent and 22 per cent of the peak flow and 60 per cent and 25 per cent of the annul silt or sediment load of the Nile. Although there are no written texts apart from mythology describing the properties and colours of the Nile waters in ancient Egypt, it is without doubt that the same scenarios that have been witnessed in later periods also took place 3000 BCE or only some 5,000 years ago. In order to understand the mythology in relation to hydrology, geology provides clues to sediment processes, and 5,000 years is a very short time geologically speaking. The Blue Nile and probably also Atbara/Tekezze originated geologically and hydrologically about 30 million years ago. Since that time, it is estimated that the rock eroded from the Ethiopian headwaters amounts to about 100,000 km^3, although some studies add an accuracy of +/- 50,000 km^3.[189] 100,000 km^3 is roughly equivalent to the volume of the Nile cone. Thus, annually there are staggering amounts of silt flowing in the Nile towards the sea, in particular given that the amount of water in the Nile is comparatively small to the other major rivers like the Amazon (with 1,200 million tonnes of silt a year), Yangste (with 480 million tonnes of silt a year) and the combined Brahmaputra-Ganges rivers in Bangladesh (with 1,700 million tonnes of silt a year). In the Nile the annual sediment load is about 230 million tonnes (+/- 20 million tonnes) where about 60 per cent (140 +/- 20 million tonnes) comes from the Blue Nile and about 25 per cent (82 +/- 10 million tonnes) from the Atbara or the Tekezze.[190] This is significantly more sediments than previous estimates suggesting an annual average silt load of 100–140 million tonnes.

In any event for this discussion, if this process started 30 million years ago and continues today, there are no geological and hydrological reasons why it should not have existed in the period 3000–2000 BCE. This means also that in all likelihood the changing colours of the Nile witnessed in recent history also were visible during the Egyptian civilization, since these are qualities of the actual deposited sediments. There could have been more or less sediments in the past, which is also dependent upon the volume of the flood, but the important factor is that throughout the Egyptian Dynasties, the White and Blue Nile tributaries carried different types of silt, since the geology of the soil composition of this part of Africa has not changed.

Although the Nile flows throughout the year, it shows a significant variation with regards to both the amount and different colours of water. Although the two main branches of the Nile are usually called the White and the Blue Nile, these colour descriptions do not accurately describe the physical properties of the river during the inundation: in Egypt the river was green, red and white.

Early travellers were well aware of the changing colours of the Nile. The contrast between the Blue and the White Nile was remarkable during the flood: the Blue Nile was reddish-brown and the waters of the White Nile were yellowish-green. The water of the Blue Nile was remarkably clear and limpid when the river was low, and it reflected the brilliant blue sky. But during the flood, it totally changed in character, becoming turbid and heavily charged with deposits and of a deep chocolate colour. The White Nile, on the other hand, contained little or no sediments, and had a greenish-grey colour throughout the year.[191]

As the waters started to rise, Lyons noted in 1905, 'the season of the lowest Nile is marked by the unusual greenness of the water, which has a marshy and putrid taste and smell, which boiling or distilling only increases'.[192] The green colour is due to large quantities of algae and decaying vegetation floating in the river. In May the White Nile supplies most of the Nile's water and the river is green. In the marshlands of Uganda the White Nile also had a poisonous odour.[193] When the Blue Nile started rising, flowing with a greater velocity, the green water was suddenly replaced by a muddy reddish-brown/red flood. In wintertime, the Blue Nile is almost clear, but during the flood period between June to October it is highly charged with alluvium and becomes reddish-brown.[194] When the Nile started to recede after the flood, the river again changed colour and became creamy-white.[195]

The first Aswan dam was completed in 1902. Work on the High Dam at Aswan started in 1960 and was completed in 1971. Since the dam's construction, the river's changing colours and qualities are not visible in Egypt. However, one can still see the differences in the Nile water at the confluence of the Blue and White Niles in Khartoum, Sudan. Until the White Nile reaches Khartoum, it is at a lower level than the Blue Nile, and there is a pronounced slope between them.[196] The Blue Nile reaches its seasonal peak flow in between July and September, and thus suppresses the White Nile's flow. The White Nile is clearly green and smells whereas the Blue Nile is reddish-brown/red during the flood season (fig. 40). Importantly, the time at which these changes in colour took place was incorporated into Egyptian mythology. Budge writes:

> The rise is felt at Khartoum about May 20, and at Aswan about June 10, and the green water announcing this rise is seen at Cairo about June 20. About June 5 the Blue Nile begins to rise quickly, and it reaches its ordinary maximum by August 25; its red, muddy water reaches Aswan about July 15. Whence once the red water has appeared the rise of the Nile is rapid, for the Atbara is in flood shortly after the Blue Nile; the Atbara floods begins early in July and is at the highest about August 20. The Nile continues to rise until the middle of September [...] In October it rises again, and attains its highest level. From this period it begins to subside.[197]

The Atbara River also has a reddish-brown colour during the inundation. Finally, the Nile goes through one more colour stage before it turns clear and blue again. When the Blue Nile starts to subside, the river turns muddy white. The White Nile got its name from this fine, whitish clay that colours the water. This whitish colour stems from the Sobat River, which is formed by two headstreams – the Baro and the Pibor – at the Ethiopian border. The Sobat is a major tributary to the Nile and joins the river above Malakāl in Sudan. The river's length from the Baro-Pibor confluence to the White Nile is 354 km. The river has its flood season in November and December, carrying enormous discharges of whitish sediment, giving the White Nile its name. The flood of the Sobat River is delayed by the plains and marshes through which the Pibor flows, which are gradually drained after the summer rains. The river reaches its peak in December, which means that historically this water would reach Egypt in January and February. From then on the Nile waters would rapidly decrease.[198]

40. The confluence of the White Nile and the Blue Nile in Khartoum, early September 2006. The light-coloured water was the green hue of the White Nile whereas the dark-coloured water was the red-brownish hue of the Blue Nile, heavily charged with silt.

It is intriguing that the cycle of the changing colours of the Nile corresponds more or less to a human pregnancy with just minor deviations. The Green Nile reached Cairo in mid-June and the Red Nile would have arrived at the end of July or beginning of August. The White Nile *being* white reached Cairo in January or February; the nine months from June to February thus represent the full term of a pregnancy. The inundation started when Osiris was killed and Isis shed a green tear and fertilizing star from heaven. Osiris was reborn through the funeral rites and the Red Nile was his efflux. Rejuvenated as a new-born child, Osiris was nursed by Isis, who fed him with Nile water as milk.

ISIS' TEAR AND OSIRIS' EXUDATIONS

In ancient Egypt green and blue would generally most likely have been described with the same word, while yellow was the same word as green. Throughout all periods, red tends to be brownish, while yellow tends to have an ochre colour. Blue is not found in the earliest materials and is introduced around 2550 BCE, while green/blue also means 'fresh' and 'papyrus stem'. It may even denote the king's 'red crown', which may be a way of avoiding red, which probably had negative connotations.[199]

Gold and green stones were closely associated with water and water deities, and green and blue pigments were based on copper.[200]

During the low period of the Nile, a sandy wind would dry the Egyptian land for a certain period before the cool winds from the north began to blow. When the Nile was at its lowest, it took on a green colour and became the 'Green Nile'. When the river started rising it became red as blood, and was seen as the 'Red Nile'. When the river subsided it remained muddy and whitish for a time before becoming blue again. MacKenzie argues:

> The 'Green Nile' was evidently of primary importance. Its greenness was the source and substance of life in human beings, in animals and vegetation. The Green Nile substance renewed life each year in the land of Egypt; it renewed life after death in Paradise. Blood and milk animated and nourished, but the green substance originated new life.[201]

The green substance in the Nile was identified with malachite, which evidently contained the 'germ of life', used for numerous purposes in the religious cult. 'The Green Osiris' was to some extent a personification of malachite, the life-giver and renewer of youth. The 'Green Nile' flowed from the pools of heaven and vitalized the 'Low Nile'. In these 'malachite pools' or 'malachite lakes' the gods dwelt as birds, which were considered to be 'Imperishable Stars' animated by malachite.[202]

The stars are the source of malachite powder which drops like dew from heaven: 'O you who stride out greatly, strewing green-stone, malachite, turquoise of(?) the stars, if you are green, then will the King be green, (even as) a living rush is green' (Pyr. 567).

As a single teardrop from Isis brought forth the inundation and blessed all of Egypt, Isis has often been described as the mistress of the region of the Eye. Isis' tears made the Nile swell, with three different stories explaining why she was crying. The most common is that she was so forlorn at the loss of Osiris that she shed a tear, which caused the Nile to flood. A second story, popular among the Greeks, tells that the Nile inundation was caused by the tears Isis shed when she discovered that she was pregnant when Hapi arrived in the summer (Plutarch 65), and 'her tears turned to joy. Their child was born at the winter solstice with the sun.'[203] Both of these descriptions fit the ecology of the rising Nile. The last explanation is more difficult to understand since, according to this myth, Isis' tears fall into the water when she was sexually violated by her son Horus. Why this incestuous rape took place is hard to say, but it must be seen in relation to Seth, because nowhere is it mentioned that mankind came from the seed of Seth's testicles.[204] Mankind came forth from the sun's Eye (CT VII, 465a), or in other words, the Nile. The water and river ideology were always superior to the absence of rain, and this water-world turned into the Osiris mythology.

Even today in Egypt, the summer night on which the Nile starts to rise is known as the Night of the Teardrop:

> The fertilising star-tear that fell into the Low-Nile on the "Night of the Drop" was evidently a malachite tear. The Green Nile was made green with malachite from the god-pools of green malachite in the celestial regions. The Green Osiris of the Green Nile was [...] the personification of malachite. The celestial malachite in the Green Nile made vegetation green. It also made the dead 'grow green again'.[205]

In the sarcophagus room in the tomb of Unas the stars are green. It seems that the theorizing priests believed copper to be the 'life of life'. The green god stone could be broken and burnt, but remained imperishable. Not least important, as the Green Nile turned red, so red copper came out of green malachite. The Green Osiris was another form of the Red Horus. 'The discovery of metal in malachite must have seemed to them as great a miracle as the annual "miracle of the Nile", which flowed now green, now red, now milk-like and now blue.'[206]

In the earliest versions of the *Book of the Dead*, the deceased says of himself: 'I am Osiris, I have come forth as thou (that is "being thou"), I have entered as thou [...] the gods live as I, I live as the gods, I live as "Grain", I grow as "Grain" [...] I am barley.'[207] With the Pyramid Text 589, the identification of Osiris with the Green Nile is complete: 'Horus comes and recognizes his father in you, you being young in your name of "Fresh Water"; Horus has split open your mouth for you' (Pyr. 589) where fresh also means green water. Osiris is 'the Green One' whose life substance is the Green Nile. It is the Green Nile that makes vegetation green.

Vegetation is green, the Egyptians argued, because Osiris' life substance is green. Because the Nile runs green the Mediterranean becomes the 'Green Sea'. 'The "beautiful green disc" of the Egyptians, which symbolized creative power, existed in the primordial waters in the night of Eternity. The sun of the Underworld was green, and the newly-risen sun was red or golden.'[208] The mysterious green substance was the very essence of life. Moreover, the Eye is also described as green or being painted green:

> I have come to my waterways which are in the bank of the flood of the Great Inundation, to the place of contentment, green of fields, which is in the horizon. I make green the herbage which is on the banks of the horizon, that I may bring greenness to the Eye of the Great One who dwells in the field. I take my seat which is in the horizon. (Pyr. 508–9):

> O my father the King, I have come and I bring to you green eye-paint; I bring to you the green eye-paint which Horus gave to Osiris. I give you to my father the King just as Horus gave you to his father Osiris; Horus has filled up his empty Eye [the eye torn out by Seth] with his full Eye [the eye-paint]. (Pyr. 1681–2)

Traditional religions are often more concerned with 'life' than 'spirits' and they are therefore more 'biocentric' or 'pantheistic' than 'theocentric'.[209] Thus, the Green Nile had the original, procreative and all-encompassing life-giving power from which all life emerged and arose. All life has its origin in this green water. Sir J. Frazer tried to explain Osiris' greenness in relation to corn, i.e. that Osiris was painted green to symbolize green corn. MacKenzie opposes James Frazer's vegetation school and turns his argument around: 'It was not the greenness of Osiris that the ancient priests had to explain when dealing with vegetation [...] the Egyptians believed the greenness of the corn came from the green Osiris. Osiris was essentially the river Nile. The Nile made Egypt green.'[210] This theme is also prevalent in the tale of the Eloquent Peasant: 'Thou art like the flood (inundation), thou art the Nile that makes green fields and furnishes the waste lands.' Moreover, Osiris is yellow before he becomes green. On the bier he is yellow when he is dead, but after he is resurrected he reigns in the Underworld as a green god. In the Judgement scene on the Ani Papyrus, Isis and Nephthys have yellow hands and faces when they are standing beside the Green Osiris. The yellow or golden colour can be seen as the golden sun that is the source of the 'vital spark'.[211]

The Green Nile does not last long, 'but generally flows in three or four days, and it is only the forerunner of the real flood [...] In eight or ten days [the Nile] has changed from greyish blue to dark red, occasionally of so intense colour as to look like newly shed blood.'[212]

The substances in the Nile which changed colour were obviously life-giving substances for the Egyptians, and as blood is 'the life thereof'; the Red Nile was seen as the blood of the slain Osiris.[213] The red hue, which is brought on by the oxide sediments during the inundations, has up to this day been compared with blood.[214] This is explicitly stated in the *Pyramid Texts*: 'which issued from [...]. The King is the blood which issued from Re, the sweet which issued from Isis' (Pyr. 1263).

As indicated, this Red Nile was also believed to purify the land: 'The canals are filled, the waterways are flooded by means of the purification which issued from Osiris' (Pyr. 848). During 'The Great Hoeing of the Earth in Busiris', there are references that the earth is hoed with blood. The companions of Seth changed themselves to goats which were sacrificed and the blood might be Seth's because the mixing of the storm-god's blood with the soil is not a unique example.[215] Rain-chiefs' blood when sacrificed and killed have been mixed with grain and this seed was believed to gain immense fertility.[216]

The efflux can also be interpreted as the secretion emitted by a decaying body – a foul-smelling liquid, which would be more brownish in colour than the red blood.[217] If the efflux is this rotting bodily fluid it has precisely this physical resemblance to the Nile during the inundation. As mentioned, the Green Nile smells rotten or putrefied whereas the Red Nile has a red-brownish colour, which may also have been seen as coagulated blood – the true efflux of Osiris.

Thus, death is the source of life, and the fluids that were lost at the moment of death were 'returned to the body of Osiris is the act of offering'.[218] This is explicitly stated in the *Coffin Texts* (Spells 94 and 96):

> I am this great soul of Osiris whom the gods commanded to copulate with him [...] I have remade Osiris from the efflux which was in his flesh, from the seed which issued from his phallus at the going into the day that he might copulate with it. I am the son Osiris, his heir with his rank, I am the soul within his blood [...] [CT Spell 94]

Also the *Pyramid Texts* say: 'Raise yourself, O spirit of this King! Your water is yours, your flood is yours, your efflux which issued from the putrefaction of Osiris is yours' (Pyr. 1360).

The rebirth of Osiris was also part of the inundation; 'the cutting of emmer wheat has been performed twice; first to indicate the death of the god manifest in vegetation [...] and second the rebirth of the god, who gives to his people a plentiful harvest.'[219] According to Plutarch, Isis realized that she was pregnant sometime in October, and '[...] Osiris is buried when the sown corn is hidden by the earth, and comes to life and show himself again when it begins to sprout' (Plutarch 65.1).

The intricate symbolic and real relations between blood and mother's milk may structure societies.[220] Blood is said to be a 'divine sanguinary substance'.[221] In general, blood is life, not only as a symbol, but very real, the veins are the life-giving arteries of humans, and hence metaphorically society. In African traditional religions, blood manifests the essence of being and is the life force permeating everything. Blood is believed to be the sanctity of every human and the source of being and becoming.[222] The fluidity of the borders between water and blood is represented by the body itself, connecting and expressing flows between the inner body and the outer world and as such also transferring meaning from one sphere to another.[223] And while there are few references to blood being purifactory, in Leviticus (17:11) when the Lord spoke to Moses, it is life-giving having purifying powers: 'For the life of the flesh *is* in the blood, and I have given it to you upon the altar to make atonement for your souls; for it *is* the blood *that* makes atonement for the soul.' Given that Moses lived and worked in an Egyptian cosmology and water-world, which will be discussed further in Chapter 6, it seems that parallel perceptions were at work in even earlier pharaonic times structured around the Osiris cult.

THE WHITE NILE OF MILK

When the Red Nile had receded, the Nile changed character, and became white. The water came from the White Nile and was muddy and creamy. The whitish, muddy Nile has most likely been seen as milk. Nile waters flowed from the breasts of Hapi and in the cavern source of the Nile at Elephantine, from where the Nile was believed to have its origin, water flowed from what were seen as human breasts. The rare geographical figure *jtrw* ('3j) is the strict personification of the Nile as these words are the normal words for the river or a delta branch. The earliest fecundity figures, which are male, are found at the valley temple of the Bent Pyramid at Dashur.

They are, however, broken, their heads are lost, and the iconography is aberrant. From the Fourth Dynasty onwards, fecundity figures are also found on royal throne sides. In the early period, fecundity figures apparently had no particular headdress, but later the figures wore long wigs, which is a divine characteristic. Moreover, fecundity figures are characterized by their long, pendulous breasts, which distinguished themselves from the breasts of normal or fat women through their pendulous character and the absence of pronounced nipples. Very few female fecundity figures or personifications are depicted, and those who are depicted are definitely fatter than average women. Three of the female depictions can be found in Sahure's temple, and it is likely that there were other such representations in the same temple, but this practice seems to have ceased after the Old Kingdom. Before the New Kingdom there are only a few isolated cases of fecundity figures carrying food offerings as well as symbolic gifts. In the Old Kingdom, it was more common to depict more 'secular' offering bearers carrying a range of material gifts, whereas in mortuary temples these are symbolic.[224] In ancient Egypt, it seems that the powers and the qualities of the Nile itself was more important than fecundity figures.

Hathor is said to have created Nut, and Hathor was also regarded as the mother of Osiris (Pyr. 466). Nut provided celestial milk – the milk of 'the Milky way' – and she had 'long hair and pendant breasts'.[225] Finally, the white colour of the Nile is also seen as Isis' nursing breast milk: 'Raise yourself, O King! You have your water, you have your inundation, you have your milk which is from the breasts of Mother Isis' (Pyr. 734). The Nile's life-giving waters were also believed to encompass divine breast milk: 'The deceased, now reborn through the sky-goddess as a god himself, is subsequently breast-fed by divine nurses and elevated to the heavens.'[226] Libations symbolically represented divine milk, and the image of the 'nursing of the child-god' most likely had its origin in the royal coronation ritual or perhaps more correctly, as an initiation rite prior to kingship, which took place before the actual coronation.

The association of the White Nile with the goddess Isis' breast milk was adopted by early Christian Copts, who called the star Sirius the 'flood-bringer' as it rose around the same time as the yearly flood. 'Undoubtedly, some form of it antedates Christianity in Egypt when a pharaoh or his priest might have actually invoked the star and the subsequent flood.'[227] The feast of Epiphany which celebrates the baptism of Jesus takes place on 19 January, which in past times marked a great celebration around the River Nile. Moreover, as mentioned above, in Cairo the Nile turned white at the end of January with the silt from Sobat River, which had its flood peak at this time. The role and continuity of the White or Milky Nile will be elaborated further with regards to early Christianity in the next chapter.

The inundation in its various forms was truly the elixir of life, as evidently shown in depictions where the water flowing out of libation vessels is simply a chain of hieroglyphs for 'life' (*ankh*).[228] All these aspects and divine capacities and qualities are eloquently described in the *Pyramid Texts*: 'You have your water, you have your flood, the fluid which issued from the god, the exudation which issued from Osiris' (Pyr. 788). Thus, the annual flood was the most important cosmogonic event in ancient Egypt. This has to be seen in relation to the actual water-world and the changes in the amount of water in the Nile and the inundation.

CLIMATE AND CHANGES IN THE ANNUAL FLOOD

Today, the desert west of the Nile is one of the driest places on earth, and as Butzer argues, 'It has become difficult to ignore the possibility that major segments of Ancient Egyptian history may be unintelligible without recourse to an ecological perspective.'[229] Climatically, the rise of the Egyptian civilization must be related to the end of the Neolithic Wet Phase and the general decline of the Nile's flood levels. In Egypt, it was a rainy interlude which ended in the 'Early Predynastic Period' (*c*. 4000 BCE). The Holocene Wet Phase affected the area that today lies within the 100–500 mm rain zone, which runs from the Senegal River to the Nile River. During the Holocene Wet Phase the Nile's catchment area became larger and consequently the river became more abundant than earlier seasonal rivers, and the Nile was a larger river than it is today, with many times the present discharge.[230] In Egypt, the maximum of moisture occurred around 5000–4000 BCE, and the overall ecological conditions worsened dramatically around 3500–2800 BCE. The substantial decline in Nile levels during the Early Dynastic period (*c*. 3000–2800 BCE) would have implied a 30 per cent reduction in the volume of water before stabilizing during the Third to the Fifth Dynasties at a slightly higher level.[231]

The difference between the average inundation from the Second to the Fifth Dynasties is 0.7 m lower than it was in the First Dynasty if one assumes that there was a fixed zero-point which rose at a uniform rate corresponding to the alluvium. The determination of a fixed zero-point is, however, complicated by the rise of the riverbed due to the annual deposits of silt. An average of 10 cm per century has been suggested, although this will vary substantially per area and time period.[232] If the rise of the alluvium was more rapid than an estimated 10 cm per century, then the decline in the flood level would have been even larger.[233]

If one assumes that the measurements on the Palermo Stone give the height of the flood in the Memphis basin, then it is reasonable to estimate that the floods had a magnitude of 130 billion m³ from the Third to the Fifth Dynasties (roughly equal to the discharge in 1878 and 1887) and the average rise of the river in the basin was around 1.8 m. The First Dynasty flood, however, would have been around 50 per cent higher, around 200 billion m³ per year. In the Second Dynasty, on the contrary, the floods were low and the discharges were around 80 billion m³ per year and consequently large areas of land must have been left uncultivated. The rains of the Holocene Wet Phase ended around the end of the Fifth Dynasty, and the level of rain in the Fifth Dynasty equals today's levels. There were periodic fluctuations, but nothing like the heavy, sustained rains of the previous period.[234] Thus, the development in Egypt was neither slow nor gradual, and when the changes took place it had the character of a crisis. It affected all aspects of life at once and all changes occurred within some few generations.[235]

THE PYRAMIDS AND CONFLICTING WATER-WORLDS

The building of pyramids started at the beginning of the Third Dynasty during the reign of Djoser (c. 2650 BCE), which was a watershed in Egyptian and world history. Djoser built a 62.5 m six-step pyramid. During the reign of Sneferu, the first king of the Fourth Dynasty (c. 2613–589 BCE), new impulses and ideas emerged. Sneferu constructed three major and two minor pyramids, which together contained more cubic metres of stone than the Great Pyramid of his son Khufu (c. 2589–66 BCE). Khufu's pyramid is the world's largest pyramid: the sides are 230.37 m and the height originally measured 146.59 m. His successor Khafre (c. 2558–32 BCE) built the second largest pyramid at Giza. The development of the pyramids was a colossal statement of divine kingship. Three generations in the Fourth Dynasty did the bulk of pyramid building, and later the pyramids became smaller and more standardized.

From the Old Kingdom 21 of the 23 major pyramids stand like sentinels on a 20-km stretch, including those at Giza.[236] The mortuary complexes in the Fifth Dynasty show a major change in focus from pyramids to funerary temples.

Today Abydos is the richest agricultural area in Upper Egypt, and most likely agriculture was the very basis of the Predynastic wealth.[237] The question is therefore which type of agricultural ideology or water religion these societies had in the Early Dynastic periods and during the Old Kingdom: rain, river or a combination? As with most archaeology, 'Most of the desirable evidence has irretrievably gone, ruling out any serious kind of quantification or deep exploration of what brought about changes.'[238] Nevertheless, by using data from mythology, climate, the archaeological material and the ritual practices which have been conducted, one may discuss and summarize some aspects of the religious development.

The very location of Abydos suggests a river adaptation and an inundation civilization, but agricultural societies may also be dependent upon rain. Mythologically, the tomb of King Zer became the shrine of Osiris in the Eighteenth Dynasty.[239] Osiris is found in the Nile, and the *Pyramid Text* generally locates this place as the banks of Nedyt at Abydos:

> Betake yourself to the waterway, fare upstream to the Thinite nome, travel about Abydos in this spirit-form of yours which the gods commanded to belong to you; may a stairway to the netherworld be set up for you to the place where Orion is, may the Bull of the sky take your hand, may you eat of the food of the gods. (Pyr. 1716–17, see Pyr. 795–9)

Moreover, the finds of two ivory objects in the grave goods in a tomb at Helwan with emblems of the Djed pillar, which is Osirian, are dated to the First Dynasty.[240] The pairing of Horus and Seth, which is essential in the later Osiris myths, is also found from the middle of the First Dynasty. King Djet's ivory comb 'presents concisely and clearly the central tenet binding together ancient Egyptian civilization, the notion that the king fulfils a role on earth under the protective wings of the celestial falcon in heaven'.[241]

The royal name was a theological statement, which expressed the relationship between the gods and the king. The Horus names of the kings of the First Dynasty are aggressive: 'Horus the fighter' (Aha), 'Horus the strong' (Djer) or 'arm-raising Horus' (Qaa), whereas in the Second and the Third Dynasties the Horus names reflect peace or divine relations. Importantly, Seth was a royal and divine titular in the earliest dynasties together with Horus.

This indicates that Seth was not totally eradicated, but still seen as an important god controlling the rain, which also strengthens the hypothesis that the former Predynastic kings were divine rainmakers.

This has to be seen in relation to the human sacrifices in the royal funerals of the First Dynasty kings. 'What might seem surprising is that the practice should begin after a formative period, not in the setting-up of the centralized state and creation of a status for the kingship but at a later point of transition, although that too can be paralleled,' John Baines argues:

> Its motivation will remain unknown, but it occurred in the same period when the titulary proliferated, along with other assertions of royal status. For reasons that have not yet been established, the king's special nature and authority – but not divinity in any simple sense – were stressed to the utmost.[242]

A dominant principle has been that 'the laws of Nature and the laws of the State are of the same kind.'[243] When offices are purely ceremonial, 'They all form part of the king's state, and the king's state is an organization for prosperity by the due observance of traditional rules.'[244]

Hierarchization was a process of divination. The water cosmology as a religious process enabled this stratification because it was ritually institutionalized in the divine kingship (fig. 41). If the kings in the Predynastic era were rainmakers, with the unification and the

41. The sacred pool at Karnak.

constitution of the ancient Egyptian civilization the kings embodied the flood as Horus through the Eye.

The success of the pharaoh was measured in the life-giving waters, to quote Amenemhet I: 'The Nile honoured me on every broad expanse', meaning that the inundations were good.[245] Hostile views of Khufu as well as other pharaohs may imply that people knew of the kings' potential or actual failures, and tomb robbing and looting were blasphemous acts against the kings.[246] In the Old Kingdom, Wainwright interprets the stories of Khufu, Khafre and Menkaure in this light as told by Herodotus, although the story is in a distorted and scarcely historical form. Khufu and Khafre were successful in the struggle against the old rainmaking ideology. Herodotus says that both of them forbade the Egyptians from conducting sacrifices (II, 124, 128) which resulted in calamites that brought the people 'to the lowest point of misery' (129). Menkaure, however, returned to the old system and allowed the people 'to resume the practice of sacrifice. His justice in the decision of causes was beyond that of all the former kings. The Egyptians praised him in this respect more highly than any of their other monarchs' (129). Menkaure built a much smaller pyramid, but he had to die after seven years, according to the oracle from Buto, who said, 'Six years only shalt thou live upon the earth, and in the seventh thou shalt end thy days' (133). This interprets Wainwright as the well-known doom of royalty under the old sky and fertility religion; when their powers failed or when they became old, they had to be sacrificed. However, the *Sed* festival was a fertility rite, and prisoners are obvious substitutes for kings. At Narmer's *Sed* festival apparently 120,000 captives were slain,[247] although most likely this number is not referring to a real event.

Seth continued to play a crucial role in the mythology of ancient Egypt. Even though he became demonized and seen as a threat to society and the welfare of the people, he did not disappear from the Egyptian pantheon. This has to do with ecological variables and his role as a rain-god. From the very beginning of the civilization the origin myth was the feud between Seth and Horus about the life-giving waters, and this theme runs through the Nile for 3,000 years, although in different forms. However, if the Nile failed successively, the last source of water was rain, and people would turn to Seth when the Nile failed. Thus, Seth could be reactivated as a god, usually a hostile one who did not give the life-giving waters, but in the absence of other bodies of water he was the last possibility.

THE WORLDS OF DEATH

In the Egyptian language the pyramid of Khufu was 'called *akhet* of Khufu. *Akhet* is the threshold region between the sky, the earth, and the underworld; in particular, *akhet* is the place where the sun rises',[248] hence the king ascends to heaven by his *akhet*. In the *Pyramid Texts* the pyramids are described as follows:

> Hail to you, daughter of Anubis, who is at the windows of the sky, the companion of Thoth, who is at the uprights of the ladder! Open my way that I may pass. Hail to you, Ostrich which is on the bank of the Winding Waterway! Open my way that I may pass. (Pyr. 468–9)

The placing of the corpse in the coffin was seen as a return to the uterus, while the comparison of the mummy with the egg points to the epitome of origin. The coffin has also been seen as the pregnant body of the sky goddess Nut or Neith who will bring forth the child.[249] In the coffin the deceased is incorporated into Nut, the great mother and goddess, and thus is regenerated for eternity. This equals the sun god. In the morning, the sun appeared between Nut's thighs. The western horizon is her mouth and the eastern horizon is her vagina.[250] Nut appears in her many facets: in the tomb and the necropolis, in the west and in the realm of the dead. All these spaces are manifestations of the womb into which the transformed dead enter. The sun god ruled the whole universe from the sky and the Duat or 'netherworld'. In the Duat the sun god underwent a transition whereby he died and was reborn the next day:[251]

> Whether as a star or in company with the sun, each day the king reenters the Duat to be born again into the sky. Given its cosmic associations, the tomb is therefore more than just the final resting place of the king. It is his personal Duat [...] And it is the womb and *3ht* that assure him daily rebirth into the sky to begin his eternal cycle of celestial life anew.[252]

This corresponds to the actual locations where the dead resided: during the night they were both in the netherworld and in the sky; while they spent their day in the sun's boat. Thus, they constantly moved in a circuit above and below the earth, but they were also capable of leaving this cosmic, eternal journey and reappearing on earth in the tomb, from which the ba could unite with the buried body or a statue.[253]

The two images of death, as both enemy and return to the womb, may seem contradictory, but they are not because 'they belong to one and the same context, they presuppose and complete one another, and they illuminate one another'.[254] The Osiris myth is the deceased's victory over his enemy – death. The solar myth is birth, particularly when the sun sets on its nocturnal journey through the netherworld. The solar immortality is illuminated through the circular path which goes from birth to death every day, again and again (fig. 42). 'The sun set an example that everyone wished to follow: a cycle course of life, return to the origin, overcoming death, consummation as conception, and restoration through (re)birth.'[255]

The netherworld is the place where the dead are dead and they have to walk upside down, eat their own excrement and urine, and wander around in dirt and filth. Beyond this realm, there is the place of eternal life where the transfigured deceased becomes an ancestral spirit. A body of water, which the deceased must cross, separates the two realms of the netherworld as either a place of death or life. In order to cross this water the deceased must wake the ferryman who is reluctant to let the dead into the spheres of the living and divine. In the netherworld, the deceased as well as the sun and the gods come into contact with the 'primeval waters' or the elements of the pre-cosmos or pre-existence. Hence, every morning the sun emerged from the primeval waters. The annual inundation of the Nile also had its origin in these waters.[256] Hence:

42. The dead's journey to eternity. From the Dendera Temple.

Without death and the descent into the deepest depths of the netherworld, regeneration cannot be achieved. The great model of regeneration is the sun god, who descends nightly into these depths to unite with his corpse, which is resting there, and to renew himself through this union.[257]

THE NILE AND REJUVENATION

In *Death and Salvation in Ancient Egypt,* Jan Assmann (2005) analysed and emphasized the role of water in death for rejuvenation and further life. While most of his examples are later than the Old Kingdom, they reveal structural insights into the dynamics and transfiguration from death to life in ancient Egypt. It is most likely a historical trajectory from earlier periods that was modified and continuously developed. Nevertheless, for analytical purposes one can treat Egyptian religion ahistorically or phenomenologically in order to illustrate certain points by using the *Pyramid Texts* and Graeco-Roman texts as sources.[258]

Water rituals, libations and purifications were fundamental throughout the history of ancient Egypt. One water ritual was 'Uniting with the Sun', which consisted first of all of the purification of the mummy as part of which water was poured over the body from *nemset*-jars. In a mortuary spell in Theban Tomb 23, the rite is described:[259]

> May you stand up on the sand of Rasetau,
> may you be greeted when the sun shines on you,
> and may your purification be carried out for you as a daily performance.
> May Nun purify you,
> may cool water come forth for you from Elephantine,
> may you be greeted with the nemset-jar.
> Take incense for yourself,
> receive natron!
> May the divine words purify you,
> may your mouth be opened by the chisel of Ptah [...]

Water from Elephantine is also mentioned in other purification spells for the dead. New Kingdom texts state that the transfigured should drink water from the 'altar of Ra' at Heliopolis. Moreover, spells and offerings were designed to make the Nile water reach the tomb. Such wishes were very common in the New Kingdom, and it was also believed that Nun, the primeval ocean from which the Nile inundation arose, flooded the tomb. Thus, in death the dead came in contact with the primeval and cosmic origin. In other contexts the inundation is seen as a stream of liquid being poured from a libation vase. Designating water as 'the discharge of the corpse of Osiris, particularly when they offered water to the deceased in the form of libation in the mortuary cult, was the central rite in the funeral rites'.[260] From the *Pyramid Texts* to Plutarch all water was seen as Osiris' efflux. In the words of Plutarch, the Egyptians call not only the Nile, but all water in general, 'the discharge of Osiris (*Osiridos aporrhoe*)'.

The Nesmin papyrus dates to the beginning of the Graeco-Roman period,[261] when the mortuary cult at Thebes was the responsibility of the choachytes (water pourers). They formed a cultic association at Medinet Habu, whose divine model was Amun of Luxor. In the Eighteenth Dynasty, Amun crossed over to the west bank every ten days to offer water to his ancestors at the temple of Medinet Habu. Hence, the choachytes were obliged to perform a similar water offering to the deceased in the tomb every ten days to unite the dead with the libations made by Amun in Luxor. In the Nesmin papyrus, this spell has the longest history going back to the *Pyramid Texts*:[262]

> O Sokar Osiris, take this libation,
> your libation from Horus,
> in your name of 'Cataract-area'.
> Take the discharges that have come out of you, which Horus gives you in that place where you were pushed into the water.

The same theme is evident in the *Pyramid Text* Spell 436 (Pyr. 788–9):

> You have your water, you have your flood, the fluid which issued from the god, the exudation which issued from Osiris. Your hands have been washed, your ears have been opened. This mighty one has been made a spririt for the benefit of(?) his soul. Wash yourself so that your double may wash himself and that your double may sit and eat bread with you without cessation for ever and ever.

'It was believed that with its annual rise, the Nile was rejuvenating itself, even as it rejuvenated the fields,' Assmann argues:

> The Nile inundation was the central symbol of cyclical time, which did not flow irreversibly toward a goal but rather ran back into itself in a cycle, thus enabling renewal, repetition, and regeneration. For this reason, water was the most important of the libation offerings. In water lay the power of return.[263]

On a late bronze libation vessel, this is explicitly stated:

> To be spoken by Nut:
> O Osiris N.,
> take the libation
> from my own arms!
> I am your affective mother,
> and I bring you a vessel containing much water
> to satisfy your heart with libation.
> Inhale the breath that goes out of me, that your flesh may live thereby,
> for it is I who give water to every mummy
> and breath to the one whose throat is empty,
> who cover the corpses of those who have no tomb.
> I shall be with you and unite you with your ba,
> I shall not depart from you, forever.
>
> O Osiris N.,
> take this libation
> that comes from Elephantine,
> this discharge that comes from Osiris,
> which Sothis (the goddess of the new year) brings with her own arms
> as she associates Khnum with you.
> A great Nile inundation has come to you,
> its arms filled with rejuvenated water,
> to bring you gifts
> of all fresh things at their time,
> with no delay [...]

The sacramental explanations of the role of water in cosmos and rituals lie in the social effects of water which connect the dead with the gods; the rejuvenating effects which made time run backwards; and its space-opening effects which provided the deceased with freedom, movement and breath. The Nile water, or more precisely the inundation, had all the qualities because the Nile flowed from the netherworld at the First Cataract at Elephantine, as stated in an inscription at Dendera: 'I purify Your Majesty with the water "Repeater of Life", which emerges from your leg, from the source-cave from which the Nile inundation springs forth, coming to your flesh, so that Your Majesty is rejuvenated.'[264] Thus, following the myth, the annual inundation came from a wound on Osiris' leg. The injury was inflicted by Seth when he murdered Osiris. The leg itself was connected to Elephantine. This correlation between Osiris' body and the actual parts of Egypt was developed and elaborated in later periods when the 42 nomes of Egypt were identified with the 42 body parts of Osiris. This is similar to the Pauline concept of the Church, which is seen as the body of Christ; in Egypt the 42 nomes constituted Osiris' complete body:

> We thus see that a correspondence of microcosm and macrocosm underlay the designation of water as the 'discharge of Osiris'. The world – or Egypt, at least – was conceived as a body, and the water of the Nile as an elixir of life that gushed forth from it [...] Elephantine [...] was the place where the life-juices flowed out of Osiris and flooded Egypt, giving rise to all the means of life. When it was offered to him in the cult, the water of the inundation, which had flowed out of the body of the slain god, made it possible to restore life to him, as well as to all dead, who were equated with him.[265]

This homology between body and water is also found in the *Pyramid Texts*:

> In your name of Dweller in the City of Lakes. What you have eaten is an Eye, and your belly is rounded with it; your son Horus has released it for you that you may live by means of it. If he lives, this King will live, etc. Your body is the body of this King, your flesh is the flesh of this King, your bones are the bones of this King; when you go, this King goes (also), and when this King goes, you go (also). (Pyr. 192–3)

The inundation was truly the elixir of life, as shown in depictions where water flowing from libation vessels is simply a chain of hieroglyphs for 'life' (*ankh*). The Nile had its origin in Nun, the primeval waters of origin but also the water that surrounded the world. Since this primeval water was ever-present, and because everything emerged and was created from this water, it also encompassed cyclical time, reversed processes, and enabled complete rejuvenation. The sun bathed in this primeval water each morning and it was this cosmic water that was poured on the deceased. Through the water the dead came in contact with the original powers of creation, impulses and energies, and it was from here that all life ultimately began and ended. Hence, these capacities could be explicitly proclaimed, as with the purification of the king which was expressed in a spell as follows: 'Pharaoh is Horus in the primeval water. Death has no power over him. The gods are satisfied with Pharaoh's purity.'[266] Thus, to sum up the cosmic qualities and capacities of the primeval water and the Nile, again in the words of Jan Assmann:

> Whoever immersed himself in the primeval water escaped death and gained strength for new life. Death was a consequence of pollution that could be erased by means of the primeval water. This water regenerated all that was decayed, and it turned back the hours. A world in which this water was effective needed no creator, for it was itself creative, divine and holy, carrying within itself the mysteries of redemption.[267]

Water was everything: it was the creator of cosmos and the world; it was self-generative and pro-creative. The Nile was hence the origin and source of everything, linking this world with the cosmic spheres. Its annual inundation secured not only life and prosperity for the living, but it also secured and renewed cosmos. This process also linked death to life or more precisely, life *through* death, which necessitated proper funeral rites and the preparation of the dead.

THE PYRAMIDS AND THE NILE IN THE SKY

Osiris and water did not only play a large role in the mortuary cult, but this procreative force where death was the source of further life included everything, in particular the growing forces. Osiris was an exceptional god. He was everywhere although he did not master any natural domains completely. He was immanent in the earth, but did not personify it; he joined the solar circuit, but did not control it, he was immanent in the Nile but the river had its own god, Hapi; and the goddess of grain was Ernutet.[268] However, it was this potential and everlasting capacity of constant rejuvenation which was Osiris' hallmark: '*being* does not emerge from *non-being* according to this ontology, creation is not creation *ex nihilo*, but a transition from that which is latently existing. In this monistic ontology, *being* originates from its own source: potential being'.[269] The most striking forces of rebirth and growth immanent in the earth were seen in the annual sprouting of vegetation, and in the earliest texts Osiris is seen as appearing as grain. In the *Mystery Play of the Succession* Osiris answers Re:

> Wherefore shall my son Horus be defrauded, seeing that it is I who make you strong, and it is I who made the barley and the emmer to

nourish the gods, and even so the living creatures after the gods, and no (other) god nor goddess found himself (able) to do it.[270]

These mortuary cults are not for the reflective commemoration of the most ancient gods, past and bygone, but for the communication with the gods whose life is going to manifest itself. The dead gods are the gods that will appear: they are the lords of latent life. Their qualification of being dead and buried is their trade-mark, so to speak: they are by definition the gods of the coming creation. Thus the gods partake in the cycle of latent and manifested life. They are not outside it – they do not transcend life and death but have integrated both states into their being.[271]

The mortuary cult's ultimate outcome was *'The utilitarian provision of rain, a "Nile in the sky", to sustain those people who do not have a share in the terrestrial Nile.'*[272] This should be understood literally and not only mythologically as I have previously argued with regards to the transformation of Seth's rainmaking powers into a river ideology in the form of Horus and the sun and then finally Osiris. The Nile became the divine river from the sky. The sky, blue during the day and black during the night, had the same qualities as the Nile, and consequently, the Egyptians believed that the sky was composed of water, which surrounded the world. This also explains the water mythology in death. King Pepi asks the ferryman to carry him to the eastern side of heaven where the Gods are born (Pyr. 1382). 'The face of the sky is washed, the celestial expanse is bright, the god is given birth by the sky upon the arms of Shu and Tefenet, upon my arms' (Pyr. 1443). The sun undergoes repeated purifications by bathing before dawn when he rises, and the dead king went through the same purifications. The water the dead crossed was also the same water they were purified with, and it was the very same water Ra bathed in before each sunrise. Hence, all ritual actions repeated the pristine emergence from the waters of chaos.[273] This was the cosmological waterworld the Egyptians lived in, but it was also a very fragile one.

The pyramids were built in a time of ecological crisis. It was a transition period in which the source of life-giving water shifted from rain to the river. When the great pyramids at Giza were built, the Nile's inundation was decreasing. The annual floods became smaller, and the whole of Egyptian society was dependent upon this diminishing river. The pyramids can therefore be seen as the ultimate testimony to the replacement of the old rain ideology by a river religion expressed through sun symbolism. Horus contained the Nile in his Solar Eye.

Horus had almost totally replaced Seth, although older perceptions still persisted, as evident in Kaphren's royal titular who addressed himself as Seth. The dimensions of the pyramids illuminate the religious struggle and seriousness of the cosmological change from a rain to a river ideology. The gigantic dimensions highlight what was at stake: life and the divinity of the pharaohs who controlled life and death through the annual inundation.

The pyramids manifest the importance of water in a desert. Water is truly life, and the pharaohs were responsible for providing it. This happened through death and the monumental pyramids. Death was inevitable, and the challenge for the pharaohs was to transform the sterile desert into life. Hence, there was a double transformation, with a single departure point: death gives life to humans and through the mortuary rituals the deceased attains eternal life and through water the barren desert becomes fertile fields. In a desert, death became the source of life through water. Ancient Egyptian religion was a perfect adaptation to the harsh realities that the desert represented for agriculturalists.

The basic mythology and the struggle between Horus and Seth and later Seth and Osiris testify to the fact that life emerges from death through water. This may also explain why there is no Nile god as such since it is the immanent life-giving power which was worshipped. The Nile was greater than any gods and therefore it could have been idolatry to have represented the Nile as one single god, or perhaps more importantly, providing and securing the annual flood was *an always ongoing process*. The Nile was the totality of cosmos from time immemorial to the present and into the future – everything was united and present in the pharaoh as Son of Ra who controlled the almighty river. The Nile legitimated everything and everything was the Nile. It was the origin and end of cosmos. Without the Nile everyone in Egypt would have died and the civilization perished. In the process of transforming death into life and recreating cosmos, the pyramids were gigantic cosmic machines securing the pharaoh's life for eternity and the life and prosperity for the commoners for one year at a time.

The pharaoh became Osiris when he died. Osiris' realm was in the underworld and the tomb. The cosmic power was where the pharaoh was, and since the living pharaoh became Osiris when dead, this father-son relationship manifested the whole Osiris-Horus mythology, which is why the pyramids lasted only one generation. When the pharaoh died, he obviously lost his life, but being a universal and eternal god, life needed to be rejuvenated, which happened through the Eye. The Osiris-Seth feud can be understood from a water perspective if water is seen as identical with life: Water is life. Life is water. As discussed earlier, the Eye contained the life-giving water, or more precisely: the Eye contained water *and* life since they were identical.

Seth killed Osiris by drowning in the Nile. As a former rain-god who had lost his life-giving waters, the drowning in water represented the intimate relationship between water and life. Death is the absence of water and further life. By human nature, every pharaoh would physically die, but there is a strong symbolism associated with the killing of Osiris. Seth did not kill Osiris in the desert, which could have been a natural place since the desert was Seth's realm. On the contrary, Seth killed Osiris in the very source of all life: the waters of the Nile. This is not a paradox because it emphasized the pervasive role of water in Egypt.

This relates to the old feud between Horus the Elder and Seth when they fought over the life-giving waters: rain or river. By drowning Osiris Seth took back the life-giving powers and water, which implies that he took the Eye. However, there were still no rains, so if Seth controlled the life-giving waters in the form of rain, there would be an absence of water and hence death. This is why Seth later became associated with the Devil who treated people malevolently. When Horus the Son killed Seth, he regained the Eye and restored it to Osiris, which is identical to the old feud in which Horus the Elder regained his Eye from which the Nile originated.

The drowning of Osiris in the Nile emphasizes that all life has its origin in death. When the Nile retreated it was mourned, but it was also a precondition for further life. Absence of water means absence of life, but the decreasing Nile created the fertile fields from where the forthcoming life would sprout. Hence, the cycle of life and death has its parallels in human life, the annual harvest and the daily birth of the sun from the cosmic waters. The pharaoh could only become eternal through death and the life-giving waters. The decreasing Nile and the sowing of grain were celebrated as Osiris' death and burial, which was the source of all further life. The sun died every evening, but was reborn the next morning. Life had its origin in death and death created life, and this cycle was the Egyptian water-world.

The new pharaoh demonstrated his cosmic powers by conquering death and restoring life. It was Horus the Son who killed Seth and made his father Osiris eternal and rejuvenated him through the life-giving waters in the Eye. Hence, the actual funeral ceremonies had a double function. The deceased Horus became eternal as Osiris and Horus the Son became the new pharaoh by killing Seth and transforming his father into the Nile and the annual, life-giving waters. Horus the Son as the pharaoh was the living God who mastered and controlled all life through the waters and the successful inundation. Since it was his father who was the actual inundation, this genealogy secured the divine status of the living pharaoh. It placed the living pharaoh in the middle of cosmos where his main task was to maintain Maat by providing and controlling the life-giving waters.

These waters came from death. The annual inundation was Osiris' efflux. As the river turned red-brownish during the summer, this was the pharaoh's blood, who now was transformed into Osiris and the forthcoming flood, which gave life and prosperity to all of Egypt. The new pharaoh as Horus the King was responsible for this transformation, and the new king was not crowned before his father was successfully transformed into the life-giving flood when his efflux covered the whole of Egypt. Osiris' discharge thus gave life to the dead king and to his people, rejuvenating Egypt and its inhabitants. The source of new life had its origin in death, which puts the emphasis on the mortuary cult.

This may also explain why the pharaohs had to build their own pyramids when they were alive. The pyramids were literally the physical 'machines' which enabled the transformation of death into life or Horus into Osiris. In other words; water and the annual inundation. This was the function of the funeral rites, and therefore, the pyramids had to be completed when the pharaoh died. Consequently, it was impossible for the ancient Egyptians to start building the pyramids after the pharaohs had died because these mortuary monuments were not commemorative sepulchres. The main function of the pyramids was as a means for the new pharaoh as Horus to transform his father's death into life-giving waters for the entire Egypt since the pharaoh was identical with Egypt, and Egypt was identical with what the annual inundation covered. This task could not be postponed to 20 or 30 years after a pharaoh's death, which would have been the case if the descendants started building pyramids after a pharaoh's death, because then all of Egypt would have perished. When the new pharaoh successfully had transformed his father as Osiris into the annual inundation through the funeral rituals, he controlled the forthcoming floods through rituals. Order was restored in cosmos. The pharaoh's death was the key threat to life in ancient Egypt as he controlled the Nile and all life. Hence, the new pharaoh could only solve this crisis of chaos by transforming death into life through the funeral rites whereby the dead pharaoh became the actual flood which possessed the life-giving powers restoring and rejuvenating life and cosmos. The religion of ancient Egypt was a water cosmogony, but how is it possible to conceptualize the very powers of the waters of the Nile? Was the water holy and how does it differ from holy water in Christianity, Islam and Hinduism? The continuity of religious beliefs in the Nile waters is also a story of the development of the monotheistic religions, which started with Akhenaten and Moses.

6 Water and World Religions Along the Nile

ORACLES PREDICTING THE NILE FLOOD OR JUST THE FASTEST RUNNERS?

After a luxury dinner in Alexandria, Julius Caesar inquired about the sources of the Nile with the Egyptian priest Acoreus, and according to Lucan, Caesar wanted to know 'the causes, hidden through such long ages, that accounts for the Nile, and the secret of its origin. Give me sure hope of setting my eyes on the head-waters of the Nile', he said 'and I shall abandon civil war'. Acoreus' answers were, if he knew the sources, as vague, elusive and mysterious as the river itself. Even if Caesar was perhaps the most powerful man on earth at that time, the priest exposed his limits to knowledge and domination; the Nile remained unconquered and no foreigner could gain this knowledge – even the Roman Emperor was inferior to the Nile and its mysteries.[1]

When Herodotus asked about the same several centuries earlier, he also got negative answers. Herodotus also refers to other wise men and oracles not knowing the sources:

> I heard from some men from Cyrene how once, in the course of a visit to the oracle of Ammon, they got into conversation with Etearchus the king of the Ammonians. The conversation happened to come around to the Nile and how no one knows about its source.[2]

Still, it seems that the Egyptians knew very well where the flood came from, and implicitly, where the sources were. Apart from the fact that cosmologically the First Cataract, with the river probably flowing in both directions, had a unique place among the ancient Egyptians and was a religious source, obviously they knew that the flood came from further upstream. After all, when they were able to build the greatest pyramids on earth, they would also know basic hydrology since they traded with the Nubians and beyond. This points to the fact that there might be several sources simultaneously, and this is not a contradiction but rather a consequence of the river itself, in particular at the First Cataract. It is worth recalling what Herodotus wrote about the priest telling him about the source of the Nile. The priest said

> that there were two mountains with sharply pointed peaks between the cities of Syene in the Thebaïd and Elephantine, which were called Crophi and Mophi; between them, he said, rise the springs of the Nile, which are bottomless, and half of their water flows north towards Egypt, while the other half flows south towards Ethiopia [...] Now, if this story of the scribe's was true, all he proved, to my mind, was that there are strong whirlpools and counter-currents there.[3]

Seneca gives a detailed description of the cataracts and the very particular and peculiar characteristics of the water and the river at this spot:

> The Cataracts receive it, a region famous for its wonderful spectacle. There the Nile surges through steep rocks which are jagged in many places, and unleashes its forces. It is broken by the rocks it runs against and, struggling through narrow places, everywhere conquers or is conquered. It swirls, and there for the first time its waters are aroused, which has been flowing without disturbance in a smooth channel. Violent and torrential, it leaps through narrow passes, unlike itself since up to this point it has been flowing muddy and heavy, but when it lashes against the boulders and the sharp points of jagged rocks it foams and its colours come not from its own properties but from its rough treatment in that place. Finally it struggles past the obstacles and, suddenly deprived of support, falls down a vast height with a great roar that fills all the regions lying around. The people established there by the Persians were unable to endure the noise. Their ears were deafened by the constant crash, and for this reason they were removed from that settlement to a quieter place.[4]

As a religious source, it has many of the specific features characterizing a source in the middle of a river; it is not ordinary water as further upstream, but it is violent and torrential – it is unnatural nature, or in the words of Seneca, it is 'unlike itself'. The sounds, intensity and even the colours are different. But there were more to this religious source. Seneca continues:

The first rise of the Nile is seen near the island of Philae, which I just mentioned. A short distance away from there the river is divided by a rock. The Greeks call it Abatos 'Untrodden', and no one sets foot on it except priests. These cliffs first feel the rise of the river. Next, after a considerable distance two crags stick out – the natives call them the Veins of the Nile – from which a great quantity of water pours, but not enough to flood over any expanse of Egypt. Into the mouth of this part the priests throw gold gifts when the sacred festival comes.[5]

The 'Veins of the Nile' came from the cliffs in the middle of the river – a holy place only for priests sacrificing gold at particular festivals. Thus, as a religious source, the First Cataract bears many similarities to the source of the White Nile, although the very shapes and specifics of the waters are different. And as with the source of the White Nile, everyone knew that water flows from further upstream as well, but the very character of the water at these particular spots made it a religious source. This directs the question to knowledge about the flood, since obviously it started further upstream and in Ethiopia. Were the ancient Egyptians aware of the specific reasons and origins of the flood? The answer is undoubtedly yes, but knowledge about the Nile and the life-giving forces of cosmos was esoteric and kept secret, and part of the mystery and oracle cult among the ancient Egyptians.

Bishop Athanasius of Alexandria (c. 296–373) has, however, one very intriguing reference. His *Life of Anthony* offers a visionary description of monks and the monastic life. These monks, living in deserts, were fundamentalists in the true sense of the word: fundamentalists since they believed in the fundamentals of the Gospel and they took the words literally. The fundamentals of the Christian faith are prayer, hospitality and charity, and the fundamentals of monasticism are love, compassion, and humility.[6] In the early days of Christianity there were religious contestations between the older and new religions, and central aspects of the ancient Egyptian religion structured around the Nile continued in practice to live on for two millennia, as will be discussed later. The ancient Egyptian religion was also an oracle religion. In his story of Saint Anthony, Bishop Athanasius presents the battle, as often in Christianity as well as in other religions, between true and false prophets. In this case he portrays the Egyptian priests and oracles as representing the false powers of the demons. While he dismisses the oracles as charlatans, cheating others because they have been able to collect knowledge of events before any other, in his discussion of why they are deceivers he also reveals astonishing information about the Egyptians and their knowledge about the flood and implicitly the sources:

> So, too, they sometimes talk nonsense in regard to the water of the River. For example, seeing heavy rains falling in the regions of Ethiopia and knowing that the flooding of the River originates there, they run ahead and tell it before the water reaches Egypt. Men could tell it too, if they could run as fast as these. And as David's look-out man […], mounting a height, got an earlier glimpse of who was coming than did the one who was staying below; and as the man who ran ahead brought tidings before the rest, not of what had not yet come to pass, but of things already on the way to be reported and actually happening, so these choose to hasten and announce things to others for the sole reason of deceiving them.[7]

The mere fact that the bishop here bluntly exposes direct contacts between Ethiopia and Egypt with regards to the hydrology of the Nile is intriguing. Not only did the Egyptians know about the flood coming from Ethiopia, but they were there themselves checking and controlling well in advance before it reached Egypt and hence they knew next year's prosperity.

At the age of 105, Anthony died in AD 356 and Athanasius probably wrote his book in AD 357, although some also argue that it was written in AD 365. If he knew in the fourth century, then this must have been common knowledge, although one cannot say anything for sure how far back in history this connection existed, including the era when the knowledge was kept in secret by the Egyptian oracles. As shown, it seems that this knowledge was not known earlier in antiquity among the scholars who theorized about the sources and the Nile flood, like Herodotus.

If it is true, which seems likely, that the Egyptian oracles, or more likely some of their assistants, went to Ethiopia and probably the highlands in Abyssinia where most of the rains fall, it opens up for several possibilities. Although this short detour is about possible or probable scenarios, of course nobody knows for sure, it is still worth pursuing different lines of reasoning with potential implications.

If one accepts Athanasius' claim that these oracles did not possess divine and magical qualities, but based their prophecies on actual observations, it might be reasonable to assume that they or some of their assistants would have been somewhere in the Lake Tana region, not necessarily by the lake itself, but at least centrally placed in areas where there traditionally would be much rain and as such be representative for the rainy season and hence the coming flood. If they were by Lake Tana, the levels of the lake would be a good indicator, but it would also have sufficed talking to farmers well aware of how the rains in one rainy season relates to another and subsequently the amount of water and the flow of the river itself. Importantly, these signs of nature would have been based on centuries of experiences, and if one assumes that the Egyptian observers were somewhere in the highlands during the rainy season, which usually spans three months from June to August, it would not have necessitated that they were there all the time. One might expect an oracle to be away for certain periods, and given the pervasive importance of the forthcoming flood, the reappearance of the oracle with divine revealed knowledge of the flood would have increased the aura and mystery. Or alternatively, if an oracle had a handful of assistants placed in Abyssinia, one after another could run back to Egypt with updated information with some weeks' intervals. This would have given the oracle valuable information on the changing flood, intensity and velocity. And if one believes Athanasius, these guys were the fastest runners, as he said: if anyone could run as fast as them they too would have been able to predict the coming flood.

Generally, in the beginning of June the Blue Nile started flooding and quickly rising in Egypt, and normally it would reach its maximum by late August. The Atbara flood would be in full flood shortly after the Blue Nile flood, and the Nile would continue rising to the middle of September and even October. Given these hydrological parameters, some good runners seeing what happened upstream would have extremely valuable knowledge for prophesies. After all, prophesies are not exact science, but it would give the oracles the necessary knowledge beforehand to know whether it would be a good year or a disastrous one – whether due to too much or too little water. If this was the case, the Egyptian oracles would be no different from rainmakers further south who were skilled observers of nature. And if intense running from the Ethiopian highlands was what was needed, they would predict the coming flood with quite some accuracy. This points to the clues of mystery traditions: nobody is supposed to know where the oracle has gained the knowledge from; divine revelation he would say – the important religious and societal role was that the oracles could predict to some extent the character of the coming flood. Certainly, this would also involve all types of blames – individual and collective responsibilities and guilt if there was too little or too much water. On the other hand, if it was a perfect or optimal flood, it would probably have been presented as the outcome of the divine powers as possessed by the oracle himself – or the pharaoh.

An oracle resembles diviners, or a specific type of healer, and sorcery and magic is part of the oracle's practices. As has been said about the Oracle at Delphi, 'that oracle which all would acknowledge to be the most ancient, most widely accepted, and most trustworthy in existence'.[8] Oracles would possess divine knowledge and represent the most trustworthy on these issues. The coming flood was of utmost importance, and the ones who could predict the flood would have immense spiritual power and religious capital, in particular when this knowledge was presented as revelations in mystery cults, although the factual knowledge being acquired from a long and fast run.

Following this speculative reasoning as it is, Egyptian observers could have followed both the Blue Nile and the Atbara Rivers, and it may have implications for other questions. One is about the route of the Beta Israel to Ethiopia, and from this perspective an Egyptian route does not seem impossible. Another question is about the knowledge about the source at Gish Abay in prehistoric times. If Egyptians were in the vicinity of the Lake Tana region, it is not unthinkable that they heard about it, but in such a case it would probably not have been important in the ancient Egyptian cosmology, since in their mythology the religious source was at the First Cataract. It may, on the other hand, have given notions to the Christian beliefs of the source from Paradise in the highlands of Ethiopia, which existed at the time Athanasius wrote about Saint Anthony, without mentioning this. In any case, mysteries were at the core of the Egyptian religion, and there was one man who was initiated into these mysteries – Moses, who married an Ethiopian princess.

MOSES – THE ONE DRAWN OUT OF WATER

In the history of religion, Moses has always been an enigma, but that enigma has been shrouded in another enigma, the role of water in religion, and with regards to Moses, how they relate – his birth and the Nile. The role of Moses in the history of ideas has had a prominent role in shaping concepts of the legendary Nile and the origin of mankind in monotheistic religions. Moses was hence a watershed in the history of religion and the origin and development of Judaism, Christianity and Islam.

Religious worldviews also shaped perceptions of the Nile, as evident in Speke's references to Moses and the holy Nile when he stood at the source of the White Nile. Writing only eight years after Darwin published *On the Origin of Species* (1859),[9] at a time when evolutionary thought and long time spans had not been generally accepted, Samuel W. Baker says:

> That great historian, general, and legislator, Moses, first cradled on the river Nile, gave us the book that describes the world's creation and origin of man: that first man, Adam, created 4004 BC, 5,870 years before present day. We are thus bound to accept as *historical* fact, that all the varying and conflicting types of the human race spread over a surface of the world at that time utterly unknown (and even now not completely known), originated in one man, Adam [...] As the account of the Creation was written by Moses, and he 'was learned in all the wisdom of the Egyptians', that account is peculiarly interesting, as emanating from one brought up in the land of Egypt, which was at that period the centre of civilization and learning.[10]

Throughout history, the centrality of Moses has intrigued scholars but more important is his role in institutionalizing monotheistic religions given the history of Judaism, Christianity and Islam. However, the very origin of Moses has been a controversial issue. Sigmund Freud, as a Jew, argued that Moses was an Egyptian and not a Jew, but as he said:

> To deny a people the man whom it praises as the greatest of his sons is not a deed to be undertaken light-heartedly – especially by one belonging to that people. No consideration, however, will move me to set aside truth in favour of supposed national interests.[11]

By claiming that Moses was an Egyptian, it posed new challenges, since the Judaic religion originated with Moses. 'My hypothesis that Moses was not a Jew but an Egyptian creates a new enigma. What he did – easily understandable if he were a Jew – becomes unintelligible in an Egyptian,' Freud says. 'But if we place Moses in Inknaton's period and associate him with that Pharaoh, then the enigma is resolved and a possible motive presents itself, answering all questions.'[12]

Jan Assmann argues that Freud also had a particular reason why he analysed and emphasized Moses as an Egyptian:

Freud wanted to discover the roots of anti-Semitism. Strikingly enough, his question was not how the Gentiles, or the Christians, or the Germans came to hate the Jews, but 'how the Jew has become what he is and why he has attracted this undying hatred.' Freud traced this 'undying hatred' back to the hostility inherent in monotheism as a religion of the father. Not the Jew but monotheism has attracted this undying hatred. By making Moses an Egyptian, he deemed himself able to shift sources of negativity and intolerance out of Judaism and back to Egypt, and to show that the defining fundamentals of Jewish monotheism and mentality came from outside. But this time the source of intolerance is enlightenment itself. Akhenaten is shown to be a figure both of enlightenment and of intolerable despotism, forcing his universal monotheism onto his people with violence and persecution.[13]

King Amenhotep IV (1352–36), who changed his name to Akhenaten (fig. 43), is seen as the founder of the first monotheistic counter religion in history. Amenhotep IV started a major building programme at Karnak, which was the centre for the Amun cult. He decided to break with all links to the traditional religious capital and the god Amun. He built a new city known today as Amarna, but at that time called Akhenathen with the cult structured around himself.[14] The sun cult during Akhenathen seems not to be a worship of the sun as Westerners usually perceive the sun, but rather the beauty of the sun and all its power in nature. However, there was a general reluctance to elaborate upon these life-giving aspects in mythology. Still, Apy requests:

> An offering which the king gives to the living Disc who brightens every land with his beauty, that he may give the sweet breath of the north wind, tasting of offerings, consumption of provisions, (granting) that I receive what is poured out for me, viz. cool water, wine, and milk upon the altar of my tomb, that there be sprinkled for me rejuvenating water each New year's day.[15]

Thus, the 'New Solar Theology reflects a deep trust in the reliability of the sun and the sun's movement.'[16] As such, they did not worship the sun, but all the all-encompassing powers of the sun.[17] Not only light, but also time, could be described as manifestations of solar energy, and hence the sun was 'the first mover' – everything could be explained as workings, 'emanations', or 'becomings' of the sun. Hence, the concept of One is not theological but physical – it is the source of cosmic existence – nothing behind and everything can be reduced, explained and related to it.[18]

43. *The Wilbour Plaque* probably depicting Akhenaten (left) and Nefertiti (right).

As Jan Assmann writes, 'Amarna theology concentrates on the one aspect of god as life and occupies itself with a uniquely explicit and forceful description of visible reality, so as to lead everything back to the one source of life in the sun.' He continues: 'We stand here at the origin less of monotheistic world religions than of a natural philosophy. If this religion had succeeded, we should have expected it to produce a Thales rather than a Moses.'[19] Thales introduced new or almost new cosmological ideas from the Near East. These may come from Egypt or Babylonia, and Thales may have heard these perceptions at the Milesian colony or even visited Egypt himself.[20] Whether Tales, the 'Father of Philosophy', actually was in Egypt and learnt from Egyptian priests is a much discussed topic, and this connection seems to occur among writers from *c.* 320 BC onwards.[21]

Thales' statement that everything is water has often been characterized as a naive answer to a question of great importance, since questions do not express propositions in the sense that they are neither true nor false. Still, Thales' question understood from his answer implies that two things are true; all things have a source, and the source of everything is one thing.[22] The essential philosophical question, or rather answer, was Thales' insistence that there was one single governing principle of the universe and the diversity of nature.[23] According to Thales, this was water; according to Akhenaten the singleness of the divine principle was the sun or the cosmic powers of the sun. This, however, also included water and the inundation. In the *Great Hymn*, it is written:

> An Inundation of your own from the sky for the foreigners
> and for the animals of every foreign land, that go on feet;
> and an Inundation coming from the Duat for Egypt;
> with your rays nursing every cultivation:
> when you rise, they live and grow for you.

Although there are few sources about the role of the Nile as such in this period, the importance of the Nile would have been the same for Akhenaten and Nefertiti as it was in the periods before or after. A fundamental aspect of the Egyptian religion was order and stability in the natural world centred around the rising and falling of the Nile, the daily return of the sun, and the successful seasons. The forces of nature were positive, ensuring life and light over-powering darkness and death.[24] From the era of the *Pyramid Texts* onwards, parts of the sky was associated with water and both the Fields of Reeds and the Fields of Offering could be flooded, and there is also one passage where it is spoken of a lake or a canal being excavated for the king in the Fields of Reeds. The most common terms suggesting that the sky is a body of water is *qbhw* or 'Fresh water'.[25] It was in this cosmology Moses was born and worked, and his origins and works are closely related to the Nile. In fact, he entered history in the Nile's reeds.

As Assmann says regarding the religious tradition of Moses, 'Moses is a figure of memory but not of history, while Akhenaten is a figure of history but not of memory.'[26] Since antiquity Moses has been identified with Akhenaten, and Clement of Alexandria wrote that the Egyptians do not reveal their religious mysteries to the commoners or the profane; only the initiated were judged as fit for this knowledge. 'State and religious secrecy are seen as interdependent [...] Without secrecy, there is no civil society or political order.' However, the monotheistic movement in the biblical narrative and theology associated with Moses and the Exodus was an anti-Egyptian revolution.[27] 'What Moses – or rather God by the mediation of Moses – did, was to translate the Egyptian premises of monotheism into revealed truth.'[28]

Many ancients as well as modern scholars have equated the Pharaoh of the Exodus with Ramses II (1279–13 BC). In antiquity, the daughter of the Pharaoh who found the baby Moses in the Nile is called Tharmuth or Thermuthis. Still, the Exodus is explicit about the fact that the Pharaoh of the Exodus is not the same as the Pharaoh at the time of Moses' birth. Moreover, although Ramses II had many daughters, none of them were named Tharmuth or Thermuthis. In any case, the name Thermuthis appears to be derived from (Ta)Renenutet; the Egyptian goddess of fertility and child nursing.[29]

Renenutet is a serpent goddess who feeds, nurses, suckles and brings up children, and she is also called a 'nurse goddess'. Some statues portray her holding a child in the position of suckling. The Egyptians also represented her in the fields erecting an altar where they had the wine and grape presses, and her cosmology was closely associated with grain, harvest, food and nursing – or the basic qualities of life. In the Ptolemaic period Renenutet or Ermuthis was assimilated with Isis and her blessings extended to the good inundation and the rejoicings following the rise of the flood. In a hymn to the Nile, it is written: 'When he (the Nile) rises then all the earth is in jubilation.'[30] If this is correct, then it was a female deity who found Moses.

Methodologically, there are a lot of problems with connecting texts and contexts, and in particular a religious text and how it relates to a person, which has caused a lot of heated debate in theology and biblical archaeology alike. According to the Old Testament scholar Thomas L. Thompson, 'It is only as history that the Bible does not make sense',[31] and 'to use the biblical traditions as the primary source for the history of Israel's origin, is to establish a hopeless situation for the historian who wants to write critical, rather than anachronistic, history'.[32] He continues:

> The problem is not that the Bible is exaggerated or unrealistic, and it is certainly not that the Bible is false. The writers of the Bible are surprisingly realistic and truthful. In their own terms – which are not the terms of critical historical scholarship – they express themselves well about the world they knew.[33]

This was to a large extent a water-world, and for Moses it was the Egyptian water-world structured around the Nile in the desert.

The birth of Moses has been a re-occurring theme throughout the ages and it has been vividly discussed whether the biblical narrative represents legends or realities.[34] Following Exodus 2:2–10:

> And a man of the house of Levi went and took *as wife* a daughter of Levi. So the woman conceived and bore a son. And when she saw that he *was* a beautiful *child*, she hid him three months. But when she could no longer

hide him, she took an ark of bulrushes for him, daubed it with asphalt and pitch, put the child in it, and laid *it* in the reeds by the river's bank. And his sister stood afar off, to know what would be done to him. Then the daughter of Pharaoh came down to bathe at the river. And her maidens walked along the riverside; and when she saw the ark among the reeds, she sent her maid to get it. And when she opened *it*, she saw the child, and behold, the baby wept. So she had compassion on him, and said, 'This is one of the Hebrews' children.' Then his sister said to Pharaoh's daughter, 'Shall I go and call a nurse for you from the Hebrew women, that she may nurse the child for you?' And Pharaoh's daughter said to her, 'Go.' So the maiden went and called the child's mother. Then Pharaoh's daughter said to her, 'Take this child away and nurse him for me, and I will give *you* your wages.' So the woman took the child and nursed him. And the child grew, and she brought him to Pharaoh's daughter, and he became her son. So she called his name Moses, saying, 'Because I drew him out of the water'.

Hence, Moses is named by the Pharaoh's daughter because he was 'drawn out of water'. In Hebrew, Moses means 'to draw out' in a similar way as a mid-wife or a water-bearer and in Egypt the name means 'to beget a child'. The latter name may also have been joined by the Egyptian deity Thut-mose;[35] Thutmose meaning the 'child of [the god] Thot'.

With regards to the Moses myth, Freud sees this in a historic perspective and in parallel to other similar myths, and the oldest of them seems to be about Sargon of Agade around 2800 BC – the very founder of Babylon. Freud quotes the king when he speaks about himself:

> I am Sargon, the mighty king, King of Agade. My mother was a Vestal; my father I knew not; while my father's brother dwelt in the mountains. In my town Azupirani – it lies on the banks of Euphrates – my mother, the Vestal, conceived me. *Secretly she bore me. She laid me in a basket of sedge*, closed the opening with pitch and *lowered me into the river*. The stream did not drown me, but carried me to Akki, the drawer of water. Akki, the drawer of water, in the goodness of his heart lifted me out of the water. *Akki, the drawer of water, as his own son he brought me up*. Akki, the drawer of water, made me his gardener. When I was a gardener, Istar fell in love with me. I became king and for forty-five years I ruled as king.[36]

Following Freud:

> The exposure in the basket is clearly a symbolical representation of birth; the basket is the womb, the stream the water at birth. In innumerable dreams the relation of the child to the parents is represented by drawing or

saving from the water. When the imagination of a people attaches this myth to a famous personage it is to indicate that he is recognized as a hero.[37]

But apart from generalization, Freud also attempts a historical explanation with regards to why there seems to be two myths, one Egyptian and one Jewish. If the original myth was Egyptian, it does not make sense that the legend makes him a hero, since according to sources the Pharaoh had a prophetic dream that his daughter's son would become a danger to him and the kingdom, and hence the child had to be delivered to the Nile as a way of getting rid of danger. The Egyptians had no reason to make Moses a hero. The Jews, on the other hand, had such reasons. According to Freud, there are two parallel stories including two families; one noble Egyptian and one humble Jewish:

> As a rule the real family corresponds with the humble one, the noble family with the fictitious one. In the case of Moses something seemed to be different [...] It is that the first family, the one from which the babe is exposed to danger, is in all comparable cases the fictitious one; the second family, however, by which the hero is adopted and in which he grows up is the real one [...] Moses is an Egyptian – probably of noble origin – whom the myth undertakes to transform into a Jew. And that would be our conclusion! The exposure in the water was in the right place [...] From means of getting rid of the child it becomes a means of its salvation.[38]

Among the Egyptians, names were magical, and there was a close and physical association between the bearer of the name and what was signified.[39] A peculiar aspect of Moses is that according to the Bible he was only given the name after three months by the Pharaoh's daughter, and three months is a lengthy time for a baby not having a name. This calls to question why the parents of Moses did not give him a name, also since double names are common for biblical characters. There are no hints of a double name in the Bible, but in the *Vision of Amram*, written in Amharic, it seems that Moses was given the Hebrew name Melchi or 'messenger of YHWA'.[40] The name thus indicated his divine role being a messenger, but it was not just a matter of naming and the Nile plays a central and fundamental role here, even on a cosmological level.

In Artapanus' description of the encounter between Moses and the Egyptian Pharaoh, Moses struck the Nile with his rod. Most translators have translated the following sentence in the same way, 'from that time on the flooding of the Nile took place', and it is hence interpreted that the annual inundation started with Moses' miraculous act. However, there might be problems with the translation, and indeed a scribal error, and it is suggested that it should read 'from that time on there took place the cataracting of the Nile'. In other words, Moses created the famous cataract from where the inundations started and the smiting of the river caused the inundation.[41] If the latter interpretation and translation is better, it testifies even more to Moses' powers, since the flood originated from the cosmic abyss at this spot, and in any case it testifies to Moses' role as cosmologically creating the life-giving flood. This act of 'drawing out' or 'bringing out', as the hand from the bosom or water from a rock, bears similarities to the very name of Moses himself being 'drawn out' of the Nile, but also of YHWH [God] who 'brought you [the Israelites] out of Egypt'.[42] This was also happening in the Wilderness of Zin where the children of Israel stayed in Kadesh:

> And Moses and Aaron gathered the assembly together before the rock; and he said to them, 'Hear now, you rebels! Must we bring water for you out of this rock?' Then Moses lifted his hand and struck the rock twice with his rod; and water came out abundantly, and the congregation and their animals drank. (Num. 20:10–11)

Thus, there are several passages and references to Moses making water, and in particular the possible cataracting of the Nile relates closely to the Egyptian cosmology. The subterranean source of the Nile from caves may have an etymological interpretation and explanation. According to Albright, the root term of 'cave, cavity' is 'hollow out, round out', meaning 'basin of a fountain, source of a spring', which resembles the meaning 'Nile source' and 'reservoir of the underworld'.[43] The name of the Nile, *itrw*, may stem from *wtr*, meaning to stretch, abound or swell.[44] And it was from the First Cataract that the Nile had its origin and source in Egyptian beliefs.

That Moses lived and worked in an Egyptian context, and also cosmology, has clear parallels also to the way God worked like an Egyptian God providing Moses with specific powers. Exodus (4:6–9) reads:

> Furthermore the LORD said to him, 'Now put your hand in your bosom.' And he put his hand in his bosom, and when he took it out, behold, his hand *was* leprous, like snow. And He said, 'Put your hand in your bosom again.' So he put his hand in his bosom again, and drew it out of his bosom, and behold, it was restored like his *other* flesh. 'Then it will be, if they do not believe you, nor heed the message of the first sign, that they

may believe the message of the latter sign. And it shall be, if they do not believe even these two signs, or listen to your voice, that you shall take water from the river and pour *it* on the dry *land*. The water which you take from the river will become blood on the dry *land*.'

The reference to the water being blood on dry land resembles closely the Osiris mythology and the fact that the fields were fertilized by the blood-red Nile. Moreover, as Lindsay points out, in Egypt Seth was also connected with both leprosy and snow (probably the snows in Ethiopia).[45] Thus, this passage in the Old Testament has clear parallels to the Egyptian cosmology, but also Moses' life-story as an infant is remarkably similar to the Horus-Osiris mythology where Osiris is slain by Seth and reborn in the Nile as Moses was found in the reeds.

The beliefs that the Nile turned to blood continued to live for a long time. In *Hermetica* it is written: 'And now I speak to thee, O River [i.e. the Nile], holiest [Stream]! I tell thee what will be. With bloody torrents shalt thou overflow thy banks. Not only shall thy streams divine be stained with blood; but they shall all flow over [with the same].'[46] In AD 216 bishop Dionysios wrote 'as in the time of Moses, the waters changed into blood', and as late as the fourth century the beliefs that the Nile also changed into wine was prevalent. In a recipe for Divine water it was said that strong vinegar should be added to sulphur until 'the liquid has the aspect of blood'.[47] Achilles Tatius did not mix wine and water when he first tasted the drink of the Nile, and it was sweet and delightful. Aristides said that the Egyptians filled their jars with water as other people fill them with wine, and kept them with pride in the homes for three or four and even more years. Epiphanius claimed in fact that at many locations and sources the water changed itself into wine. This, however, seems to be the only reference of transformation of Nile water to wine, and the author may have confused other accounts like the one of Achilles Tatius and Aristides, but it may also relate to Osiris' identification with Dionysus.[48] In any event, turning water into wine is also a prominent theme in another more famous religion.

That the water of Nile was as fine as wine, tasting sweet, has been held throughout most of known history. In the nineteenth century, Gérad de Nervall writes that in Constantinople Nile water was very much praised and appreciated and was sold in bottles at a high price. Indeed, the Sultan apparently drank no other water than from the Nile, which was believed to be good for fecundity.[49] These beliefs of the life-giving qualities of the Nile go, however, far back in history to time immemorial, and they seem to be one of the main reasons one of the greatest conquerors searched for the sources.

ALEXANDER THE GREAT

Alexander the Great had a fascination for Egypt. He was particularly careful in paying respect to the local gods and the priestly traditions, and he also undertook expensive restorations in the southern temples, which depicted him as a legitimate successors of the pharaonic rulers.[50] Alexander is said to have been searching for the water of life through which one gains immortality, and although not the only reason for Alexander's many conquests in Africa and elsewhere, it seems to have been one of them, and in the Babylonian Talmud he is believed to have found the water of a well coming from the Garden of Eden on the way to Africa.[51]

Alexander dreamt of finding the sources of the Nile and understanding the river's behaviour and fluctuation. His conquest of Egypt in 332 BC enabled him to investigate these questions that had been central in the pre-Socratic tradition stretching back to Thales. He made two attempts to settle the question about the sources, but in vain. Still, Alexander worked in a tradition where scientific inquiry and colonial conquest worked hand in hand, very much in the same way albeit in different forms as the later Nile explorers: 'If the river and its mysteries were part of Egypt's appeal for Alexander, it is also true that the Greek tradition about the river assumed a directly colonial function.'[52]

The Hellenistic geographers connect the Indus and the Nile, since both had a summer flood. Agatharkhides noted that shortly after the rains had swelled the Hydaspes, the heavy summer rains began in Egypt. Moreover, the mud of both rivers was also taken as an indication of their being linked.[53] Artaxerxes Ochus thought there was a lake that connected India and Ethiopia and that the Indus was the Upper Nile.[54] It was further believed that the Ethiopians had previously lived in India before migrating to Ethiopia, as Philostratos notes in his *Life of the Apollonius*. The Ethiopians were sons of the River Ganges and the subjects of King Ganges. However, they murdered the king and were compelled to migrate, and Heliodorus perhaps suggested that they accepted the sovereignty of another river-related ruler similar to their former overlords: in other words, connecting the Hydaspes and the Nile flood.[55]

Years after Alexander left Egypt and waged war in India, the question about the Nile sources came up again. In the academic discussion there is still an ongoing debate with regards to how much Alexander knew about the Ganges if he knew anything at all.[56] In any case, for a while Alexander was certain that the Indus tributary Hydaspes and the Nile were connected and that he had found the sources of the Nile in India. Nearchus of Crete, Alexander's boyhood friend and admiral, was well schooled in the antique tradition and exerted influence on Alexander. Following Herodotus, crocodiles were found in both the Indus and the Nile, but a crucial find was the discovery of the Egyptian beans growing, which was the lotus, although not an indigenous species in Egypt. Moreover, the summer monsoon in India could explain the rains giving rise to the flood in Egypt, it was believed for a while. However, the explorations showed that the Indus ended in the ocean and the theory had to be abandoned.[57]

Still, the beliefs that the Nile stretched beyond the African continent was widely held and long lived whether the sources were in Africa interior or beyond. In the Roman period with the expansion of the Isis cult, Isis was not only bringing forth the flood of the Nile in Egypt, but also the floods of the rivers Eleutheros in Tripolis and Ganges in India. Isis was the 'Mistress of the earth, you bring the flooding of rivers,'[58] but also Osiris was ascribed with similar omnipotent and global powers. According to Diodorus Siculus, Osiris was 'the one who campaigned over every land as far as the uninhabited regions of the Indians and those lying to the north, as far as the well-springs of the Danube River and again over the other parts as far as the Ocean'.[59] Even some Muslim geographers held that the Nile had its source in the Indus, although strongly rejected by most.[60] Mythologically, the Nile connected people and continents even in different religions and the most important aspect of the river itself was the dependency of the water and the annual flow shaping continuities in these beliefs and practices.

The transformation of the Egyptian religion from the ancient Egyptians to the Christians and later the Muslims, and its overall continuity in ritual practices and beliefs in the lay religion, pose analytical challenges. While the high religion often has doomed the prevailing practices as 'pagan' or 'heretic', David Frankfurter proposes another approach. 'Religion in Roman Egypt should be understood first as a local, collective endeavor to negotiate fertility, safety, health, misfortune, identity, and collective solidarity.'[61] This relates to the role of economy in relation to religion, or more precisely farming as a livelihood from the cradle to the grave:

> The rites around the Nile's surge display a different dynamic of persistence [...] as a popular tradition bound up so inescapably with the rhythms of the agricultural cycle that neither priestly nor imperial, nor, ultimately, Christian institutions could alter its cultural significance.[62]

Frankfurter elaborates further on with regards to the all-empowering and structuring role of the Nile:

> Nile cult should be understood as tradition in its deepest sense: as community-sustaining ritual patterns that inevitably determine those local activities sponsored by any 'great' or institutional religion. Thus we may understand why the veneration for the Nile flood constitutes one of the best documented 'survivals' in Coptic culture.

The Nile was simply too important for any great or transcendental religion to alter; they had to incorporate it: 'it was a tradition too intertwined with popular economic mentality.'[63]

COPTIC CHRISTIANITY

Upon the introduction of a new religion, the ancient Egyptian religion with regards to the Nile was Christianized at least on the surface. The Nile rose through the power of Christ or by the intercession of the Archangel Michael and the saints.[64] Coptic Christianity is truly syncretic, mingling remnants of Pharaonic practices with elements of Hellenistic, Byzantine Egyptian and Arab civilization as well as being one of the most ancient forms of Christianity. The word 'Copt' is interpreted as an Egyptian Christian, although it refers to all Egyptians, including both Christians and Muslims.[65] The word itself comes from the ancient *Hikaptah* (house of the *ka* or spirit of Ptah).[66] By the turn of the millennia, the government estimated that approximately 6 per cent of the population were Copts, or approximately 3.5 million people. However, the church claimed that the number was considerably higher, approximately 10 million or more (fig. 44).[67] The Christians in Egypt have faced many challenges from the

44. Saint Virgin Mary's Coptic Church or the Hanging Church in Old Cairo built on top of the Water Gate of Roman Babylon.

very beginning. As a Coptic priest in the United States said, 'The Coptic people's problems in Egypt have never been solved by talk of rights and laws. It is only by fasting and prayer that we may solve our problems. We know that fasting and prayer move mountains; this is our only choice.'[68]

According to Egyptian Christians, St Mark, who was Egyptian by birth, was the first apostle of Egypt and arrived in Egypt in approximately AD 60. He became a martyr in AD 68.[69] The martyrdom built for the relics of Johan the Baptist in Alexandria in the fourth century was also believed to contain the relic of the prophet Elisha, a disciple of Elijah.[70] The martyrs and the persecutions have played a central role in the Coptic Christianity.

A central core in Coptic Christianity is Jesus' flight to Egypt, and indeed as shown, in a similar way also central in Ethiopian Orthodox Church when the Holy family was in Ethiopia. In Egypt, Jesus found refuge on the banks of the Nile with his family who were fleeing persecution at the hands of Herod the Great, King of Judea, according Matthew (2:12–15):

> And having been warned by God in a dream not to return to Herod, the magi left for their own country by another way. Now when they had gone, behold, an angel of the Lord appeared to Joseph in a dream and said, 'Get up! Take the Child and His mother and flee to Egypt, and remain there until I tell you; for Herod is going to search for the Child to destroy Him.' So Joseph got up and took the Child and His mother while it was still night, and left for Egypt. He remained there until the death of Herod.

The Egyptian tradition makes a great deal of the holy family's stay, and along the Nile there are many pilgrimage sites, including the Church of the Virgin at Daqadus, the church at Sakha, the crypt of Musturud, the balsam tree at Mataria known as the Tree of the Virgin, and the monasteries of Gebel el-Tair and Deir el-Muharraq.[71]

The Coptic era begins on 29 August, AD 284, which is the date the Roman emperor Diocletan came to reign. Diocletan published four edicts of persecution, which struck the eastern Christians hard. The church in Egypt was so devastated that it later started the time era – The Era of Martyrs – with the tyrant's reign. A soldier in service of the Romans named Menas met his death and became a martyr in AD 296. On 11 November he was apparently executed for his Christian faith. According to legend, his body was miraculously transferred from his deathbed to a spot approximately 20 km south of Alexandria. It is believed that he said his body should be placed on a camel and sent out into the desert, and that he should be buried at the spot where the camel halted. His remains were interred, and soon afterwards Menas' fame spread among the Christians in Egypt. Around AD 324 the Roman empress Helena (c. 248–c. 328) erected a shrine at his grave after her daughter had been cured of elephantiasis by drinking from a nearby spring.[72] The grave became an important pilgrimage centre, on which a small limestone church was built during the fourth century. In the fifth century a large basilica was constructed, but this was destroyed in the seventh century. The fundamental religious commodity at Abu Menas was water. The pilgrimage place was like an Egyptian Lourdes, and the water was believed to have strong curative properties. Long after the cult of St Menas' declined, a large 150 m-square pool was the foci for the cult in the town of Abu Menas. Before leaving the town, pilgrims filled vessels or ampullae with this water to take with them, and water and sanctity is a common pilgrimage motif.[73]

Other Christian groups developed other approaches to religion in Egypt. The movement of the 'Desert Fathers' initiated by St Anthony (251–356) consisted of Christian hermits living in isolation and extreme poverty resisting temptation. St Pachomius (286–346) developed communal monastic settlements, which became monasteries in every sense of the word.[74] 'The Copts believe that monks in the desert are superior to virtuous men in the world. Even the novice monk is believed to surpass the virtuous man in righteousness.'[75] The hardship in the desert and rewards were explained in this way by Thomas Merton, who was a great monastic figure of the twentieth-century western Church:

> He [the monk] withdraws from [the world] in order to place himself more intensively at the divine source from which the forces that drive the world onwards originate, and to understand in this light the great designs of mankind. For it is in the desert that the soul most often receives its deepest inspirations. It was in the desert that God fashioned his people. It was to the desert he brought his people back after their sin [...] It was in the desert, too, that the Lord Jesus, after he had overcome the devil, displayed all his power and foreshadowed the victory of his Passover.[76]

'One of these desert monasteries was the White Monastery.' Although situated in the desert, water and the Nile had a prominent role. Shenoute was a Coptic abbot at the White Monastery from the latter part of the fourth into the third quarter of the fifth century, but the writings which are preserved from Shenoute are fragmentary copies made long after he died.[77] The White Monastery was located close to today's Sohag. Although the copies are difficult to date, it is generally believed that the various parts were written between the eighth and eleventh centuries.[78] Around AD 385, the monk Shenoute who was then in his mid-thirties became the third head of the White Monastery. He had been living in the monastery since he was seven years old, and is believed to have died in 464 at the age of somewhere between 115 and 118 years old.[79] Shenoute practised for more than 80 years, and it seems that at one point his disciples numbered as many as 2,200 monks and 1,800 nuns. Although he is labelled as authoritarian, harsh and violent, Shenoute plays a crucial role in the history of monasticism.[80] Shenoute's hatred of paganism and heresy in all its forms resulted in attacks on the local deities and he played a crucial role in erasing these former religious traditions as he envisaged and established Coptic Christianity in all areas and sectors of Upper Egypt.[81]

In *The Angel of the Waters* Shenoute wrote about the tense wait for the annual flooding of the Nile. Shenoute called the annual inundation of the Nile God's 'yearly mercy'.[82] Besa, who was his disciple and successor at the White Monastery, writes in his *The Life of Shenoute*:

> It happened one year that [the Nile] did not flood, and our father apa Shenoute knew from God the hidden reason for it. He also revealed the matter to the brothers with tears flowing from his eyes, and said to us: 'Pray to God. I, too, will go into the desert and spend this week praying to the Lord. See that no-one at all comes to me.' Shenoute said to his disciples; 'You know what I said to you, that God has commanded that there should be no flooding of the land this year. Behold, then, I prayed to him, and he, as the good and merciful God, promised me that this year again he would cause the waters to come and cover the face of the land.'[83]

Thus, water had an important role in the religious life and 'Shenoute's self-proclaimed relationship with God gave him knowledge of what God required for salvation,'[84] which in daily life was water. Even after Shenoute's death his divine powers were so great that he was still believed to be able to control the annual inundation. In prayers, he was invoked to cause the Nile to rise to its 'full measure' and thereby multiplying 'the harvests of the earth'. In fact, according to a heavenly vision attributed to him, he beholds the very angel in charge of the river and the flood.[85]

The coming of the flood was an important Christian event. The Copts call the star Sirius the 'flood-bringer' due to the proximity of its rising and the yearly rise of the Nile:

> As it appears, the monks intone the *owshia*, the special liturgical prayer which distinguishes each of the three Coptic seasons. A new Coptic year has begun [...] Undoubtedly, some form of it antedates Christianity in Egypt when a pharaoh or his priest might have actually invoked the star and the subsequent flood.[86]

11 September is New Year's Day:

> Near the end of October, forty days after the New Year has begun, the flood waters ordinarily begin to subside. The prayers of the Church turn

to concerns about vegetation. Likewise, from the third week in January to mid-June, alternative prayers are chanted for the coming of seasonable winds, not so strong as to damage crops, but constant enough to assist pollenization and fruitfulness.[87]

Thus, the Copts continued the Pharaonic calendar with three seasons of four months; the season of the flood, the season of the cultivation and the season of the harvest.[88]

Thousands of wooden statuettes were called 'wives of the Nile' and seen as concubines of Hapi probably representing human sacrifices in a symbolic form. However, while there are few evidences of human sacrifices to the Nile in the early Egyptian history, it seems that this practice gained importance in later periods whether symbolic or not.[89] In the fourth century among the Copts, as documented by a Christian source:

> There was a huge temple in one of the villages which housed a very famous idol, though in reality this image was nothing but a wooden statue. The priests together with the people [...] used to carry it in procession through the villages, no doubt performing the ceremony to ensure the flooding of the Nile.[90]

As will be seen later, this tradition continued for one and a half millennium and was fundamental also for Muslims.

In the first centuries of Coptic Christianity, death continued also the pharaonic perceptions in a Christianized way. On the epitaph of Cosmas from an area near Cairo, it was written: 'His short life faded in a moment. It acted as the grass which dries up and whose flowers withers.' This seems parallel to the Nile, which after receding and the crops grown and harvested, the field lay bare waiting for the new flood and the rebirth of nature, humans included.[91]

The feast of the Epiphany or baptism of Jesus is celebrated on 19 January, which was previously a great celebration of the Nile. Before most festivals there is a period of fasting and abstinence. During fast, no food or drink is taken between sunrise and sunset. Another major celebration, The Feast of the Cross,

> was a procession from the church that used to tour the village before ending at the Nile, or its nearest tributary, with the throwing of the cross into the river [...] there is little doubt that this festival was related to the Pharaonic feast of the Bride of the Nile.[92]

HOLY WATER, *LOGOS* AND VIRGIN MARY'S BREAST MILK

Virgin Mary has a fundamental place in Coptic Christianity. 'Mary's perpetual virginity is especially emphasized in all these feasts as a special means of her total dedication to God. She is thereby regarded as a favourite model of monastic holiness by the monks who celebrate her feasts.'[93] The *galaktotrophousa* or nursing image has a crucial role in Coptic Christianity. *Galaktotrophousa* means 'she who nourishes with milk'. The nursing period in Late Antiquity and Early Byzantine Egypt lasted normally for two or three years, and most often it was not the child's mother who nursed the baby but a wet nurse. Hence, this image, which is depicted in Coptic iconography in monasteries, does not represent a symbol of mother and child intimacy as such. Clement of Alexandria described in the second century AD the milk in Virgin Mary's breast as having its origin from God, and more precisely *logos*, since it has the same composition as the flesh and blood of Christ. The milk does not originate from the Virgin's own body, because this blood is 'liquid flesh'. The milk is 'the drink of immortality'.[94] According to Clement:

> What a surprising mystery! There is a single Father in the universe, a single *Logos* in the universe, and also a single Holy Spirit, everywhere identical. There is also a single virgin become mother, and I like to call her the Church. This mother, alone, did not have milk because, alone, she did not become a woman; she is at the same time virgin and mother, intact as a virgin, full of love as a mother; she draws to her the little children and nurses them with sacred milk, the Logos of nursling.[95]

Early in the fifth century, Cyril, another Alexandrian, followed this line and argued that Mary deserved to have the flesh and blood of Christ placed in her body since this milk is given 'in the heavens'. Heaven contained rivers of milk and honey, and milk was given as a reward to Christian martyrs. In Egypt the newly baptized infants were given a special Eucharist consisting of milk mixed with honey. Following the 'Canons of Hippolytus', the baptismal Eucharist should consist of milk and honey since it is the flesh of Christ which 'dissolves the bitterness of the heart through the sweetness of the *logos*'. This understanding of Virgin Mary's milk as the nectar of immortality also has a parallel in an Egyptian tale called the 'History of Aur', where a family of wealthy magicians addresses and asks her: 'deign to give us a little milk from thy breasts, so that we might drink it and never die.'[96]

45. The divine breast milk. From the Dendera Temple, Egypt.

These depictions of the nursing Virgin Mary in monasteries may have had a political function from the seventh century onward. While the Muslims claimed that Christ was simply a human prophet and not the divine son of God, the iconographic message would have underlined the divine aspects. Moreover, although this practice of using milk and honey in the baptismal Eucharist was never established in Syria and declined in Rome after the sixth century, it continued in Christian Egypt and Ethiopia in an unbroken tradition at least until the nineteenth century, and most likely into the twentieth century as well.[97]

The most interesting aspect of *galaktotrophousa* in this discussion is the explicit reference to milk being the cosmic *logos* which incorporates everything. The close relation to Isis is intriguing (fig. 45), and in particular the contemporary interpretations by Christians that the breast milk – the ultimate life giving water – was *logos*. Following Plutarch, these were exactly the divine qualities he described:

> In the Soul [of cosmos], then, Mind and reason (*Logos*), the guide and lord of all the best in it, is Osiris; and so in earth and air and water and heaven and stars, that which is ordered and appointed and in health, is the efflux of Osiris, reflected in seasons and temperatures and periods.[98]

As shown in Chapter 5, the actual waters of the Nile turns white and this was a central part of the Isis mythology when she suckled the infant Osiris.

Altogether, the number of miracles grew with time to a total of 316.[99] Virgin Mary's breast milk was not limited to nursing Jesus, but the holy substance could cure any disease; among other things it could heal the blind. John Bakansi was a priest in Cairo. He was more than 100 years old and had become blind in both eyes. In the church there was a picture of the Virgin Mary, and in a dream he saw her coming out of the painting, 'And she drew nigh unto him and took out her breasts from inside her apparel, and she pressed milk out from them upon his eyes,' and straightaway his eyes were opened. In Upper Egypt, she cured a blind girl by sprinkling 'upon her from her breasts some drops of milk of healing mercy; and straightway the eyes of the maiden were opened'.[100] Her milk also cured a monk who suffered from lip cancer.

The continuity of Nile beliefs was impossible to evade although it created controversies since it also represented continuity in older Parthenon of gods:

> In the fourth century AD the cult of the Nile, which lost nothing of its popularity during the final epoch of the Ancient Egyptian religion, became an object of controversy between the Christian authorities and the pagan party in Alexandria. After the victory of the new religion the beliefs concerning the Nile were, at least on the surface, Christianized. The Nile rises through the power of Christ and at the intercession of the archangel Michael and the saints.[101]

Hence, it also seems reasonable to interpret the *galaktotrophousa* or nursing image as a historic trajectory of ancient Egyptian beliefs and in particular the nursing Isis. This goes back to the *Pyramid Texts* where the White Nile was also seen as Isis' nursing breast milk: 'Raise yourself, O King! You have your water, you have your inundation, you have your milk which is from the breasts of Mother Isis.' Moreover, when Theodosius outlawed paganism and the temples were closed in AD 379, the Egyptians continued to see their beloved Isis and her son Horus in the images of Mary and Jesus.[102]

In Ethiopia, the image of the Virgin breastfeeding the Child is rare in pictorial representations although common in the *One Hundred and Ten Miracles of Our Lady Mary*. Still, in the main church of the monastery of Daga Istafanos in Lake Tana, there is such a painting (fig. 46). This image was repainted after a

46. The Virgin Mary breastfeeding Jesus, Daga Istafanos Monastery, Lake Tana.

fire in the mid-nineteenth century destroyed the much older original image. In the church of Abreha Atsbeha, just north of Wukro, there is another fresco of this scene. Mary sits on her throne and Jesus is suckling her breast.[103] In Ethiopia, there are three icons attributed to St Luke. One is in the monastery of Dabra Jamado Maryam in Lasta, and depicts a small curly-haired Jesus suckling at the breast of the Virgin Mary, which he supports with both hands. This icon is called Se'el Gebsawit, 'The Egyptian picture', and it has miraculous powers and can both speak and shed tears. The monks argued that the icon's miraculous powers would be transmitted to the photograph taken of it in the early 1970s, and that if the picture was widely distributed, it would lead to a spiritual revival and cause people to come to the monastery and venerate the original.[104]

In most Ethiopian churches, priests deny that Virgin Mary breastfed him on account of Jesus' divine character. Others, however, agree that Jesus was breastfed based on logical inference, even though this is not mentioned in the Bible. Since Jesus lived on earth as a normal person and did what people usually do, except commit sinful acts, he must also have been breastfed. However, this reasoning was made only on logical grounds and the Ethiopian tradition evident in both iconography and older texts seems to have changed and disappeared. These beliefs relate, however, to the flood in Egypt going back to the Pharaonic civilization and the particular characteristics the inundation had in this context. The Nile connected Egyptian and Ethiopian beliefs, and the waters in Egypt came from upstream, and apart from the Blue Nile one of the main tributaries was the Atbara River.

THE ATBARA DELUGE

Noah and the Deluge is part of a larger corpus of flood myths, of which the Babylonian tradition from Gilgamesh is the oldest documented. In Mesopotamian, Hebrew and ancient Greek traditions, mythologies of a Great Flood have been prominent.[105] This flood myth is so central and common that in the 1950s it was estimated that there were around 80,000 works in 72 languages only about Noah and the Ark alone.[106] However, conceptions of a Universal Deluge, at least based on the biblical narratives, are not generally found in Africa. Still, the annual inundation in ancient Egypt enabled interpretations connecting this flood with the Biblical Deluge. Although not widely held interpretations today, in the nineteenth century and before, the coffin made for Osiris' body after he was drowned has been compared with Noah's Ark.[107] Christians also saw the flood as a collective baptism.[108] Philo from Alexandria perceived Noah as a preliminary stage in the advance of the soul where Abraham and Moses represented higher stages. The deluge was a flood of passion cleansing souls. In the Nag Hammadi collection, found in 1945, God destroys all flesh in the flood, according to The Apocalypse of Adam. And while it is commonly perceived that Noah's ark came to rest at Mt Ararat after the flood,[109] there is seemingly an absence of references connecting the Deluge to the Nile and its floods, with some few exceptions. In Muslim traditions there are some specific flood myths in relation to the pyramids. According to one legend, there was a king named Sūrīd who dreamt of a catastrophe. A priest named Philemon reinterpreted this as a dream about a catastrophic flood, and Sūrīd then ordered the pyramids built as his own tomb and storerooms for treasures, magic statues and precious sciences of Egyptian wisdom. Philemon was the only survivor of the forthcoming flood, and the priest's wisdom was handed down for many generations.[110] This flood myth does not relate directly to the biblical narrative, but it seems that there has been such beliefs surrounding the Atbara flood.

Despite the voluminous research on the Nile, the Atbara River as a main tributary has largely been under-researched although not forgotten in past and present analyses. The Atbara has no lake as its headwater or source, but stems from thousands of mountain streams that flow from the annual rains in the Ethiopian highlands. The Atbara or Tekezze River is about 880 km long and the highest point in the catchment reaches more than 3,500 m above sea level and the larger part of the eastern watershed is situated at altitudes higher than 2,500 m. The strong seasonality creates an exceptional intense flood during the rainy season (generally June–October), and the river may rise more than 5 m above its normal levels. Importantly, it also brings millions of tonnes of silt each year and, as such, it hugely contributes to the fertile plains of Egypt. However, in 1966 the Khashm al-Girba Dam on the Atbara was completed, erasing and controlling the flood.[111] Given that little research has been conducted on this river, there are not many written sources with regards to perceptions of this mighty, albeit very seasonal, river. One reason for this is the very hostile and desolate climate in the region around the Atbara River where few people historically have lived.

Given the ecology, agriculture has never been a major subsistence strategy along the lower parts of the Atbara. Even the Atbara Bisharin, who in the 1930s had lived there for eight generations, were seen as poor and idle cultivators despite that the rich alluvial islands could have enabled them to become more dependent on farming:

> They have fine wadi lands where the business of cultivation is reduced to a minimum and the harvest is phenomenally heavy when rainfall is even moderate. They thus tend to ignore their river lands where the preliminaries of cleaning and tillage are onerous.

Even along the river, agriculture was mainly dependent upon the rains and sacrifices part of rainmaking rituals, since 'prayers of rain' were part of being a good Muslim.[112]

When Baker was on his tour exploring Africa on the way to the Nile sources, he also spent time at other places in the basin. In 1861 he was travelling in the deserts by the shores of the river Atbara, and on 23 June he writes that the party almost suffocated by a whirlwind that buried everything within the tents by several inches of dust. The heat was intense and as usual the sky was spotless. That night, when the coolness arrived and he tried to sleep around half-past eight, he heard a rumbling like a distant thunder, a sound far away which grew stronger. The Arabs started shouting, 'El Bahr! El Bahr!' (the river! the river!):

We were up in an instant, and my interpreter, Mahomet, in a state of intense confusion, explained that the river was coming down, and that the supposed thunder was the roar of approaching water [...] the water had arrived, and the men, dripping with wet, had just sufficient time to drag their heavy burdens up the bank [...] the river had arrived 'like a thief in the night'.

Baker writes:

On the morning of the 24th June, I stood on the banks of the noble Atbara river, at the break of day. The wonder of the desert! – yesterday there was a barren sheet of glaring sand [...] For days we had journeyed along the exhausted bed: all Nature, even in Nature's poverty, was poor [...] In one night there was a mysterious change – wonders of the mighty Nile! – an army of water was hastening to the wasted river: there was no drop of rain, no thunder-cloud on the horizon to give hope, all had been dry and sultry [...] The rains were pouring in Abyssinia! *these were the sources of the Nile!*[113]

James Bruce also described the Atbara, and the role and importance of the water can best be understood in light of the burning heat in the desert. Starting with Sennar in Sudan, he first describes what he means by *cold, temperate, warm, hot* and *very hot*. But it can get worse:

I call it *excessive hot*, when a man, in his shirt, at rest, sweats excessively, when all motion is painful, and the knees feel feeble as if after fever. I call it *extreme hot*, when the strengths fails, a disposition to faint comes on [...] This, I apprehend, denotes death at hand.

This extreme hotness is not only because of the sun, but in combination with the poisonous winds

which pursued us through Atbara, and will be more particularly described in our journey down the desert, to which Heaven, in pity to mankind, has confined it, and where it has, no doubt, contributed to the total extinction of everything that hath the breath of life.[114]

If Bruce felt the heat more like hell than heaven, he still referred to myths concerning the annual flood of the Atbara:

It is a tradition among the Abyssinians, which they say they have had from time immemorial, and which is equally received among the Jews and Christians, that almost immediately after the flood, Cush, grandson of Noah, with his family, passing through Atbara from the low country of Egypt, then without inhabitants, came to the ridge of mountains which still separates the flat country of Atbara from the more mountainous high-land of Abyssinia.

He continues after describing the Abyssinian Mountains:

> Their tradition say that, terrified with the late dreadful event the flood, still recent in their minds, and apprehensive of being again involved in similar calamity, they chose for their habitation caves in the sides of these mountains, rather than trust themselves again on the plains.

This was a safe choice, according to Bruce, and they preferred to live high up being dependent upon the rains:

> They chose to stop at the first mountain, rather than proceeding farther at the risk of involving themselves, perhaps in the land of floods, that might prove as fatal to their posterity as that of Noah had been to their ancestors.[115]

Thus, it seems that in a distant past there were stories and legends connecting the violent flow of the Atbara River with the Biblical Deluge, if one is to believe Bruce that these stories were shared by Christians and Jews alike. That the coming of the flood was an impressing event, such as Baker described, is without any doubt, and his men were almost swept away by the flood, and other flashfloods in the region may also have evoked similar experiences. Then, as now, in Sudan, such flashfloods are extremely dangerous and may cause havoc and death as they suddenly come from apparently nowhere with intense force and speed. Following the Abyssinian history that Cush with his family came to Atbara shortly after the flood, it gives testimonies to beliefs that the actual deluge was related to the Nile's annual flooding, and more specifically to the Atbara, since the Blue Nile flood is slowly expanding and increasing although to intensive velocity and volumes, but not as a gigantic flash flood.

Still, the Atbara, or the Tekeze as it is known in Ethiopia, has connected other parts of biblical stories and Christianity in different ways, some more curious than others, but they somehow share the importance of Moses. In the process of mythmaking, Graham Hancock, who wrote the controversial *The Sign and the Seal: The Quest for the Lost Ark of the Covenant*, put forward another reason for James Bruce's searches for the sources of the Nile. The Scotsman was a freemason, and therefore a member of the group that knew about the Templar Knights, and hence his real mission was to search for the Ark. According to Hancock, the search for the source of the Nile was a masquerade and plausible alibi for him going to Ethiopia, and evidence for his hidden agenda is that he hardly mentions the Ark, although that was one of the few facts known about Ethiopia in his days.[116] And according to legends, the ark resided, and still does, in Aksum.

The great Ethiopian civilization may also be seen as having its origin water. Aksum is situated at the water-divide between two main drainage systems; the Tekeze/Atbara River and the Märäb/Gas River. The name Aksum seems to be derived from 'ak', which is possibly the Cushitic root word for 'water', and 'šum', the Semitic word for chief. It seems that springs and water cisterns fed by rain and groundwater were the main water resources for the city, although today none of the man-made structures firmly date older than the fifteenth century. The most famous pond and water resource is May Šum, which originally was 65 m in diameter and 5 m deep and enlarged at various stages. Still, another well is mentioned by Saint Yared who lived there in the sixth century.[117] Hence, also this civilization was based on changing concepts of water as time passed on and religions evolved, and closely developed to the particular water-world where the annual rainfall is usually less than 650 mm per year.

Moving from the borders of the Nile basin to Nile proper, the river has structured all societies and civilizations throughout the ages. Whether mythologies or realities, the Nile has it all, and the river combines religions and beliefs transferred from one religion to another because of ecological logics and limitations, but also possibilities, given the absolute necessity of water and the spectacular character of the Nile itself. This is further testified by the Islamic succession of Nile cosmologies in the desert regions of Egypt.

NILE MUSLIMS

The Qur'an (21:30) says: 'We made from water every living thing,' summing up the all importance of water in Islam. The word 'water' occurs more than 60 times in the Qur'an, 'rivers' over 50 and 'the sea' over 40, whereas 'fountains', 'springs', 'rain' and 'hail' are less frequent. Statements concerning water often begin with 'It is God [...] It is He Who [...]' reminding humans that the origin of fresh water is with God and not humans.[118] As it says in the Qur'an: 'Consider the water which you drink. Was it you that brought it down from the rain cloud or We? If We had pleased, We could make it bitter: why then do you not give thanks?' (56:68–70). Water is a divine gift and the benefits are clearly expressed: 'We send down pure water from the sky, that We may thereby give life to a dead land and provide drink for what We have created – cattle and men in great numbers' (25:48–9).

Before prayers five times each day, purification by ablution is necessary, and the rules of purification are based on the Qur'an, particularly 5:6:

> O you who are faithful! When you undertake ritual worship, then wash your faces, your hands to the elbows, rub your heads and legs to the ankles. And if you are precluded [from ritual worship etc.], cleanse. If you are sick, or on a journey, or one of you come from the privy, or you have had [physical] contact with women, and you do not find water, then take good topsoil and rub your faces and hands with it. God does not want place a burden on you but He wants to cleanse you and complete His benefaction for you, perhaps you will acknowledge your obligation.

Water is the preferred, but in the absence of water sand is also a proper medium, stressing that purification is not cleanliness in a hygienic sense but rather in a ritual sense emphasizing spiritual purity.[119]

Islam is a desert religion, and the concepts and beliefs of water should be seen in relation to its place of origin and the areas where the religion spread, including Egypt where the Nile was everything. The Islamic invasion of Egypt took place in AD 639. Apart from the Nile, there was little continuity from ancient to Islamic Egypt due to a double cultural break; first with the victory of Christianity and then three centuries later with Islam. Hence, in the Islamic area the knowledge of the pyramids, rituals and symbols, and indeed the whole civilization was gone.[120] Still, the almighty Nile shaped the beliefs of Muslims in Egypt (fig. 47).

In the second half of the first millennium, there was an Islamic tradition highlighting the religious Nile:

> The Nile of Egypt is the lord of rivers. God has subordinated to it every river, from east to west. For when God wishes to make the Nile of Egypt flood, He commands every other river to lower, and they lower their waters. God cleaves the earth into springs, and they make the river flow as God will – may He be glorified and praised. And when its flood is finished, He inspires every water to return to its own.[121]

Not only were all the rivers in the world under the control of God, but the Nile was the most important of them all, and when it flooded, it was because all the other rivers had been lowered.

In a lost work by the Fatimid envoy Ibn Sulaym al-Aswānī there are numerous references to the Nile. Although the original work is lost, he is quoted by many writers including al-Maqrīzī, and probably he presented

47. Al-Azhar mosque, Cairo.

his book to the second Fatimid Caliph in Egypt, al-Azizi, in the second half of the tenth century. His descriptions of the Nile seem to have been popular among medieval writers because of their unique and precise descriptions. During the flood, he described the colours of the Nile as muddy as well as white and green.[122] As indicated earlier, the 'Blue Nile' is a misnomer and mistranslation, and the original Arabic word signifies 'dark'.

Bahr al-Nīl (The sea of Nile) is the name Arab Egyptians usually use when describing the Nile. Although this word does not appear explicitly in the Qur'an, it appears at least metaphorically as a poetical allusion in the word Yamm (Sea) in the story of Moses and the Egyptian Pharaoh. Although it was shared by Muslim geographers that there were four rivers issuing from Paradise, there was no consensus with regards to where, but the Nile often had a prominent role. The rivers of Paradise were also often connected with the Fountain of Life itself, a belief which originated in the Jewish and Christian traditions.[123] The peculiarities of the Nile were summed up in this way:

> The learned are all agreed that there is not in the world a river of greater length than the Nile. For its course through the land of Muslims amounts to more than a month's journey; and it its course through Nubia to two month's journey; and for a journey of four months it flows through uninhabited waste land, until the source is reached in the Mountain of the Moon, south of equator. There is no other river again which runs from south to north except the Nile.[124]

The uniqueness of the Nile in the Islamic era was the same as in earlier periods, and the importance of the flood for tax and all wealth was as important then as it was from the earliest periods documented on the Palermo stone.

Throughout history, different authors have referred to the various measures and their importance for Egypt. According to Pliny: 'When the Nile rise reaches twelve cubits, there is hunger; at thirteen there is still scarcity, fourteen bring joy, fifteen security and sixteen abundance and delights or pleasure.' Following Denys (Dionysius) of Tell Mahrê in Syria, who visited Egypt in AD 824 and 832, if the waters were less than 14 cubits, only a small part of Egypt was watered, and no crop was grown and no tax collected. If the waters rose to 15 or 16 cubits, the harvest was medium and the tax likewise. If the waters rose to 17 or 18 cubits, all of Egypt was watered and the harvest and tax were successful. If the volume of water rose to 20 cubits it caused damage and there would be no harvest. The actual levels of cubits have varied, and according to 'Amr at the time of the conquest of Egypt; at 12 cubits there was drought; 14 cubits was enough to avoid drought; 16 cubits meant that all cultivable land was flooded and there could even be reserves for the following year; at 18 cubits there was flooding. 'Abd al-Latîf of Baghdad, who visited Egypt around AD 1200, called 16 cubits 'water of the sultan' since the land tax became payable at this volume. At that level half of the land was irrigated, producing enough crops to feed the whole population for a year. If the water was between 16 and 18 cubits, the crops could sustain the population for two years. In general, land tax became mandatory when the Nile rose to 16 cubits. Below that, it could not be exacted. If the lands were not inundated, the peasants were not obliged to pay tax, but the government could open the canals, causing sufficient levels of flooding to make the tax obligatory after all (fig. 48).[125]

In Islam, ancient Egypt was seen as the embodiment of paganism, and the ninth-century book-dealer and bibliographer Ibn al-Nadīm labelled ancient Egypt as the 'Babel of sorcerers'. Nevertheless, there were scholars who aimed to integrate the pagan pre-history into the salvation patterns of Islam. Moreover, the pyramids played a fundamental role in the Islamic eschatology. According to the Shi'i theologian Ibn Bābūyah (d. AD 991), at the end of history the pyramids which had served as talismans against the inundations would be destroyed by the Twelfth Immam. In the Ottoman period, in the final days of the world

48. The Roda Nilometer in Cairo with records from AD 641 to AD 1890.

the cruel King Nebuchadnezzar was believed to use black powder to blow up the pyramids, ensuring that Egypt is open to the demise in the floods of the Nile. The pyramids were also important in Islam with regards to another watershed in history: the Deluge which divided this period of paganism into two halves. Abū Ja'far al-Idrīsī of the thirteenth century worked on this treatise. He consulted 22 authorities on this question, of which 18 favoured an antediluvian date, because as one of them said, 'Otherwise their story would have been preserved.' Thus, the pyramids survived the flood, but not without damage, and the Deluge precipitated the Sphinx and broke it into pieces.[126]

Known in Arabic as the Ghitās, the most important Coptic Nile festival coincided with the rising of the waters, commemorating baptism and the unity with the Holy Spirit. The festival took place shortly after the winter solstice when the Nile water is most pure. The most important ritual was submersion into the Nile, a rite of water purification. In 367 AH (AD 977–8) the caliph al 'Azīz prohibited the festival.[127] Although he allowed the festival for a period of time, the Fatimid caliph al-Hakim banned the collective ritual of submersion, and in 403–5 AH (AD 1012–15) ordered a banishment of Copts and Jews to Byzantine territories. Fourteen years later, however, the festival flourished under the patronage of the caliph who used it to articulate Fatimide authority, a tradition which seems to have lasted until as late as 517 AH (AD 1123–4).[128]

A very unusual event in the history of Islam is the participation of a Muslim governor in a Christian religious feast – the feast of baptism celebrated by the Copts every year on 19 January. al-Mas'ūdi described the event elaborately:

> I attended in the year 330 A.H. [AD 941–2] the feast of baptism in Cairo. During that time the governor of Egypt, al-Ikhshīd Muhammad ibn Turghj was in his palace, called al-Mukhtar, on al-Roda Island which is surrounded by the water of the Nile. He ordered that ten thousand torches be lightened on the island along the Nile shore of al-Fustāt. This was over and above the [number of] torches that the people had lightened in the city. Thousands of Muslims and Christians came to the Nile shore, others came in boats and others watched from their homes overlooking the river. Many on the shores of the Nile, who did not disapprove of eating and drinking in public, showed up in their gold and silver jewellery and played music to entertain themselves. During that evening the gates remained open and many people immersed themselves in the Nile claiming that it gave them protection from illness and prevented the spread of disease.[129]

The rule of al-Hakim was harsh and cruel. In 400 AH (AD 1009–10) Christian feasts were cancelled and celebration forbidden throughout the country. Three years later an order was issued to loot and destroy the remaining churches and monasteries in Egypt. Finally, al-Hakim came up with the last choice: death or conversion. However, the historian al-Antākī mentions that al-Hakim had attended the celebration several times in disguise, and 'after dinner Christians and Muslims alike dipped into the water of the Nile. They claimed whoever dipped into the water that night would be safe from weakness of the body during that year.'[130] When al-Zahir succeeded al-Hakim, he allowed the celebration of the feast in 405 AH (AD 1014–15). Maqrīzī writes:

> The emir al-Mu'aminīn [the Prince of the Faithful] al-Zahir li-'Izāz Dīn Allah, the son of al-Hakim, went to the palace of his grandfather al-'Azīz bi-Allah to look upon the al-Ghitās festival with his harem. It was announced that Muslims should not join the Christians when they dipped into the water of the river Nile on that night. [Even so,] the caliph ordered the torches to be lit at night, and there were a great many

of them. The monks and priests carried crosses and candles, and prayed and sang hymns for a long time until they dipped into the Nile.[131]

Muslims also worshipped the Nile and consequently two of the most controversial issues between the Christians and the Muslims were the Coptic festivals and who was in control of the Nilometer and the flood. As long as one follows the 'true' religion, the land will prosper. The Copts were therefore deprived their privilege of announcing the rise of the Nile waters. 'Measuring the Nile water became a tradition that was followed religiously by subsequent states, not the least of which was the Mamluk state.'[132] The Coptic Nile festivals in Egypt also mobilized collective social and religious reaction by the Muslims, and hence it was seen as a threat to the Mamluk leaders who had to recast it to accommodate dominant Muslim structures.

Based on Maqrīzī's historical texts from fifteenth-century Cairo, Huda Lufti has analysed how the Coptic festival as a social and cultural event and hence the Copts as an ethnic minority became marginalized in the official Mamluk narratives. Rather than giving a full account of the Coptic Nile festival itself or analysing the suppressive means employed by the Mamluks, Lufti has emphasized how the Nile and the former rituals and perceptions even overpowered the Muslims. Maqrīzī constructs two cultures in tension; a hegemonic Arab-Muslim culture and a declining but nevertheless resilient Coptic culture. Maqrīzī starts his treaty of the Coptic Nile festivals with the famous story of the first Arab Muslim governor of Egypt who forbade the practice of sacrificing a female virgin to the Nile. However, due to this ritual sanction, the Nile did not rise for three months. The governor was in despair and wrote to the pious caliph 'Umar I, asking him for advice. The caliph proclaimed that instead of virgins being sacrificed, the governor should throw a piece of paper into the Nile on which the caliph had inscribed:

> Allah alone can cause the Nile water to flow. [The governor] threw the paper in the Nile, one day before the festival of al-Salīb, but in the meantime, the people of Egypt were preparing to depart, because their welfare rested only on the Nile. However, on the day of the Salīb festival, Allah, the Almighty, caused the Nile to flow, reaching 16 cubits in one night, thus preventing harm from happening to the people of Egypt.[133]

Later on, the Copts used to throw a finger which belonged to a male Coptic martyr into the Nile. On this Maqrīzī comments:

The finger of the martyr was taken in a box to al-Malik al-Sālih to be burnt in front of him in the *maydān*. He then ordered that its ashes be thrown in the Nile, so that the Copts would not be able to take it back. From that day on, 'Īd al-Shahīd was discontinued until this period. To Allah we owe gratitude and strength.[134]

There are very few references to Mamluk state ceremonials of the Wafā festival. Wafā al-Nīl was the date when the Nile reached 16 cubits. Nevertheless, Maqrīzī gives an account of the state's celebration of such an event, constructing a glamorous picture of the Fatimids' celebrations:

> Wafā al-Nīl was of great importance for them, and they celebrated it with excessive joy, for it was the cause of the land's prosperity and the creatures' harmony before Allah's grace. This explains why the caliph paid much greater attention to it than any of the other festivals.[135]

Qur'an reciters and the religious leaders of the most important mosques were ordered to spend the night in the Nilometer mosque, and when the Nile reached the 16 cubit mark, the ritual of anointing the Nilometer was performed, signifying a desire to bring life to the Nilometer, a ritual the caliph attended. In contrast to the Coptic festival of the Nile in the Mamluk period, the Wafā had undergone a fuller process of Islamization:

> Thus Wafā al-Nīl seems to have been displaced as a Coptic festival, only to reappear as an official Muslim event. Notorious for their patronage of popular religious festivals, it is quite possible that it was the Fatimids who pushed for the Islamisation of the Wafā rituals.[136]

Not only the river, but all types of water belonged to the divine realms. Rain prayers also took place, but only when the Nile failed and showed signs of drought:

> The communal performance of rain rituals may be said to express a collective desire to pass from a state of sin to a state of virtue in order to bring about forgiveness and mercy, thus effecting a reversal of the drought situation. Underlying the performance of these rituals is the common belief that natural catastrophes are caused by human transgressions of God's laws, which may be reversed only if people repent their sins.[137]

Maqrīzī writes about a Nile decrease in 810 AH (AD 1407–8): 'The Nile water stopped increasing for three days, beginning Thursday, and several amirs rode in order to attack the sites where people congregated for rejoicing. They were forbidden to commit abominations, so it started to increase on Sunday and the increase continued.'[138] In 823 AH (AD 1420–1) he reports of a drought:

> The Nile stopped increasing for several days. Grain prices rose and merchants stopped selling it. People's worry increased. They were called upon to stop committing what Allah forbade, and instead to commit themselves to virtue. They were asked to fast for three days and to go out to the desert. Many people fasted the next day, including the sultan. So it was announced that there was an increase of one digit.[139]

The Muslim rulers had to control the Nile and, in other words, it should be in the hands of Allah and not the Christian God, but this was not only a religious contest in Egypt since the Nile connects people and beliefs and Egypt's water came from Ethiopia. Those who controlled the Nile controlled the people, and according to a story about King Dawit of Ethiopia, it was clearly stated that Christian control was a threat to the Muslim people (see below), their rulers and their God – Allah. Nevertheless, it was essentially the Pharaonic and Christian rituals which became Islamized, and thus, Nile Islam was a syncretism of the previous religions and worship of the river, with roots going back to ancient Egypt, which is also seen in the opening of the canal.

The opening of the seasonal canals and the Canal of the Commander of the Faithful used to take place on the Coptic festival of the veneration of the Cross on the seventeenth day of the Coptic month of Tut, or around 17 September, but in the Islamic era it could also take place some few days earlier. The opening usually took place when the level of the Nile averaged just over 15 cubits on the Roda Nilometer, indicating the plentitude to come.[140]

Edward William Lane described manners and customs among the Egyptians in the years between 1833 and 1835. Not only were prayers performed for rain when needed, but he elaborates in great detail how Muslims observed specific religious periods in accordance with the Coptic religious calendar concerning changes in the weather, and in particular the annual flood. The night of 17 June, which is called Leylet en-Nuktah or the Night of the Drop, was believed to be when a miraculous drop fell into the Nile causing the flood to start rising. Astrologers calculated the exact time when the 'drop' was expected to fall, which coincided with the night. Not only in Cairo but also in other parts of Egypt, many inhabitants spent the night on the banks of the Nile. It was also a custom, especially among women, to place upon the terrace of their house the same number of lumps of dough as there were members living in the household. Each lump of dough for each person had a personal mark, and at daybreak the next morning each lump was checked to see if it had cracked. If a lump of dough for a specific member was cracked, it was a sign that he or she may have a long life, or at least live throughout the year. On the contrary, if the lumps were not cracked, it was inferred that the life of that person would be terminated in the following year. Some also believed that this was a way of predicting if the Nile would rise high in the ensuing season, and in Egypt the annual inundation was a matter of life or death.[141]

The rise of the Nile usually coincided with the period of the summer solstice. From or about 3 July the rise was daily proclaimed in the streets of Cairo. This was a specific task ascribed to a special group of functionaries called the Criers of the Nile. Each particular district had its own crier who, accompanied by a boy, announced the rise of the Nile. When the flood started, he proclaimed: 'God hath been propitious to the lands! The day of good news!' The daily announcements included proclamations such as:

> Mohammad is the Prophet of guidance [...] He will prosper who blesseth him! [...] The treasuries of the Bountiful are full! [...] I extol the perfection of Him who spread out the earth! [and the boy replies] And hath given running rivers! Through whom the fields have become green! [...] God hath given abundance, and increased [the river] and watered the high lands! [...] May he abundantly bless them with his perfect abundance, and pour abundantly the Nile over the country! O Bountiful! O God! [...] Five [or six, etc., digits] to-day, and the Lord is bountiful!

These last proclamations were ended by the boy uttering 'Bless ye Mohammad!' in 'the fear lest the rising of the river should be affected by malicious wish or evil eye, which is supposed to be rendered ineffectual if the malicious person bless the Prophet'.[142]

Although the Crier of the Nile sometimes got his daily piece of bread from people, most did not give him much before the day of opening the Canal of Cairo. Still, although he was often uninformed or misinformed by those who actually measured the height of the rising Nile, people listened with interest to his cries, which lasted until the day before the dam that controlled the canal of Cairo was opened. On this day, the crier went around and announced the 'Completion, or Abundance, of the Nile', which was when the Nile had reached the sufficient height of 16 cubits of the Nilometer. This level, however, was also the level which the ancient laws stated that land-tax can be collected by the government, implying that the blessings of the waters came with obligations. The Crier of the Nile announced: 'The river hath given abundance, and completed [its measure]! [and the boys reply] God hath given abundance! [...] And the canals flow! [...] By permission of the Mighty, the Requiter!' The cutting of the dam attracted a huge group of spectators, partly because of the political importance it used to have in the past, although in the 1830s it was mainly an occasion for a public festival. The dam was constructed before or just after the flood started to increase with a height of 22 or 23 ft above the Nile when at its lowest, and the depth of the canal was a bit more so the top of the dam was a few feet lower than the banks of the canal.[143]

In front of the dam a round pillar of earth was raised with a truncated cone and not as high as the dam. This pillar was called the 'bride'. Upon the top of the pillar as well as the dam, some millet or maize were usually sown. The 'bride'-pillar was always washed down before the inundation had reached its summit and often a week or fortnight before the dam was cut. It was believed that this tradition originated among the ancient Egyptians when they sacrificed a young virgin to the Nile to secure a plentiful inundation. This practice was stopped by the Arab conquest of Egypt.[144]

Still, the ancient Egyptian tradition continued with not only the 'bride', but also the procession leading to the cutting of the dam. Preceding the actual cutting, private parties in numerous boats were on the river, and it included hired professional musicians, although the dancing-girls who used to take part in the past had been forbidden. It was a time of festivities with fireworks and guns in the dark hours and together with the lamps on the boats it formed a picturesque scene. There was also one large boat, and this vessel was believed to represent the magnificent boat in which the ancient Egyptians used from where the virgin was thrown into the river. Before sun-rise a great number of workmen started to cut the dam. These were paid Jews and Muslim grave-diggers. Huge crowds stood at the banks of the rivers, including dignitaries from the government. The Governor himself threw a small purse of gold to the labourers and in the past money was thrown into the canal and picked up by the commoners. People used to die when the water started flowing, and in 1834 one drowned in the Canal and two others in a lake. In any event, people continued for days after the opening to enjoy the view and marvel of the rising and expanding waters. The Crier of the Nile continued his cries, and he came back on other occasions later in September when the Nile had reached its greatest height, concluding that 'The fortunate Nile of Egypt hath taken leave of us in prosperity; in its increase it hath irrigated all the country.'[145]

The total dependency of the Nile for prosperity and all life is evident in the ritual continuity throughout the centuries. The long continuity of beliefs and traditions has a double explanation relating to functional and substantive aspects of religion. On one hand, if the rituals had worked and functioned for centuries and millennia, there were no reasons to doubt that they would continue to work in the future. This points to the extreme long historic trajectories going back to ancient Egypt and the fundamental role and importance of the inundation in all societies situated along the banks of the Nile in Egypt. On the other, the yearly flood was the divine miracle ever occurring, and without the divinities it was believed that it would not take place. The gods changed, but not the fundamental contents and importance of the rituals and their function. From this perspective, at least in Egypt, it was the rituals and their outcomes that shaped the perceptions of the powers of the gods and the divinities rather than the other way around, continuing at least to the nineteenth century and then gradually changing in the age of modernization.

Thus, as it has been pointed out, seeing Egypt as 'the gift of the Nile' is misleading because it reflects

> both ancient and modern Orientalist perspectives of an inherently passive Egypt: it would surely be preferable to understand past Egyptian society not as a 'gift' – for which, implicitly, no exertion or payment is required – but rather as an ongoing dialectic between Egypt's human inhabitants and the landscape in which they found themselves.[146]

The Muslim Nile created by Allah originating from Paradise has yet had other political uses in more recent times. Anwar Sadat offered Jews and other believers in 'monotheistic religions' Nile waters as a good gesture if Israel would withdraw from Gaza and the west Bank. Sadat also said:

> In the name of Egypt and its great Al-Azhar and in the name of defending peace, the Nile water will become the new 'Zamzam well' for believers in the three monotheistic religions [...] The water will serve all pilgrims visiting the holy shrines in Jerusalem.[147]

This caused indignation and protests from the upstream countries, but it also shows how relics of religious water still lingered on even among revolutionaries. The Zamzam well is the Holy well in Mecca central during the Hajj and refers to the biblical story of how Hagar and Ismail were saved from thirst. The Zamzam spring has it origin, as recorded in both the Jewish and the Islamic tradition, when Abraham following God's command sent his second wife Hagar, an Egyptian slave woman, into the desert with their son Ishmael. Almost dying of thirst in the desert, God revealed a 'well of water' when he heard the child cry, and Hagar let the child drink from its waters.[148] In Islam water is also a symbol of paradise, and indeed containing moral qualities of God's grace and paradise. The Qur'an (88:1–12) says: 'In the garden is no idle talk; there is a gushing fountain.' The Zamzam spring in Mecca is a source of life-giving waters also curing illness.

Rules and regulations regarding water are very important in Islam since the religion originated in arid regions. In some versions of Islamic law, water cannot be sold since it is a gift of God, although limited ownership is permitted if individuals for instance have made a well and created specific access to water.[149] Sharia law originally has a very specific meaning – 'the path to water' or 'the path to God' – and hence, sharia is a moral compass guiding a Muslim's public and personal life.[150] In a broader perspective, sharia is 'the religious law of God: consisting of such ordinances as those of fasting and prayer and pilgrimage and the giving of the poor rate and marriage and other acts of piety, or of obedience to God, or duty to Him and to men.'[151] Sharia is a divine law in origin and transcendent with regards to the aims, and here is where 'the path to the water' comes in more spiritually and metaphorically than mere shares and needs of physical water. The 'path' or 'way' indicates movement in a direction, and sharia carries the idea of direction into something: it is a path with aims and purposes. Sharia 'shows you what you *ought to do* ("walk this way") to access the source of *that which you need* (water) in order to bring about the desired *state* (satiety and purity)'.[152]

If Egypt has used the religious Nile in political contexts and disputes, so too has Sudan to illustrate challenges between the two countries. Hasan al-Turabi was the chairman of the Muslim Brotherhood. In November 1982 Hasan al-Turabi and the Muslim Brotherhood insisted that the reformation of the Sudanese law in accordance with sharia was the most urgent task. In September 1983 President al-Numayri announced the implementation of sharia in Sudan and symbolically thousands of bottles of whiskey and other alcoholic drinks were poured into the Nile, worth an estimated 3 million Sudanese pounds.[153] A new regime had started.[154] Hasan al-Turabi, as a religious and political leader, said in 1995: 'Egypt is today experiencing a drought in faith and religion [...], [but] Allah wants Islam to be received from Sudan and flow along with the waters of the Nile to purge Egypt from obscenity.'[155] Purity of faith and beliefs may be seen as flowing with and like the Nile, although obviously Mecca is the heart of Islam and Allah as an almighty God can appear wherever and in whatever form.

As Naguib Mahfouz said in his *Adrift on the Nile*, 'They do not know that it is the Nile which has condemned us to ourselves [...] And that the real malady is fear of life, not death.'[156] In this book he was writing about the Egyptians; the Nile has been the destiny of Egypt – not only physical life but also spiritual life has been dependent upon the river's water. And while all religions have provided answers for life after death; the all-dependencies and uncertainties of the Nile's inundations have created fears of life – or the continuity of life. This is at the core of water in rituals and religion, not only in Egypt but in all the other Nile countries as well, including the beliefs at the sources.

CONNECTING THE SOURCES AND THE SEA – BACK TO ETHIOPIA

With regards to the religious Nile, Islam continued large parts of Coptic Christianity, which again was a continuity of ancient Egyptian beliefs and practices. And as with Christian and Islamic beliefs, they also spread beyond the Nile basin, which happened also in earlier periods when Greek and Roman cultures and religions were highly influenced by Nile cosmologies, like the Isis-Sarapis cult. Thus, rather than following the spread of the beliefs through time to other continents and places, I will return to the sources, because the total cosmologies are not only a historic product or development in a given ecology, like the deserts in Egypt, but are also a result of the flow of the river itself combining the waters from sources to the sea, and religious perceptions at the source are part of the religious corpus at the sea since religion, although relating and working historically in given ecologies, has no borders. Obviously, mythology and cosmology are not determined by ecology, but often related, since it may create a closer and more intimate relation between beliefs and practices. Still, cosmological water like the Deluge may have a prominent role in Christianity world-wide without contemporary references to actual floods and physical water landscapes (apart from, for instance, vague references to the Atbara flood in a distant past hardly known today), precisely because such a religion is believed to be universal and hence beyond historic time.

A river like the Nile binds people, ideas and the spread of beliefs together through time in little investigated ways, and part of the reason for the complexities is that it combines all existing theories, such as original development (or evolution), diffusion and migration; it relates to and is structured around the flow of the river, but it does not follow the flow from the sources to the sea or the other way around in a straightforward way, and in many cases it does not follow the river at all but still refers to the river as the ultimate reference point. As seen with the searches for the sources, from the earliest travellers and philosophers to the spread of Christianity in Ethiopia, which came from north via Aksum to the Lake Tana region and then to Gish Abay, and later Speke from the East Coast to Uganda and many others, the *idea* that there was a source and that the waters originating from there connected everyone together – physically and spiritually – enabled also the spread of these beliefs, which are incorporated into cosmologies and rich myriads of webs of significance far from the original source. Not only is this a rich symbolic resource for specific religions like Christianity, but it may also create conflicts between religions, as evident between Ethiopian Christianity and Islam, where the source of the Blue Nile is also holy for Muslims, but they are denied access to the very water since they may, like Western Christians, pollute it. But the flows of water and beliefs being connected may also work in more dramatic ways.

DIVERTING OR WITHHOLDING THE NILE

Even though Egyptian Muslims Islamized beliefs about the Nile and saw it as a gift from Allah, throughout the Middle Ages one of the greatest tensions between Egypt and Ethiopia and Islam and Christianity was the belief that Christian Ethiopians could divert or withhold the Nile water from Muslim Egyptians.

During medieval times, the Nile was perceived as a wondrous, divine creation. It was associated with Gihon, one of the heavenly rivers. The thirteenth-century chronicler Jean de Joinville wrote in his *Life of Saint Louis* that 'nobody knows how these inundations occur, unless it be by God's will', and the products 'come from the heavenly paradise'. He also referred to a Mamluk expedition that searched for the source of the Nile: 'After they had gone a considerable distance up the river they had come to a great mass of rock, so high and sheer that no one could get by. From these rocks the river fell streaming down.' Thus, the source of the Nile was the unreachable earthly paradise, and 'the Nile was the Gihon of the Scriptures'.[157]

This is evident in *The Liturgy of the Nile* at the British Museum (Or. 4951), written in a Palestinian Syriac dialect, which contains services of the church in Alexandria. The Patriarch of Alexandria, the metropolitan and all the priests and deacons declare the object of the service with the words: 'We have come to prepare a good season and an acceptable year; risen in the well-spring of God, the Nile, and by the command of God has it mounted upwards.'[158]

The holiness of the Nile was reckoned in Europe already in the fourteenth century. In 1338, Pope Benedict XII sent Franciscan Friar Giovanni da Marignolli together with three other legates to the Mongol court in Peking. When he returned 15 years later, he wrote that the River Gihon flowed around the land of Abyssinia and descended into Egypt through a crack called Abasty. He also commented that the people there were Christians of the Apostle Matthew and that the Sultan of Egypt paid them tribute since they could cut off the water to his country. Egypt's fear of the Nile related not only to the absence of water but also to too much water, and there were similar myths regarding Ethiopia's ability to inundate Egypt. In 1384, Simone Sigoli visited Egypt, the Sinai and Palestine. He was told the sultan paid tribute to Prester John in Ethiopia. The latter controlled the sluices of the Nile, which were opened only a little, but if he wanted to drown the whole of Egypt, he could open them completely. This myth continued to flourish, and as late as the seventeenth century Milton wrote that the Egyptians believed there was a sluice in the Nile that the Ethiopians opened on 12 June, when the rainy season started, widening the passage each day until 14 September.[159]

This common myth was evident from the eleventh century, when the question of Ethiopia's alleged ability to interrupt the Nile's flow became generally acknowledged.[160] During a famine that lasted nearly seven years (AD 1066–72), the Egyptian caliph sent an embassy bearing valuable gifts to the king of Ethiopia, who was believed to be withholding the water. The Ethiopians accepted the gifts, and in the following years received tribute for sending the Nile waters. For centuries, the Christians had kept alive the idea that the coming of the Nile waters was one of the miracles of the Virgin Mary.[161] During the reign of the Fatimid Sultan al-Mustansir, around 1089–90, the flood failed and did not reach Egypt. The Arab writer al-Makin reports that the sultan sent the Patriarch Michael of Alexandria to Ethiopia to ask the Ethiopians to restore the flood, which they accordingly did.[162]

During a war between Christians and Muslims, the Virgin appeared saying that God had given the Christian Emperor Dawit of Ethiopia (1380–1412) the wisdom to divert the Nile. With this power, the Muslims became scared since they could not harvest without the Nile waters, and they declared that they were not enemies of the Christians. When Dawit heard this news, he praised the Virgin. 'Since that time it was commonly accepted, not only by the Egyptians but also by European rulers, that the Ethiopians were the masters of the Nile.'[163] Thus, it has generally been believed that the Ethiopians could control the Nile flow,[164] and droughts occurred when God 'restrained the heavens' so it 'could not rain'.[165]

In November 1443, a letter from Zar'a Ya'cob was given by a delegation to the Egyptian Sultan Jaqmaq saying:

> And are you not aware, you and your Sultan, that the River Nile is flowing to you from our country and that we are capable of preventing the floods that irrigate your country? Nothing keeps us from so doing, only the belief in God and the care for his slaves. We have presented to you what you need to know and you should know what you have to do.[166]

In the nineteenth century the 'idea of diverting the Nile' was again seen as a Miracle of the Virgin Mary, a theme which had been a challenging topic in the relationship between Egypt and Ethiopia since early times. The Miracle 268 of the corpus *Tä'amrä Maryam* [Miracles of Mary] concerns the Nile and Dawit, the King of Ethiopia:

And on this day at Midnight Our Lady Mary, the holy twofold Virgin, bearer of God, appeared to the King of Ethiopia Dawit and she said to him: O my beloved and beloved of my son Jesus Christ, and now I have asked my son on behalf of you that you will go and rescue my nation, the Christians, and thus He has granted and made even for you your way. Get up and go. And He will perform through your hand many miracles [...] And God gave him wisdom and he stopped the river [Nile], so it did not descend into the land of Egypt, because there are no rains in the land of the people of Egypt; unless the water of the [Nile], which flows from Ethiopia, reaches them, they do not plough, they do not sow seed and they do not get water at all [... King Dawit said] Was it not said once: To restrain the water is like beginning a war, but the will of God, the Lord of the Christians, may come about.[167]

Thus, for centuries it was generally accepted not only by Egyptians but also European rulers that the Ethiopians were the masters of the Nile. The oldest Arab source referring to Ethiopia's alleged ability to control and divert the Nile is probably the *Kitab al-Jawahir al-buhur*, written by Ibn Wasif Shah al-Misri (d. 1202–3). Of the Ethiopian sources the earliest is the *Gad log King Lalibela*. In Europe, the myth was known from at least 1335 when Jacob of Verona travelled to Palestine and reported back about Ethiopia's power over the Nile.[168] Thus, the fear Egypt faced was perceived to be real. And sometimes even nature played its tricks, and mere coincidences may have strengthened these beliefs. It was not only the Blue Nile the Ethiopian Emperors were believed to control. During the Zagwe dynasty, their last king is said to have blocked the Tekeze River. Apparently he was furious because the Egyptians did not send a new *abun* and also for refusing to pay tributes. He prayed to God to stop the river, and according to tradition, it so happened. Either by coincidence or divine intervention, more or less at the same time Egypt suffered a famine lasting for three years and seven months.[169] With regard to whether it was possible to divert the Nile into the Red Sea and thereby famish Egypt, Bruce argued in 1790 that 'there seems to be no doubt but that it is possible'.[170]

However, the belief that the Ethiopian emperor had the power to control the Nile was a double-edged sword. In 1522, during the reign of Lebna Dengel (1508–40), a monk told the Venetian scholar Alessandro Zorzi that the emperor could take Nile water 'so that it did not reach Cairo', but that he refrained from doing so for fear that the Muslims 'would ruin the churches and the Christian monks who are in Jerusalem and those in Egypt of which there are many'.[171] Moreover, 'if Ethiopia was the source of the Nile for Egypt, Egypt was the source of the *abun*, the Egyptian metropolitan bishop, for Ethiopia',[172] and the *abun* was second only to the emperor. 'The Egyptian card was the sultan's or the Coptic patriarch's ability to delay or avoid sending an *abun*.'[173]

For the Muslims living along the Nile, it was intolerable that the Christians controlled the Nile and had the religious legitimacy of the precious life-giving water. Therefore, many of the controversies between the Christians and the Muslims were concerned with the Nile, both politically and religiously. These perceptions continued for a long time and have also been present in more recent times. In 1924 when the Anglo-Ethiopian interests in the Tana dam were a burning issue, Tafari (Haile Selassie) visited Cairo. While the Egyptians could do nothing about the plans and were kept in the dark about this cardinal question, numerous journalists discussed and repeated Egypt's old fear that Ethiopia could possibly block the Nile, and they even referred to medieval incidents.[174]

Egypt's quest for water security can be seen in this context. By building the High Dam at Aswan, Egypt sent a signal that it was not dependent upon Ethiopian Lake Tana, but on Lake Nasser, which the Egyptians controlled.[175] 'In 1959, a few months after the breaking of the church connection, Nasser signed a water agreement with the Sudanese, bluntly ignoring Ethiopia, as if declaring it irrelevant in this context, too.'[176] Thus, although Egyptian rulers could deny the Ethiopians the *abun*, 'for Nasser and his new revolutionary concepts, however, this religious card was of secondary importance. It was sacrificed for the sake of other regional interests and to undermine further the institutions of the Coptic community at home.'[177] However, as seen, even Sadat used the role of religious waters in the geopolitical context, and from this perspective, historically, relations between Egypt and Ethiopia were to a large extent defined within a religious setting as a struggle over who controlled and defined the life-giving resources of the Nile.

It is not, however, only the source of the Blue Nile that has connected religions and beliefs from the source to the sea; also beliefs at the source of the White Nile have shaped beliefs further downstream and vice versa.

GOD PREPARED UGANDA A SPECIAL ROLE IN THE SALVATION HISTORY

From one perspective, Speke was more right than he could have known and anticipated when he came to the source of the White Nile in Uganda or the outlet of Lake Victoria. Speke described the source as 'the cradle of Moses – the waters of which, sweetened with sugar, men carry all the way from Egypt to Mecca, and sell to the pilgrims' and 'the N'yanza [Lake Victoria] is the great reservoir that floated Father Moses on his first adventurous sail – the Nile'. There are in particular two aspects worth commenting on this quotation. Although Sadat was criticized by his contemporaries, it seems in fact that he was building on century older religious perceptions stressing that indeed pilgrims did carry holy Nile waters from Egypt to Mecca. That these perceptions were outdated in the middle of the twentieth century is another matter, but it points to the fact that the religious Nile has had important divine roles far away from its banks throughout history. The other aspect is that Speke was also right when, although this is perhaps the loops of history creating new realities, he connected the source of the White Nile with Egypt and the role of Christianity through Moses.

One hundred and fifty years later, a Catholic priest made this connection between the source and Christianity's salvation history stronger and more explicit than what Speke did. The River Nile is a history of salvation in Christianity. Moses the law maker and liberator drank of the waters from the Nile, so did other biblical figures like Abraham and Jacob. And Jesus too with his family drank waters from the Nile. Uganda in general and Busoga in particular have therefore a special role in Christianity and the salvation history. The Nile connects the religious beliefs since without the waters from Lake Victoria and the historic source of the White Nile identified by Speke, the biblical history could not have evolved and unfolded as it did. Still, the water at the source is not holy from a Christian perspective and the waters from the very source itself is not used in baptism because of the strong currents, but the flow of the river binds the biblical Egypt and Israel to Uganda. And it was the search for the sources and the confirmation of this millennia long Nile quest, which also brought Christianity to Uganda.

The first Christian missionaries came to Uganda in 1877 as a result of Stanley's request. As it was written back in Britain in 1903:

> Stanley's challenge to the Christian world to send forth missionaries to the Court of Mutesa appeared in the columns of the *Daily Telegraph* of 15 November 1875, and probably no single letter to a newspaper has ever brought about such extraordinary results.

Mockler-Ferryman writes: 'The sum of £24,000 was almost immediately offered to the Church Missionary Society for the establishment of a special mission in Uganda.'[178] Indeed, one English Christian alone gave £5,000 anonymously.

The execution of the Christians in 1885–7 by the Buganda political leadership took place less than ten years after the introduction of Christianity, with ever-lasting implications for not only the development of the Church in Uganda, but also the country itself. The 22 martyrs were beatified in 1920, which is a formal recognition by the Catholic Church of their entrance into Heaven and their capacity to intercede if individuals pray in their name.[179] Among the killed was Bishop James Hannington, the first Anglican bishop of East Africa. His grave is in the Kyondo village, and his martyrdom connects and increases the role and importance of Christianity in the Busoga Kingdom. More than being killed as Christians becoming martyrs, their blood connects them to Christianity at large and Uganda specifically as a means of spreading the gospel. The Nile itself was also seen as the veins of evangelization. In a text from the Archdiocese of Gulu it is written:

> That way of witnessing to the faith seems to follow mysteriously the flow of the Nile symbolically from Namugongo at the source of the Nile where the blood of the twenty two martyrs mixes with the waters of the Nile to flow north wards touching the Acholi land home of the two new martyrs to continue on its saving course over all the lands touched by the Nile. The course of the gospel cannot be stopped until the whole continent is evangelised. Thus, Blessed Daudi Okelo and Jildo Irwa become a sign of the Catholicity of the faith which does not stop until new people, new regions, new cultures, are gathered together and recognised as integrals and living parts of society and of the church.[180]

In this process of becoming Christian, baptism is the essential rite opening the gates to the kingdom of God, and although there are many practices and beliefs, some denominations still baptize in the Nile River itself.

BAPTISM NEXT TO THE SOURCE OF THE WHITE NILE

The Nile in general and the source in particular may provide wealth to Christians specifically, along with everyone else. The role of rivers is eloquently described in Ezekiel 47:7, a passage that is appropriate to the Nile and the source: 'And it shall be *that* every living thing that moves, wherever the rivers go, will live. There will be a very great multitude of fish, because these waters go there; for they will be healed, and everything will live wherever the river goes.'

Although the water at the source or in the Nile is not holy in Christian cosmology, it does have important religious significance. The water that flowed in Egypt in biblical times came from the upper sources. Thus, the Nile plays a fundamental role in the Old Testament and it was from Egypt that Moses led the Israelites to the Promised Land. In the New Testament too, the Holy Family resided along the banks of the Nile. One may recall again what Speke wrote in 1862: 'I told my men they ought to shave their heads and bathe in the holy river, the cradle of Moses.' Although the role of the White Nile and the source among Christians today is not precisely what Speke described, the biblical narrative does play an important role, since the water in Egypt originated at the source at Jinja. Hence, then as now, biblical narratives are directly linked to the source by the very flow of the river itself.

The role and importance of water and baptism in Christianity has been discussed at length elsewhere.[181] Suffice it to add that throughout the history of Christianity, the significance and function of baptism has been discussed avidly: is the baptismal water holy or not, is child or adult baptism more appropriate, and should it be ablution, aspersion or full immersion? Seventh Day Adventists conduct baptism and full immersion in the river, but other denominations may collect water from the source and use it in their baptisms. Baptism has not been conducted at the source because the water is too deep and strong, but the bubbling water flowing strongly from the source has been seen as God's water and used in the liturgy.

Born Again Christians practise immersion in the Nile and perform adult baptism (fig. 49). Already being a Christian is no impediment to being baptized again by Born Again Christians. On the contrary, re-baptism is a premise and promise of being a good and true Christian. Whereas, when a child is baptized, it has no free will and did not decide of itself to be a Christian. Moreover, throughout life humans sin, hence another cleansing baptism is appropriate as a way of denouncing the acts of a former life and starting anew. Adult baptism involves an active and deliberate choice to partake in Christ and denounce Satan and his works. By choosing Christ and being committed to the Ten Commandments as an adult, one may be saved, the Pentecostals argue.

Hence, although the main rationale for being baptized is the same in all Christian denominations – enabling a presence in the Kingdom of Heaven and the purification of sins – there are important differences regarding when and how it should be done. This has serious implications as to who are the proper Christians, if the disagreements among Christian denominations are any indication. One pastor in a Born Again church argued strongly in favour of adult baptism, claiming that all other Christian denominations were wrong. According to him, in the Bible there are only references to adult baptism with full immersion, and not the Catholic ablution. When he challenges bishops and clerics about where in the Bible child baptism takes place, he gets no answers and the priests change the subject, he said. Adult baptism is the only true baptism in the Bible, as when John the Baptist baptized Jesus in the Jordan. Moreover, Jesus only baptized adults. Although he gathered the children unto him, he only *blessed* them. That is why everybody can be baptized again – in fact, should be baptized again, preferably in his church by him, the pastor argued.

49. Baptism in the Nile close to the source.

During baptisms, which do not happen each Sunday but only when there are sufficient numbers of newly converted, one candidate after another is baptized by being fully immersed in the Nile, while a small group of congregants sing and clap along the shore. The water in the Nile is not holy in itself, but is free floating like the spirit of Christ or the Holy Ghost. When the pastor prays, however, the water becomes holy. By praying before a baptism, the water becomes purified and holy, just as prayer before a meal purifies the food and makes it blessed.

Thus, although not holy in itself in Christianity, the water and the source are still important cosmologically. Comparatively, though, the water religion par excellence is Hinduism, with its great mythologies of the river goddess Ganga and its divinities, which has implications for perceptions of holiness of other rivers. In Uganda and Jinja there is a large Hindu population and diaspora, but the Nile is not holy as such.

SPEKE AND HINDUS AT THE SOURCE OF THE WHITE NILE

Speke did not credit the Arabs with the knowledge of the source, but the Hindus:

> I came, at the same time, to the conclusion that all our previous information concerning the hydrography of these regions, as well as the Mountains of the Moon, originated with the ancient Hindus, who told it to the priests of the Nile; and that all those busy Egyptian geographers, who disseminated their knowledge with a view to be famous for their long-sightedness, in solving the deep-seated mystery which enshrouded the source of the holy river, were so many hypothetical humbugs.[182]

Speke's belief that the Hindus were at the source caused him a lot of problems and in fact part of the reason why he was discredited with having found the source back in London, and in an odd twist of history points to how completely wrong religious belief of the Nile could still have great impact on the Nile discourse. Not only shaped hydrological perceptions of the Ganga the Nile discourse and searches for the source, but the holiness of Ganga also had relevance for understanding religious perceptions of the Nile.

Speke's travails began in part more than 50 years earlier, with another captain in colonial India, Captain Francis Wilford. The only map of the Nile in Speke's *Journal of the Discovery* is one he got from Colonel

Rigby. It bears the title: 'The Course of the River Cali or Great Krishna', extracted from the Puranas by Francis Wilford. 'It is remarkable that the Hindus have christened the source of the Nile Amara, which is the name of a country at the north-east corner of the Victoria N'yanza,' Speke says. 'This, I think, shows clearly that the ancient Hindus must have had some kind of communication with both the northern and southern ends of the Victoria N'yanza.'[183] The Nile was the river Kali or Great Krishna.

If Speke was criticized for inaccuracy by his contemporaries, his inaccuracies were as nothing compared to Wilford's. Wilford resided in Benares in India from 1788 to 1822. He retired in 1794 and spent most of his time studying Hindu scriptures. As a scholar, Wilford never attained fame. In part this was because of his extreme diffusionist approach: he claimed that all European myths had a Hindu origin and that India even had its own Christ, whose works and deeds resembled those of the biblical Christ. His interpretations were criticized even in his own day. His gullibility was recognized by his contemporaries, and his texts are today largely incomprehensible, even to those with a knowledge of Hinduism and ancient sacred texts. In *On Egypt and other Countries, Adjacent to the Cali River, or Nile of Ethiopia. From the Ancient Books of the Hindus*, his thesis was that Indians had been living along the Nile and that Hindu knowledge had been transferred to Egyptian priests, who subsequently transferred the knowledge to the Greeks and hence the rest of Europe.[184]

In a humiliating article in 1808,[185] Wilford had to apologize and swallow the bitter pill of being publicly exposed for fraud and deceit. One may feel some pity for him for his naive trust in his translator, and some admiration for his courage in admitting blunders and for taking responsibility for the damage done. Between 1793 and 1805 he had systematically been misled by his priest and informant. He starts his 1808 article thus: 'At the moment of appearing before the tribunal of the Asiatic Society, and the public, it would be in vain to attempt to conceal my emotion and anxiety.' He was thunderstruck to realize his faults, but as he said, 'I shall not trouble the Society with a description of what I felt, and of my distress at this discovery.' Devoted to and passionate about Oriental and Hindu mythology, he wanted to study the sacred Hindu books in depth. This was an immense task, since there are many such books, and they are thick. But as he conversed with his pandit and many others, they told him the most amazing and intriguing legends, which closely resembled Western mythologies. Thus, he engaged the priest to make extracts of the key texts, in particular the Puranas, and also provided the priest with a number of assistants and scribes. Wilford trusted the priest, and he even considered him his own guru or spiritual teacher. After a few years of work, the collections of extracts had become very voluminous, and Wilford aimed to ensure their quality: 'At our commencement, I enjoined him to be particular cautious in his extracts and quotations; and informed him, that if I should, at a future period, determine to publish any thing, the strictest scrutiny would take place in the collection.'[186] The priest assured him that the greatest care had been taken.

But not all was well – in fact nothing was. The priest was more than eager to please and fulfil the wishes of his employer and all too willing to give Wilford what he believed Wilford wanted. Wilford wrote: 'His forgeries were of three kinds; in the first there was only a word or two altered; in the second were such legends as had undergone a more material alteration; and in the third all those which he had written from memory.'[187] Not only had the priest altered the original texts where they existed, but more damaging was the fact that most of what he had written had no firm basis in the texts whatever. And it was in this third class of material that fraud was most prevalent – in fact, there were 12,000 instances of it. These were not just minor mistakes: the priest had heroically composed 12,000 new Sanskrit verses![188]

The priest had connected all the legends together, and Wilford says:

> I used to translate the extracts which he made for me, by way of exercise; and never thought, at that time, of comparing them with the originals; first, because I had no reason to doubt their authenticity, secondly, because it would have been soon enough to make the collection when I had determined upon publishing any part of them.

Wilford explains: 'This apparently lulled him into security; but, being afterwards sensible of the danger of his defection, he was intended to attempt the most daring falsification of the originals, in order, if possible, to extricate himself.' When Wilford confronted the priest with his fraud, the reaction was as alarming as one might imagine: 'When discovered, he flew into the most violent paroxysms of rage, calling down the vengeance of heaven, with the most horrid and tremendous imprecations upon himself and his children, if the extracts were not true.'[189] And what first prompted Wilford's suspicions was the unlikely 'discovery' that Noah's drunkenness was also recorded in the Puranas.[190]

Wilford and his pandit with their 12,000 new verses were also the background to the map of the Kali Nile that Speke included in the *Journal* in 1863. This inclusion helped undermine the scientific integrity of Speke's work. The map was already viewed as a notorious forgery, and Speke was criticized by eminent theoretical geographers like W. D. Cooley and Dr Charles Beke for referring to it. Blackwood dropped the map in the second edition of Speke's *Journal*, but the damage was already done, and difficult to repair.[191]

There are many lessons to be learned from this for ethnography, interviews and checking and double-checking information. And in defence of the pandit, depending upon his status and holiness, the way in which he reinterpreted and presented the truth, for money, has also to be understood in context. The Puranas are sacred texts, not holy texts or direct divine revelations like the Rig Veda or the Baghavad Gita (the Christian and Muslim equivalent would be the Bible or Qur'an). Their ontology is not divine: they are composed by seers and sages at a later stage – mainly in the first half of the first millennium AD – and open to interpretation by qualified ritual specialists like the pandit.

Thus, it illustrates in a very profound way the difference between holy and sacred, although the pandit in this case crossed the line. Although any perception of holiness is by definition an interpretation or understanding, it is still believed to be external and representing an objective divinity apart and beyond humans. Sacred things, as venerated, can be shaped in accordance to what is perceived to capture a holy essence, or with the cross an example. If there are remnants of the original cross existing (although the relics of this are numerous), this cannot be altered. In other churches, on the other hand, artists have a great freedom to make the cross and Jesu suffering according to taste and tradition. The latter would be sacred, the former holy.

The story about Wilford also illustrates another aspect of how ideas of holy water spreads from one place to another shaping new beliefs in new contexts. Ideas about Ganges was not only hydrologically a source for Speke's searchers for the sources of the Nile in Africa, where he believed that it originated in high mountains similar to the Himalayas. The holiness of Ganga itself also shaped beliefs about the legendary status of the Nile, making the river even more fabled. That these ideas of holiness had no factual basis is another issue, but in the process of mythologizing a river as the Nile has been for millennia, one new myth inevitably partakes in previous mythologies whether knowing it explicitly or not. This is also to a large extent how myths work, subtle and explicit at the same time, nobody knows everything but still there is a feeling of a shrouded totality to identify with, which continues on new premises and inherited traditions. In this case it was the perception of holiness of a very different river that shaped new understanding of the Nile. It created a hydro-psychological mentality connecting beliefs because of the fluidity of ideas similar to the rivers themselves. In any event, the Hindu Nile had no ancient role, but certainly it has in recent times, but it is not as holy as the holiest of the Hindu rivers: Ganges.

HINDUS AND GANDHI ON THE NILE

In Hinduism it is believed that there are 330 million gods or facets of the divine – all of these are present in Varanasi, the city existing in a constant stage of purity, whereas the rest of the world is decaying and deteriorating. The rivers of India are 'Mother Rivers' and the nurturing waters are compared to milk of cow-mothers.[192] The river nourishes and fertilizes the land through which it flows and Ganga's maternal character is especially seen in her nourishing aspect. Ganga water is sometimes called milk or the drink of immortality. She nourishes her children with water as a mother feeds her infant with milk.[193] Water and milk become identical since they are vital life-givers and Goddess Ganga is worshipped as a source of life and regeneration, and Ganga is one with all life-giving waters or fluids in their many facets.[194]

The intimate connection between water, life and death is explicit in Hindu texts. When the harvest is collected and eaten, it becomes sperm, and when finally injected into the vagina it becomes new life. Sacrifices give new life in the form of rain from the clouds guaranteeing a successful harvest. This link is most specifically expressed in funerals when the fire that dissolves the deceased creates clouds, which will bring new life. Thus, the hydrological cycle produces the sperm that in metaphorical terms is 'planted in the fields', eventually creating new humans. The hydrological and cosmological cycle are identical and symbolized by the process of cooking rice, which illustrates the dual character of both fire and water: they are different, but inseparable.[195] In the *Siva-Purana* it is written:

> In the cooking vessel the rice and water remain separate. Water is above fire. The rice is above water. The wind slowly blows against the fire

beneath the water. The fire kindled by the wind makes the water boil. The rice with hot-boiling water all around it becomes cooked. When cooked it becomes separated into sediment and juice. (More or less a similar process takes place in the body):[196]

The semen is secreted from the food eaten. From the semen, the birth of another body is made possible. When the semen unalloyed is deposited in the vaginal passage during the prescribed period of cohabitation after the monthly menses, then the semen blow by the vital wind mingles with the blood of the woman. At the time when the semen is discharged the individual soul with the causal body or unit of sense-organs etc. enters the vaginal passage fully covered and urged by its past actions. The semen and blood in the unified state becomes foetus in a day.[197]

The hydrological cycle of the year, which includes rain and a successful harvest in the form of rice, has its parallel in the human cycle, which includes copulation and the creation of an offspring. These two cycles of metaphors work together and give each other strength and rationale, and in practice it is impossible to separate the two because they are parts of the same cosmogonic process linking microcosm to macrocosm. Copulation and cosmogony are two parallel life-giving processes expressed and created by fire and water. Beliefs in the same cosmology and how cosmos work can be shared by believers of the same religion across continents although the very water in these processes may not be the same and possess the same holiness. There is only one Ganga, and that river is in India.

The Hindu temple on Bell Avenue in Jinja, where there is also a Gandhi statue where he holds a stick in his right hand and a book in the left, is primarily a temple to Vishnu, but there are also numerous other gods. Nile water is used in this and other Hindu temples, and the priests bless the water before it is ritually used. Still, the Nile is very different from the Ganges, and there are different perceptions of the spiritual qualities of its waters.

One Hindu priest was explicit that the Nile is altogether different from the holy Indian rivers. Ganges is holy and divine whereas the Nile is not. The Nile only flows and floats, whereas the Ganges flows to the heavens thereby connecting all three realms of the cosmos: this world, the underworld and heaven; the past, the present and the future. Ganges endows other rivers with sanctity: 'Not only is the Ganges said to be present in other rivers, but other rivers are present in her.' It is the 'nectar of immortality', which brings life to the cremated on the banks of the River of Heaven. 'The Ganges is the liquid essence of the scriptures, the gods, and the wisdom of the Hindu tradition. She is the liquid essence, in sum, of Shakti – the energy and power of the Supreme, flowing in the life of the world.'[198]

There is no god or goddess in the Nile, and its water collected in a bottle will become foul within a few days, being full of worms and parasites. This is not so with Ganga water, which will forever remain pure and clear, the priest said (although this is myth, for the real Ganges is highly polluted). By drinking Ganga water, mind and body become healed and healthy, but not so with the Nile's waters. Moreover, water from the Nile is used to brew beer, one priest pointed out with contempt, and that would never have happened with the holy Ganges. This practice is indeed evident on the billboard at the source, where Bell beer is advertised as the heritage of Uganda. Moreover, 'Nile Special, 5,6 ABV, Premium Lager' is marketed as the 'True Reward from the Source.' From a Hindu perspective with Ganga in mind, this is not a reward, but sacrilege, the priest said.

Common Hindus may perceive the Nile as holy at an abstract level not referring particularly to the Nile, simply because all water, including fresh running water, is holy. Still, it was claimed, the source has no specific meaning relative to other water in the river. All water is holy, no matter in what country. And although living in Jinja, one can close one's eyes and believe and feel that one is living in a cave in the Himalayas, one Hindu said. This works also for water and Ganga. Nobody can see the gods, but it is possible to imagine them and make statues in different forms and shapes. Thus, one may also imagine and experience the holiness of water, including the waters of the Nile, one devotee said. However, although the water might be perceived as holy and used in water rituals, the qualities of the Nile differ fundamentally from the holy waters of the Ganges. As such, devotees do not take holy baths in the Nile, but use water from the taps at the temples. In a ritual context, the Nile water fulfils religious roles, but as water in itself it is not holy.

The great fame of the Nile and the source of the White Nile among Hindus derives not from perceptions of the qualities of the water itself, but from Mahatma Gandhi (fig. 50). Gandhi was truly universal and his philosophy of peace has inspired not only Hindus: Nelson Mandela, for instance, called Gandhi his 'political guru'. Gandhi said:

I live and move and have my being in the pursuit of this goal [...] If we believe in God, not merely with our intellect but with our whole being, we will love all mankind without any distinction of race, or class, nation or religion. We will work for the unity of mankind [...] I have no distinction between relatives and strangers, countrymen and foreigners, white or colored, Hindus, and Indians of other faiths whether Muslims, Parsees, Christians or Jews. I may say that my heart has been incapable of making any such distinctions.[199]

Gandhi spent 21 years of his early life in South Africa (1893–1914) and for the Hindu diaspora this is important, because Africa's struggle for independence and freedom is symbolized by Gandhi. He was devoted to African justice and freedom, and the Nile as the longest river in the world, traversing many countries, was a symbol of peace. Given the role of cremation in Hinduism, Gandhi fought for a crematorium in South Africa, and he saw this issue as yet another example of discrimination against the Hindu diaspora. In 1918 the Hindu community opened its first crematorium in Johannesburg.[200]

Gandhi was shot and killed by Nathuram Godse, a Hindu extremist, on 30 January 1948. On 31 January, his body was cremated at Rajghat, a cremation ground along the holy Yamuna River in New Delhi. His was

50. Gandhi symbolically overlooking the Nile as the river flows by.

a spectacular cremation. Although Nehru was asked to light the pyre, it was Gandhi's son Ramdas who did so:

> Very soon, the pyre was ablaze. The wind fanned the fire and the flames soared high. The fire became too hot for people to stay near it. It seemed as if the flames were reprimanding us for our sins and telling us that the great world citizen whom it was now transporting to another world, was a victim of the wicked passions that consume us humans. The flames seemed to be telling us that we had no right to go near one who had tried to rid society of its passions, but had, alas! died in the attempt. And so the flames kept us away from Bapuji.[201]

It was Gandhi's wish that most of his ashes be given to the major rivers of the world: the Ganges (in Allahabad at the confluence with the Yamuna River and the mythological Saraswati River), the Nile, the Volga (the longest river in Europe) and the Thames, among others. Apparently, before his execution it was the wish of Nathuram Godse, Gandhi's murderer, that his ashes should only be immersed in the Sindhu River in Pakistan, since Gandhi was associated with all the other rivers in the world. The Pakistan Government refused to pollute the Sindhu River with the ashes of the murderer.[202]

The urn with Gandhi's ashes for Africa went first to Nairobi. After homage was paid to Gandhi in the Kenyan capital, the urn was transported to Kampala and then to Jinja, where it was kept in the Hindu temple on Bell Avenue for two days before the ashes were immersed in the Nile at the source on 14 August 1948.[203]

At the source of the Nile there is a huge grey-brown bust of Gandhi looking out at the visitors, pilgrims and tourists who come to see his likeness. The statue was unveiled on 5 October 1997 by the then prime minister of India, Inder Kumar Gujral. According to the director of the bank financing the statue, 'by putting up the statue, we commemorate a great man, who worked hard to spread a message of peace in the world, but also whose virtues of non-violence influenced leaders like Nelson Mandela and other rulers'. Annually on Gandhi's birthday, 2 October, the Hindu community pays homage to its spiritual father by visiting the statue and laying flowers.[204]

According to the Hindu community in Jinja, the statue of Gandhi has enhanced the importance of the source, and annually some 25,000 Hindus come to the source and the statue, but that is because of Gandhi and not because the water is holy. Nevertheless, the Hindu diaspora or community conducts their rituals as they would have done in India, which include the water cosmology and all its rich mythologies. On the river, they give pujas to the water by floating banana leaves with rice. In the temples, the priests bless the water, but as it was emphasized by the priests, the water is not holy and it is not like Ganga. Still, the rituals are carried out in the same ways as Hindus do other places, and the fact that the water itself at a given place is not holy does not decrease the importance of the rituals. This shows part of the complex nature and relation between water and rituals found in religious cosmologies; holy water may enable and be the reason for the rituals, but rituals may work without holy water and normal water may have the same ritual function – in some spheres at some times, but not others. Nevertheless, when I was back at the source in 2017 a huge billboard was placed next to the statue of Gandhi explaining that his ashes were 'immersed here in [the] Holy River Nile at Jinja' – showing that perceptions of holiness might be fluid.

WATER AS SOURCES OF RELIGION AND LIFE

Water is thus both the origin, within, around and beyond life in its broadest sense from the minutest aspects to cosmos as a whole. Although different religions give various importance to these ever changing and grading scales of life-giving properties, all religions do, however, emphasize water, since it is the source of the most precious and fundamental element or medium of the essence of humans and divinities alike: life. The waters of the religious Nile are at all time and from time immemorial to now the same and different in the course of the river's flow. The ever-changing and fluid character and the ultimate dependency for everyone on this vital and precious resource have made and enabled this myriad of overlapping and omnipresence of beliefs throughout all times and in all cosmologies. Precisely because some challenges and hardships are shared by all and other needs and dependencies are very specific and localized in particular ecological contexts, the use of religious waters and the role of water in religion is part of a very wide cultural and cosmological repertoire of possibilities. What is shared along the whole Nile is that water is a religious source for humanity throughout the ages, and the religious uses and conceptions of the waters have more than anything else elevated the Nile to the most legendary of all rivers in the world, because water is intrinsic to all religions, their mysteries and enigmas. As it has been said:

> The Nile, as both the site of the early beginnings as well as the space of mysterious diversity, has captured the human imagination since the earliest civilizations have resided along its banks. The enigma of its sources, the life it gave to barren areas, and the capricious nature of its vital flow have produced endless speculations and legends. The realities and myths of the river personified have been retold and reproduced from the early ancient times to the present.[205]

And it has shaped humans, the perceptions of their gods and hence their religions. The religious Nile from the sources to the sea is therefore a source for understanding humans and their religions, their historic developments through time and what matters most for all at all times: life, and water for life, in this world and beyond.

Notes

1 SOURCES OF RELIGION

1. Speke, J. H. 1863. *Journal of the Discovery of the Source of the White Nile*. Blackwood and Sons. Edinburgh and London, p. 461.
2. Speke 1863: 467.
3. Speke 1863: 469.
4. Speke 1864: 259.
5. Oestigaard, T. & Gedef, A. F. 2013. *The Source of the Blue Nile – Water Rituals and Traditions in the Lake Tana Region*. Cambridge Scholars Publishing. Newcastle.
6. Bradt 2010. *The Bradt Travel Guide. Uganda*. The Globe Pequot Press Inc. Guildford, CT, p. 480.
7. Jeal, T. 2011. *Explorers of the Nile: The Triumph and the Tragedy of a Great Victorian Adventure*. Yale University Press. New Haven, CT, p. 7.
8. Nwauwa, A. O. 2000. The Europeans in Africa: prelude to colonialism. In Falola, T. (ed.), *Africa. Volume 2. African Cultures and Societies before 1888*. Carolina Academic Press. Durham, pp. 303–18, p. 304.
9. Jeal 2011: 7.
10. Ayrton, F. 1848. Observations upon M. d'Abbadies' account of his discovery of the sources of the White Nile, and upon certain objections and statements in relation thereto, by Dr. Beke. *Journal of the Royal Geographical Society of London*, Vol. 18: 48–74, p. 48.
11. Ayrton 1848: 48.
12. Baker, S. W. 1869. *Albert N'yanza. Great Basin of the Nile, and Exploration of the Nile Sources*. Lippincott. Philadelphia, p. vii.
13. Maitland, A. 2010 [1971]. *Speke and the Discovery of the Source of the Nile*. Faber and Faber. London, p. 177.
14. Murchison, R. 1863. Address to the Royal Geographical Society. *Journal of the Royal Geographical Society of London*, Vol. 33, No. cxiii–cxcii, p. clxxiv.
15. Burton, R. F. & Speke, J. H. 1858–9. Explorations in Eastern Africa. *Proceedings of the Royal Geographical Society in London*, Vol. 3, No. 6: 348–85, p. 355.
16. Schlichter, H. 1891. Ptolemy's topography of eastern equatorial Africa. *Proceedings of the Royal Geographical Society and Monthly Record of Geography*, Vol. 13, No. 9: 513–53, p. 514.
17. Relano, F. 1995. Against Ptolemy: the significance of the Lopes-Pigafetta Map of Africa. *Imago Mundi*, Vol. 47: 49–66, pp. 49–50.
18. Johnston, H. 1903. *The Nile Quest*. Lawrence and Bullen. London, p. 293.
19. Stone, C. P. 1884. The navigation of the Nile. *Science*, Vol. 4, No. 93: 456–7.
20. NBI 2012. *State of the River Nile Basin 2012*. The Nile Basin Initiative. Entebbe, p. 5.
21. Dawson, C. 1957. *The Dynamics of World History*. Sheed and Ward. London, p. 128.

22. Herodotus. 2008, *Herodotus. The Histories. A New Translation by Robin Waterfield*. Oxford World's Classics. Oxford University Press, Book II.19.
23. Herodotus 2008, Book II.28.
24. Herodotus 2008, Book II.12.
25. Philostratus. 1912. *Philostratus. The Life of Apollonius of Tyana. The Epistles of Apollonius and the Treatise of Eusebius*, with an English translation by F. C. Conybeare, Vol. 2. Harvard University Press. Cambridge, MA, 1912. Book VI, I, p. 3.
26. Dickson, D. R. 1987. *The Fountain of Living Waters. The Typology of the Waters of Life in Herbert, Vaughan, and Traherne*. University of Missouri Press. Columbia, p. 11.
27. Wainwright, G. A. 1953. Herodotus II, 28 on the Sources of the Nile. *The Journal of Hellenic Studies*, Vol. 73: 104–7.
28. Albright, W. F. 1919. The mouth of rivers. *The American Journal of Semitic Languages and Literatures*, Vol. 35, No. 4: 161–95, p. 175.
29. Albright 1919: 165 fn. 3 and 167.
30. Schlichter 1891.
31. Kidd, I. G. 1998. *Posidonius. Volume II. The Commentary (ii) Fragments 150-293. Cambridge Classical Texts and Commentaries. 14b*. Cambridge University Press. Cambridge, p. 796, Strabo, XVII. 1.5. §5.
32. Pliny the Elder. 2004. *Natural History. A Selection*. Translated by J. F. Healy. Penguin Classics. London, p. 59.
33. Kidd 1998: 797.
34. Diadji, I. N. 2003. From 'life-water' to 'death-water' or on the foundation of African artistic creation from yesterday to tomorrow. *Leonardo*, Vol. 36, No. 4: 273–7, p. 274.
35. Hogg, J. E. 1926. 'Living water' – 'water of Life'. *The American Journal of Semitic Languages and Literatures*, Vol. 42, No. 2: 131–3.
36. Dickson 1987: 32.
37. Stevenson, W. 1973. 'Kubla Khan' as symbol. *Texas Studies in Literature and Language*, Vol. 14, No. 4: 605–30, p. 615.
38. Dickson 1987: 29.
39. Dickson 1987: 30.
40. Dickson 1987: 50.
41. Fulke, W. 1537. *Praelections upon the Sacred and Holy Revelation of S. John*. Thomas Purfoote. London, fol. 145v.
42. Williams, R. 1980. *Keywords. A Vocabulary of Culture and Society*. Fontana/Croom Helm. London.
43. Crosby, D. 2002. *Religion of Nature*. State University of New York Press. New York, p. 21.
44. Crosby 2002: 21.
45. Seneca. 1971. *Seneca in Ten Volumes. VII. Naturales Quaestiones. II.*, with an English translation by T. H. Corcoran, PhD. William Heineman Ltd. London, 3.26.8.
46. Tvedt, T. & Oestigaard, T. 2006. Introduction. In Tvedt, T. & Oestigaard, T. 2006. (eds), *A History of Water Vol. 3. The World of Water*: ix–xxii. I.B.Tauris. London, and Tvedt, T. & Oestigaard. 2010. A history of the ideas of water: deconstructing nature and constructing society. In Tvedt, T. & Oestigaard, T. (eds), *A History of Water. Series 2, Vol. 1. The Ideas of Water from Antiquity to Modern Times*: 1–36. I.B.Tauris. London.
47. See Bachelard, G. 1968. *The Psychoanalysis of Fire*. Beacon Press. Boston, MA; Bachelard, G. 1988. *The Flame of a Candle*. The Bachelard Translations. The Dallas Institute Publications. The Dallas Institute of Humanities and Culture. Dallas, TX; Bachelard, G. 1990. *Fragments of a Poetics of Fire*. The Bachelard Translations. The Dallas Institute Publications. The Dallas Institute of Humanities and Culture. Dallas, TX, and Bachelard, G. 1994. *Water and Dreams. An Essay on the Imagination of Matter*. The Dallas Institute of Humanities and Culture. Dallas, TX.

48. Bachelard 1994: 93, 134, 139.
49. Pliny the Elder 2004: 4.
50. Tvedt, T. 1997. *En reise i vannets historie – fra regnkysten til Muscat.* Cappelens Forlag AS. Oslo, and Tvedt, T. 2002. *Verdenbilder og selvbilder. En humanitær stormakts intellektuelle historie.* Universitetsforlaget. Oslo, pp. 166–8.
51. Pliny the Elder 2004: 272.
52. Eliade, M. 1993. *Patterns in Comparative Religion.* Sheed and Ward Ltd. London, p. 188.
53. Turner, V. 1975. *Revelation and Divination in Ndembu Ritual.* Cornell University Press. Cornell, p. 21.
54. Eliade 1993: 193.
55. Hocart, A. M. 1987. *Imagination and Proof. Selected Essays of A. M. Hocart.* The University of Arizona Press. Tuscon, p. 52.
56. Hocart, A. M. 1968. *Caste. A Comparative Study.* Russel & Russel. New York, p. 18.
57. Hocart, A. M. 1954. *Social Origins.* Watts & Co. London, p. 123.
58. Wild, R. A. 1981. *Water in the Cultic Worship of Isis and Sarapis.* E. J. Brill. Leiden, p. 86.
59. Hocart 1954: 25.
60. Lindsay, J. 1968. *Men and Gods on the Roman Nile.* Frederick Muller Ltd. London.
61. Heliodorus. 1895. *Æthiopica, An Æthiopian History Written by Helidorus* / Translated by Thomas Underdowne, anno 1587. With an Introduction by Charles Whibley. David Nutt. London, p. 251.
62. Lindsay 1968: 39.
63. Jones, M. 2005. The wisdom of Egypt. Base and heavenly magic in Heliodoros' *Aithiopika*. *Ancient Narrative* 4: 79–98.
64. Seneca 1971: 3.1.2, p. 213.
65. Seneca 1971: III, 22.1, pp. 253–5.
66. Seneca 1971: III, 23.1, p. 255.
67. Seneca 1971: III, 15.1, p. 233.
68. Philostratus 1912: Book VI, VI, p. 21.
69. Seneca. 1972. *Seneca in Ten Volumes. X. Naturales Quaestiones. II.*, with an English translation by T. H. Corcoran. William Heineman Ltd. London, 4a.2.2–10, pp. 21, 29.
70. Philostratus 1912: Book VI, XVII, p. 75.
71. Philo. 1935. *De Vita Mosis*, with an English translation by translated by F. H. Colson. William Heinemann Ltd, London, Book 1.5–6, p. 279.
72. Philo. 1962. *Philo* with an English translation by F. H. Coulson & Whitaker, G. H., in ten volumes, Vol. 1. William Heinemann Ltd, London. Allegorical Interpretation, I.XIX.64–5, p. 189.
73. Philo 1962: On the Creation, 1.XIII, p. 33.
74. Diodorus. 1960. *Diodorus of Sicily*, with an English translation by C. H. Oldfather, in 12 volumes. I. Books I and II, 1–34. William Heinemann Ltd. London, Book I.36.2, p. 121.
75. Diodorus 1960: Book I.36.3–5, pp. 121–3.
76. Diodorus 1960: Book I.36.10–12, p. 125.
77. Crosby, D. 2001. *Religion of Nature.* State University of New York Press. New York, p. 82.
78. Campbell, J. 1959. *The Mask of God: Primitive Mythology.* The Viking Press. New York, p. 177.
79. Mbogoni, L. E. Y. 2013. *Human Sacrifice and the Supernatural in African History.* Mkiki Na Nyota. Dar-es-Salaam.
80. Ruel, M. 1990. Non-sacrificial ritual killing. *Man*, New Series, Vol. 25, No. 2: 323–35, p. 323.
81. Hocart 1954: 30.
82. Hocart 1954: 31.
83. Weber, M. 1964. *The Sociology of Religion.* Beacon Press. Boston.

84. Obeyesekere, G. 1984. *The Cult of the Goddess Pattini*. The University of Chicago Press. Chicago, p. 51, original emphasis.
85. Campbell 1959: 21.
86. Goa, D., Plate, S. B. & Paine, C. 2005. 'Editorial statement', *Material Religion*, Vol. 1, No. 1: 4–9, p. 4.
87. This section and the chronological ordering of the various scholars on religion is inspired by Morris, B. 1987. *Anthropological Studies of Religion. An Introduction*. Cambridge University Press. Cambridge.
88. Merleau-Ponty, M. 1964. *Sense and Non-Sense*. Northwestern University Press. Illinois, p. 63.
89. Hegel, G. W. F. 2007 [1899]. *The Philosophy of History*. Cosimo. New York, p. 99.
90. Hegel 2007 [1899]: 98.
91. Hegel 2007 [1899]: 99.
92. Trevor-Roper, H. 1965. *The Rise of Christian Europe*. Thames and Hudson. London, p. 9.
93. Baker, S. W. 1867. *The Races of the Nile Basin*. Transactions of the Ethnological Society of London. London, p. 231.
94. Mbiti, J. 1969. *African Religions and Philosophy*. Heinemann. London.
95. Marx, K. & Engels, F. 1957. *On Religion*. Progress. Moscow, p. 38.
96. Verner, M. 2003. *The Pyramids. Their Archaeology and History*. Atlantic Books. London.
97. Pliny the Elder 2004: 352.
98. Kipling, R. 1920. *Letters of Travel, 1892–1913*. Doubleday, Page & Company. New York, p. 269.
99. Fagan, G. 2004. *The Rape of the Nile. Tomb Robbers, Tourists, and Archaeologists in Egypt*. Westview Press. Boulder, p. 17.
100. Herodotus 2008: II.126.
101. Darby, L. et al. 1977. *Food: The Gift of Osiris. Volume 1*. Academic Press. London, p. 32.
102. Parsons, T. 1964. Introduction. In Weber, M. *The Sociology of Religion*: xix–lxvii. Beacon Press. Boston, p. lxvii.
103. Weber 1964: 1.
104. Weber, M. 2006 [1930]. *The Protestant Ethic and the Spirit of Capitalism*. Routledge. London.
105. Oestigaard, T. 2013. *Water, Christianity and the Rise of Capitalism*. I.B.Tauris. London.
106. Thomas, K. 1971. *Religion and the Decline of Magic. Studies in Popular Beliefs in Sixteenth and Seventeenth Century in England*. Weidenfeld and Nicolson. London, p. 89.
107. Oestigaard, T. 2009. The materiality of hell: the Christian hell in a world religion context. *Material Religion*, Vol. 5, No. 3: 312–31; Oestigaard, T. 2010a. Purification, purgation and penalty: Christian concepts of water and fire in heaven and hell. In Tvedt, T. & Oestigaard, T. (eds), *A History of Water. Series 2, Vol. 1. The Ideas of Water from Antiquity to Modern Times*: 298–322. I.B.Tauris. London.
108. Morris 1987: 59–61.
109. Morris 1987: 106–7.
110. Durkheim, E. 1904. *The Rules of Sociological Method*. Free Press. New York. 3rd ed. 1966.
111. Snow, C. P. 1966. *The Two Cultures*. Cambridge University Press. Cambridge.
112. Durkheim, E. 1915. *The Elementary Forms of Religious Life*. George Allen & Unwin Ltd. London, p. 3.
113. See for instance Freud, S. 1913. *The Interpretation of Dreams*. The Macmillan Company. New York and Freud, S. 1920. *Three Contributions to the Theory of Sex*. Nervous and Mental Disease Publishing Co. New York and Washington.
114. Otto, R. 1958. *The Idea of The Holy*. Oxford University Press. Oxford.
115. Eliade, M. 1954. *The Myth of the Eternal Return*. Pantheon Books. New York; Eliade, M. 1958. *Yoga – Immortality and Freedom*. Bollingen Series LVI. Pantheon Books. New York; Eliade,

M. 1987 [1959]. *The Sacred and Profane. The Nature of Religion*. Harcourt Brace. New York; Eliade, M. 1959. Methodological remarks on the study of religious symbolism. In Eliade, M. & Kitagawa, J. M. (eds), *The History of Religions*: 86–107. University of Chicago Press. Chicago, and Eliade, M. 1993. *Patterns in Comparative Religion*. Sheed and Ward Ltd. London.

116. Berger, A. 1986. Cultural hermeneutics: the concept of imagination in the phenomenological approaches of Henry Corbin and Mircea Eliade. *The Journal of Religion*, Vol. 66, No. 2: 141–56, p. 151.
117. Allen, D. 1988. Eliade and history. *The Journal of Religion*, Vol. 68, No. 4: 545–65, p. 552.
118. Schilbrack, K. 2014. *Philosophy and the Study of Religions. A Manifesto*. Wiley-Blackwell. Oxford, p. 75.
119. Geertz, C. 1973. *The Interpretation of Cultures*. HarperCollins. New York, pp. 88–125.
120. World Bank. 2003. *Accountability at the World Bank: The Inspection Panel 10 Years On*. World Bank. Washington, p. 84.
121. See for instance Obeyesekere, G. 1981. *Medusa's Hair*. The University of Chicago Press. Chicago, with regards to holy men, healers or diviners and psychology.
122. World Bank. 2008. *Report No. 44977-UG. The Inspection Panel. Investigation Report. Uganda: Private Power Generation (Bujagali) Project (Guarantee No. B0130-UG). August 29, 2008*. World Bank, Washington, p. 180.
123. Parsons, T. 1944. The theoretical development of the sociology of religion: a chapter in the history of modern social science. *Journal of the History of Ideas*, Vol. 5, No. 2: 176–90.
124. Davies, C. 1999. The fragmentation of the religious tradition of the creation, after-life and morality: modernity not post-modernity. *Journal of Contemporary Religion* Vol. 17. No. 3: 339–60.
125. Nash, H. S. 1913. The nature and definition of religion. *The Harvard Theological Review*, Vol. 6, No. 1: 1–30, p. 1.
126. Dworkin, R. 2013. *Religion Without God*. Harvard University Press. Cambridge, p. 1.
127. Augustine. 1957. *Saint Augustine. The City of God Against the Pagans*, with an English translation by G. E. McCracken, in seven volumes. William Heinemann Ltd. London.
128. Schilbrack, K. 2013. What Isn't Religion. *The Journal of Religion*, Vol. 93, No. 3: 291–318, p. 313.
129. Trigger, B. 2003. *Understanding Early Civilizations. A Comparative Study*. Cambridge University Press. Cambridge, p. 473.
130. Long, C. 1993. Cosmogony. In Eliade, M. (ed.), *The Encyclopedia of Religion*. Vol. 3: 94–100. Macmillian Publishing Company. New York, p. 94.
131. Trigger 2003: 473.
132. Faherty, R. L. 1974. Sacrifice. *The New Encyclopaedia Britannica*. 15th ed. Macropaedia. Vol. 16: 128–35.
133. Lugira, A. 2009. *African Traditional Religion*. Chelsea House. New York.
134. Tanner, R. E. S. 1956a. An introduction to the spirit being of the Northern Basukuma. *Anthropological Quarterly*, Vol. 29, No. 2: 45–56; Wijsen, F. & Tanner, R. 2000. *Seeking a Good Life. Religion and Society in Usukuma, Tanzania*. Paulines Publications Africa. Nairobi, p. 9.
135. Wlodarczyk, N. 2013. African traditional religion and violence. In Juergensmeyer, M. et al. (eds), *The Oxford Handbook of Religion and Violence*: 153–66, p. 157.
136. Oestigaard, T. 2014. *Religion at Work in Globalised Traditions. Rainmamking, Witchcraft and Christianity in Tanzania*. Cambridge Scholars Publishing. Newcastle.
137. Rappaport, R. A. 2001. *Ritual and Religion in the Making of Humanity*. Cambridge University Press. Cambridge, p. 2.
138. Tvedt 1997.
139. Raglan, L. 1954. Foreword. In Hocart, A. M. *Social Origins*: vii–ix. Watts & Co. London.
140. Weber 1964: 57.

141. Weber 1964: 3, 57.
142. Piketty, T. 2014. *Capital in the Twenty-First Century*. Belknap Press. London, pp. 32–3.
143. Mauss, M. 1990. *The Gift*. Routledge. London.
144. Weber, M. 1951. *The Religion of China. Confucianism and Taoism*. The Free Press. Illinois, p. 196, my emphasis.
145. Weber, M. 2006 [1930].
146. Shipton, P. M. 2007. *The Nature of Entrustment: Intimacy, Exchange, and the Sacred in Africa*. Yale University Press. New Haven, p. 107.
147. Weber 1964: 83
148. Hocart 1954: 19.
149. Hocart 1954: 15.
150. Barth, F. 1987 [1993]. *Cosmologies in the Making. A Generative Approach to Cultural Variation in Inner New Guinea*. Cambridge University Press. Cambridge, p. 84.
151. http://oxforddictionaries.com/definition/tradition (accessed 28 May 2012).
152. Barth, F. 1990. The Guru and the Conjurer: transactions in knowledge and the shaping of culture in Southeast Asia and Melanesia. *Man* Vol. 25: 640–53.
153. Haleem, M. A. 1999. *Understanding the Qur'an. Themes and Styles*. I.B.Tauris. London, pp. 26–9.
154. Oxtoby, W. G. 1987. Holy, Idea of the. In M. Eliade (ed.), *The Encyclopaedia of Religion*. Vol. 6: 431–8. Macmillian, New York, p. 434.
155. Thomas, K. 1971. *Religion and the Decline of Magic. Studies in Popular Beliefs in Sixteenth and Seventeenth Century in England*. Weidenfeld and Nicolson. London.
156. Finnestad, R. B. 1985. *Image of the World and Symbol of the Creator. On the Cosmological and Iconological Values of the Temple of Edfu*. Otto Harrassowitz. Wiesbaden.
157. Tvedt & Oestigaard 2010: 16.
158. Beke, C. T. 1847. On the Nile and its tributaries. *Journal of the Royal Geographical Society of London*, Vol. 17: 1–84, p. 2.
159. Lucas, G. 1995. Interpretation in contemporary archaeology: some philosophical issues. In Hodder, I. et al. (eds), *Interpreting Archaeology: Finding Meaning in the Past*: 37–44. Routledge. London.
160. Thomson, J. 1884. *A Voice from the Nile and Other Poems*. Reeves and Turner. London.

2 THE SOURCE OF THE BLUE NILE AND LAKE TANA IN ETHIOPIA

1. Simoons, F. J. 1960. Snow in Ethiopia: a review of the evidence. *Geographical Review*, Vol. 50, No. 3: 402–11, p. 403.
2. Crawford, O. G. S. 1949. Some Medieval theories about the Nile. *The Geographical Journal*, Vol. 114, No. 1/3: 6–23.
3. Lynam, E. et al. Some Medieval theories about the Nile: discussion. *The Geographical Journal*, Vol. 114, No. 1/3: 24–9.
4. Johnston, H. 1903. *The Nile Quest*. Lawrence and Bullen. London, p. 47.
5. Blundell, H. W. 1906. Exploration in the Abai Basin, Abyssinia. *The Geographical Journal*, Vol. 27, No. 6: 529–51, p. 548.
6. Markham, C. R. 1868. The Portuguese expeditions to Abyssinia in the fifteenth, sixteenth, and seventeenth centuries. *Journal of the Royal Geographical Society of London*, Vol. 38: 1–12, pp. 4–6.
7. Friedlander, M. J. 2007. *Ethiopia's Hidden Treasures: A Guide to the Paintings of the Remote Churches of Ethiopia*. Shama Books. Addis Ababa, p. 67.

8. Johnston 1903: 51.
9. Bruce, J. 1790. *Travels to Discover the Source of the Nile, in the Years 1768, 1769, 1770, 1771, 1772, and 1773 in Five Volumes*. J. Ruthven. London, Vol. 3, p. 619.
10. Lobo, J. 1789. *A voyage to Abyssinia, by Father Jerome Lobo, a Portuguese Missionary. Containing the history, natural, civil, and ecclesiastical, of that remote and unfrequented country, continued down to the beginning of the eighteenth century: With fifteen dissertations ... relating to the antiquities, government, religion, manners, and natural history, of Abyssina*. By M. Le Grand, translated from the French by Samuel Johnson, LL.D. To which are added, various other tracts by the same author, not published by Sir John Hawkins or Mr Stockdale. Elliot and Kay, London and C. Elliot, Edinburgh, pp. 110–11.
11. Johnston 1903: 64
12. Lobo 1789: 111–12.
13. Lobo 1789: 66.
14. Beckingham, C. F. & Huntingford, G. W. B. 1954. *Some Records of Ethiopia 1593–1646: Being Extracts from the History of High Ethiopia or Abassia by Manoel De Almeida. Together with Bahrey's History of the Galla*. Printed for the Hakluyt Society, London, pp. 23–4.
15. Markham 1868: 11–12.
16. See footnote 9.
17. Johnston 1903: 78–81.
18. Cheesman, R. E. 1928. The Upper Waters of the Blue Nile. *Geographical Journal*, Vol. 85, No. 6: 358–74, p. 361.
19. Johnston 1903: 78–81.
20. Bruce 1790, Vol. 3: 603–4.
21. Bruce 1790, Vol. 3: 597–8.
22. Bruce 1790, Vol. 3: 598.
23. Bruce 1790, Vol. 3: 599.
24. Bruce 1790, Vol. 3: 600.
25. Moorehead, A. 1962. *The Blue Nile*. Hamish Hamilton. London, p. 41.
26. Bruce 1790, Vol. 3: 638.
27. Bruce 1790, Vol. 3: 735.
28. Bruce 1790, Vol. 3: 633.
29. Bruce 1790, Vol. 3: 636.
30. Bruce 1790, Vol. 3: 730.
31. Bruce 1790, Vol. 3: 731.
32. Bruce 1790, Vol. 3: 732.
33. Bruce 1790, Vol. 3: 732
34. Bruce 1790, Vol. 3: 733.
35. Bruce 1790, Vol. 3: 733.
36. Bruce 1790, Vol. 3: 744.
37. Beke, C. T. 1844. Abyssinia: being a continuation of routes in that country. *Journal of the Royal Geographical Society of London*, Vol. 14:1–76, p. 13.
38. Beke 1844: 34.
39. Beke 1844: 34.
40. Beke 1844: 35.
41. Cheesman, R. E. 1928. The upper waters of the Blue Nile. *Geographical Journal*, Vol. 85, No. 6: 358–74, and Cheesman, R. E. 1935. Lake Tana and its Island. *Geographical Journal*, Vol. 71, No. 4: 489–502.

42. Cheesman, R. E. 1968 [1936]. *Lake Tana and the Blue Nile: An Abyssinian Quest*. Frank Cass. London, p. 16.
43. Beckingham and Huntingford 1954: 29, fn. 1.
44. Cheesman 1968 [1936]: 73.
45. Cheesman 1968 [1936]: 74.
46. Philo, 1962. *Philo*, with an English translation by F. H. Coulson and G. H. Whitaker, in ten volumes, Vol. 1. William Heinemann Ltd, London, p. 409.
47. Lobo 1789: 110.
48. Tafla, B. 2000. The father of rivers: the Nile in Ethiopian literature. In Erlich, H. & Gershoni, I. (eds), *The Nile: Histories, Cultures, Myths*: 153–70. Lynne Rienner Publishers. London, pp. 155, 167–8.
49. See Finneran, N. 2007. *The Archaeology of Ethiopia*. Routledge. London; Finneran, N. 2009. Holy Water: pre-Christian and Christian water association in Ethiopia. In Oestigaard, T. (ed.), *Water, Culture and Identity: Comparing Past and Present Traditions in the Nile Basin Region*: 165–87. BRIC Press. Bergen, and Finneran, N. 2014. Holy wells, hot springs, and royal baths: water and sociocultural developments in Medieval and Post-Medieval Ethiopia c. AD 700–900. In Tvedt, T. & Oestigaard, T. (eds), *A History of Water. Series 3, Vol. 1. Water and Urbanization*: 262–82. I.B.Tauris. London.
50. Messerschmidt, D. 1992. *Muktinath: Himalayan Pilgrimage, A Cultural & Historical Guide*. Sahayogi Press. Kathmandu. Nepal, p. 16.
51. Gold, A. G. 1988. *Fruitful Journeys: The Ways of Rajasthani Pilgrims*. University of California Press. Berkeley, p. 301.
52. Hayes, A. J. 1905. *The Source of the Blue Nile: A Record of a Journey Through the Soudan to Lake Tsana in Western Abyssinia, and the Return to Egypt by the Valley of Atbara*. Smith, Elder & Co. London, p. 226.
53. Lobo 1789: 113–14.
54. Bruce 1790, Vol. 3: 422, 572.
55. Bruce 1790, Vol. 3: 425–7.
56. Tamrat, T. 1972a. A short note on the traditions of pagan resistance to the Ethiopian Church (14th and 15th Centuries). *Journal of Ethiopian Studies*, Vol. X, No. 1: 137–50, p. 137. See also Tamrat, T. 1972b. *Church and State in Ethiopia: 1270–1527*. Clarendon Press. Oxford.
57. Tamrat 1972a: 138.
58. Tamrat 1972a: 139.
59. Tamrat 1972a: 139–41.
60. Henze, P. 2000. Consolidation of Christianity around the source of the Blue Nile. In Erlich, H. & Gershoni, I. (eds), *The Nile: Histories, Cultures, Myths*: 39–56. Lynne Rienner Publishers. London.
61. Beke 1844: 47.
62. Beke 1847: 15.
63. Budge, E. A. W. 1928. *A History of Ethiopia: Nubia and Abyssinia*. Methuen. London, p. 128.
64. Cheesman 1935: 490.
65. Johnston 1903: 55.
66. Munro-Hay, S. 2005. *The Quest for the Ark of the Covenant: The True History of the Tablets of Moses*. I.B.Tauris. London, pp. 31–7.
67. Bruce 1790, Vol. 3: 328.
68. Bruce 1790, Vol. 3: 332
69. Bruce 1790, Vol. 3: 328.

70. Bruce 1790, Vol. 3: 328.
71. Kaplan, S. 2000. Did Jewish influence reach Ethiopia via the Nile? In Erlich, H. & Gershoni, I. (eds), *The Nile: Histories, Cultures, Myths*: 57–69. Lynne Rienner Publishers. London.
72. Parfitt, T. 1999. Rabbi Nahoum's anthropological mission to Ethiopia. In Parfitt, T. & Semi, E. T. (eds), *The Beta Israel in Ethiopia and Israel*: 1–14. Curzon Press. Surrey.
73. Quirin, J. 1992. *The Evolution of the Ethiopian Jews: A History of the Beta Israel (Falasha) to 1920*. University of Philadelphia Press. Philadelphia, p. 10.
74. Budge, E. A. W. 1932. *The Queen of Sheba and Her Only Son Menylek (I)*. Oxford University Press. London, pp. 142–3.
75. Budge 1932: 17.
76. Budge 1932: 29.
77. Budge 1932: 30–1.
78. Budge 1932: 142–3.
79. Seeman, D. 2000. The question of kinship: bodies and narratives in the Beta Israel-European encounter (1860–1920). *Journal of Religion in Africa*, Vol. 30, Fasc. 1: 86–120, p. 88.
80. Ribner, D. S. & Schindler, R. 1996. The crisis of religious identity among Ethiopian immigrants in Israel. *Journal of Black Studies*, Vol. 27, No. 1: 104–17, p. 110.
81. Seeman 2000: 91–5, p. 110.
82. Quirin, J. 1998. Caste and class in historical north-west Ethiopia: the Beta Israel (Falasha) and Kemant, 1300–1900. *The Journal of African History*, Vol. 39, No. 2 (1998): 195–220, p. 210.
83. Quirin 1992: 162.
84. Kaplan, S. 1992. *The Beta Israel (Falasha) in Ethiopia*. New York University Press. New York, p. 113.
85. Ribner & Schindler 1996.
86. Karadawi, A. 1991. The smuggling of the Ethiopian Falasha to Israel through Sudan. *African Affairs*, Vol. 90, No. 358: 23–49.
87. Kaplan, S. 1993. The invention of Ethiopian Jews: three models (Trois approches de l' 'invention' des Juifs éthiopiens). *Cahiers d'Études Africaines*, Vol. 33, Cahier 132 (1993): 645–58.
88. Tegegne, M. 1993. *'Gojjam' the Stigma: An Abyssinian Pariah*. Guihon Books. Addis Ababa, p. 17.
89. Gedef, A. F. 2014. *Archaeological Fieldwork Around Lake Tana Area of Northwest Ethiopia and the Implication for an Understanding of Aquatic Adaptation*. Dissertation for the degree of philosophiae doctor (PhD). University of Bergen. Bergen, pp. 235, 245.
90. Blundell 1906: 532.
91. Cheesman 1968 [1936]: 93.
92. Tegegne 1993: 17.
93. Beckingham & Huntingford 1954: 35, fn. 4.
94. Cheesman 1968 [1936]: 163–4.
95. See also Gedef 2014.
96. Cheesman 1968 [1936]: 93.

3 FROM LAKE VICTORIA TO MURCHISON FALLS IN UGANDA

1. Reid, R. J. 2002. *Political Power in Pre-Colonial Buganda*. Fountain Publishers. Kampala, pp. 68–9.
2. Speke, J. H. 1863. *Journal of the Discovery of the Source of the White Nile*. Blackwood and Sons. Edinburgh and London, p. 569.
3. See also Reid, A. 2016. The lake, bananas and ritual power in Uganda. In Tvedt, T. & Oestigaard, T. (eds), *A History of Water, Series 3, Vol. 3. Water and Food: From Hunter-Gatherers to Global Production in Africa*: 277–98. I.B.Tauris. London.
4. Speke 1863: 394–5.
5. Speke 1863: 396.
6. Kenny, M. G. 1988. Mutesa's crime: Hubris and the control of African kings. *Comparative Studies in Society and History*, Vol. 30, No. 4: 595–612, pp. 605–7.
7. Bridges, R. C. 1970. John Hanning Speke: negotiating a way to the Nile. In Rotberg, R. I. (ed.), *Africa and Its Explorers: Motives, Methods, and Impact*: 95–137. Harvard University Press. Cambridge, MA, p. 127.
8. Johnston, H. 1902. *The Uganda Protectorate*. Hutchinson. London, p. 693.
9. Nyakatura 1973: 44, op. cit. Kenny, M. G. 1977. The powers of Lake Victoria. *Anthropos*, Bd. 72, H. 5/6: 717–33, p. 722.
10. Northrop, H. D. 1889. *Wonders of the Tropics or Explorations and Adventures of Henry M. Stanley*. National Publishing. Philadelphia, p. 391.
11. Kenny 1977: 724–8.
12. Kenny 1977: 724.
13. Speke, J. H. 1864. *What Led to the Discovery of the Source of the Nile*. Blackwood and Sons. Edinburgh and London, p. 321.
14. Speke 1863: 295–6, 420.
15. Speke 1863: 441.
16. Roscoe, J. 1911. *The Baganda: An Account of Their Native Customs and Beliefs*. Macmillan and Co. London, p. 290.
17. Roscoe 1911: 294.
18. Stam, N. 1908. The religious conceptions of some tribes of Buganda (British Equatorial Africa). *Anthropos*, Bd. 3, H. 2: 213–18, pp. 214–15, 217.
19. Roscoe 1911: 300.
20. Roscoe 1911: 314–15.
21. Kenny, M. G. 1977. The powers of Lake Victoria. *Anthropos*, Bd. 72, H. 5/6: 717–33.
22. Tvedt, T. 2012. *Nilen – historiens elv*. Aschehoug. Oslo.
23. Kenny 1977.
24. Condon, M. A. 1911. Contribution to the ethnography of Basogabatamba Uganda Protectorate, Br. E. Africa (continued). *Anthropos*, Bd. 6, H. 2: 366–84, p. 381.
25. Condon 1911: 382–3.
26. Roscoe 1911: 318.
27. Roscoe, J. 1909. Python worship in Uganda. *Man*, Vol. 9: 88–90.
28. Roscoe 1911: 18.
29. Roscoe 1911: 241.
30. Roscoe 1911: 458–9.
31. Schoenbrun, D. L. 1998. *A Green Place, A Good Place: Agrarian Change, Gender, and Social Identity in the Great Lakes Region to the 15th Century*. James Currey. Oxford. See also

Stephens, R. 2013. *A History of African Motherhood: The Case of Uganda, 700–1900.* Cambridge University Press. Cambridge.
32. Thomas, L. M. 2003. Politics of the Womb. Women, reproduction, and the State of Kenya. University of California Press. Berkeley, pp. 3–4.
33. Behrend, H. 2011. *Resurrecting Cannibals: The Catholic Church, Witch-Hunts, & The Production of Pagans in Western Uganda.* James Currey. London, pp. 3, 4.
34. Hocart, A. M. 1954. *Social Origins.* Watts & Co. London, p. 68.
35. Behrend 2011: 27.
36. Behrend 2011: 22.
37. Behrend 2011: 34.
38. Colvile, H. 1895. *The Land of the Nile Springs: Being Chiefly an Account of How We Fought Kabarega.* Edward Arnold. London, p. 32.
39. Heien, K. H. 2007. *Local Livelihoods and the Bujagali Hydro-Power Dam, Uganda. MA-thesis.* Faculty of Economics and Social Sciences. Agder University College. Kristiansand.
40. Byerley, A. 2005. *Becoming Jinja: The Production of Space and Making of Place in an African Industrial Town.* Department of Human Geography. Stockholm University. Stockholm, p. 1.
41. Stanley, H. M. 1878. A geographical sketch of the Nile and Livingstone (Congo) Basins. *Proceedings of the Royal Geographical Society of London*, Vol. 22, No. 6 (1877–8): 382–410, p. 392.
42. Stanley 1878: 390.
43. Churchill, W. S. 1909. *My African Journey.* William Briggs. Toronto, p. 120.
44. Oestigaard, T. 2015. *Dammed Divinities: The Water Powers at Bujagali Falls, Uganda.* Current African Issues No. 62. The Nordic Africa Institute. Uppsala.
45. See Oestigaard 2015 for an in-depth discussions regarding the controversies of the dam project and the global discourse, and World Bank, 2008. *Report No. 44977-UG. The Inspection Panel. Investigation Report. Uganda: Private Power Generation (Bujagali) Project (Guarantee No. B0130-UG). August 29, 2008.* World Bank. Washington.
46. World Bank 2008: 186–7.
47. Burnside. 2006. *Bujagali Hydropower Project: Social and Environmental Assessment Report: Executive Summary.* R.J. Burnside International. Guelph, p. 44.
48. World Bank 2008: 176.
49. World Bank 2008: 179.
50. World Bank 2008: 177.
51. World Bank 2008: 167.
52. World Bank 2008: 178.
53. World Bank 2008: 179.
54. Oweyegha-Afunaduula, F. C. and Isaac, A. 2004. Environmental hydropolitics of the Nile Basin's Bujagali Dam, Uganda: an annotated bibliography. Working to Protect River Nile, Fighting for Justice Occasional Paper No.7 NAPE/SBC-2004 February 6 2004.
55. Lacey 2001.
56. World Bank 2008: 172.
57. Kitimbo, I. 2007. *The Monitor.* 9 September 2007. Uganda: Bujagali Spirits Relocated. http://allafrica.com/stories/200709100646.html (accessed 21 February 2014).
58. Kitimbo 2007.
59. Kitimbo 2007.
60. Mugabi, F. 2011. Bujagali spirits moved to new place. *New Vision*, 6 July.

61. Musinguzi, B. 2011. 'Budhagali' water spirits find a new resting place. The East African, 24 July 2011.
   http://www.theeastafrican.co.ke/magazine/Budhagali+water+spirits+find+a+new+resting+place/-/434746/1206588/-/e6n3tvz/-/index.html (accessed 21 February 2014).
62. Gonza, R. K. et al. 2001. *Reconciliation Among the Busoga*. Cultural Research Centre. Jinja.
63. Stanley 1878: 390.
64. Cohen, D. W. 1972. *The Historical Tradition of Busoga: Mukama and Kintu*. Clarendon Press. Oxford, p. 23.
65. Gonza, R. K. et al. 2003. *Witchcraft, Divination and Healing Among the Basoga*. Cultural Research Centre. Jinja, p. 114.
66. Gonza et al. 2003: 117–18.
67. Gonza et al. 2003: 117–18.
68. See Oestigaard 2015.
69. Akiiki, R. K. 2012. People-centred development. In Johnston, R. B. et al. (eds), *Water, Cultural Diversity, and Global Environmental Change: Emerging Trends, Sustainable Futures?*: 341–3. Springer/UNESCO. Paris.
70. Gonza R. K. et al. 2010. *The Concept of Good Luck and Bad Luck Among the Basoga*. Marianum Publishing Company. Kisubi, p. 6.
71. Gonza et al. 2010: 111.
72. Chief Waguma Yasin, pers. com.
73. EIB-CM 2012: 106.
74. Gonza, R. K. et al. 2002. *Traditional Religion and Clans Among the Busoga*. Vol. 1. Cultural Research Centre. Jinja, pp. 152–3.
75. For literature on witchcraft, see for instance Abrahams, R. (ed.), 1994. *Witchcraft in Contemporary Tanzania*. Cambridge African Monographs. Cambridge; Behringer, W. 2004. *Witches and Witch-Hunts*. Polity Press. Oxford; Comaroff, J. and Comaroff, J. (eds), 1993. *Modernity and Malcontents; Rituals and Power in Postcolonial Africa*. University of Chicago Press. Chicago; Geschiere, P. 1997. *The Modernity of Witchcraft: Politics and the Occult in Postcolonial Africa*. University Press of Virginia. Charlottesville; Haar, G. T. (ed.), 2006. *Imagining Evil: Witchcraft Beliefs and Accusations in Contemporary Africa*. Africa World Press, inc. Trenton and Asmara; Kiernan, J. (ed.), 2006. *The Power of the Occult in Modern Africa: Continuity and Innovation in the Renewal of African Cosmologies*. Lit Verlag. Berlin; Levack, B. P. 2006. *The Witch-Hunt in Early Modern Europe*. Third edition. Longman. London; Levack, B. P. 2008. *Witch-Hunting in Scotland: Law, Politics and Religion*. Routledge. London; Mesaki, S. 1993. *Witchcraft and Witch-Killings in Tanzania*. PhD thesis. University of Minnesota. Minnesota; Oestigaard, T. 2014. *Religion at Work in Globalised Traditions: Rainmaking, Witchcraft and Christianity in Tanzania*. Cambridge Scholars Publishing. Newcastle, and Stroeken, K. 2010. *Moral Power: The Magic of Witchcraft*. Berghahn Books. Oxford.
76. Gonza et al. 2003: 9.
77. Werbner, R. 2015. *Divination's Grasp: African Encounters with the Almost Said*. Indiana University Press. Bloomington and Indianapolis.
78. Gonza et al. 2003: 83.
79. Gonza et al. 2003: 9.
80. Gonza et al. 2003: 13.
81. Gonza et al. 2003: 15.
82. Gonza et al. 2003: 37.
83. Gonza et al. 2003: 41.
84. Gonza et al. 2003: 41.

85. Gonza et al. 2003: 44.
86. Gonza et al. 2002: 175–6.
87. Gonza et al. 2003: 87.
88. Gonza et al. 2003: 101.
89. Gonza et al. 2003: 108.
90. Oestigaard 2014.
91. *Electricity Regulatory Authority: Developments and Investment Opportunities in Renewable Energy Resources in Uganda*. June 2012, p. 13.
92. Heike Behrend, pers. com.
93. Behrend, H. 1999. *Alice Lakwena & the Holy Spirits*. James Currey. Oxford, p. 30.
94. Behrend 1999: 62–3.
95. Behrend 1999: 25–6.
96. Allen, T. 1991. Understanding Alice: Uganda's Holy Spirit movement in context. *Africa: Journal of the International African Institute*, Vol. 61, No. 3: 370–99, pp. 392–3.
97. Behrend 1999: 134.
98. Behrend 1999: 134.
99. Meier, B. 2013. Powerful spirits and weak rulers: prophets' authority in Acholi conflict. In Meier, B. & Steinforth, A. S. (eds), *Spirits in Politics: Uncertainties of Power and Healing in African Societies*: 223–45. Campus Verlag. Frankfurt.
100. Behrend 1999: 91, 97.
101. Behrend 1999: 179, 185.
102. Doom, R. & Vlassenroot, K. 1999. Kony's message: a New Koine? The Lord's Resistance Army in Northern Uganda. *African Affairs*, Vol. 98, No. 390: 5–36, pp. 20–3.
103. Weber, M. 1964. *The Sociology of Religion*. Beacon Press. Boston, p. 1.
104. Meier, B. & Offermann, P. 2010. Fighting spirits. A film production of the Cluster of Excellence, Religion and Politics. WWU Münster.

4 THE SOURCES IN THE SKY AND RAINMAKING

1. Warburg, G. R. 2007. The search for the sources of the White Nile and Egyptian-Sudanese relations. *Middle Eastern Studies*, Vol. 43, No. 3: 475–86, pp. 475, 484 fn. 1.
2. Kerisel, J. 2001. *The Nile and its Masters: Past, Present, Future. Source of Hope and Anger*. A.A. Balkema. Rotterdam, p. 5.
3. Collins, R. 2002. *The Nile*. Yale University Press. New Haven, pp. 27–9.
4. http://news.nationalgeographic.com/news/2006/04/0419_060419_nile.html (accessed 10 July 2014).
5. Homer. 1998. *Homer the Odyssey*. Translated by Samuel Butler. Orange Street Press Classics, online pdf, p. 47; Homer. 1891. *The Odyssey of Homer*. Translated by Herbert Palmer. Houghton, Mifflin and Company, Boston.
6. Griffith, R. D. 1997. Homeric ΔΙΙΠΕΤΕΟΣΠΟΤΑΜΟΙΟ and the Celestial Nile. *The American Journal of Philology*, Vol. 118, No. 3: 353–62.
7. Daly, C. P. 1875. Remarks on Stanley's verification of Ptolemy's Geography. *Journal of the Geographical Society of New York*, Vol. 7: 290–5.
8. Randles, W. G. L. 1956. South-East Africa as shown on selected printed maps of the sixteenth century. *Imago Mundi*, Vol. 13: 69–88, pp. 75–6.
9. Randles 1956: 75–6.

10. Stanley, H. M. 1890. *In Darkest Africa or the Quest Rescue and Retreat of Emin Governor of Equatoria*. Sampson Low, Marston, Searle and Rivington. London.
11. Stanley 1890: 280–1.
12. Stanley 1890: 282.
13. Stanley 1890: 285.
14. Stanley 1890: 286.
15. Baker, S. W. 1869. *Albert N'yanza: Great Basin of the Nile, and Exploration of the Nile Sources*. Lippincott. Philadelphia, p. 308.
16. Baker 1869: 313.
17. Stanley 1890: 290, 299.
18. Stanley 1890: 304–5, my italics.
19. Hochschild, A. 1998. *King Leopold's Ghost: A Story of Greed, Terror, and Heroism in Colonial Africa*. Houghton Mifflin. Boston.
20. Philipps, T. 1947. Etymology of some African names. *The Geographical Journal*, Vol. 110, No. 1/3: 142–4.
21. Collins 2002: 33.
22. Goodenough, W. & Gowers, W. 1933. Ruwenzori: flights and further exploration: discussion. *The Geographical Journal*, Vol. 82, No. 6: 511–14, p. 511.
23. Eggermont, H. et al. 2009. Ruwenzori Mountains (Mountains of the Moon): headwaters of the White Nile. In Dumont, H. J. (ed.), *The Nile: Origin, Environments, Limnology and Human Use*: 243–61. Springer. Leiden, p. 245.
24. Chamberlain, P. 2009. Nile Basin climates. In Dumont, H. J. (ed.), *The Nile: Origin, Environments, Limnology and Human Use*: 307–33. Springer. Leiden, p. 314.
25. Jacobs, L. et al. 2016. The Rwenzori Mountains, a landslide-prone region? *Landslides*, Vol. 13, No. 3: 519–36.
26. Johnston, H. 1902. The Uganda Protectorate, Ruwenzori, and the Semliki Forest. *The Geographical Journal*, Vol. 19, No. 1: 1–39, pp. 37–8.
27. Hogarth, D. G. et al. 1927. New routes on Ruwenzori: discussion. *The Geographical Journal*, Vol. 69, No. 6: 525–31, p. 527.
28. Packard, R. M. 1982. Chiefship and the history of Nyavingi possession among the Bashu of Eastern Zaire. *Africa: Journal of the International African Institute*, Vol. 52, No. 4: 67–86 + 90.
29. Bright, R. G. T. 1909. Survey and exploration in the Ruwenzori and Lake Region. *The Geographical Journal*, Vol. 34, No. 2: 128–53, p. 145.
30. Fisher, A. B. 1904. Western Uganda. *The Geographical Journal*, Vol. 24, No. 3: 249–63, p. 254.
31. Fisher 1904: 262.
32. Stacey, T. 2003. *Tribe: The Hidden History of the Mountains of the Moon: An Autobiographical Study*. Stacey International. London, pp. 236–7.
33. http://www.westminster-abbey.org/our-history/people/david-livingstone (accessed 15 February 2016).
34. http://www.newworldencyclopedia.org/entry/David_Livingstone#cite_note-2 (accessed 17 February 2016).
35. Hill, R. 1956. The search for the White Nile's sources: two explorers who failed. *The Geographical Journal*, Vol. 122. No. 2: 247–50, p. 247.
36. Burton, R. F. 1859. The Lake Regions of Central Africa. *Journal of the Royal Geographical Society of London*, Vol. 29: 1–454, p. 17.
37. Waller, H. 1875. *The Last Journals of David Livingstone in Central Africa: From Eighteen Hundred and Sixty-Five to His Death*. Harper & Brothers Publishers. New York.

38. Livingstone, D. 1874. Letters of the late Dr. Livingstone. *Proceedings of the Royal Geographical Society of London*, Vol. 18, No. 3 (1873–4): 255–81, p. 258.
39. Jeal, T. 1973. *Livingstone*. Heinemann. London.
40. Findlay, A. G. 1867. On Dr. Livingstone's last journey, and the probable ultimate sources of the Nile. *Journal of the Royal Geographical Society of London*, Vol. 37: 193–212, p. 211.
41. Jeal 1973: 287.
42. Baker 1869: xxi.
43. Mill, J. S. 1887. *Principles of Political Economy*. D. Appleton and Company. New York, p. 390.
44. Baker 1869: xxii.
45. Baker 1869: xxi, my emphasis.
46. Bennet, N. R. 1970. David Livingstone: exploration for Christianity. In Rotberg, R. I. (ed.), *Africa and Its Explorers: Motives, Methods, and Impact*: 39–62. Harvard University Press. Cambridge, MA, p. 43.
47. Bennet 1970: 59.
48. Johnston, H. 1913. Livingstone as an explorer. *The Geographical Journal*, Vol. 41, No. 5: 423–46, p. 445.
49. Jeal 1973: 1–2.
50. Johnston 1913: 437.
51. Livingstone 1874: 280.
52. Tvedt, T. 2012. *Nilen – Historiens elv*. Aschehoug. Oslo, p. 354.
53. Reade, W. 1864. *Savage Africa; Being the Narrative of a Tour in Equatorial, Southwestern, and Northwestern Africa*. Harper. New York, p. 136.
54. Obeyesekere, G. 2005. *Cannibal Talk: The Man-Eating Myth and Human Sacrifice in the South Seas*. University of California Press. Berkeley; Behrend, H. 2011. *Resurrecting Cannibals: The Catholic Church, Witch-Hunts, & The Production of Pagans in Western Uganda*. James Currey. London.
55. Stocking, G. W. 1987. *Victorian Anthropology*. The Free Press. New York, pp. 252–3.
56. Livingstone 1874: 259.
57. Jeal 1973: 81.
58. Livingstone, D. 1858. *Missionary Travels and Researches in South Africa*. Harper & Brothers Publishers. New York, pp. 20, 22.
59. See Tvedt, T. 2010a. Why England and not China and India? Water systems and the history of the industrial revolution. *Journal of Global History* Vol. 5: 29–50; Tvedt, T. 2010b. Water: a source of wars or a pathway to peace? An empirical critique of two dominant schools of thought on water and international politics. In Tvedt, T. et al. (eds), *A History of Water, Series 3, Vol. 3 Water, Geopolitics and the New World Order*: 78-108. I.B.Tauris. London; Tvedt, T. 2010c. Water systems, environmental history and the deconstruction of nature, *Environment and History*, Vol. 16: 143–66; Tvedt, T. 2011. Hydrology and empire: The Nile, water imperialism and the partition of Africa. *The Journal of Imperial and Commonwealth History*, Vol. 39, No. 2: 173–94; Tvedt, T. 2016. *Water and Society – Changing Perceptions of Societal and Historical Development*. I.B.Tauris. London.
60. Livingstone 1858: 21–2.
61. Livingstone 1858: 24.
62. Livingstone 1858: 25–7.

63. Landau, P. S. 1993. When rain falls: rainmaking and community in a Tsawa Village, c. 1870 to recent times. *The International Journal of African Historical Studies*, Vol. 26, No. 1: 1–30, p. 3.
64. Cory, H. 1951a. *The Ntemi: The Traditional Rites of a Sukuma Chief in Tanganyika*. Macmillan. London, p. 47.
65. Brandström, P. 1990. Seeds and soil: the quest for life and the domestication of fertility in Sukuma-Nyamwezi thought and social reality. In Jacobson-Widding, A. & van Beek, W. (eds), *The Creative Communion: African Folk Models of fertility and the Regeneration of Life*: 167–86. Almquist and Wiksell. Uppsala, p. 168.
66. Sanders, T. 2001. Save our skins. Structural adjustment, morality and the occult in Tanzania. In Moore, H. & Sanders, T. (eds), *Magical Interpretation, Material Realities: Modernity, Witchcraft and the Occult in Postcolonial Africa*: 160–83. Routledge. London, p. 169.
67. Oestigaard, T. 2005. *Death and Life-Giving Waters – Cremation, Caste, and Cosmogony in Karmic Traditions*. BAR International Series 1353. Oxford, p. 145.
68. Wijsen, F. & Tanner, R. 2000. *Seeking a Good Life: Religion and Society in Usukuma, Tanzania*. Paulines Publications Africa. Nairobi, p. 33.
69. Scribner, R. W. 1987. *Popular Culture and Popular Movements in Reformation Germany*. Hambledon Press. London.
70. Wijsen & Tanner 2000: 30.
71. Gombrich, R. F. 1988. *Theravada Buddhism: A Social History from Ancient Benares to Modern Colombo*. Routledge. London, p. 118.
72. Wijsen & Tanner 2000: 47.
73. Westerlund, D. 2006. *African Indigenous Religions and Disease Causation: Studies of Religion in Africa 28*. E. J. Brill. Leiden, p. 86.
74. Wijsen, F. & Tanner, R. 2002. *"I am just a Sukuma": Globalization and Identity Construction in Northwest Tanzania*. Rodopi. Amsterdam, p. 57.
75. Wijsen & Tanner 2002: 58.
76. Wijsen & Tanner 2002: 57.
77. Brandström, P. 1998. Lolandi – se jag är! En historia om det berättande namnet hos sukuma-nyamwezi i Tanzania. In Andersson, T. et al. (eds), *Personnamn och social identitet*. Konferanser 42. Kung. Vitterhets Historie och Antikvitets Akademien. Stockholm.
78. Brandström 1990: 169.
79. Westerlund 2006: 95.
80. Westerlund 2006: 94.
81. Tanner, R. E. S. 1959. The spirits of the dead: an introduction to the ancestor worship of the Sukuma of Tanganyika. *Anthropological Quarterly*, Vol. 32, No. 2: 108–24, p. 121.
82. Tanner, R. E. S. 1955. Hysteria in Sukuma Medical Practice. *Africa: Journal of International African Institute*, Vol. 25, No. 3: 274–9, p. 274.
83. Wijsen & Tanner 2000: 63.
84. Wijsen & Tanner 2002: 51, 56.
85. Sanders, T. 1998. Making children, making chiefs: gender, power and ritual legitimacy. *Africa: Journal of the International African Institute*, Vol. 68, No. 2: 238–62, pp. 240–1.
86. Drangert, J. O. 1993. *Who Cares About Water? Household Water Development in Sukumaland, Tanzania*. Linköping Studies in Arts and Science 85. Linköping, p. 84.
87. Cory, H. 1951b. *Traditional Rites in Connection with the Burial, Election, Enthronement and Magic Powers of a Sukuma Chief*. MacMillian and Co. Ltd. London, p. 328.
88. Sanders, T. 2008. *Beyond Bodies: Rainmaking and Sense Making in Tanzania*. Toronto University Press. Toronto, pp. 119–20.

89. Kollmann, P. 1899. *The Victoria Nyanza: The Land, the Races and their Customs, with Specimens of Some of the Dialects*. Swan Sonnenschein & Co, Ltd. London, p. 168.
90. See Oestigaard, T. 2014. *Religion at Work in Globalised Traditions: Rainmaking, Witchcraft and Christianity in Tanzania*. Cambridge Scholars Publishing. Newcastle, for discussion of the reason for the disappearance of rainmaking and other traditions.
91. For cross-cultural references, see for instance Frazer, J. G. 1996 [1922]. *The Golden Bough: A Study in Magic and Religion*. A Touchstone Book, Simon & Schuster. New York, pp. 788–9.
92. Gansum, T. 2003. Hår og stil og stilig hår. Om langhåret maktsymbolikk. In Stylegar, F–A. & Rolfsen, P. (eds), *Snartemofunnene i nytt lys*: 191–222. Universitetets kulturhistoriske museer Skrifter nr. 2. Oslo.
93. Sanders, T. 2000. Rains gone bad, women gone mad: rethinking gender rituals of rebellion and patriarchy. *The Journal of the Royal Anthropological Institute*, Vol. 6, No. 3: 469–86; Sanders, T. 2002. Reflections on two sticks: gender, sexuality and rainmaking. *Cahiers d'Études Africaines*, Vol. 42, Cahier 166: 285–313.
94. Saetersdal, T. et al. 2009. If the Vagina had Teeth. The NAFA Film Collection. 1 hour.
95. Sanders 2000: 479.
96. Lakoff, G. & Johnson, M. 1999. *Philosophy on the Flesh: The Embodied Mind and Its Challenge to Western Thought*. Basic Books. New York.
97. Leach, E. 1954. *Political Systems of Highland Burma: A Study of Kachin Social Structure*. Beacon Press. Boston, p. 13ff.
98. Brück, J. 1999. Ritual and rationality: some problems of interpretation in European archaeology. *European Journal of Archaeology*, Vol. 2, No. 3: 313–44, p. 326.
99. Hocart, A. M. 1922. Myths in the making. *Folklore*, Vol. 33, No. 1: 57–71, p. 57.
100. Raglan, L. 1970. Introduction. In Hocart, A. M. *The Life-Giving Myth*: 6–8. Grove Press. New York, p. 6, my emphasis.
101. Campbell, J. 1964. *The Masks of God: Occidental Mythology*. The Viking Press. New York, pp. 519–21.
102. Mann, T. 1936. *Joseph and His Brothers*. Alfred A. Knopf. New York, p. 3.
103. Campbell, J. 1959. *The Masks of God: Primitive Mythology*. The Viking Press. New York, p. 42.
104. Kaspin, D. 1996. A Chewa cosmology of the body. *American Ethnologist*, Vol. 23, No. 3: 561–78.
105. Jacobs, N. 1996. The flowing eye: water management in the Upper Kuruman Valley, South Africa, c. 1800–1962. *The Journal of African History*, Vol. 37, No. 2: 237–60.
106. Oestigaard 2014: 70.
107. Lonsdale, J. 2008. Soil, work, civilisation, and citizenship in Kenya. *Journal of Eastern Africa Studies*, Vol. 2, No. 2: 305–14.
108. Bjerk, P. K. 2006. They poured themselves into the milk: Zulu political philosophy under Shaka. *The Journal of African History*, Vol. 47, No. 1: 1–19, p. 8.
109. Kjerland, K. A. 1995. *Cattle Breed; Shillings Don't: The Belated Incorporation of the abaKuria into Modern Kenya*. PhD thesis, University of Bergen. Bergen.
110. See for instance Rutten, M. 2016. Dying cows due to climate change? Drought can never finish the Maasai cattle, only the human mouth can (Maasai saying). In Tvedt, T. & Oestigaard, T. (eds), *A History of Water, Series 3, Vol. 3. Water and Food: From Hunter-Gatherers to Global Production in Africa*: 299–331. I.B.Tauris. London.
111. Spencer, P. 1991. The Loonkidongi Prophets and the Maasai: protection racket or incipient state? *Africa: Journal of the International Africa Institute*, Vol. 61, No. 3: 334–42.
112. Talle, A. 2007. 'Serious games': licenses and prohibitions in Maasai sexual Life. *Africa: Journal of the International Africa Institute*, Vol. 77, No. 3: 351–70.

113. Århem, K. 1989. Maasai food symbolism: the cultural connotations of milk, meat, and blood in the pastoral diet. *Anthropos*, Bd. 84, H. 1./3.: 1–23.
114. Lévi-Strauss, C. 1968. *Structural Anthropology*. Allen Lane The Penguin Press. London; Lévi-Strauss, C. 1969. *The Raw and the Cooked*. The University of Chicago Press. Chicago; Lévi-Strauss, C. 1981. *Introduction to a Science of Mythology Vol. 4. The Naked Man*. Cape. London; Lévi-Strauss, C. 1983. *Introduction to a Science of Mythology Vol. 2. From Honey to Ashes*. Cape. London; Lévi-Strauss, C. 1990. *Introduction to a Science of Mythology Vol. 3. The Origin of Table Manners*. The University of Chicago Press. Chicago.
115. Lévi-Strauss 1990: 484.
116. See for instance Mafeje, A. 1998. *Kingdoms of the Great Lakes Region: Ethnography of African Social Formations*. Fountain Publishers. Kampala.
117. Mamdani. M. 2001. *When Victims Becomes Killers: Colonialism, Nativism, and the Genocide in Rwanda*. Fountain Publishers. Kampala, pp. 82–6.
118. Taylor, C. C. 1999. *Sacrifice as Terror: The Rwandan Genocide of 1994*. Berg. Oxford; Taylor, C. C. 2009. The sovereign as savage. The pathos of ethno-nationalist passion. In Kapferer, B. & Bertelsen, B. E. (eds), *Crisis of the State: War and Social Upheaval*: 163–86. Berghahn. New York and Oxford; Taylor, C. C. 2013. Genocide and the religious imaginary in Rwanda. In Juergensmeyer, M. et al. (eds), *The Oxford Handbook of Religion and Violence*: 269–79. Oxford University Press. Oxford.
119. Taylor 1999: 126.
120. Taylor 1999: 130.
121. Gwassa, G. C. K. & Iliffe, J. 1968. *Records of the Maji Maji Rising*. Part One. East African Publishing House. Dar es Salaam, p. 3.
122. Middleton, J. 1963. The Yakan or Allah water cult among the Lugbara. *The Journal of Anthropological Institute of Great Britain and Ireland*, Vol. 93, No. 1: 80–108, pp. 92–3.
123. Mbogoni, L. E. Y. 2013. *Human Sacrifice and the Supernatural in African History*. Mkiki Na Nyota. Dar-es-Salaam, pp. 160–1.
124. Kyemba, H. 1997. *A State of Blood: The Inside story of Idi Amin*. Fountain Publishers Ltd. Kampala, pp. 108–10.
125. Kyemba 1997: 59.
126. Hutchinson, S. E. & Pendle, N. R. 2015. Violence, legitimacy, and prophecy: Nuer struggles with uncertainty in South Sudan. *American Ethologist*, Vol. 42, No. 3: 415–30.
127. Jonglei Investigation Team, 1953. The Equatorial Nile Project and its effects in Sudan. *Geographical Journal*, Vol. 119: 33–48, p. 35.
128. Green, J. & El-Moghraby, A. I. J. 2009. Swamps of the Upper Nile. In Dumont, H. J. (ed.), *The Nile: Origin, Environments, Limnology and Human Use*: 193–204. Springer. Leiden, p. 194.
129. NBI 2012. *State of the River Nile Basin 2012*. The Nile Basin Initiative. Entebbe, p. 38.
130. Johnson, D. H. 1986. The historical approach to the study of societies and their environment in the eastern Upper Nile plains. *Cashiers d'Études Africaines*, Vol. 26, cashier 101/102: 131–44, pp. 134, 138.
131. Seide, W. M. 2016. Lease the land, but use the water: the case of Gambella, Ethiopia. In Sanström, E. et al. (eds), *Land and Hydropolitics in the Nile River Basin: Challenges and New Investments*: 166–88. Routledge. London, p. 182.
132. Seligman, C. G. 1932. *Pagan Tribes of the Nilotic Sudan*. Routledge & Kegan Paul. London, pp. 126–7.
133. Seligman 1932: 131.
134. Evans-Pritchard, E. E. 1937. *Witchcraft, Oracles and Magic Among the Azande*. Oxford at the Clarendon Press. Oxford, pp. 470–4.

135. Evans-Pritchard, E. E. 1956. *Nuer Religion*. Oxford at the Clarendon Press. Oxford, pp. 1–2, 141.
136. Evans-Pritchard 1956: 299.
137. Seligman 1932: 232–4.
138. Evans-Pritchard, E. E. 1969 [1940]. *The Nuer: A Description of the Modes of Livelihood and Political Institutions of a Nilotic People*. Oxford University Press. Oxford, p. 36.
139. Evans-Pritchard 1969: 57.
140. Evans-Pritchard 1969: 59.
141. Evans-Pritchard 1969: 61.
142. Saetersdal, T. 2009. Manica rock-art in contemporary society. In Oestigaard, T. (ed.), 2009. *Water, Culture and Identity: Comparing Past and Present Traditions in the Nile Basin Region*: 55– 82. BRIC Press. Bergen; Saetersdal, T. 2010. Rain, snakes and sex – making rain: rock art and rain-making in Africa and America. In Tvedt, T. & Oestigaard, T. (eds), 2010. *A History of Water. Series 2, Vol. 1. Ideas of Water from Antiquity to Modern Times*: 378– 404. I.B.Tauris. London.
143. Wainwright, G. A. 1938. *The Sky-Religion in Egypt: Its Antiquity and Effects*. Cambridge at the University Press. Cambridge, p. 7.
144. Yuzbashi, X. 1905. Tribes on the Upper Nile: The Bari. *Journal of the Royal African Society*, Vol. 4, No. 14: 226–31.
145. Wainwright 1938: 64.
146. Spire, F. 1905. Rain-making in equatorial Africa. *Journal of the Royal African Society*, Vol. 5, No. 17: 15–21, p. 19.
147. Seligman 1932: 295.
148. Beaton, A. C. 1939. Fur rain cults and ceremonies. *Sudan Notes and Records*, Vol. XXII, Part II: 186–203.
149. Seligman 1932: 281.
150. Simonse, S. 1992. *Kings of Disaster: Dualism, Centralism and the Scapegoat King in Southeastern Sudan*. E J. Brill. Leiden, pp. 6–8.
151. Simonse 1992: 191.
152. Simonse 1992: 199.
153. Simonse 1992: 202.
154. Simonse 1992: 249.
155. Simonse 1992: 321–2.
156. Simonse 1992: 331.
157. Wainwright 1938: 4.
158. Seligman 1932: 75.
159. Seligman 1932: 195.
160. Seligman 1932: 196.
161. Seligman, C. G. 1934. *Egypt and Negro Africa: A Study in Divine Kingship*. George Routledge and Sons. London, p. 30.
162. Seligman 1934: 31.
163. Seligman 1934: 41.
164. Simonse 1992: 386.
165. Simonse 1992: 386–9.
166. Seligman, C. G. & Seligman, B. Z. 1928. The Bari. *The Journal of the Royal Anthropological Institute of Great Britain and Ireland*, Vol. 58: 409–79.
167. Seligman 1932: 281.
168. Seligman & Seligman 1928: 464, 468.

169. Cooke, M. C. 1939. Bari Rain Cults. *Sudan Notes and Records*, Vol. XXII, Part II: 181–6.
170. Insoll, T. 2015. *Material Exploration in African Archaeology*. Oxford University Press. Oxford, p. 185.
171. Seligman & Seligman 1928: 463, 472.
172. Seligman & Seligman 1928: 475–6.
173. Lienhardt, G. 1961. *Divinity and Experience: The Religion of the Dinka*. Oxford at the Clarendon Press, pp. 92, 161.
174. Lienhardt 1961: 207.
175. Seligman, C. G. 1931. The religion of the pagan tribes of the White Nile. *Journal of the International African Institute*, Vol. 4, No. 1: 1–21, pp. 6, 12.
176. Seligman 1932: 142.
177. Seligman 1932: 147–8.
178. Seligman & Seligman 1932: 178.
179. Geertz, C. 1973. *The Interpretation of Cultures*. HarperCollins. New York, p. 119.
180. Seligman 1932: 179–96.
181. Seligman 1932: 196–8.
182. Bedri, I. E. 1939. Notes on Dinka religious beliefs in their hereditary chiefs and rain makers. *Sudan Notes and Records*, Vol. XXII, Part I: 125–31, p. 131.
183. Lienhardt 1961: 21–3.
184. Seligman 1932: 198–9.
185. Bedri 1939: 125.
186. Seligman 1931: 4–5, 11.
187. Howell, P. P. 1952. Observations on the Shilluk of the Upper Nile: the laws of homicide and the legal functions of the 'reth'. *Africa: Journal of the International African Institute*, Vol. 22, No. 2: 97–119, p. 102.
188. Schnepel, B. 1991. Continuity despite and through death: regicide and royal shrines among the Shilluk of Southern Sudan. *Africa: Journal of the International African Institute*, Vol. 61, No. 1: 40–70, p. 43.
189. Howell, P. P. 1944. The installation of the Shilluk king. *Man*, Vol. 44: 146–7, p. 146.
190. Simonse 1992: 388.
191. Schnepel, B. 1988. Shilluk Royal ceremonies of death and Installation. *Anthropos* Bd 83, H. 4./6.: 433–52, p. 434.
192. Lienhardt, G. 1955. Nilotic kings and their mothers' kin. *Africa: Journal of the International African Institute*, Vol. 25, No. 1: 29–42.
193. Schnepel, B. 1991. Continuity despite and through death: regicide and Royal Shrines among the Shilluk of Southern Sudan. *Africa: Journal of the International African Institute*, Vol. 61, No. 1: 40–70, p. 47.
194. Schnepel 1991: 57.
195. Schnepel 1991: 59.
196. Seligman 1931.
197. Schnepel 1991: 62.
198. Hunt, R. 1997. Frazer, Sir James (1854–1941). In Barfield, T. (ed.), *The Dictionary of Anthropology*: 206–8. Blackwell Publishing. Oxford.
199. Frazer, J. G. 1996 [1922]. *The Golden Bough: A Study in Magic and Religion*. A Touchstone Book, Simon & Schuster. New York, pp. 1–2.
200. Simonse 1992: 397.

201. Frankfort, H. 1948. *Kingship and the Gods: A Study of Ancient Near Eastern Religion as the Integration of Society & Nature*. The University of Chicago Press. Chicago, p. 200.
202. Wenke, R. 2009. *The Ancient Egyptian State: The Origins of Egyptian Culture (c. 8000–2000 bc)*. Cambridge University Press. Cambridge, p. 80.
203. Gemmill, P. F. 1928. Egypt is the Nile. *Economic Geography*, Vol. 4, No. 3: 295–312, p. 296.
204. Gordon, D. L. 1902. *Letters from Egypt*. McClure, Phillips & Co. New York, pp. 56, 67–8.
205. Bell, B. 1971. The Dark Ages in Ancient History. I. The First Dark Age in Egypt. *American Journal of Archaeology*, Vol. 75, No. 1: 1–26, p. 20.
206. Aldred, C. 1984. *The Egyptians*. Thames and Hudson. London, p. 69.
207. Aldred 1984: 69.
208. Wainwright 1938: 65.
209. Wainwright 1938: 71.
210. Aldred, C. 1965. *Egypt: To the End of the Old Kingdom*. Thames and Hudson. London, p. 50.

5 THE RIVER CIVILIZATION IN THE DESERT

1. Moorehead, A. 1960. *The White Nile*. HarperCollins Publishers. New York, p. vii.
2. MacQuitty, W. 1976. *Island of Isis: Philae, Temple of the Nile*. Macdonald and Jane's. London, p. 50.
3. Baines, J. 1985a. *Fecundity Figures*. Aris & Phillips Ltd. Warminster.
4. Baines 1985a: 113–15.
5. Hornung, E. 1982. *Conceptions of God in Ancient Egypt: The One and the Many*. Translated by John Baines. Cornell University Press. New York, pp. 77–9.
6. Kemp, B. 2006. *Ancient Egypt: Anatomy of a Civilization*. Routledge. London. Second edition, pp. 8–10.
7. Carneiro, R. 1970. A theory of the origin of the state. *Science*, Vol. 169: 733–8.
8. Said, R. 1993. *The River Nile: Geology, Hydrology and Utilization*. Pergamon Press. Oxford, p. 193.
9. Kemp 2006: 11–12.
10. Childe, G. V. 1934. *New Light on the Most Ancient East: The Oriental Prelude to European Prehistory*. Kegan Paul. London, p. 42.
11. Kemp 2006: 12.
12. Hornblower, G. D. 1945. The establishing of Osiris. *Man*, Vol. 45: 59–63, p. 60.
13. Wenke, R. 1989. Egypt: origins of complex societies. *Annual Review of Anthropology*, Vol. 18: 129–55, p. 134.
14. Tvedt, T. 2004. *The River Nile in the Age of the British: Political Ecology and the Quest for Economic Power*. I.B.Tauris. London; Tvedt, T. 2016. *Water and Society – Changing Perceptions of Societal and Historical Development*. I.B.Tauris. London.
15. Bard, K. 1994. The Egyptian Predynastic: a review of the evidence. *Journal of Field Archaeology*, Vol. 21, No. 3: 265–88; Bard, K. A. 1999a. Predynastic period, overview. In Bard, K. A. (ed.), *Encyclopaedia of the Archaeology of Ancient Egypt*: 23–30. Routledge. London; Bard, K. A. 1999b. Early Dynastic period, overview. In Bard, K. A. (ed.), *Encyclopaedia of the Archaeology of Ancient Egypt*: 31–5. Routledge. London.
16. Kemp 2006: 74.
17. Erman, A. 1971 [1894]. *Life in Ancient Egypt*. Dover. New York, p. 425.

18. Leibovitch, J. 1953. Gods of agriculture and welfare in ancient Egypt. Egyptian theology in the third millennium B.C. *Journal of Near Eastern Studies*, Vol. 18, No. 2: 73–113, p. 110.
19. Park, T. K. 1992. Early trends towards stratification: chaos, common property, and flood recession agriculture. *American Anthropologist*, New Series, Vol. 94, No. 1: 90–117, p. 107.
20. Wilson, J. A. 1951. *The Culture of Ancient Egypt*. Chicago University Press. Chicago, p. 13.
21. Verner, M. 2003. *The Pyramids: Their Archaeology and History*. Atlantic Books. London, p. 23.
22. Finnestad, R. B. 1985. *Image of the World and Symbol of the Creator: On the Cosmological and Iconological Values of the Temple of Defu*. Otto Harrassowitz. Wiesbaden, p. 51.
23. Finnestad 1985: 11–12.
24. Assmann, J. 2002. *The Mind of Egypt: History and Meaning in the Time of the Pharaohs*. Metropolitan Books. New York, p. 39.
25. Weber, M. 1968. *The Religion of China: Confucianism and Taoism*. The Free Press. New York, p. 68.
26. Clagett, M. 1989. *Ancient Egyptian Science Vol. 1*. American Philosophical Society. Philadelphia, pp. 264–5.
27. Finnestad 1985: 122.
28. Frankfort, H. 1961. *Ancient Egyptian Religion: An Interpretation*. Harper & Row. New York, p. 20.
29. Clagett 1989: 264–5.
30. Frankfort, H. 1948. *Kingship and the Gods: A Study of Ancient Near Eastern Religion as the Integration of Society & Nature*. The University of Chicago Press. Chicago, p. 154.
31. Frankfort 1948: 182.
32. Frankfort 1948: 151–3.
33. Frankfort 1948: 66.
34. Clagett 1989: 265–6.
35. Frankfort 1948: 177.
36. *The Ancient Egyptian Book of the Dead*. Translated by Faulkner, R. O. 1972. The British Museum Press. London.
37. Assmann, J. 2001. *The Search for God in Ancient Egypt*. Cornell University Press. Ithaca, p. 5.
38. Frankfort 1948: 15–17.
39. Frankfort 1948: 19–20.
40. Wilkinson, T. A. H. 1999. *Early Dynastic Egypt*. Routledge. London, pp. 49, 192–6.
41. Said 1993: 191.
42. Wilkinson 1999: 142.
43. Baines, J. 1995. Origins of Egyptian kingship. In O'Connor, D. & Silverman, D. P. (eds), *Ancient Egyptian Kingship*: 95–156. E. J. Brill. Leiden, p. 139.
44. Hornung 1982: 263.
45. Wilkinson 1999: 27, 60–1.
46. Hoffman, M. A. 1980. *Egypt before the Pharaohs*. Routledge. London, p. 272.
47. Petrie, W. M. F. 1900. *Royal Tombs of the First Dynasty I*. Egypt Exploration Fund. Memoir 18. London, p. 2.
48. Petrie, W. M. F. 1925. *Tombs of the Courtiers and Oxyrhynkhos*. British School of archaeology in Egypt. London, p. 1.
49. Petrie 1925.

50. Wilkinson 1999: 234; Petrie, W. M. F. 1901. *Royal Tombs of the Earliest Dynasties II*. Egypt Exploration Fund. Memoir 21. London, pls. LVIII, LIX–LXI.
51. Petrie 1925: 3.
52. Petrie 1925: 2–3.
53. Wilkinson, T. A. H. 2000. What a king is this: Narmer and the concept of the ruler. *The Journal of Egyptian Archaeology*, Vol. 86: 23–32, p. 31.
54. Baines 1995: 106.
55. Petrie 1925: 8.
56. Petrie 1925: 8
57. Wilkinson 1999: 80.
58. Petrie 1925: 8.
59. Wilkinson 1999: 83–90.
60. Wilkinson 1999: 91–3.
61. Wilkinson 1999: 95–6.
62. Lubbock, J. 1870. *The Origin of Civilisation and the Primitive Condition of Man: Mental and Social Condition of Savages*. Longmans, Green. London, 315.
63. Wainwright, G. A. 1938. *The Sky-Religion in Egypt: Its Antiquity and Effects*. Cambridge at the University Press. Cambridge, p. 75.
64. Meyerowitz, E. L. R. 1960. *The Divine Kingship in Ghana and Ancient Egypt*. Faber and Faber. London, p. 75.
65. Wainwright 1938: 1–2.
66. Kemp 2006: 81.
67. Kemp 2006: 81.
68. Petrie 1901. *Royal Tombs II*, Pl. 27, nos. 96, 128, 129.
69. Wilkinson 1999: 202.
70. Griffiths, J. G. 1960. *The Conflict of Horus and Seth: From Egyptian and Classical Sources*. Liverpool University Press. Liverpool, p. 121.
71. Gardiner, A. 1950. The baptism of Pharaoh. *The Journal of Egyptian Archaeology*, Vol. 36: 3–12.
72. Griffiths 1960: 138.
73. Emery, W. B. 1961. *Archaic Egypt*. Penguin. Harmondsworth, p. 119.
74. Kemp 2006: 21.
75. Bell, B. 1971. The Dark Ages in ancient history. I. The First Dark Age in Egypt. *American Journal of Archaeology*, Vol. 75, No. 1: 1–26, p. 24.
76. Griffiths 1960: 16, 23–6.
77. Quirke, S. 1992. *Ancient Egyptian Religion*. British Museum Press. London, p. 61.
78. Saad, Z. Y. 1947. *Royal Excavations at Helwan (1941–1945)*. IFAO. Cairo, p. 27.
79. Wilkinson 1999: 295.
80. Assmann, J. 2005. *Death and Salvation in Ancient Egypt*. Cornell University Press. Ithaca, p. 70.
81. Griffiths 1960: 15.
82. Wainwright, G. A. 1963. The origin of storm-gods in Egypt. *The Journal of Egyptian Archaeology*, Vol. 49: 13–20, p. 19.
83. Griffiths 1960: 16.
84. Griffiths 1960: 13–14
85. Griffiths 1960: 20.

86. Assmann 2005: 23.
87. Griffiths 1960: 21.
88. Griffiths 1960: 12–15.
89. te Velde, H. 1967. *Seth, God of Confusion: A Study of His Role in Egyptian Mythology and Religion*. E. J. Brill. Leiden, pp. 54, 109.
90. Dundes, A. 1981. Wet and dry, the evil eye: an essay in Indo-European and Semitic worldview. In Dundes, A. (ed.), *The Evil Eye: A Folklore Casebook*: 257–98. Garland Publishing. New York, p. 267.
91. Maloney, C. 1976. Introduction. In Maloney, C. (ed.), *The Evil Eye: Outgrowth of a Symposium on the Evil Eye Belief Held at the 1972 Meeting of the American Anthropological Association*: i–xvi. Columbia University Press. New York.
92. Dundes 1981: 258.
93. Dundes 1981: 274.
94. Borghouts, J. F. 1973. The evil eye of Apopis. *The Journal of Egyptian Archaeology*, Vol. 59: 114–50, p. 143.
95. Dundes 1981: 282.
96. Griffiths 1960: 48–9.
97. te Velde 1967: 36.
98. Griffiths 1960: 41, 125.
99. Wainwright, G. A. 1935. Some celestial associations of Min. *The Journal of Egyptian Archaeology*, Vol. 21, No. 2: 152–70, p. 154.
100. Wainwright 1935: 170.
101. te Velde 1967: 58.
102. te Velde 1967: 55.
103. el-Saady, H. 1994. Reflections on the Goddess Tayet. *The Journal of Egyptian Archaeology*, Vol. 80: 213–17.
104. Dundes 1981: 274.
105. Griffiths 1960: 120.
106. Gardiner, A. 1944. Horus the Behdetite. *The Journal of Egyptian Archaeology*, Vol. 30: 23–60, p. 24.
107. Frankfort 1948: 24, 352.
108. Quoted in Frankfort 1948: 26.
109. Frankfort 1961: 129.
110. Quirke, S. 2001. *The Cult of Ra: Sun-worship in Ancient Egypt*. Thames & Hudson. London.
111. Anthes, R. 1959. Egyptian theology in the third millennium B.C. *Journal of Near Eastern Studies*. Vol. 18, No. 3: 169–212, p. 171.
112. Wainwright 1935: 170.
113. Anthes 1959: 180.
114. Assmann, J. 1995. *Egyptian Solar Religion in the New Kingdom: Re, Amun and the Crisis of Polytheism*. Kegan Paul International. London, p. 50.
115. Frankfort 1948: 159.
116. Blackman, A. M. 1925. Osiris or the Sun-God? *The Journal of Egyptian Archaeology*, Vol. 11, No. 3/4: 201–9, pp. 206–7.
117. Assmann 1995: 181.
118. Griffiths 1960: 125.
119. Anthes 1959: 199.

120. Anthes 1959: 178.
121. Hornblower, G. D. 1937. Osiris and his Rites: I. *Man*, Vol. 37: 153–8, p. 155.
122. Hornblower, G. D. 1941. Osiris and the fertility-rite. *Man*, Vol. 41: 94–103, p. 103.
123. Blackman, A. M. 1998. Purification (Egyptian). In *Gods, Priests and Men: Studies in the Religion of Pharaonic Egypt by Aylward M. Blackman*: 3–21. Kegan Paul International. London.
124. Griffiths 1960.
125. David, R. 1981. *A Guide to Religious Ritual at Abydos*. Aris & Phillips Ltd. War-minster, pp. 119–20.
126. Frankfort 1948: 212.
127. Anthes 1959: 175, 180.
128. Anthes 1959: 183.
129. Mojsov, B. 2005. *Osiris: Death and Afterlife of a God*. Blackwell. Oxford.
130. Assmann, J. 1989. Death and Initiation in the funerary religion of ancient Egypt. In Simpson, W. K. (ed.), *Religion and Philosophy in Ancient Egypt*: 135–59. Yale Egyptological Studies 3: New Haven, Connecticut, p. 138.
131. Anthes 1959: 199.
132. te Velde 1967: 86, 95.
133. Frankfort 1948: 198.
134. Anthes 1959: 200.
135. Anthes 1959: 202.
136. Frankfort 1948: 30–1.
137. te Velde 1967: 66.
138. Troy, L. 1986. *Patterns of Queenship in Ancient Egyptian Myth and History*. Acta Universitatis Upsaliensis. Uppsala Studies in Ancient Mediterranean and Near Eastern Civilizations 14. Uppsala, p. 36.
139. McKittrick, M. 2006. 'The wealth of these nations': rain, rulers and religion on the Cuvelai floodplain. In Tvedt, T. & Oestigaard, T. (eds), *A History of Water Vol. 3. The World of Water*: 449–69. I.B.Tauris. London.
140. Plutarch. 2001. *Concerning the Mysteries of Isis and Osiris*, by Mead, G. R. S., and Plutarch. From Mead, G. R. S. *Thrice Greatest Hermes Part 1*. Reed Wheel. York Beach, 54: 1–2.
141. Assmann 2001: 1.
142. Hornblower 1937: 153.
143. Smith, W. S. 1962. *The Old Kingdom in Egypt and the Beginning of the First Intermediate Period*. Cambridge at the University Press. Cambridge, p. 61.
144. Beth, K. 1916. 'El und Neter'. *ZAW* 36: 129–86, p. 183.
145. Le Page Renouf, P. 1880. *Lectures on the Origin and Growth of Religion as Illustrated by the Religion of Ancient Egypt* (The Hibbert Lectures 1879.) London. 4th edition 1897, p. 92.
146. Hornung 1982: 42, 86, 93, 176.
147. Kemp 2006: 69.
148. Baines, J. 1996. Myth and literature. In Loprieno, A. (ed.), *Ancient Egyptian Literature: History and Forms*: 361–78. E. J. Brill. Leiden, p. 361.
149. Finnestad 1985: 23.
150. Assmann 2001: 109.
151. Hornung 1982: 179.
152. Assmann 2001: 7.
153. Hornung 1982: 181.

154. O'Connor, D. & Silverman, D. P. 1995. Introduction. In O'Connor, D. & Silverman, D. P. (eds), *Ancient Egyptian Kingship*: xvii–xxvii. E. J. Brill. Leiden, p. xix.
155. Hornung 1982: 182.
156. Finnestad 1985: 13.
157. Hornung 1982: 213.
158. te Velde 1968: 37–8.
159. Frankfort 1948: 51.
160. Frankfort 1948: 157.
161. Frankfort, H. 1951. *The Birth of Civilization in the Near East*. Williams & Norgate Ltd. London, p. 79.
162. Frankfort 1948: 191.
163. Plutarch 33:1.
164. Dundes 1981: 266–7.
165. Frankfort 1948: 391, footnote 38.
166. Lange, H. O. & Neugebauer, O. 1940. *Papyrus Carlsberg No. 1. Ein Hieratisch-Demotischer Kosmologischer Text*. Det Kongelige Danske Videnskabernes Selskab. Historisk-filologiske Skrifter, Bind 1, Nr. 2. Copenhagen, pp. 22–3.
167. Frankfort 1948: 395, footnote 101.
168. Aldred, C. 1984. *The Egyptians*. Thames and Hudson. London, p. 59.
169. Frankfort 1948: 190.
170. Gardiner, A. H. 1961. *Egypt of the Pharaohs: An Introduction*. Clarendon Press. Oxford, p. 403.
171. Frankfort 1948: 191.
172. Frankfort 1948: 34, 136.
173. Plutarch 36.1.
174. Breasted, J. H. 1959. *Development of Religion and Thought in Ancient Egypt*. P. Smith. Gloucester, Mass, p. 103.
175. Blackman 1925: 208.
176. Frankfort 1948: 193.
177. Assmann 2005: 19.
178. Meyerowitz 1960: 113.
179. Assmann 2005: 32–9.
180. Assmann 2005: 70.
181. Wild 1981: 28.
182. Faulkner, R. O. 1982. A coffin text miscellany. *The Journal of Egyptian Archaeology*, Vol. 68: 27–30, p. 27.
183. Assmann 2005: 356–7.
184. Assmann 2005: 357.
185. Assmann 2005: 357–8.
186. Meskell, L. & Joyce, R. A. 2003. *Embodied Lives: Figuring Ancient Maya and Egyptian Experience*. Routledge. London, p. 95.
187. Assmann 2005: 358.
188. Vijverberg, J. et al. 2009. Lake Tana: source of the Blue Nile. In Dumont, H. J. (ed.), *The Nile: Origin, Environments, Limnology and Human Use*: 163–92. Springer. Leiden, p. 183.

189. Talbot, M. R. & Williams, A. J. 2009. Cenozoic evolution of the Nile Basin. In Dumont, H. J. (ed.), *The Nile: Origin, Environments, Limnology and Human Use*: 37–60. Springer. Leiden, p. 50.
190. Garzanti, E. et al. 2006. Petrology of Nile River sands (Ethiopia and Sudan): sediment budgets and erosion patterns. *Earth and Planetary Science Letters* 252: 327–41; Williams, M. 2012. River sediments. *Philosophical Transactions of the Royal Society*, 370: 2093–122.
191. Hume, W. F. 1906. Notes on the history on the Nile and its valley. *The Geographical Journal*, Vol. 27, No. 1: 52–9, p. 55; Garstin, W. 1909. Fifty years of exploration, and some of its results. *The Geographical Journal*, Vol. 33, No. 2: 117–47, p. 137.
192. Lyons, H. G. 1905. On the Nile and its variation. *The Geographical Journal*, Vol. 26, No. 3: 249–72, p. 252.
193. Long, C. C. 1876. Uganda and the White Nile. *Journal of the American Geographical Society of New York*, Vol. 8: 285–304, p. 285.
194. Budge, E. A. W. 1912. *The Nile: Notes for Travellers in Egypt and the Egyptian Sudan*. Thos. Cook & Sons, Ltd. London, p. 169.
195. Lyons 1908.
196. Berry, L. & Whiteman, A. J. 1968. The Nile in the Sudan. *The Geographical Journal*, Vol. 134, No. 1: 1–33, p. 15.
197. Budge 1912: 172–3.
198. Lyons, H. G. 1908. Some geographical aspects of the Nile. *The Geographical Journal*, Vol. 32, No. 5: 449–75, pp. 454, 459.
199. Baines, J. 1985b. Color terminology and color classification: ancient Egyptian color terminology and polychrony. *American Anthropologist*, Vol. 87, No. 2: 282–97, pp. 284–6.
200. MacKenzie, D. A. 1922. Colour symbolism. *Folklore*, Vol. 33, No. 22: 136–69, p. 140.
201. MacKenzie 1922: 160.
202. MacKenzie 1922: 160–2.
203. Mojsov 2005: 37.
204. te Velde 1967: 55.
205. MacKenzie 1922: 162.
206. MacKenzie 1922: 164.
207. Breasted, J. H. 1959. *Development of Religion and Thought in Ancient Egypt*. P. Smith. Gloucester, Mass, pp. 22–3.
208. MacKenzie 1922: 156.
209. Morris, B. 1998. *The Power of Animals*. Berg. Oxford, p. 211.
210. MacKenzie 1922: 154.
211. MacKenzie 1922: 151–2.
212. Maspero, G. 1903–4. *History of Egypt, Chaldea, Syria, Babylonia, and Assyria. Volume IV*. The Grolier Society Publishers. London, pp. 29–30.
213. MacKenzie 1922: 156–7.
214. Mojsov 2005: 7.
215. Wainwright 1938: 13.
216. Seligman, C. G. 1934. *Egypt and Negro Africa*. George Routledge and Sons, Ltd. London, pp. 30–1.
217. Winkler, A. 2006. The efflux that issued from Osiris: a study on rdw in the pyramid texts. *Göttinger Miszellen*, No. 211: 125–39.
218. Winkler 2006: 129.
219. Meyerowitz 1960: 184 fn. 1.

220. Haaland, G. 1998: Beer, blood and mother's milk. The symbolic context of economic behaviour in fur society. *Sudan Notes and Records,* New Series, Vol. 2: 53–76.
221. McCarthy, D. J. 1969. The symbolism of blood and sacrifice. *Journal of Biblical Literature,* Vol. 88, No. 2: 166–7.
222. Nabofa, M. Y. 1985. Blood symbolism in African religion. *Religious Studies,* Vol. 21, No. 3: 389–405.
223. See Strang, V. 2004. *The Meaning of Water.* Berg. Oxford; Strang, V. 2005. Common senses: water, sensory experience and the generation of meaning. *Journal of Material Culture,* Vol. 10, No. 1: 92–120; Strang, V. 2014. Fluid consistencies. Material relationality in human engagements with water. *Archaeological Dialogues,* Vol. 21, No. 2: 133–50.
224. Baines, J. 1995b. Origins of Egyptian kingship. In O'Connor, D. & Silverman, D. P. (eds), *Ancient Egyptian Kingship*: 95–156. E. J. Brill. Leiden.
225. MacKenzie 1922: 157–8.
226. Assmann 1989: 140.
227. Gruber, M. 2003. *Sacrifice in the Desert: A Study of an Egyptian Minority Through the Prism of Coptic Monasticism.* University Press of America. New York, p. 179.
228. Assmann 2005: 362.
229. Butzer, K. W. 1976. *Early Hydraulic Civilization in Egypt: A Study in Cultural Ecology.* University of Chicago Press. Chicago, p. 56.
230. Said 1993: 55, 128–9.
231. Butzer, K. 1995. Environmental change in the Near East and human impact on the land. In Sasson, J. M. (ed.), *Civilizations of the Ancient Near East.* Vol. 1: 123–51. Schribner. New York, pp. 132–5.
232. Butzer, K. 1959. Environment and human ecology in Egypt during predynastic and early dynastic times. *Bulletin de la Societé de Géographie* d'Egypte, Vol. 32: 43–87.
233. Bell, B. 1970. The oldest records of the Nile Floods. *The Geographical Journal,* Vol. 136, No. 4: 569–73.
234. Said 1993: 138.
235. Frankfort 1951.
236. Lehner, M. 1997. *The Complete Pyramids.* Thames and Hudson. London, pp. 14–15.
237. Bard, K. A. 1987. The geography of excavated Predynastic sites and the rise of complex society. *Journal of the American Research Center in Egypt,* 24: 81–93, p. 90.
238. Kemp 2006: 7.
239. Petrie 1901: 8.
240. Saad 1947: 27.
241. Quirke 1992: 21–2.
242. Baines 1995: 137.
243. Hocart, A. M. 1968. *Caste: A Comparative Study.* Russell & Russell. New York, p. 37.
244. Hocart 1968: 97.
245. Bell 1971: 18.
246. Silverman, D. P. 1995. The nature of Egyptian kingship. In O'Connor, D. & Silverman, D. P. (eds), *Ancient Egyptian Kingship*: 49–92. E. J. Brill. Leiden, pp. 58–60.
247. Wainwright 1938: 60–8.
248. Assmann 2002: 58.
249. Assmann 2005: 95, 165.
250. Meskell & Joyce 2003: 16.
251. O'Connor & Silverman 1995: xix.

252. Allen, J. 1989. The cosmology of the pyramid texts. In Allen, J. (ed.), *Religion and Philosophy in Ancient Egypt*: 1–28. Yale Egyptological Seminar, Dept. of Near Eastern Languages and Civilizations, the Graduate School, Yale University. New Haven, pp. 25–6.
253. Frankfort 1948: 120.
254. Assmann 2005: 173.
255. Assmann 2005: 174.
256. Assmann 2005: 131–3, 184.
257. Assmann 2005: 183.
258. Assmann 2001: 149.
259. Assmann 2005: 323.
260. Assmann 2005: 355, my emphasis.
261. Haikal, F. M. H. 1970. *Two Hieratic Funerary Papyri of Nesmin 1*. Foundation Egyptologique Reine Elisabeth. Bruxelles.
262. Assmann 2005: 356.
263. Assmann 2005: 359, the spell on pages 359–60.
264. Assmann 2005: 361.
265. Assmann 2005: 361.
266. Assmann 2005: 363.
267. Assmann 2005: 363.
268. Frankfort 1948: 185.
269. Finnestad 1985: 109.
270. Frankfort 1948: 185.
271. Finnestad 1985: 110.
272. Assmann 2001: 59, my emphasis.
273. Frankfort 1948: 154–7.

6 WATER AND WORLD RELIGIONS ALONG THE NILE

1. Williams, G. 2008. Reading the waters: Seneca on the Nile in 'Natural Questions', Book 4A. *The Classic Quarterly, New Series*, Vol. 58, No. 1: 218–42, p. 231.
2. Herodotus. 2008. *Herodotus: The Histories. A New Translation by Robin Waterfield*. Oxford University Press. Oxford, Book II.32.
3. Herodotus. n.d., Book II.28.
4. Seneca. 1972. *Seneca in Ten Volumes. X. Naturales Quaestiones. II.*, with an English translation by T. H. Corcoran, PhD. William Heineman Ltd. London, 4a.2.4–5.
5. Seneca 1972: 4a.2.7.
6. Vivian, T. 1994. Introduction: hearing God's call. In Athanasius. 'Life of Anthony'. Translated by T. Vivian. *Society of Coptic Studies. Coptic Church Review*, Vol. 15, No. 1 & 2: 99–101.
7. Meyer, R. T. 1950. *St. Athanasius: The Life of Saint Anthony*. Ancient Christian Writers 10. Newman. Westminster, para. 32, pp. 47–8.
8. Walsh, L. 2003. The rhetoric of oracles. *Rhetoric Society Quarterly*, Vol. 33, No. 3: 55–78, p. 62. See also, for instance, Blackman, A. 1925. Oracles in ancient Egypt. *The Journal of Egyptian Archaeology*, Vol. 11, No. 3/4: 249–55; Blackman, A. 1925. Oracles in ancient Egypt. II. *The Journal of Egyptian Archaeology*, Vol. 12, No. 3/4: 176–85, and Hayes, J. H. 1968. The usage of oracles against foreign nations in ancient Israel. *Journal of Biblical Literature*, Vol. 87, No. 1: 81–92.

9. Darwin, C. 2006 [1859]. *The Origin of Species* (original title 1859, On the origin of species by means of natural selection). University of Pennsylvania Press. Philadelphia.
10. Baker, S. W. 1867. The races of the Nile Basin. *Transactions of the Ethnological Society of London*, Vol. 5: 228–38, p. 228.
11. Freud, S. 1939. *Moses and Monotheism*. Hogarth Press. Hertfordshire, p. 11.
12. Freud 1939: 46.
13. Assmann, J. 1997. *Moses the Egyptian: The Memory of Egypt in Western Monotheism*. Harvard University Press. Boston, MA, p. 167.
14. Dijk, J. v. 2000. The Amarna Period and the Later New Kingdom. In Shaw, I. (ed.), *The Oxford History of Ancient Egypt*: 272–313. Oxford University Press. Oxford.
15. Redford, D. B. 1980. The sun-disc in Akhenaten's program: its worship and antecedents, II. *Journal of the American Research Center in Egypt*, Vol. 17: 21–38, p. 27.
16. Hornung, E. 1992. The rediscovery of Akhenaten and his place in religion. *Journal of the American Research Center in Egypt*, Vol. 29: 43–9, p. 47.
17. Asante, M. K. & Ismail, S. 2009. Akhenaten to Origen: characteristics of philosophical thought in ancient Africa. *Journal of Black Studies*, Vol. 40, No. 2: 296–309, p. 299.
18. Assmann, J. 1992. Akhanyati's theology of light and time. *Proceedings of the Israel Academy of Sciences and Humanities*, VII 4: 143–76.
19. Assmann, J. 1984. *Ägypten: Theologie und Frömmigkeit einer frühen Hochkultur*. Urban-Taschenbücher, 366. W. Kohlhammer. Stuggart, pp. 248–9.
20. Stokes, M. C. 1963. Hesiodic and Milesian cosmogonies: II. *Phronesis*, Vol. 8, No. 1: 1–34, pp. 16–17.
21. Dicks, D. R. 1959. Thales. *The Classical Quarterly*, Vol. 9, No. 2: 294–309.
22. Allen, R. E. (ed.), 1966. *Greek Philosophy: Thales to Aristotle*. The Free Press. New York, pp. 1–2.
23. Allen, J. 1989. The natural philosophy of Akhenaten. In Allen, J. (eds), *Religion and Philosophy in Ancient Egypt*: 89–101. Yale Egyptological Seminar, Dept. of Near Eastern Languages and Civilizations, the Graduate School, Yale University. New Haven, CT.
24. Vincent, A. T. 1988. Mytho-theology in ancient Egypt. *Journal of American Research Center in Egypt*, Vol. 25: 169–83.
25. Allen, J. 1989. The cosmology of the Pyramid Texts. In Allen, J. (eds), *Religion and Philosophy in Ancient Egypt*: 1–28. Yale Egyptological Seminar, Dept. of Near Eastern Languages and Civilizations, the Graduate School, Yale University. New Haven, CT, pp. 7–9.
26. Assmann 1997: 2.
27. Assmann 1997: 24, 83, 101, 211.
28. Assmann 1997: 102.
29. Day, J. 1995. The Pharaoh of the Exodus, Josephus and Jubilees. *Vetus Testamentum*, Vol. 45, Fasc. 3: 377–9.
30. Leibovitch, J. 1953. Gods of agriculture and welfare in ancient Egypt. *Journal of Near Eastern Studies*, Vol. 12, No. 2: 73–113, p. 108.
31. Thompson, T. L. 1999. *The Bible in History: How Writers Create a Past*. Jonathan Cape. London, p. 210.
32. Thompson, T. L. 1987. *The Origin Tradition of Ancient Israel*. Sheffield Academic Press. Sheffield, p. 26.
33. Thompson 1999: 104.
34. Childs, B. S. 1965. The birth of Moses. *Journal of Biblical Literature*, Vol. 84, No. 2: 109–22.
35. Guenther, L. 2006. 'Like a maternal body': Emmanuel Levinas and the motherhood of Moses. *Hypatia*, Vol. 21, No. 1: 119–36, p. 125 and fn. 7.

36. Freud 1939: 17.
37. Freud 1939: 18.
38. Freud 1939: 22–3.
39. Hord, J. K. 1997. Two problems regarding Moses. *Comparative Civilizations Review*, No. 37: 16–49.
40. Duke, R. 2007. Moses' Hebrew name: the evidence of the 'Vision of Amram'. *Dead Sea Discoveries*, Vol. 14: 34–48.
41. Jacobson, H. 2006. Artapanus and the flooding of the Nile. *The Classical Quarterly*, Vol. 56, No 2: 602–3.
42. Marks, H. 1995. Biblical naming and poetic etymology. *Journal of Biblical Literature*, Vol. 114, No. 1: 21–42, p. 32.
43. Albright, W. F. 1918. Notes on Egypto-Semitic etymology. II. *The American Journal of Semitic Languages and Literatures*, Vol. 24, No. 4: 215–55, p. 254.
44. Albright, W. F. 1927. Notes on Egypto-Semitic etymology III. *Journal of the American Oriental Society*, Vol. 47: 198–237, p. 208.
45. Lindsay, J. 1968. *Men and Gods on the Roman Nile*. Frederick Muller Ltd. London, p. 309.
46. *Hermetica*. 2010. Being English Translations of Hermetic Discourses and Fragments by G. R. S. Mead. *Comprising Corpus Hermeticum* I–XIV, XVI–XVIII, The Perfect Sermon (Asclepius), Hermetic Excerpts from Stobæus. Celephaïs Press. Ulthar, p. 106.
47. Lindsay 1968: 194.
48. Wild, R. A. 1981. *Water in the Cultic Worship of Isis and Sarapis*. E. J. Brill. Leiden, pp. 90–1, and fn. 44, p. 231.
49. Nerval, G. 1884. *Voyage en Orient II*. Ancienne Maison Michel Lévy Frères. Paris, p. 59.
50. Vasunia, P. 2001. *The Gift of the Nile: Hellenizing Egypt from Aeschylus to Alexander*. University of California Press. Berkeley, p. 268.
51. Wheeler, B. M. 1998. Moses or Alexander. Early Islamic Exegesis of Qur'ān. *Journal of near Eastern Studies*, Vol. 57, No. 3: 191–215, pp. 194, 206.
52. Vasunia 2001: 275.
53. Elmer, D. F. 2008. Heliodoros's 'Sources': intertextuality, paternity, and the Nile River in the 'Aithiopika'. *Transactions of the American Philological Association*, Vol. 138, No. 2: 411–50, pp. 439–40.
54. Tarn, W. W. 1923. Alexander and the Ganges. *Journal of Hellenistic Studies*, Vol. 43, Part 2: 93–101, p. 99.
55. Elmer 2008: 442.
56. Bosworth, A. B. 1996. *Alexander and the East: The Tragedy of Triumph*. Clarendon Press. Oxford, pp. 187–200.
57. Bosworth, A. B. 1993. Aristotle, India and the Alexander Historians. *Topoi*, Vol. 3/2: 407–24.
58. Dousa, T. 2002. Imagining Isis: on some continuities and discontinuities in the image of Isis in Greek Isis hymns and demotic texts. In Ryholt, K. (ed.), *Acts of the Seventh International Conference of Demotic Studies Copenhagen 23–27 August 1999 (Cni Publications, 27)*: 149–84. Museum Tusculanum Press. Copenhagen, p. 160, fn. 43; Lindsay 1968: 59.
59. Dousa 2002: 160, fn. 43, Diodorus, Bibl., 1.27.5.
60. Namzi, A. 2004. The Nile River in Muslim geographical sources. *Studia Arabistyczne i Islamistyczne* 12: 28–54, pp. 33–24.
61. Frankfurter, D. 1998. *Religion in Roman Egypt: Assimilation and Resistance*. Princeton University Press. Princeton, pp. 5–6.
62. Frankfurter 1998: 42.

63. Frankfurter 1998: 45.
64. Kakosy, L. 1982. The Nile, Euthenia, and the Nymphs. *The Journal of Egyptian Archaeology*, Vol. 68: 290–8, p. 297.
65. Finneran, N. 2002. *The Archaeology of Christianity in Africa*. Tempus. Gloucestershire, p. 62.
66. Kamil, J. 2002. *Christianity in the Land of the Pharaohs: The Coptic Orthodox Church*. The American University in Cairo Press. Cairo, p. 1.
67. Cannuyer, C. 2001. *Coptic Egypt: The Christians of the Nile*. Thames & Hudson. London, p. 110.
68. Shenoda, M. 2007. Displacing Dhimmī, maintaining hope: unthinkable Coptic representations of Fatimid Egypt. *International Journal of Middle East Studies*, Vol. 39, No. 4: 587–606, p. 587.
69. Meinardus, O. F. A. 2002. *Two Thousand Years of Coptic Christianity*. The American University in Cairo Press. Cairo, pp. 26–8.
70. Frankfurter, D. 1994. The cult of the martyrs in Egypt before Constantine: the evidence of the Coptic 'Apocalypse of Elijah'. *Vigiliae Christianae*, Vol. 48, No. 1: 25–47, p. 36.
71. Cannuyer 2001: 15.
72. Cannuyer 2001: 26.
73. Finneran 2002: 87–8.
74. Finneran 2002: 21.
75. Gruber, M. 2003. *Sacrifice in the Desert: A Study of an Egyptian Minority Through the Prism of Coptic Monasticism*. University Press of America. New York, p. 38.
76. Merton, T. 1977. *The Monastic Journey*. Sheed Andrews and McMeel. Kansas City, MI, p. 175.
77. Young, D. W. 1993. *Coptic Manuscripts from the White Monastery: Works of Shenute*. Hollinek. Wien, p. 17.
78. Young 1993: 19.
79. Krawiec, R. 2002. *Shenoute & the Women of the White Monastery: Egyptian Monasticism in Late Antiquity*. Oxford University Press. Oxford, p. 3.
80. Veilleux, A. 1983. Shenoute or the pitfalls of Monasticism. Preface in Bell, D. N. 1983. *Besa. The Life of Shenoute: Introduction, Translation, and Notes by David N. Bell*: vxv. Cistercian Publications. Kalamazoo, MI, p. v.
81. Bell, D. N. 1983. *Besa. The Life of Shenoute: Introduction, Translation, and Notes by David N. Bell*. Cistercian Publications. Kalamazoo, MI, pp. 18–19.
82. Bell 1983: 107.
83. Besa. 1983. *The Life of Shenoute: Introduction, translation, and notes by David N. Bell*. Cistercian Publications. Kalamazoo, MI, pp. 72–3.
84. Krawiec 2002: 56.
85. Frankfurter 1998: 46.
86. Gruber 2003: 179.
87. Gruber 2003: 180.
88. Kamil 2002: 33.
89. Kákosy, L. 1982. The Nile, Euthenia, and the Nymphs. *The Journal of Egyptian Archaeology*, Vol. 68: 290–8, pp. 290–1, 297.
90. Frankfurter 1998: 44.
91. Ward, W. A. 1957. The philosophy of death in Coptic epitaphs. *Journal of Bible and Religion*, Vol. 25, No. 1: 34–40, p. 37.

92. Bishop Thomas. 2004. The Coptic Orthodox Church and folk traditions. In Immerzeel, M. & Vliet, J. V. D. (eds), *Coptic Studies on the Threshold of a New Millennium: Proceedings of the Seventh International Congress of Coptic Studies, Leiden, 27 August – 2 September 2000*: 983–8. Peeters Publishers & Department of Oriental Studies. Leuven, p. 985.
93. Gruber 2003: 182.
94. Bolman, E. S. 2004. The Coptic Galaktotrophousa revisited. In Immerzeel, M. & Vliet, J. V. D. (eds), *Coptic Studies on the Threshold of a New Millennium: Proceedings of the Seventh International Congress of Coptic Studies, Leiden, 27 August – 2 September 2000*: 1173–84. Peeters Publishers & Department of Oriental Studies. Leuven.
95. Bolman 2004: 1179.
96. Bolman 2004: 1179–80.
97. Bolman 2004: 1179–82.
98. Plutarch. *Concerning the Mysteries of Isis and Osiris, by Mead, G R S, and Plutarch*. From Mead, G. R. S. 2001. Thrice Greatest Hermes Part 1. Reed Wheel. York Beach, ME, 49.3.
99. Six, V. 1999. Water, the Nile, and the Tä'amrä Maryam: miracles of Virgin Mary in the Ethiopian version. *Aethiopica*, Vol. 2: 53–68, p. 55.
100. Budge, E. A. W. 1933. *One Hundred and Ten Miracles of Our Lady Mary*. Oxford University Press. London, pp. 47–8, 54.
101. Kákosy 1982: 297.
102. Kamil 2002: 18.
103. Friedlander, M. J. 2007. *Ethiopia's Hidden Treasures: A Guide to the Paintings of the Remote Churches of Ethiopia*. Shama Books. Addis Ababa, pp. 51–2.
104. Spencer, D. 1972. In search of St Luke icons in Ethiopia. *Journal of Ethiopian Studies*, Vol. X, No. 2: 67–103, p. 80.
105. Frazer, J. G. 1916. Ancient stories of a great flood. *The Journal of the Royal Anthropological Institute of Great Britain and Ireland*, Vol. 46: 231–83.
106. Tvedt, T. 2016. *Water and Society – Changing Perceptions of Societal and Historical Development*. I.B.Tauris. London, p. 77.
107. Farrar, F. W. 1865. Traditions, real and fictitious. *Transactions of the Ethnological Society of London*, Vol. 3: 298–307, p. 303.
108. Literature on the deluge and flood myths is extensive, but see for instance Allen, D. C. 1963. *The Legend of Noah: Renaissance, Rationalism in Art, Science, and Letters*. University of Illinois Press. Urbana; Cohn, N. 1996. *Noah's Flood: The Genesis Story in Western Thought*. Yale University Press. New Haven, CT and London; Dundes, A. (ed.), 1988. *The Flood Myth*. University of California Press. Berkeley; Kramer, S. N. & Maier, J. 1989. *Myths of Enki, the Crafty God*. Oxford University Press. Oxford; Leach, E. 1969. *Genesis as Myth and Other Essays*. Jonathan Cape. London.
109. Lewis, J. P. 1984. Noah and the flood: in Jewish, Christian, and Muslim tradition. *The Biblical Archaeologist*, Vol. 47, No. 4: 224–39.
110. Dykstra, D. 1994. Pyramids, prophets, and progress: ancient Egypt in the writings of 'yra Mubārak. *Journal of the American Oriental Society*, Vol. 114, No. 1: 54–65, p. 58.
111. Eman Hasan, E. & Elshamy, M. 2011. Application of hydrological models for climate sensitivity estimation of the Atbara sub-basin. In Melesse, A. M. (ed.), *Nile River Basin: Hydrology, Climate and Water Use*. Springer. Dordrecht, pp. 227–40, p. 213.
112. Clark, W. T. 1938. Manners, customs and beliefs of the northern Bega. *Sudan Notes and Records*, Vol. XXI, Part 1: 1–29, p. 20.
113. Baker, S. W. 1868. *The Nile Tributaries of Abyssinia, and the Sword Hunters of the Hamran Arabs*. J. B. Lippincott and Co. Philadelphia, pp. 36–8.
114. Bruce, J. 1790. *Travels to Discover the Source of the Nile, in the Years 1768, 1769, 1770, 1771, 1772, and 1773 in Five Volumes*. J. Ruthven. London, p. 401.

115. Bruce 1790, Vol. I: 376–7.
116. See Munro-Hay 2005: 143–4. Others have also argued along these lines.
117. Sulas, F. 2014. Aksum: water and urbanization in northern Ethiopia. In Tvedt, T. & Oestigaard, T. (eds), 2014. *A History of Water. Series 3, Vol. 1. Water and Urbanization*: 175–97. I.B.Tauris. London.
118. Haleem, M. A. 1999. *Understanding the Qur'an: Themes and Styles*. I.B.Tauris. London, pp. 29–30.
119. Reinhart, A. K. 1990. Impurity/no danger. *History of Religions*, Vol. 30, No. 1: 1–24, pp. 5–6.
120. Haarmann, U. 1996. Medieval Muslim perception of pharaonic Egypt. In Loprieno, A. (ed.), *Ancient Egyptian Literature: History and Forms*: 605–27. E. J. Brill. Leiden, p. 606.
121. Cooper, J. P. 2014. *The Medieval Nile: Route, Navigation, and Landscape in Islamic Egypt*. The American University in Cairo Press. Cairo, p. xviii.
122. Kheir, El-Hag H. M. 1989. A contribution to a textual problem: 'Ibn Sulaym al-Aswānī's Kitāb Akhbār al-Nūba wa-l-Maqurra wa-l-Beja wa-l-Nīl.' *Arabica*, T. 36, Fasc. 1 (March 1989): 36–80.
123. Nazmi, A. 2004. The Nile River in Muslim geographical sources. *Studia Arabistyczne i Islamistyczne* Vol. 12: 28–54.
124. Nazmi 2014: 35.
125. Popper, W. 1951. *The Cairo Nilometer: Studies in Ibn Taghrî Birdî's Chronicles of Egypt 1*. University of California Press. Berkeley, pp. 79–81, see also Mikhail, A. 2016. The Nile and Flood in Early Modern Ottoman Empire. In Tvedt, T. & Oestigaard, T. (eds), *A History of Water, Series 3, Vol. 3. Water and Food: From Hunter-Gatherers to Global Production in Africa*: 163–84. I.B.Tauris. London.
126. Haarmann 1996: 607–9.
127. Year 1 AH in the Islamic calendar starts AD 622, but the Islamic year which follows the moon is shorter than the year used in the Gregorian calendar.
128. Lutfi, H. 1998. Coptic festivals of the Nile: aberrations of the past? In Philipp, T. & Haarmann, U. (eds), *The Mamluks in Egyptian Politics and Society*: 254–82. Cambridge University Press. Cambridge, pp. 259–62.
129. Tagher, J. 1998. *Christians in Muslim Egypt: An Historical Study of the Relations between Copts and Muslims from 640 to 1922*. Oros Verlag. Altenberge, pp. 91–2.
130. Tagher 1998: 120.
131. Tagher 1998: 119.
132. Lutfi 1998: 258.
133. Lutfi 1998: 256.
134. Lutfi 1998: 268.
135. Lutfi 1998: 269.
136. Lutfi 1998: 270.
137. Lutfi 1998: 273.
138. Lutfi 1998: 273.
139. Lutfi 1998: 274.
140. Cooper 2014: 118.
141. Lane, E. W. 1895. *An Account of the Manners and Customs of the Modern Egyptians: Written in Egypt During the Years 1833–1835*. Alexander Gardner. London, pp. 495–6.
142. Lane 1895: 496–7.
143. Lane 1895: 498–500.
144. Lane 1895: 498–500.
145. Lane 1895: 502–5.

146. Cooper 2014: 1.
147. Warburg, G. R. 1982. Islam and Politics in Egypt: 1952–80. *Middle Eastern Studies*, Vol. 18, No. 2: 131–57, p. 144.
148. Châtel, F. 2010. Bathing in divine waters: water and purity in Judaism and Islam. In Tvedt, T. & Oestigaard, T. (eds), *A History of Water. Series 2, Vol. 1. Ideas of Water from Antiquity to Modern Times*: 273–97. I.B.Tauris. London, p. 277.
149. Dellapenna, J. & Gupta, J. 2008. Toward global law on water. *Global Governance*, Vol. 14, No. 4: 437–53, p. 439.
150. Ciftci, S. 2013. Secular-Islamist cleavage, values and support for democracy and Shari'a in the Arab world. *Political Research Quarterly*, Vol. 66, No. 4: 781–93, fn. 1, p. 792.
151. Moad, E. O. 2007. A path to the oasis: 'Shari'ah' and reason in Islamic moral epistemology. *International Journal for Philosophy of Religion*, Vol. 62, No. 3: 135–48, p. 138.
152. Moad 2007: 140.
153. Warburg, G. R. 1990. The Sharia in Sudan: implementation and repercussions, 1983–1989. *Middle East Journal*, Vol. 44, No. 4: 624–37.
154. See also Tvedt, T. 2012. *Nilen – historiens elv*. Aschehoug. Oslo, p. 154ff.
155. Warburg, G. 2000. The Nile in Egyptian-Sudanese relations, 1956–1995. In Erlich, H. & Gershoni, I. (eds), *The Nile: Histories, Cultures, Myths*: 227–34. Lynne Rienner Publishers. Boulder, CO and London.
156. Mahfouz, N. 1993 [1966]. *Adrift of the Nile*. Doubleday. New York, p. 87.
157. Arbel, B. 2000. Renaissance geographical literature on the Nile. In H. Erlich & L. Gershoni (eds), *The Nile: Histories, Cultures, Myths*: 105–20. Lynne Rienner. London, pp. 106–7.
158. Margoliouth, G. 1896. The liturgy of the Nile. *Journal of the Royal Asiatic Society of Great Britain and Ireland*: 677–731, p. 684.
159. Donzel, E. v. 2000. The legend of the Blue Nile in Europe. In Erlich, H. & Gershoni, I. (eds), *The Nile: Histories, Cultures, Myths*: 121–30. Lynne Rienner Publishers. Boulder, CO and London, p. 122.
160. Pankhurst, R. 2000. Ethiopia's alleged control of the Nile. In Erlich, H & Gershoni, I. (eds), *The Nile: Histories, Cultures, Myths*: 25–38. Lynne Rienner Publishers. Boulder, CO.
161. Six 1999: 53.
162. Pankhurst 2000: 26.
163. Six 1999: 58.
164. E.g. Donzel 2000.
165. Pankhurst 2000: 26.
166. Erlich, H. 2002. *The Cross and the River: Ethiopia, Egypt, and the Nile*. Lynne Rienner Publishers. Boulder, CO, p. 46.
167. Six 1999: 66.
168. Donzel 2000: 121–2.
169. Erlich 2002: 38.
170. Bruce 1790 Vol. 3: 712.
171. Pankhurst 2000: 30.
172. Erlich 2002: 9.
173. Erlich 2002: 22
174. Erlich 2002: 97.
175. Erlich 2000: 38.
176. Erlich 2000: 39.
177. Erlich 2000: 42.

178. Mockler-Ferryman, A. F. 1903. Christianity in Uganda. *Journal of the Royal African Society*, Vol. 2, No. 7: 276–91, p. 276.
179. Kassimir, R. 1991. Complex martyrs: symbols of Catholic Church formation and political differentiation in Uganda. *African Affairs*, Vol. 90, No. 360: 357–82.
180. Archdiocese of Gulu 2012. Renewed hope of Christianity in Uganda. From Namugongo to Paimol Two more Martyrs. Daudi Okelo and Jildo Irwa, Martyrs of Evangelization. Archdiocese of Gulu. Gulu.
181. Oestigaard, T. 2013. *Water, Christianity and the Rise of Capitalism*. I.B.Tauris. London.
182. Speke, J. H. 1863. *Journal of the Discovery of the Source of the White Nile*. Blackwood and Sons. Edinburgh and London, p. 264.
183. Speke 1863: 13.
184. Bayly, C. A. 2000. Orientalists, informants and critics in Benares, 1790–1860. In Malik, J. (ed.), *Perspectives of Mutual Encounters in South Asian History, 1750–1860*: 97–127. E. J. Brill. Leiden.
185. Wilford, F. 1808. An essay on the sacred isles in the west, with other essays connected with that work. *Asiatic Researches*, Vol. 8: 245–54.
186. Wilford 1808: 250.
187. Wilford 1808: 251.
188. Bayly 2000: 105.
189. Wilford 1808: 252–3.
190. Bayly 2000: 106.
191. Maitland, A. 2010 [1971]. *Speke and the Discovery of the Source of the Nile*. Faber and Faber. London, p. 189.
192. Eck, D. E. 1983. *Banaras – City of Light*. Penguin Books. New Delhi, pp. 73–4.
193. Kinsley, D. 1989. *The Goddesses' Mirror: Visions of the Divine from East and West*. State University of New York Press. Albany, p. 194.
194. Darian, S. G. 1978. *The Ganges in Myth and History*. The University Press of Hawaii. Honolulu, p. 81.
195. Oestigaard, T. 2005. *Death and Life-Giving Waters – Cremation, Caste, and Cosmogony in Karmic Traditions*. BAR International Series 1353. Oxford.
196. *The Siva-Purana Part III*, trans. by a board of scholars. 1970. In Shastri, J. L. (ed.), *Ancient Indian Tradition & Mythology Vol. 3*. Montilal Banarsidass. Delhi, 22.3–5, p. 1541.
197. *Siva-Purana III*, 22.14–16, p. 1542.
198. Eck 1983: 214, 215, 219.
199. Zikra, A. B. 2009. *One Home, One Family, One Future*. AuthorHouse. Bloomington, p. 88.
200. Dennie, G. M. 2003. Flames of race, ashes of death: re-inventing cremation in Johannesburg, 1910–1945. *Journal of South African Studies*, Vol. 29, No. 1: 177–92.
201. Gandhi. M. 1962. *The End of an Epoch*. Navajivan Publishing House. Ahmedabad, pp. 61–2.
202. http://defence.pk/threads/why-godse-murdered-gandhi.49897/#ixzz43YLCW1zy (accessed 22 March 2016).
203. Patel, Z. 2006. *Unquiet: The Life and Times of Makhan Singh*. Zand Graphics. Nairobi, p. 159.
204. Ssenkaaba, S. 2013. The symbolic Gandhi statue in Jinja. *The New Vision*, 31 October 2013. http://www.newvision.co.ug/news/648956-the-symbolic-gandhi-statue-in-jinja.html (accessed 19 June 2014).
205. Erlich, H. & Gershoni, I. 2000. Introduction. In Erlich, H. & Gershoni, I. (eds), *The Nile: Histories, Cultures, Myths*: 1–14. Lynne Rienner Publishers. Boulder, CO and London.

Bibliography

Abrahams, R. (ed.), *Witchcraft in Contemporary Tanzania* (Cambridge: Cambridge African Monographs, 1994).
Akiiki, R. K., 'People-centred development', in R. B. Johnston, L. Hiwasaki, I. J. Klaver, A. R. Castillo & V. Strang (eds), *Water, Cultural Diversity, and Global Environmental Change: Emerging Trends, Sustainable Futures?* (Paris: Springer/UNESCO, 2012), pp. 341–3.
Albright, W. F., 'Notes on Egypto-Semitic etymology. II', *The American Journal of Semitic Languages and Literatures* 24/4 (1918), pp. 215–55.
—— 'The mouth of rivers', *The American Journal of Semitic Languages and Literatures* 35/4 (1919), pp. 161–95.
—— 'Notes on Egypto-Semitic etymology III', *Journal of the American Oriental Society* 47 (1927), pp. 198–237.
Aldred, C., *Egypt. To the End of the Old Kingdom* (London: Thames and Hudson, 1965).
—— *The Egyptians* (London: Thames and Hudson, 1984).
Allen, D., *The Legend of Noah. Renaissance, Rationalism in Art, Science, and Letters* (Urbana: University of Illinois Press, 1963).
—— 'Eliade and history', *The Journal of Religion* 68/4 (1988), pp. 545–65.
Allen, J., 'The cosmology of the Pyramid Texts', in J. Allen (eds), *Religion and Philosophy in Ancient Egypt* (New Haven, CT: Yale Egyptological Seminar, Dept. of Near Eastern Languages and Civilizations, the Graduate School, Yale University, 1989a), pp. 1–28.
—— 'The natural philosophy of Akhenaten', in J. Allen (eds), *Religion and Philosophy in Ancient Egypt* (New Haven, CT: Yale Egyptological Seminar, Dept. of Near Eastern Languages and Civilizations, the Graduate School, Yale University, 1989b), pp. 89–101.
Allen, R. E. (ed.), *Greek Philosophy: Thales to Aristotle* (New York: The Free Press, 1966).
Allen, T., 'Understanding Alice: Uganda's Holy Spirit movement in context', *Africa: Journal of the International African Institute* 61/3 (1991), pp. 370–99.
The Ancient Egyptian Book of the Dead, trans. by R. O. Faulkner (London: The British Museum Press, 1972).
Anthes, R., 'Egyptian theology in the third millennium B.C.', *Journal of Near Eastern Studies* 18/3 (1959), pp. 169–212.
Arbel, B., 'Renaissance geographical literature on the Nile', in H. Erlich and L. Gershoni (eds), *The Nile. Histories, Cultures, Myths* (London: Lynne Rienner, London, 2000), pp. 105–20.
Archdiocese of Gulu. *Renewed Hope of Christianity in Uganda. From Namugongo to Paimol Two More Martyrs. Daudi Okelo and Jildo Irwa, Martyrs of Evangelization* (Gulu: Archdiocese of Gulu, 2012).
Århem, K., 'Maasai food symbolism: the cultural connotations of milk, meat, and blood in the pastoral diet', *Anthropos* 84/1–3 (1989), pp. 1–23.
Asante, M. K. and S. Ismail, 'Akhenaten to Origen: characteristics of philosophical thought in ancient Africa', *Journal of Black Studies* 40/2 (2009), pp. 296–309.

BIBLIOGRAPHY

Assmann, J., Ägypten: Theologie und Frömmigkeit einer frühen Hochkultur (Stuggart: Urban-Taschenbücher, 366. W. Kohlhammer, 1984).

—— 'Death and initiation in the funerary religion of ancient Egypt', in W. K. Simpson (ed.), *Religion and Philosophy in Ancient Egypt* (New Haven, CT: Yale Egyptological Studies 3, 1989), pp. 135–59.

—— 'Akhanyati's theology of light and time', *Proceedings of the Israel Academy of Sciences and Humanities* VII/4 (1992), pp. 143–76.

—— *Egyptian Solar Religion in the New Kingdom. Re, Amun and the Crisis of Polytheism* (London: Kegan Paul, 1995).

—— *Moses the Egyptian. The Memory of Egypt in Western Monotheism* (Boston, MA: Harvard University Press, 1997).

—— *The Search for God in Ancient Egypt* (Ithaca, NY: Cornell University Press, 2001).

—— *The Mind of Egypt. History and Meaning in the Time of the Pharaohs* (New York: Metropolitan Books, 2002).

—— *Death and Salvation in Ancient Egypt* (Ithaca, NY: Cornell University Press, 2005).

Augustine, *Saint Augustine: The City of God Against the Pagans*, with an English translation by G. E. McCracken, in seven volumes (London: William Heinemann Ltd, 1957).

Ayrton, F., 'Observations upon M. d'Abbadies's account of his discovery of the sources of the White Nile, and upon certain objections and statements in relation thereto, by Dr. Beke', *Journal of the Royal Geographical Society of London* 18 (1848), pp. 48–74.

Bachelard, G., *The Psychoanalysis of Fire* (Boston, MA: Beacon Press, 1968).

—— *The Flame of a Candle* (Dallas, TX: The Dallas Institute of Humanities and Culture, 1988).

—— *Fragments of a Poetics of Fire* (Dallas, TX: The Dallas Institute of Humanities and Culture, 1990).

—— *Water and Dreams. An Essay on the Imagination of Matter* (Dallas, TX: The Dallas Institute of Humanities and Culture, 1994).

Baines, J., *Fecundity Figures* (Warminster: Aris & Phillips Ltd, 1985a).

—— 'Color terminology and color classification: ancient Egyptian color terminology and polychrony', *American Anthropologist* 87/2 (1985b), pp. 282–97.

—— 'Origins of Egyptian kingship', in D. O'Connor and D. P. Silverman (eds), *Ancient Egyptian Kingship* (Leiden: E. J. Brill, 1995), pp. 95–156.

—— 'Myth and literature', in A. Loprieno (ed.), *Ancient Egyptian Literature. History and Forms* (Leiden: E. J. Brill, 1996), pp. 361–78.

Baker, S. W., 'The races of the Nile basin', *Transactions of the Ethnological Society of London* 5 (1867), pp. 228–38.

—— *The Nile Tributaries of Abyssinia, and the Sword Hunters of the Hamran Arabs* (Philadelphia, PA: J. B. Lippincott and Co., 1868).

—— *Albert N'yanza. Great Basin of the Nile, and Exploration of the Nile Sources* (Philadelphia, PA: Lippincott, 1869).

Bard, K. A., 'The geography of excavated Predynastic sites and the rise of complex society', *Journal of the American Research Center in Egypt* 24 (1987), pp. 81–93.

—— 'The Egyptian predynastic: a review of the evidence', *Journal of Field Archaeology* 21/3 (1994), pp. 265–88.

—— 'Predynastic period, overview', in K. A. Bard (ed.), *Encyclopaedia of the Archaeology of Ancient Egypt* (London: Routledge, 1999), pp. 23–30.

—— 'Early Dynastic period, overview', in K. A. Bard (ed.), *Encyclopaedia of the Archaeology of Ancient Egypt* (London: Routledge, 1999), pp. 31–5.

Barth, F., *Cosmologies in the Making: A Generative Approach to Cultural Variation in Inner New Guinea* (Cambridge: Cambridge University Press, 1993 [1987]).

―――― 'The guru and the conjurer: transactions in knowledge and the shaping of culture in southeast Asia and Melanesia', *Man* 25 (1990), pp. 640–53.

Bayly, C. A., 'Orientalists, informants and critics in Benares, 1790-1860', in J. Malik (ed.), *Perspectives of Mutual Encounters in South Asian History, 1750–1860* (Leiden: E. J. Brill, 2000), pp. 97–127.

Beaton, A. C., 'Fur rain cults and ceremonies', *Sudan Notes and Records* XXII/II (1939), pp. 186–203.

Beckingham, C. F. and G. W. B. Huntingford, *Some Records of Ethiopia 1593-1646. Being Extracts from the History of High Ethiopia or Abassia by Manoel De Almeida. Together with Bahrey's History of the Galla* (London: Printed for the Hakluyt Society, 1954).

Bedri, I. E., 'Notes on Dinka religious beliefs in their hereditary chiefs and rain makers', *Sudan Notes and Records* XXII/I (1939), pp. 125–31.

Behrend, H., *Alice Lakwena & the Holy Spirits* (Oxford: James Currey, 1999).

―――― *Resurrecting Cannibals. The Catholic Church, Witch-Hunts, & The Production of Pagans in Western Uganda* (London: James Currey, 2011).

Behringer, W., *Witches and Witch-Hunts* (Oxford: Polity Press, 2004).

Beke, C. T., 'Abyssinia: being a continuation of routes in that country', *Journal of the Royal Geographical Society of London* 14 (1844), pp. 1–76.

―――― 'On the Nile and its tributaries', *Journal of the Royal Geographical Society of London* 17 (1847), pp. 1–84.

Bell, B., 'The oldest records of the Nile floods', *The Geographical Journal* 136/4 (1970), pp. 569–73.

―――― 'The Dark Ages in ancient history, I: the first Dark Age in Egypt', *American Journal of Archaeology* 75/1 (1971), pp. 1–26.

Bell, D. N., *Besa. The Life of Shenoute: Introduction, Translation, and Notes* (Kalamazoo, MI: Cistercian Publications, 1983).

Bennet, N. R., 'David Livingstone: exploration for Christianity', in R. I. Rotberg (ed.), *Africa and Its Explorers. Motives, Methods, and Impact* (Cambridge, MA: Harvard University Press, 1970), pp. 39–62.

Berger, A., 'Cultural hermeneutics: the concept of imagination in the phenomenological approaches of Henry Corbin and Mircea Eliade', *The Journal of Religion* 66/2 (1986), pp. 141–56.

Berry, L. and A. J. Whiteman, 'The Nile in the Sudan', *The Geographical Journal* 134/1 (1968), pp. 1–33.

Besa, *The Life of Shenoute: Introduction, Translation, and Notes by David N. Bell* (Kalamazoo, MI: Cistercian Publications, 1983).

Beth, K., 'El und Neter', *ZAW* 36 (1916), pp. 129–86.

Bishop Thomas, 'The Coptic Orthodox Church and folk traditions', in M. Immerzeel and J. V. D. Vliet (eds), *Coptic Studies on the Threshold of a New Millennium. Proceedings of the Seventh International Congress of Coptic Studies, Leiden, 27 August–2 September 2000* (Leuven: Peeters Publishers & Department of Oriental Studies, 2004), pp. 983–8.

Bjerk, P. K., 'They poured themselves into the milk: Zulu political philosophy under Shaka', *The Journal of African History* 47/1 (2006), pp. 1–19.

Blackman, A. M., 'Osiris or the Sun-God?', *The Journal of Egyptian Archaeology* 11/3–4 (1925a), pp. 201–9.

―――― 'Oracles in ancient Egypt', *The Journal of Egyptian Archaeology* 11/3–4 (1925b), pp. 249–55.

―――― 'Oracles in ancient Egypt. II', *The Journal of Egyptian Archaeology* 12/3–4 (1925c), pp. 176–85.

―――― 'Purification (Egyptian)', in *Gods, Priests and Men. Studies in the Religion of Pharaonic Egypt by Aylward M. Blackman* (London: Kegan Paul International, 1998), pp. 3–21.

Blundell, H. W., 'Exploration in the Abai Basin, Abyssinia', *The Geographical Journal* 27/6 (1906), pp. 529–51.

Bolman, E. S., 'The Coptic Galaktotrophousa revisited', in M. Immerzeel and J. V. D. Vliet (eds), *Coptic Studies on the Threshold of a New Millennium. Proceedings of the Seventh International Congress of Coptic Studies, Leiden, 27 August–2 September 2000* (Leuven: Peeters Publishers & Department of Oriental Studies, 2004), pp. 1173–84.

Borghouts, J. F., 'The evil eye of Apopis', *The Journal of Egyptian Archaeology* 59 (1973), pp. 114–50.

Bosworth, A. B., 'Aristotle, India and the Alexander Historians', *Topoi* 3/2 (1993), pp. 407–24.

―― *Alexander and the East. The Tragedy of Triumph* (Oxford: Clarendon Press, 1996).

Bradt, *The Bradt Travel Guide. Uganda* (Guildford, CT: The Globe Pequot Press Inc., 2010).

Brandström, P., 'Lolandi – se jag är! En historia om det berättande namnet hos sukuma-nyamwezi i Tanzania', in T. Andersson, E. Brylla & A. Jacobson-Widding (eds), *Personnamn och social identitet* (Stockholm: Konferanser 42. Kung. Vitterhets Historie och Antikvitets Akademien, 1998).

―― 'Seeds and soil: the quest for life and the domestication of fertility in Sukuma-Nyamwezi thought and social reality', in A. Jacobson-Widding and W. van Beek (eds), *The Creative Communion: African Folk Models of Fertility and the Regeneration of Life* (Uppsala: Almquist and Wiksell, 1990), pp. 167–86.

Breasted, J. H., *Development of Religion and Thought in Ancient Egypt* (Gloucester, MA: P. Smith, 1959).

Bridges, R. C., 'John Hanning Speke: negotiating a way to the Nile', in R. I. Rotberg (ed.), *Africa and Its Explorers. Motives, Methods, and Impact* (Cambridge, MA: Harvard University Press, 1970), pp. 95–137.

Bright, R. G. T., 'Survey and exploration in the Ruwenzori and Lake region', The Geographical Journal 34/2 (1909), pp. 128–53.

Bruce, J., *Travels to Discover the Source of the Nile, in the Years 1768, 1769, 1770, 1771, 1772, and 1773 in Five Volumes* (London: J. Ruthven, 1790).

Brück, J., 'Ritual and rationality: some problems of interpretation in European archaeology', *European Journal of Archaeology* 2/3 (1999), pp. 313–44.

Budge, E. A. W., *The Nile. Notes for Travellers in Egypt and the Egyptian Sudan* (London: Thos. Cook & Sons, Ltd, 1912).

―― *A History of Ethiopia. Nubia and Abyssinia* (London: Methuen, 1928).

―― *The Queen of Sheba and Her Only Son Menyelek (I)* (London: Oxford University Press, 1932).

―― *One Hundred and Ten Miracles of Our Lady Mary* (London: Oxford University Press, 1933).

Burnside, *Bujagali Hydropower Project: Social and Environmental Assessment Report: Executive Summary* (Guelph: R.J. Burnside International, 2006).

Burton, R. F., 'The Lake Regions of Central Equatorial Africa', *Journal of the Royal Geographical Society of London* 29 (1859), pp. 1–454.

Burton, R. F. and J. H. Speke, 'Explorations in Eastern Africa', *Proceedings of the Royal Geographical Society in London* 3/6 (1858–9), pp. 348–85.

Butzer, K., 'Environment and human ecology in Egypt during predynastic and early dynastic times', *Bulletin de la Societé de Géographie d'Egypte* 32 (1959), pp. 43–87.

―― *Early Hydraulic Civilization in Egypt. A Study in Cultural Ecology* (Chicago, IL: The University of Chicago Press, 1976).

―― 'Environmental change in the Near East and human impact on the land', in J. M. Sasson (ed.), *Civilizations of the Ancient Near East*, Vol. 1 (New York: Schribner, 1995), pp. 123–51.

Byerley, A., *Becoming Jinja: The Production of Space and Making of Place in an African Industrial Town* (Stockholm: Department of Human Geography, Stockholm University, 2005).

Campbell, J., *The Masks of God: Primitive Mythology* (New York: The Viking Press, 1959).
────── *The Masks of God: Occidental Mythology* (New York: The Viking Press, 1964).
Cannuyer, C., *Coptic Egypt. The Christians of the Nile* (London: Thames & Hudson, 2001).
Caplan, P., *Feasts, Fasts, Famine: Food for Thought* (Oxford: Berg Occasional Papers in Anthropology, 1994).
Carneiro, R., 'A theory of the origin of the state', *Science* 169 (1970), pp. 733–8.
Chamberlain, P., 'Nile Basin Climates', in H. J. Dumont (ed.), *The Nile. Origin, Environments, Limnology and Human Use* (Leiden: Springer, 2009), pp. 307–33.
Châtel, F., 'Bathing in divine waters: water and purity in Judaism and Islam', in T. Tvedt and T. Oestigaard (eds), *A History of Water. Series 2, Vol. 1. Ideas of Water from Antiquity to Modern Times* (London: I.B.Tauris, 2010), pp. 273–97.
Cheesman, R. E., 'The upper waters of the Blue Nile', *Geographical Journal* 85/6 (1928), pp. 358–74.
────── 'Lake Tana and its island', *Geographical Journal* 71/4 (1935), pp. 489–502.
────── *Lake Tana and the Blue Nile. An Abyssinian Quest* (London: Frank Cass, 1968 [1936]).
Childe, G. V., *New Light on the Most Ancient East: The Oriental Prelude to European Prehistory* (London: Kegan Paul, 1934).
Childs, B. S., 'The birth of Moses', *Journal of Biblical Literature* 84/2 (1965), pp. 109–22.
Churchill, W. S., *My African Journey* (Toronto: William Briggs, 1909).
Ciftci, S., 'Secular-Islamist cleavage, values and support for democracy and Shari'a in the Arab world', *Political Research Quarterly* 66/4 (2013), pp. 781–93.
Clagett, M., *Ancient Egyptian Science*, Vol. 1 (Philadelphia, PA: American Philosophical Society, 1989).
Clark, W. T., 'Manners, customs and beliefs of the Northern Bega', *Sudan Notes and Records* XXI/1 (1938), pp. 1–29.
Cohen, D. W., *The Historical Tradition of Busoga: Mukama and Kintu* (Oxford: Clarendon Press, 1972).
Cohn, N., *Noah's Flood: The Genesis Story in Western Thought* (New Haven, CT and London: Yale University Press, 1996).
Collins, R., *The Nile* (New Haven, CT: Yale University Press, 2002).
Colvile, H., *The Land of the Nile Springs: Being Chiefly an Account of How We Fought Kabarega* (London: Edward Arnold, 1895).
Comaroff, J. and J. Comaroff, J. (eds), *Modernity and Malcontents; Rituals and Power in Postcolonial Africa* (Chicago, IL: The University of Chicago Press, 1993).
Condon, M. A., 'Contribution to the ethnography of Basogabatamba Uganda Protectorate, Br. E. Africa (continued)', *Anthropos* 6/2 (1911), pp. 366–84.
Cooke, M. C., 'Bari rain cults', *Sudan Notes and Records* XXII/II (1939), pp. 181–6.
Cooper, J. P., *The Medieval Nile: Route, Navigation, and Landscape in Islamic Egypt* (Cairo: The American University in Cairo Press, 2014).
Cory, H., *The Ntemi: The Traditional Rites of a Sukuma Chief in Tanganyika* (London: Macmillan, 1951a).
────── *Traditional Rites in Connection with the Burial, Election, enthronement and Magic Powers of a Sukuma Chief* (London: Macmillan, 1951b).
Crawford, O. G. S., 'Some Medieval theories about the Nile', *The Geographical Journal* 114/1–3 (1949), pp. 6–23.
Crosby, D., *Religion of Nature* (New York: State University of New York Press, 2002).
Daly, C. P., 'Remarks on Stanley's verification of Ptolemy's geography', *Journal of the Geographical Society of New York* 7 (1875), pp. 290–5.
Darby, L., P. Ghalioungui and L. Grivetti, *Food: The Gift of Osiris*, Vol. 1 (London: Academic Press, 1977).

Darian, S. G., *The Ganges in Myth and History* (Honolulu: The University Press of Hawaii, 1978).
Darwin, C., *The Origin of Species* (Philadelphia: University of Pennsylvania Press, 2006 [1859]).
David, R., *A Guide to Religious Ritual at Abydos* (Warminster: Aris & Phillips Ltd, 1981).
Davies, C., 'The fragmentation of the religious tradition of the creation, after-life and morality: modernity not post-modernity', *Journal of Contemporary Religion* 17/3 (1999), pp. 339–60.
Davies, V. and R. Friedman, 'The Narmer palette: an overlooked detail', in M. Eldmaty and M. Trad (eds), *Egyptian Museum Collections around the World, Studies for the Centennial of the Egyptian Museum*, Vol. 1 (Cairo: American University Press in Cairo, 2002), pp. 243–6.
Dawson, C., *The Dynamics of World History* (London: Sheed and Ward, 1957).
Day, J., 'The Pharaoh of the Exodus, Josephus and Jubilees', *Vetus Testamentum* 45/3 (1995), pp. 377–9.
Dellapenna, J. and J. Gupta, 'Toward global law on water', *Global Governance* 14/4 (2008), pp. 437–53.
Dennie, G. M., 'Flames of race, ashes of death: re-inventing cremation in Johannesburg, 1910–1945', *Journal of South African Studies* 29/1 (2003), pp. 177–92.
Diadji, I. N., 'From "life-water" to "death-water" or on the foundation of African artistic creation from yesterday to tomorrow', *Leonardo* 36/4 (2003), pp. 273–7.
Dicks, D. R., 'Thales', *The Classical Quarterly* 9/2 (1959), pp. 294–309.
Dickson, D. R., *The Fountain of Living Waters: The Typology of the Waters of Life in Herbert, Vaughan, and Traherne* (Columbia: University of Missouri Press, 1987).
Dijk, J. v., 'The Amarna Period and the Later New Kingdom', in I. Shaw (ed.), *The Oxford History of Ancient Egypt* (Oxford: Oxford University Press, 2000), pp. 272–313.
Diodorus, *Diodorus of Sicily*, with an English translation by C. H. Oldfather, in 12 volumes. I. Books I and II (London: William Heinemann Ltd, 1960), pp. 1–34.
Donzel, E. v., 'The legend of the Blue Nile in Europe', in H. Erlich and I. Gershoni (eds), *The Nile. Histories, Cultures, Myths* (Boulder, CO: Lynne Rienner Publishers, 2000), pp. 121–30.
Doom, R. and K. Vlassenroot, 'Kony's message: a New Koine? The Lord's Resistance Army in Northern Uganda', *African Affairs* 98/390 (1999), pp. 5–36.
Doré, G., *The Bible Gallery* (London: Cassell, Petter, Galpin & Co, 1880).
Dousa, T., 'Imagining Isis: on some continuities and discontinuities in the image of Isis in Greek Isis hymns and demotic texts', in K. Ryholt (ed.), *Acts of the Seventh International Conference of Demotic Studies Copenhagen 23–27 August 1999 (Cni Publications, 27)* (Copenhagen: Museum Tusculanum Press, 2002), pp. 149–84.
Drangert, J. O., *Who Cares About Water? Household Water Development in Sukumaland, Tanzania* (Linköping: Linköping Studies in Arts and Science 85, 1993).
Duke, R., 'Moses' Hebrew name: the evidence of the "Vision of Amram"', *Dead Sea Discoveries* 14 (2007), pp. 34–48.
Dundes, A., 'Wet and dry, the evil eye: an essay in Indo-European and Semitic worldview', in A. Dundes (ed.), *The Evil Eye: A Folklore Casebook* (New York: Garland Publishing, 1981), pp. 257–98.
—— (ed.), *The Flood Myth* (Berkeley: University of California Press, 1988).
Durkheim, E., *The Rules of Sociological Method*, 3rd edition (New York: Free Press, 1966 [1904]).
—— *The Elementary Forms of Religious Life* (London: George Allen & Unwin Ltd, 1915).
Dworkin, R., *Religion Without God* (Cambridge: Harvard University Press, 2013).
Dykstra, D., 'Pyramids, prophets, and progress: ancient Egypt in the writings of ʿAlī Mubārak', *Journal of the American Oriental Society* 114/1 (1994), pp. 54–65.
Eck, D. E., *Banaras – City of Light* (New Delhi: Penguin Books, 1983).
Eggermont, H., K. Van Damme and J. M. Russel, 'Ruwenzori Mountains (Mountains of the Moon): headwaters of the White Nile', in H. J. Dumont (ed.), *The Nile: Origin, Environments, Limnology and Human Use* (Leiden: Springer, 2009), pp. 243–61.

BIBLIOGRAPHY

Electricity Regulatory Authority. Developments and Investment Opportunities in renewable Energy Resources in Uganda. June 2012.

Eliade, M., *The Myth of the Eternal Return* (New York: Pantheon Books, 1954).

—— *Yoga – Immortality and Freedom* (New York: Pantheon Books, 1958).

—— 'Methodological remarks on the study of religious symbolism', in M. Eliade and J. M. Kitagawa (eds), *The History of Religions* (Chicago, IL: The University of Chicago Press, 1959), pp. 86–107.

—— *The Sacred and Profane. The Nature of Religion* (New York: Harcourt Brace, 1987 [1959]).

—— *Patterns in Comparative Religion* (London: Sheed and Ward Ltd, 1993).

Elmer, D. F., 'Heliodoros's "sources": intertextuality, paternity, and the Nile River in the "Aithiopika"', *Transactions of the American Philological Association* 138/2 (2008), pp. 411–50.

el-Saady, H., 'Reflections on the Goddess Tayet', *The Journal of Egyptian Archaeology* 80 (1994), pp. 213–17.

Eman Hasan, E. and M. Elshamy, 'application of hydrological models for climate sensitivity estimation of the Atbara Sub-basin', in A. M. Melesse (ed.), *Nile River Basin. Hydrology, Climate and Water Use* (Dordrecht: Springer, 2011), pp. 227–40.

Emery, W. B., *Archaic Egypt* (Harmondsworth: Penguin, 1961).

Erlich, H., *The Cross and the River: Ethiopia, Egypt, and the Nile* (Boulder, CO: Lynne Rienner Publishers, 2002).

Erlich, H. and I. Gershoni, 'Introduction', in H. Erlich and I. Gershoni (eds), *The Nile: Histories, Cultures, Myths* (Boulder, CO and London: Lynne Rienner Publishers, 2000), pp. 1–14.

Erman, A., *Life in Ancient Egypt* (New York: Dover, 1971 [1894]).

European Investment Bank Complaints Mechanism (EIB-CM). *Bujagali Hydroelectric Project, Jinja, Uganda. Complaint SG/E/2009/09.* Conclusion Report. 30 August 2012.

Evans-Pritchard, E. E., *Witchcraft, Oracles and Magic Among the Azande* (Oxford: Oxford at the Clarendon Press, 1937).

—— *Nuer Religion* (Oxford: Oxford at the Clarendon Press, 1956).

—— *The Nuer: A Description of the Modes of Livelihood and Political Institutions of a Nilotic People* (Oxford: Oxford University Press, 1969 [1940]).

Fagan, G., *The Rape of the Nile: Tomb Robbers, Tourists, and Archaeologists in Egypt* (Boulder, CO: Westview Press, 2004).

Faherty, R. L., 'Sacrifice', in *The New Encyclopaedia Britannica*, 15th edition. Macropaedia. Vol. 16 (Chicago, IL: Encyclopædia Britannica, Inc., 1974), pp. 128–35.

Farrar, F. W., 'Traditions, real and fictitious', *Transactions of the Ethnological Society of London* 3 (1865), pp. 298–307.

Faulkner, R. O., 'A coffin text miscellany', *The Journal of Egyptian Archaeology* 68 (1982), p. 27.

Findlay, A. G., 'On Dr. Livingstone's last journey, and the probable ultimate sources of the Nile', *Journal of the Royal Geographical Society of London* 37 (1867), pp. 193–212.

Finneran, N., *The Archaeology of Christianity in Africa* (Gloucestershire: Tempus, 2002).

—— *The Archaeology of Ethiopia* (London: Routledge, 2007).

—— 'Holy Water: pre-Christian and Christian water association in Ethiopia', in T. Oestigaard (ed.), *Water, Culture and Identity: Comparing Past and Present Traditions in the Nile Basin Region* (Bergen: BRIC Press, 2009), pp. 165–87.

—— 'Holy wells, hot springs, and royal baths: water and sociocultural developments in medieval and post-medieval Ethiopia c. AD 700–900', in T. Tvedt and T. Oestigaard (eds), *A History of Water. Series 3, Vol. 1. Water and Urbanization* (London: I.B.Tauris, 2014), pp. 262–82.

Finnestad, R. B., *Image of the World and Symbol of the Creator: On the Cosmological and Iconological Values of the Temple of Edfu* (Wiesbaden: Otto Harrassowitz, 1985).

Fisher, A. B., 'Western Uganda', *The Geographical Journal* 24/3 (1904), pp. 249–63.
Frankfort, H., *Kingship and the Gods: A Study of Ancient Near Eastern Religion as the Integration of Society & Nature* (Chicago, IL: The University of Chicago Press, 1948).
—— *The Birth of Civilization in the Near East* (London: Williams & Norgate Ltd, 1951).
—— *Ancient Egyptian Religion. An Interpretation* (New York: Harper & Row, 1961).
Frankfurter, D., 'The cult of the martyrs in Egypt before Constantine: the evidence of the Coptic "Apocalypse of Elijah"', *Vigiliae Christianae* 48/1 (1994), pp. 25–47.
—— *Religion in Roman Egypt. Assimilation and Resistance* (Princeton, NJ: Princeton University Press, 1998).
Frazer, J. G., 'Ancient stories of a great flood', *The Journal of the Royal Anthropological Institute of Great Britain and Ireland* 46 (1916), pp. 231–83.
—— *The Golden Bough: A Study in Magic and Religion* (New York: Simon & Schuster, 1996 [1922]).
Freud, S., *The Interpretation of Dreams* (New York: The Macmillan Company, 1913).
—— *Three Contributions to the Theory of Sex* (New York and Washington: Nervous and Mental Disease Publishing Co., 1920).
—— *Moses and Monotheism* (Hertfordshire: Hogarth Press, 1939).
Friedlander, M. J., *Ethiopia's Hidden Treasures: A Guide to the Paintings of the Remote Churches of Ethiopia* (Addis Ababa: Shama Books, 2007).
Friedman, J., 'Marxism, structuralism, and vulgar materialism', *Man* 9 (1974), pp. 444–69.
Fulke, W., *Praelections upon the Sacred and Holy Revelation of S. John* (London: Thomas Purfoote, 1537).
Gandhi, M., *The End of an Epoch* (Ahmedabad: Navajivan Publishing House, 1962).
Gansum, T., 'Hår og stil og stilig hår: Om langhåret maktsymbolikk', in F-A.Stylegar and P. Rolfsen (eds), *Snartemofunnene i nytt lys* (Oslo: Universitetets kulturhistoriske museer Skrifter nr. 2, 2003), pp. 191–222.
Gardiner, A., 'Horus the Behdetite', *The Journal of Egyptian Archaeology* 30 (1944), pp. 23–60.
—— 'The baptism of Pharaoh', *The Journal of Egyptian Archaeology* 36 (1950), pp. 3–12.
—— *Egypt of the Pharaohs: An Introduction* (Oxford: Clarendon Press, 1961).
Garstin, W., 'Fifty years of exploration, and some of its results', *The Geographical Journal* 33/2 (1909), pp. 117–47.
Garzanti, E., S. Andò, G. Vezzoli, A. Ali, A. Megid & A. El Kammar, 'Petrology of Nile River sands (Ethiopia and Sudan): sediment budgets and erosion patterns', *Earth and Planetary Science Letters* 252 (2006), pp. 327–41.
Gedef, A. F., 'Archaeological fieldwork around Lake Tana area of northwest Ethiopia and the implication for an understanding of aquatic adaptation' (PhD thesis, University of Bergen, 2014).
Geertz, C., *The Interpretation of Cultures* (New York: HarperCollins, 1973).
Gemmill, P. F., 'Egypt is the Nile', *Economic Geography* 4/3 (1928), pp. 295–312.
Geschiere, P., *The Modernity of Witchcraft: Politics and the Occult in Postcolonial Africa* (Charlottesville: University Press of Virginia, 1997).
Goa, D., S. B. Plate and C. Paine, 'Editorial statement', *Material Religion* 1/1 (2005), pp. 4–9.
Godelier, M., *The Enigma of the Gift* (Chicago, IL: The University of Chicago Press, 1999).
Goedicke, H., 'Neilos – an etymology', *The American Journal of Philology* 100/1 (1979), pp. 69–72.
Gold, A. G., *Fruitful Journeys: The Ways of Rajasthani Pilgrims* (Berkeley: University of California Press, 1988).
Gombrich, R. F., *Theravada Buddhism: A Social History from Ancient Benares to Modern Colombo* (London: Routledge, 1988).
Gonza, R. K. et al., *Reconciliation Among the Busoga* (Jinja: Cultural Research Centre, 2001).

Gonza, R. K. et al., *Traditional Religion and Clans Among the Busoga*, Vol. 1 (Jinja: Cultural Research Centre, 2002).

Gonza, R. K. et al., *Witchcraft, Divination and Healing Among the Basoga* (Jinja: Cultural Research Centre, 2003).

Gonza R. K. et al. *The Concept of Good Luck and Bad Luck Among the Basoga* (Kisubi: Marianum Publishing Company, 2010).

Goodenough, W. and W. Gowers, 'Ruwenzori: flights and further exploration: discussion', *The Geographical Journal* 82/6 (1933), pp. 511–14.

Gordon, D. L., *Letters from Egypt* (New York: McClure, Phillips & Co., 1902).

Green, J. and A. I. J. El-Moghraby, 'Swamps of the Upper Nile', in H. J. Dumont (ed.), *The Nile. Origin, Environments, Limnology and Human Use* (Leiden: Springer, 2009), pp. 193–204.

Griffith, R. D., 'Homeric ΔΙΙΠΕΤΕΟΣΠΟΤΑΜΟΙΟ and the Celestial Nile', *The American Journal of Philology* 118/3 (1997), pp. 353–62.

Griffiths, J. G., *The Conflict of Horus and Seth: From Egyptian and Classical Sources* (Liverpool: Liverpool University Press, 1960).

Gruber, M., *Sacrifice in the Desert: A Study of an Egyptian Minority Through the Prism of Coptic Monasticism* (New York: University Press of America, 2003).

Guenther, L., '"Like a maternal body": Emmanuel Levinas and the motherhood of Moses', *Hypatia* 21/1 (2006), pp. 119–36.

Gwassa, G. C. K. and J. Iliffe, *Records of the Maji Maji Rising: Part One* (Dar es Salaam: East African Publishing House, 1968).

Haaland, G., 'Beer, blood and mother's milk: the symbolic context of economic behaviour in fur society', *Sudan Notes and Records* 2 (1998), pp. 53–76.

Haar, G. T. (ed.), *Imagining Evil. Witchcraft Beliefs and Accusations in Contemporary Africa* (Trenton and Asmara: Africa World Press, Inc., 2006).

Haarmann, U., 'Medieval Muslim perception of pharaonic Egypt', in A. Loprieno (ed.), *Ancient Egyptian Literature: History and Forms* (Leiden: E. J. Brill, 1996), pp. 605–27.

Haikal, F. M. H., *Two Hieratic Funerary Papyri of Nesmin 1* (Bruxelles: Foundation Egyptologique Reine Elisabeth, 1970).

Haleem, M. A., *Understanding the Qur'an. Themes and Styles* (London: I.B.Tauris, 1999).

Hayes, A. J., *The Source of the Blue Nile: A Record of a Journey through the Soudan to Lake Tsana in Western Abyssinia, and the Return to Egypt by the Valley of Atbara* (London: Smith, Elder & Co., 1905).

Hayes, J. H., 'The usage of oracles against foreign nations in ancient Israel', *Journal of Biblical Literature* 87/1 (1968), pp. 81–92.

Hegel, G. W. F., *The Philosophy of History* (New York: Cosimo, 2007 [1899]).

Heien, K. H., 'Local livelihoods and the Bujagali hydro-power dam, Uganda' (MA thesis, Kristiansand, Agder University College, 2007).

Heliodorus, *Æthiopica, An Æthiopian History Written By Helidorus / Englished by Thomas Underdowne, anno 1587. With an Introduction by Charles Whibley* (London: David Nutt, 1895).

Henze, P., 'Consolidation of Christianity around the source of the Blue Nile', in H. Erlich and I. Gershoni (eds), *The Nile. Histories, Cultures, Myths* (London: Lynne Rienner Publishers, 2000), pp. 39–56.

Hermetica, Being English Translations of Hermetic Discourses and Fragments by G. R. S. Mead. Comprising Corpus Hermeticum I–XIV, XVI–XVIII, The Perfect Sermon (Asclepius), Hermetic Excerpts from Stobæus (Ulthar: Celephaïs Press, 2010).

Herodotus, *Herodotus. The Histories. A New Translation by Robin Waterfield* (Oxford: Oxford University Press, 2008).

Hill, R., 'The search for the White Nile's sources: two explorers who failed', *The Geographical Journal* 122/2 (1956), pp. 247–50.

Hocart, A. M., 'Myths in the making', *Folklore* 33/1 (1922), pp. 57–71.

—— *Social Origins* (London: Watts & Co., 1954).

—— *Caste. A Comparative Study* (New York: Russel & Russel, 1968).

—— *The Life-Giving Myth and Other Essays* (London: Methuen & Co Ltd, 1970).

—— *Imagination and Proof: Selected Essays of A. M. Hocart* (Tuscon, AZ: The University of Arizona Press, 1987).

Hochschild, A., *King Leopold's Ghost: A Story of Greed, Terror, and Heroism in Colonial Africa* (Boston, MA: Houghton Mifflin, 1998).

Hoffman, M. A., *Egypt before the Pharaohs* (London: Routledge, 1980).

Hogarth, D. G., D. Freshfield, E. H. Armitage, E. M. Jack, A. L. Mumm and A. B. Fisher, 'New routes on Ruwenzori: discussion', *The Geographical Journal* 69/6 (1927), pp. 525–31.

Hogg, J. E., '"Living water" – "water of life"', *The American Journal of Semitic Languages and Literatures* 42/2 (1926), pp. 131–3.

Homer, *The Odyssey of Homer*, trans. by H. Palmer (Boston: Houghton, Mifflin and Company, 1891).

—— *Homer the Odyssey*, trans. by S. Butler (Orange Street Press Classics, online pdf, 1998).

Hord, J. K., 'Two problems regarding Moses', *Comparative Civilizations Review* 37 (1997), pp. 16–49.

Hornblower, G. D., 'Osiris and his rites: I', *Man* 37 (1937), pp. 153–8.

—— 'Osiris and the fertility-rite', *Man* 41 (1941), pp. 94–103.

—— 'The establishing of Osiris', *Man* 45 (1945), pp. 59–63.

Hornung, E., *Conceptions of God in Ancient Egypt. The One and the Many*, trans. by J. Baines (New York: Cornell University Press, 1982).

—— 'The rediscovery of Akhenaten and his place in religion', *Journal of the American Research Center in Egypt* 29 (1992), pp. 43–9.

Howell, P. P., 'The installation of the Shilluk king', *Man* 44 (1944), pp. 146–7.

—— 'Observations on the Shilluk of the Upper Nile: the laws of homicide and the legal functions of the "reth"', *Africa: Journal of the International African Institute* 22/2 (1952), pp. 97–119.

Hume, W. F., 'Notes on the history on the Nile and its valley', *The Geographical Journal* 27/1 (1906), pp. 52–9.

Hunt, R., 'Frazer, Sir James (1854–1941), in T. Barfield (ed.), *The Dictionary of Anthropology* (Oxford: Blackwell Publishing, 1997), pp. 206–8.

Hutchinson, S. E. and N. R. Pendle, 'Violence, legitimacy, and prophecy: Nuer struggles with uncertainty in South Sudan', *American Ethnologist* 42/3 (2015), pp. 415–30.

Insoll, T., *Material Exploration in African Archaeology* (Oxford: Oxford University Press, 2015).

Jacobs, L., O. Dewitte, J. Poesen, D. Delvaux, W. Thiery and M. Kervyn, 'The Rwenzori Mountains, a landslide-prone region? *Landslides* 13/3 (2016), pp. 519–36.

Jacobs, N., 'The flowing eye: Water management in the Upper Kuruman Valley, South Africa, c. 1800–1962', *The Journal of African History* 37/2 (1996), pp. 237–60.

Jacobson, H., 'Artapanus and the flooding of the Nile', *The Classical Quarterly* 56/2 (2006), pp. 602–3.

Jeal, T., *Livingstone* (London: Heinemann, 1973).

—— *Explorers of the Nile: The Triumph and the Tragedy of a Great Victorian Adventure* (New Haven, CT: Yale University Press, 2011).

Johnson, D. H., 'The historical approach to the study of societies and their environment in the Eastern Upper Nile Plains', *Cashiers d'Études Africaines* 26/101–102 (1986), pp. 131–44.

Johnston, H., *The Uganda Protectorate* (London: Hutchinson, 1902a).

—— 'The Uganda Protectorate, Ruwenzori, and the Semliki Forest', *The Geographical Journal* 19/1 (1902b), pp. 1–39.

—— *The Nile Quest* (London: Lawrence and Bullen, 1903).

—— 'Livingstone as an explorer', *The Geographical Journal* 41/5 (1913), pp. 423–46.

Jones, M., 'The wisdom of Egypt: base and heavenly magic in Heliodoros', *Aithiopika: Ancient Narrative* 4 (2005), pp. 79–98.

Jonglei Investigation Team, 'The Equatorial Nile Project and its effects in Sudan', *Geographical Journal* 119 (1953), pp. 33–48.

Kákosy, L., 'The Nile, Euthenia, and the Nymphs', *The Journal of Egyptian Archaeology* 68 (1982), pp. 290–8.

Kamil, J., *Christianity in the Land of the Pharaohs: The Coptic Orthodox Church* (Cairo: The American University in Cairo Press, 2002).

Kaplan, S., *The Beta Israel (Falasha) in Ethiopia* (New York: New York University Press, 1992).

—— 'The invention of Ethiopian Jews: three models (Trois approches de l' "invention" des Juifs éthiopiens)', *Cahiers d'Études Africaines* 33/132 (1993), pp. 645–58.

—— 'Did Jewish influence reach Ethiopia via the Nile?', in H. Erlich and I. Gershoni (eds), *The Nile. Histories, Cultures, Myths* (London: Lynne Rienner Publishers, 2000), pp. 57–69.

Karadawi, A., 'The smuggling of the Ethiopian Falasha to Israel through Sudan', *African Affairs* 90/358 (1991), pp. 23–49.

Kaspin, D., 'A Chewa cosmology of the body', *American Ethnologist* 23/3 (1996), pp. 561–78.

Kassimir, R., 'Complex martyrs: symbols of Catholic Church formation and political differentiation in Uganda', *African Affairs* 90/360 (1991), pp. 357–82.

Kemp, B., *Ancient Egypt: Anatomy of a Civilization* (London: Routledge, 2006).

Kenny, M. G., 'The powers of Lake Victoria', *Anthropos* 72/5–6 (1977), pp. 717–33.

—— 'Mutesa's crime: hubris and the control of African kings', *Comparative Studies in Society and History* 30/4 (1988), pp. 595–612.

Kerisel, J., *The Nile and its Masters: Past, Present, Future. Source of Hope and Anger* (Rotterdam: A.A. Balkema, 2001).

Kheir, El-Hag H. M., 'A contribution to a textual problem: "Ibn Sulaym al-Aswānī's Kitāb Akhbār al-Nūba wa-l-Maqurra wa-l-Beja wa-l-Nīl"', *Arabica* 36/1 (1989), pp. 36–80.

Kidd, I. G., *Posidonius. Volume II. The Commentary (ii) Fragments 150–293. Cambridge Classical Texts and Commentaries. 14b* (Cambridge: Cambridge University Press, 1998).

Kiernan, J. (ed.), *The Power of the Occult in Modern Africa: Continuity and Innovation in the Renewal of African Cosmologies* (Berlin: Lit Verlag, 2006).

Kinsley, D., *The Goddesses' Mirror. Visions of the Divine from East and West* (Albany: State University of New York Press, 1989).

Kipling, R., *Letters of Travel, 1892–1913* (New York: Doubleday, Page & Company, 1920).

Kjerland, K. A., 'Cattle breed; shillings don't: the belated incorporation of the abaKuria into modern Kenya' (PhD thesis, University of Bergen, 1995).

Kollmann, P., *The Victoria Nyanza: The Land, the Races and Their Customs, with Specimens of Some of the Dialects* (London: Swan Sonnenschein & Co, Ltd, 1899).

Kramer, S. N. and J. Maier, *Myths of Enki, the Crafty God* (Oxford: Oxford University Press, 1989).

Krawiec, R., *Shenoute & the Women of the White Monastery. Egyptian Monasticism in Late Antiquity* (Oxford: Oxford University Press, 2002).

Kyemba, H., *A State of Blood: The Inside story of Idi Amin* (Kampala: Fountain Publishers Ltd, 1997).

Lakoff, G. and M. Johnson, *Philosophy on the Flesh: The Embodied Mind and Its Challenge to Western Thought* (New York: Basic Books, 1999).

Landau, P. S., 'When rain falls: rainmaking and community in a Tsawa village, c. 1870 to recent times', *The International Journal of African Historical Studies* 26/1 (1993), pp. 1–30.

Lane, E. W., *An Account of the Manners and Customs of the Modern Egyptians: Written in Egypt during the Years 1833-1835* (London: Alexander Gardner, 1895).

Lange, H. O. and O. Neugebauer, *Papyrus Carlsberg No. 1. Ein Hieratisch-Demotischer Kosmologischer Text*. Historisk-filologiske Skrifter, Bind 1, Nr. 2. (Copenhagen: Det Kongelige Danske Videnskabernes Selskab, 1940).

Leach, E., *Political Systems of Highland Burma: A Study of Kachin Social Structure* (Boston: Beacon Press, 1954).

Lehner, M., *The Complete Pyramids* (London: Thames and Hudson, 1997).

Leibovitch, J., 'Gods of agriculture and welfare in ancient Egypt: Egyptian theology in the third millennium B.C.', *Journal of Near Eastern Studies* 18/2 (1953), pp. 73–113.

Levack, B. P., *The Witch-Hunt in Early Modern Europe*, 3rd edition (London: Longman, 2006).

—— *Witch-Hunting in Scotland: Law, Politics and Religion* (London: Routledge, 2008).

Lévi-Strauss, C., *Structural Anthropology* (London: Allen Lane the Penguin Press, 1968).

—— *The Raw and the Cooked* (Chicago, IL: The University of Chicago Press, 1969).

—— *Introduction to a Science of Mythology Vol. 4: The Naked Man* (London: Cape, 1981).

—— *Introduction to a Science of Mythology Vol. 2: From Honey to Ashes* (London: Cape, 1983).

—— *Introduction to a Science of Mythology Vol. 3: The Origin of Table Manners*. (Chicago, IL: The University of Chicago Press, 1990).

Lewis, J. P., 'Noah and the flood: in Jewish, Christian, and Muslim tradition', *The Biblical Archaeologist* 47/4 (1984), pp. 224–39.

Lienhardt, G., 'Nilotic kings and their mothers' kin', *Africa: Journal of the International African Institute* 25/1 (1955), pp. 29–42.

—— *Divinity and Experience: The Religion of the Dinka* (Oxford: Oxford at the Clarendon Press, 1961).

Lindsay, J., *Men and Gods on the Roman Nile* (London: Frederick Muller Ltd, 1968).

Livingstone, D., *Missionary Travels and Researches in South Africa* (New York: Harper & Brothers Publishers, 1858).

—— 'Letters of the late Dr. Livingstone', *Proceedings of the Royal Geographical Society of London* 18/3 (1873–4), pp. 255–81.

Lobo, J. *A Voyage to Abyssinia, by Father Jerome Lobo, a Portuguese Missionary. Containing the History, Natural, Civil, and Ecclesiastical, of that Remote and Unfrequented Country, Continued Down to the Beginning of the Eighteenth Century: With Fifteen Dissertations ... Relating to the Antiquities, Government, Religion, Manners, and Natural History, of Abyssina. By M. Le Grand, translated from the French by Samuel Johnson, LL.D. To which are added, various other tracts by the same author, not published by Sir John Hawkins or Mr Stockdale* (London: Elliot and Kay / Edinburgh: C. Elliot, 1789).

Long, C., 'Cosmogony', in M. Eliade (ed.), *The Encyclopedia of Religion*, Vol. 3 (New York: Macmillan Publishing Company, 1993), pp. 94–100.

Long, C. C., 'Uganda and the White Nile', *Journal of the American Geographical Society of New York* 8 (1876), pp. 285–304.

Lonsdale, J., 'Soil, work, civilisation, and citizenship in Kenya', *Journal of Eastern Africa Studies* 2/2 (2008), pp. 305–14.

Lubbock, J., *The Origin of Civilisation and the Primitive Condition of Man: Mental and Social Condition of Savages* (London: Longmans, Green, 1870).

Lucas, G., 'Interpretation in contemporary archaeology: some philosophical issues', in I. Hodder, M. Shanks, A. Alexandri, V. Buchli, J. Carman, J. Last, et al. (eds), *Interpreting Archaeology: Finding Meaning in the Past* (London: Routledge, 1995), pp. 37–44.

Lugira, A., *African Traditional Religion* (New York: Chelsea House, 2009).
Lutfi, H., 'Coptic festivals of the Nile: aberrations of the past?', in T. Philipp and U. Haarmann (eds), *The Mamluks in Egyptian Politics and Society* (Cambridge: Cambridge University Press, 1998), pp. 254–82.
Luther, M., *Selections from his Writing*, edited and with an introduction by J. Dillenberger (New York: Anchor Books, 1962).
Lynam, E., M. Letts, J. W. Crowfoot, R. A. Skelton, E. G. R. Taylor, O. G. S. Crawford, et al., 'Some Medieval theories about the Nile: discussion', *The Geographical Journal* 114/1–3 (1949), pp. 24–9.
Lyons, H. G., 'On the Nile and its variation', *The Geographical Journal* 26/3 (1905), pp. 249–72.
——— 'Some geographical aspects of the Nile', *The Geographical Journal* 32/5 (1908), pp. 449–75.
MacKenzie, D. A., 'Colour symbolism', *Folklore* 33/22 (1922), pp. 136–69.
MacQuitty, W., *Island of Isis: Philae, Temple of the Nile* (London: Macdonald and Jane's, 1976).
Mafeje, A., *Kingdoms of the Great Lakes Region: Ethnography of African Social Formations* (Kampala: Fountain Publishers, 1998).
Mahfouz, N., *Adrift of the Nile*. (New York: Doubleday, 1993 [1966]).
Maitland, A., *Speke and the Discovery of the Source of the Nile* (London: Faber and Faber, 2010 [1971]).
Maloney, C., 'Introduction', in C. Maloney (ed.), *The Evil Eye: Outgrowth of a Symposium on the Evil Eye Belief Held at the 1972 Meeting of the American Anthropological Association* (New York: Columbia University Press, 1976), pp. i–xvi.
Mamdani, M., *When Victims Becomes Killers: Colonialism, Nativism, and the Genocide in Rwanda* (Kampala: Fountain Publishers, 2001).
Mann, T., *Joseph and His Brothers* (New York: Alfred A. Knopf, 1936).
Margoliouth, G., 'The liturgy of the Nile', *Journal of the Royal Asiatic Society of Great Britain and Ireland* (1896), pp. 677–731.
Markham, C. R., 'The Portuguese expeditions to Abyssinia in the fifteenth, sixteenth, and seventeenth centuries', *Journal of the Royal Geographical Society of London* 38 (1868), pp. 1–12.
Marks, H., 'Biblical naming and poetic etymology', *Journal of Biblical Literature* 114/1 (1995), pp. 21–42.
Marx, K. and F. Engels, *On Religion* (Moscow: Progress, 1957).
Maspero, G., *History of Egypt, Chaldea, Syria, Babylonia, and Assyria*, Vol. 2 (London: The Grolier Society Publishers, 1903–4).
Mauss, M., *The Gift* (London: Routledge, 1990).
Mbiti, J., *African Religions and Philosophy* (London: Heinemann, 1969).
Mbogoni, L. E. Y., *Human Sacrifice and the Supernatural in African History* (Dar-es-Salaam: Mkiki Na Nyota, 2013).
McCarthy, D. J., 'The symbolism of blood and sacrifice', *Journal of Biblical Literature* 88/2 (1969), pp. 166–7.
McKittrick, M., '"The wealth of these nations": rain, rulers and Religion on the Cuvelai Floodplain', in T. Tvedt and T. Oestigaard (eds), *A History of Water Vol. 3: The World of Water* (London: I.B.Tauris, 2006), pp. 449–69.
Meier, B., 'Powerful spirits and weak rulers: prophets' authority in Acholi Conflict', in B. Meier and A. S. Steinforth (eds), *Spirits in Politics: Uncertainties of Power and Healing in African Societies* (Frankfurt: Campus Verlag, 2013), pp. 223–45.
Meier, B. and P. Offermann, 'Fighting spirits', A film production of the Cluster of Excellence, Religion and Politics (WWU Münster, 2010).
Meinardus, O. F. A., *Two Thousand Years of Coptic Christianity* (Cairo: The American University in Cairo Press, 2002).

Merleau-Ponty, M., *Sense and Non-Sense* (Evanston, IL: Northwestern University Press, 1964).
Merton, T., *The Monastic Journey* (Kansas City, MI: Sheed Andrews and McMeel, 1977).
Mesaki, S., 'Witchcraft and witch-killings in Tanzania' (PhD thesis, University of Minnesota, 1993).
Meskell, L. and R. A. Joyce, *Embodied Lives: Figuring Ancient Maya and Egyptian Experience* (London: Routledge, 2003).
Messerschmidt, D., *Muktinath: Himalayan Pilgrimage, A Cultural & Historical Guide* (Kathmandu, Nepal: Sahayogi Press, 1992).
Meyer, R. T., *St. Athanasius: The Life of Saint Anthony* (Ancient Christian Writers 10) (Westminster, MD: Newman Press, 1950).
Meyerowitz, E. L. R., *The Divine Kingship in Ghana and Ancient Egypt* (London: Faber and Faber, 1960).
Middleton, J., 'The Yakan or Allah Water Cult among the Lugbara', *The Journal of Anthropological Institute of Great Britain and Ireland* 93/1 (1963), pp. 80–108.
Mikhail, A., 'The Nile and flood in early modern Ottoman Empire', in T. Tvedt and T. Oestigaard (eds), *A History of Water Vol. 3: Water and Food: From Hunter-Gatherers to Global Production in Africa* (London: I.B.Tauris, 2016), pp. 163–84.
Mill, J. S., *Principles of Political Economy* (New York: D. Appleton and Company, 1887).
Moad, E. O., 'A path to the oasis: "Shari'ah" and reason in Islamic moral epistemology', *International Journal for Philosophy of Religion* 62/3 (2007), pp. 135–48.
Mockler-Ferryman, A. F., 'Christianity in Uganda', *Journal of the Royal African Society* 2/7 (1903), pp. 276–91.
Mojsov, B., *Osiris. Death and Afterlife of a God* (Oxford: Blackwell, 2005).
Moorehead, A., *The White Nile* (New York: HarperCollins Publishers, 1960).
—— *The Blue Nile* (London: Hamish Hamilton, 1962).
Morris, B., *Anthropological Studies of Religion: An Introduction* (Cambridge: Cambridge University Press, 1987).
—— *The Power of Animals* (Oxford: Berg, 1998).
Munro-Hay, S., *The Quest for the Ark of the Covenant: The True History of the Tablets of Moses* (London: I.B.Tauris, 2005).
Murchison, R., 'Address to the Royal Geographical Society', *Journal of the Royal Geographical Society of London* 33 (1863), pp. cxiii–cxcii.
Nabofa, M. Y., 'Blood symbolism in African religion', *Religious Studies* 21/3 (1985), pp. 389–405.
Nash, H. S., 'The nature and definition of religion', *The Harvard Theological Review* 6/1 (1913), pp. 1–30.
Nazmi, A., 'The Nile River in Muslim geographical sources', *Studia Arabistyczne i Islamistyczne* 12 (2004), pp. 28–54.
NBI, *State of the River Nile Basin 2012* (Entebbe: The Nile Basin Initiative, 2012).
Nerval, G., *Voyage en Orient II* (Paris: Ancienne Maison Michel Lévy Frère, 1884).
Northrop, H. D., *Wonders of the Tropics or Explorations and Adventures of Henry M. Stanley* (Philadelphia, PA: National Publishing Co., 1889).
Nwauwa, A. O., 'The Europeans in Africa: prelude to Colonialism', in T. Falola (ed.), *Africa. Volume 2: African Cultures and Societies before 1888* (Durham: Carolina Academic Press, 2000), pp. 303–18.
Obeyesekere, G., *Medusa's Hair* (Chicago, IL: The University of Chicago Press, 1981).
—— *The Cult of the Goddess Pattini* (Chicago, IL: The University of Chicago Press, 1984).
—— *Cannibal Talk: The Man-Eating Myth and Human Sacrifice in the South Seas* (Berkeley: University of California Press, 2005).

O'Connor, D. and D. P. Silverman, 'Introduction', in D. O'Connor and D. P. Silverman (eds), *Ancient Egyptian Kingship* (Leiden: E. J. Brill, 1995), pp. xvii–xxvii.

Oestigaard, T., *Death and Life-giving Waters – Cremation, Caste, and Cosmogony in Karmic Traditions* (Oxford: BAR International Series 1353, 2005).

―― 'The materiality of hell: the Christian hell in a world religion context', *Material Religion* 5/3 (2009a), pp. 312–31.

―― (ed.), *Water, Culture and Identity: Comparing Past and Present Traditions in the Nile Basin Region* (Bergen: BRIC Press, 2009b).

―― 'Purification, purgation and penalty: Christian concepts of water and fire in heaven and hell', in T. Tvedt and T. Oestigaard (eds), *A History of Water. Series 2, Vol. 1: The Ideas of Water from Antiquity to Modern Times* (London: I.B.Tauris, 2010), pp. 298–322.

―― *Horus' Eye and Osiris' Efflux: The Egyptian Civilisation of Inundation ca. 3000-2000 BCE* (Oxford: Archaeopress, 2011).

―― *Water, Christianity and the Rise of Capitalism* (London: I.B.Tauris, 2013).

―― *Religion at Work in Globalised Traditions: Rainmamking, Witchcraft and Christianity in Tanzania* (Newcastle: Cambridge Scholars Publishing 2014).

―― *Dammed Divinities: The Water Powers at Bujagali Falls, Uganda* (Current African Issues No. 62) (Uppsala: The Nordic Africa Institute, 2015).

Oestigaard, T. and A. F. Gedef, *The Source of the Blue Nile – Water Rituals and Traditions in the Lake Tana Region* (Newcastle: Cambridge Scholars Publishing, 2013).

Otto, R., *The Idea of The Holy* (Oxford: Oxford University Press, 1958).

Oxtoby, W. G., 'Holy, idea of the', in M. Eliade (ed.), *The Encyclopaedia of Religion*, Vol. 6 (New York: Macmillian, 1987), pp. 431–8.

Packard, R. M., 'Chiefship and the history of Nyavingi possession among the Bashu of Eastern Zaire'. *Africa: Journal of the International African Institute* 52/4 (1982), pp. 67–86+90.

Pankhurst, R., 'Ethiopia's alleged control of the Nile', in H. Erlich and I. Gershoni, (eds), *The Nile: Histories, Cultures, Myths* (Boulder, CO: Lynne Rienner Publishers, 2000), pp. 25–38.

Parfitt, T., 'Rabbi Nahoum's anthropological mission to Ethiopia', in T. Parfitt and E. T. Semi (eds), *The Beta Israel in Ethiopia and Israel* (Surrey: Curzon Press, 1999), pp. 1–14.

Park, T. K., 'Early trends towards stratification: chaos, common property, and flood recession agriculture', *American Anthropologist* 94/1 (1992), pp. 90–117.

Parsons, T., 'The theoretical development of the sociology of religion: a chapter in the history of modern social science', *Journal of the History of Ideas* 5/2 (1944), pp. 176–90.

―― 'Introduction', in M. Weber, *The Sociology of Religion* (Boston, MA: Beacon Press, 1964), pp. xix–lxvii.

Patel, Z., *Unquiet: The Life and Times of Makhan Singh* (Nairobi: Zand Graphics, 2006).

Petrie, W. M. F., *Royal Tombs of the First Dynasty I* (London: Egypt Exploration Fund. Memoir 18, 1900).

―― *Royal Tombs of the Earliest Dynasties II* (London: Egypt Exploration Fund. Memoir 21, 1901).

―― *Tombs of the Courtiers and Oxyrhynkhos* (London: British School of Archaeology in Egypt, 1925).

Philipps, T., 'Etymology of some African names', *The Geographical Journal* 110/1–3 (1947), pp. 142–4.

Philo, *De Vita Mosis*, trans. by F. H. Colson (London: William Heinemann Ltd, 1935).

Philo, *Philo*, with an English translation by F. H. Colson and G. H. Whitaker, in ten volumes, Vol. 1 (London: William Heinemann Ltd, 1962).

Philostratus, *Philostratus: The Life of Apollonius of Tyana: The Epistles of Apollonius and the Treatise of Eusebius*, Vol. 2, trans. by F. C. Conybeare (Cambridge, MA: Harvard University Press, 1912).

Piketty, T., *Capital in the Twenty-First Century* (London: Belknap Press, 2014).
Pliny the Elder, *Natural History: A Selection*, trans. by J. F. Healy (London: Penguin Classics, 2004).
Plutarch, 'Concerning the mysteries of Isis and Osiris', in G. R. S. Mead, *Thrice Greatest Hermes, Part 1* (York Beach, ME: Reed Wheel, 2001).
Popper, W., *The Cairo Nilometer: Studies in Ibn Taghrî Birdî's Chronicles of Egypt 1* (Berkeley: University of California Press, 1951).
Quirin, J., *The Evolution of the Ethiopian Jews: A History of the Beta Israel (Falasha) to 1920* (Philadelphia, PA: University of Philadelphia Press, 1992).
—— 'Caste and class in historical north-west Ethiopia: The Beta Israel (Falasha) and Kemant, 1300–1900', *The Journal of African History* 39/2 (1998), pp. 195–220.
Quirke, S., *Ancient Egyptian Religion* (London: British Museum Press, 1992).
—— *The Cult of Ra. Sun-worship in Ancient Egypt* (London: Thames & Hudson, 2001).
Raglan, L., 'Foreword', in A. M. Hocart, *Social Origins* (London: Watts & Co., 1954), pp. vii–ix.
—— 'Introduction', in M. Hocart, *The Life-Giving Myth* (New York: Grove Press, 1970), pp. 6–8.
Randles, W. G. L., 'South-East Africa as shown on selected printed maps of the sixteenth century', *Imago Mundi* 13 (1956), pp. 69–88.
Ranger, T., 'Territorial cults in the history of Central Africa', *Journal of African History* 14/4 (1973), pp. 581–97.
Rappaport, R. A., *Ritual and Religion in the Making of Humanity* (Cambridge: Cambridge University Press, 2001).
Reade, W., *Savage Africa; Being the Narrative of a Tour in Equatorial, Southwestern, and Northwestern Africa* (New York: Harper, 1864).
Redford, D. B., 'The sun-disc in Akhenaten's program: its worship and antecedents, II', *Journal of the American Research Center in Egypt* 17 (1980), pp. 21–38.
Reid, A., 'The lake, bananas and ritual power in Uganda', in T. Tvedt and T. Oestigaard (eds), *A History of Water, Series 3, Vol. 3. Water and Food: From Hunter-Gatherers to Global Production in Africa* (London: I.B.Tauris, 2016), pp. 277–98.
Reid, R. J., *Political Power in Pre-Colonial Buganda* (Kampala: Fountain Publishers, 2002).
Reinhart, A. K., 'Impurity/no danger', *History of Religions* 30/1 (1990), pp. 1–24.
Relano, F., 'Against Ptolemy: the significance of the Lopes-Pigafetta Map of Africa', *Imago Mundi* 47 (1995), pp. 49–66.
Ribner, D. S. and R. Schindler, 'The crisis of religious identity among Ethiopian immigrants in Israel', *Journal of Black Studies* 27/1 (1996), pp. 104–17.
Rinbochay, L. and J. Hopkins, *Death, Intermediate State and Rebirth in Tibetan Buddhism* (Ithaca, NY: Snow Lion Publications, Inc., 1985).
Roscoe, J., 'Python worship in Uganda', *Man* 9 (1909), pp. 88–90.
—— *The Baganda: An Account of Their Native Customs and Beliefs* (London: Macmillan and Co., 1911).
Ruel, M., 'Non-sacrificial ritual killing', *Man*, 25/2 (1990), pp. 323–35.
Rutten, M., 'Dying cows due to climate change? Drought can never finish the Maasai cattle, only the human mouth can (Maasai saying)', in T. Tvedt and T. Oestigaard (eds), *A History of Water, Series 3, Vol. 3: Water and Food: From Hunter-Gatherers to Global Production in Africa* (London: I.B.Tauris, 2016), pp. 299–331.
Saad, Z. Y., *Royal Excavations at Helwan (1941–1945)* (Cairo: IFAO, 1947).
Saetersdal, T., 'Manica rock-art in contemporary society', in T. Oestigaard (ed.), *Water, Culture and Identity: Comparing Past and Present Traditions in the Nile Basin Region* (Bergen: BRIC Press, 2009), pp. 55–82.

───── 'Rain, snakes and sex – making rain: rock art and rain-making in Africa and America', in T. Tvedt and T. Oestigaard (eds), *A History of Water. Series 2, Vol. 1: Ideas of Water from Antiquity to Modern Times* (London: I.B.Tauris, 2010), pp. 378–404.

Saetersdal, T., L. Niglas and F. Storaas, 'If the Vagina had Teeth'. The NAFA Film Collection. 1 hour (2009).

Said, R., *The River Nile. Geology, Hydrology and Utilization* (Oxford: Pergamon Press, 1993).

Sanders, T., 'Making children, making chiefs: gender, power and ritual legitimacy', *Africa: Journal of the International African Institute* 68/2 (1998), pp. 238–62.

───── 'Rains gone bad, women gone mad: rethinking gender rituals of rebellion and patriarchy', *The Journal of the Royal Anthropological Institute* 6/3 (2000), pp. 469–86.

───── 'Save our skins: structural adjustment, morality and the occult in Tanzania', in H. Moore and T. Sanders (eds), *Magical Interpretation, Material Realities: Modernity, Witchcraft and the Occult in Postcolonial Africa* (London: Routledge, 2001), pp. 160–83.

───── 'Reflections on two sticks: gender, sexuality and rainmaking', *Cahiers d'Études Africaines* 42/166 (2002), pp. 285–313.

───── *Beyond Bodies: Rainmaking and Sense Making in Tanzania* (Toronto: Toronto University Press, 2008).

Schapera, I., *Rain-Making Rites of Tswana Tribes* (African Social Research Documents – Volume 3) (Cambridge: African Studies Centre, 1971).

Schilbrack, K., 'What isn't religion', *The Journal of Religion* 93/3 (2013), pp. 291–318.

───── *Philosophy and the Study of Religions: A Manifesto* (Oxford: Wiley-Blackwell, 2014).

Schlichter, H., 'Ptolemy's topography of Eastern Equatorial Africa', *Proceedings of the Royal Geographical Society and Monthly Record of Geography* 13/9 (1891), pp. 513–53.

Schnepel, B., 'Shilluk royal ceremonies of death and Installation', *Anthropos* 83/4–6 (1988), pp. 433–52.

───── 'Continuity despite and through death: regicide and Royal Shrines among the Shilluk of Southern Sudan', *Africa: Journal of the International African Institute* 61/1 (1991), pp. 40–70.

Schoenbrun, D. L., *A Green Place, A Good Place: Agrarian Change, Gender, and Social Identity in the Great Lakes Region to the 15th Century* (Oxford: James Currey, 1998).

Scribner, R. W., *Popular Culture and Popular Movements in Reformation Germany* (London: The Hambledon Press, 1987).

Seeman, D., 'The question of kinship: bodies and narratives in the beta Israel-European encounter (1860–1920)', *Journal of Religion in Africa* 30/1 (2000), pp. 86–120.

Seide, W. M., 'Lease the land, but use the water: the case of Gambella, Ethiopia', in E. Sanström, A. Jägerskog and T. Oestigaard (eds), *Land and Hydropolitics in the Nile River Basin: Challenges and New Investments* (London: Routledge, 2016), pp. 166–88.

Seligman, C. G., 'The religion of the pagan tribes of the White Nile', *Journal of the International African Institute* 4/1 (1931), pp. 1–21.

───── *Pagan Tribes of the Nilotic Sudan* (London: Routledge & Kegan Paul, 1932).

───── *Egypt and Negro Africa* (London: George Routledge and Sons, Ltd, 1934).

Seligman, C. G. and B. Z. Seligman, 'The Bari', *The Journal of the Royal Anthropological Institute of Great Britain and Ireland* 58 (1928), pp. 409–79.

Seneca, *Seneca in Ten Volumes. VII. Naturales Quaestiones. I.*, with an English translation by T. H. Corcoran (London: William Heinemann Ltd., 1971).

───── *Seneca in Ten Volumes. X. Naturales Quaestiones. II.*, with an English translation by T. H. Corcoran (London: William Heineman Ltd., 1972).

Shenoda, M., 'Displacing Dhimmī, maintaining hope: unthinkable Coptic representations of Fatimid Egypt', *International Journal of Middle East Studies* 39/4 (2007), pp. 587–606.

Shipton, P. M., *The Nature of Entrustment: Intimacy, Exchange, and the Sacred in Africa* (New Haven, CT: Yale University Press, 2007).

Silverman, D. P., 'The nature of Egyptian kingship', in D. O'Connor and D. P. Silverman (eds), *Ancient Egyptian Kingship* (Leiden: E. J. Brill, 1995), pp. 49–92.

Simonse, S., *Kings of Disaster. Dualism, Centralism and the Scapegoat King in Southeastern Sudan* (Leiden: E. J. Brill, 1992).

Simoons, F. J., 'Snow in Ethiopia: a review of the evidence', *Geographical Review* 50/3 (1960), pp. 402–11.

'The Siva-Purana Part III, trans. by a board of scholars', in J. L. Shastri (ed.), *Ancient Indian Tradition & Mythology Vol. 3* (Delhi: Montilal Banarsidass, 1970).

Six, V., 'Water, the Nile, and the Tä'amrä Maryam: miracles of Virgin Mary in the Ethiopian version', *Aethiopica* 2 (1999), pp. 53–68.

Smith, W. S., *The Old Kingdom in Egypt and the Beginning of the First Intermediate Period* (Cambridge: Cambridge University Press, 1962).

Snow, C. P., *The Two Cultures* (Cambridge: Cambridge University Press, 1966).

Speke, J. H., *Journal of the Discovery of the Source of the White Nile* (Edinburgh and London: Blackwood and Sons, 1863).

—— *What Led to the Discovery of the Source of the Nile* (Edinburgh and London: Blackwood and Sons, 1864).

Spencer, D., 'In search of St Luke icons in Ethiopia', *Journal of Ethiopian Studies* X/2 (1972), pp. 67–103.

Spencer, P., 'The Loonkidongi Prophets and the Maasai: protection racket or incipient state?', *Africa: Journal of the International Africa Institute* 61/3 (1991), pp. 334–42.

Spire, F., 'Rain-making in Equatorial Africa', *Journal of the Royal African Society* 5/17 (1905), pp. 15–21.

Stacey, T., *Tribe: The Hidden History of the Mountains of the Moon: An Autobiographical Study* (London: Stacey International, 2003).

Stam, N., 'The religious conceptions of some tribes of Buganda (British Equatorial Africa)', *Anthropos* 3/2 (1908), pp. 213–18.

Stanley, H. M., 'A geographical sketch of the Nile and Livingstone (Congo) basins', *Proceedings of the Royal Geographical Society of London*, 22/6 (1877–8), pp. 382–410.

—— *In Darkest Africa or the Quest Rescue and Retreat of Emin Governor of Equatoria*, Vol. 2 (London: Sampson Low, Marston, Searle and Rivington, 1890).

Stephens, R., *A History of African Motherhood: The Case of Uganda, 700-1900* (Cambridge: Cambridge University Press, 2013).

Stocking, G. W., *Victorian Anthropology* (New York: The Free Press, 1987).

Stokes, M. C., 'Hesiodic and Milesian cosmogonies: II', *Phronesis* 8/1 (1963), pp. 1–34.

Stone, C. P., 'The navigation of the Nile', *Science* 4/93 (1884), pp. 456–7.

Strang, V., *The Meaning of Water* (Oxford: Berg, 2004).

—— 'Common senses: water, sensory experience and the generation of meaning', *Journal of Material Culture* 10/1 (2005), pp. 92–120.

—— 'Fluid consistencies: material relationality in human engagements with water', *Archaeological Dialogues* 21/2 (2014), pp. 133–50.

Stroeken, K., *Moral Power: The Magic of Witchcraft* (Oxford: Berghahn Books, 2010).

Sulas, F., 'Aksum: water and urbanization in northern Ethiopia', in T. Tvedt and T. Oestigaard (eds), *A History of Water. Series 3, Vol. 1: Water and Urbanization* (London: I.B.Tauris, 2014), pp. 175–97.

Tafla, B., 'The father of rivers: the Nile in Ethiopian literature', in H. Erlich and I. Gershoni (eds), *The Nile: Histories, Cultures, Myths* (London: Lynne Rienner Publishers, 2000), pp. 153–70.

Tagher, J., *Christians in Muslim Egypt: An Historical Study of the Relations between Copts and Muslims from 640 to 1922* (Altenberge: Oros Verlag, 1998).

Talbot, M. R. and A. J. Williams, 'Cenozoic evolution of the Nile basin', in H. J. Dumont (ed.), *The Nile: Origin, Environments, Limnology and Human Use* (Leiden: Springer, 2009), pp. 37–60.

Talle, A., '"Serious games": licenses and prohibitions in Maasai sexual life', *Africa: Journal of the International Africa Institute* 77/3 (2007), pp. 351–70.

Tamrat, T., 'A short note on the traditions of pagan resistance to the Ethiopian church (14th and 15th Centuries)', *Journal of Ethiopian Studies* X/1 (1972a), pp. 137–50.

—— *Church and State in Ethiopia: 1270–1527* (Oxford: Clarendon Press, 1972b).

Tanner, R. E. S., 'Hysteria in Sukuma medical practice', *Africa: Journal of International African Institute* 25/3 (1955), pp. 274–9.

—— 'An introduction to the spirit being of the Northern Basukuma', *Anthropological Quarterly* 29/2 (1956), pp. 45–56.

—— 'The spirits of the dead: an introduction to the ancestor worship of the Sukuma of Tanganyika', *Anthropological Quarterly* 32/2 (1959), pp. 108–24.

Taylor, C. C., *Sacrifice as Terror: The Rwandan Genocide of 1994* (Oxford: Berg, 1999).

—— 'The sovereign as savage: the pathos of ethno-nationalist passion', in B. Kapferer and B. E. Bertelsen (eds), *Crisis of the State: War and Social Upheaval* (New York and Oxford: Berghahn, 2009), pp. 163–86.

—— 'Genocide and the religious imaginary in Rwanda', in M. Juergensmeyer, M. Kitt and M. Jerryson (eds), *The Oxford Handbook of Religion and Violence* (Oxford: Oxford University Press, 2013), pp. 269–79.

Tegegne, M., *'Gojjam' the Stigma: An Abyssinian Pariah* (Addis Ababa: Guihon Books, 1993).

te Velde, H., *Seth, God of Confusion: A Study of His Role in Egyptian Mythology and Religion* (Leiden: E. J. Brill, 1967).

Thomas, K., *Religion and the Decline of Magic: Studies in Popular Beliefs in Sixteenth and Seventeenth Century in England* (London: Weidenfeld and Nicolson, 1971).

Thomas, L. M., *Politics of the Womb: Women, reproduction, and the State of Kenya* (Berkeley: University of California Press, 2003).

Thompson, T. L., *The Origin Tradition of Ancient Israel* (Sheffield: Sheffield Academic Press, 1987).

—— *The Bible in History: How Writers Create a Past* (London: Jonathan Cape, 1999).

Thomson, J., *A Voice from the Nile and Other Poems* (London: Reeves and Turner, 1884).

Trevor-Roper, H., *The Rise of Christian Europe* (London: Thames and Hudson, 1965).

Trigger, B., *Understanding Early Civilizations: A Comparative Study* (Cambridge: Cambridge University Press, 2003).

Troy, L., *Patterns of Queenship in Ancient Egyptian Myth and History* (Uppsala: Acta Universitatis Upsaliensis. Uppsala Studies in Ancient Mediterranean and Near Eastern Civilizations 14, 1986).

Turner, V., *Revelation and Divination in Ndembu Ritual* (Cornell, NY: Cornell University Press, 1975).

Tvedt, T., *En reise i vannets historie – fra regnkysten til Muscat* (Oslo: Cappelens Forlag AS, 1997).

—— *Verdenbilder og selvbilder. En humanitær stormakts intellektuelle historie* (Oslo: Universitetsforlaget, 2002).

—— *The River Nile in the Age of the British: Political Ecology and the Quest for Economic Power* (London: I.B.Taurus, 2004).

―――― 'Why England and not China and India? Water systems and the history of the industrial revolution', *Journal of Global History* (2010a), pp. 29–50.

―――― 'Water: a source of wars or a pathway to peace? An empirical critique of two dominant schools of thought on water and international politics', in T. Tvedt, G. Chapman and R. Hagen (eds), *A History of Water, Series 3, Vol. 3: Water, Geopolitics and the New World Order* (London: I.B.Tauris, 2010b), pp. 78–108.

―――― 'Water systems, environmental history and the deconstruction of nature', *Environment and History* 16 (2010c), pp. 143–66.

―――― 'Hydrology and empire: the Nile, water imperialism and the partition of Africa', *The Journal of Imperial and Commonwealth History* 39/2 (2011), pp. 173–94.

―――― *Nilen – historiens elv* (Oslo: Aschehoug, 2012).

―――― *Water and Society – Changing Perceptions of Societal and Historical Development* (London: I.B.Tauris, 2016).

Tvedt, T. and T. Oestigaard, 'Introduction', in T. Tvedt and T. Oestigaard (eds), *A History of Water Vol. 3: The World of Water* (London: I.B.Tauris, 2006), pp. ix–xxii.

―――― 'A history of the ideas of water: deconstructing nature and constructing society', in T. Tvedt and T. Oestigaard (eds), *A History of Water. Series 2, Vol. 1: The Ideas of Water from Antiquity to Modern Times* (London: I.B.Tauris, 2010), pp. 1–36.

Vasunia, P., *The Gift of the Nile: Hellenizing Egypt from Aeschylus to Alexander* (Berkeley: University of California Press, 2001).

Veilleux, A., 'Shenoute or the pitfalls of Monasticism: preface', in D. N. Bell, *Besa: The Life of Shenoute: Introduction, Translation, and Notes* (Kalamazoo, MI: Cistercian Publications, 1983), p. vxv.

Verner, M., *The Pyramids: Their Archaeology and History* (London: Atlantic Books, 2003).

Vijverberg, J., F. A. Sibbing and E. Dejen, 'Lake Tana: source of the Blue Nile', in H. J. Dumont (ed.), *The Nile. Origin, Environments, Limnology and Human Use* (Leiden: Springer, 2009), pp. 163–92.

Vincent, A. T., 'Mytho-theology in ancient Egypt', *Journal of American Research Center in Egypt* 25 (1988), pp. 169–83.

Vivian, T., 'Introduction: hearing God's call', in Athanasius, 'Life of Anthony', trans. by T. Vivian, *Society of Coptic Studies: Coptic Church Review* 15/1–2 (1994), pp. 99–101.

Wainwright, G. A., 'Some celestial associations of Min', *The Journal of Egyptian Archaeology* 21/2 (1935), pp. 152–70.

―――― *The Sky-Religion in Egypt: Its Antiquity and Effects* (Cambridge: Cambridge at the University Press, 1938).

―――― 'Herodotus II, 28 on the sources of the Nile', *The Journal of Hellenic Studies* 73 (1953), pp. 104–7.

―――― 'The origin of storm-gods in Egypt', *The Journal of Egyptian Archaeology* 49 (1963), pp. 13–20.

Waller, H., *The Last Journals of David Livingstone in Central Africa: From Eighteen Hundred and Sixty-Five to His Death* (New York: Harper & Brothers Publishers, 1875).

Walsh, L., 'The rhetoric of oracles', *Rhetoric Society Quarterly* 33/3 (2003), pp. 55–78.

Warburg, G. R., 'Islam and politics in Egypt: 1952–80', *Middle Eastern Studies* 18/2 (1982), pp. 131–57.

―――― 'The Sharia in Sudan: implementation and repercussions, 1983–1989', *Middle East Journal* 44/4 (1990), pp. 624–37.

―――― 'The Nile in Egyptian-Sudanese relations, 1956–1995', in H. Erlich and I. Gershoni (eds), *The Nile. Histories, Cultures, Myths* (Boulder, CO and London: Lynne Rienner Publishers, 2000), pp. 227–34.

―――― 'The search for the sources of the White Nile and Egyptian-Sudanese relations', *Middle Eastern Studies* 43/3 (2007), pp. 475–86.

Ward, W. A., 'The philosophy of death in Coptic epitaphs', *Journal of Bible and Religion* 25/1 (1957), pp. 34–40.
Weber, M., *The Religion of China: Confucianism and Taoism* (Glencoe, IL: The Free Press, 1951).
—— *The Sociology of Religion* (Boston, MA: Beacon Press, 1964).
—— *The Protestant Ethic and the Spirit of Capitalism* (London: Routledge, 2006 [1930]).
Werbner, R., *Divination's Grasp: African Encounters with the Almost Said* (Bloomington and Indianapolis: Indiana University Press, 2015).
Wheeler, B. M., 'Moses or Alexander: early Islamic exegesis of Qur'ān', *Journal of Near Eastern Studies* 57/3 (1998), pp. 191–215.
Wenke, R., 'Egypt: origins of complex societies', *Annual Review of Anthropology* 18 (1989), pp. 129–55.
—— *The Ancient Egyptian State: The Origins of Egyptian Culture (c. 8000–2000 BC)* (Cambridge: Cambridge University Press, 2009).
Westerlund, D., *African Indigenous Religions and Disease Causation: Studies of Religion in Africa* 28 (Leiden: E. J. Brill, 2006).
Wijsen, F. and R. Tanner, *Seeking a Good Life: Religion and Society in Usukuma, Tanzania* (Nairobi: Paulines Publications Africa, 2000).
—— *'I am Just a Sukuma': Globalization and Identity Construction in Northwest Tanzania* (Amsterdam: Rodopi, 2002).
Wild, R. A., *Water in the Cultic Worship of Isis and Sarapis* (Leiden: E. J. Brill, 1981).
Wilford, F., 'An essay on the sacred isles in the west, with other essays connected with that work', *Asiatic Researches* 8 (1808), pp. 245–54.
Wilkinson, T. A. H., *Early Dynastic Egypt* (London: Routledge, 1999).
—— 'What a king is this: Narmer and the concept of the ruler', *The Journal of Egyptian Archaeology* 86 (2000), pp. 23–32.
Williams, G., 'Reading the waters: Seneca on the Nile in "Natural Questions" Book 4A', *The Classic Quarterly* 58/1 (2008), pp. 218–42.
Williams, M., 'River sediments', *Philosophical Transactions of the Royal Society* 370 (2012), pp. 2093–122.
Williams, R., *Keywords: A Vocabulary of Culture and Society* (London: Fontana/Croom Helm, 1980).
Wilson, J. A., *The Culture of Ancient Egypt* (Chicago, IL: The University of Chicago Press, 1951).
Winkler, A., 'The efflux that issued from Osiris: a study on rdw in the Pyramid Texts', *Göttinger Miszellen* 211 (2006), pp. 125–39.
Wittfogel, K. A., *Oriental Despotism: A Comparative Study of Total Power* (New Haven, CT: Yale University Press, 1957).
Wlodarczyk, N., 'African traditional religion and violence', in M. Juergensmeyer, M. Kitt and M. Jerryson (eds), *The Oxford Handbook of Religion and Violence* (Oxford: Oxford University Press, 2013), pp. 153–66.
World Bank, *Accountability at the World Bank: The Inspection Panel 10 Years On* (Washington: World Bank, 2003).
World Bank, *Report No. 44977-UG. The Inspection Panel. Investigation Report. Uganda: Private Power Generation (Bujagali) Project (Guarantee No. B0130-UG). August 29, 2008* (Washington: World Bank, 2008).
Young, D. W., *Coptic Manuscripts from the White Monastery: Works of Shenute* (Wien: Hollinek, 1993).
Yuzbashi, X., 'Tribes on the Upper Nile: the Bari', *Journal of the Royal African Society* 4/14 (1905), pp. 226–31.
Zikra, A. B., *One Home, One Family, One Future* (Bloomington, IN: AuthorHouse, 2009).

Index

Please note that page references to Figures will be in *italics*. Page references to Notes will be followed by the letter 'n' and number of the Note.

Abay Ras (source of Abay) 117
ABBA (Swedish group) 205–6, 207
Abinas (river spirit) 59, 117, 118, 122–4, 127
    Woyto of Lake Tana, among 108–16
ablution 83, 107, 115, 380
Abo Monastery, Tis Abay 86
Abuna Thadeos 113
Abydos, Egypt 267, 268, 269, 272, 312
Abyssinia 2, 17, 64, 65, 356
    see also Blue Nile, Abyssinia; Ethiopia
d'Accoramboni, Marchese Flippo 70
Achilles Tatius 341
Adam and Eve 20, 78, 97
Adrift on the Nile (Mahfouz) 371
Aeschylus (525–456 BC) 64
Africa 31, 37, 44, 88
    see also Ethiopia; Kenya; Lake Tana, Ethiopia; Lake Victoria, Uganda; Tanzania; Uganda
    cosmology 19, 213
    Equatorial 241
    sub-Saharan Africa 60, 136
    traditional religions 33, 43, 149, 308
    traditional societies 240
Agatharchides 18, 342
agriculture 49, 50, 262
Aha, King of Egypt 269, 270
Aigyptos (Nile) 24
Aire River, Bradford (UK) 56
Akagera River 230
Akhenaten 336
Aksum, Ethiopia 357
Albright, William F. 16, 340, 393n28
Aldred, C. 257, 412n206, 412n210, 417n168
Alexander the Great 342–4
Ali, Abdul Hassan 199
Alice Auma/Lakwena 184–6, 188–90, 193, 234
Allah 42, 43, 55, 110, 366, 369, 371
Allah Water Cult (Yakan) 232–4
Almeida, Father Manoel de 67
Alvarez, Father 65, 103

ambrosia 23
Amda-Seyon rule (1314–44), Lake Tana region 88–9
Amenemhet I, King 314
Amenhotep IV, King 334
Amin, Idi 232, 233, 234
Anaxagoras (*c.* 500–428 BC) 18, 64
ancestors 43, 215, 216, 217, 240
ancestral spirits 43, 163, 173, 194, 244, 248, 316
ancient Egypt *see* Egypt/ancient Egypt
Ancient Greeks 18, 19, 23, 197
    see also Aristotle
Ancient Romans 18, 19
Angel Gabriel 96
The Angel of the Waters (Shenoute) 348
animal sacrifice 121
    see also sacrifices
    cattle 101, 133
    Ethiopia 71, 92, 115–18
    Great Sacrifice (calf sacrifice) 116–18
    Uganda 132–3
Ankoli Kingdom 204
al-Antākī 363
Anthes, R. 285, 286, 415n111
St Anthony 347
anthropology 222
Apollonius 26
appeasement ceremonies 141–2, 163
Archangel Michael 344
Aristides 341
Aristotle 18, 23, 197
Ark of Noah 99, 100, 103
Ark of St Michael 103
Ark of the Covenant 89, 99, 100, 103, 106
Artapanus 339
Ashe, Robert 130
A'shihi St Michael church (Gish Abay) 74
Assmann, Jan 317, 321, 333–5, 336
al-Aswāni, Ibn Sulaym 359–60
Aswan High Dam 16, 26, 302, 376
Atbara River 300, 302, 332, 372, 424n111

climate 355, 356
deluge 331, 354–8
  Khashm al-Girba Dam on 355
Athanasius of Alexandria, Bishop 329, 330, 331
atheists *see* non-believers
Atlas Mountains 197–8
Atum (sun god) 265–6
Augustine (Saint) 41
Auma, Alice *see* Alice Auma/Lakwena
Axum, Northern Ethiopia 68, 89, 91, 92, 93, 106
Azande tribe, South Sudan 236–7

Babylonian Talmud 342
Bachelard, G. 22
Bahima (pastoral people) 204
Bahir Dar, Lake Tana 95, 98–101
  Woyto of Lake Tana living in 108, 109
Bahire Timiket (baptismal pool) 98–102
Bahr al-Nīl (The sea of Nile) 360
Baines, John 259
Baker, Samuel W. 9, 31, 200, 207, 333, 355–6
Banda, Hastings (Malawi's first president) 7
baptism 126, 165, 379, 380
  of Jesus 53, 95–8, 100
  at Timkat festival 95–104
  water and religion 48–9
  Western versus Eastern churches 96
  and White Nile source 379–81
Bari tribe, Equatorial Africa 241, 243, 248
  iron-workers 244
  rainmaking 244, 245
Barnabas, Abune 101
Barth, F. 50, 51, 397n150
Behrend, Heike 136
Beke, Charles T. 72, 73–6, 383
Bell Lager Beer 4
Benedict XII, Pope 373
Bent Pyramid, Dashur 308
Besa 348
Beta Israel (Ethiopian Jews) 77, 89, 104–8
Bible *see* Deuteronomy; Genesis; Hebrew Bible; New Testament; Old Testament
Bicolo, Gish Abay 76
blood 61, 233, 308
  see also sacrifices
  animal 74, 112, 117, 132–3, 156–7, 165, 216–17
  and Christ/Christianity 350, 378
  coagulated 307
  on dry land 341
  female 308, 386
  fluidity 107, 285

human 134, 176, 178, 226, 233
menstruation 119, 229
milk, mixed with 227
Red Nile 306, 307, 341
sacrifices 92, 112, 114, 117, 132–4, 143, 178, 182, 184, 234
bloodthirsty spirits 59, 174–8
Blue Nile, Abyssinia (Ethiopia) 10, 18, 58, 80, 81, 111, 300, 301
  see also Ethiopia
  Abay (Ethiopian name for) 78, 79, 80, 114, 115, 117, 118, 124
  compared to White Nile 301
  rituals 73–4
  source 58, 59, 65–8, 376
    difficulties presented by canyons 67
    Gish Abay as 2, 28, 77–8
    'God of Peace' 71
    length 74–5
    visits by Beke (1842) 73, 74
body fluid metaphors
  see also blood; menstruation; milk
  and Maasai (Kenyan pastoralists) 225–7
  semen 226
  sexuality 219–21, 226
  and water 219–23
  wetness, of women 221
boiling 227
Book of the Dead 279, 293
Born Again Christians 379
Brandström, Per 213
breast milk 227, 309
  Virgin Mary 350–3
'bride'-pillar 368
Bridges, R. C. 130–1
Bruce, James 66, 68–71, 72–3, 76, 103–4, 108, 125, 127, 356, 357
Brück, Joanna 222
Bubembe Island, Lake Victoria 132
Budge, E. A. W. 302
Budhagaali (water spirit) 6–7, 38, 39, 40, 55, 150, 155, 166, 189, 237
  Bujagali Dam, blocking 139–44
  as a Busoga spirit 152
  compared to other spirits 178
  importance of 146, 169
  Jaja Bujagali as 39th incarnation 128, 171, 231
  miracles of 160–1
  mythology 172
  relocating of 145
Buganda, Lake Victoria 128, 129, 134
  see also Lake Victoria, Uganda; Uganda

Bugeta tributary 76
Bujagali, Jaja (healer) 55, 59, 139, 141–7, 160, 163, 165, 167, 168, 170–6, 183, 234
  as 39th incarnation of Budhagaali 128, 171, 231
  perceptions of 171, 174
  powers 38–40, 193, 194
Bujagali Dam, Uganda 38–40, 59, 165, 169, 182
  Budhagaali (water spirit) blocking 139–44
  rituals 153, 182
Bujagali Energy Limited (BEL) 142
Bujagali Falls, Uganda 39, 55–6, 59, 128, 129, 143, 144, 150, 164, 174, 176, 181, 192, 231, 233
Bujagali hydropower project 143, 165, 402n47
Bujet (female donor of money for church at Gish Abay) 75–6
Bunyoro, Kingdom of 137
Burton, Richard 208
Burundi 15
Busoga Kingdom, Uganda 2, 4, 6, 49, 139, 140, 141, 145, 169
  witchcraft 178–9
Butzer, K. 310, 419n229, 419n231, 419n232

Callisthenes 18
Calvinism 53
Campbell, Joseph 27, 29, 222, 223
Canal of the Commander of the Faithful 366
cannibalism 208, 233
Carneiro, Robert 260
Cataracts, ancient Egypt 26
  First Cataract 15, 16, 54, 294, 319, 327, 328, 332, 340
catfish 110, 118–19
Catherine, Empress of Russia 70
Catholicism 149
cattle 232, 236, 238, 239, 244, 246, 249, 250, 358
  fertility issues 53, 120, 254
  versus hippos 124
  and Maasai (Kenyan pastoralists) 225–7
  sacrifices 101, 133
celestial milk 309
ceremonies
  see also death and death practices; funerals
  appeasement 141–2, 163
  cult 232
  death 252
  rainmaking 212, 216, 245
  Timkat festival, Ethiopia see Timkat festival, Ethiopia
Chadzuka, chiefdom of 219–20
Champollion 259

Chaos 263, 264
  Order from 265
Che Abinas see Abinas (river spirit)
Cheesman, R. E. 73, 75–6, 110, 118
Chélu, M. 15–16
Cheops 32
Chikondo (fishing village) 158
child sacrifice 174, 176, 183
Childe, V. Gordon 260–1
Christianity
  see also baptism; Jesus Christ; New Testament; Virgin Mary
  and African traditional religions 149
  and blessing of water 83–4
  and Blue Nile 81
  Born Again Christians 379
  Calvinism 53
  Catholicism 149
  conversion to 209
  Coptic see Coptic Christianity
  cosmology 59, 158
  Ethiopian Orthodox 82, 85, 88
  fasting in 116, 344, 349
  and Gihon River 78
  God in 42, 46, 159
  and here and now 214
  history 19
  Lake Tana, Ethiopia 85, 88–94
  and Moses 333
  mythology 19, 59
  Pauline concept of the Church 320
  Pentecostal 149, 195
  pre-Christian practices at Gish (1770) 70–3
  Protestantism 53
  revelation 97
  role of Nile in history 2, 11
  salvation 83, 93, 95, 96, 100–1
  as transcendental religion 42
  Trinity (Father, Son and Holy Spirit) 97, 102
  water, place of 20, 75
  as world religion 51
Christianization 88
Christmas Day 96
Churchill, Winston 138
civilization, river 257, 258–326
  see also Egypt/ancient Egypt
  commerce, role in civilization process 207
  Egyptian water-world 260–3
  Nile and Egyptian gods 258–9
  primeval waters 263–6
  Seth (traditional sky fertility god) 273–6
Clement of Alexandria 350

climate
    see also rain; rainmaking; rain-stopping; snow
    and annual flood, changes in 310–11
    Atbara River 355, 356
    Egypt 257
    Ruwenzori Mountains, eastern Africa 202, 203
    Uganda 152
Coffin Texts 297, 307
commerce, role in civilization process 207
Condon, M. A. 134–5, 401n24
construction accidents 182
cooking 227
Cooley, W. D. 384
Coptic Christianity 309, 344–9, 371
    beginning of Coptic era (AD 284) 346
    iconography 350
    martyrdom 345, 346
    Nile festivals, in Egypt 362, 364
    and Virgin Mary 350
corpses 137, 206, 215, 233, 234, 245, 287, 297, 315, 317
    see also death and death practices
    decaying 61, 296
    in lakes/rivers 114, 231, 233
    of Osiris 61, 296, 299, 318
    washing of 249
Cory, Hans 216–17
cosmogonic religions 42
cosmology 4, 10, 29–30, 136, 149
    African 18, 213
    approaching 49
    Christianity 59
    Egyptian 16, 32, 332, 340
    Greek 197
    invisible world 213
    rainmaking 211, 223, 230
    and Rwanda 228
    traditional 158, 159
    water 2, 6, 7, 8, 18, 71, 127, 231, 248, 313
    Woyto of Lake Tana 114, 115
Cosmos (sixth-century Egyptian monk) 64
cosmos, creation of 263–6
creation waters 19
Criers of the Nile 367–9
Crophi mountain 14
crucifixion 28, 51, 93, 98, 107
Crusaders 65
culture
    definition challenges 30

Gish Abay, cultural and religious significance 2
'two cultures' 34
cyclical concept 300

Da Gama, Christopher 65
Daga Istafanos monastery 352
dams
    Aswan High Dam 16, 26, 302, 376
    Bujagali *see* Bujagali Dam
    damming of Lake Victoria 138
    Owen Falls *see* Owen Falls Dam, Uganda
d'Angelo, Jacopo 10
D'Anville (French geographer) 68
Darkest Africa (Stanley) 198
Darwin, Charles 333
David (Dawit), King 98, 106
Dawit of Ethiopia (1380–1412) 374
Dawson, C. 13, 392n21
de Joinville, Jean 373
de Nervall, Gérad 341
death and death practices 133, 315–17
    see also corpses; funerals
    among Sukuma ethnic group 215
    killing of rainmaker 241–5, 249–51
    and Rwanda 229
    in Uganda 135, 137, 178–9
    witchcraft 178–9
    worlds of death 315–17
Death and Salvation in Ancient Egypt (Assmann) 317
Debra Mariam Church, Debra Mariam Island 113
Debra Qusquam Monastery, Egypt 93
Debre Maryam Monastery, Lake Tana 113
Deluge, the 29, 34, *35*, 53, 354, 362, 372
    see also floods
    Universal 354
Deng/Dengit (great rain) 246
Dengel, Lebna 375
'Desert Fathers' 346
Deuteronomy 45
Devil 34, 73, 83, 111, 116, 187, 276, 278, 324
    Adam as servant of/Eve as slave of 97
    and pre-Christian practices 70, 72
Diadji, I. N. 19, 393n34
Dicaearchus 18
Dickson, D. R. 15, 20, 393n26
Dimisqi (Arab geographer) 197
Dinka people, Upper Nile 246–7, *247*, 248, 250, 253–4

Agar Dinka 232
  rainmaking 237, 242, 244, 246, 248
  religious beliefs 244, 246, 248, 411n182
Diocletan (Roman emperor) 346
Diodorus Siculus 27, 343
Dionysios (bishop) 341, 361
divination 135
divine revelations 52
divine water 9, 20, 231, 234, 341
  divine water agency and holy, sacred and neutral waters 52–63
  Gish Abay, Ethiopia 82
  rainmaking 243–56
diviners *see* healers/diviners
Djed pillar 312
Djoser, King of Egypt 258, 268, 272, 273, 283, 311
Doran, S. S. 243
Douglas, Mary 34
Dumbbell Island 140, 171
Durkheim, Émile 33, 34–5, 37, 39
  atheism of 34, 36
Dworkin, Ronald 41

Earthly Paradise 65
Eastern Orthodox Church 96
eating 136
Eden, Garden of 19, 20, 77, 342
Egypt/ancient Egypt xiv, 10, 16, 17, 19, 60, 61, 71, 221, 255–7, 289, 300, 303, 309, 325, 326, 329, 352, 354
  see also Horus (ancient Egyptian god); Nile Basin; Nile River; Osiris (ancient Egyptian king); Seth (traditional sky fertility god)
  Abydos 267, 268, 269, 272, 312
  and Africa 31
  as 'black land' 289
  civilization (*c.* 3000–332 BCE) ix, 58, 260, 267, 273, 312, 314
  climate 257, 310–11
  and Coptic Christianity 371
  cosmology 17, 32, 332, 340
  Dynasties 27, 301, 311
    Pre-dynastic (*c.* 5500–3100 BCE) 263, 267, 270, 274, 312
    First (3000–2890 BCE) 262, 266–71, 272, 275, 312, 313
    Second (2890–686 BCE) 267, 268, 271–3, 276, 310, 311
    Third (2686–613 BCE) 268, 271–3, 310, 311
    Fourth (2613–498 BCE) 269, 274, 309, 310, 311
    Fifth (2465–323 BCE) 269, 275, 276, 310, 311
    Sixth (2345–181 BCE) 286
    Old Kingdom (2686–2181 BCE) 263, 267, 268, 298, 309, 312, 314, 317
    Middle Kingdom (2040–1797 BCE) 298
    New Kingdom (1567–1070 BCE) 309, 317
    Eighteenth Dynasty (1570–1293 BCE) 260, 312
    Nineteenth Dynasty (1293–1185 BCE) 280
    Twentieth Dynasty (1185–1070 BCE) 280
  economy 262
  and Ethiopia 330
  First Cataract 15, 16, 54, 294, 319, 327, 328, 332, 340
  flows of continuity in 256–7
  Gerzean period (*c.* 3500–3200 BCE) 285
  as 'gift of the Nile' 369
  Holy Family in 91, 92, 94, 344
  ideology 291
  and Islam 359, 361–2
  language 290
  literature 290
  Lower Egypt 25, 267, 272–5, 282, 283, 290
  mythology 283–4, 291, 314
  natural features 265
  Nile and Egyptian gods 258–9
  nomes, division into 267, 320
  origin of Egyptian state 262
  Pharaonic period 258, 260, 261, 263, 264, 274
  pyramids *see* pyramids
  red crown 266–7
  regulation of the Nile 47
  religion 15, 260, 290–3, 294, 323, 329, 343, 344, 352
  Royal Tombs 268, 269
  and Shilluk beliefs 256
  sun and water
    Crown as Eye 284–5
    Eye as water 284
    movement and cosmic demarcation 283–4
    purity 106
  sun as god in 258

Upper Egypt 25, 262, 266, 273–5, 282, 283, 290, 312, 347, 352
warmth and heat 285
water-world 260–3
white crown 266, 267
Egyptian Delta 15
The Elementary Forms of Religious Life (Durkheim) 34–5
Elephantine, Nile source at 287, 294–6, 308, 317, 319, 320, 328
and Cataracts 15, 26, 319
Eliade, Mircea 23, 36, 40, 41, 394n52, 394n54
Elijah 46
energy 28
Ennead 264
Epiphany 95, 96, 309–10
Western Church on 103
Equatorial Zone 202
Eratosthenes 18
Erman, Adolf 262
Ermuthis 337
Ernutet (goddess of grain) 321
eschatology, universal 51
Ethiopia 14, 15, 18, 52, 72, 88, 103, 105, 330, 372
see also Ethiopian Orthodox Church; Gish Abay, Ethiopia; Lake Tana, Ethiopia
animal sacrifice 71, 92, 115–18
Axum, Northern Ethiopia 68, 89, 91, 92, 93, 106
Beta Israel (Ethiopian Jews) 77, 89, 104–8
flag 88
Gambella region 236
Holy Family in 91, 92, 93
Timkat festival 74, 81, 94, 95–104
Ethiopian Orthodox Church xvi, 93–7, 100, 105, 106, 116, 345
and Blue Nile 82, 85
and holy water 52–3, 59, 94
and Lake Tana, Ethiopia 88, 91
Tewahedo Church 97
Timkat festival *see* Timkat festival, Ethiopia
ethnologists, British Victorian 208
Eucharist 350
Euripides (*c.* 484–407 BC) 64
Euthymenes 18
Evans-Pritchard, E. E. 34, 236–9
Witchcraft, Oracles and Magic Among the Azande 236
Eve *see* Adam and Eve
existentialism 30

Exodus 336, 337–8, 340
exorcism of spirits 83
eye metaphors 279
Eye of Horus 278–83, 284, 297, 298
Ezekiel 379

Falasha (Ethiopian Jews) 89, 107
farming 225
see also agriculture
fasting 82, 100, 101, 106, 112, 345, 349
in Christianity 116, 344, 349
fat 136
Feast of the Cross 349
fecundity figures 259, 309
fertility 80, 119, 156, 220, 241, 245, 259, 264, 273, 292, 295, 297, 307, 314
cattle 53, 120, 254
fertility-gods 273, 278, 280, 283, 336
land 25, 200, 215, 241, 288
rituals 221, 276, 314
'Fighting spirits' (film) 189
Finnestad, Ragnild 264
First Cataract, ancient Egypt 15, 16, 54, 294, 319, 327, 332, 340
fish and fishing 109, 118–19, 158
floods
see also rain; rainmaking; water
annual 61, 71, 235, 259, 310–11, 357
Atbara River 331, 354–8
Blue Nile, Abyssinia 10
Deluge, the 29, 34, *35*, 53, 354
flashfloods 357
mythology 354
Nile River 18, 265, 301, 327–32, 357
oracles predicting 327–32
and Paradise 65
and religious activities 27
and snow 64
variability 263
fountain 19–20
Frankfort, Henri 256, 266, 286
Frankfurter, David 344
Frazer, Sir James G. 255, 256, 306
Freud, Sigmund 36, 37, 39–40, 333–4, 338, 339
Fulke, William 20
functionalism 44, 45, 46, 47
funerals 179
see also corpses; death and death practices
ceremonies 325
of kings/chiefs 60, 176, 270, 271, 272, 313
rites/rituals 303, 318, 321, 325, 326

INDEX

St Gabriel 110
galaktotrophousa (nursing image) 350, 351, 352
Gandhi, Mahatma 386, 387, 388, 389
Ganga (goddess) 55, 381, 384, 385, 386
Ganges 56, 385, 386, 387, 389
Garden of Eden 19, 20, 77, 342
Geertz, Clifford 37, 40, 248
Geesh 71
Genesis 19, 51, 77, 228
genesis 42
genocide, Rwanda 228–31
Geography (Ptolemy) 10
George III, King 69
Ghitās (Coptic Nile festival) 362
Gibtsawit Anbesamit Mariam, Dera District 92
Giesh St Michael church (Gish Abay) 74
Gihon River (Book of Genesis) 2, 21, 28, 52–3, 65, 77–8, 79, 80, 125
 see also Blue Nile, Abyssinia; Gish Abay, Ethiopia
 and Christianity 78
 milk, turning to 78
Gilgamesh 354
Gish, St Michael 75
Gish Abay, Ethiopia 2, 18, 21, 51, 54, 66, 68, 75, 77, 79, 80, 82, 372
 see also Gihon River (Book of Genesis)
 church 74, 75–6, 80
 and Gihon River 77–8
 heavenly nature of 76–85, 94
 and Mountains of the Moon 199
 origins 79, 80
 as pilgrimage site 81, 82
 pre-Christian practices (1770) 70–3, 76
 religious water from 125–7
 as source of Blue Nile 2, 28, 77–8
 spring 2, 3, 56, 66, 74–7, 125
 Wetet Abay/Milk Abay (Gish Abay local area) 76, 78
Gish Mikael monastery 76, 82
The Glory of the Kings (Budge) 105
God 33, 55, 65, 80, 95, 96
 belief in 42, 83, 96, 97, 159, 374
 in Christianity 42, 46, 159
 divine control, or rainmaking 212–13
 God of Peace 71
 Kingdom of God 20, 95, 96, 97, 126, 190, 378
 and sinners 82, 87, 92
 water and religion 41, 42, 43, 45
 worship of 41, 99, 105, 217
gods 46, 114, 224
 Egyptian 258–9

healers' bodies, inhabiting 148–9
Jaja Bujagali and powers of 38–40
'Kiyira' spirit 6
Seth *see* Seth (traditional sky fertility god)
Godse, Nathuram 388
The Golden Bough (Frazer) 255
Gonder (capital of Tana region) 75, 76, 88, 92
 Fasiladas' bath in 81–2
good and evil 73, 83, 135
Gordon, Captain Robert James 206
Gordon, Lady Duff 256–7
Gospel 329
Gragn, Mohammed (Ahmad) 65, 110
Grant, James Augustus 9, 57
Great Hymn 336
Great Pyramid of Khufu 31–2, 258, 311, 315
Green Nile 303–7
Griffiths, J. G. 274, 275
gruel 227
Gujral, Inder Kumar 389
guru 50, 51

Haile Selassie 76, 124
hair
 see also hair-cutting sacrifices
 of healers 165, 173–5
 long 175, 219, 309
 symbolic meaning 219
hair-cutting sacrifices 165, 174–8, 219
al-Hakim 363
hallucinogenic plants 232
Ham (son of Noah) 105, 228
Hamites 228
Hancock, Graham 357
Hannington, James 378
Hathor 309
healers/diviners 7, 50, 130, 147–50, 156, 168, 178, 181, 183, 194, 204, 332
 see also Alice Auma/Lakwena; Bujagali, Jaja (healer); diviners; healers; Kiyira, Jaja (healer); Nfuudu, Benedicto (chief spirit medium)
 and Budhagaali spirit/Bujagali Dam 140, 141
 hair 165, 173–5, 219
 possession by spirits 136, 148–9, 150, 153–4, 163, 171
 traditional 163–4, 166
Hebrew Bible 51
Hecataeus of Miletus 32–3
Hegel, Georg Wilhelm Friedrich 30, 31, 37

455

Helena (Roman empress) 346
Heliodorus (Bishop of Tricca) 24
Heliopolis, Nine Gods of 264
Hellenistic geographers 342
heresy *see* paganism
Herod the Great 92, 93, 346
Herodotus (Father of History) 13–16, 18, 32–3, 266, 297, 314, 327, 328, 330, 343
Herodotus. The Histories 14, 393n22
Hesiod 24
Hetepsekhemwy, King of Egypt 272
Hierakonpolis (site) 274
Hinduism 47, 259, 381–5
    and Gandhi 385–90
    Mother Ganga 52
    texts 385
hippos, in Lake Tana and Blue Nile 118–25
    versus cattle 124
    hide 119, 120
    hunting of 121, 124
    killing of 121–4
    meat 119, 120, 122, 123
    and non-Woyto societies 120
    sounds, significance 120
    teeth 119–20
    waste 120
historical materialism 33
historical sources of rivers 3
History of Ethiopia (Kircher) 66
History of High Ethiopia or Abassia (Almeida) 67
Hocart, Arthur Maurice 23–4, 28, 46, 49, 394n56
holiness/holy water 52, 53, 55, 71, 127, 373
    bringing impurity to/polluting 82
    effects of holy water 84
    at Lake Tana 94, 99
    powers of holy water 84
Holocene Wet Phase 310
Holy Spirit Mobile Forces 188
Holy Spirit Movement 186, 188, 189
Holy Spirit Soldiers 186
Homer 24, 197
Hornung, E. 259, 267, 292, 412n5, 421n16
Horus (ancient Egyptian god) 60, 273, 274, 275, 322–3
    Eye of 278–83, 284, 297, 298
    homosexual violation by Seth 280, 281
    Horus-Seth feud 275, 276–8, 280, 282, 314, 323
    mythology 286
    as son of Osiris 256, 283
Howell, P. P. 251, 411n187, 411n189

human sacrifices 133, 173, 174, 175, 176, 182, 183, 348–9
Humphrey, Captain 203
Hutus 228, 230
Hydaspes (Indus tributary) 343
hydrology 2–3, 15, 18, 151, 328, 385
hydropower
    Bujagali hydropower project 143, 165, 402n47
    Murchison Falls, Uganda 184

idealism (Hegel) 31
ideology, religion as 31
al-Idrīsī, Abū Ja'far 362–3
If the Vagina had Teeth (film) 220
immortality 23
incorporation, forms of 136–7
Indus 342, 343
Internally Displaced People 142
International Criminal Court 188–9
interpretative challenges 58
invisible world 213
Isimba Falls, Uganda 167
Isis, tear of 303–8
Islam 11, 61
    see also Muslims
    and cosmology 158
    as desert religion 359
    and Egypt 359, 361–2
    and Moses 333
    Sharia law 370
    water and religion 42, 43
    as world religion 51
Itanda (spirit) 150, 155, 160, 163, 178
    as a Busoga spirit 152, 159–60
Itanda, Jaja 159–67, 170, 175, 194
Itanda, Mary 159, 163, *164*, 166, 167, 170, 176–7, 194–5, 223
Itanda Dam, plans for 139
Itanda Falls, Uganda 6, 59, 159, *160*, 165, 167, 181, 184, 193
    and rainmaking 223, 224
St Iyasu 99

Japhet (son of Noah) 105, 228
Jeal, Tim 207–8
Jerusalem 91
Jesuit priests, Portuguese 66, 67
Jesus Christ 20, 46
    see also Christianity
    baptism 53, 95–9, 100

birth 78, 81
body of 320
breastfeeding of 353
crucifixion 28, 51, 93, 98, 107
Egypt, flight to 91, 92, 94, 344
footprint 91
immersion in Jordan River 100, 101
as Messiah 96
persecution of 92
as Son of God 93
Jewish people 89, 104
see also Beta Israel (Ethiopian Jews); Hebrew Bible; Old Testament
Jinja, southern Uganda 3, 4, 15, 137, 142, 161, 174
Bell Avenue, Hindu temple on 386
Cultural Research Centre 175
John the Baptist 20, 46, 52–3, 95, 97
John the Holy (John I, 1667–82) 75
Johnson, Douglas 235
Johnston, Harry 10, 203, 207–8
Jordan River 53, 95, 97–102, 380
immersion of Jesus in 100, 101
Journal of the Discovery of the Source of the Nile (Speke) 1, 381, 384
Juba 18
Judaism 11, 42, 46, 333
see also Old Testament
Julius Caesar 327
Juok (god) 251

Kafipa, Chief Charles 217
Kaghango (rain spirit) 180
'Kaitabaloga' (craters) 204
Kakwa tribe, Uganda 233
Kalagala Dam, plans for 139
Kalagala Falls, Uganda 159, 165, 167, 184
Kalagala spirit 159
Kamanzi, Stanislas 11
Kaplan, Steven 104
Karuma Falls, Uganda 129, 233
Katigo (spirit) 162
Katonda (god) 134
Kemp, Barry 261
Kenya 15, 48
Khartoum, Sudan 302
Khasekhemwy, King of Egypt 272, 274
Khufu pyramid *see* Great Pyramid of Khufu
Kiir, President Salva 234
King Solomon's Palace 91
Kingdom of God 20, 95, 96, 97, 126, 190, 378
Kipling, Rudyard 32

Kircher, Athanasius 66
Kiyira (water spirit) 6, 7, 147, 149, 150, 153, 155, 178
as a Busoga spirit 152
versus Nalubaale (water spirit) 151–2
sacrifices to 157
Kiyira, Jaja (healer) xi, 149–59, 164, 165, 175–6, 177, 234
knowledge transfer 50, 51
Kony, Joseph 168, 188–9, 193, 234
kosmos 42

Lake Albert, east-central Africa 31, 200
Lake Ashangi, Ethiopia 64
Lake Tana, Ethiopia 52, 58, 64, *90*, 330–1, 372, 376
see also Woyto of Lake Tana
Abay Ras (source of Abay) 117
Bahir Dar 95, 98, 99, 100
Beta Israel in 104
blessing of water 94
Christianity 85, 88–94
Debre Maryam Monastery 113
Gonder (capital) 75, 76, 81, 88, 92
holy water at 94, 99
Lake Tana Dambia 94
monasteries 75, 88, 89
non-Christian resistance 89
and non-Woyto societies 120
religious significance 59
Tana Kirkos island 89, *90*, 91, 92, 93, 94
visits by Cheesman 75
Lake Victoria, Uganda 4, 128–36, 231
see also Uganda
Bubembe Island 132
damming of 138
as Nalubaale 134
sea python 131
size 192
as source of White Nile 1–3, 6–8, 9, 54, 57
Sukama people *see* Sukuma ethnic group, Tanzania
Lakshmi (Hindu goddess) 47
Lakwena (Holy Spirit) 185, 186, 187
Lakwena, Alice (healer) *see* Alice Auma/Lakwena
Lane, Edward William 366
al-Latîf of Baghdad, 'Abd 361
Leach, Edmund 34, 222
Lent, sacrifice before 112, 115
Lévi-Strauss, Claude 34, 227
Leviticus 308

INDEX

lexicography 80
Life of Anthony (Bishop Athanasius) 329
Life of Saint Louis (de Joinville) 373
The Life of Shenoute (Besa) 348
life-giving properties of water 19, 23, 235, 254, 260, 309, 324, 325
lightning 132, 133, 137, 161, 162, 179, 180, 191, 244, 246
Lindsay, J. 341
The Liturgy of the Nile (British Museum) 373
Livingstone, David 8, 205–11, 234–5
    commemoration by ABBA 205
    Egyptology, drawn to 208
    Missionary Travels and Researches in South Africa 207
    statue 206
Lobo, Father 66–7, 68, 80
logos 350, 351
'lords of the plains' (Maasai) 225–7
Lord's Resistance Army 168, 188, 189
LSD 232
Lubaale, Jaja 167, 168, 169, 177, 184
Lugbara (Sudanic-speaking group) 232
Luo language 134
Luxor 318
Lyons, H. G. 301

Maasai 225–7
Maat, goddess 266, 292, 293
Mabira rainforest 172, 173
McGrigor, Neil 196
Machar, Riek 234
MacKay (missionary) 130
MacKenzie, D. A. 304, 306, 418n200
Mahfouz, Naguib 371
Maji Maji rebellion (1905–07), Tanzania 232, 234
al-Makin 374
malignity 155, 172, 179, 216
Mamluk state ceremonials 364
Manbebya Kifle Church (Gish Abay) 83
Mandela, Nelson 387
Manica, Mozambique 219–20
Mann, Thomas 223
Maqrīzī 363, 364
Mariette, Auguste 32
St Mark 345
martyrdom 345, 346, 378
Marx, Karl 30, 31
al-Masʿūdi 363
Master of Disaster (rainmaker King) 241
materialism (of Marx) 31, 32, 38
materiality 23, 32

Matthew (Biblical) 96, 345–6
Mauss, Marcel 47
meat 72, 227
    of hippos 119, 120, 122, 123
Mecca 377
Memphis city 266, 267, 288
Memphite Theology 282
Menelik I (son of Queen Sheba and King Solomon) 106
Menes, King of Egypt 266, 267
menstruation 119, 135–6, 229
Merleau-Ponty, Maurice 30
Merneit, Queen of Egypt 269
Merton, Thomas 347
Meshiha (divinity, Lake Tana) 115
Mesoké (god of rain and thunder) 151, 161–2, 163, 169, 180, 223, 224, 225
Messiah 20
methodological collectivism 34
methodological individualism 34
Mgussa (spirit) *see* Mukasa (Mgussa, Ugandan lake god)
St Michael 75
Middleton, J. 232, 409n122
St Mikael 115
St Mikael Church 82
mikvah (Jewish ritual bath) 106
milk
    blood, mixed with 227
    breast milk 227, 309, 350, 352
    celestial 309
    curdled 227
    and Gihon River 78
    and Maasai (Kenyan pastoralists) 226–7
Milky Nile *see* White Nile source (Uganda)
Min (fertility god) 280, 283
al-Misri, Wasif Shah 375
Mockler-Ferryman, A. F. 378, 427n178
monotheistic religions 326, 333
Moors, Muslim 65
Mophi mountain 14
Moses 2, 6, 61, 77, 105, 208, 308, 332–41, 357, 360, 379
    Ethiopian wife 104, 105
    as hero 339
    mythology 338–9
    naming by Pharaoh's daughter 338, 339
    origins 333
    powers 340
    tablets of 99
Moubarek, H. E. Ali Pasha 198
Mount Carmel 46
Mount Gish 75

INDEX

Mountains of the Moon, Abyssinia 10, 200, 381
   see also Ruwenzori Mountains
   Arabic name 197
   cosmological significance 197–8
   documentation 197
   perceptions as Rain-Maker 202–5
   Ruwenzori Mountains perceived as 64
   and source of the Nile 64–70
Mugesera, Leon 230
Mukasa (Mgussa, Ugandan lake god) 129–31, 151
   medium 130, 133
   sacrifices to 132–3
Mukirane, Isaya 205
Murchison, Sir Roderick 9
Murchison Falls, Uganda 31, 59, 184–95, 234
   National Park 192
   natural phenomena 191
   Wang Jok 185, 193
   water spirits at 184–5, 189
Museveni, Yoweri Kaguta (Ugandan politician) 141, 146, 187
Muslim Brotherhood 370
Muslims 30, 61, 65
   see also Islam
   in Bahir Dar 111
   healers as 158
   of the Nile 358–71
   Orthodox 110, 111
   Woyto of Lake Tana 109, 110, 112–13
al-Mustansir, Fatimid Sultan 374
Mutyaba, James Christopher 143
Muwereza, Jaja 153
Mystery Play of the Succession 321
mythology
   Budhagaali (water spirit) 172
   Bujagali, Jaja (healer) 171
   Christianity 19, 59
   Egypt/ancient Egypt 283–4, 291, 314
   floods 354
   functions 222–3
   Hamitic 228
   Horus (ancient Egyptian god) 286
   and hydrological sources 18
   Moses 338–9
   Osiris (ancient Egyptian king) 274–7, 286, 287, 316, 341
   and rituals 222
   and Rwanda 228
   Seth (Egyptian sky fertility god) 273–6, 288–90

Nabamba (Budhagaali spirit twin brother) 172, 173, 175
al-Nadīm, Ibn 361–2
Nadiope, William Gabula 146
Nalubaale (water spirit) 55, 129, 134, 170
   see also Lake Victoria, Uganda
   as a Buganda spirit 152
   versus Kiyira (water spirit) 151–2
Nambaga (female river spirit) 153, 154
Namweni (water spirit) 147, 154–5
Nangendo, Florence 142
Nanina, Abyssinia 65
Naqada, Predynastic Egypt 262, 267
Narmer, King of Egypt 270
Narmer Palette 267, 273
Nash, Henry S. 41
National Geographic 196
National Resistance Army, Uganda 187, 188
Natural History (Pliny the Elder) 22
natural phenomena 13–30, 191
nature
   see also natural phenomena
   definition challenges 30
   qualities of 21–30
   worship of 28, 29
Nearchus of Crete 343
Nebuchadnezzar, King 362
Negedie Woyto see Woyto of Lake Tana
Neolithic Wet Phase 257, 273, 275, 310
Nero, Emperor 17
Nesmin papyrus 318
netherworld 316, 319
Netjerikhet see Djoser, King of Egypt
New Testament 46, 77, 379
Nfuudu, Benedicto (chief spirit medium) 38, 59, 142–4, 147, 167–70, 182
   hair-cutting 184
   imposter claim 145, 170, 175
   witchcraft 183
Nfuudu, Jajja Lubaale 140, 142, 165
Nietzsche, Friedrich 30
Niglas, Liivo 219–20
Nile Basin 3, 8, 10, 358
   see also Nile River
   Nile Basin Initiative 11, 235
   rainfall 202
   Upper Nile 60
Nile River
   see also floods; Nile Basin
   awe inspired by 201
   Blue Nile see Blue Nile, Abyssinia
   civilization 258–326

INDEX

colours 300–3, 360
  see also Blue Nile, Abyssinia (Ethiopia); Green Nile; Red Nile; White Nile source (Uganda)
  diverting or withholding 372–6
  as divine river from the sky 322
  and Egyptian gods 258–9
  floods 18, 265, 301, 327–32, 357
  flow of 5, 198, 257, 301, 331, 371, 372, 377–9
  global relevance 1–2, 11
  green, red and white 300–3
  Green Nile , 303–7
  and holy water 56
  life-giving properties 201
  map of 12
  Muslims 358–71
  'Nile god' 259
  'Nile is Wealth' proverb 137
  Nilotic people along see Nilotic tribes
  Red Nile 303, 304, 307, 308, 341
  regulation, in Egypt 47
  and rejuvenation 317–21
  religious status 259
  River Nile Basin Report 11
  role in Old Testament 2
  snows feeding 64
  sources
    Blue Nile see Blue Nile, Abyssinia
    heaven and God, associated with 65
    and Moses 336
    and Mountains of the Moon 64–70
    in Paradise (Muslim perceptions) 199
    quest for, by Livingstone 206, 208
    White Nile see under White Nile, source of
  'Vains of the Nile' 329
  water of see water of the Nile 24, 78
  White Nile see White Nile
  'wives of the Nile' (statuettes) 349
  world religions along 327–90
  worship of 25, 71, 81, 110, 113, 115, 366
Nile Valley 260
Nilometers 27, 362, 364, 365, 368
  Roda 366
Nilotic tribes 31, 229, 242, 254, 256, 411n192
  and pastoralism 235, 239
Nilus 26
Nine Gods of Heliopolis 264
Noah and the Ark 87, 228
non-ancestral spirits 43
non-believers 36, 40

non-existence 291–2
Nordén (Swedish traveller) 16
Northrop, H. D. 131, 401n10
Ntembe, Chief 145
Nuer tribe, Sudd 237, 239, 248
Nun (primeval waters of origin) 244, 264, 295, 298, 320
nursing image 350
nursing period 350–1
Nut (sky goddess) 264, 276, 296, 299, 309, 315, 319
Nyakang (god) 251
Nyalic (God in the Firmament) 246
N'yanza reservoir 1, 2, 382
Nyavingi ('mother of abundance') 203
Nyikang (king) 252–3
Nyungwe Forest, Rwanda 196

Obeyesekere, G. 28–9
Obuzzinga Nalubale (two small islands) 4, 5
ocean, and sources 18, 371–2
The Odyssey (Homer) 24
Odyssey (Homer) 197
Oedipus complex 36
Ojok, Isaac 190
Old Testament 2, 19, 46, 77, 228, 341
  see also Deuteronomy; Exodus; Ezekiel; Genesis; Hebrew Bible; Jewish people; Leviticus; Moses
  Adam and Eve 20, 78, 97
  and Lake Tana, Ethiopia 89, 91
  role of Ethiopia in 105
Omugga Kiyira 6
On the Origin of Species (Darwin) 333
One Hundred and Ten Miracles of Our Lady Mary 352–3
'Operation Moses' (1983–1985) 107
'Operation Solomon' (1991) 108
oracles, predicting of Nile flood 327–32
Oriental Despotism (Wittfogel) 260
Oris, Juma 188
Osiris (ancient Egyptian king) 24, 256, 264–6, 266, 275, 276, 284
  all waters as 293–7
  coffin 354
  corpse of 61, 296, 299, 318
  as dead King of the netherworld 60–1
  dismembering of body 287, 289, 293
  as divine power 61
  efflux (discharge) 61, 287–9, 296, 303, 307, 318, 325, 351, 418n217
  emblems 275

exudations 303–8
Horus as son of 256, 283
murder by Seth (drowning) 277, 278, 285–8, 297, 299, 303, 324, 341
mythology 274–7, 286, 287, 316, 341
Osiris-Seth feud 278, 323, 324
rebirth 308
rejuvenation 289, 293, 321
Otto, Rudolf 36, 40, 41, 222
Ottoman period 361
Owen Falls Dam, Uganda 4, 5, 6, 128, 138, 139, 147, 163, 233
female river spirit 153
ox sacrifice 71
Oxtoby, W. G. 397n154

St Pachomius 347
Paez, Pedro 66, 67, 68
paganism 116, 348, 352, 361, 362
Paradise 19, 20, 28, 65, 98, 199, 360
Park, Thomas K. 262, 263
pastoralism 225, 226, 250
and Nilotic people 235, 239
Pentecostals 149, 195
Permanent Committee on Geographical Names 93
Petrie, Sir William Matthew Flinders 267–71, 274, 413n47
Pharaonic calendar 349
Pharaonic period 258, 260, 261, 263, 264, 274
phenomenology 30, 36
Philo of Alexandria 26, 76, 354
Philostratus 14, 25
Piketty, Thomas 47–8, 397n142
pilgrimage sites 81, 82, 346
pillars, sacrificial 89, *90*, 91, 92
Pitia (blacksmith) 245
Pliny the Elder 17, 22, 23, 32, 361, 393n32
Plutarch 289, 296, 308, 318
polygamy 218
Poncet (physician) 68
Prester John (Christian monarch) 64, 65, 373
priests 52, 73, 75, 76, 88, 115
Jesuit priests, Portuguese 66, 67
lack of, among the Woyto 114
and sacrifices, Uganda 132–3
Primeval Hill 264, 265
primeval waters 263–6
procreation 226
The Protestant Ethic (Weber) 33, 48
Protestantism 53
psychoanalysis 30, 36

Ptah (creator of universe) 264, 265
Ptolemaic period 337
Ptolemy, Claudius (geographer) 8, 10, 64
Puranas 383
purification 83, 106, 359
purity 284
pyramids 31, 32, 196
Bent Pyramid, Dashur 308
building in time of ecological crisis 321–2
and conflicting water-worlds 311–14
Great Pyramid of Khufu 31, 32, 258, 311, 315
and importance of water in a desert 323
land on which built 265
and the Nile 321–6
Pyramid Age 268, 273, 296
Pyramid Texts 274, 276–7, 279, 280, 282, 287, 290, 298, 307, 310, 317, 318, 320, 352
Step Pyramid, Saqqara 258, 272, 273, 283
python-snake 131, 161, 223, 224

Qa, King of Egypt 271
Qur'an 51, 53, 358

Ra (sun god) 258, 267, 279, 317
rain 47, 50, 86, 115, 132
see also rainmaking
Deng/Dengit (great rain) 246
failure 240
and holy water 53–4, 57, 60
low and erratic rainfalls 225
prayer for 216
scarcity of 209
unpredictability 239
rainbow 87, 88, 223, 224
rain-god 224
rainmaking 46, 60, 137, 156, 210–11, 219
see also rain; rain-stopping; Seth (Egyptian sky fertility god)
in Africa 240
Bari tribe, Equatorial Africa 244, 245
ceremonies 212, 216, 245
cosmology 211, 223, 230
Dinka people, Upper Nile 237, 242, 244, 246, 248
or divine control 212–13
as ecological technique 212
killing of rainmaker 241–5, 249–51
Mountain of the Moon perceived as Rain-Maker 202–5
rainmaker king as Master of Disaster 241

INDEX

rituals 22, 43, 44, 50, 72, 161, 209, 212, 216–19, 221, 225, 235, 247, 251, 255
   and sacrifices of divine rainmakers 243–56
   and Sukuma cosmology 214–19
rain-stones 244–5
rain-stopping 179, 239
Ramses II (1279–13 BC) 336
Rappaport, Roy 44
Rassam, Hormuzd 110
rationalization 33
Reade, Winwood 208
Red Nile 303, 304, 307, 308, 341
regicide 242
Reid, Richard 128
rejuvenation 288, 292, 300
   and Nile 317–21
   of Osiris 289, 293, 321
religion
   see also specific religions
   'abolition as the illusory happiness of the people' 31, 38
   definition challenges 30, 40–1
   Egypt/ancient Egypt 15, 260, 290–3, 294, 323, 329, 343, 344, 352
   functional and substantive approaches to 42–3
   main questions 40–1
   Marx on 31
   monotheistic 326, 333
   origins 34–5
   theories of religion without water 30–7
   totality of 40
   world religions 51
Religion Without God (Dworkin) 41
religious communities 42
religious quest 10–13
religious sources of rivers 3
Renenutet (serpent goddess) 337
reproductive difficulties 136
revelation 97
Ripon Falls, Lake Victoria 1–6, 128, 138, 147
rites, cosmic 49
Ritual and Religion in the Making of Humanity (Rappaport) 45
ritual baths 83, 106
ritual purity 106
rituals 7, 55, 61, 126, 176, 184, 193, 195, 213, 215, 220–2, 229, 237
   agrarian 49
   and beliefs 70, 110, 111
   benevolent 184, 192
   blood 233

   at Blue Nile 73–4
   and Budhagaali spirit/Bujagali Dam 59, 141–3, 145, 146, 153, 182
   Christian 92
   extreme 175
   food 227
   and healers/diviners 148, 151, 153, 157–9, 164, 166, 169, 171
   and medicine 24
   mocking 219
   and mythology 222
   opposition to 72
   pre-Christian practices at Gish (1770) 72, 76
   protective 216
   rainmaking 22, 43, 44, 50, 72, 161, 209, 212, 216–19, 221, 225, 235, 247, 251, 255
   rain-stopping 239
   and religion 41, 92, 115–16, 118
   ritual practices 21, 73, 112, 113, 312, 343
   sacrifice 250
   and Sirius (star) 71
   traditional 44, 124
   water 81, 82, 84, 94, 96, 235, 276, 317, 387
   and witchcraft 177, 179, 180, 182
   witchcraft 184
   Woyto of Lake Tana 119
River Nile *see* Nile River
River Nile Basin Report 11
river spirits 128–9, 139, 147
   see also Abinas (river spirit); water spirits
   female 153
   importance of 158
   sacrifices to 156
rivers 230, 231
   see also river spirits; *specific rivers*
roasting 227
Roscoe, John 132, 133, 135
The Rules of Sociological Method (Durkheim) 34
Ruwenzori Mountains, eastern Africa 11, 15, 60
   see also Mountains of the Moon, Abyssinia
   climate 202, 203
   Mountains of the Moon perceived as 64
   people living on slopes of 204–5
   as Rain-Maker 202
   Stanley and Mount Ruwenzori 197–202
   terminology 202, 204
Rwanda 11
   genocide in 228–31
   Hutus 228
   monarchy 229, 230
   Nyungwe Forest 196
   Tutsis 228

INDEX

sacredness 52
sacrifices 60, 92, 116, 230, 250
   animal *see* animal sacrifice
   blood 92, 112, 114, 117, 118, 132–4, 143, 178, 182, 184, 234
   children 174, 176, 183
   of divine rainmakers 243–56
   Ethiopian Orthodox Church on 116
   Great Sacrifice (calf sacrifice) 116–18
   hair-cutting 165, 174–8, 219
   human 133, 173, 174, 175, 176, 182, 183, 349
   before Lent 112, 115
   to Mukasa 132–3
   as 'pagan practices' 116
   pillars 89, *90*, 91, 92
   sacrificial stones 89
   and sources of the Nile 7, 66–7
   to spirits 155–7, 162–3
   Woyto of Lake Tana 111–12, 114
Saeteresdal, Tore 219–20
salvation 83, 93, 95, 96, 100–1
   salvation history and Uganda 377–8
Samaritan women, in Christianity 20
Samson 219
Sargon of Agade 338
scarcity 135, 227, 238, 361
Scheabeddin (Arab geographer) 199
Schilbrack, Kevin 36, 41, 42
Schnepel, B. 253, 411n188, 411n191, 411n193
scriptures 52
sea python, Lake Victoria 131
Sechele (chief of Bakwain tribe, Limpopo area) 209–10
sediment processes 300
Selama, Abune 91, 92
Selassie, Haile 76, 124
Seligman, B. Z. 244, 248
Seligman, C. G. 244, 248
semen 226
Semerkhet, King of Egypt 271
Semien province 64
   Jew's Mountain 65
Semra, Christos 94
Seneca 21, 25
Senecio rainforest 202
Seth (Egyptian sky fertility god)
   in history 273–6
   Horus-Seth feud 275, 276–8, 280, 282, 314, 323
   as incarnation of evil 283

   meanings 278
   mythology 273–6, 288–90
   Osiris, murder of by drowning 277, 278, 285–8, 297, 299, 303, 324, 341
   Osiris-Seth feud 278, 323, 324
   rainmaking powers 322
   testicles, abduction by Horus 280, 281, 305
   as trickster 293
Sethe, Hans 259, 274
Severino (father of Alice Auma/Lakwena) 185, 187, 189, 190, 191
sexuality 136–7
   metaphors 219–21
Shakti 387
Sharia law 370
Sheba, Queen 105, 106, 109
Sheik Abinas *see* Abinas (river spirit)
Shem (son of Noah) 105, 228
Shenoute (monk) 347–8
Sher Abinas 114
Shilluk people, Sudan 237, 242, 244, 246, 254–6, 411n187, 411n188
   kings 248, 251, 252, 253, 411n189
Shipton, P. M. 48, 397n146
shrines 157, 159, 165, 170
Shum (river priest) 73, 76
The Sign and the Seal (Hancock) 357
Sigoli, Simone 373
sinners 186, 188
   Adam and Eve as 97–8
   cleansing of sin 84, 92
   and God 82, 87, 92
   punishment of 92, 183
Sirius (star) 71, 348
Siva-Purana 385
snakes/snake forms 131, 154, 161, 223, 224, 236
snow 64
Snow, C. P. 34
Sobat River 302
Social Origins (Hocart) 46
The Sociology of Religion (Weber) 33
Solomon, King 105, 106, 108
soteriology, cosmic 51
sources
   of the Nile *see* Nile River
   and the ocean 18, 371–2
   of religion 1–63
      approaching 1–10
      challenges and contents 57–63
      importance of finding 1–2

and natural phenomena 13–30
religious quest 10–13
before the sky 196–7
Speke, John Hanning 9, 128–30, 132, 147, 197, 234–5, 333, 376
Journal of the Discovery of the Source of the Nile 1, 381, 383
on Lake Victoria outlet as source of White Nile 1–3, 6–8, 57, 379, 381–5
spirits 43, 59, 83, 133, 140, 155
see also river spirits; water spirits
ancestral 43, 163, 173, 194, 244, 248, 316
appearance of 153–4
benevolent 149, 155, 180
bloodthirsty 59, 133, 134, 172–8, 181
characteristics 155
malevolent 149, 155
messages, delivery of 153–4
possession by 137–8, 148–9, 150, 153–4, 163, 171
powers 150–1, 155
and rainmaking 212
requests from 156
resident 135
sacrifices to 155–7, 162–3, 234
shrines for 157
twin 172, 173
violence as invasion of 190
Ssese Islands, Uganda 129, 131, 132
Stanley, Henry M. 9, 138, 147, 154, 197–202, 208, 378
Darkest Africa 198
Step Pyramid, Saqqara 258, 272, 273, 283
Storaas, Frode 219–20
Strabo 17, 18
Strates (assistant to James Bruce) 69–70, 72, 73
stratification/stratified systems 262
sub-Saharan Africa 60
'politics of the belly' 136
Sudd (barrier), Sudan 57, 234, 235, 236, 237
Sukuma ethnic group, Tanzania 43, 223
and rainmaking 212, 213, 214–19, 220
sun
Ra (sun god) 258, 267, 279, 317
and rainbows 224
and water 283–5
'willing the sun' 239–43
worship of 258, 273, 285, 334
Supreme Being 43
see also God
swamps 235
symbolism 20, 40, 219, 229, 281

taboos 135, 165, 176, 227
Tafla, B. 80, 399n48
Talmudic law 107
Tana, Lake *see* Lake Tana, Ethiopia
Tana Kirkos island, Lake Tana 90, 91, 92, 93
monastery 89
monks at 94
Tanner, R. 214, 396n134, 407n68, 407n74
Tanzania 15, 45, 51
Tara Gedam monastery, Ethiopia 92
Taylor, Christopher C. 228, 229, 230
Tekeze River *see* Atbara River
Tellez, Balthazar 66
Templar Knights 357
Ten Commandments 51
Thales 18, 335
theodicy 33, 34
Theogony (Hesiod) 24
theology 51
Thomas, K. 33, 395n106
Thomas, L. M. 136, 402n32
Thompson, Thomas L. 337
Thomson, James 61–2
Thrasyalces 18
Timkat festival, Ethiopia 74, 81, 94
baptism 95–104
Bahire Timiket (baptismal pool) 98–102
as not a sacrament 96
properties of water 97
of repentance 96
sprinkler system 102
duration 103
Meskel Square ceremony 98–9, 100, 101, 102
purpose 95–6
tabot (replica of Ark and tablets of the law) 99, 100
Tis Abay
religious water 125–7
'smoking waters' 86, 87
waterfalls at 72, 85, 86, 87, 125
and Woyto of Lake Tana 110
Tooro, Kingdom of 137
Toro Kingdom, Ankole 204
transcendental religions 42
Travels to Discover the Source of the Nile (Bruce) 68
tree of knowledge 97
Trevor-Roper, Hugh 31
Trigger, Bruce 42
Trinity (Father, Son and Holy Spirit) 97, 102

Tsima Silasie 79, 80
al-Turabi, Hasan 370
Turner, Victor 23, 34
Tutsis, Rwanda 228
twin spirits 172, 173
Tylor, Edward 41

Uganda 4, 8, 15, 135, 152, 234
   see also Bujagali Dam, Uganda; Bujagali Falls, Uganda; Lake Victoria, Uganda
   Acholi people 236
   animal sacrifice 132–3, 156, 157
   Busoga Kingdom 2, 4, 6, 49, 139, 140, 141, 145, 169
   Jinja, southern Uganda 3, 4, 15, 137, 142, 161, 174, 175, 386
   Murchison Falls *see* Murchison Falls, Uganda
   National Resistance Army 187, 188
   Owen Falls Dam 4, 5, 6, 128, 138, 139, 147, 153, 163, 233
   Ripon Falls, Lake Victoria 1, 2, 3–4, 5, 6, 128, 138, 147
   and salvation history 377–8
   Ssese Islands 129, 131, 132
   wells 135–6
universe, creation of 264, 265

Varanasi, India 55, 385
Victoria, Lake *see* Lake Victoria, Uganda
Victoria N'yanza 1, 382
violence, as invasion of spirits 190
Virgin Mary 69–70, 88, 91
   breast milk 350–2, 353
   and Coptic Christianity 349
   persecution of 92, 93
   scarf 87, 126
A Voice from the Nile (Thomson) 62–3
volcanoes 191, 204

Wafā festival 364
Wainright, G. A. 241, 276, 283, 314, 393n27, 410n143, 414n63, 414n82, 415n99
Wakooli, Kawunhe 144
Waldecker, Burchardt 196
Waldiba monastery, Ethiopia 92
Walumbe (water god) 161, 162, 163
Wamala (deity) 134
water 19, 20, 22, 54, 60, 107, 149, 235, 284
   see also floods; rain; rainmaking
   blessing of 83–4, 94, 322
   and body fluid metaphors 219–23
   and Christianity 20, 75
   cosmology 2, 6, 7, 8, 18, 71, 127, 231, 248, 313
   in a desert 323
   divine *see* divine water
   flow of 21, 151, 152
   holy *see* holiness/holy water
   life-giving properties 19, 22, 235, 254, 260, 309, 324, 325
   of the Nile *see* water of the Nile
   and Osiris (Egyptian king) 293–7
   power of 19, 23, 33, 150
   primeval waters 263–6
   pyramids and conflicting water-worlds 311–14
   and qualities of nature 21–30
   and religion as function or substance 40–52
   rituals 81, 82, 84, 94, 96, 235, 276, 317, 387
   as sources of religion and life 390–1
   and sun 283–5
   theories of religion without 30–7
   and witchcraft 178–84
water cults 128
water of the Nile 8, 24, 62, 287, 288, 295, 302, 303, 317, 319, 319, 341, 359, 362, 363, 364, 365, 369, 372, 375, 386, 387, 406n59
   and Blue Nile 72, 78, 110, 127
   as covenant between humans and God 78
   Muslim perceptions 198–9
water spirits 6, 7, 55, 129, 135, 148, 150–1, 154–5, 161
   see also Budhagaali (water spirit); Kiyira (water spirit); Namweni (water spirit); river spirits
   at Murchison Falls 184–5
waterfalls 72, 85, 138, 139, 161, 166, 173, 223
   see also Bujagali Falls, Uganda; Isimba Falls, Uganda; Itanda Falls, Uganda; Kalagala Falls, Uganda; Karuma Falls, Uganda; Owen Falls Dam, Uganda; Ripon Falls, Lake Victoria
water-worlds
   Egypt 260–3, 311–14
   pyramids and conflicting water-worlds 311–14
   and religion 30
   Woyto of Lake Tana *108*, 111, 126
wealth 6, 47, 48, 181, 194
Weber, Max 33, 34, 37, 39, 47, 189
wells 135–6

INDEX

Wenke, Robert 256, 261
Western Island, White Nile 3
Wetet Abay/Milk Abay (Gish Abay local area) 76, 78
White Monastery (desert monastery) 347
White Nile source (Uganda) 3, 5, 6, 87, 235, 301, 302, 308–10
   baptism next to 379–81
   compared to Blue Nile 301
   Jinja, southern Uganda 3, 4, 15, 137, 142, 161, 386
   Lake Victoria outlet 1–3, 6–8, 9, 15, 54, 57
   odour 301, 302
   Omugga Kiyira 5–6
   southernmost hydrological source 196, 197
   Speke and Hindus at 381–5
Wijsen, F. 214, 396n134, 407n68, 407n74
Wilford, Francis 381, 382, 383
Williams, Roy 21
Wilson, John 263
witchcraft 133, 135, 163, 187, 188, 194
   defining 178
   evidence of existence, for the Busoga 178–9
   and Mountains of the Moon, Abyssinia 203, 204
   and rituals 177, 179, 180, 182
   and water 178–84
Wittfogel, Karl 260
Word, the 53
world religions 51
worship
   acts of 42
   of Ark 89
   by Bari tribe, Equatorial Africa 248
   of God 41, 99, 105, 217
   idols 106
   of nature 28, 29
   of Nile River 25, 71, 81, 110, 113, 115, 366
   ritual 91–2, 359
   of spirits 144
   by Sukuma ethnic group, Tanzania 214, 215
   sun 258, 273, 285, 334
   of water 81, 111
Woyto of Lake Tana 72
   see also hippos, in Lake Tana and Blue Nile; Lake Tana, Ethiopia
   Abinas (river spirit) among 108–16, 127
   at Bahir Dar 108, 109
   Christian opposition to practices of 113, 115–16
   cosmology 114, 115
   diet 118–19
   economy 118
   hippo-cult among 118–25
   initiation rites 120
   killing of hippos 121
   marriage 120–3
   Muslims 108, 110, 113
   origin of name 109
   priests, lack of 114
   religion 111–12, 114
   sacrifice 111–12, 114
   water-worlds *108*, 111, 126

Ya'cob, Zar'a 374
Yahweh 46, 47
Yakan (Allah Water Cult) 232–4
St Yared (Ethiopian composer) 91, 358
Yasin, Waguma 145, 173
Yeshaq, Emperor (1413–30) 106
Yohannes Kadus 75

al-Zahir 363
Zer, King of Egypt 269, 270, 312
Zerabruk 75
   church 81, 82
   holy day 82
   miracles of 78, 80, 81
Zerabruk, Abune 78, 79
   death of 80
   holy books of 80
Zerufael, Aba 79
Zet, King of Egypt 269
Zeus 197